MW01620655

Parish Book of Psalms

Arlene Oost-Zinner

Parish Book of Psalms

The Church Music Association
of America

Cover design by Chad Parish
Engraving by Richard Chonak and Ben Yanke
Layout by Mary C. Weaver
Indexing by Richard Chonak

ISBN 978-0-9848652-7-7
Second printing

Contents

Introduction

This collection of plainchant Responsorial Psalm settings in English is intended for Ordinary Form Masses. The texts of these psalms correspond with those found in the *Lectionary for Mass* for the dioceses of the United States of America and provide an accessible, tradition-based option for singing the Responsorial Psalms at Mass on Sundays and selected solemnities and feasts.

Each of these settings can be led by an unaccompanied schola or single cantor; members of the congregation should be able to repeat their parts after one or two hearings. All of the verses are fully pointed and notated to facilitate ease in performance by the cantor or schola.

Plainchant is text driven. Though modal in form, neither the melodies nor the mode choices for these settings are based on those of their corresponding Graduals, which are sometimes considered the predecessors of the Responsorial Psalm. The melodies of these antiphons are original and were inspired by the abrupt but ultimately delightful sonority and rhythms of the English language.

The verses are set to the Gregorian Office tone formulas that not only correspond in terms of mode but also best complement the English idiom. With a few exceptions, I have opted to treat each cycle of verses with only one mediant and final cadence. This allows the congregation to hear the final cadence only one time per cycle and sends a clear signal when it is time to repeat the antiphon.

Finally, spending a good deal of time on the reciting tone translates into fewer interruptions in the flow of the text and, by way of contrast, renewed attention to the antiphon melody.

My hope is that this collection fosters prayer in the minds and hearts and on the lips of individuals and communities who sing from it—

and that its foundation in Gregorian structures gives rise to a greater appreciation of our musical heritage as Catholics in both cognitive and auditory ways.

Many thanks are due my friends and colleagues in the Church Music Association of America and beyond who have provided me with a great deal of encouragement: David Hughes, Paul Weber, Aristotle Esguerra, Jeffrey Ostrowski, Adam Bartlett, Richard Rice, Ryan Murphy, Wilko Brouwers, William Mahrt, Scott Turkington, Mary Jane Ballou, and many more. I am also indebted to the Reverend Monsignor William J. Skoneki, the St. Cecilia Schola, and parishioners of St. Michael the Archangel Catholic Church in Auburn, Alabama, for helping me to see, week after week, what works and what does not.

Special thanks are also due Jeffrey Tucker, Richard Chonak, Ben Yanke, and Mary Weaver as well as the many donors who have made this book a reality. As always, I am grateful to my family, and I remain in humble service to our Lord, to whom all prayers are lifted and for whom all songs are sung.

Arlene Oost-Zinner

Advent

First Sunday of Advent

Ps. 122: 1-2, 3-4, 4-5, 6-7, 8-9 **YEAR A**

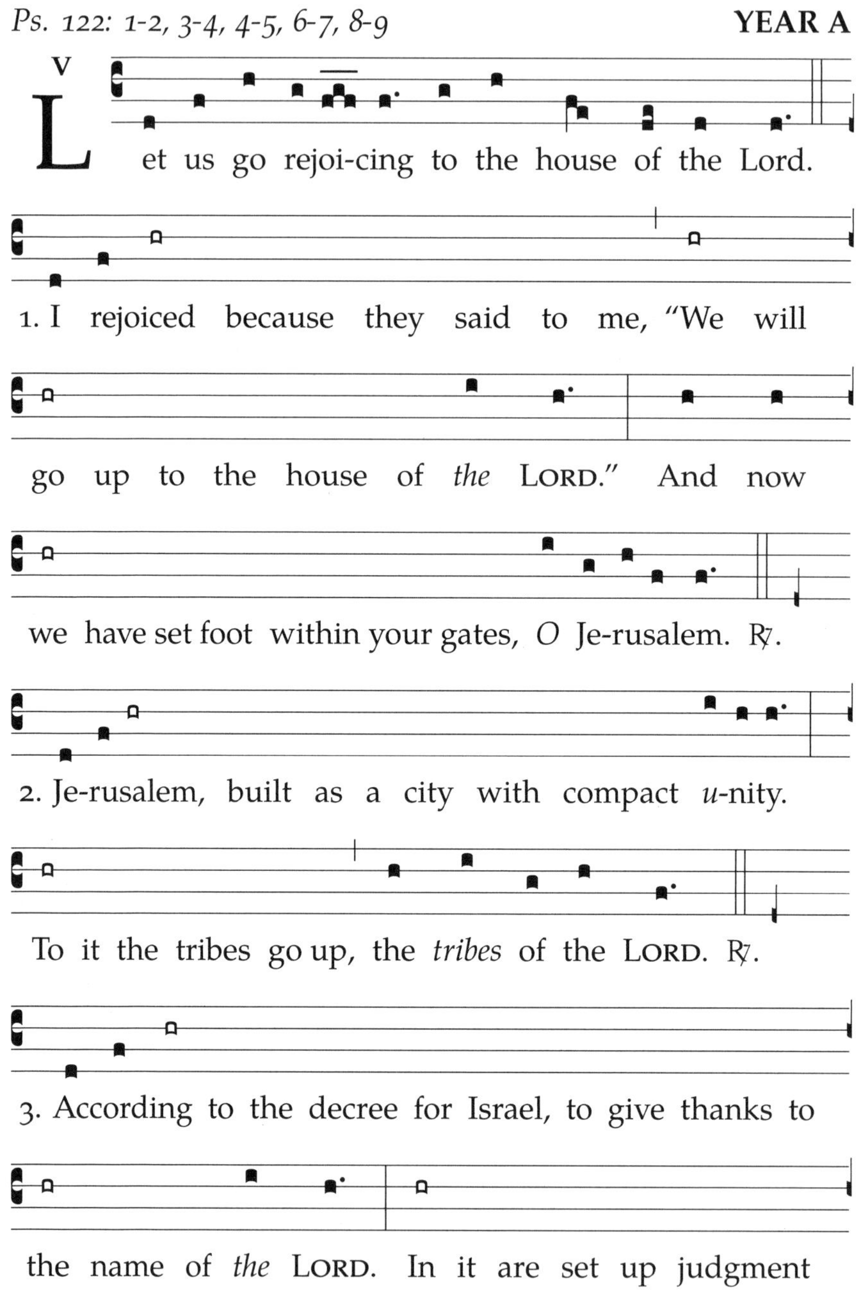

℣
Let us go rejoi-cing to the house of the Lord.
1. I rejoiced because they said to me, "We will
go up to the house of *the* LORD." And now
we have set foot within your gates, *O* Je-rusalem. ℟.
2. Je-rusalem, built as a city with compact *u*-nity.
To it the tribes go up, the *tribes* of the LORD. ℟.
3. According to the decree for Israel, to give thanks to
the name of *the* LORD. In it are set up judgment

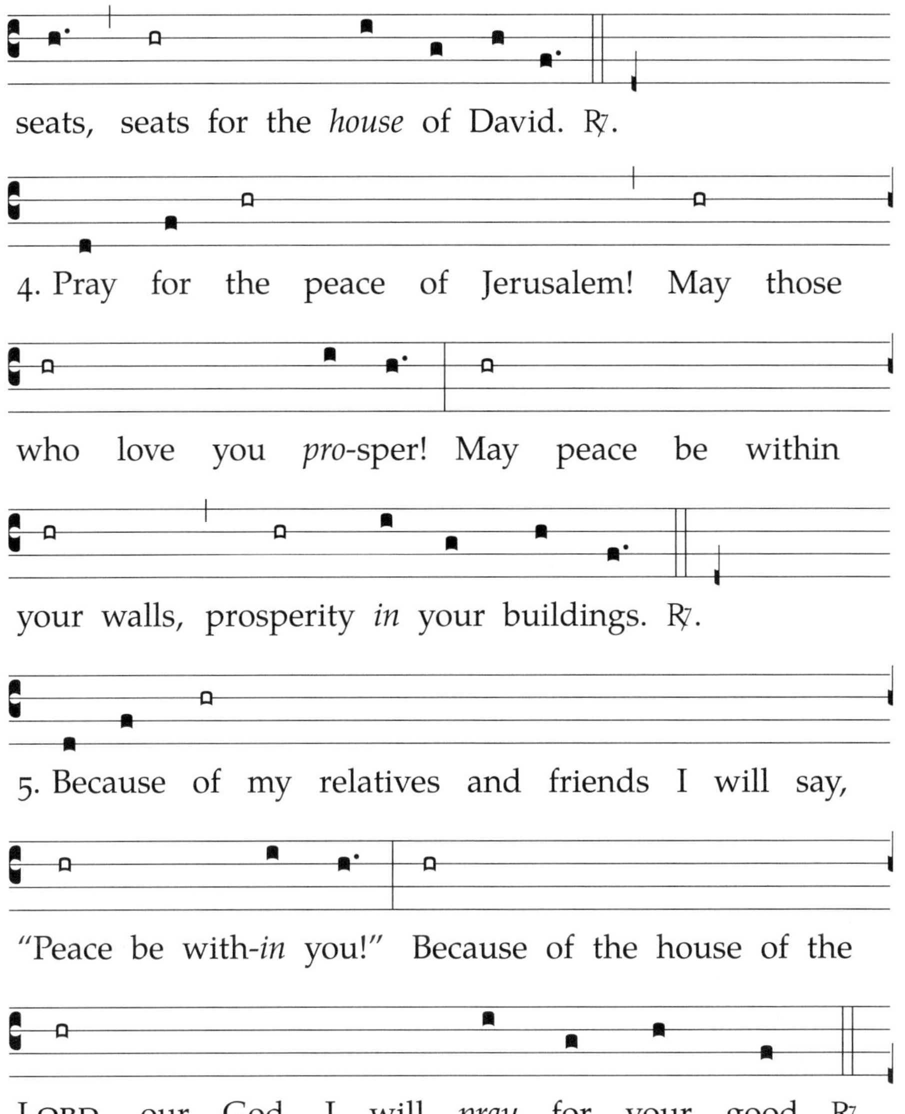
seats, seats for the *house* of David. ℟.
4. Pray for the peace of Jerusalem! May those
who love you *pro*-sper! May peace be within
your walls, prosperity *in* your buildings. ℟.
5. Because of my relatives and friends I will say,
"Peace be with-*in* you!" Because of the house of the
Lord, our God, I will *pray* for your good. ℟.

First Sunday of Advent

Ps. 80: 2-3, 15-16, 18-19 **YEAR B**

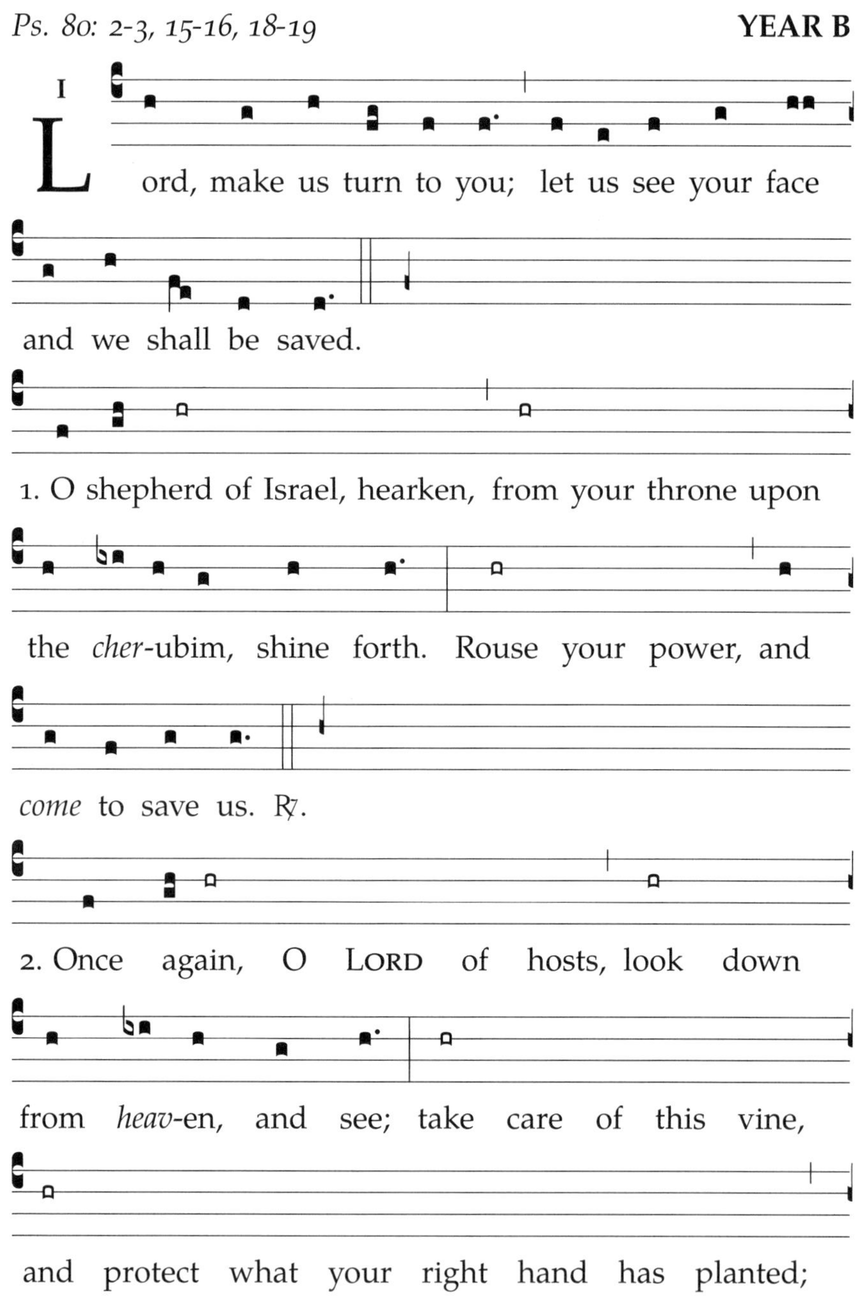

I
Lord, make us turn to you; let us see your face
and we shall be saved.
1. O shepherd of Israel, hearken, from your throne upon
the *cher*-ubim, shine forth. Rouse your power, and
come to save us. ℟.
2. Once again, O Lord of hosts, look down
from *heav*-en, and see; take care of this vine,
and protect what your right hand has planted;

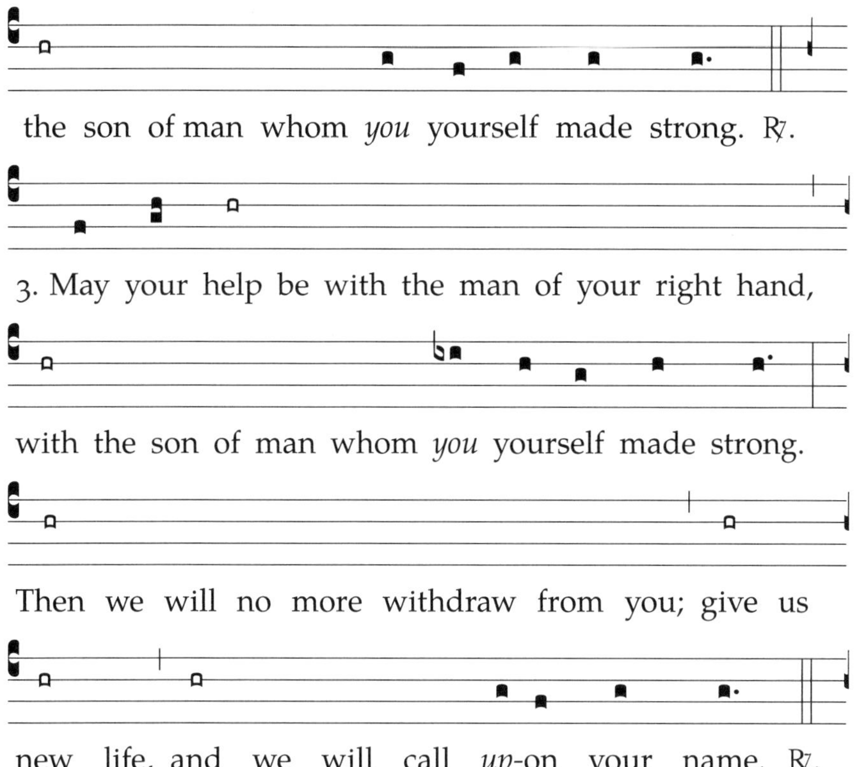
the son of man whom *you* yourself made strong. ℟.
3. May your help be with the man of your right hand,
with the son of man whom *you* yourself made strong.
Then we will no more withdraw from you; give us
new life, and we will call *up*-on your name. ℟.

First Sunday of Advent

Ps. 25: 4-5, 8-9, 10, 14 **YEAR C**

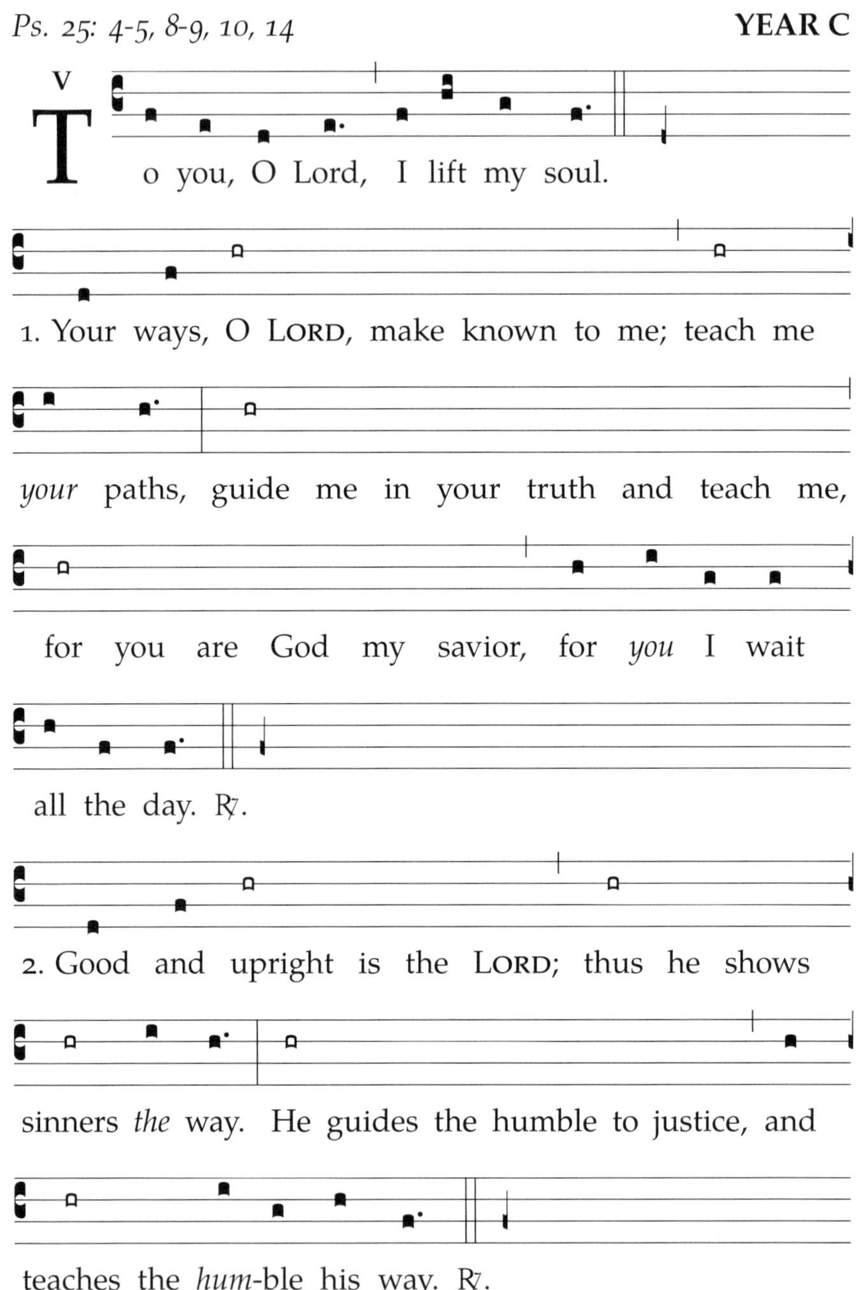

℣
To you, O Lord, I lift my soul.
1. Your ways, O Lord, make known to me; teach me
your paths, guide me in your truth and teach me,
for you are God my savior, for *you* I wait
all the day. ℟.
2. Good and upright is the Lord; thus he shows
sinners *the* way. He guides the humble to justice, and
teaches the *hum*-ble his way. ℟.

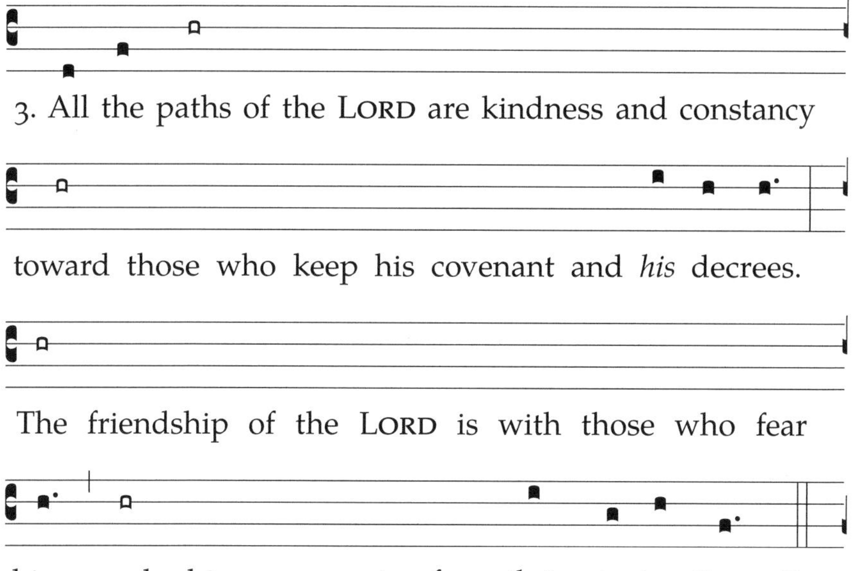
3. All the paths of the LORD are kindness and constancy
toward those who keep his covenant and *his* decrees.
The friendship of the LORD is with those who fear
him, and his covenant, for *their* instruction. ℟.

Second Sunday of Advent

Ps. 72: 1-2, 7-8, 12-13, 17 **YEAR A**

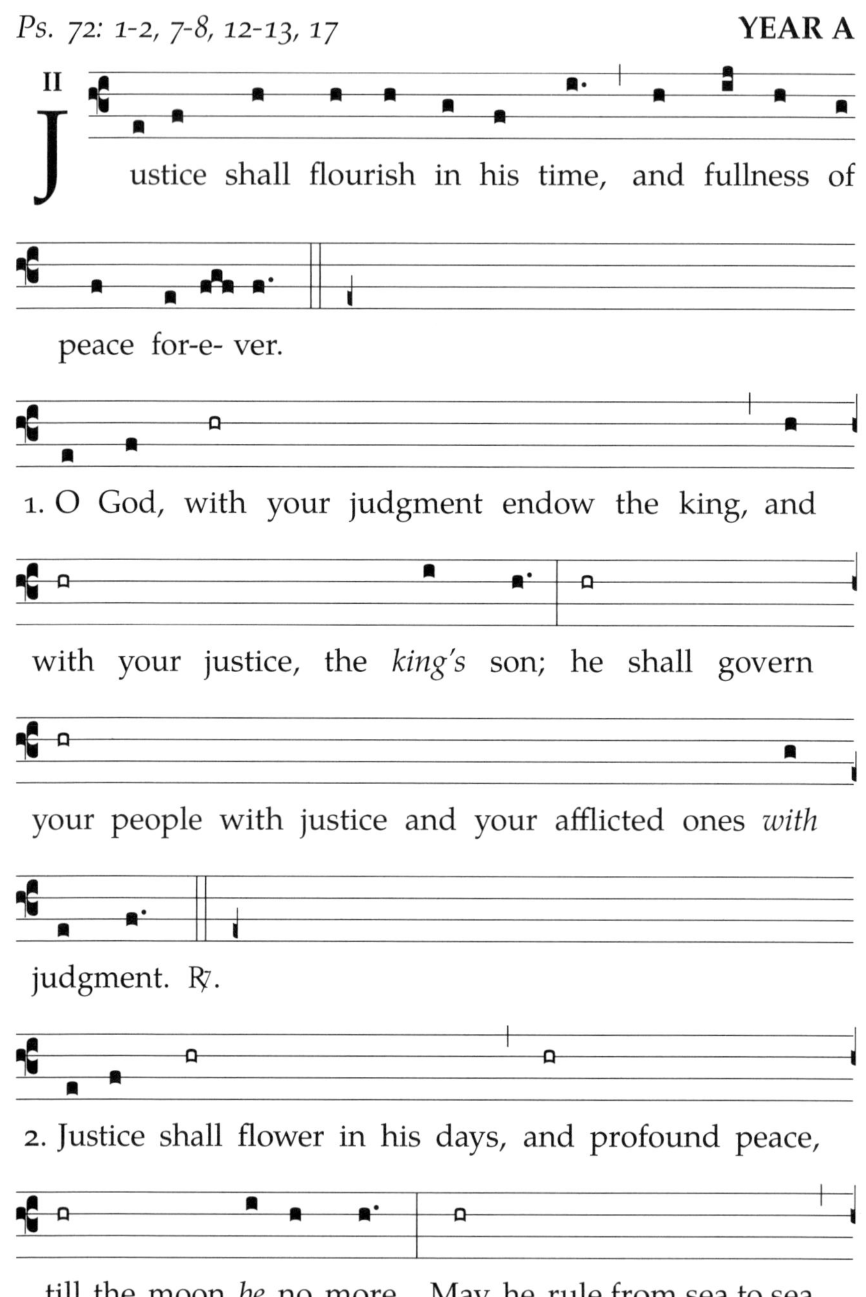

II
Justice shall flourish in his time, and fullness of
peace for-e- ver.
1. O God, with your judgment endow the king, and
with your justice, the *king's* son; he shall govern
your people with justice and your afflicted ones *with*
judgment. ℟.
2. Justice shall flower in his days, and profound peace,
till the moon *be* no more. May he rule from sea to sea,

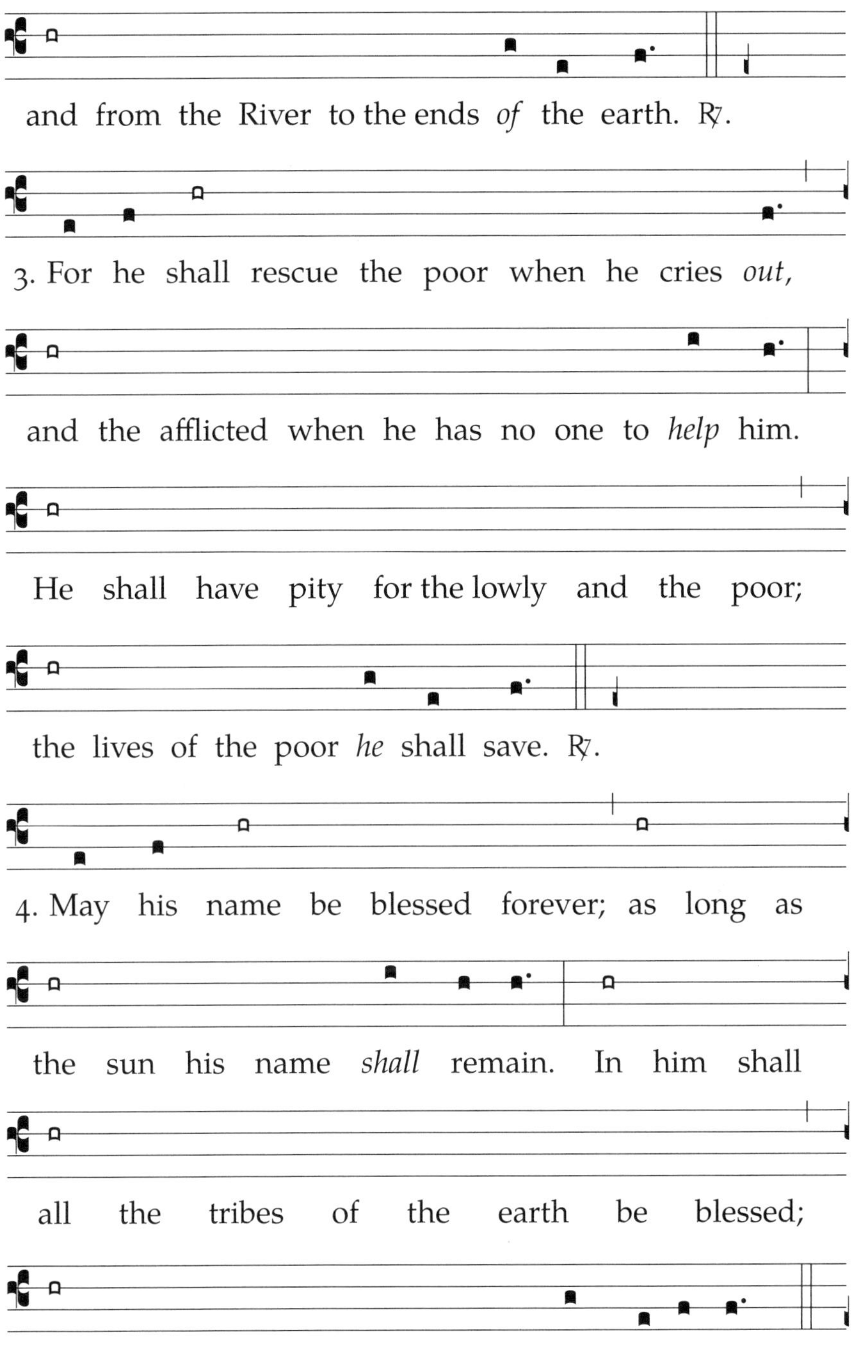
and from the River to the ends *of* the earth. ℟.
3. For he shall rescue the poor when he cries *out,*
and the afflicted when he has no one to *help* him.
He shall have pity for the lowly and the poor;
the lives of the poor *he* shall save. ℟.
4. May his name be blessed forever; as long as
the sun his name *shall* remain. In him shall
all the tribes of the earth be blessed;
all the nations shall proclaim *his* happiness. ℟.

SECOND SUNDAY OF ADVENT

Ps. 85: 9-10, 11-12, 13-14 **YEAR B**

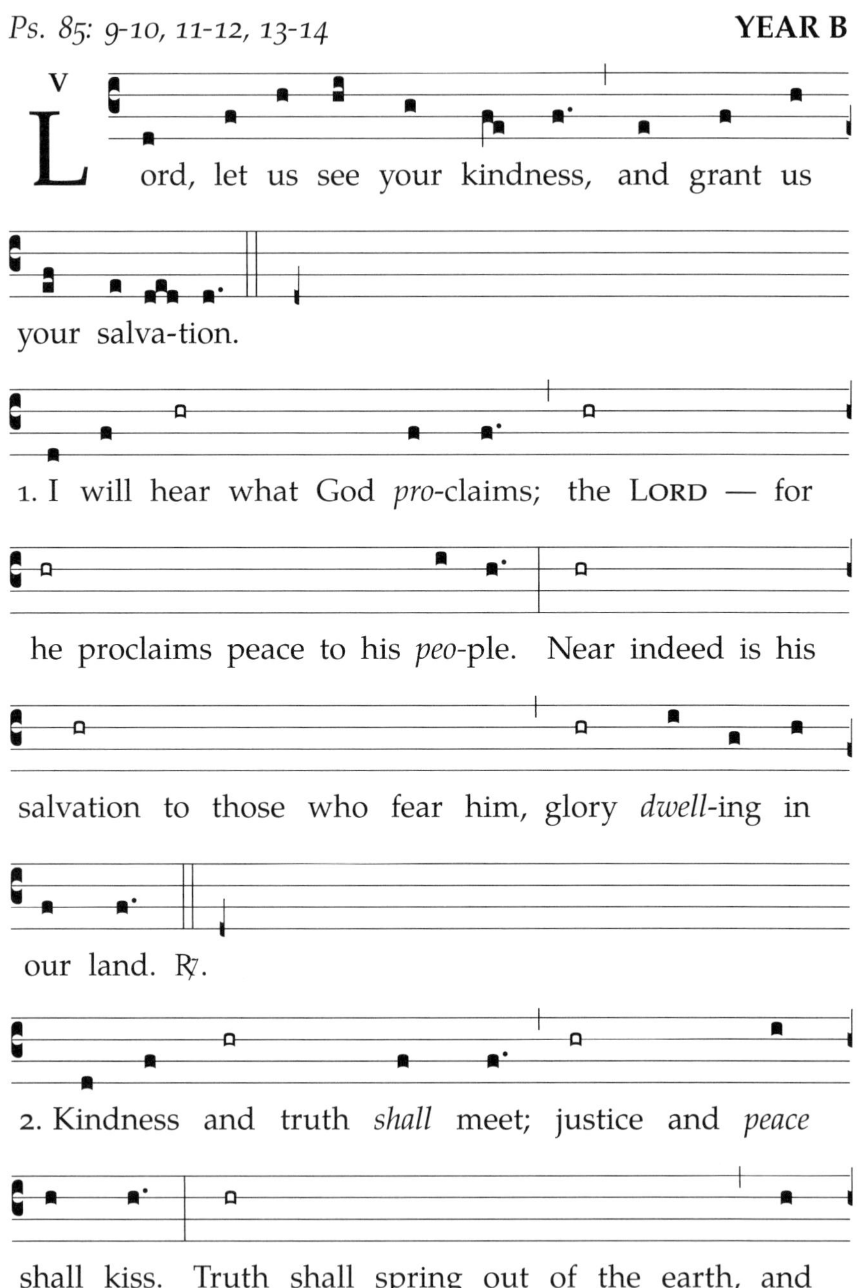
V
Lord, let us see your kindness, and grant us your salvation.
1. I will hear what God *pro*-claims; the LORD — for he proclaims peace to his *peo*-ple. Near indeed is his salvation to those who fear him, glory *dwell*-ing in our land. ℟.
2. Kindness and truth *shall* meet; justice and *peace* shall kiss. Truth shall spring out of the earth, and

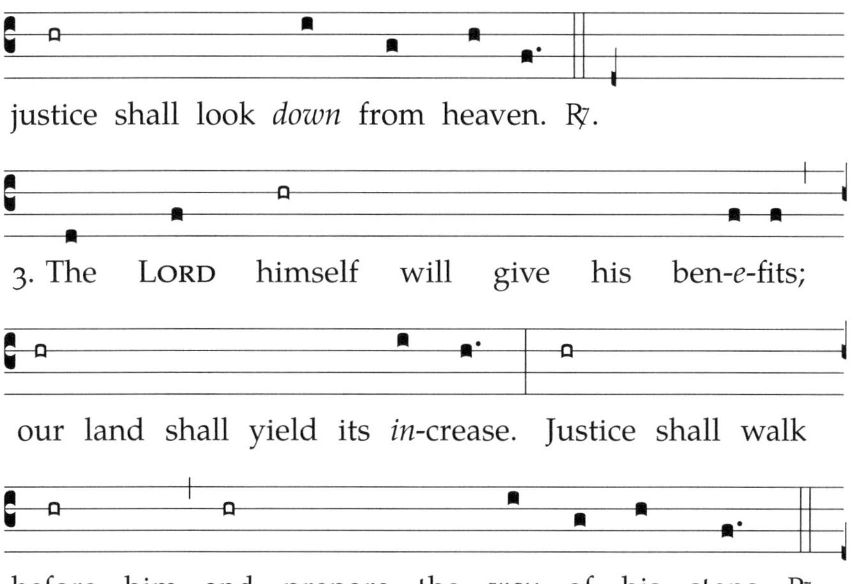
justice shall look *down* from heaven. ℟.
3. The LORD himself will give his ben-*e*-fits;
our land shall yield its *in*-crease. Justice shall walk
before him, and prepare the *way* of his steps. ℟.

Second Sunday of Advent

Ps. 126: 1-2, 2-3, 4-5, 6 **YEAR C**

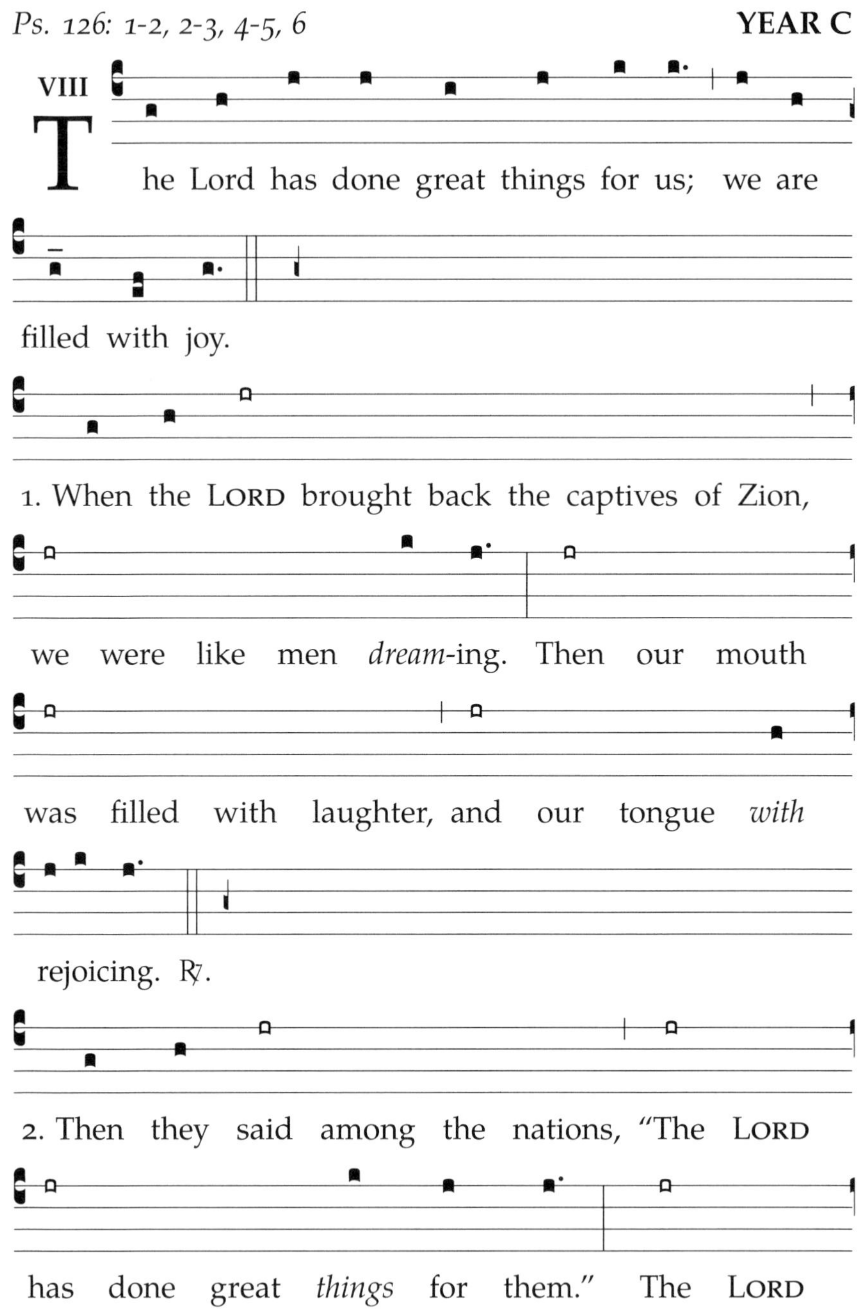
VIII
The Lord has done great things for us; we are
filled with joy.
1. When the LORD brought back the captives of Zion,
we were like men *dream*-ing. Then our mouth
was filled with laughter, and our tongue *with*
rejoicing. ℟.
2. Then they said among the nations, "The LORD
has done great *things* for them." The LORD

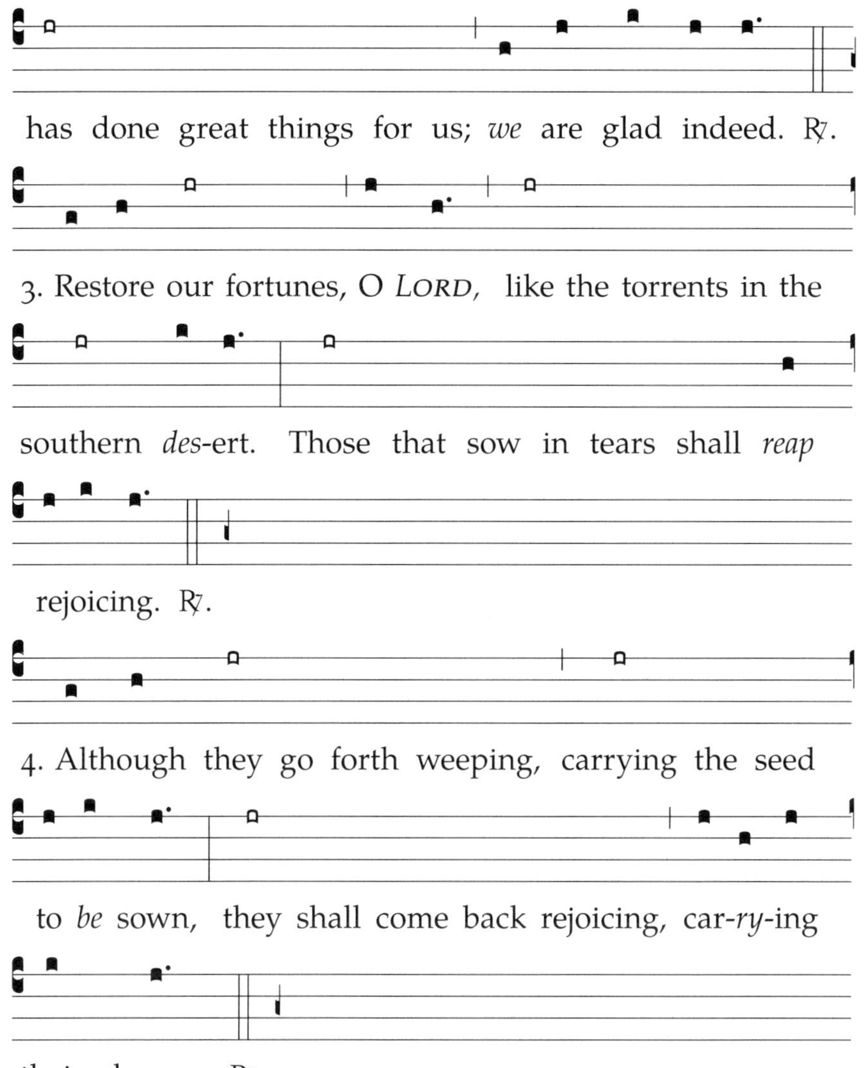
has done great things for us; *we* are glad indeed. ℟.
3. Restore our fortunes, O *LORD,* like the torrents in the
southern *des*-ert. Those that sow in tears shall *reap*
rejoicing. ℟.
4. Although they go forth weeping, carrying the seed
to *be* sown, they shall come back rejoicing, car-*ry*-ing
their sheaves. ℟.

Third Sunday of Advent

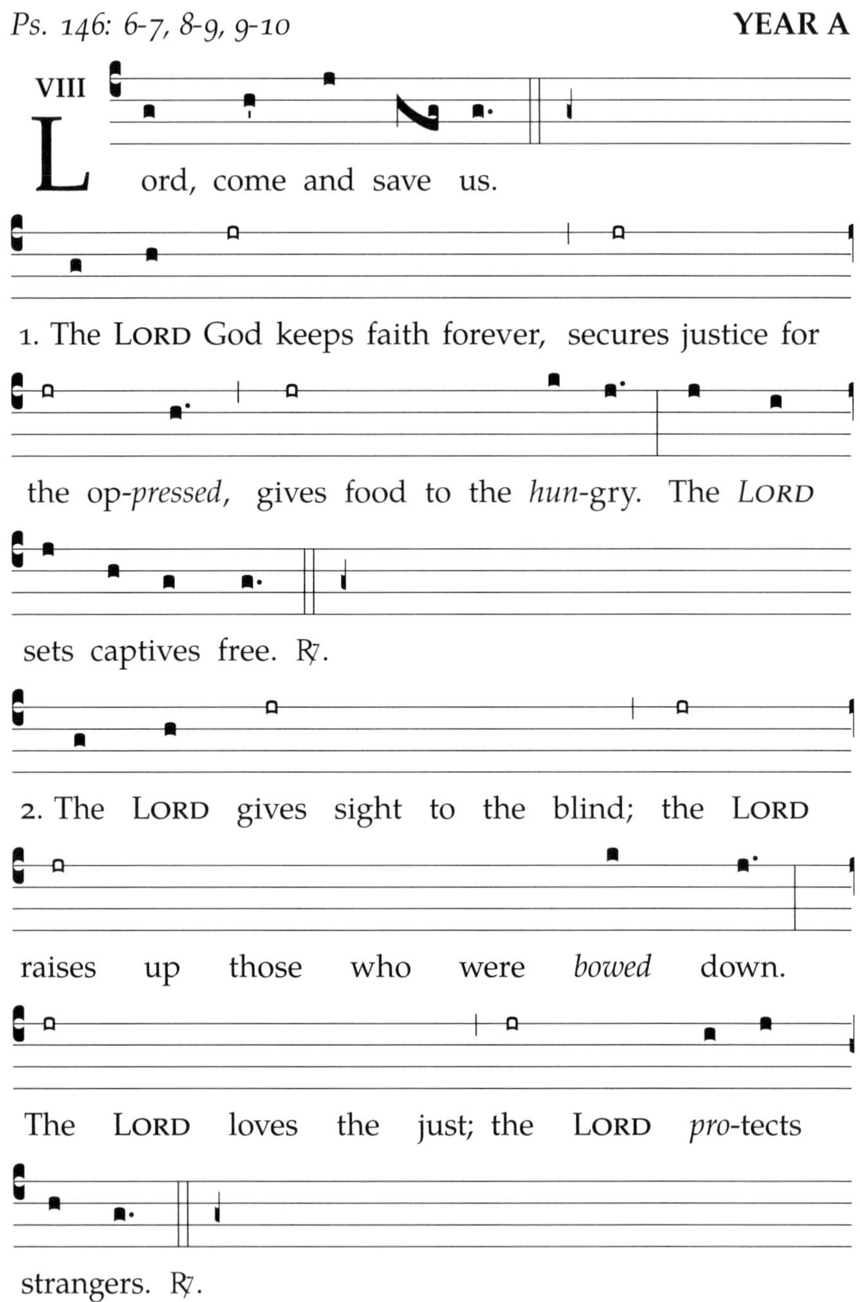

Ps. 146: 6-7, 8-9, 9-10
YEAR A
VIII
Lord, come and save us.
1. The LORD God keeps faith forever, secures justice for
the op-pressed, gives food to the hun-gry. The LORD
sets captives free. ℟.
2. The LORD gives sight to the blind; the LORD
raises up those who were bowed down.
The LORD loves the just; the LORD pro-tects
strangers. ℟.

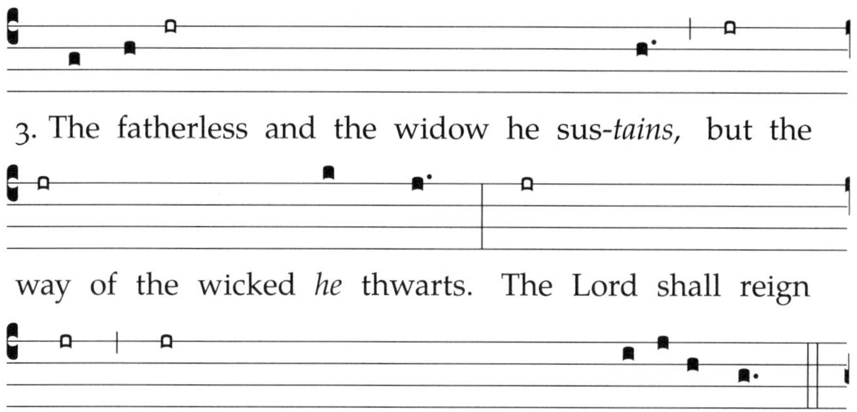
3. The fatherless and the widow he sus-*tains*, but the
way of the wicked *he* thwarts. The Lord shall reign
forever; your God, O Zion, through all *ge*-nerations. ℟.

Third Sunday of Advent

Lk. 1: 46-48, 49-50, 53-54 **YEAR B**

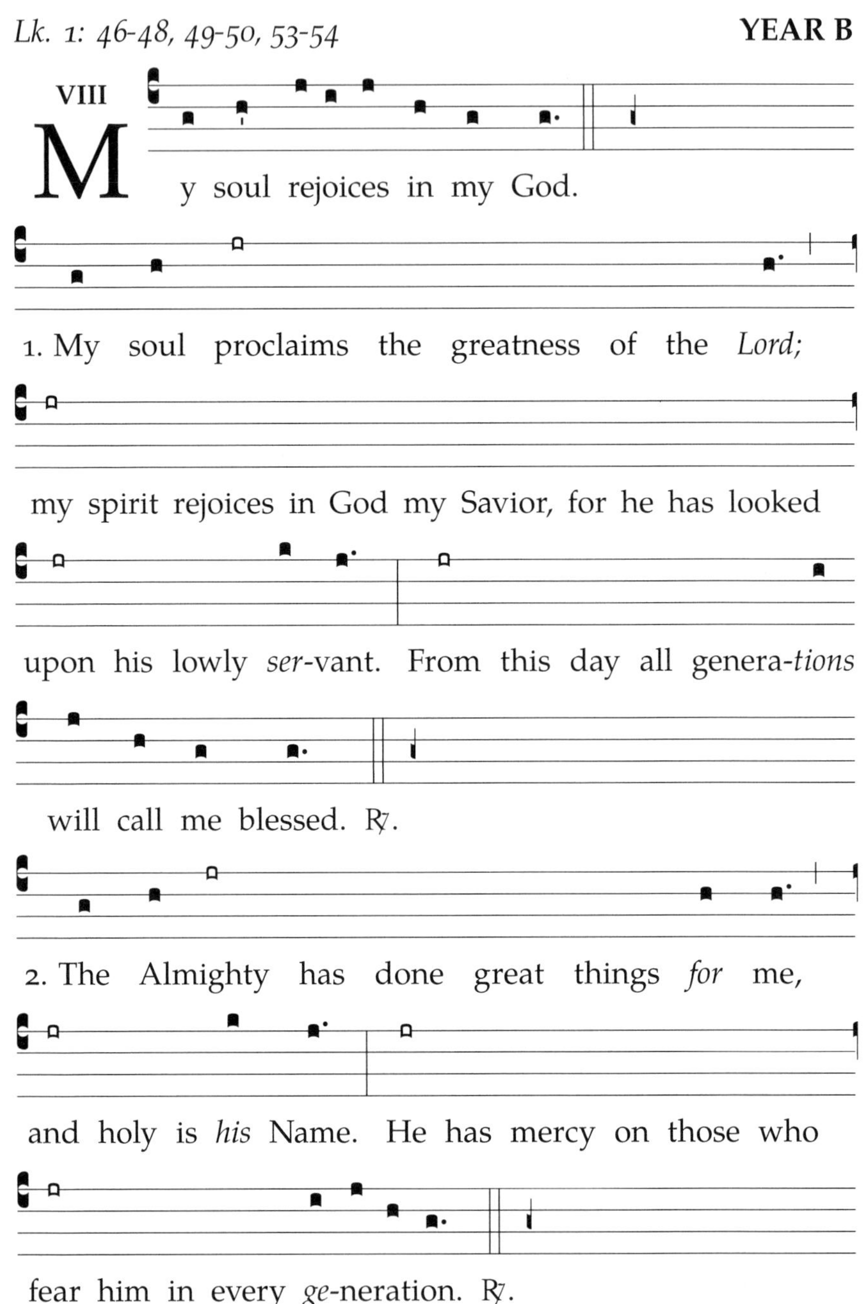
VIII
My soul rejoices in my God.
1. My soul proclaims the greatness of the *Lord;*
my spirit rejoices in God my Savior, for he has looked
upon his lowly *ser*-vant. From this day all genera-*tions*
will call me blessed. ℟.
2. The Almighty has done great things *for* me,
and holy is *his* Name. He has mercy on those who
fear him in every *ge*-neration. ℟.

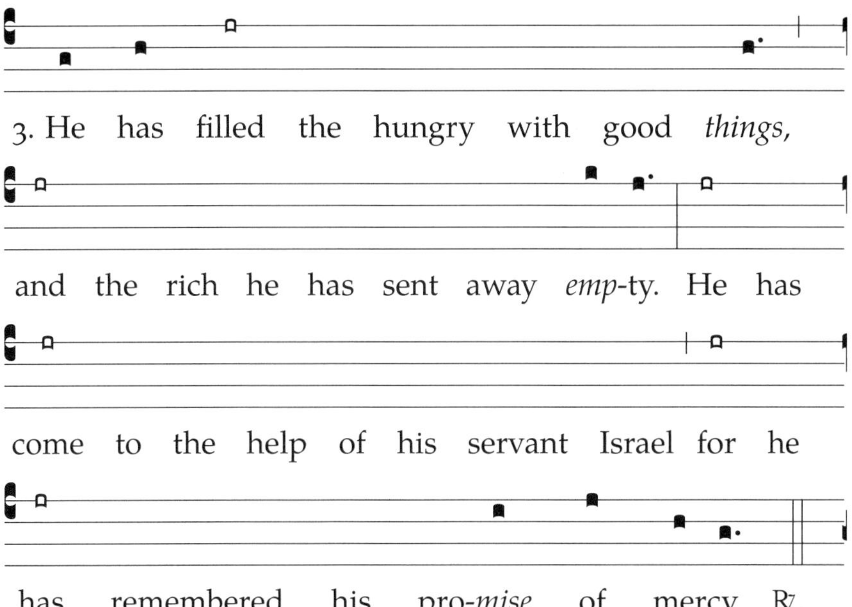
3. He has filled the hungry with good *things,*
and the rich he has sent away *emp*-ty. He has
come to the help of his servant Israel for he
has remembered his pro-*mise* of mercy. ℟.

Third Sunday of Advent

Is. 12: 2-3, 4, 5-6 **YEAR C**

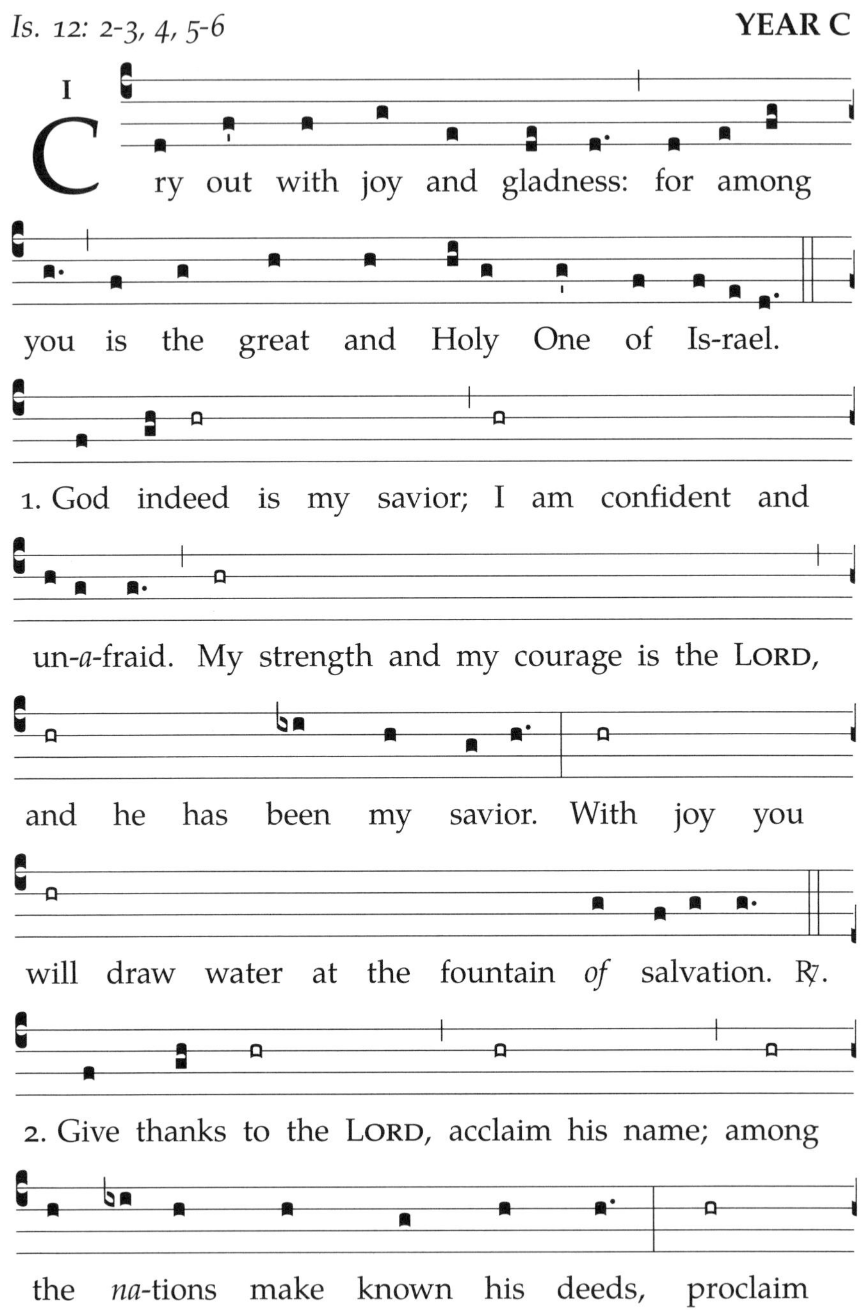
I
Cry out with joy and gladness: for among
you is the great and Holy One of Is-rael.
1. God indeed is my savior; I am confident and
un-*a*-fraid. My strength and my courage is the LORD,
and he has been my savior. With joy you
will draw water at the fountain *of* salvation. ℟.
2. Give thanks to the LORD, acclaim his name; among
the *na*-tions make known his deeds, proclaim

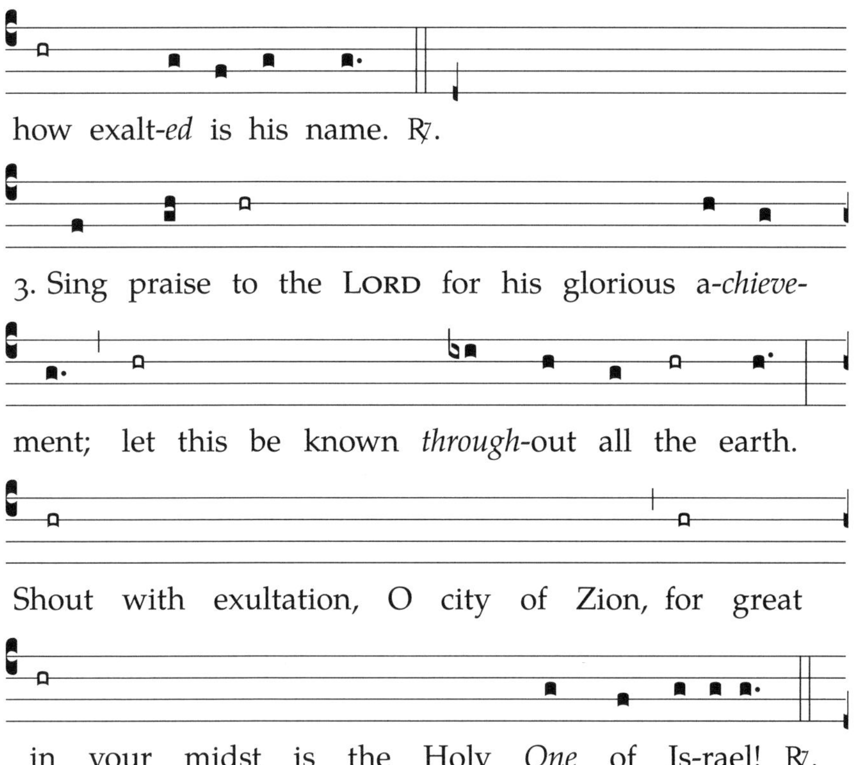
how exalt-*ed* is his name. ℟.
3. Sing praise to the LORD for his glorious a-*chieve*-
ment; let this be known *through*-out all the earth.
Shout with exultation, O city of Zion, for great
in your midst is the Holy *One* of Is-rael! ℟.

Fourth Sunday of Advent

Ps. 24: 1-2, 3-4, 5-6 **YEAR A**

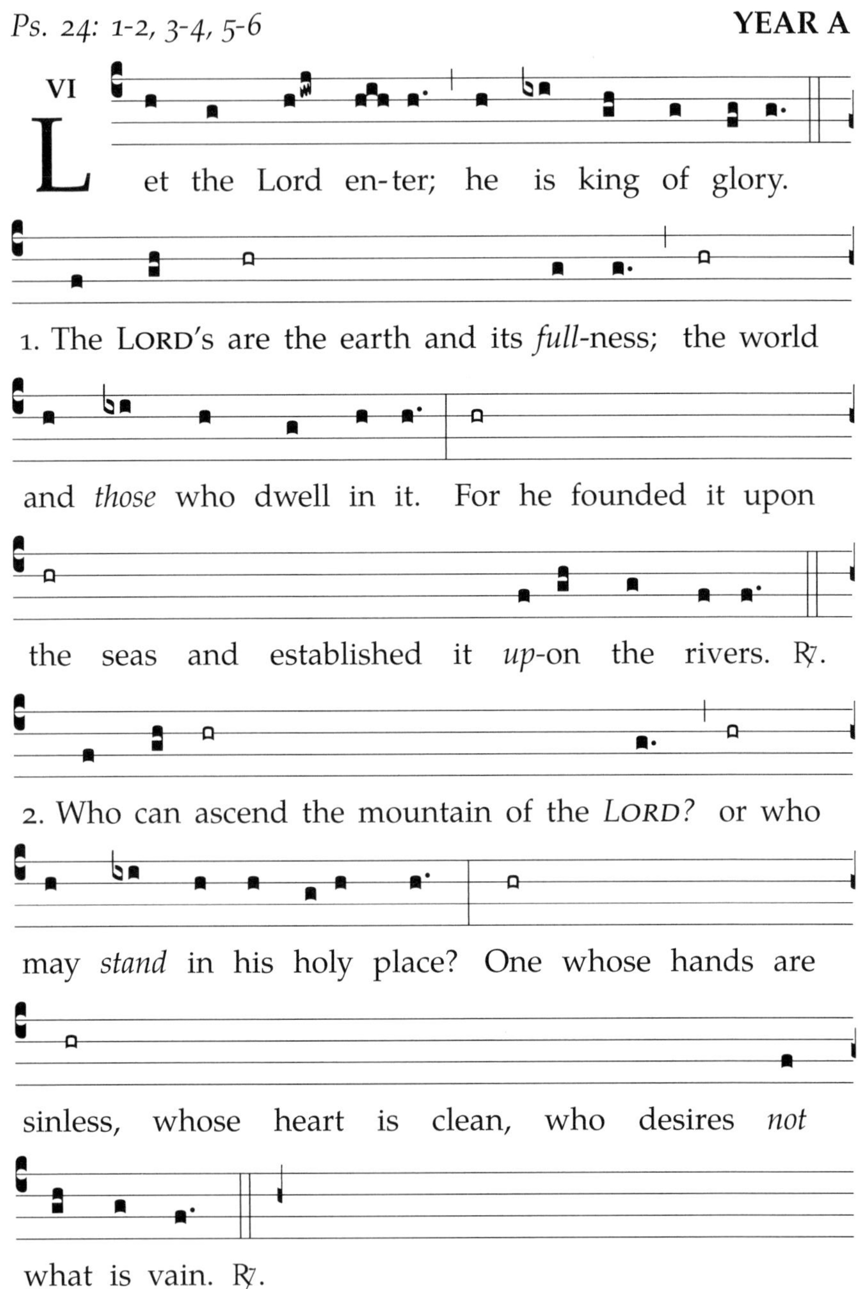
VI
Let the Lord en-ter; he is king of glory.
1. The LORD's are the earth and its *full*-ness; the world
and *those* who dwell in it. For he founded it upon
the seas and established it *up*-on the rivers. ℟.
2. Who can ascend the mountain of the *LORD?* or who
may *stand* in his holy place? One whose hands are
sinless, whose heart is clean, who desires *not*
what is vain. ℟.

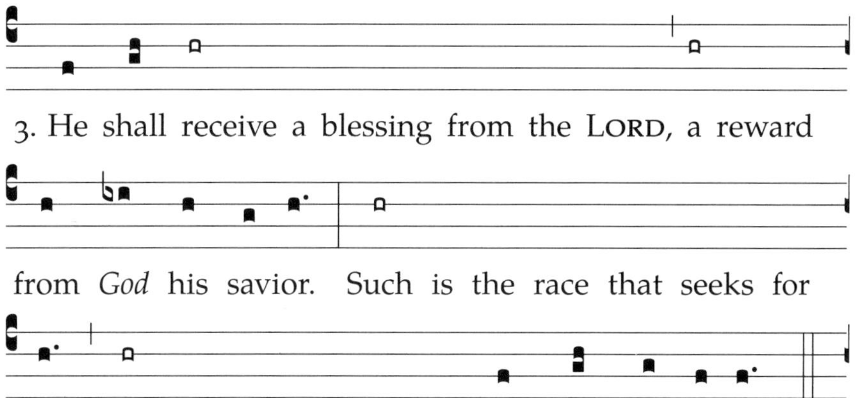
3. He shall receive a blessing from the LORD, a reward
from *God* his savior. Such is the race that seeks for
him, that seeks the face of *the* God of Jacob. ℟.

Fourth Sunday of Advent

Ps. 89: 2-3, 4-5, 27, 29 **YEAR B**

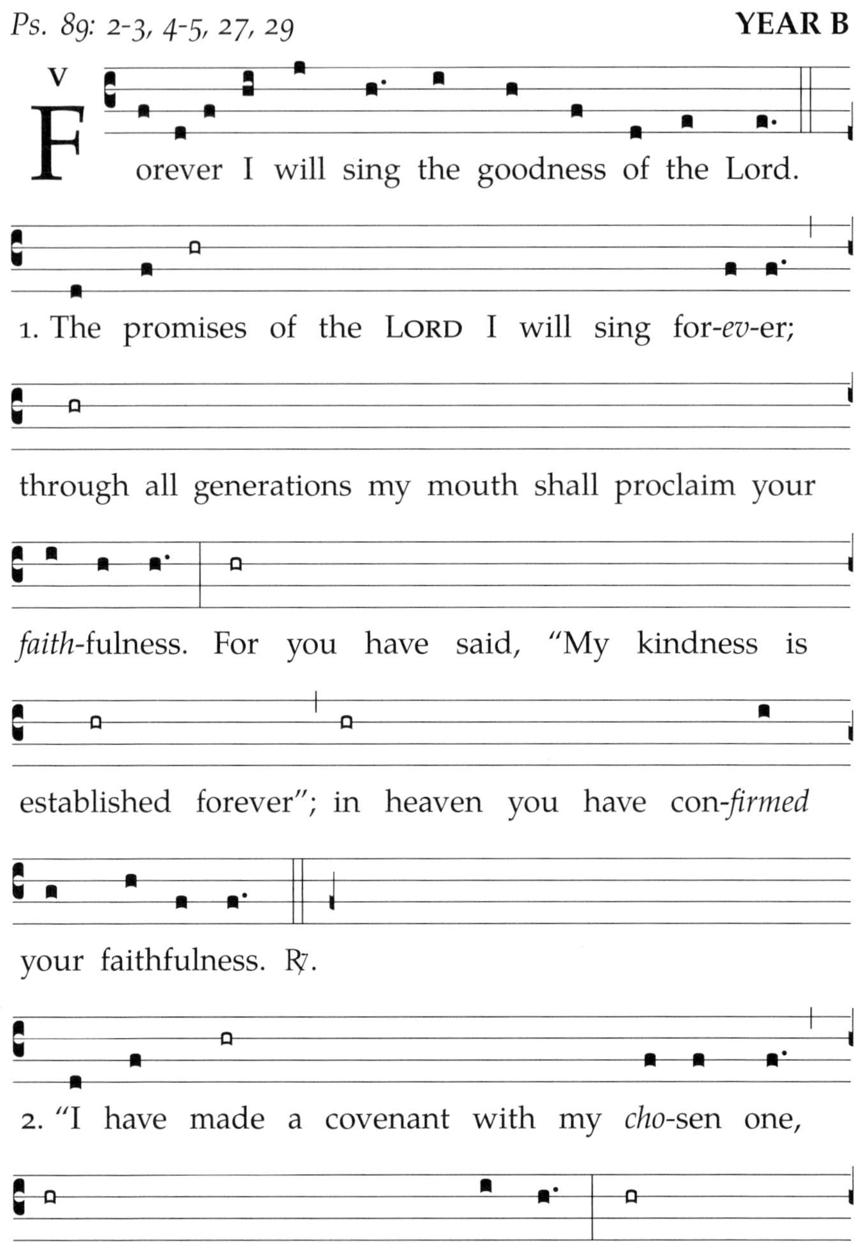

V
Forever I will sing the goodness of the Lord.
1. The promises of the LORD I will sing for-*ev*-er;
through all generations my mouth shall proclaim your
faith-fulness. For you have said, "My kindness is
established forever"; in heaven you have con-*firmed*
your faithfulness. ℟.
2. "I have made a covenant with my *cho*-sen one,
I have sworn to David my *ser*-vant: Forever will I

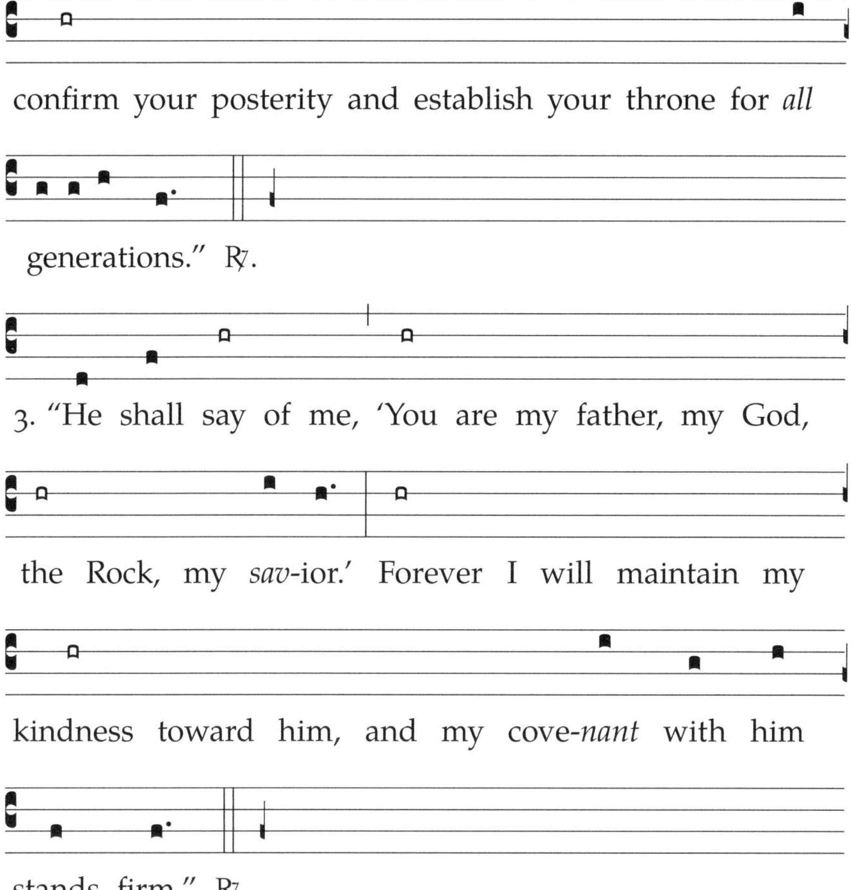
confirm your posterity and establish your throne for *all*
generations." ℟.
3. "He shall say of me, 'You are my father, my God,
the Rock, my *sav*-ior.' Forever I will maintain my
kindness toward him, and my cove-*nant* with him
stands firm." ℟.

Fourth Sunday of Advent

Ps. 80: 2-3, 15-16, 18-19 **YEAR C**

I
Lord, make us turn to you; let us see your face
and we shall be saved.
1. O shepherd of Israel, hearken, from your throne
upon the *cher*-ubim, shine forth. Rouse your power,
and *come* to save us. ℟.
2. Once again, O Lord of hosts, look down from *heav*-en,
and see; take care of this vine, and protect what your
right hand has planted; the son of man whom *you*

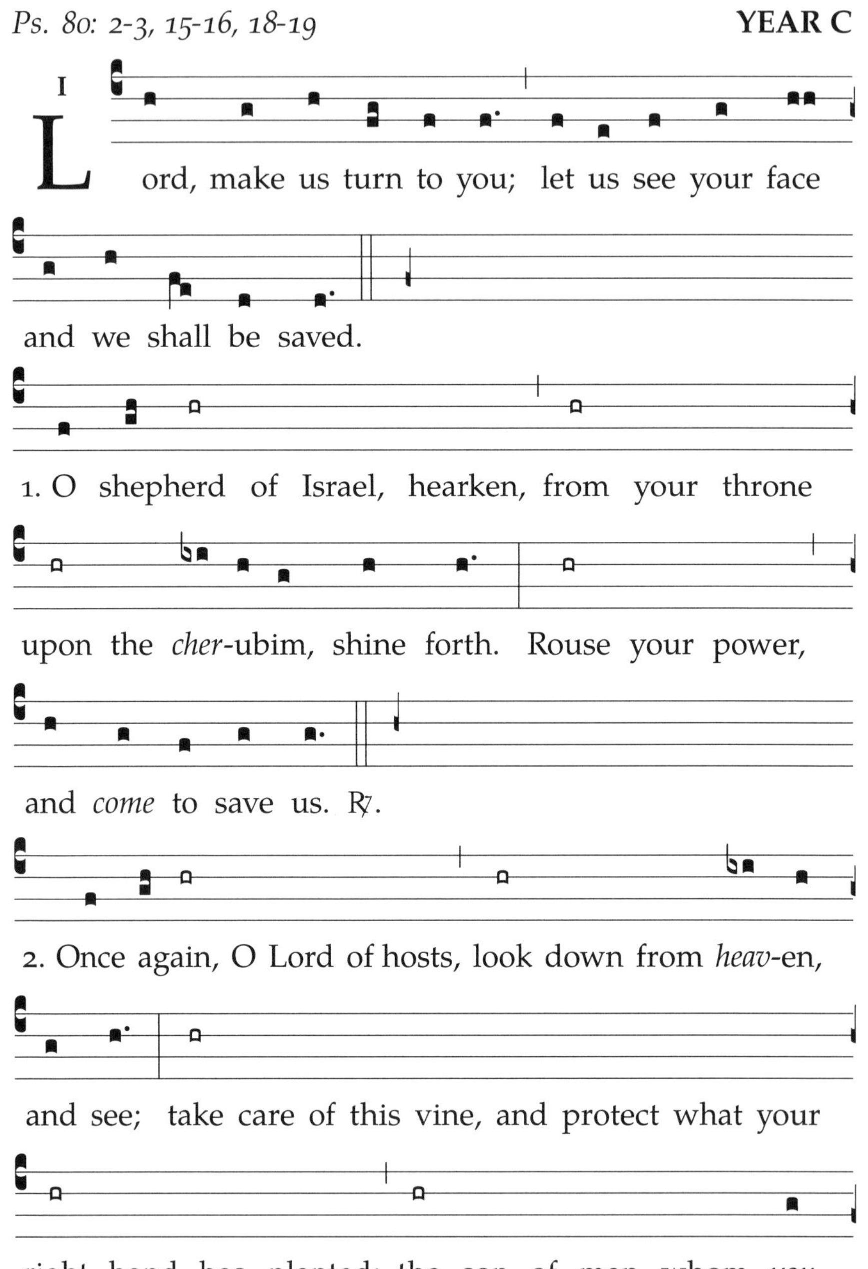

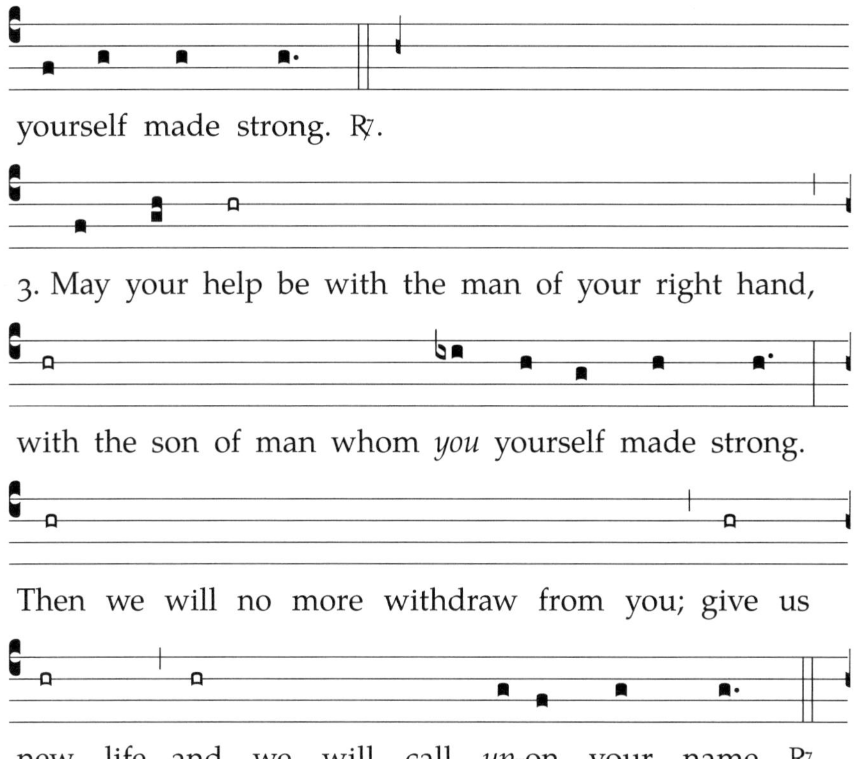
yourself made strong. ℟.
3. May your help be with the man of your right hand,
with the son of man whom *you* yourself made strong.
Then we will no more withdraw from you; give us
new life, and we will call *up*-on your name. ℟.

Christmas

Christmas Vigil Mass

Ps. 89: 4-5, 16-17, 27, 29 **YEAR ABC**

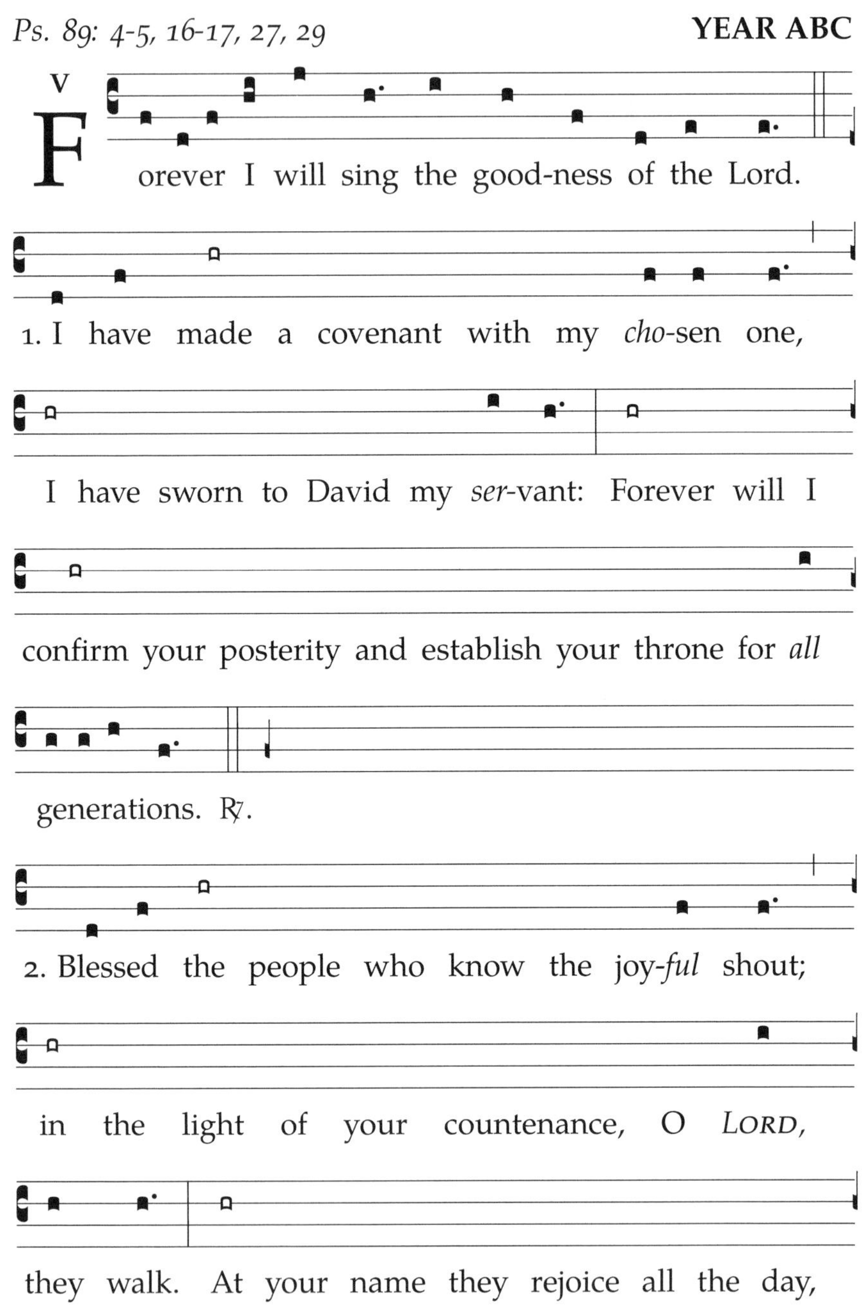

℣
Forever I will sing the good-ness of the Lord.
1. I have made a covenant with my *cho*-sen one,
I have sworn to David my *ser*-vant: Forever will I
confirm your posterity and establish your throne for *all*
generations. ℟.
2. Blessed the people who know the joy-*ful* shout;
in the light of your countenance, O LORD,
they walk. At your name they rejoice all the day,

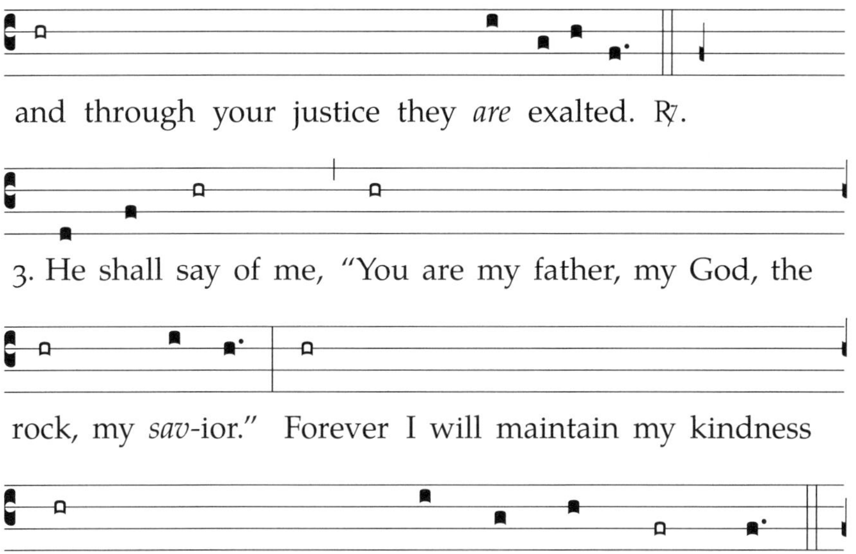
and through your justice they *are* exalted. ℟.
3. He shall say of me, "You are my father, my God, the
rock, my *sav*-ior." Forever I will maintain my kindness
toward him, and my cove-*nant* with him stands firm. ℟.

Christmas
Mass during the Night

Ps. 96: 1-2, 2-3, 11-12, 13 **YEAR ABC**

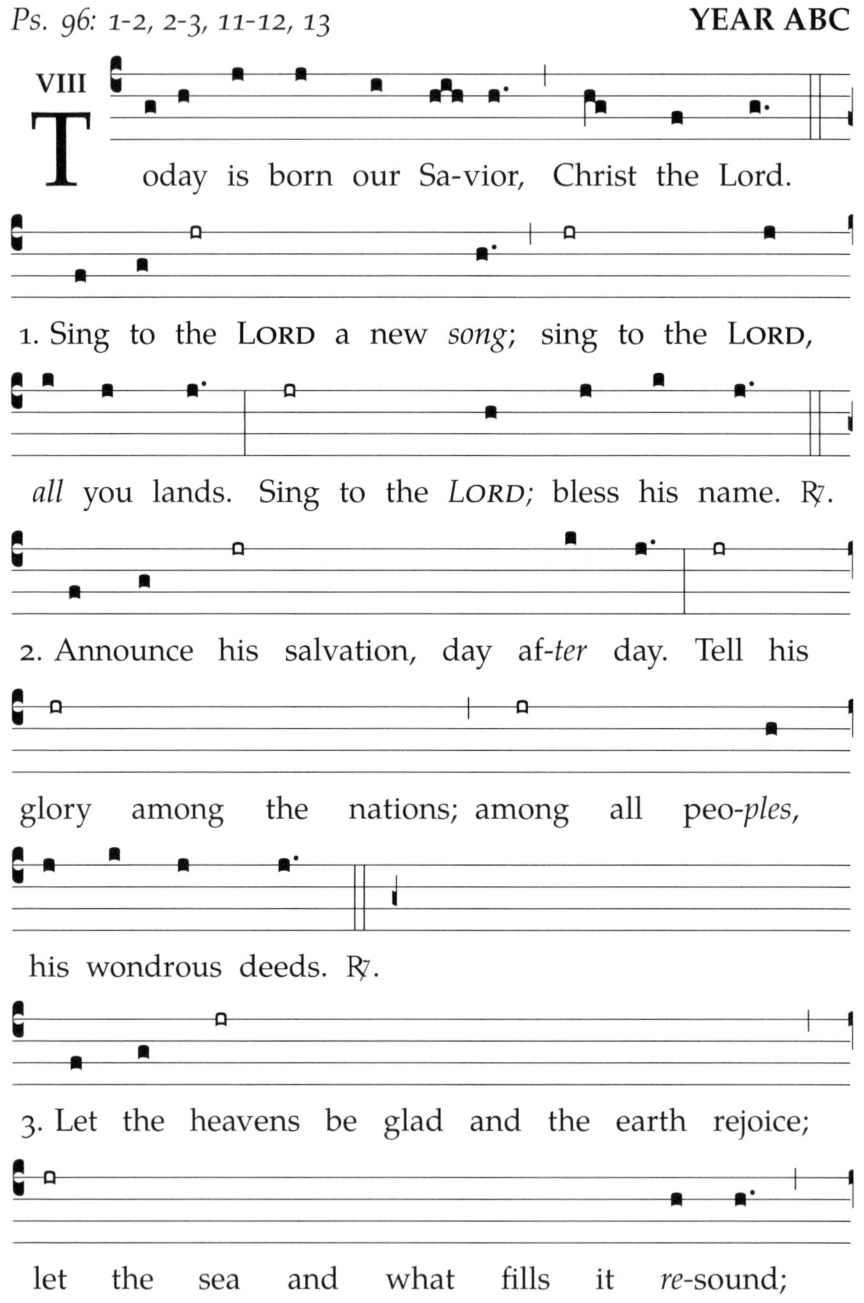
VIII
Today is born our Sa-vior, Christ the Lord.
1. Sing to the LORD a new *song;* sing to the LORD,
all you lands. Sing to the *LORD;* bless his name. ℟.
2. Announce his salvation, day af-*ter* day. Tell his
glory among the nations; among all peo-*ples,*
his wondrous deeds. ℟.
3. Let the heavens be glad and the earth rejoice;
let the sea and what fills it *re*-sound;

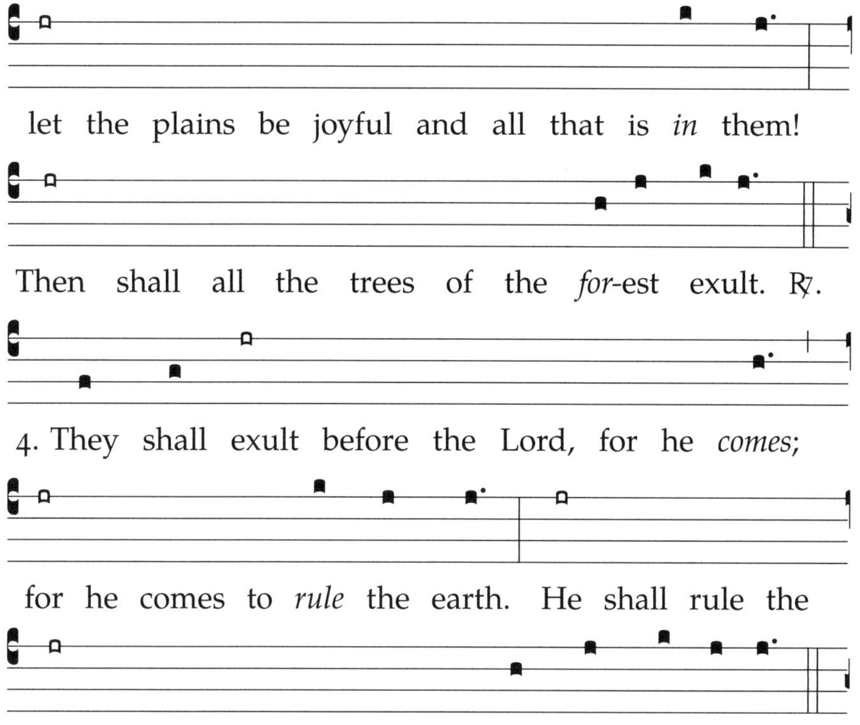
let the plains be joyful and all that is *in* them!
Then shall all the trees of the *for*-est exult. ℟.
4. They shall exult before the Lord, for he *comes;*
for he comes to *rule* the earth. He shall rule the
world with justice and the peo-*ples* with constancy. ℟.

Christmas
Mass at Dawn

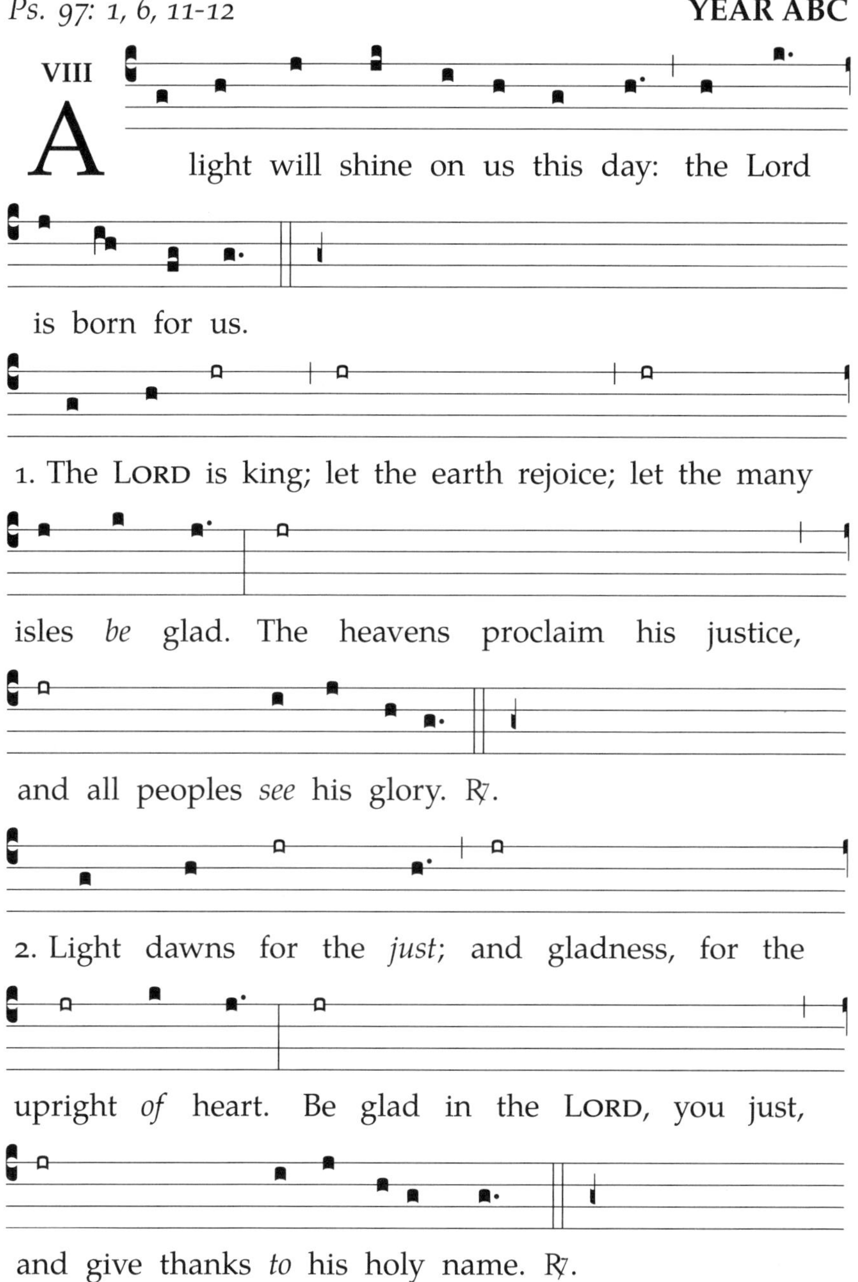
Ps. 97: 1, 6, 11-12
YEAR ABC
VIII
A light will shine on us this day: the Lord
is born for us.
1. The LORD is king; let the earth rejoice; let the many
isles *be* glad. The heavens proclaim his justice,
and all peoples *see* his glory. ℟.
2. Light dawns for the *just*; and gladness, for the
upright *of* heart. Be glad in the LORD, you just,
and give thanks *to* his holy name. ℟.

CHRISTMAS
MASS DURING THE DAY

Ps. 98: 1, 2-3, 3-4, 5-6 **YEAR ABC**

VIII
All the ends of the earth have seen the saving
power of God.
1. Sing to the LORD a new song, for he has done
won-*drous* deeds; his right hand has won victory for
him, his holy arm. ℟.
2. The LORD has made his salvation known:
in the sight of the nations he has revealed
his *jus*-tice. He has remembered his kindness

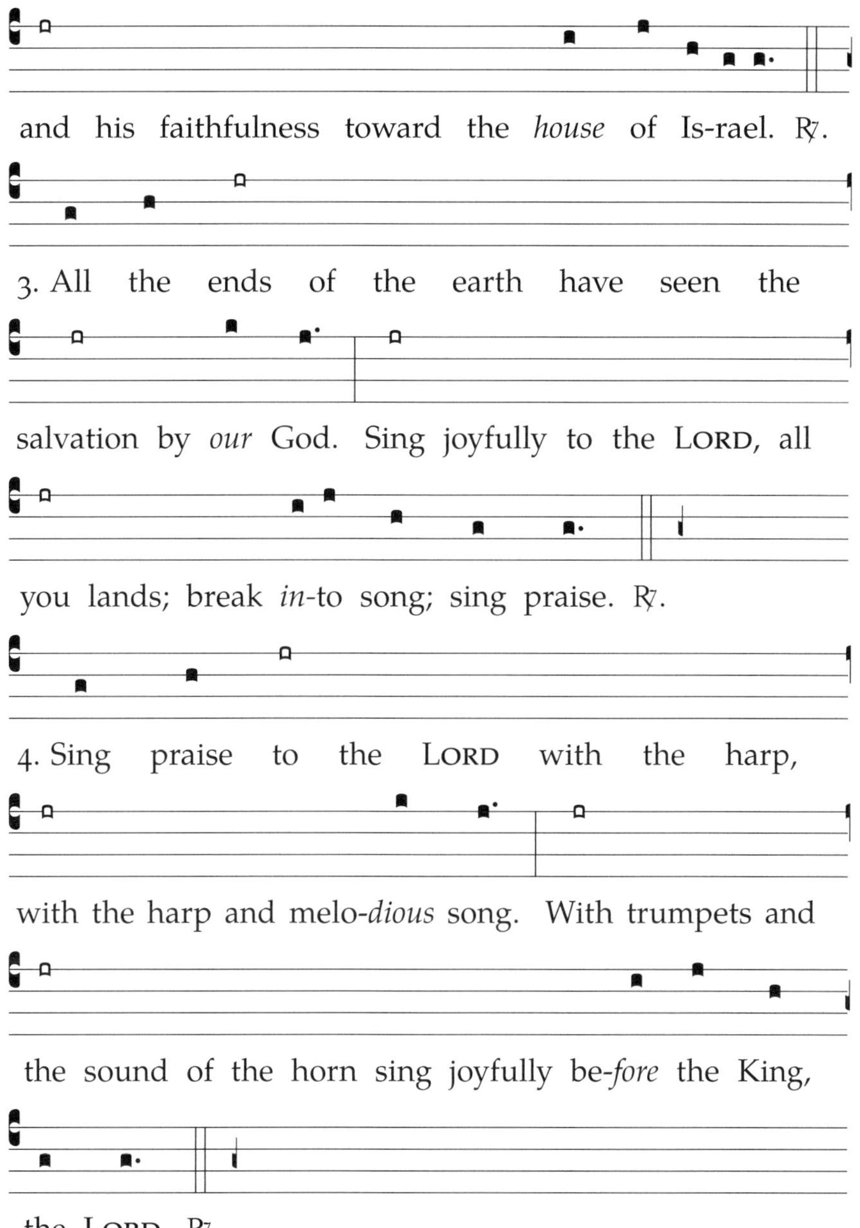

and his faithfulness toward the *house* of Is-rael. ℟.
3. All the ends of the earth have seen the
salvation by *our* God. Sing joyfully to the LORD, all
you lands; break *in*-to song; sing praise. ℟.
4. Sing praise to the LORD with the harp,
with the harp and melo-*dious* song. With trumpets and
the sound of the horn sing joyfully be-*fore* the King,
the LORD. ℟.

Holy Family

Ps. 128: 1-2, 3, 4-5 **YEAR ABC**

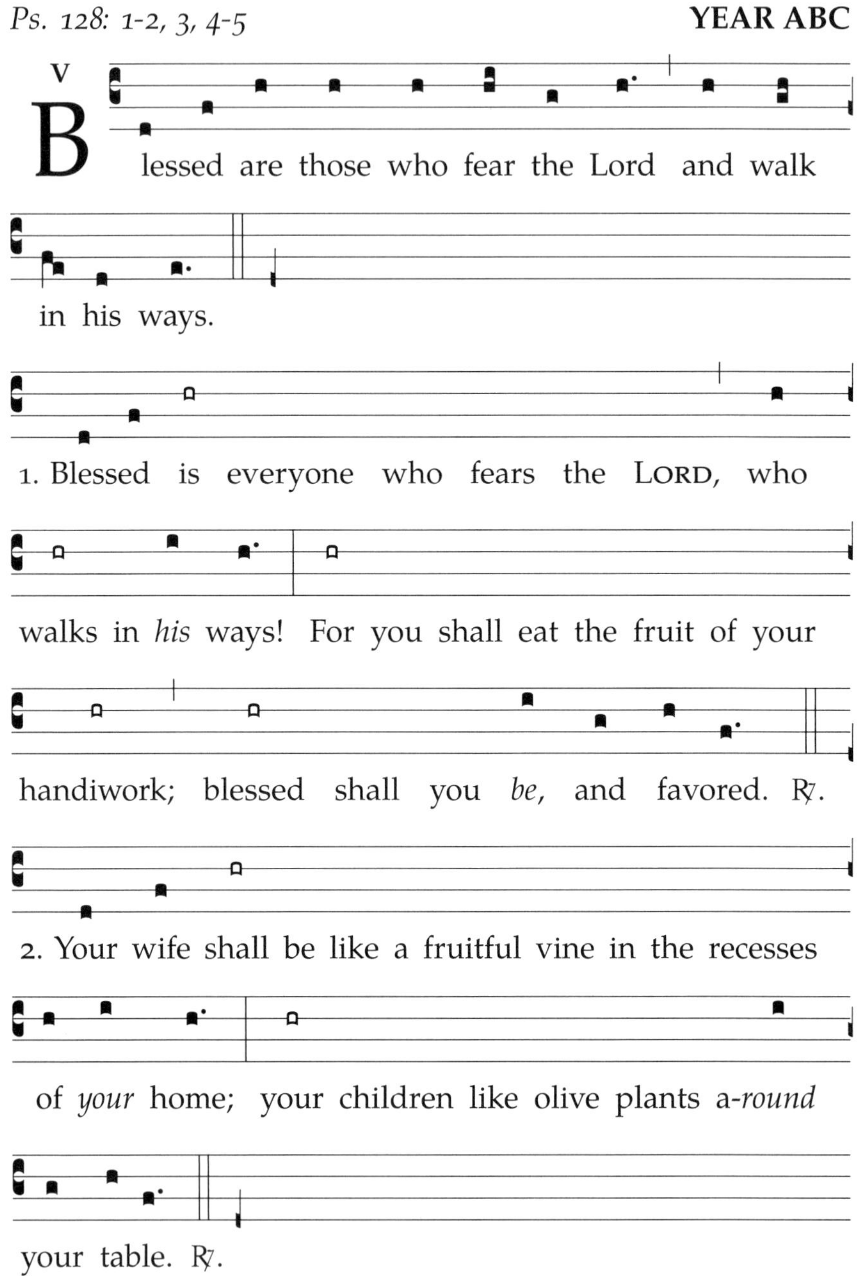

V
Blessed are those who fear the Lord and walk in his ways.
1. Blessed is everyone who fears the LORD, who walks in *his* ways! For you shall eat the fruit of your handiwork; blessed shall you *be,* and favored. ℟.
2. Your wife shall be like a fruitful vine in the recesses of *your* home; your children like olive plants a-*round* your table. ℟.

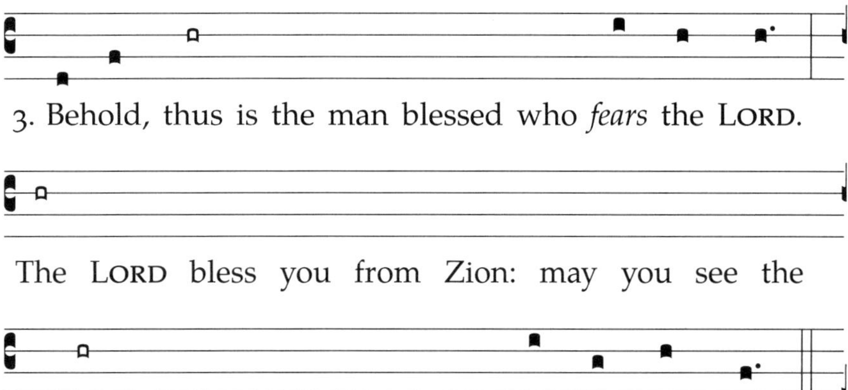

3. Behold, thus is the man blessed who *fears* the LORD.

The LORD bless you from Zion: may you see the

prosperity of Jerusalem all the *days* of your life. ℟.

Holy Family (alternate text)

Ps. 105: 1-2, 3-4, 6-7, 8-9 **YEAR B**

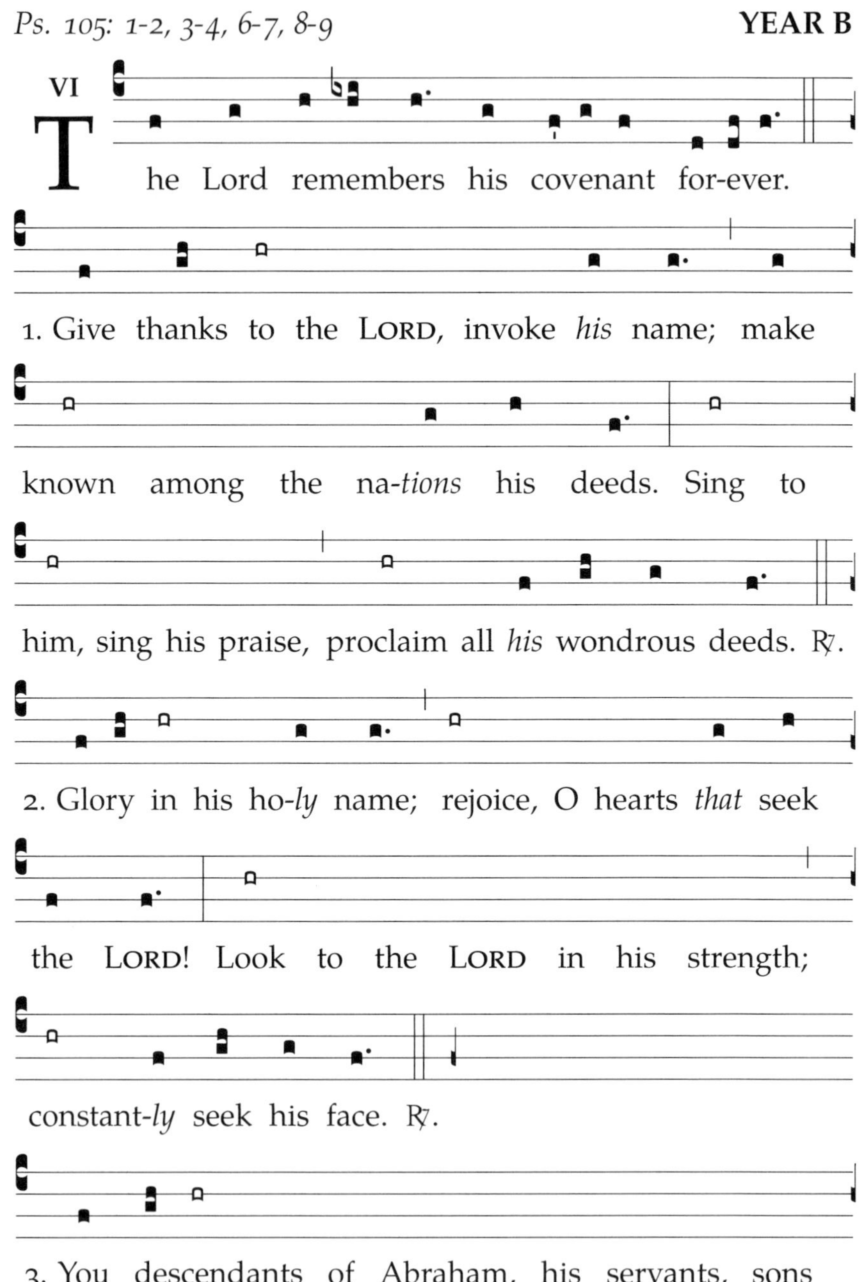
VI
The Lord remembers his covenant for-ever.
1. Give thanks to the LORD, invoke *his* name; make
known among the na-*tions* his deeds. Sing to
him, sing his praise, proclaim all *his* wondrous deeds. ℟.
2. Glory in his ho-*ly* name; rejoice, O hearts *that* seek
the LORD! Look to the LORD in his strength;
constant-*ly* seek his face. ℟.
3. You descendants of Abraham, his servants, sons

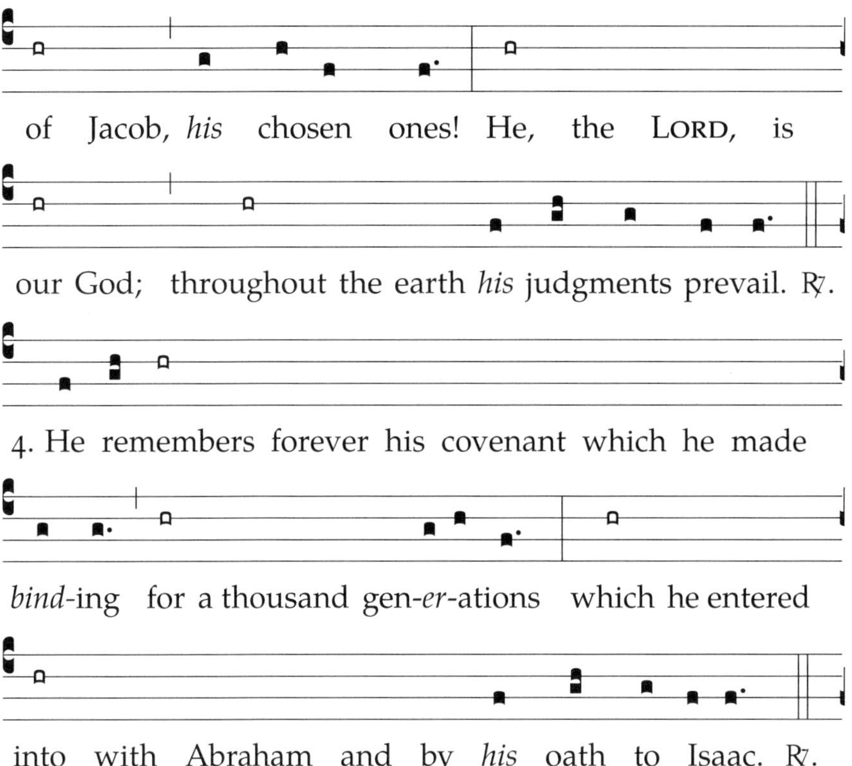
of Jacob, *his* chosen ones! He, the LORD, is
our God; throughout the earth *his* judgments prevail. ℟.
4. He remembers forever his covenant which he made
bind-ing for a thousand gen-*er*-ations which he entered
into with Abraham and by *his* oath to Isaac. ℟.

Holy Family (alternate text)

Ps. 84: 2-3, 5-6, 9-10 **YEAR C**

VI
Blessed are they who dwell in your house,
O Lord.
1. How lovely is your dwelling place, O Lord of hosts!
My soul yearns and pines for the courts *of* the
Lord. My heart and my flesh cry out *for* the
living God. ℟.
2. Happy they who dwell in your house. Continual-*ly*
they praise you. Happy the men whose strength

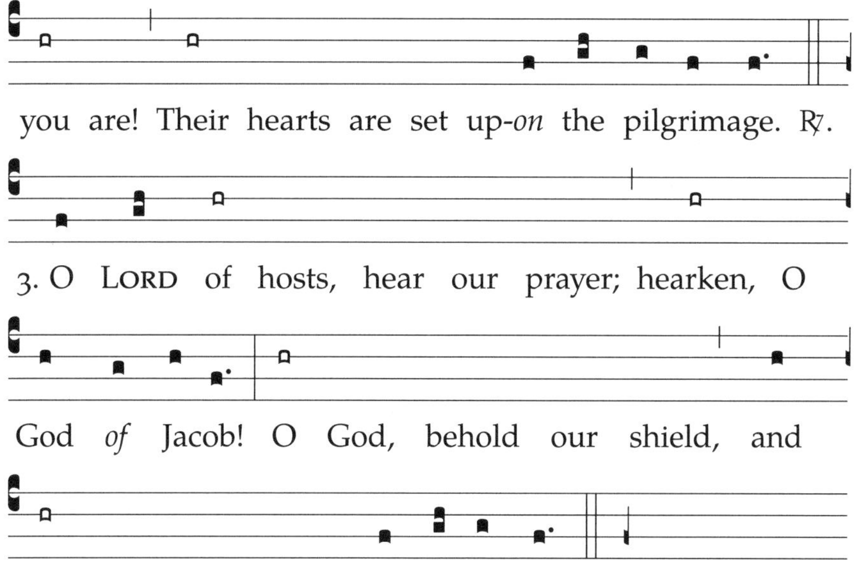
you are! Their hearts are set up-*on* the pilgrimage. ℟.
3. O LORD of hosts, hear our prayer; hearken, O
God *of* Jacob! O God, behold our shield, and
look upon the face of *your* anointed. ℟.

Mary, Mother of God

Ps. 67: 2-3, 5, 6, 8 **YEAR ABC**

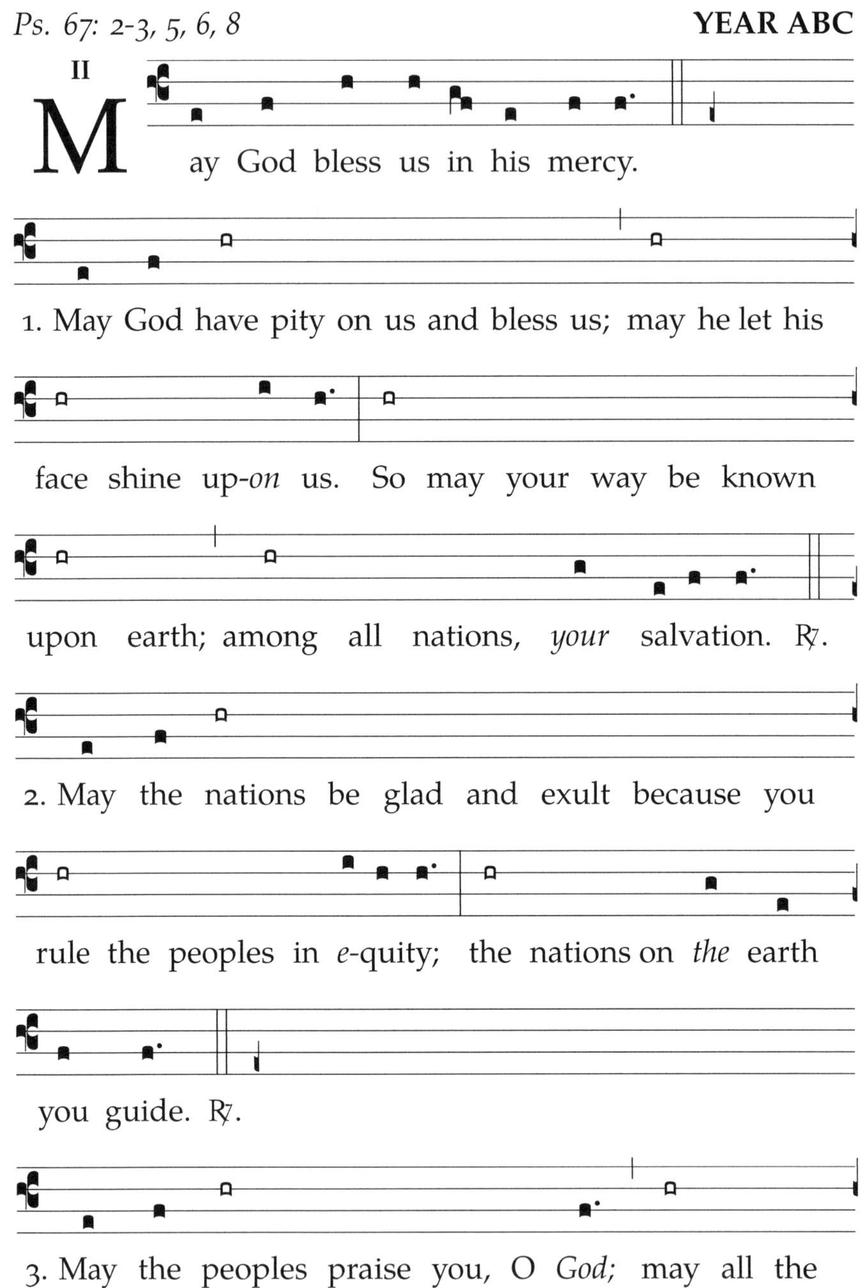
II
May God bless us in his mercy.
1. May God have pity on us and bless us; may he let his
face shine up-*on* us. So may your way be known
upon earth; among all nations, *your* salvation. ℟.
2. May the nations be glad and exult because you
rule the peoples in *e*-quity; the nations on *the* earth
you guide. ℟.
3. May the peoples praise you, O *God;* may all the

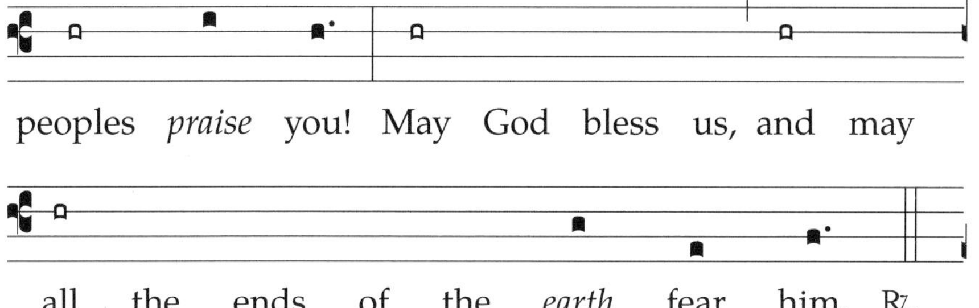
peoples praise you! May God bless us, and may
all the ends of the earth fear him. ℟.

Second Sunday after the Nativity

Ps. 147: 12-13, 14-15, 19-20 **YEAR ABC**

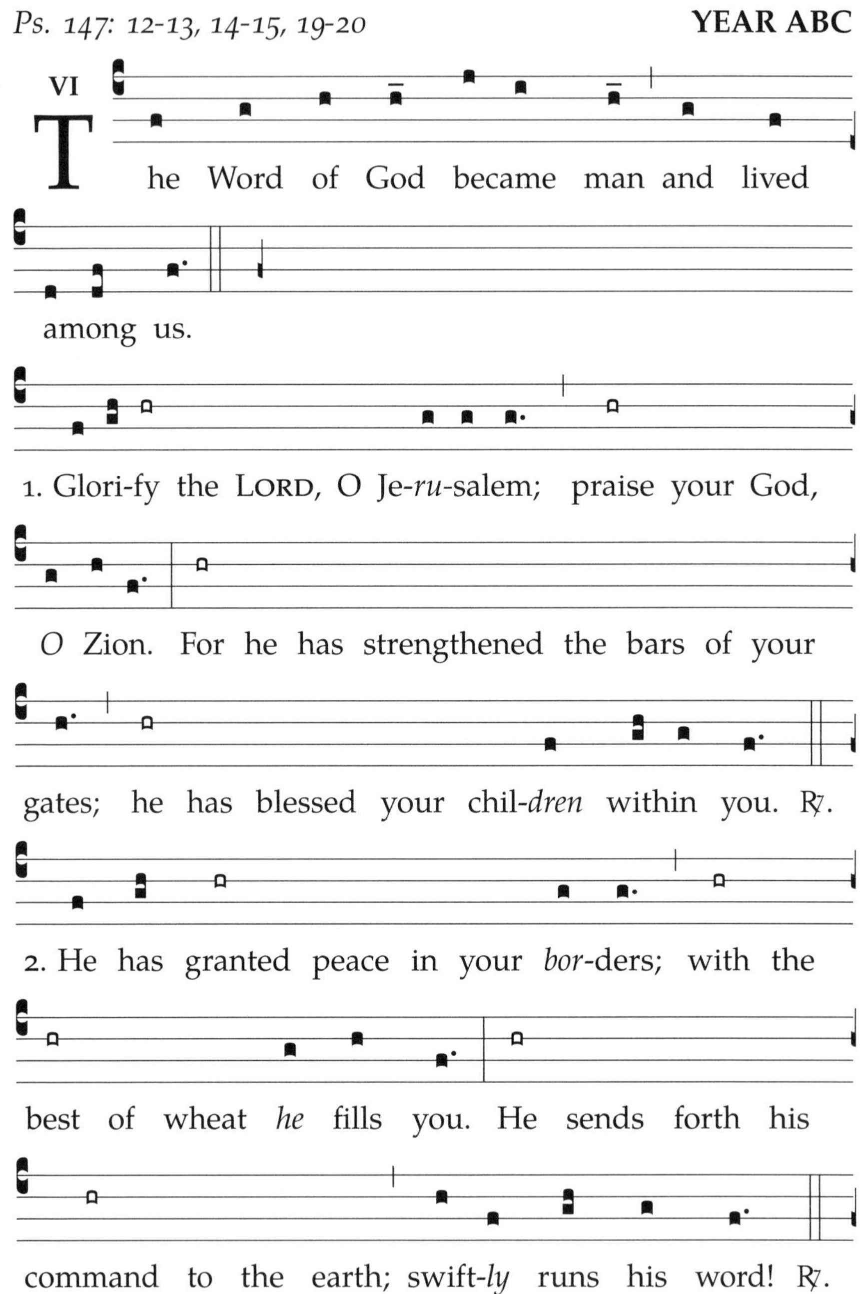
VI
The Word of God became man and lived among us.
1. Glori-fy the LORD, O Je-*ru*-salem; praise your God, O Zion. For he has strengthened the bars of your gates; he has blessed your chil-*dren* within you. ℟.
2. He has granted peace in your *bor*-ders; with the best of wheat *he* fills you. He sends forth his command to the earth; swift-*ly* runs his word! ℟.

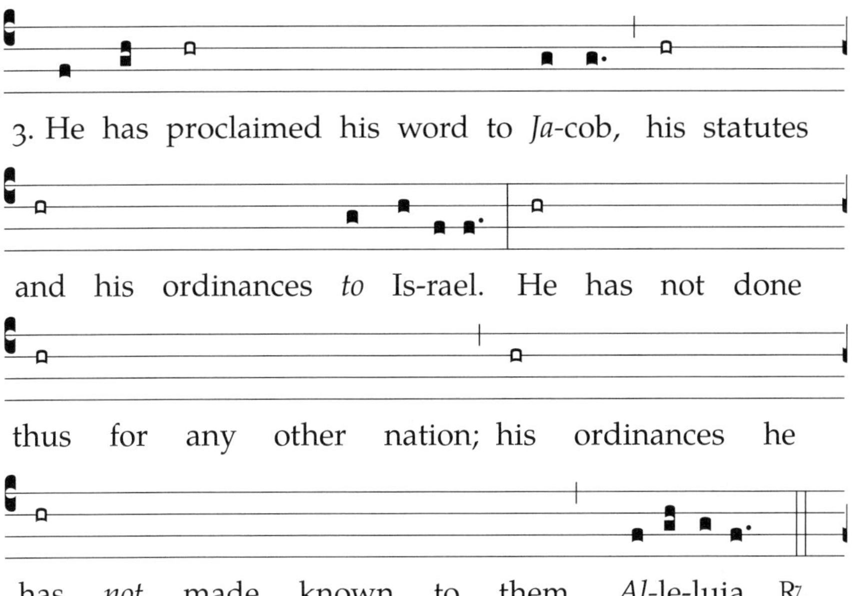
3. He has proclaimed his word to *Ja*-cob, his statutes
and his ordinances *to* Is-rael. He has not done
thus for any other nation; his ordinances he
has *not* made known to them. *Al*-le-luia. ℟.

The Epiphany of the Lord

Ps. 72: 1-2, 7-8, 10-11, 12-13 **YEAR ABC**

IV
Lord, every nation on earth will adore you.
1. O God, with your judgment endow the *king*,
and with your *jus*-tice, the king's son; He shall govern
your people with justice and your af-*flic*-ted ones with
judgment. ℟.
2. Justice shall flower in his days, and profound peace,
till the *moon* be no more. May he rule from sea
to sea, and from the River *to* the ends of the earth. ℟.

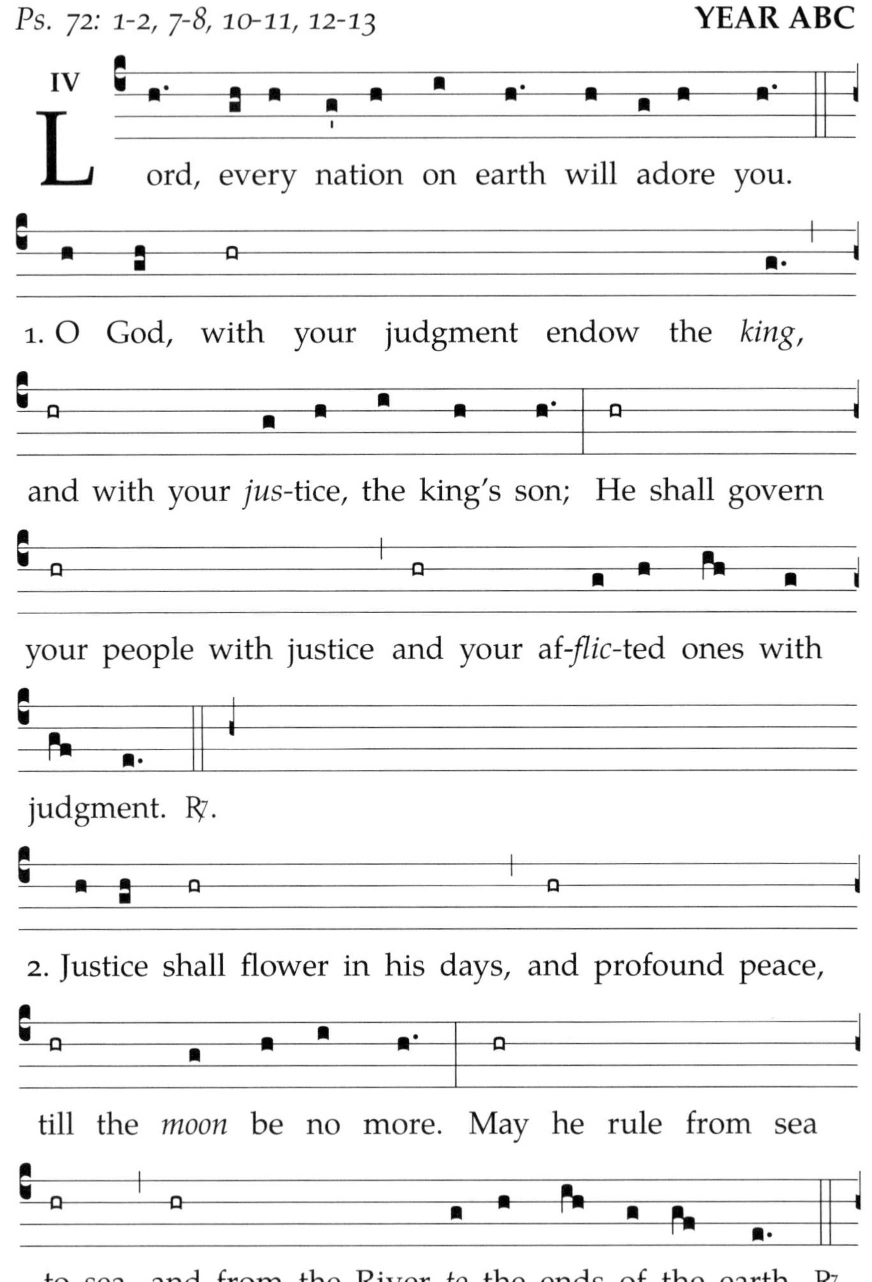

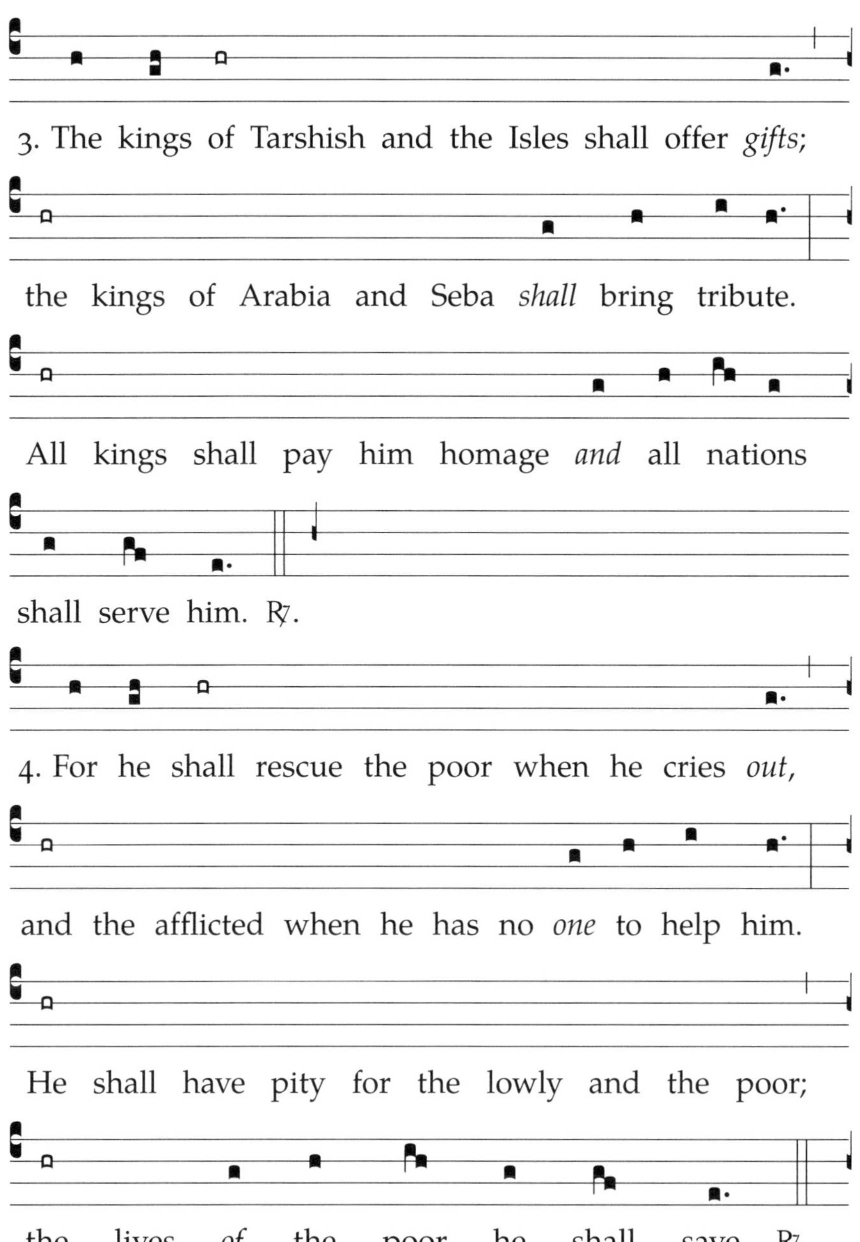
3. The kings of Tarshish and the Isles shall offer *gifts;*
the kings of Arabia and Seba *shall* bring tribute.
All kings shall pay him homage *and* all nations
shall serve him. ℟.
4. For he shall rescue the poor when he cries *out,*
and the afflicted when he has no *one* to help him.
He shall have pity for the lowly and the poor;
the lives *of* the poor he shall save. ℟.

The Baptism of the Lord

Ps. 29: 1-2, 3-4, 3, 9-10 **YEAR A**

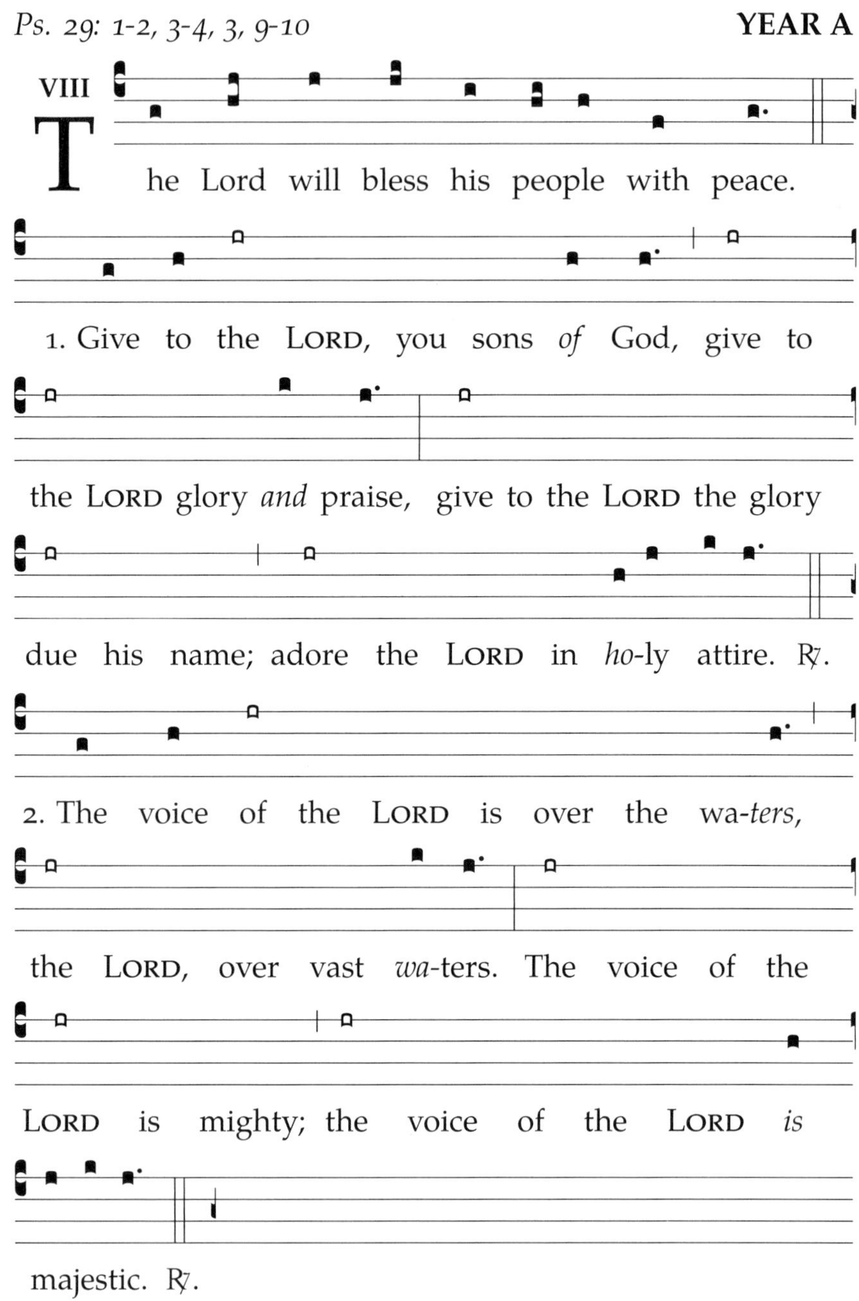

VIII
The Lord will bless his people with peace.
1. Give to the LORD, you sons *of* God, give to
the LORD glory *and* praise, give to the LORD the glory
due his name; adore the LORD in *ho*-ly attire. ℟.
2. The voice of the LORD is over the wa-*ters*,
the LORD, over vast *wa*-ters. The voice of the
LORD is mighty; the voice of the LORD *is*
majestic. ℟.

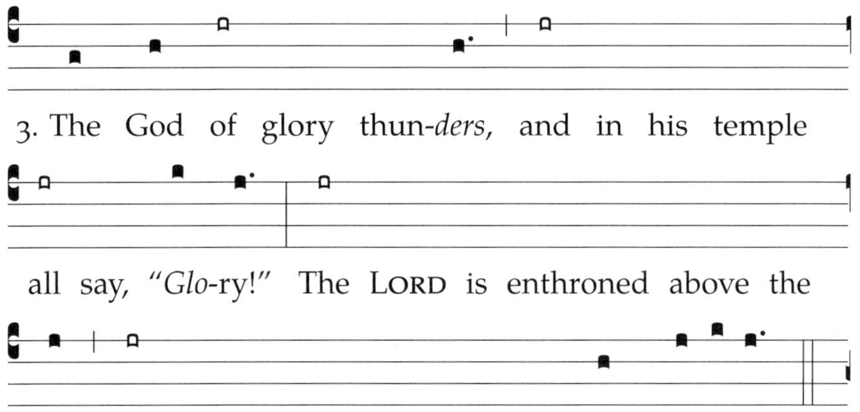
3. The God of glory thun-*ders,* and in his temple
all say, "*Glo*-ry!" The LORD is enthroned above the
flood; the LORD is enthroned as *king* forever. ℟.

The Baptism of the Lord

Is. 12: 2-3, 4, 5-6 **YEAR B**

℣
You will draw water joyfully from the springs
of salvation.
1. God indeed is my savior; I am confident and
un-*a*-fraid. My strength and my courage is the
Lord, and he has been my *sav*-ior. With joy
you will draw water at the fountain *of* salvation. ℟.
2. Give thanks to the Lord, acclaim *his* name; among
the nations make known his deeds, proclaim how

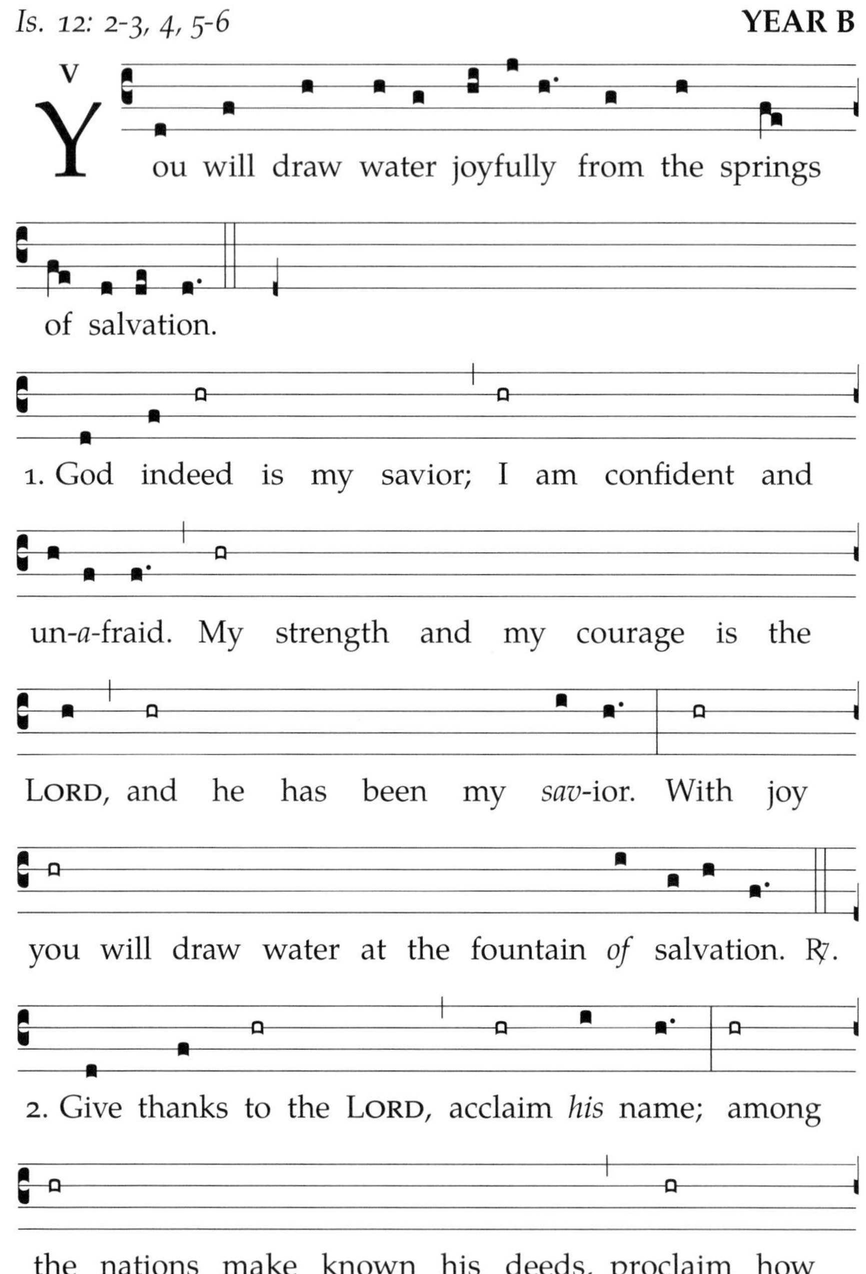

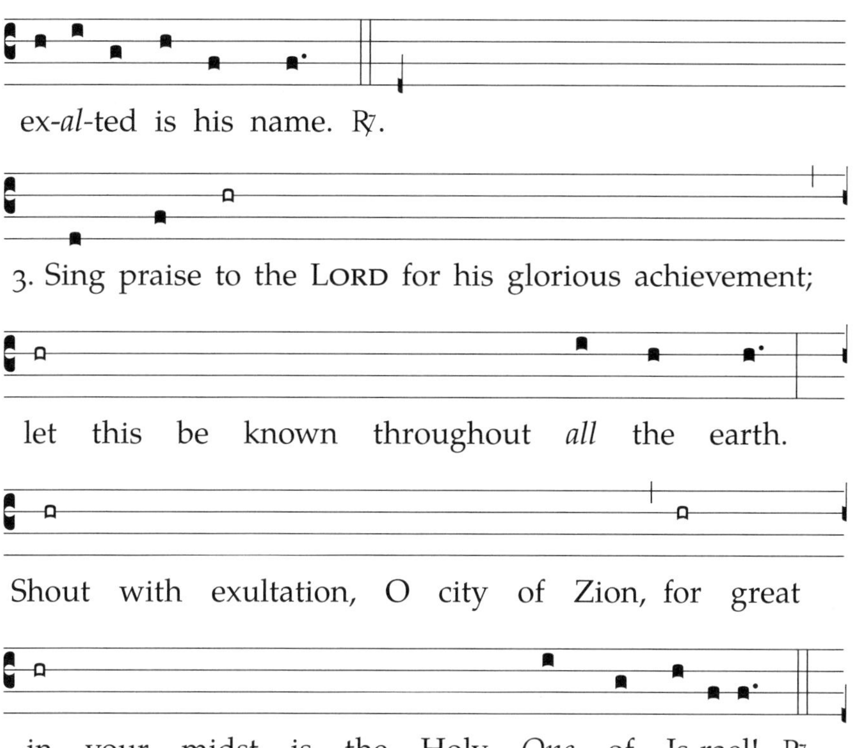
ex-*al*-ted is his name. ℟.
3. Sing praise to the LORD for his glorious achievement;
let this be known throughout *all* the earth.
Shout with exultation, O city of Zion, for great
in your midst is the Holy *One* of Is-rael! ℟.

THE BAPTISM OF THE LORD

Ps. 104: 1b-2, 3-4, 24-25, 27-28, 29-30 **YEAR C**

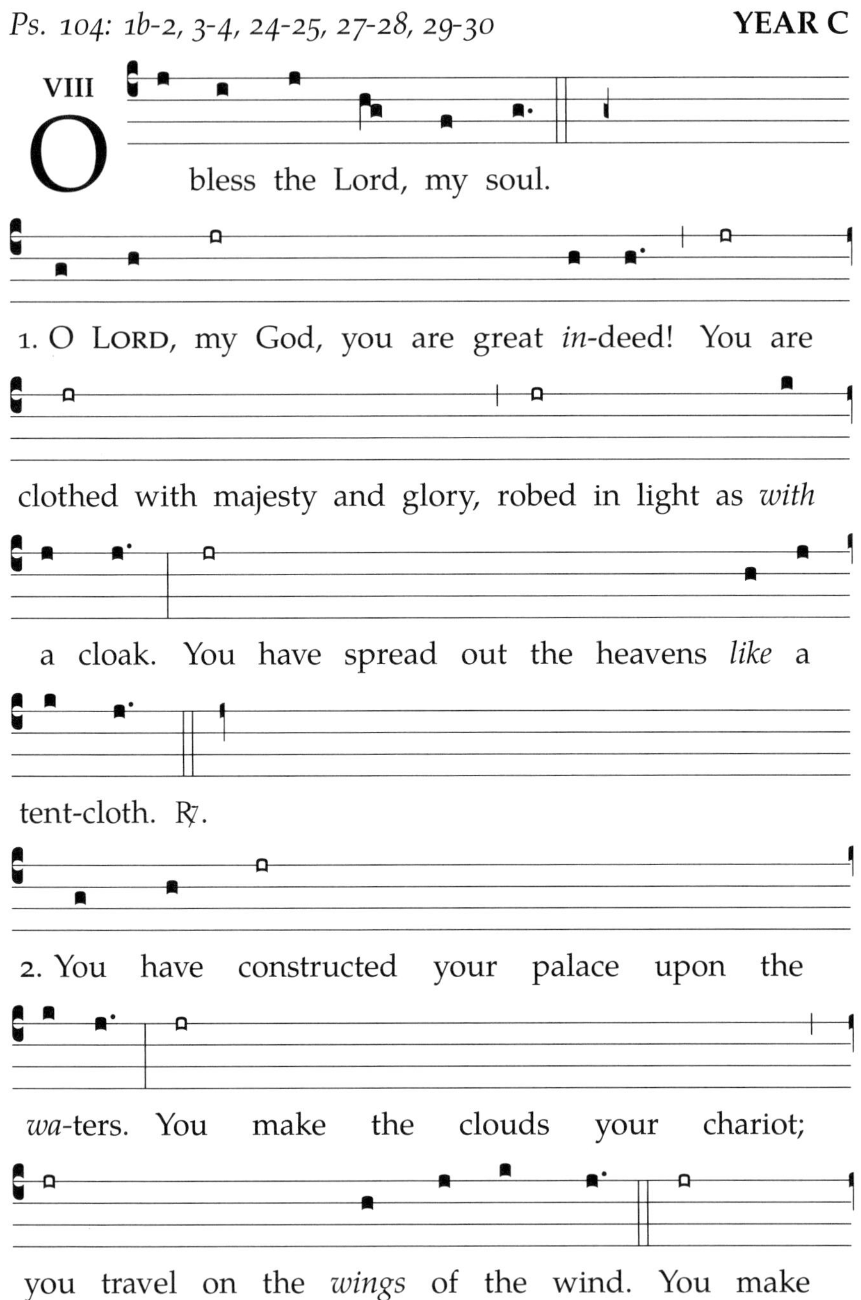
VIII
O bless the Lord, my soul.
1. O LORD, my God, you are great *in*-deed! You are
clothed with majesty and glory, robed in light as *with*
a cloak. You have spread out the heavens *like* a
tent-cloth. ℟.
2. You have constructed your palace upon the
wa-ters. You make the clouds your chariot;
you travel on the *wings* of the wind. You make

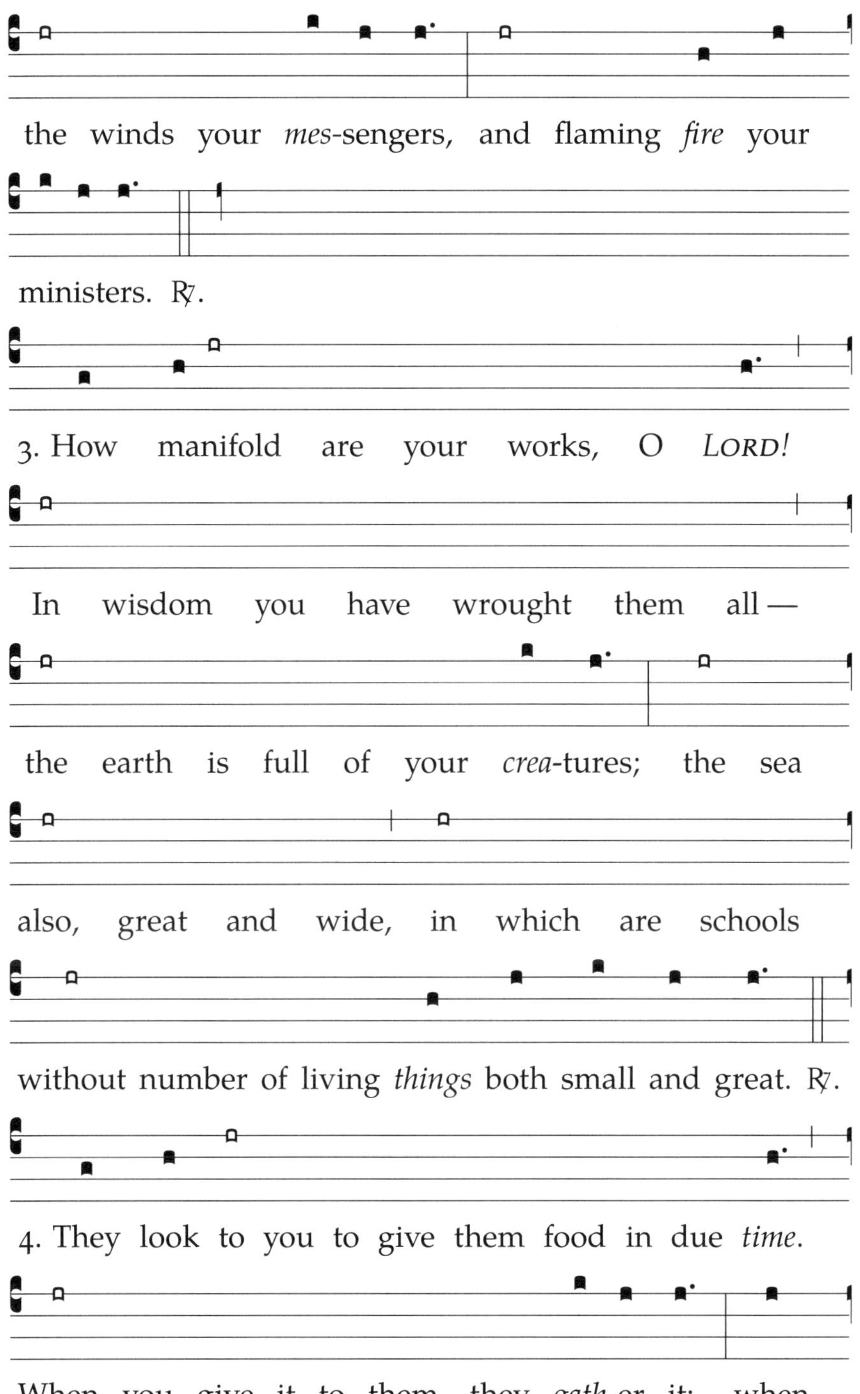
the winds your *mes*-sengers, and flaming *fire* your
ministers. ℟.
3. How manifold are your works, O *Lord!*
In wisdom you have wrought them all —
the earth is full of your *crea*-tures; the sea
also, great and wide, in which are schools
without number of living *things* both small and great. ℟.
4. They look to you to give them food in due *time.*
When you give it to them, they *gath*-er it; when

you open your hand, they are *filled* with good things. ℟.
5. If you take away their breath, they perish and return
to the dust. When you send forth your spirit, they
are created, and you renew the *face* of the
earth. ℟.
Antiphon:
℟. O bless the Lord, my soul.

Lent

Ash Wednesday

Ps. 51: 3-4, 5-6, 12-13, 14, 17 **YEAR ABC**

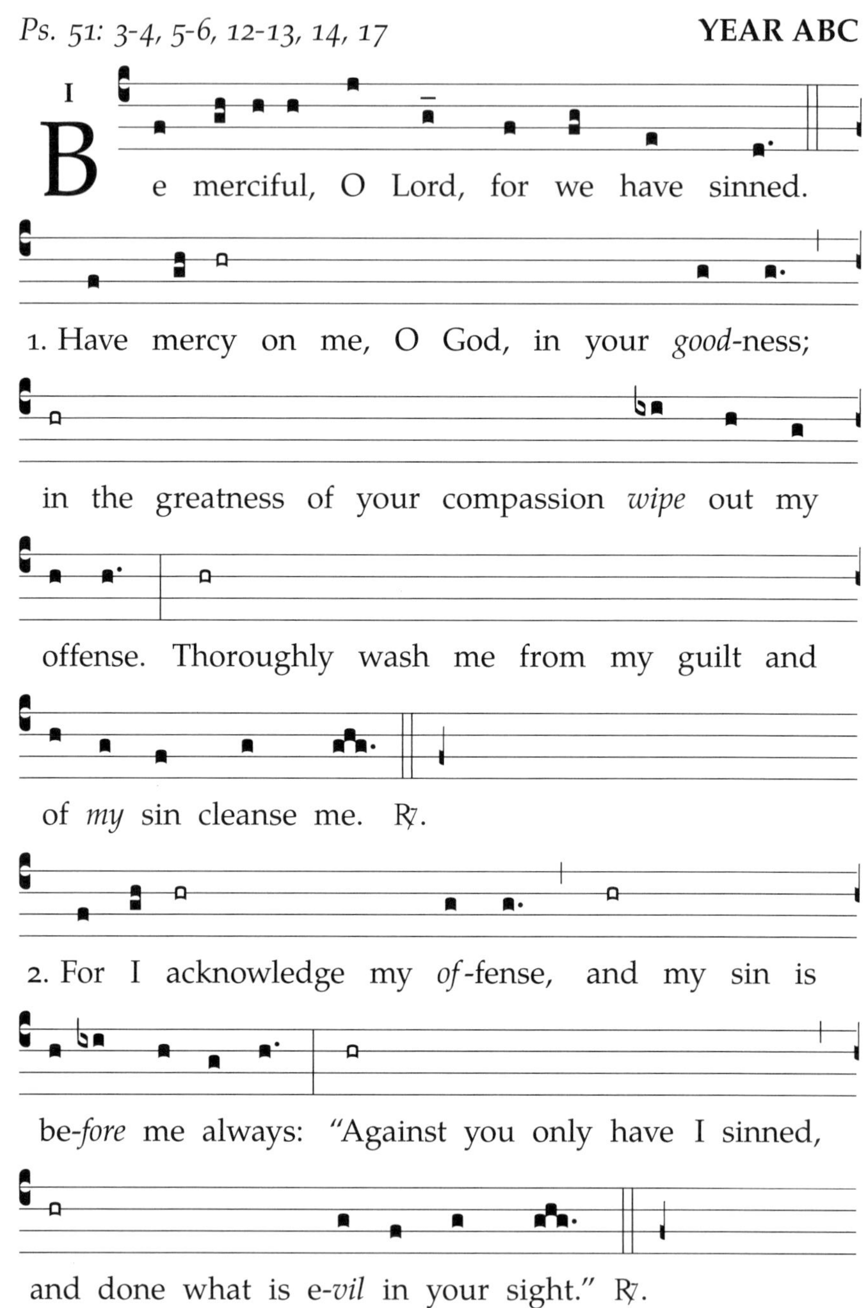
I
Be merciful, O Lord, for we have sinned.
1. Have mercy on me, O God, in your *good*-ness;
in the greatness of your compassion *wipe* out my
offense. Thoroughly wash me from my guilt and
of *my* sin cleanse me. ℟.
2. For I acknowledge my *of*-fense, and my sin is
be-*fore* me always: "Against you only have I sinned,
and done what is e-*vil* in your sight." ℟.

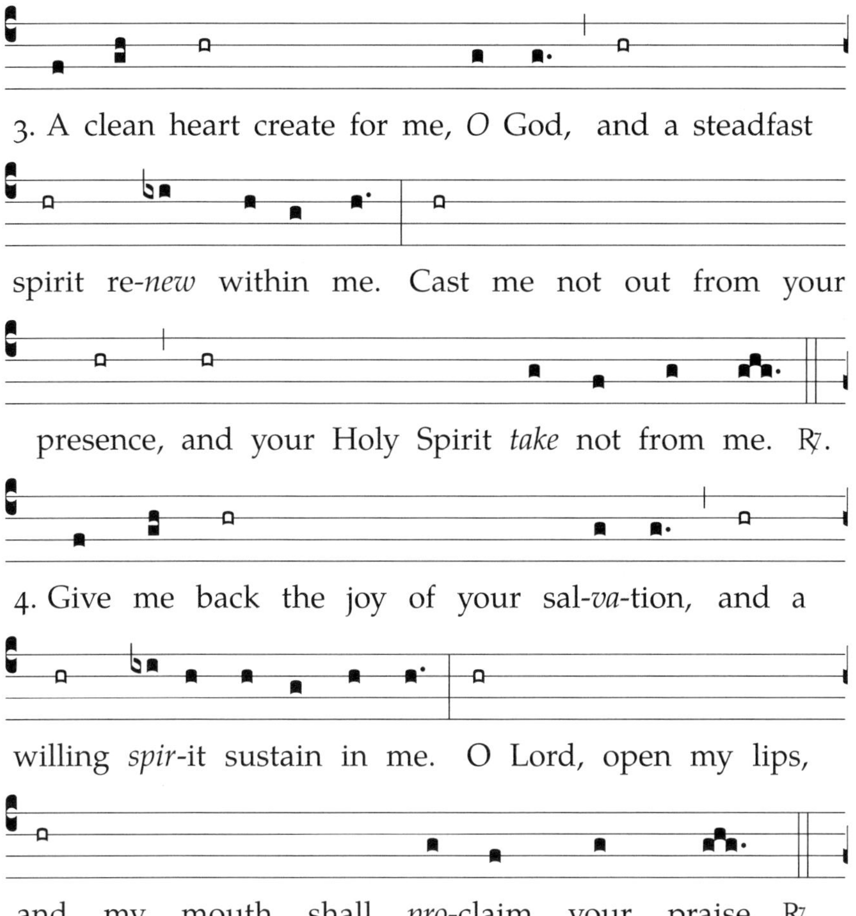
3. A clean heart create for me, *O* God, and a steadfast
spirit re-*new* within me. Cast me not out from your
presence, and your Holy Spirit *take* not from me. ℟.
4. Give me back the joy of your sal-*va*-tion, and a
willing *spir*-it sustain in me. O Lord, open my lips,
and my mouth shall *pro*-claim your praise. ℟.

First Sunday of Lent

Ps. 51: 3-4, 5-6, 12-13, 14, 17 **YEAR A**

I
Be merciful, O Lord, for we have sinned.
1. Have mercy on me, O God, in your *good*-ness; in the
greatness of your compassion *wipe* out my offense.
Thoroughly wash me from my guilt and of *my* sin
cleanse me. ℟.
2. For I acknowledge my *of*-fense, and my sin is
be-*fore* me always: "Against you only have I
sinned, and done what is e-*vil* in your sight." ℟.

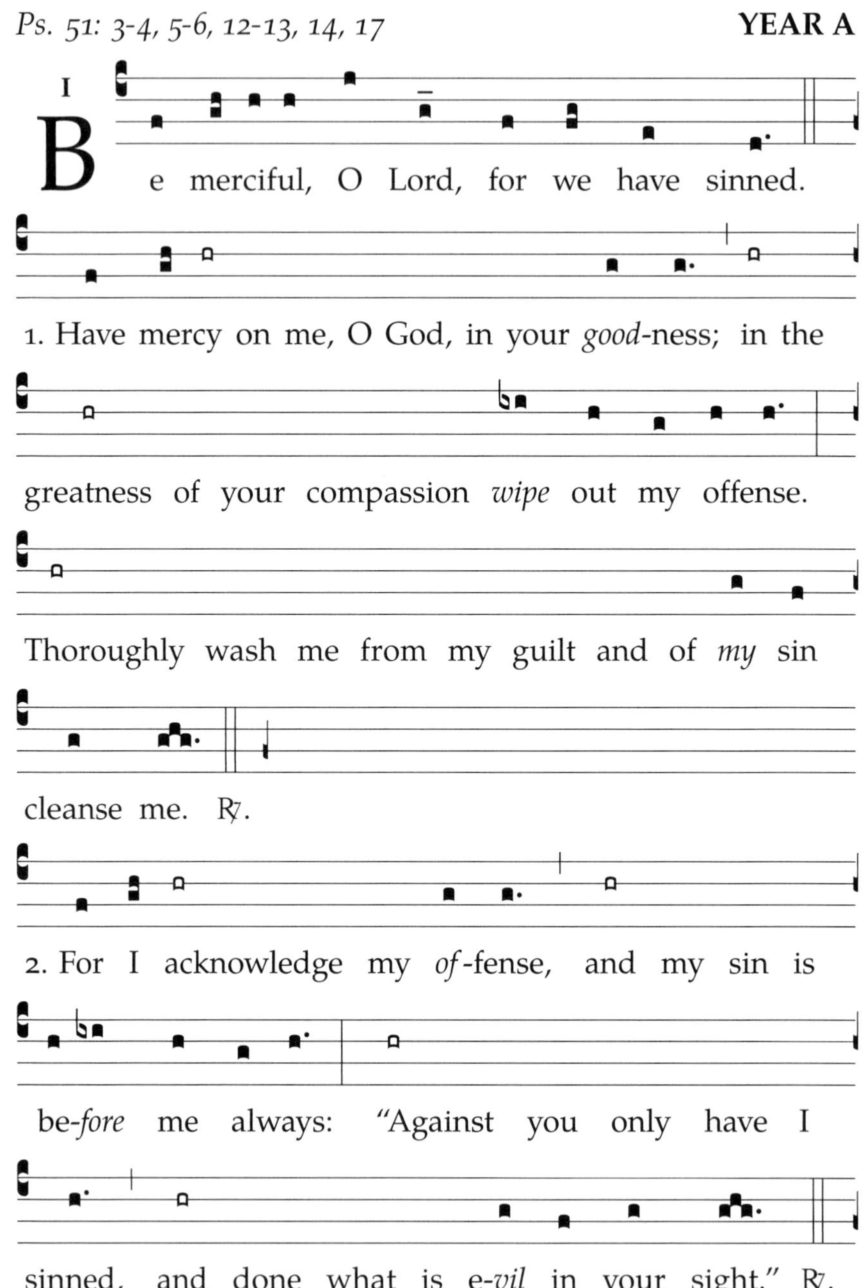

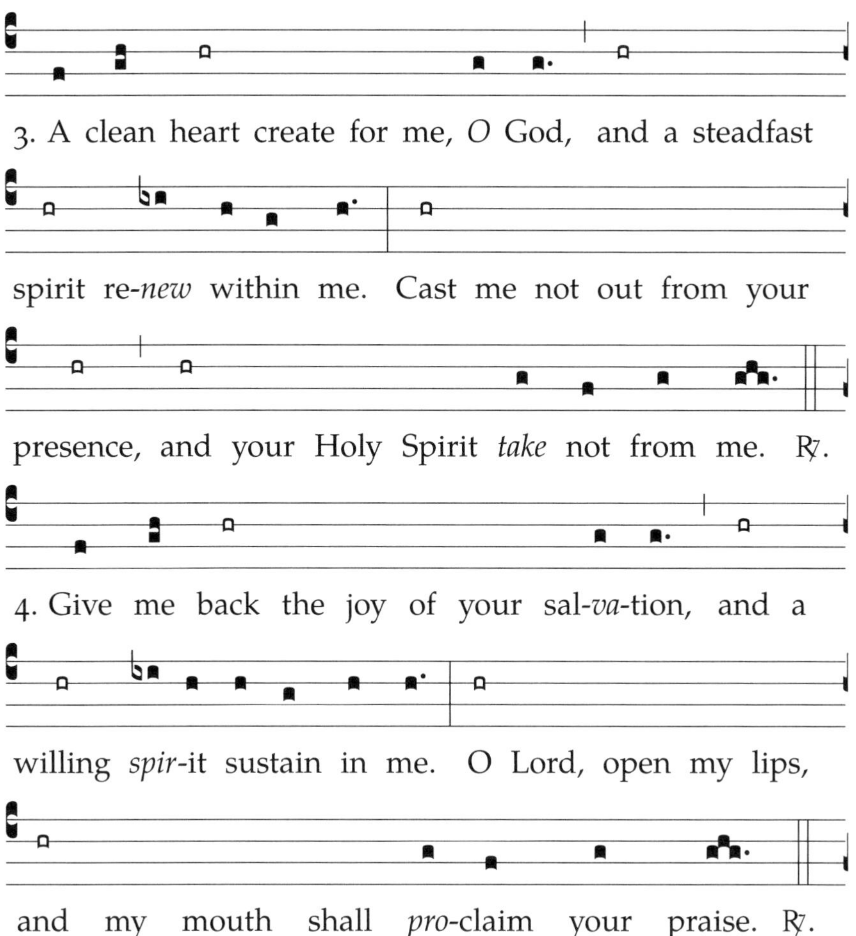
3. A clean heart create for me, *O* God, and a steadfast
spirit re-*new* within me. Cast me not out from your
presence, and your Holy Spirit *take* not from me. ℟.
4. Give me back the joy of your sal-*va*-tion, and a
willing *spir*-it sustain in me. O Lord, open my lips,
and my mouth shall *pro*-claim your praise. ℟.

First Sunday of Lent

Ps. 25: 4-5, 6-7, 8-9 **YEAR B**

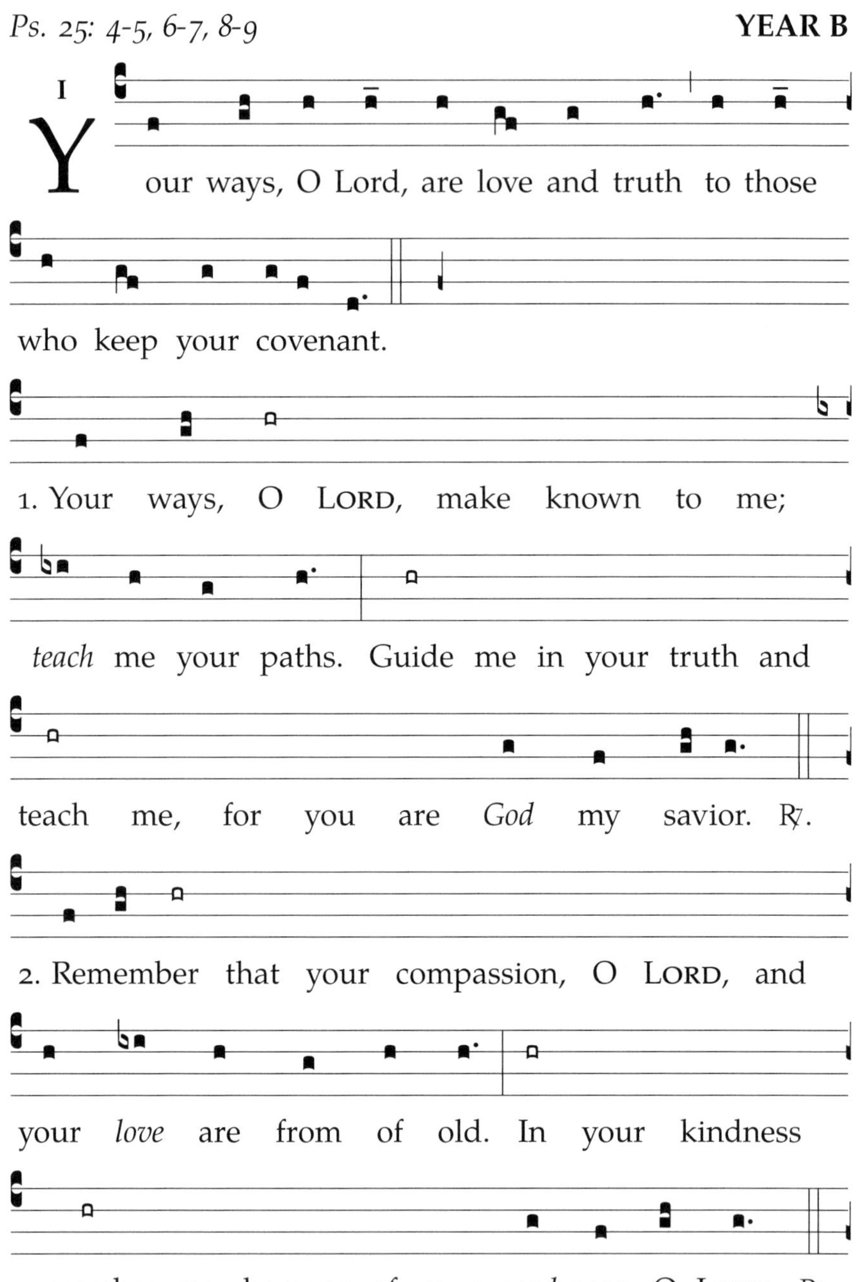

I
Your ways, O Lord, are love and truth to those
who keep your covenant.
1. Your ways, O LORD, make known to me;
teach me your paths. Guide me in your truth and
teach me, for you are *God* my savior. ℟.
2. Remember that your compassion, O LORD, and
your *love* are from of old. In your kindness
remember me, because of your *good*-ness, O LORD. ℟.

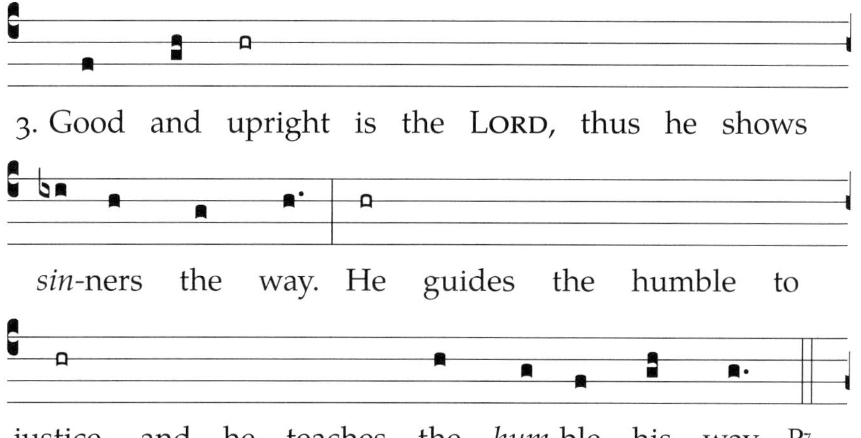
3. Good and upright is the LORD, thus he shows
sin-ners the way. He guides the humble to
justice, and he teaches the *hum*-ble his way. ℟.

First Sunday of Lent

Ps. 91: 1-2, 10-11, 12-13, 14-15 **YEAR C**

I
Be with me, Lord, when I am in trouble.
1. You who dwell in the shelter of the Most *High,* who
abide in the shadow of the Almighty, *say* to the Lord,
"My refuge and fortress, my God *in* whom I trust." ℟.
2. No e-vil shall befall you, nor shall affliction *come*
near your tent, for to his angels he has given
command about you, that they guard you *in* all your
ways. ℟.

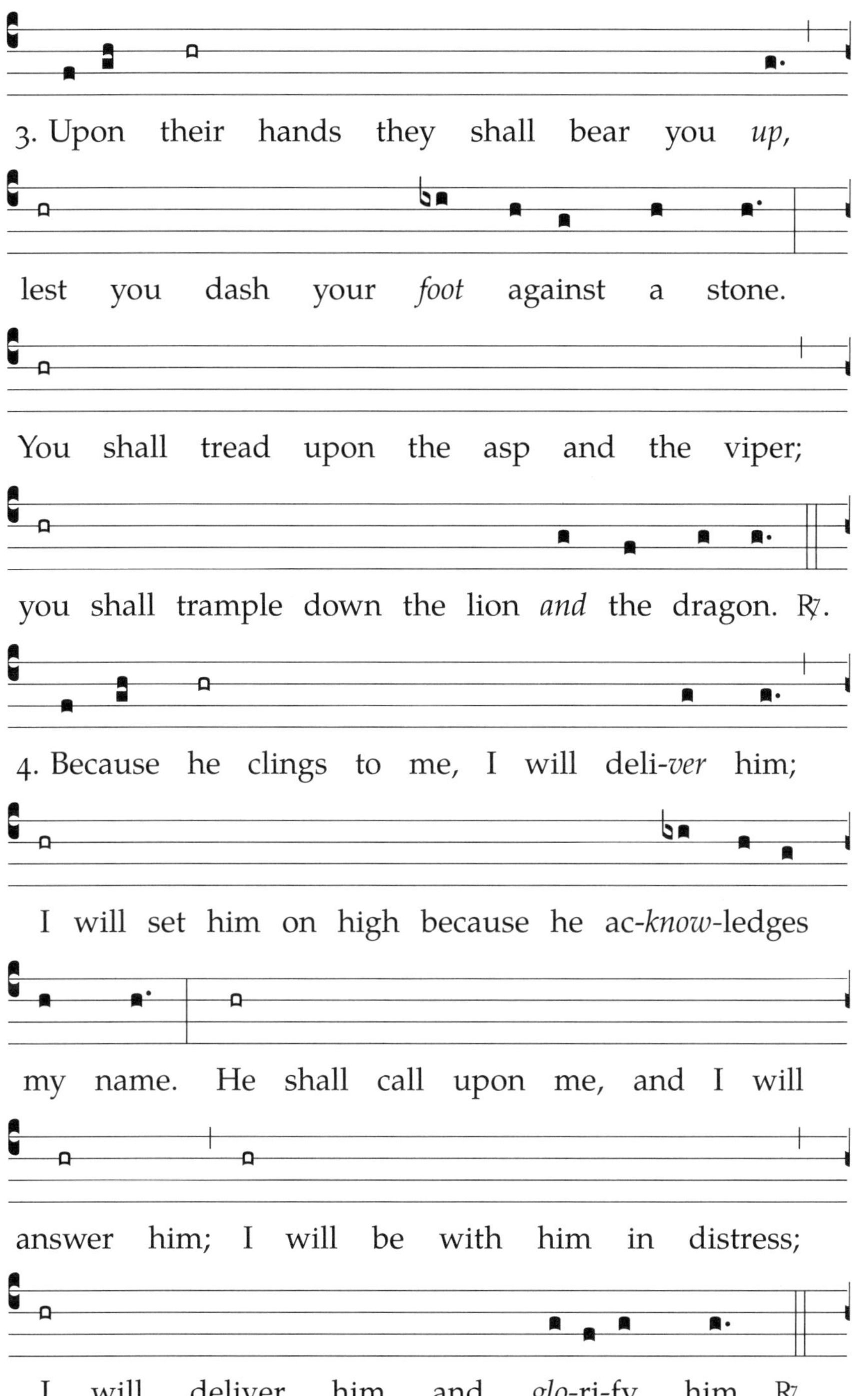
3. Upon their hands they shall bear you *up,*
lest you dash your *foot* against a stone.
You shall tread upon the asp and the viper;
you shall trample down the lion *and* the dragon. ℟.
4. Because he clings to me, I will deli-*ver* him;
I will set him on high because he ac-*know*-ledges
my name. He shall call upon me, and I will
answer him; I will be with him in distress;
I will deliver him and *glo*-ri-fy him. ℟.

Second Sunday of Lent

Ps. 33: 4-5, 18-19, 20, 22 **YEAR A**

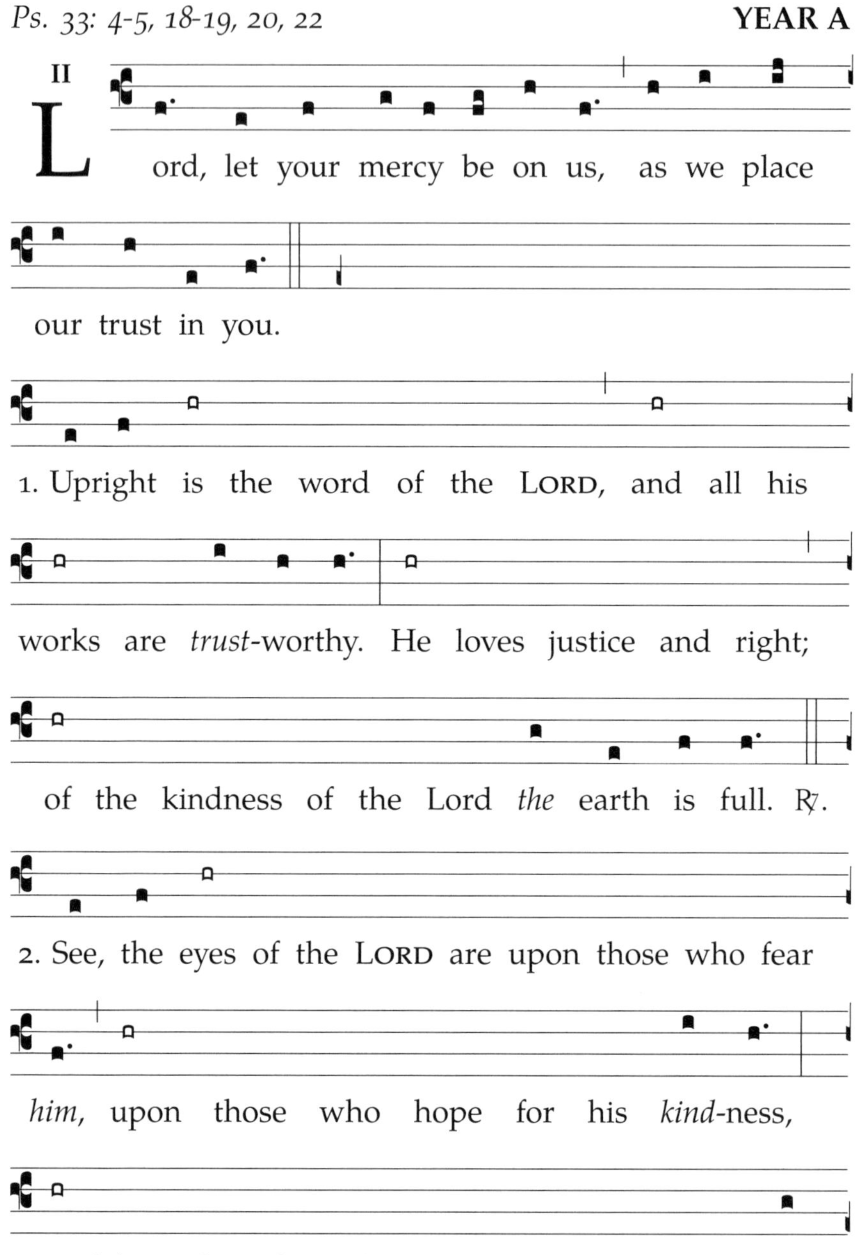

II
Lord, let your mercy be on us, as we place
our trust in you.
1. Upright is the word of the LORD, and all his
works are *trust*-worthy. He loves justice and right;
of the kindness of the Lord *the* earth is full. ℟.
2. See, the eyes of the LORD are upon those who fear
him, upon those who hope for his *kind*-ness,
to deliver them from death and preserve them in *spite*

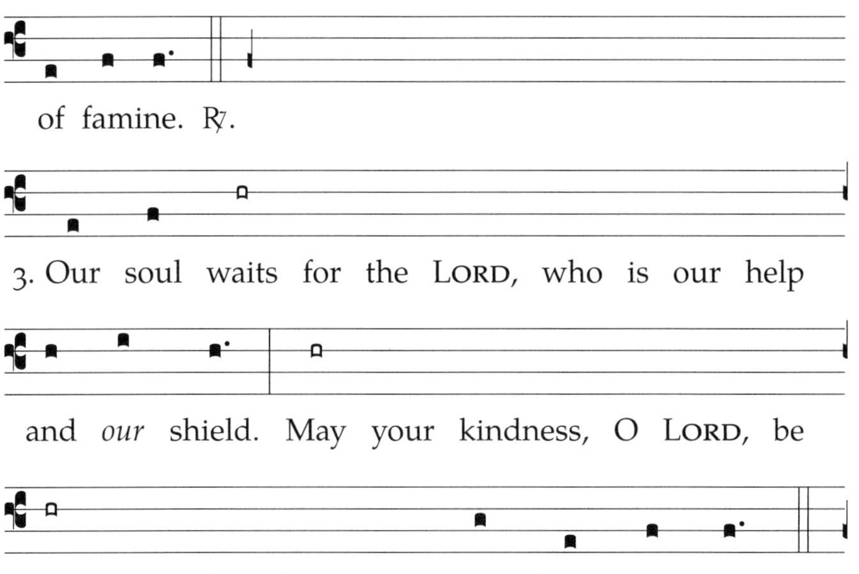
of famine. ℟.
3. Our soul waits for the Lord, who is our help
and *our* shield. May your kindness, O Lord, be
upon us who have put *our* hope in you. ℟.

Second Sunday of Lent

Ps. 116: 10, 15, 16-17, 18-19 **YEAR B**

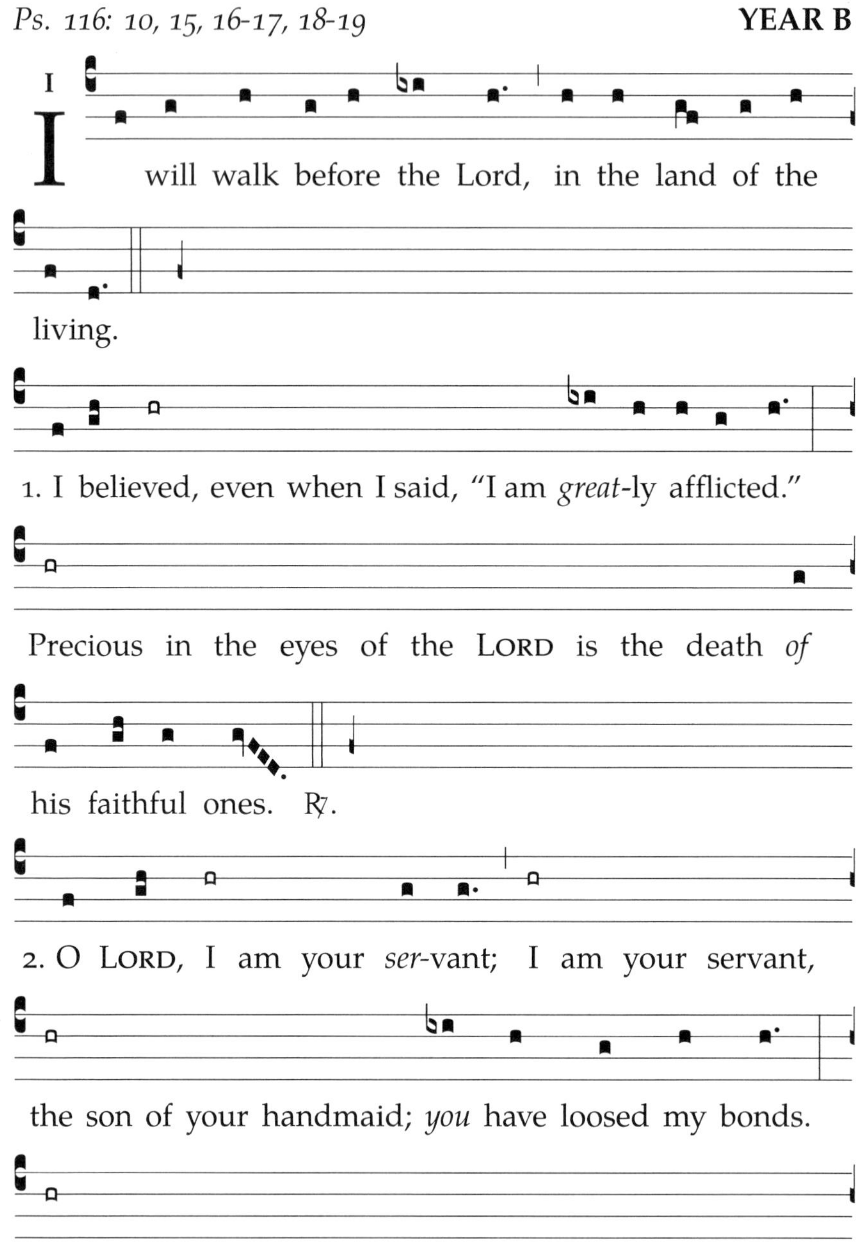

I
I will walk before the Lord, in the land of the
living.
1. I believed, even when I said, "I am *great*-ly afflicted."
Precious in the eyes of the LORD is the death *of*
his faithful ones. ℟.
2. O LORD, I am your *ser*-vant; I am your servant,
the son of your handmaid; *you* have loosed my bonds.
To you will I offer sacrifice of thanksgiving, and

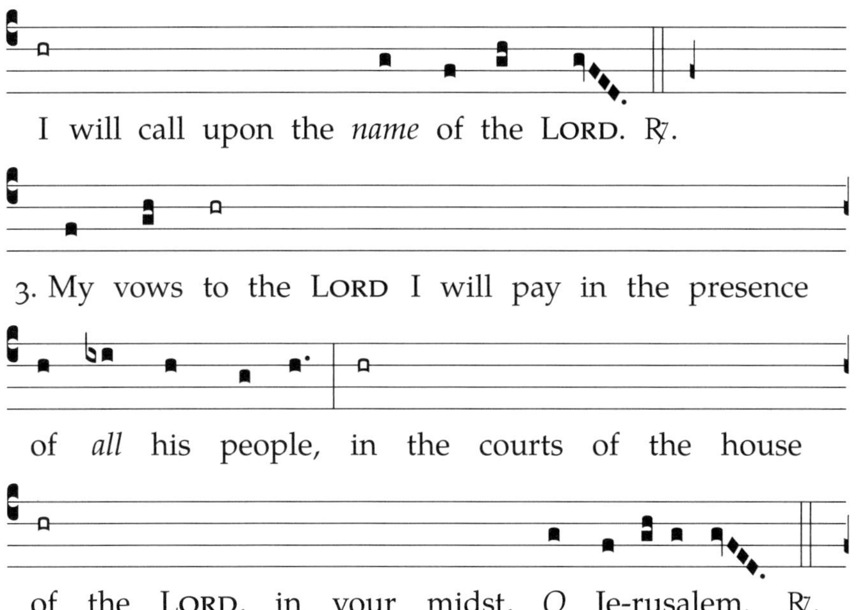
I will call upon the *name* of the Lord. ℟.
3. My vows to the Lord I will pay in the presence
of *all* his people, in the courts of the house
of the Lord, in your midst, *O* Je-rusalem. ℟.

Second Sunday of Lent

Ps. 27: 1, 7-8, 8-9, 13-14 **YEAR C**

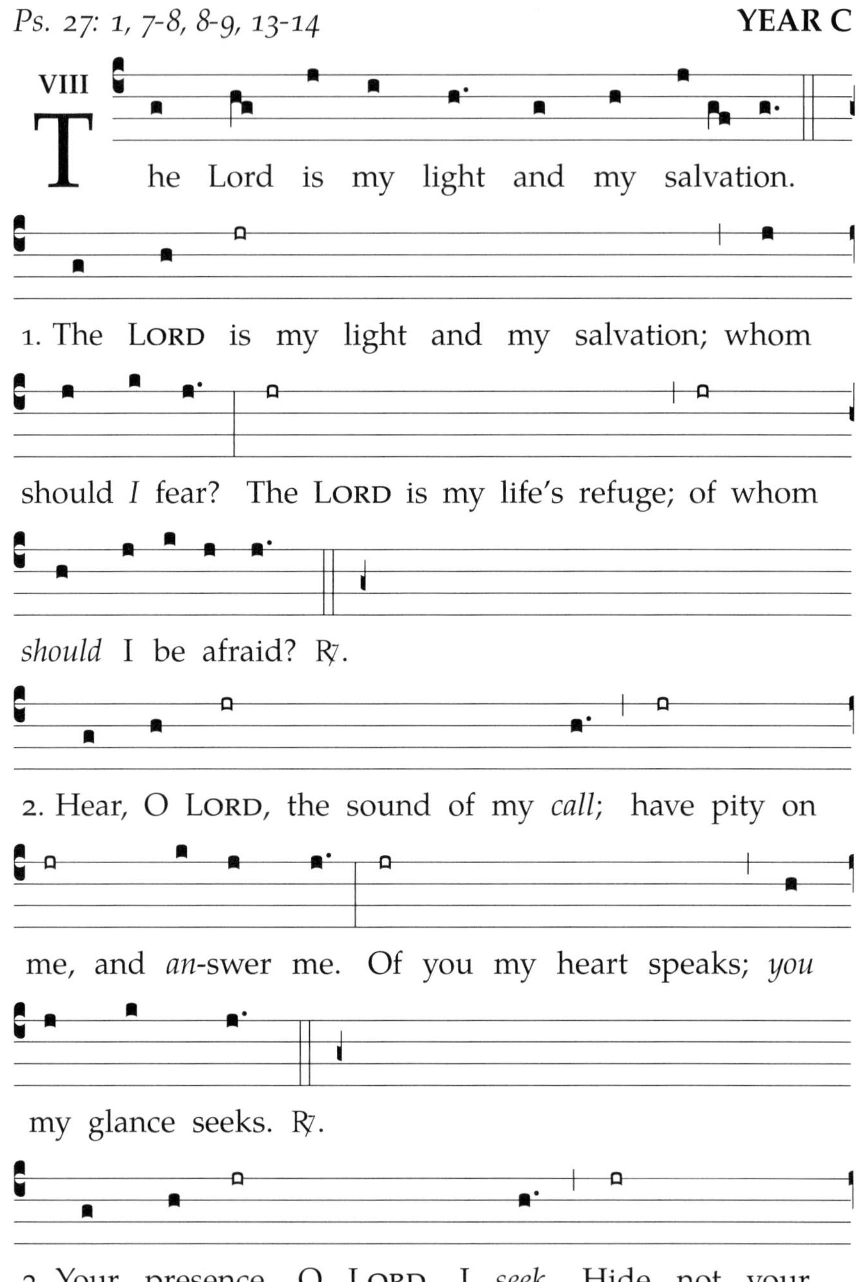
VIII
The Lord is my light and my salvation.
1. The LORD is my light and my salvation; whom
should *I* fear? The LORD is my life's refuge; of whom
should I be afraid? ℟.
2. Hear, O LORD, the sound of my *call;* have pity on
me, and *an*-swer me. Of you my heart speaks; *you*
my glance seeks. ℟.
3. Your presence, O LORD, I *seek.* Hide not your

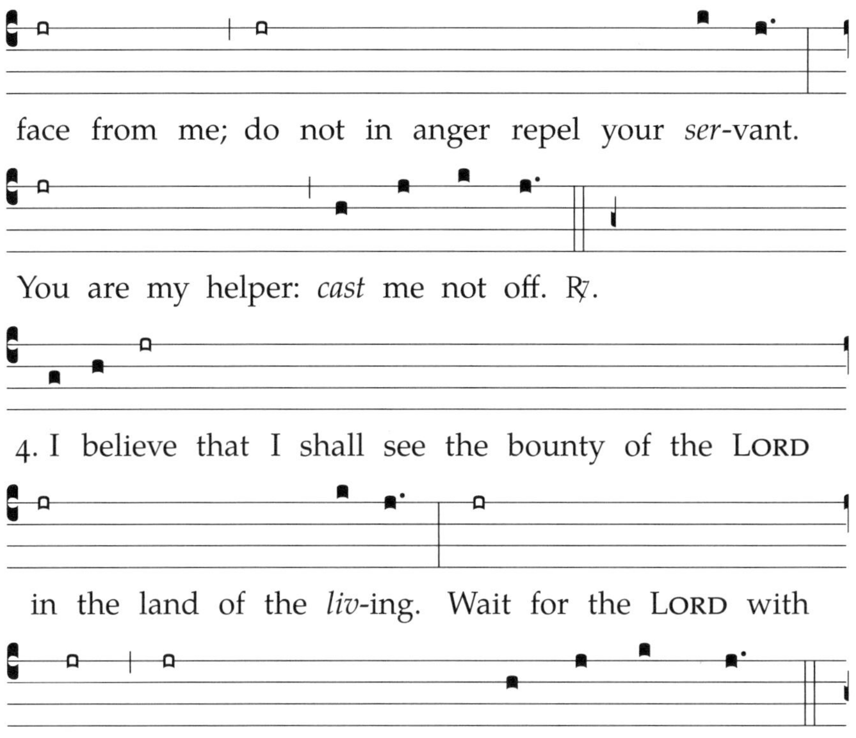
face from me; do not in anger repel your *ser*-vant.
You are my helper: *cast* me not off. ℟.
4. I believe that I shall see the bounty of the LORD
in the land of the *liv*-ing. Wait for the LORD with
courage; be stouthearted, and *wait* for the LORD. ℟.

THIRD SUNDAY OF LENT

Ps. 95: 1-2, 6-7, 8-9 **YEAR A**

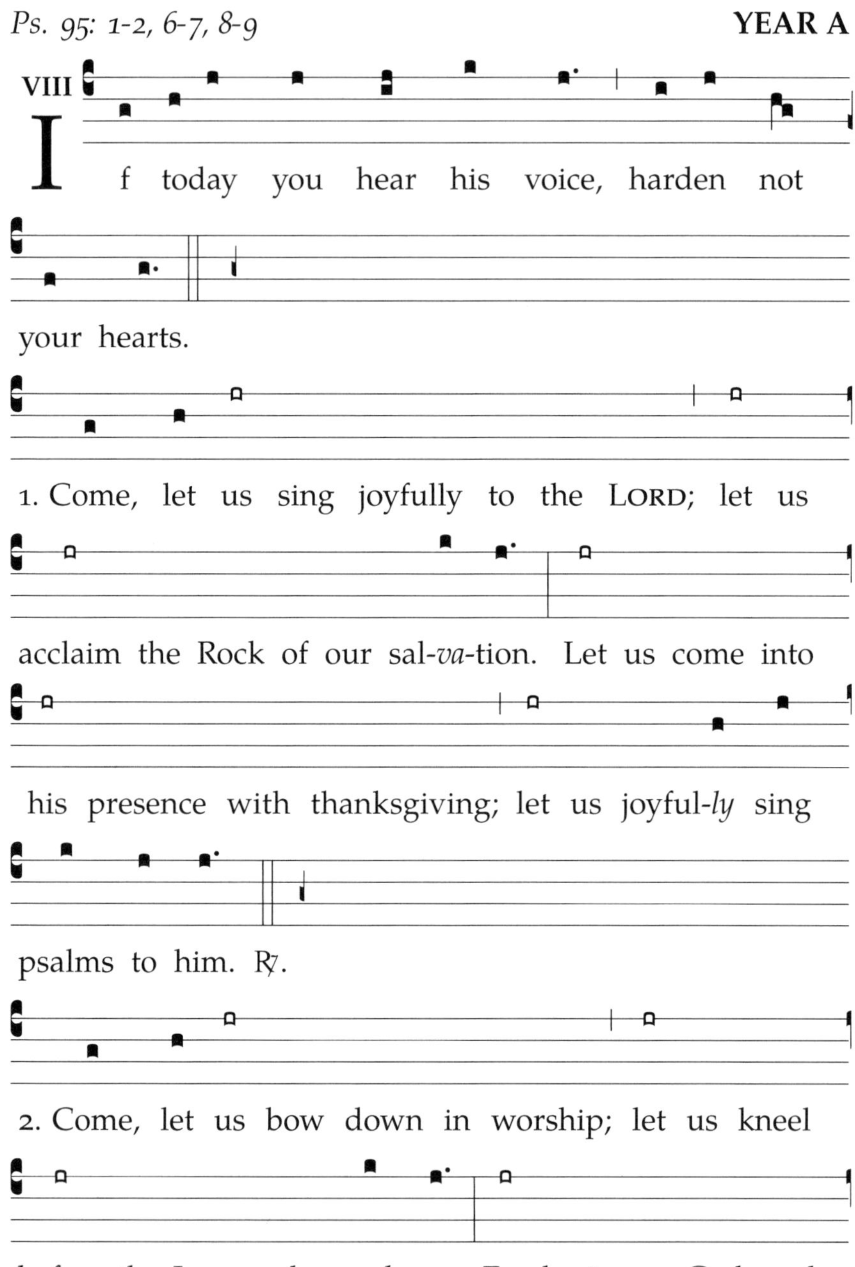
VIII
If today you hear his voice, harden not
your hearts.
1. Come, let us sing joyfully to the LORD; let us
acclaim the Rock of our sal-*va*-tion. Let us come into
his presence with thanksgiving; let us joyful-*ly* sing
psalms to him. ℟.
2. Come, let us bow down in worship; let us kneel
before the LORD who *made* us. For he is our God, and

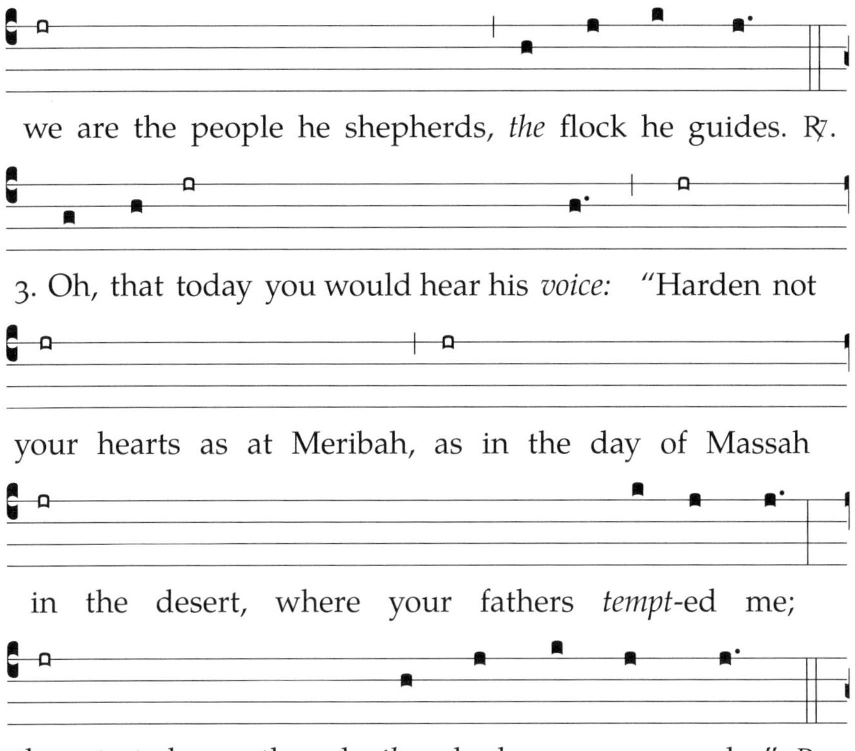
we are the people he shepherds, *the* flock he guides. ℟.
3. Oh, that today you would hear his *voice:* "Harden not
your hearts as at Meribah, as in the day of Massah
in the desert, where your fathers *tempt*-ed me;
they tested me though *they* had seen my works." ℟.

Third Sunday of Lent

Ps. 19: 8, 9, 10, 11 **YEAR B**

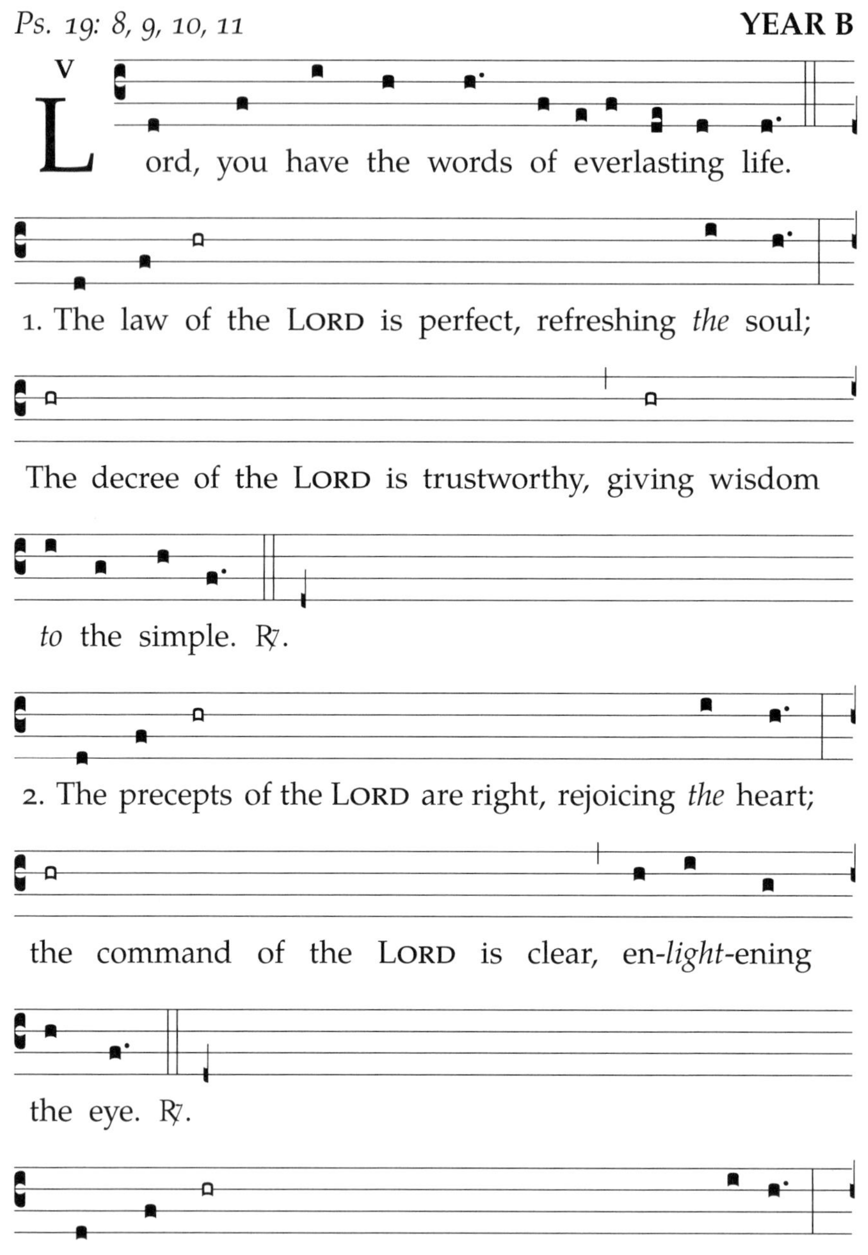
V
Lord, you have the words of everlasting life.
1. The law of the Lord is perfect, refreshing *the* soul;
The decree of the Lord is trustworthy, giving wisdom
to the simple. ℟.
2. The precepts of the Lord are right, rejoicing *the* heart;
the command of the Lord is clear, en-*light*-ening
the eye. ℟.
3. The fear of the Lord is pure, enduring for-*ev*-er;

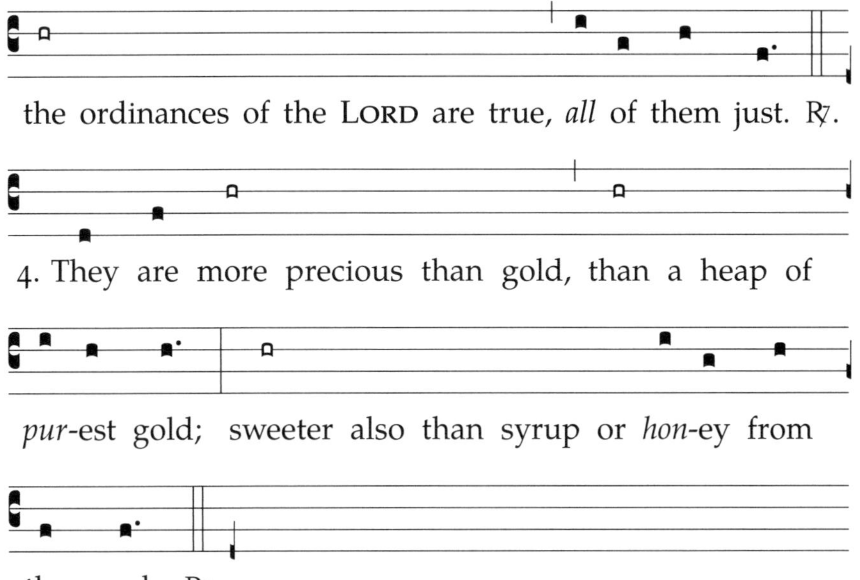
the ordinances of the LORD are true, *all* of them just. ℟.
4. They are more precious than gold, than a heap of
pur-est gold; sweeter also than syrup or *hon*-ey from
the comb. ℟.

THIRD SUNDAY OF LENT

Ps. 103: 1-2, 3-4, 6-7, 8, 11 **YEAR C**

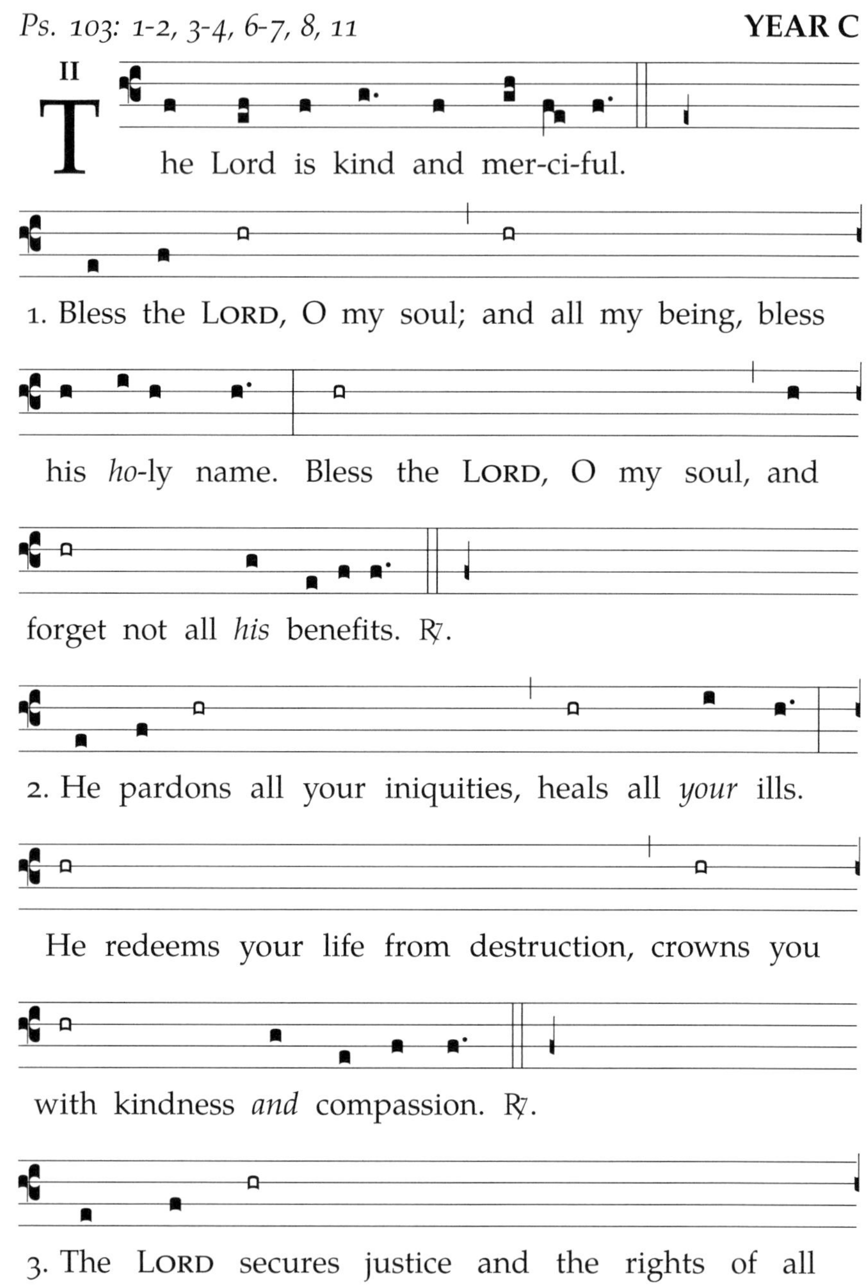

II
The Lord is kind and mer-ci-ful.
1. Bless the LORD, O my soul; and all my being, bless
his *ho*-ly name. Bless the LORD, O my soul, and
forget not all *his* benefits. ℟.
2. He pardons all your iniquities, heals all *your* ills.
He redeems your life from destruction, crowns you
with kindness *and* compassion. ℟.
3. The LORD secures justice and the rights of all

the *op*-pressed. He has made known his ways
to Moses, and his deeds to the children *of*
Is-rael. ℟.
4. Merciful and gracious is the *LORD,* slow to anger
and abounding in *kind*-ness. For as the heavens
are high above the earth, so surpassing is
his kindness toward those *who* fear him. ℟.

Fourth Sunday of Lent

Ps. 23: 1-3a, 3b-4, 5, 6 **YEAR A**

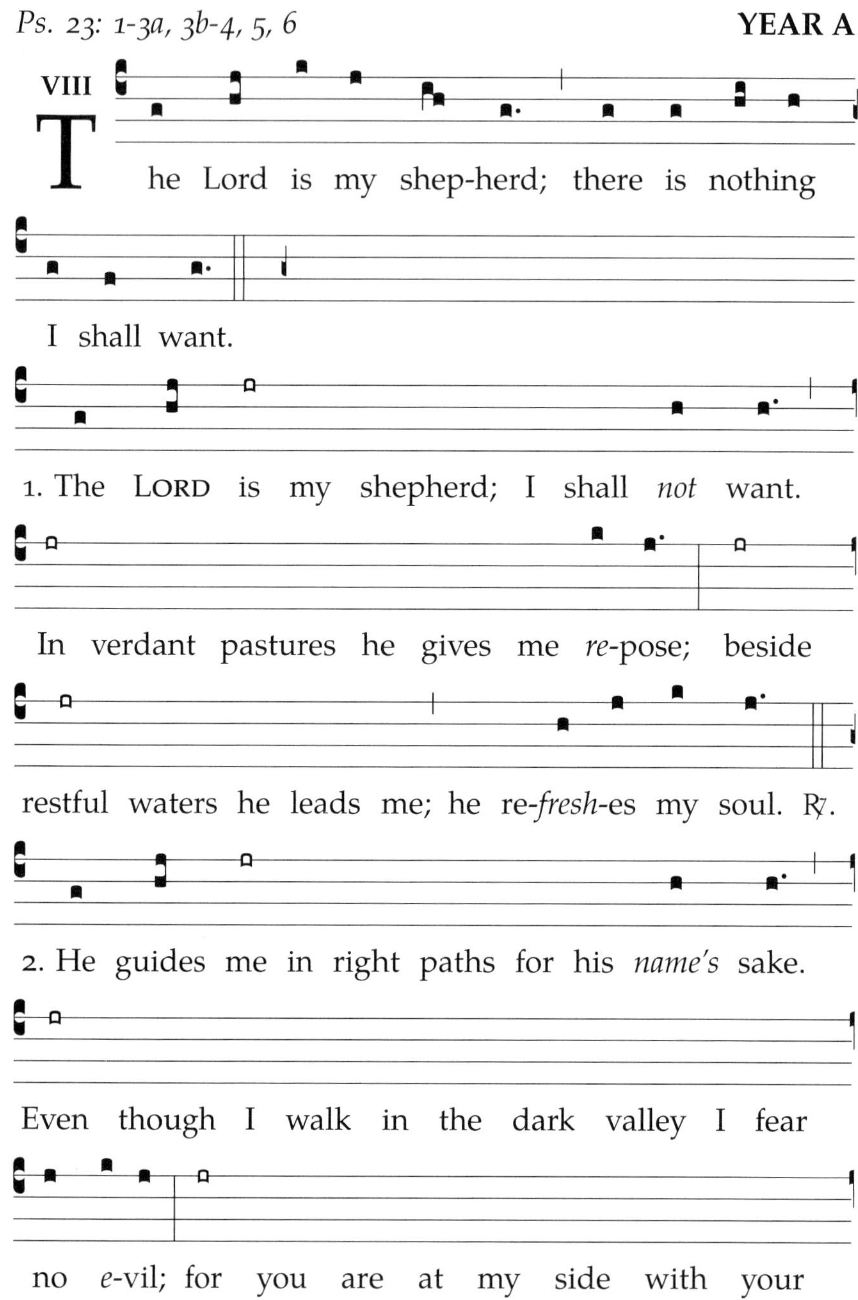
VIII
The Lord is my shep-herd; there is nothing
I shall want.
1. The LORD is my shepherd; I shall *not* want.
In verdant pastures he gives me *re*-pose; beside
restful waters he leads me; he re-*fresh*-es my soul. ℟.
2. He guides me in right paths for his *name's* sake.
Even though I walk in the dark valley I fear
no *e*-vil; for you are at my side with your

rod and your staff that *give* me courage. ℟.
3. You spread the table before me in the sight of
my foes; you anoint my head with oil; my
cup overflows. ℟.
4. Only goodness and kindness follow me all the
days of *my* life; and I shall dwell in the
house of the *LORD* for years to come. ℟.

Fourth Sunday of Lent

Ps. 137: 1-2, 3, 4-5, 6 **YEAR B**

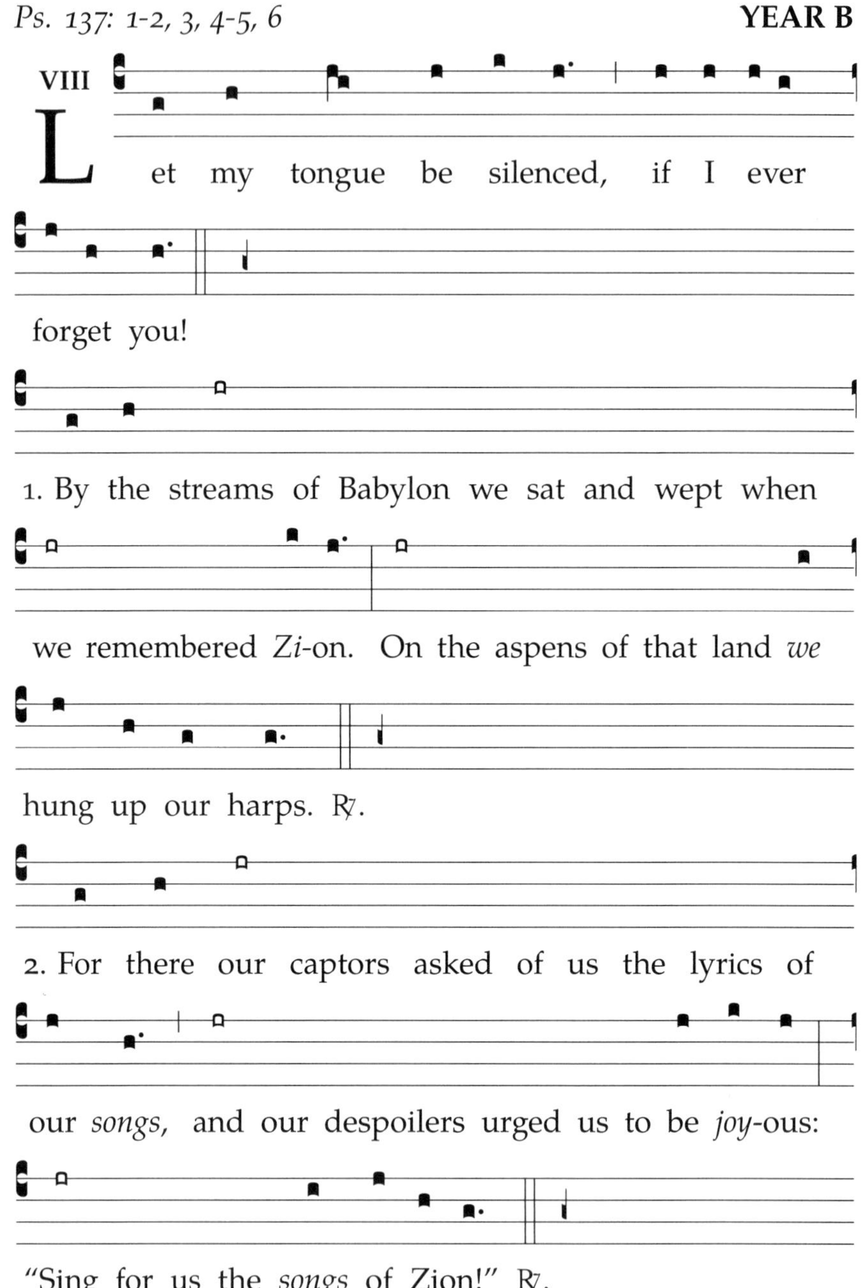

VIII
Let my tongue be silenced, if I ever forget you!
1. By the streams of Babylon we sat and wept when we remembered *Zi*-on. On the aspens of that land *we* hung up our harps. ℟.
2. For there our captors asked of us the lyrics of our *songs,* and our despoilers urged us to be *joy*-ous: "Sing for us the *songs* of Zion!" ℟.

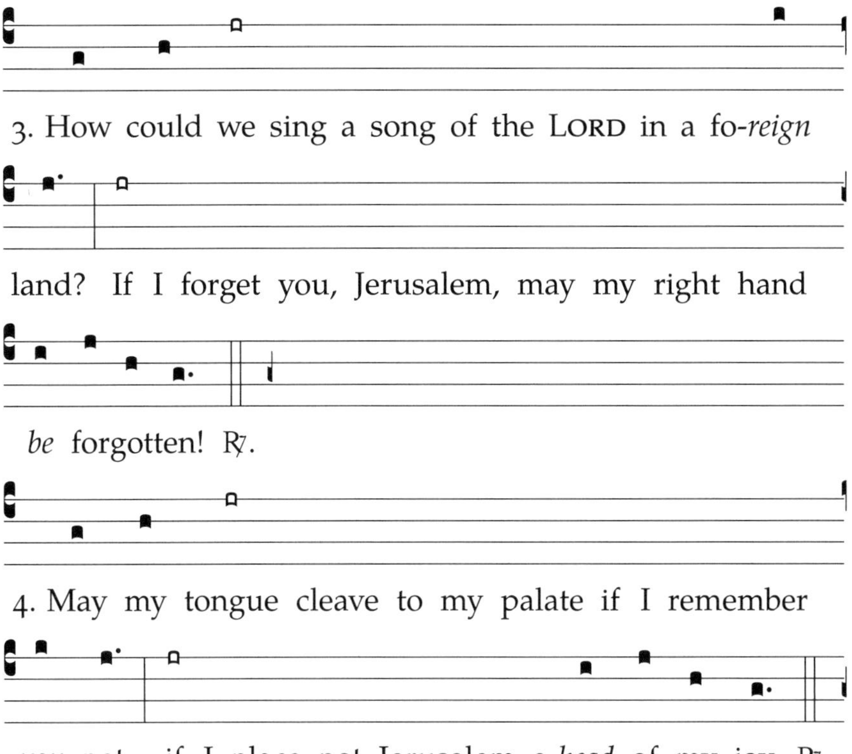
3. How could we sing a song of the LORD in a fo-*reign*
land? If I forget you, Jerusalem, may my right hand
be forgotten! ℟.
4. May my tongue cleave to my palate if I remember
you not, if I place not Jerusalem a-*head* of my joy. ℟.

Fourth Sunday of Lent

Ps. 34: 2-3, 4-5, 6-7 **YEAR C**

VIII
Taste and see the goodness of the Lord.
1. I will bless the LORD at all times; his praise shall
be ever in *my* mouth. Let my soul glory in
the LORD; the lowly will *hear* me and be glad. ℟.
2. Glori-fy the LORD with me, let us together
extol *his* name. I sought the Lord, and he
answered me and delivered *me* from all
my fears. ℟.

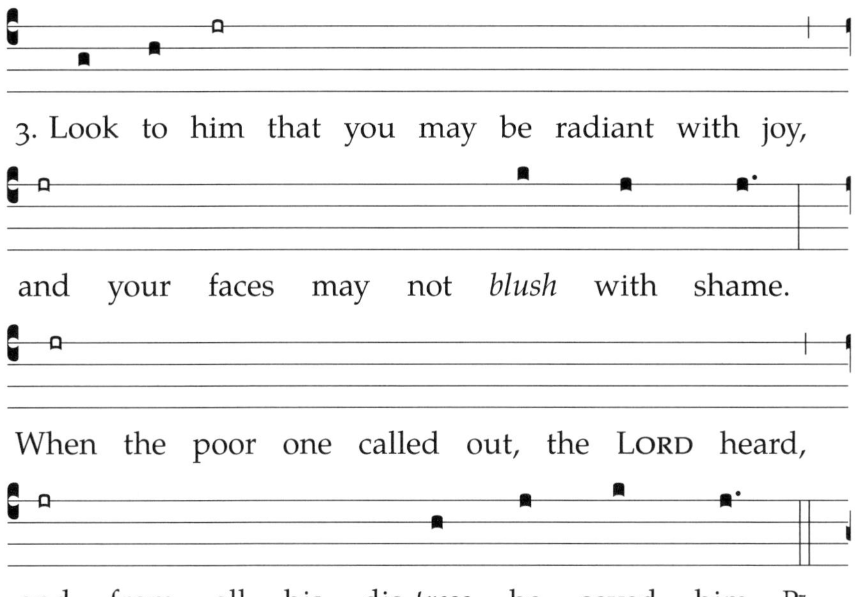
3. Look to him that you may be radiant with joy,
and your faces may not *blush* with shame.
When the poor one called out, the LORD heard,
and from all his dis-*tress* he saved him. ℟.

Fifth Sunday of Lent

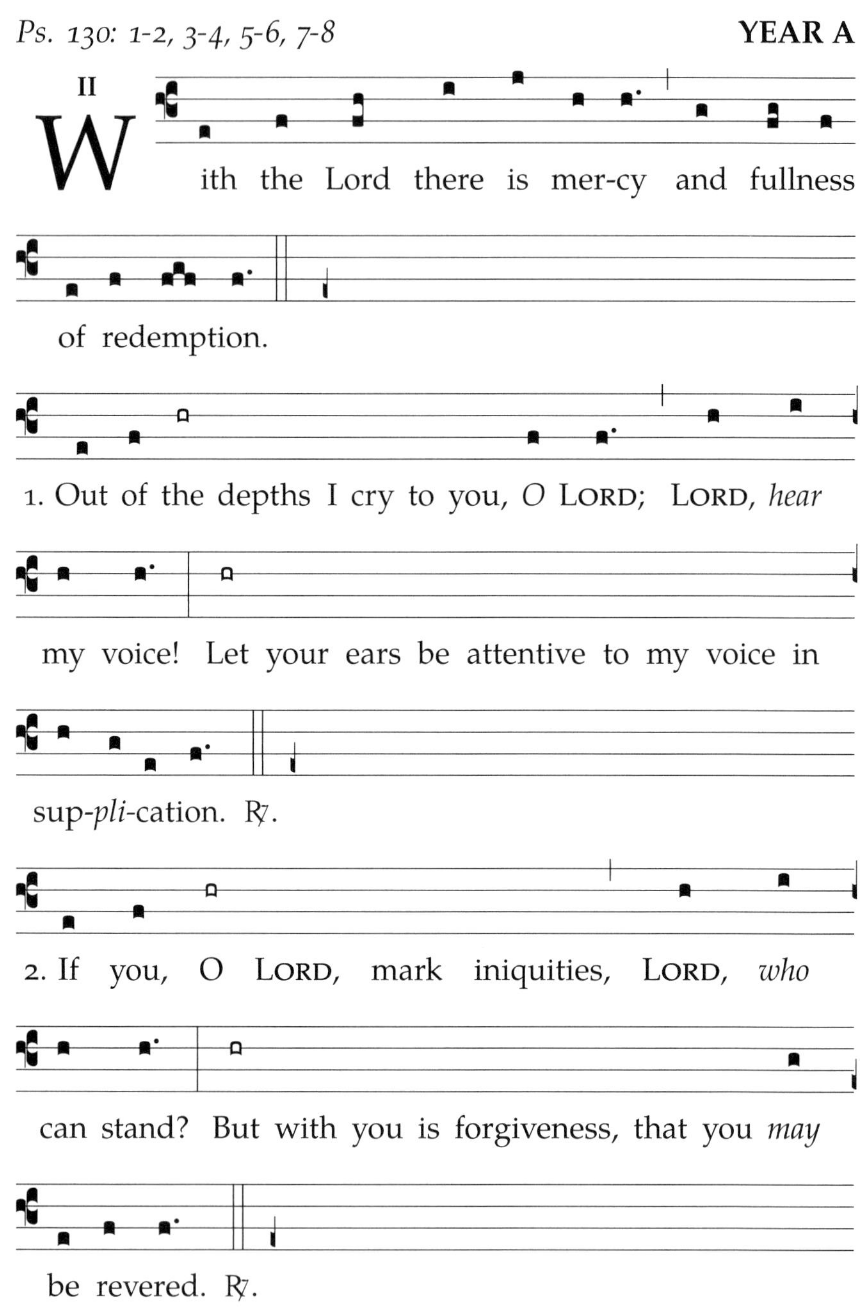

Ps. 130: 1-2, 3-4, 5-6, 7-8
YEAR A
II
With the Lord there is mer-cy and fullness
of redemption.
1. Out of the depths I cry to you, O LORD; LORD, hear
my voice! Let your ears be attentive to my voice in
sup-pli-cation. ℟.
2. If you, O LORD, mark iniquities, LORD, who
can stand? But with you is forgiveness, that you may
be revered. ℟.

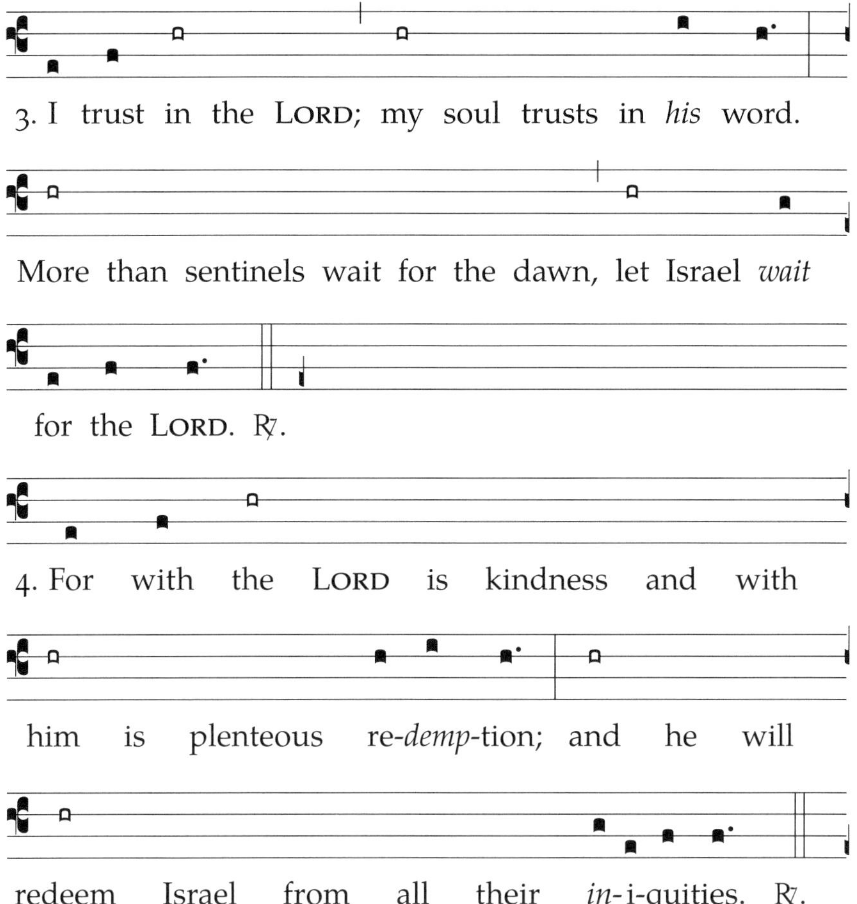
3. I trust in the LORD; my soul trusts in *his* word.
More than sentinels wait for the dawn, let Israel *wait*
for the LORD. ℟.
4. For with the LORD is kindness and with
him is plenteous re-*demp*-tion; and he will
redeem Israel from all their *in*-i-quities. ℟.

Fifth Sunday of Lent

Ps. 51: 3-4, 12-13, 14-15 **YEAR B**

VIII
Create a clean heart in me, O God.
1. Have mercy on me, O God, in your *good*-ness; in the
greatness of your compassion wipe out my *of*-fense.
Thoroughly wash me from my guilt and of *my* sin
cleanse me. ℟.
2. A clean heart create for me, O God, and a steadfast
spirit renew with-*in* me. Cast me not out from your
presence, and your Holy Spirit *take* not from me. ℟.

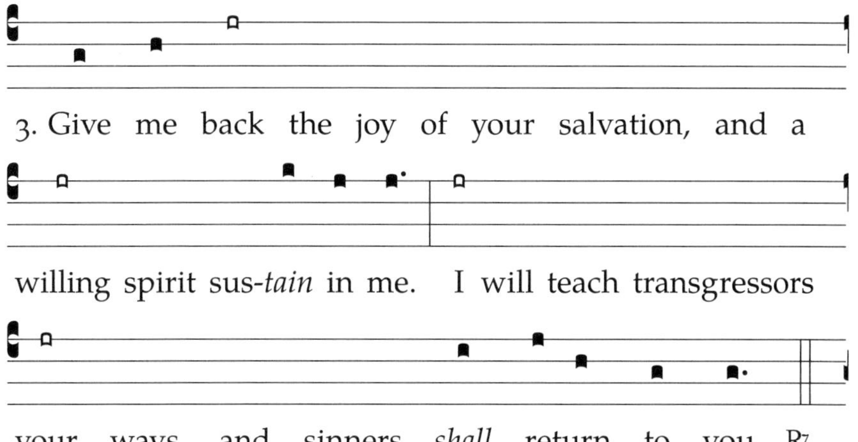
3. Give me back the joy of your salvation, and a
willing spirit sus-*tain* in me. I will teach transgressors
your ways, and sinners *shall* return to you. ℟.

Fifth Sunday of Lent

Ps. 126: 1-2, 2-3, 4-5, 6 **YEAR C**

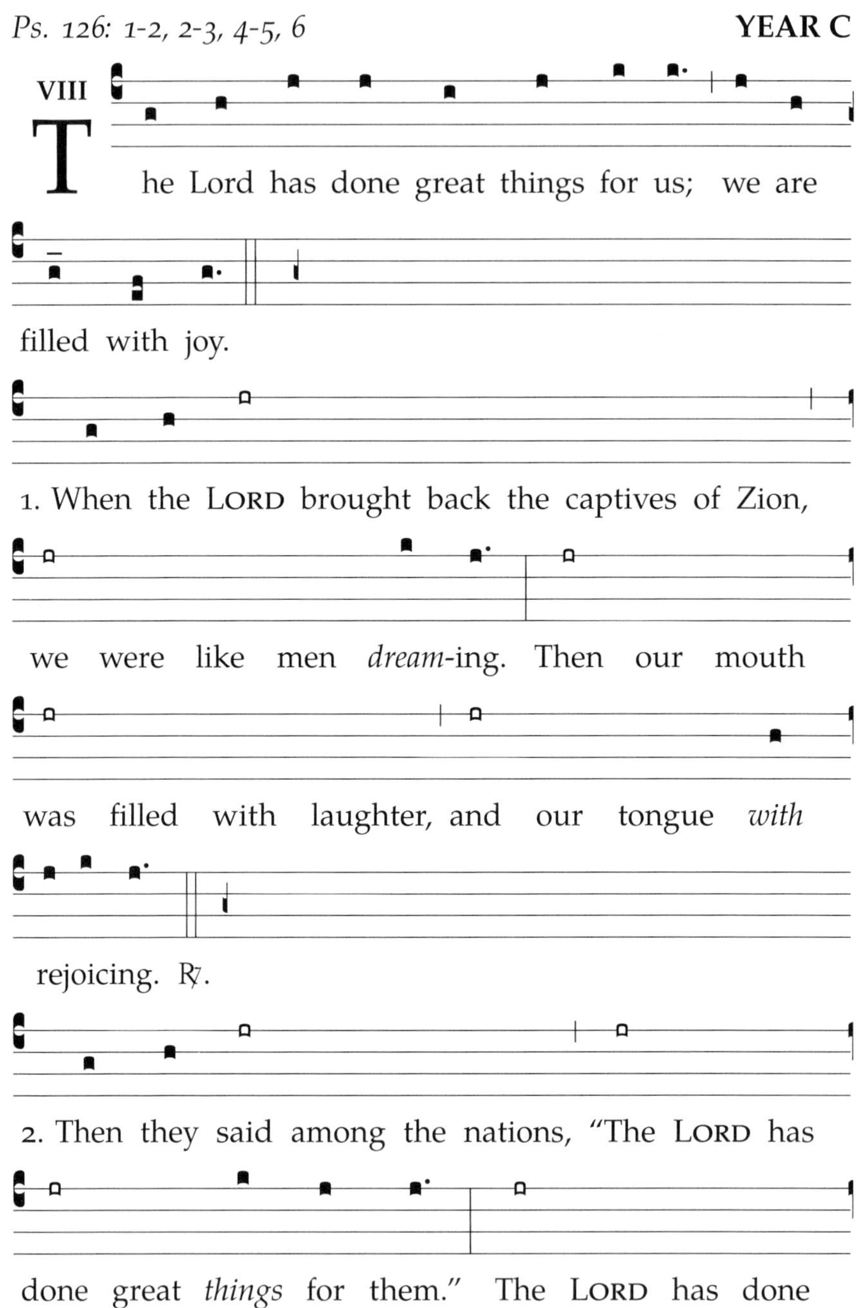

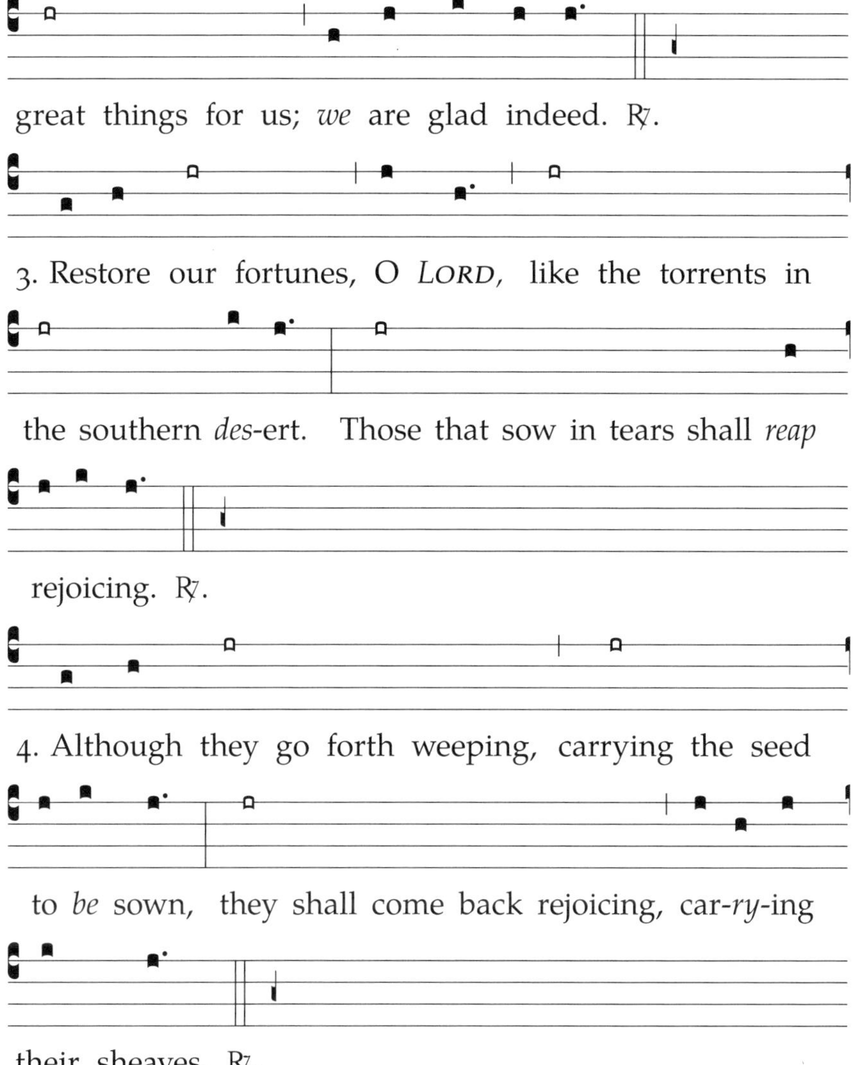
great things for us; *we* are glad indeed. ℟.
3. Restore our fortunes, O LORD, like the torrents in
the southern *des*-ert. Those that sow in tears shall *reap*
rejoicing. ℟.
4. Although they go forth weeping, carrying the seed
to *be* sown, they shall come back rejoicing, car-*ry*-ing
their sheaves. ℟.

Holy Week

Palm Sunday

Ps. 22: 8-9, 17-18, 19-20, 23-24 **YEAR ABC**

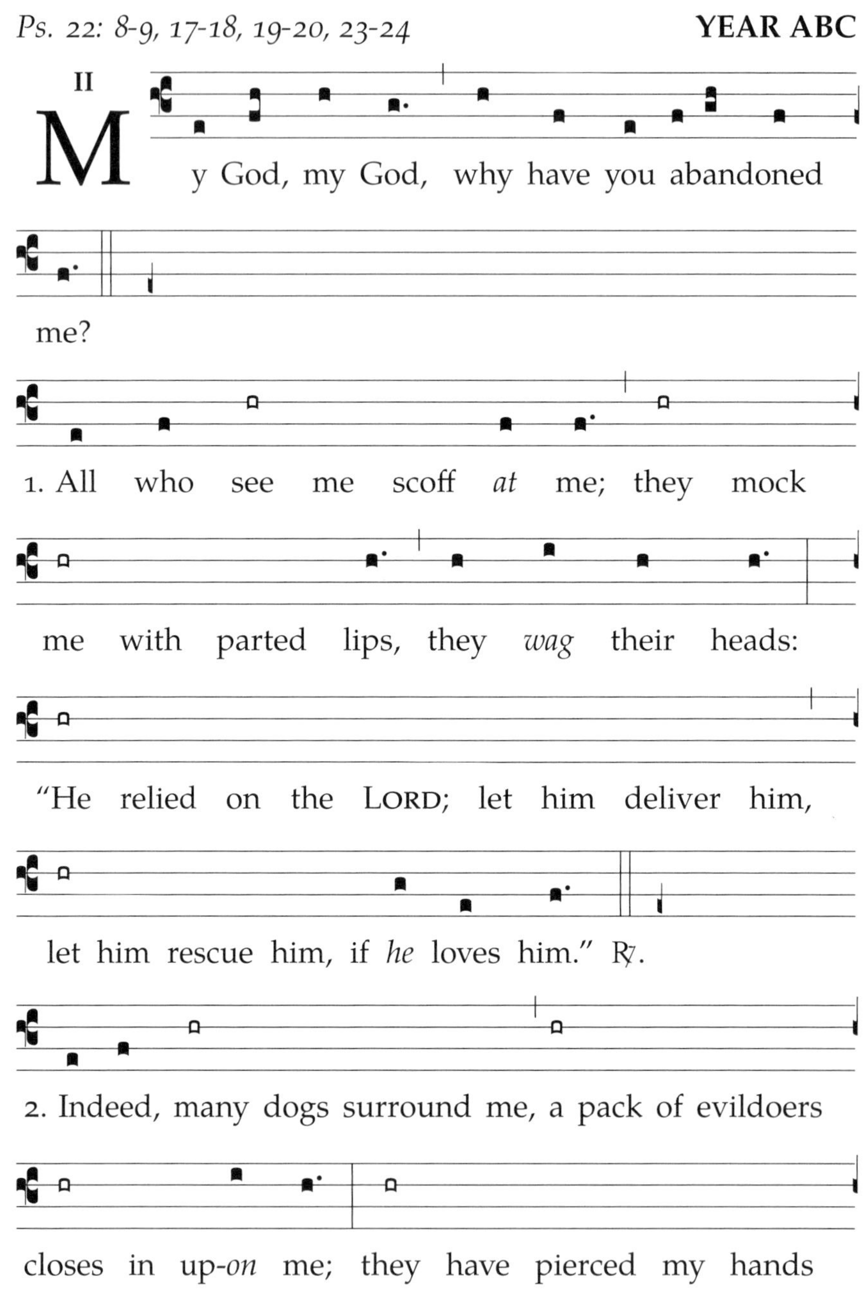
II
My God, my God, why have you abandoned me?
1. All who see me scoff *at* me; they mock me with parted lips, they *wag* their heads:
"He relied on the LORD; let him deliver him, let him rescue him, if *he* loves him." ℟.
2. Indeed, many dogs surround me, a pack of evildoers closes in up-*on* me; they have pierced my hands

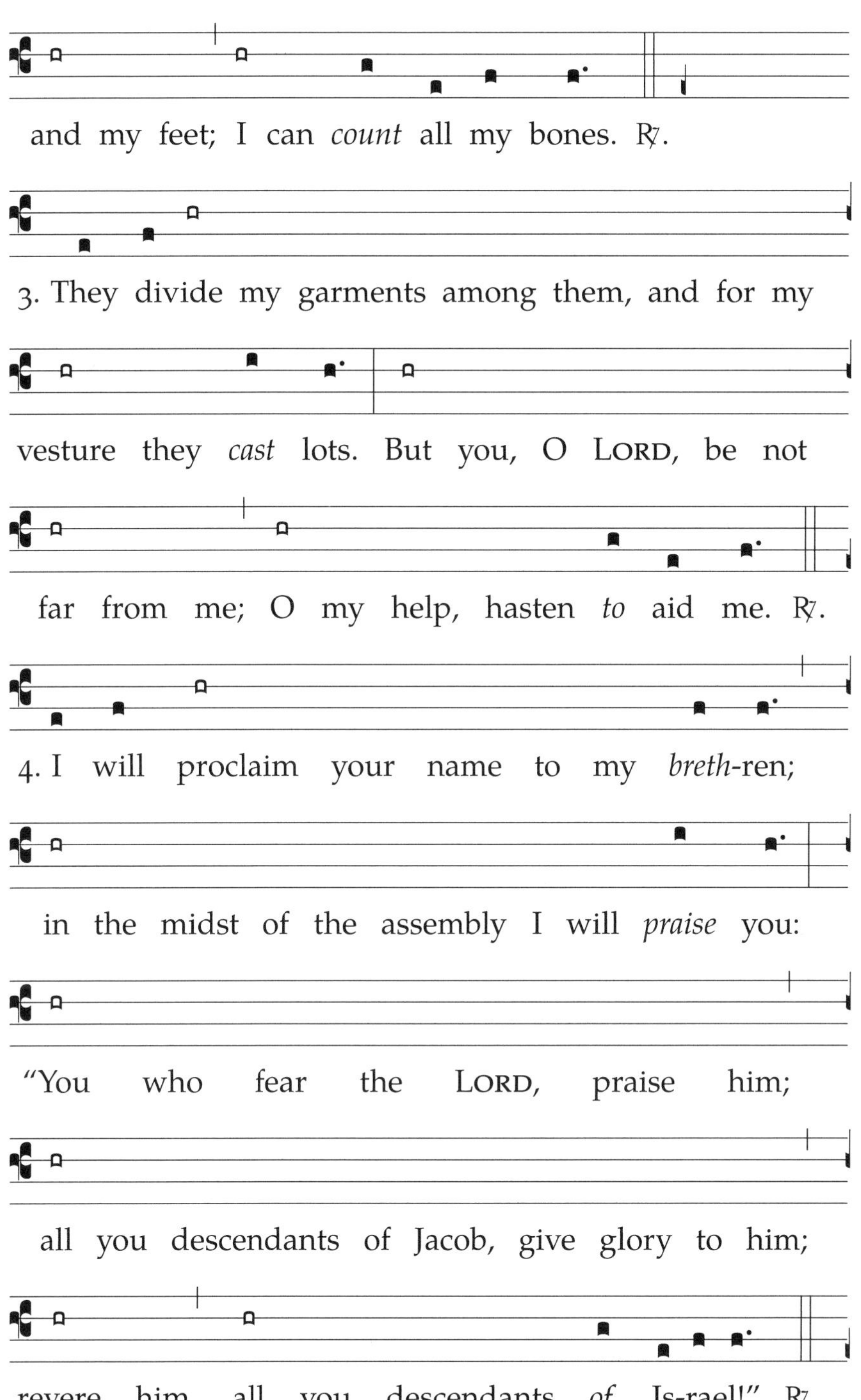
and my feet; I can *count* all my bones. ℟.
3. They divide my garments among them, and for my
vesture they *cast* lots. But you, O LORD, be not
far from me; O my help, hasten *to* aid me. ℟.
4. I will proclaim your name to my *breth*-ren;
in the midst of the assembly I will *praise* you:
"You who fear the LORD, praise him;
all you descendants of Jacob, give glory to him;
revere him, all you descendants *of* Is-rael!" ℟.

Thursday of the Lord's Supper

Ps. 116: 12-13, 15-16bc, 17-18 **YEAR ABC**

VIII
Our blessing-cup is a communion with the
Blood of Christ.
1. How shall I make a return to the LORD for all the
good he has *done* for me? The cup of salvation
I will take up, and I will call upon the *name* of
the LORD. ℟.
2. Pre-cious in the eyes of the LORD is the death
of his *faith*-ful ones. I am your servant, the son

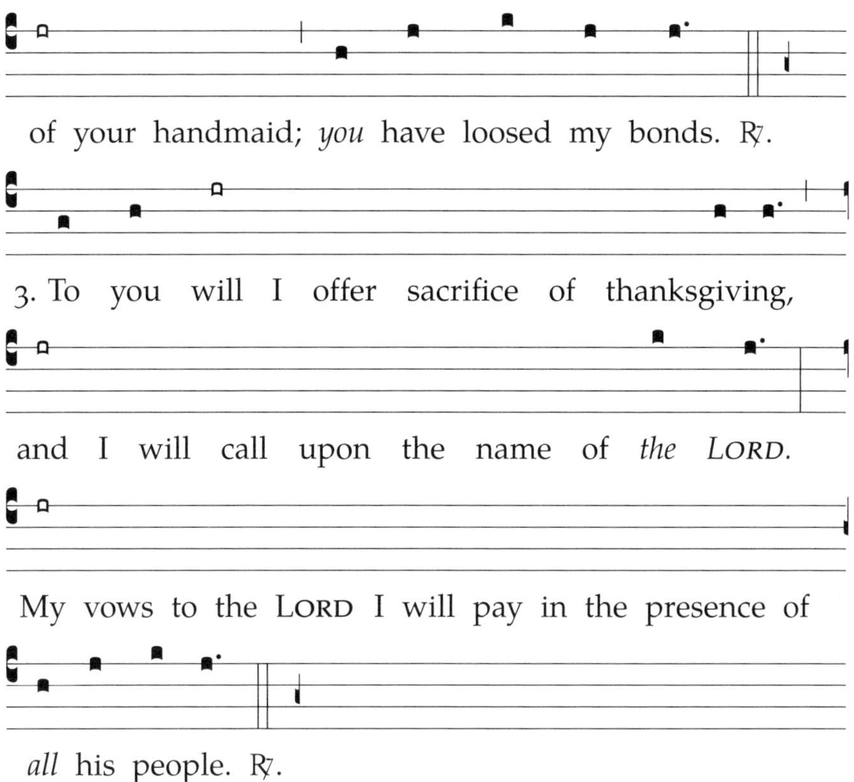
of your handmaid; you have loosed my bonds. ℟.
3. To you will I offer sacrifice of thanksgiving,
and I will call upon the name of the LORD.
My vows to the LORD I will pay in the presence of
all his people. ℟.

Friday of the Passion of the Lord

Ps. 31: 2, 6, 12-13, 15-16, 17, 25 **YEAR ABC**

IV
Father, in-to your hands I commend
my spirit.
1. In you, O LORD, I take refuge; let me never
be put *to* shame. In your *jus*-tice rescue me.
Into your hands I commend my spirit; you will redeem
me, O *LORD*, O faith-ful God. ℟.
2. For all my foes I am an object of reproach,
a laughingstock to my neighbors, and a dread to my

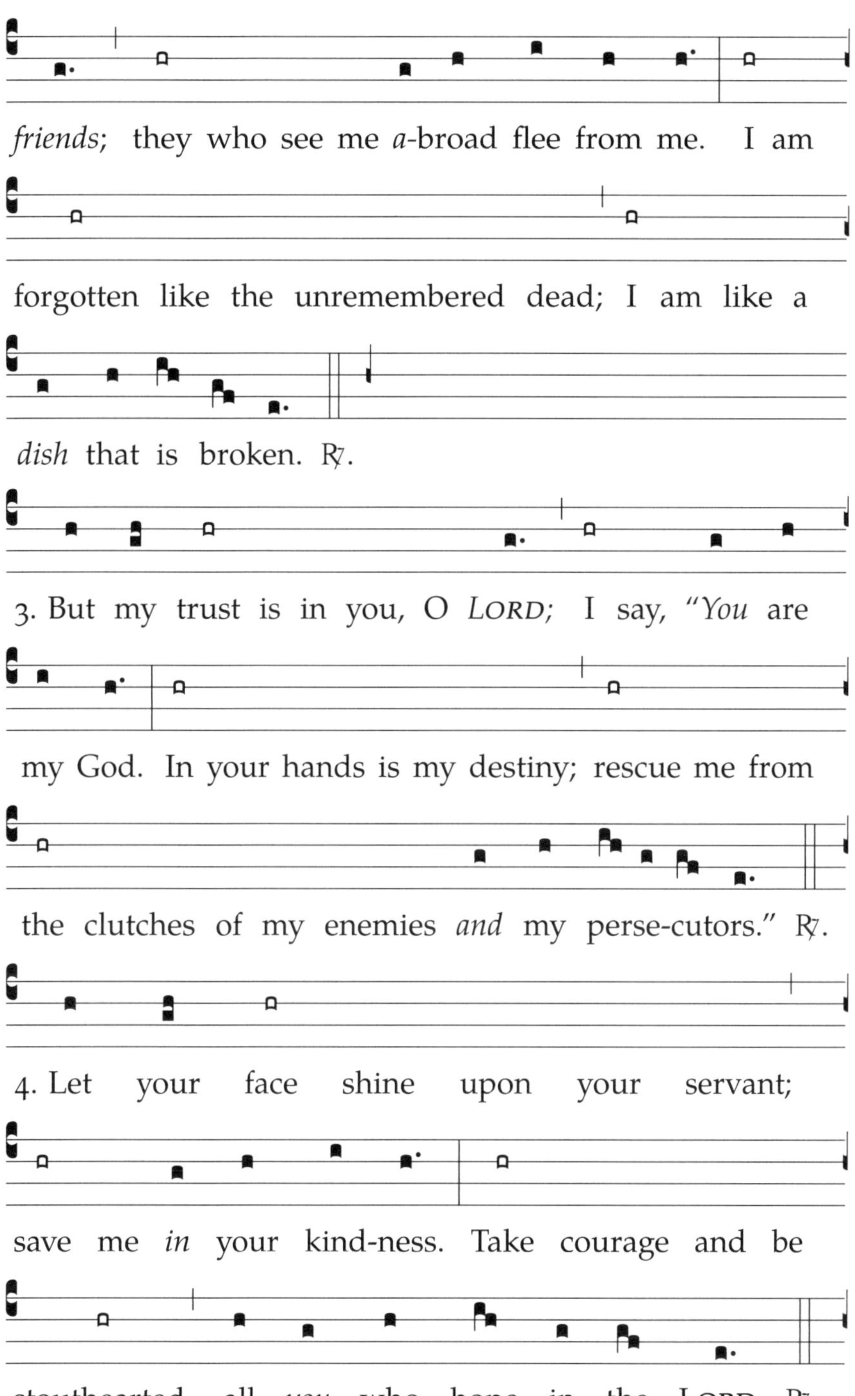
friends; they who see me a-broad flee from me. I am
forgotten like the unremembered dead; I am like a
dish that is broken. ℟.
3. But my trust is in you, O LORD; I say, "You are
my God. In your hands is my destiny; rescue me from
the clutches of my enemies and my perse-cutors." ℟.
4. Let your face shine upon your servant;
save me in your kind-ness. Take courage and be
stouthearted, all you who hope in the LORD. ℟.

Easter

Easter Vigil, after Reading 1 (Option 1)

Ps. 104: 1-2, 5-6, 10, 12, 13-14, 24, 35 **YEAR ABC**

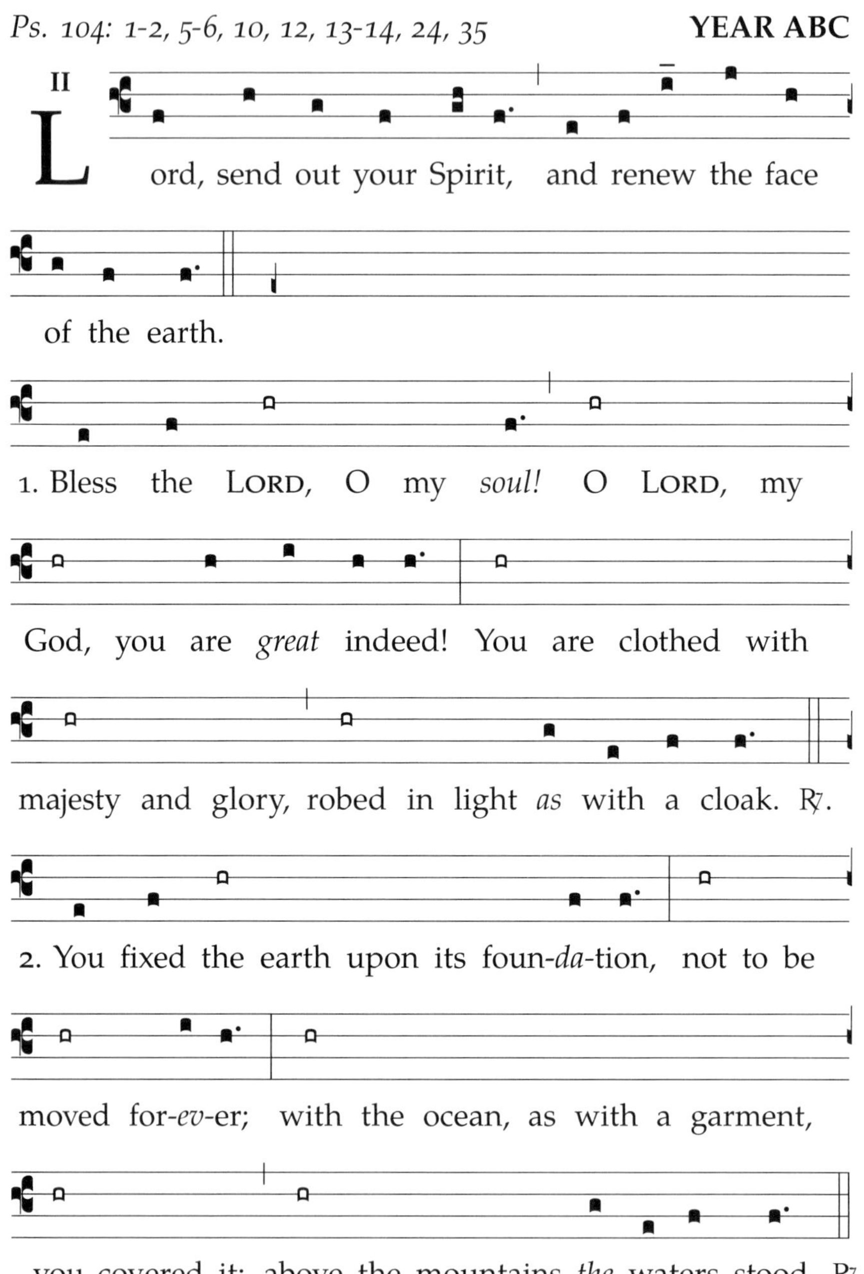
II
Lord, send out your Spirit, and renew the face
of the earth.
1. Bless the LORD, O my *soul!* O LORD, my
God, you are *great* indeed! You are clothed with
majesty and glory, robed in light *as* with a cloak. ℟.
2. You fixed the earth upon its foun-*da*-tion, not to be
moved for-*ev*-er; with the ocean, as with a garment,
you covered it; above the mountains *the* waters stood. ℟.

3. You send forth springs into the watercourses
that wind among the *moun*-tains. Beside them the
birds of heaven dwell; from among the branches they
send forth their song. ℟.
4. You water the mountains from your *pal*-ace;
the earth is replete with the fruit of *your* works.
You raise grass for the cattle, and vegetation
for man's use, producing bread *from* the earth. ℟.

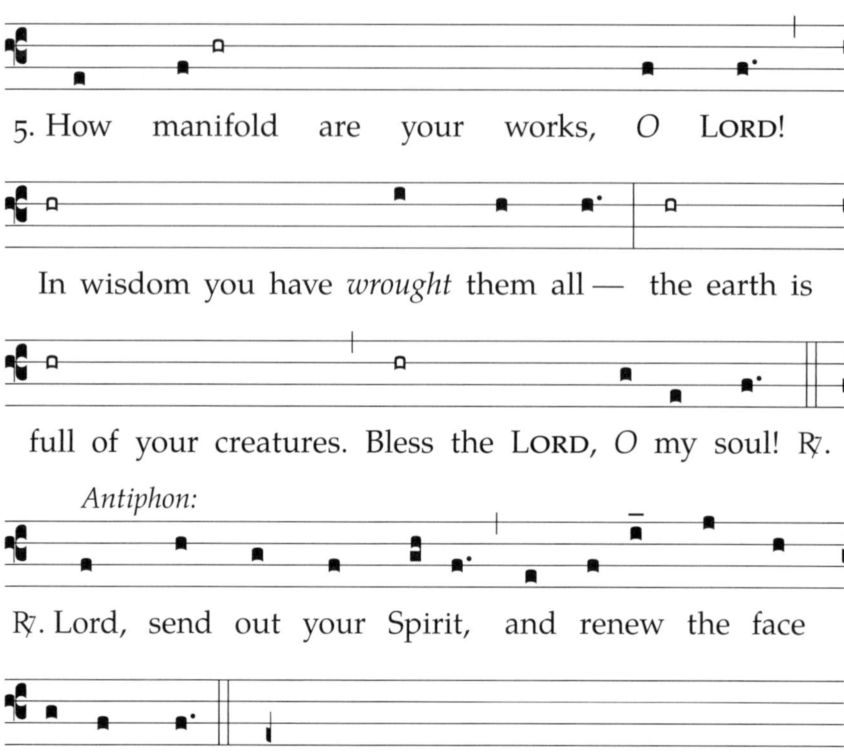
5. How manifold are your works, O LORD!
In wisdom you have wrought them all — the earth is
full of your creatures. Bless the LORD, O my soul! ℟.
Antiphon:
℟. Lord, send out your Spirit, and renew the face
of the earth.

Easter Vigil, after Reading 1 (option 2)

Ps. 33: 4-5, 6-7, 12-13, 20, 22 **YEAR ABC**

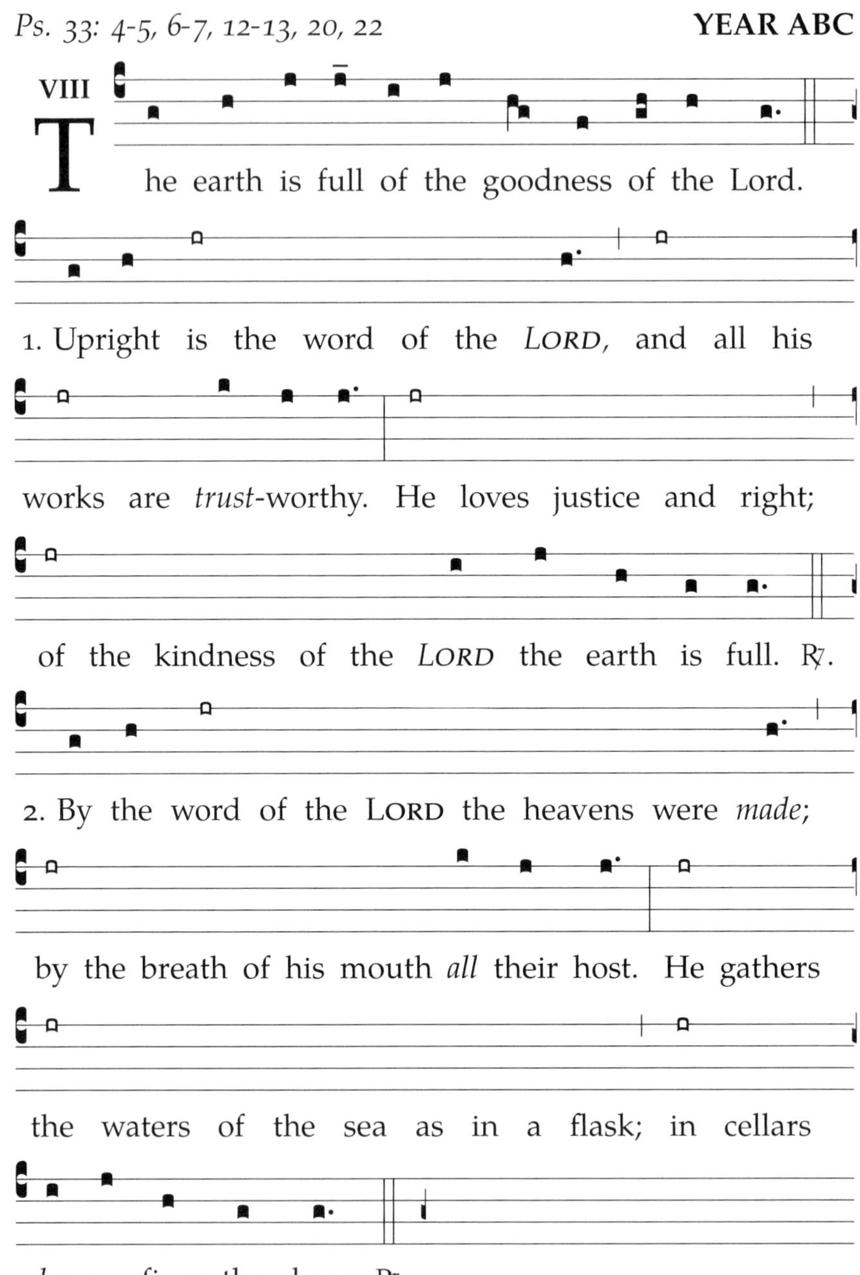
VIII
The earth is full of the goodness of the Lord.
1. Upright is the word of the *LORD,* and all his
works are *trust*-worthy. He loves justice and right;
of the kindness of the *LORD* the earth is full. R̸.
2. By the word of the LORD the heavens were *made;*
by the breath of his mouth *all* their host. He gathers
the waters of the sea as in a flask; in cellars
he con-fines the deep. R̸.

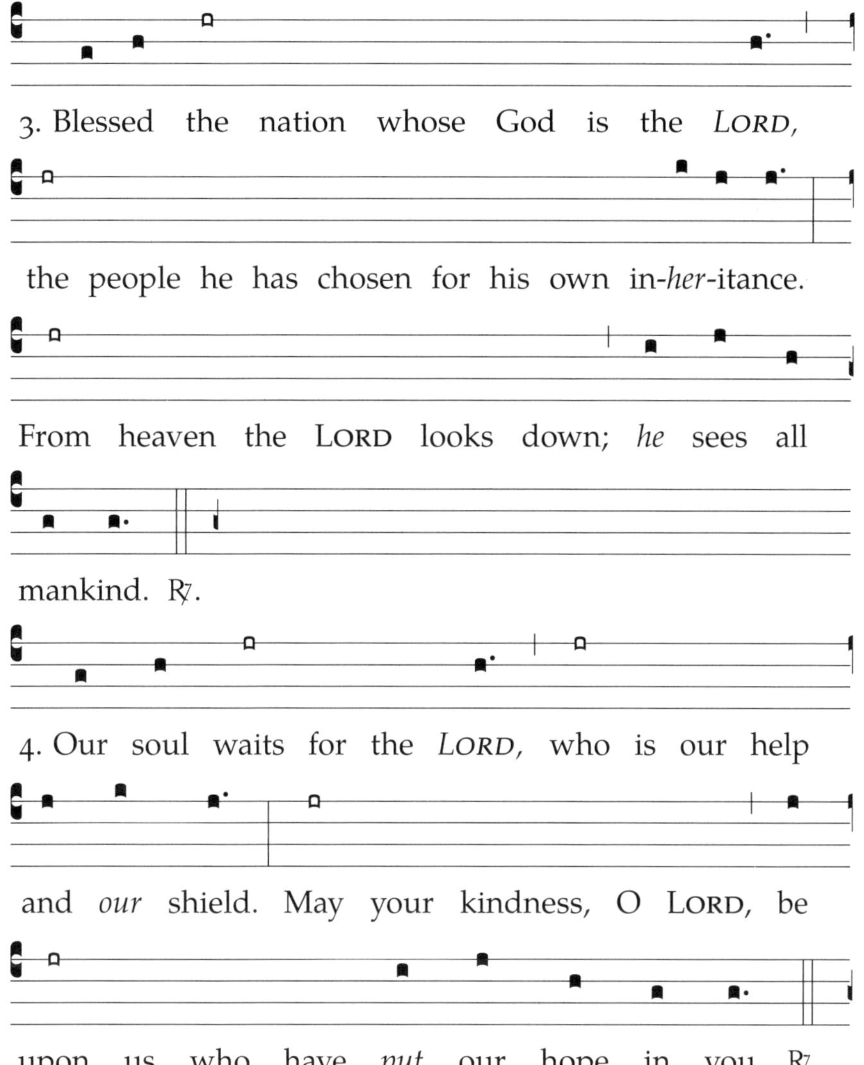
3. Blessed the nation whose God is the *LORD,*
the people he has chosen for his own in-*her*-itance.
From heaven the LORD looks down; *he* sees all
mankind. ℟.
4. Our soul waits for the *LORD,* who is our help
and *our* shield. May your kindness, O LORD, be
upon us who have *put* our hope in you. ℟.

Easter Vigil, after Reading 2

Ps. 16: 5, 8, 9-10, 11 **YEAR ABC**

II
You are my inhe-ritance, O Lord.
1. O LORD, my allotted portion and my *cup,* you it is
who hold fast *my* lot. I set the LORD ever before
me; with him at my right hand I shall *not* be
disturbed. ℟.
2. Therefore my heart is glad and my soul re-*joic*-es,
my body, too, abides in *con*-fidence; because you
will not abandon my soul to the netherworld,

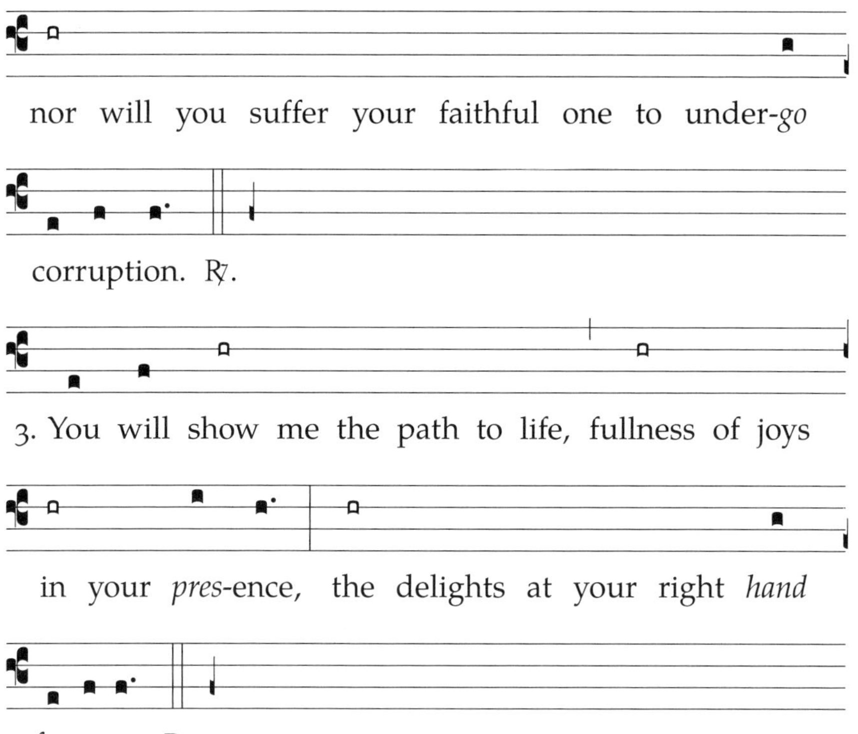
nor will you suffer your faithful one to under-*go*
corruption. ℟.
3. You will show me the path to life, fullness of joys
in your *pres*-ence, the delights at your right *hand*
for-ever. ℟.

Easter Vigil, after Reading 3

Ex. 15: 1-2, 3-4, 5-6, 17-18 **YEAR ABC**

VI
Let us sing to the Lord; he has covered himself
in glo-ry.
1. I will sing to the LORD, for he is gloriously
tri-*um*-phant; horse and chariot he has cast *in*-to
the sea. My strength and my courage is the LORD,
and he *has* been my savior. He is my God,
I praise him; the God of my fa-*ther*, I extol him. ℟.

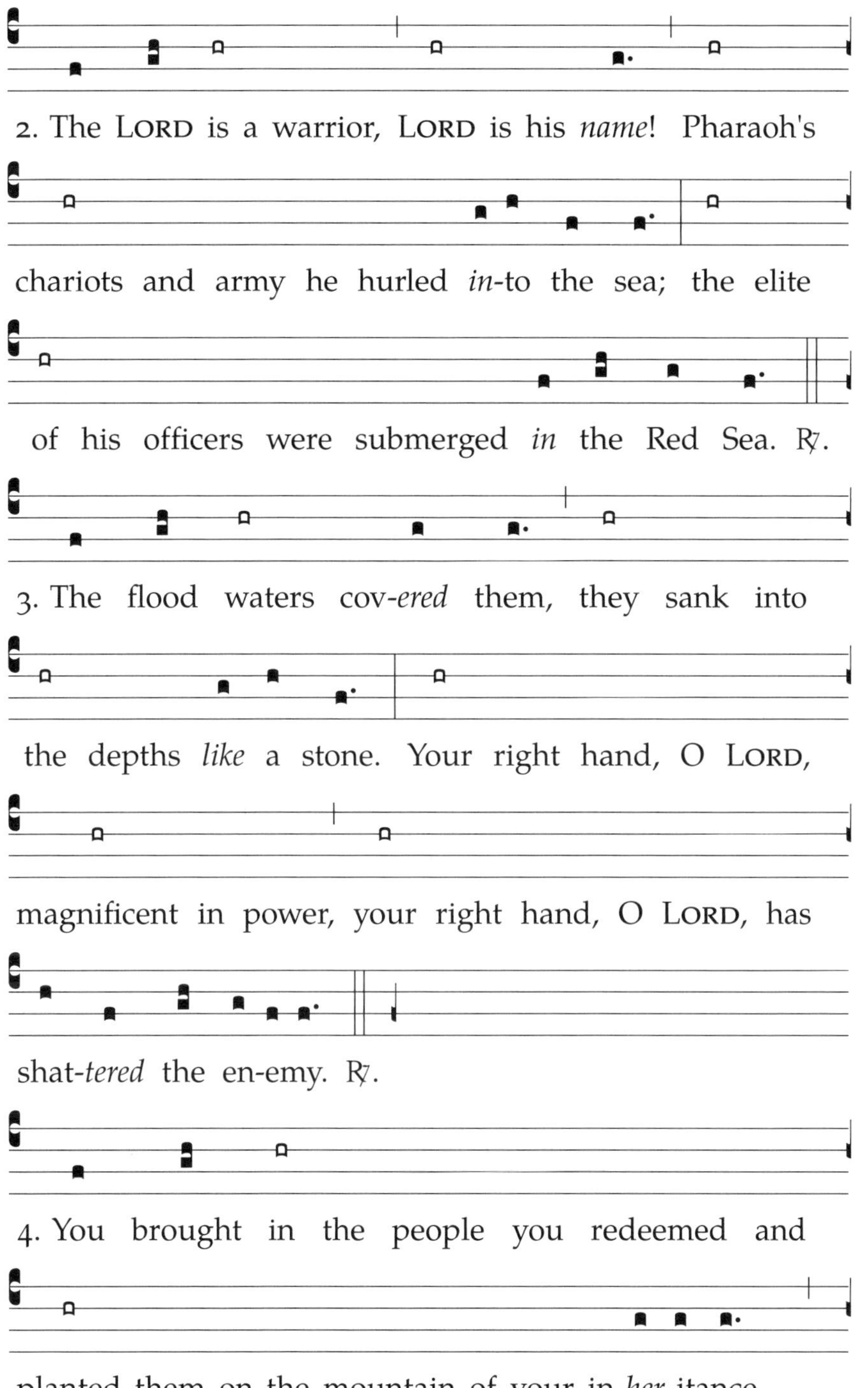
2. The LORD is a warrior, LORD is his *name*! Pharaoh's
chariots and army he hurled *in*-to the sea; the elite
of his officers were submerged *in* the Red Sea. ℟.
3. The flood waters cov-*ered* them, they sank into
the depths *like* a stone. Your right hand, O LORD,
magnificent in power, your right hand, O LORD, has
shat-*tered* the en-emy. ℟.
4. You brought in the people you redeemed and
planted them on the mountain of your in-*her*-itance —

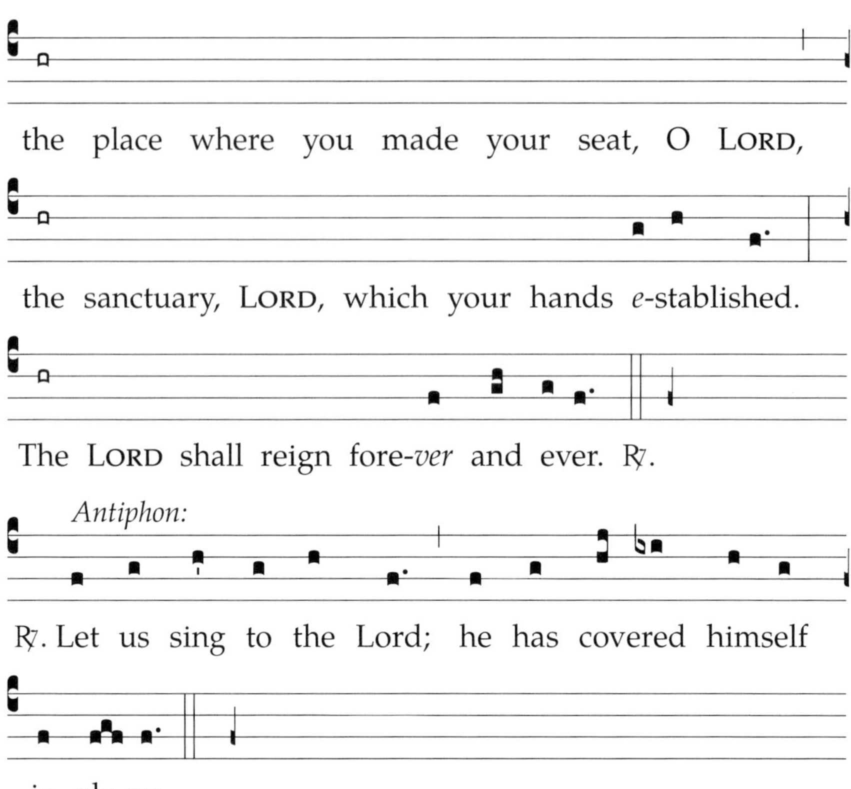
the place where you made your seat, O LORD,
the sanctuary, LORD, which your hands *e*-stablished.
The LORD shall reign fore-*ver* and ever. ℟.
Antiphon:
℟. Let us sing to the Lord; he has covered himself
in glo-ry.

Easter Vigil, after Reading 4

Ps. 30: 2, 4, 5-6, 11-12, 13 **YEAR ABC**

II
I will praise you, Lord, for you have rescued me.
1. I will extol you, O LORD, for you drew me clear and did not let my enemies rejoice *o*-ver me. O LORD, you brought me up from the netherworld; you preserved me from among those going down *in*-to the pit. ℟.
2. Sing praise to the LORD, you his faith-*ful* ones,

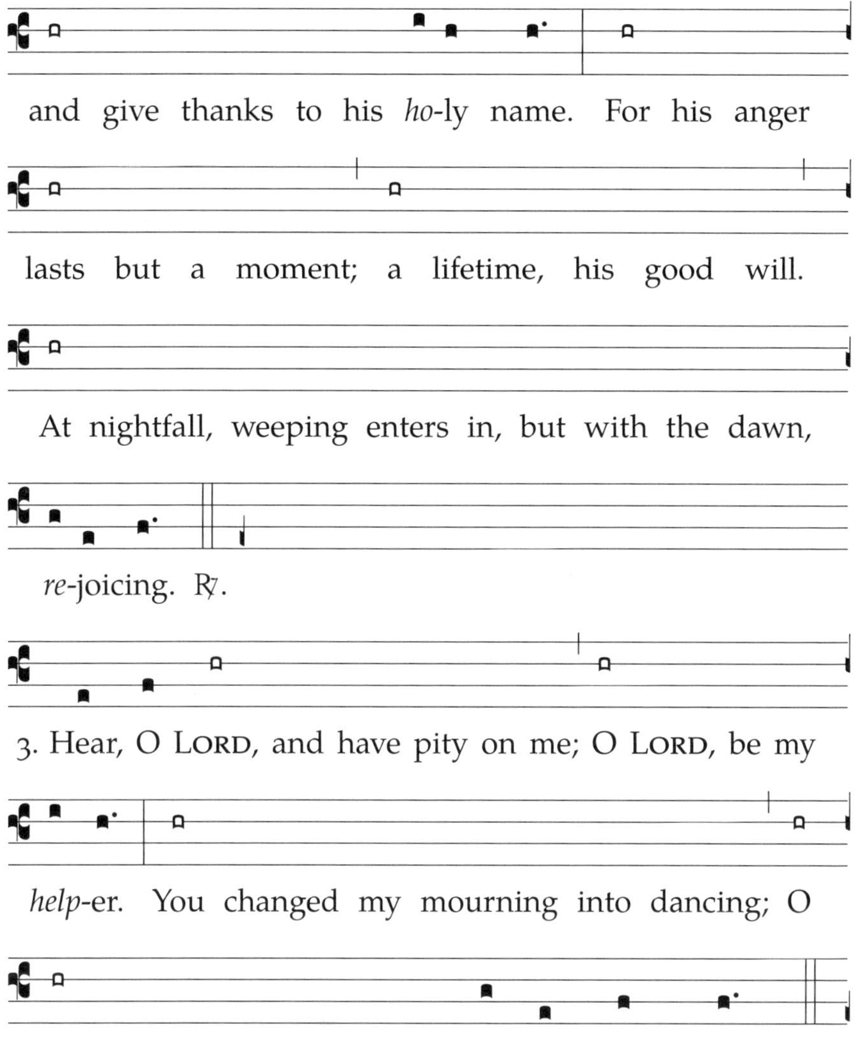
and give thanks to his ho-ly name. For his anger
lasts but a moment; a lifetime, his good will.
At nightfall, weeping enters in, but with the dawn,
re-joicing. R7.
3. Hear, O LORD, and have pity on me; O LORD, be my
help-er. You changed my mourning into dancing; O
LORD, my God, forever will I give you thanks. R7.

EASTER VIGIL, AFTER READING 5

Is. 12: 2-3, 4, 5-6 **YEAR ABC**

℣
You will draw water joyfully from the springs
of salvation.
1. God indeed is my savior; I am confident and
un-*a*-fraid. My strength and my courage is the
LORD, and he has been my *sav*-ior. With joy
you will draw water at the fountain *of* salvation. ℟.
2. Give thanks to the LORD, acclaim *his* name; among
the nations make known his deeds, proclaim how

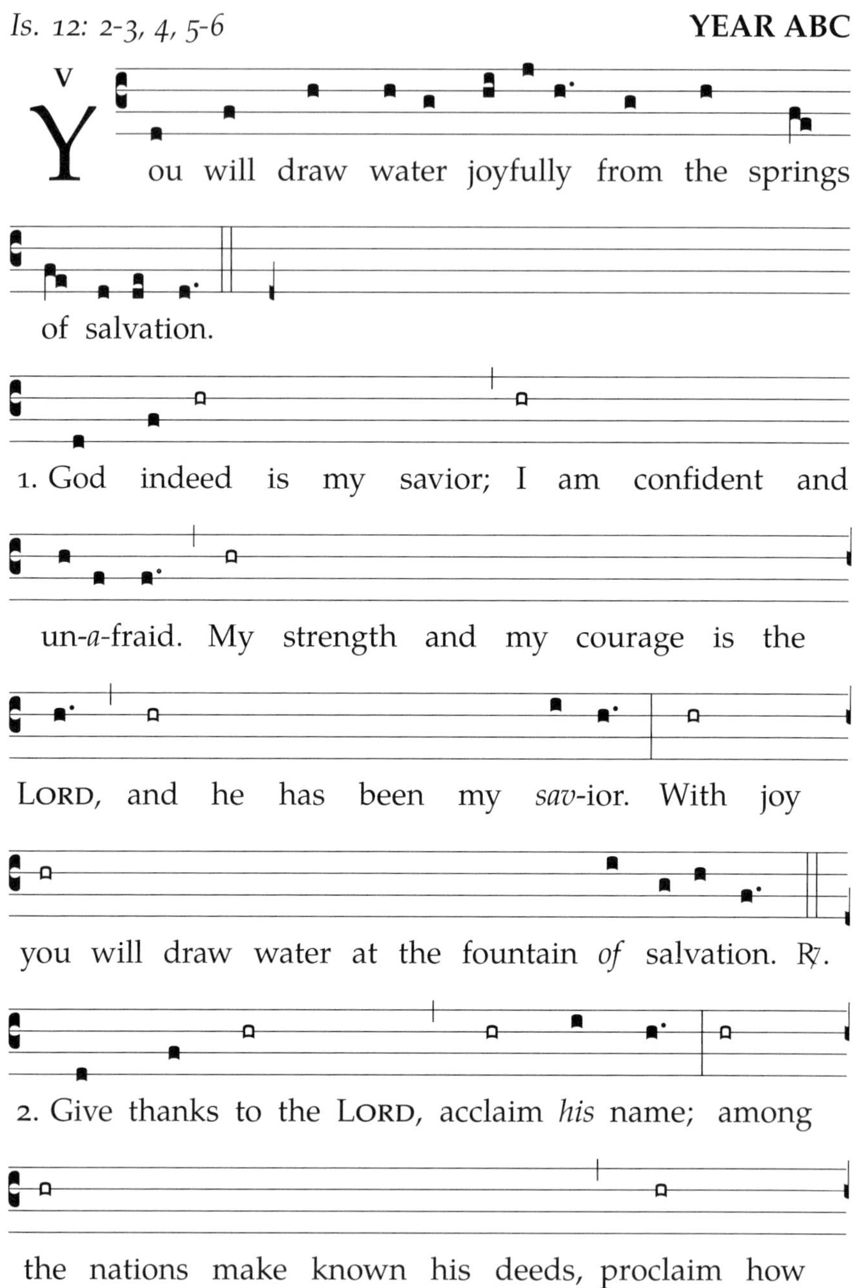

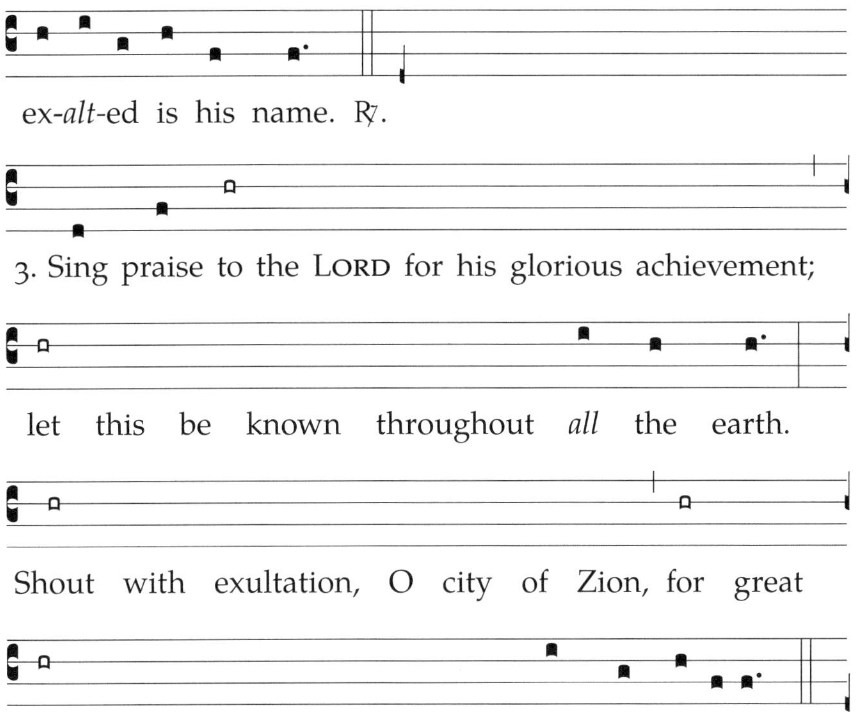
ex-*alt*-ed is his name. ℟.
3. Sing praise to the LORD for his glorious achievement;
let this be known throughout *all* the earth.
Shout with exultation, O city of Zion, for great
in your midst is the Holy *One* of Is-rael! ℟.

Easter Vigil, after Reading 6

Ps. 19: 8, 9, 10, 11 **YEAR ABC**

℟
Lord, you have the words of everlasting life.
1. The law of the LORD is perfect, refreshing *the* soul;
the decree of the LORD is trustworthy, giving wisdom
to the simple. ℟.
2. The precepts of the LORD are right, rejoicing *the*
heart; the command of the LORD is clear, en-*light*-ening
the eye. ℟.
3. The fear of the LORD is pure, enduring for-*ev*-er;

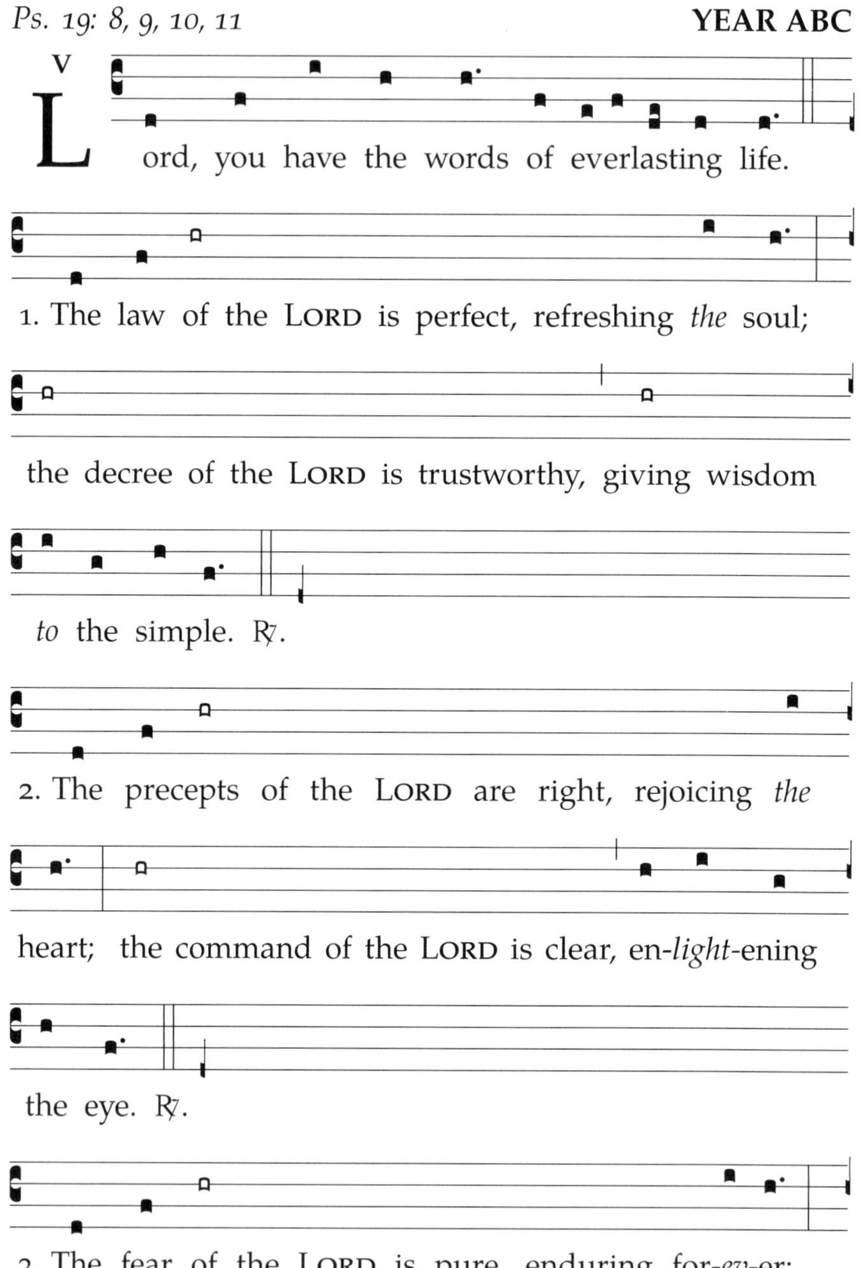

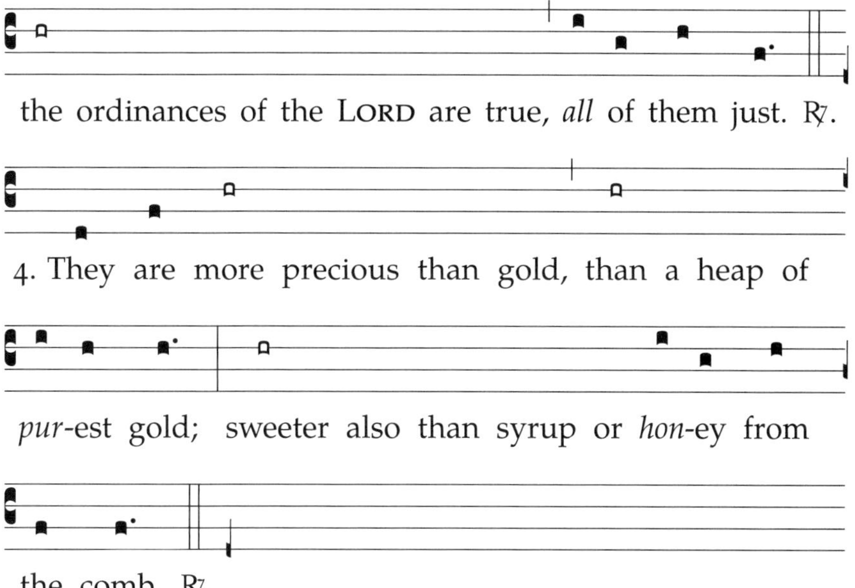
the ordinances of the LORD are true, *all* of them just. ℟.
4. They are more precious than gold, than a heap of
pur-est gold; sweeter also than syrup or *hon*-ey from
the comb. ℟.

Easter Vigil, after Reading 7 (if baptism is celebrated)

Ps. 42: 3, 5; 43:3, 4 **YEAR ABC**

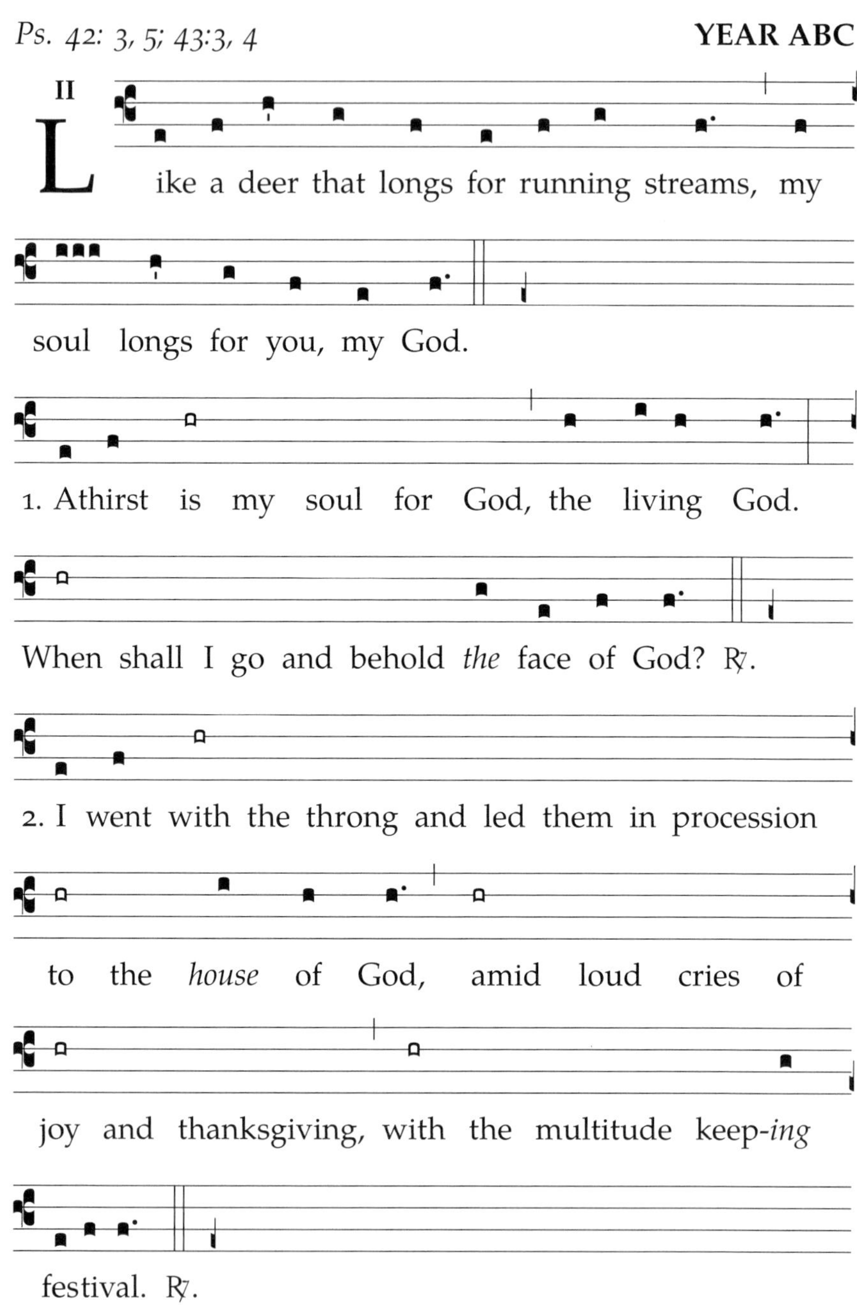
II
Like a deer that longs for running streams, my
soul longs for you, my God.
1. Athirst is my soul for God, the living God.
When shall I go and behold *the* face of God? ℟.
2. I went with the throng and led them in procession
to the *house* of God, amid loud cries of
joy and thanksgiving, with the multitude keep-*ing*
festival. ℟.

3. Send forth your light and your fi-*del*-i-ty; they shall
lead me on and bring me to your holy mountain,
to *your* dwelling-place. ℟.
4. Then will I go in to the altar of God, the God
of my gladness *and* joy; then will I give you
thanks upon the harp, *O* God, my God! ℟.

Easter Vigil, after Reading 7 (option 1 when baptism is not celebrated)

Is. 12: 2-3, 4, 5-6 **YEAR ABC**

℣
You will draw water joyfully from the springs of salvation.
1. God indeed is my savior; I am confident and un-*a*-fraid. My strength and my courage is the LORD, and he has been my *sav*-ior. With joy you will draw water at the fountain *of* salvation. ℟.
2. Give thanks to the LORD, acclaim *his* name; among the nations make known his deeds, proclaim how

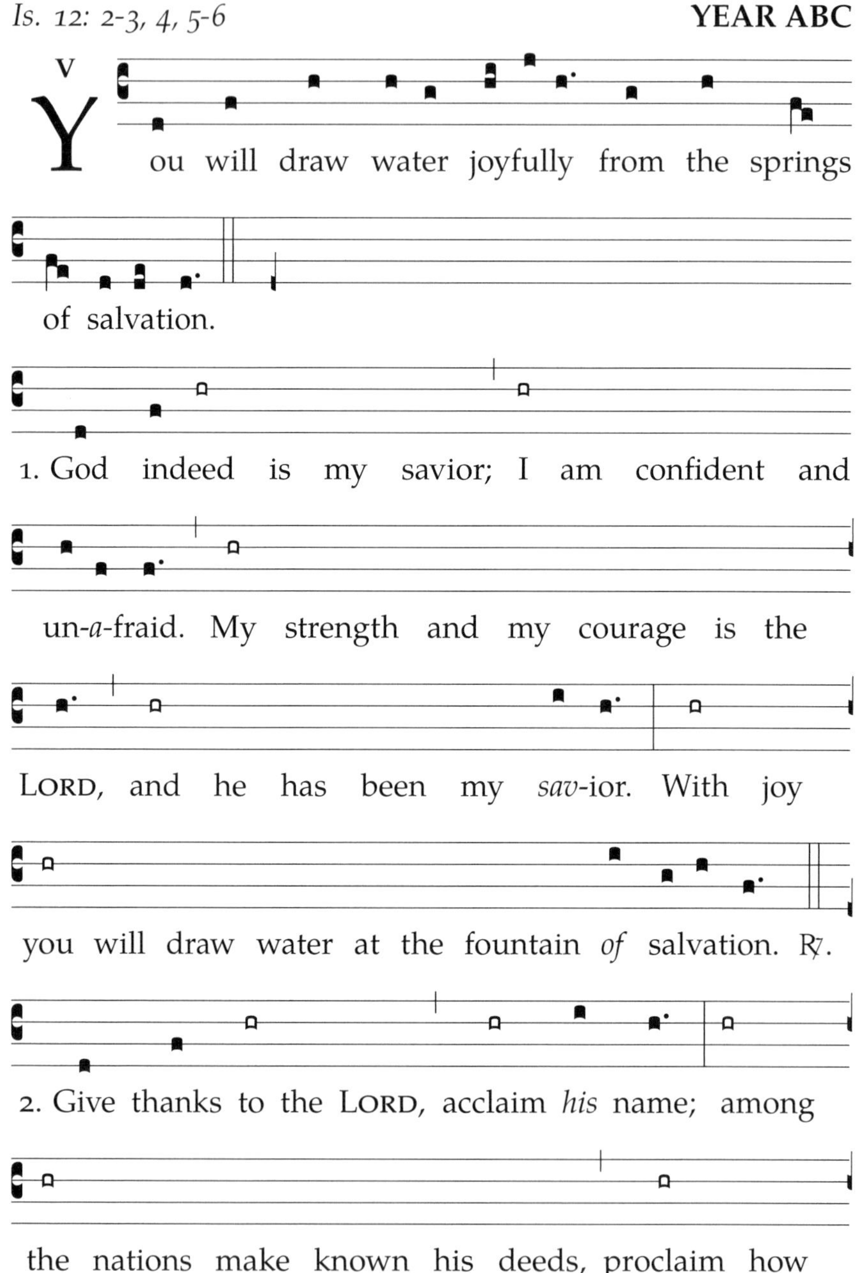

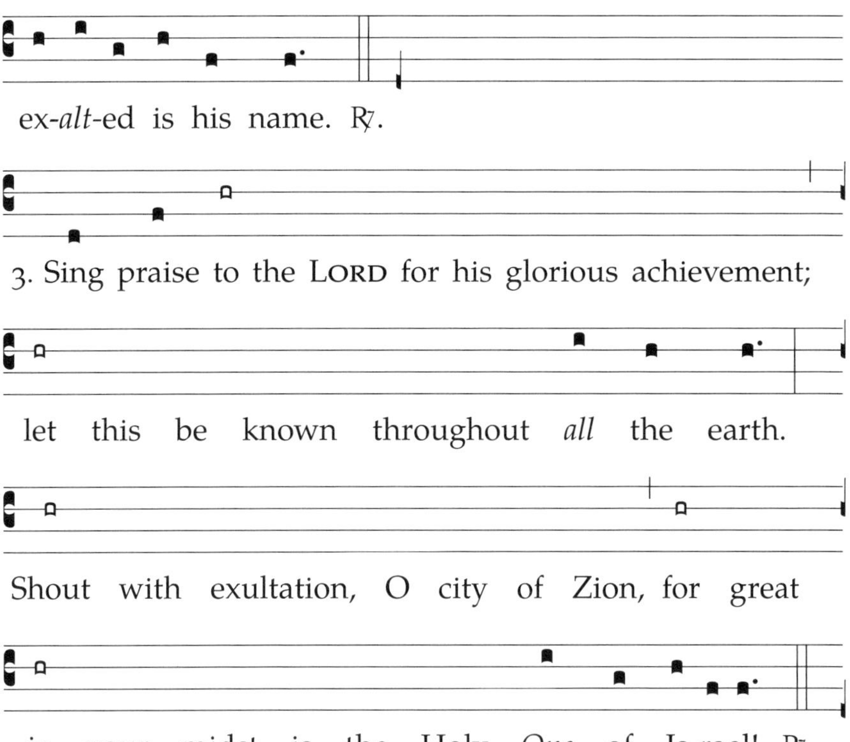
ex-*alt*-ed is his name. ℟.
3. Sing praise to the LORD for his glorious achievement;
let this be known throughout *all* the earth.
Shout with exultation, O city of Zion, for great
in your midst is the Holy *One* of Is-rael! ℟.

Easter Vigil, after Reading 7 (option 2 when baptism is not celebrated)

Ps. 51: 12-13, 14-15, 18-19 **YEAR ABC**

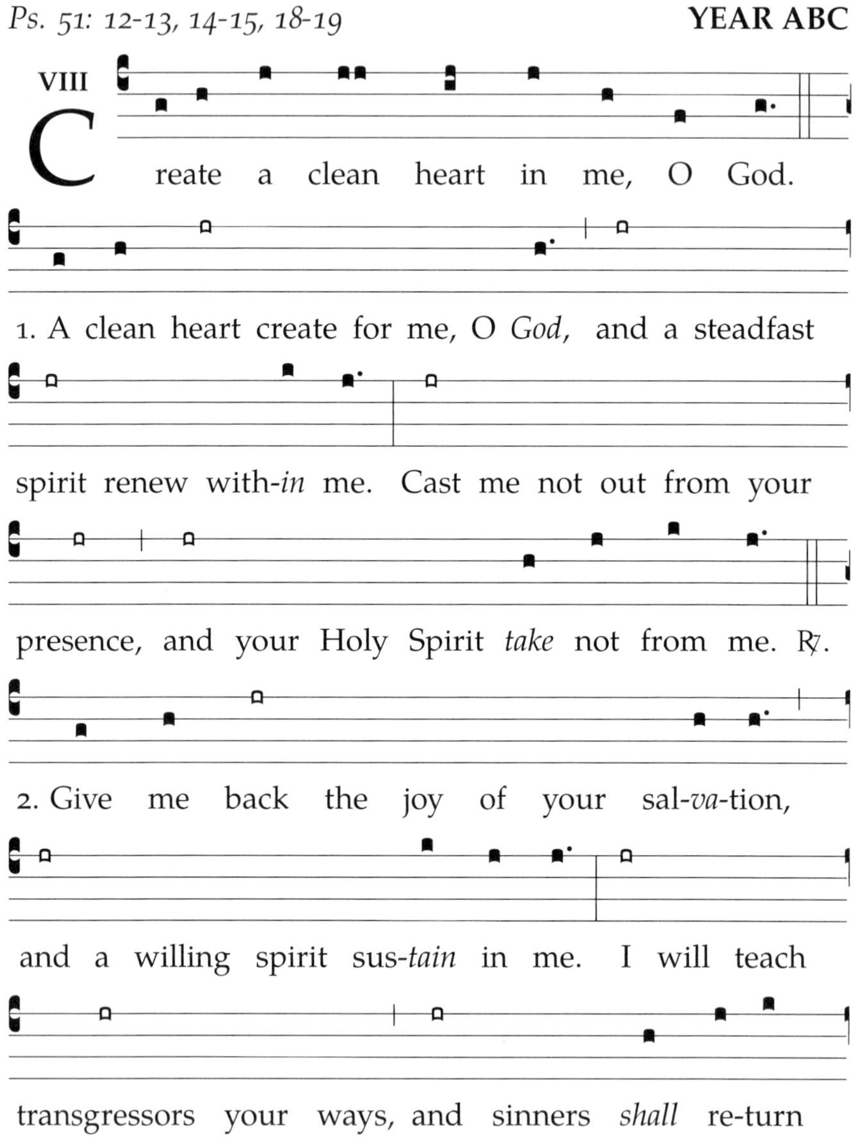
VIII
Create a clean heart in me, O God.
1. A clean heart create for me, O *God,* and a steadfast
spirit renew with-*in* me. Cast me not out from your
presence, and your Holy Spirit *take* not from me. ℟.
2. Give me back the joy of your sal-*va*-tion,
and a willing spirit sus-*tain* in me. I will teach
transgressors your ways, and sinners *shall* re-turn

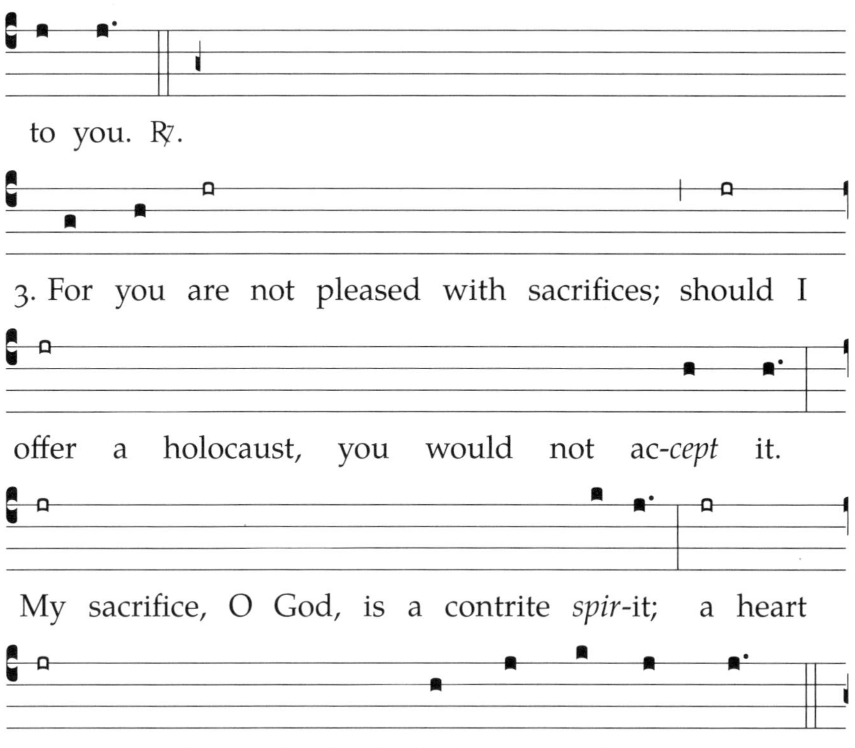
to you. ℟.
3. For you are not pleased with sacrifices; should I
offer a holocaust, you would not ac-*cept* it.
My sacrifice, O God, is a contrite *spir*-it; a heart
contrite and humbled, O *God*, you will not spurn. ℟.

Easter Vigil: Alleluia

Ps. 118: 1-2, 16-17, 22-23 **YEAR ABC**

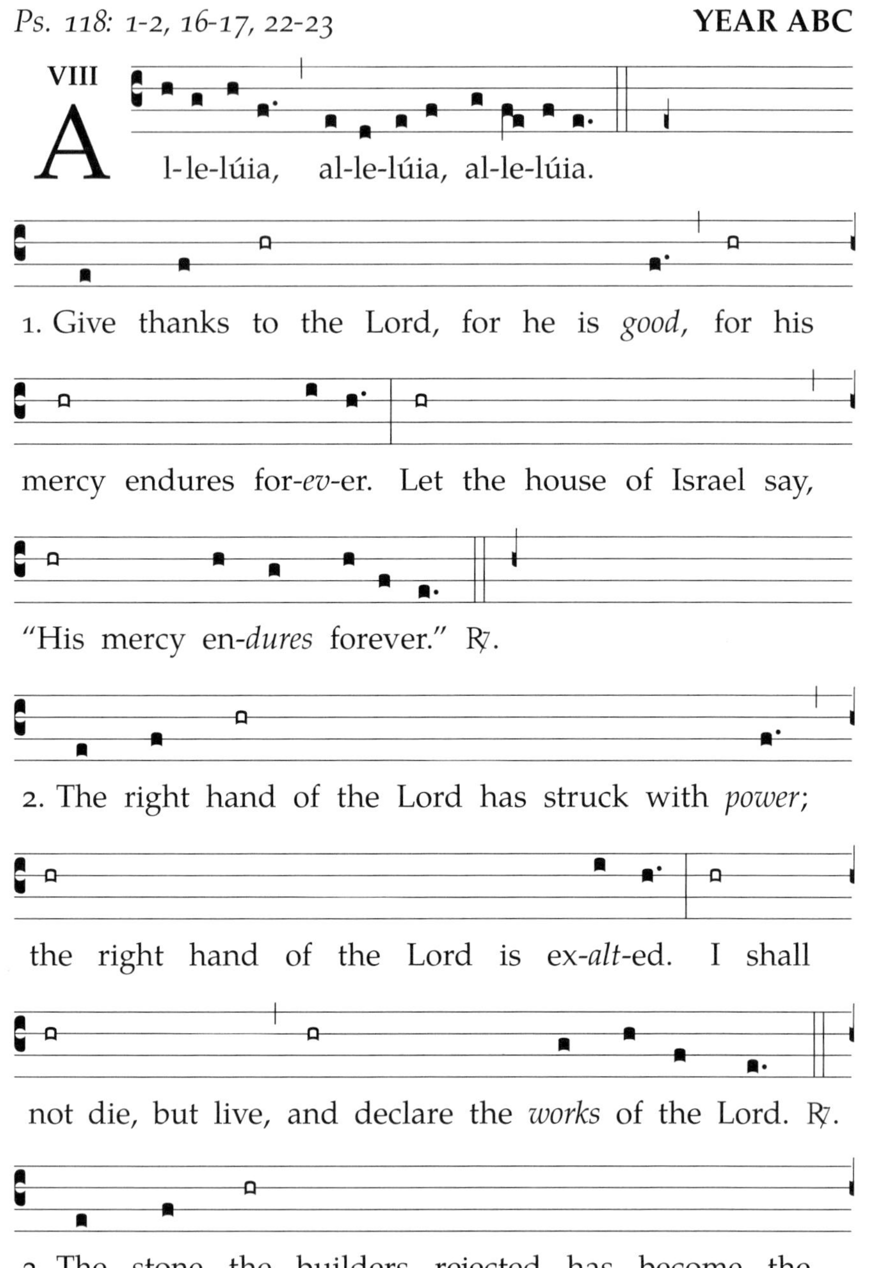
VIII
A l-le-lúia, al-le-lúia, al-le-lúia.
1. Give thanks to the Lord, for he is *good,* for his
mercy endures for-*ev*-er. Let the house of Israel say,
"His mercy en-*dures* forever." ℟.
2. The right hand of the Lord has struck with *power;*
the right hand of the Lord is ex-*alt*-ed. I shall
not die, but live, and declare the *works* of the Lord. ℟.
3. The stone the builders rejected has become the

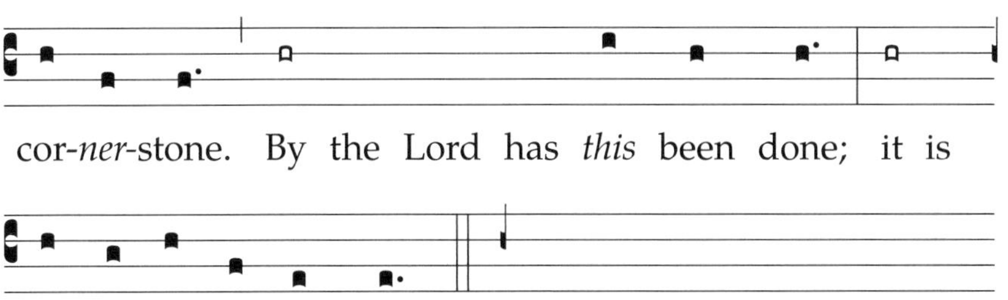
cor-*ner*-stone. By the Lord has *this* been done; it is

won-*der*-ful in our eyes. ℟.

Easter Sunday of the Resurrection

Ps. 118: 1-2, 16-17, 22-23 **YEAR ABC**

V
This is the day the Lord has made; let us rejoice
and be glad.
1. Give thanks to the LORD, for he is *good,* for his
mercy endures for-*ev*-er. Let the house of Israel say,
"His mercy en-*dures* forever." ℟.
2. "The right hand of the LORD has struck with *pow*-er;
the right hand of the LORD is ex-*alt*-ed. I shall not
die, but live, and declare the *works* of the LORD." ℟.

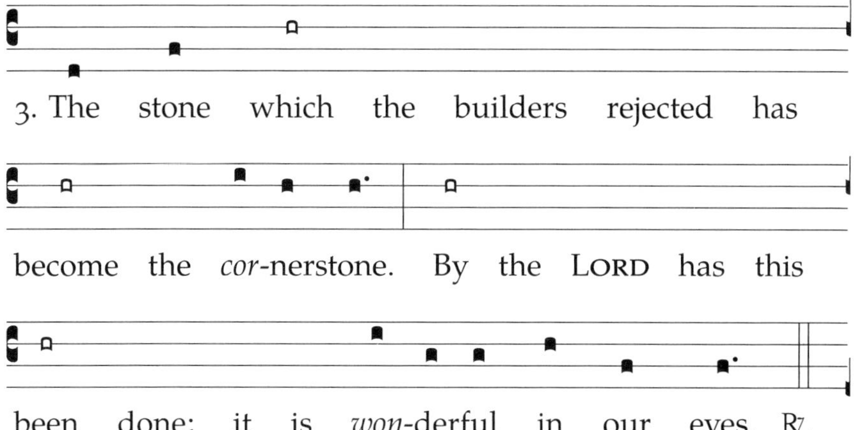
3. The stone which the builders rejected has
become the *cor*-nerstone. By the LORD has this
been done; it is *won*-derful in our eyes. ℟.

Second Sunday of Easter, or Divine Mercy Sunday

Ps. 118: 2-4, 13-15, 22-24 **YEAR ABC**

II
Give thanks to the Lord, for he is good, his
love is everlasting.
1. Let the house of Israel say, "His mercy endures
for-*ev*-er." Let the house of Aaron say, "His mercy
endures for-*ev*-er." Let those who fear the LORD say,
"His mercy en-*dures* forever." ℟.
2. I was hard pressed and was falling, but the
LORD *helped* me. My strength and my courage

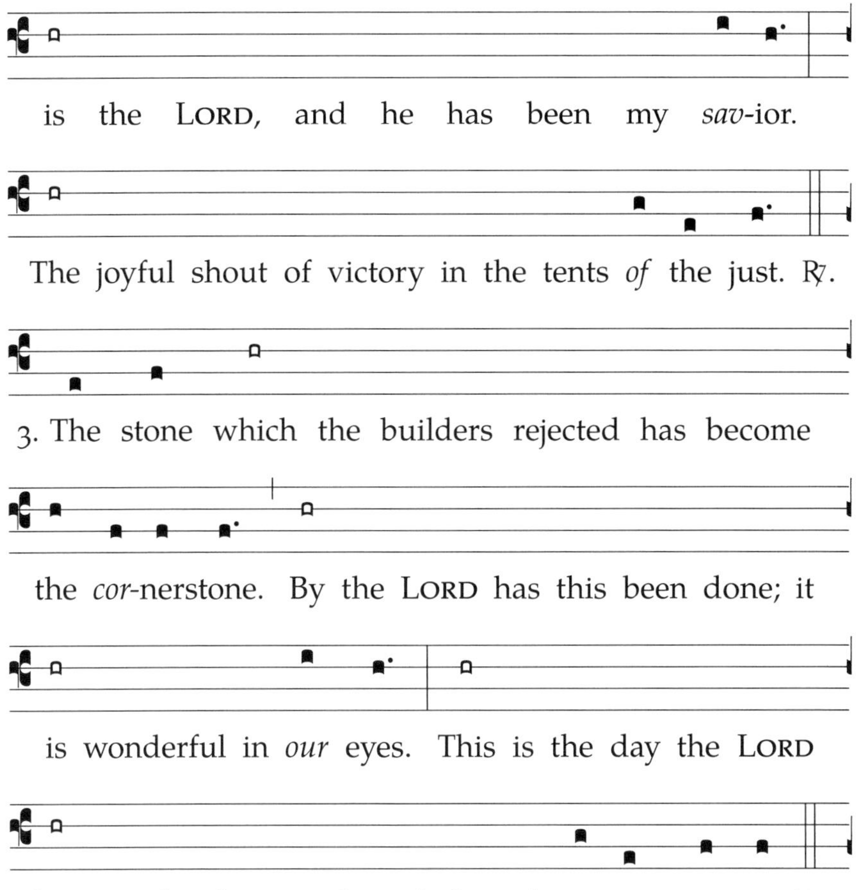

is the LORD, and he has been my *sav*-ior.
The joyful shout of victory in the tents *of* the just. ℟.
3. The stone which the builders rejected has become
the *cor*-nerstone. By the LORD has this been done; it
is wonderful in *our* eyes. This is the day the LORD
has made; let us be glad and *re*-joice in it. ℟.

THIRD SUNDAY OF EASTER

Ps. 16: 1-2, 5, 7-8, 9-10, 11 **YEAR A**

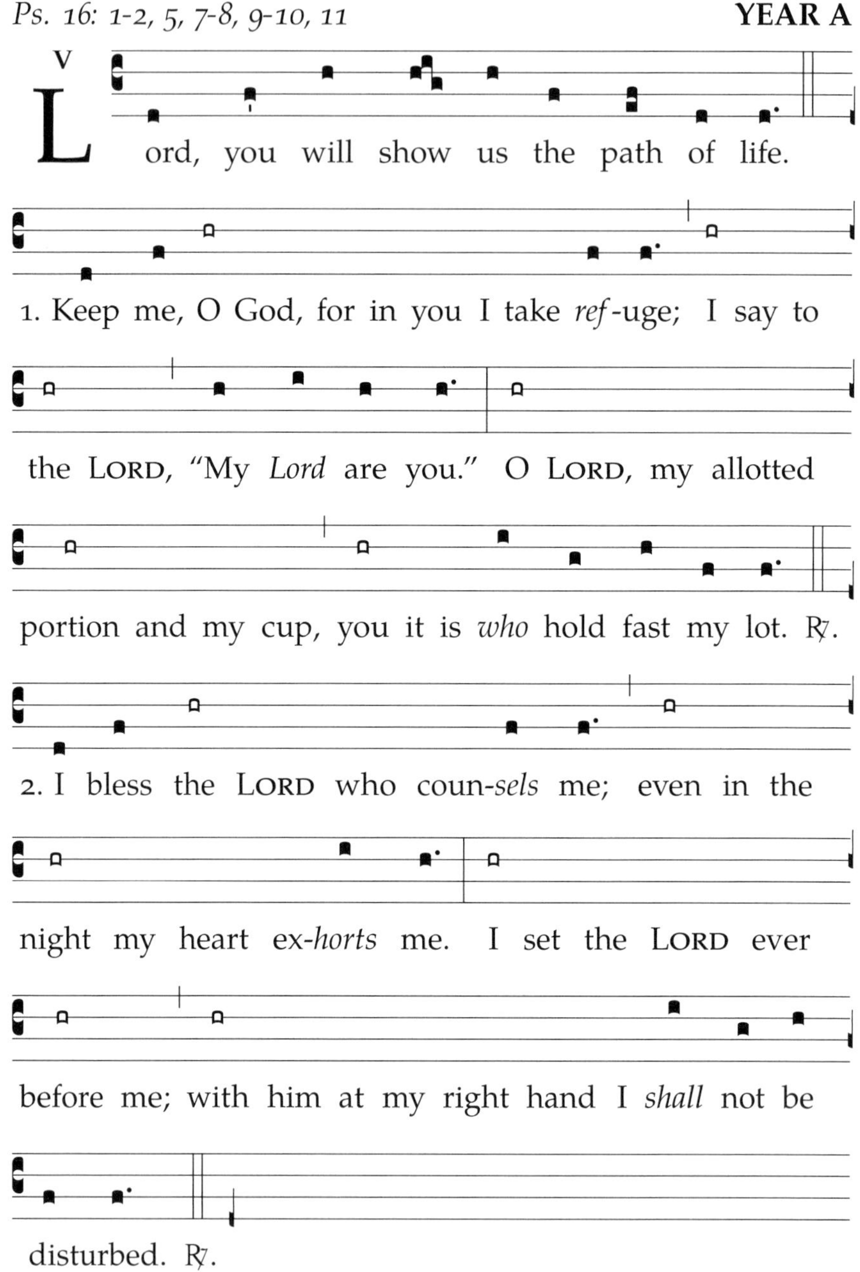

V
Lord, you will show us the path of life.
1. Keep me, O God, for in you I take *ref*-uge; I say to
the LORD, "My *Lord* are you." O LORD, my allotted
portion and my cup, you it is *who* hold fast my lot. ℟.
2. I bless the LORD who coun-*sels* me; even in the
night my heart ex-*horts* me. I set the LORD ever
before me; with him at my right hand I *shall* not be
disturbed. ℟.

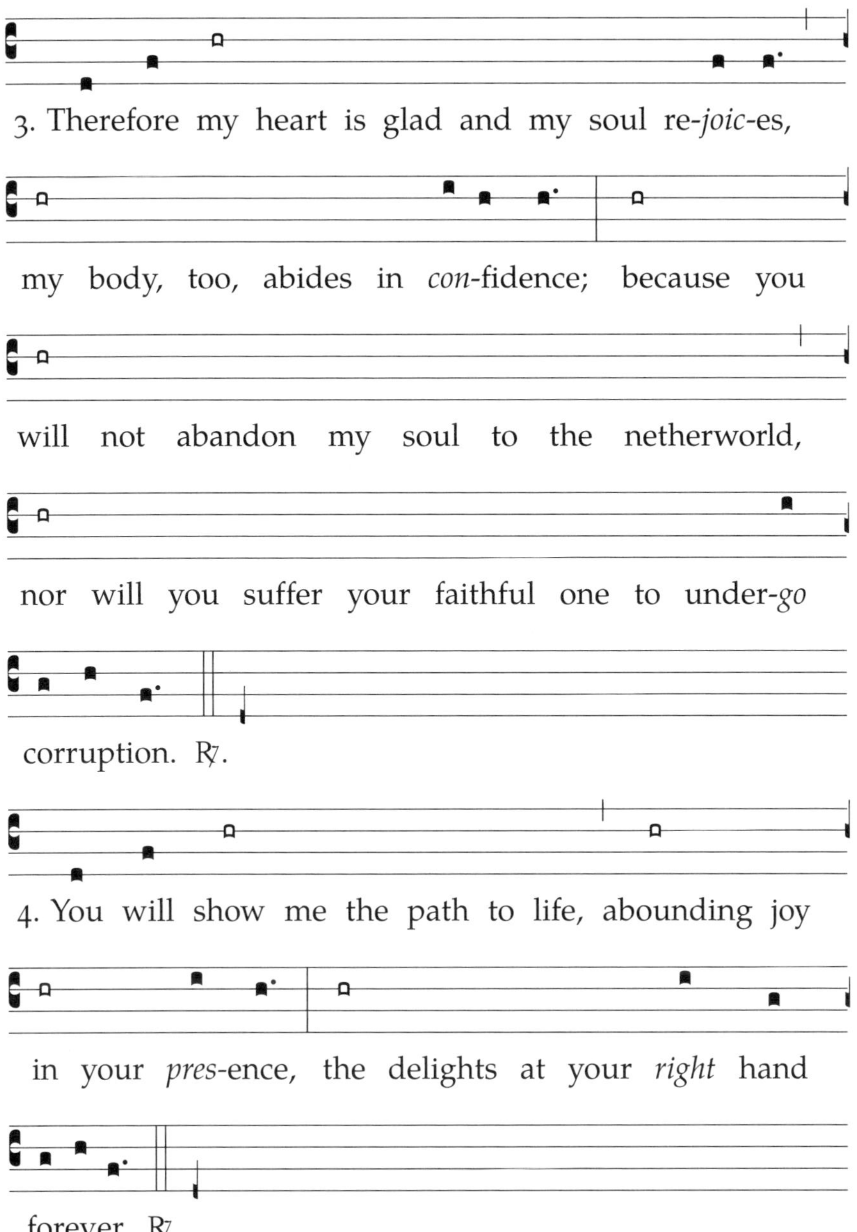
3. Therefore my heart is glad and my soul re-*joic*-es,
my body, too, abides in *con*-fidence; because you
will not abandon my soul to the netherworld,
nor will you suffer your faithful one to under-*go*
corruption. ℟.
4. You will show me the path to life, abounding joy
in your *pres*-ence, the delights at your *right* hand
forever. ℟.

Third Sunday of Easter

Ps. 4: 2, 4, 7-8, 9 **YEAR B**

II
Lord, let your face shine on us.
1. When I call, answer me, O my just *God,* you who
relieve me when I am in *dis*-tress; have pity on me,
and hear my prayer! ℟.
2. Know that the LORD does wonders for his *faith*-ful
one; the LORD will hear me when I call *up*-on him. ℟.
3. O LORD, let the light of your countenance shine
up-*on* us! You put gladness into *my* heart. As soon

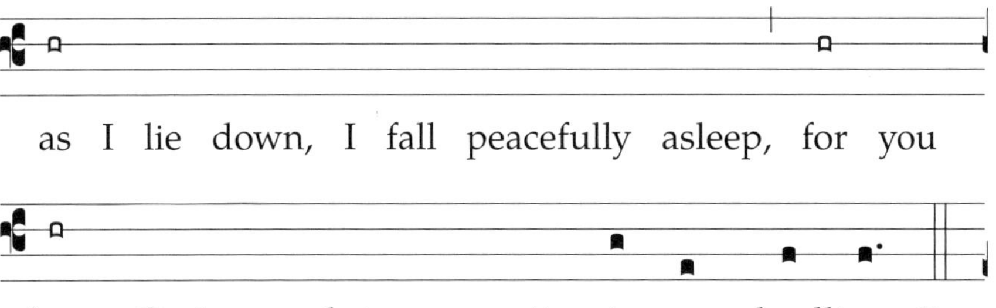
as I lie down, I fall peacefully asleep, for you

alone, O LORD, bring security *to* my dwelling. ℟.

Third Sunday of Easter

Ps. 30: 2, 4, 5-6, 11-12, 13 **YEAR C**

II
I will praise you, Lord, for you have rescued me.
1. I will extol you, O LORD, for you drew me clear
and did not let my enemies rejoice *o*-ver me.
O LORD, you brought me up from the netherworld;
you preserved me from among those going down
in-to the pit. ℟.
2. Sing praise to the LORD, you his faith-*ful* ones,

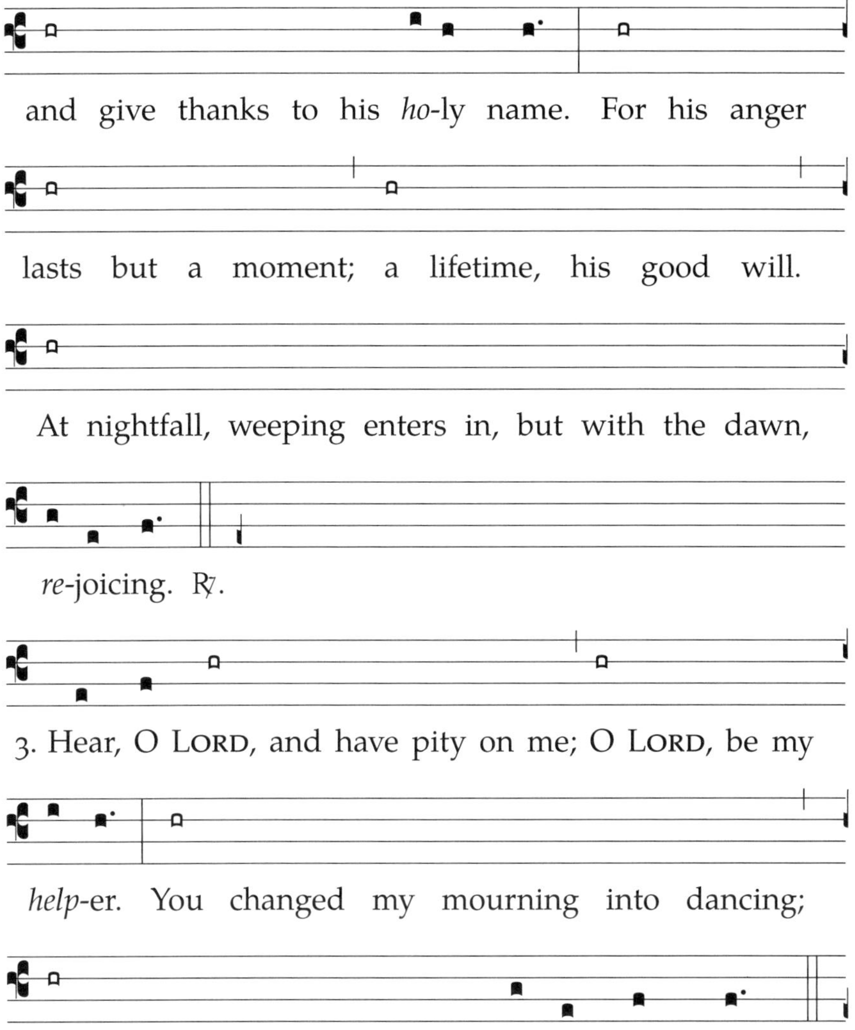
and give thanks to his *ho*-ly name. For his anger
lasts but a moment; a lifetime, his good will.
At nightfall, weeping enters in, but with the dawn,
re-joicing. ℟.
3. Hear, O LORD, and have pity on me; O LORD, be my
help-er. You changed my mourning into dancing;
O LORD, my God, forever will *I* give you thanks. ℟.

Fourth Sunday of Easter

Ps. 23: 1-3a, 3b-4, 5, 6 **YEAR A**

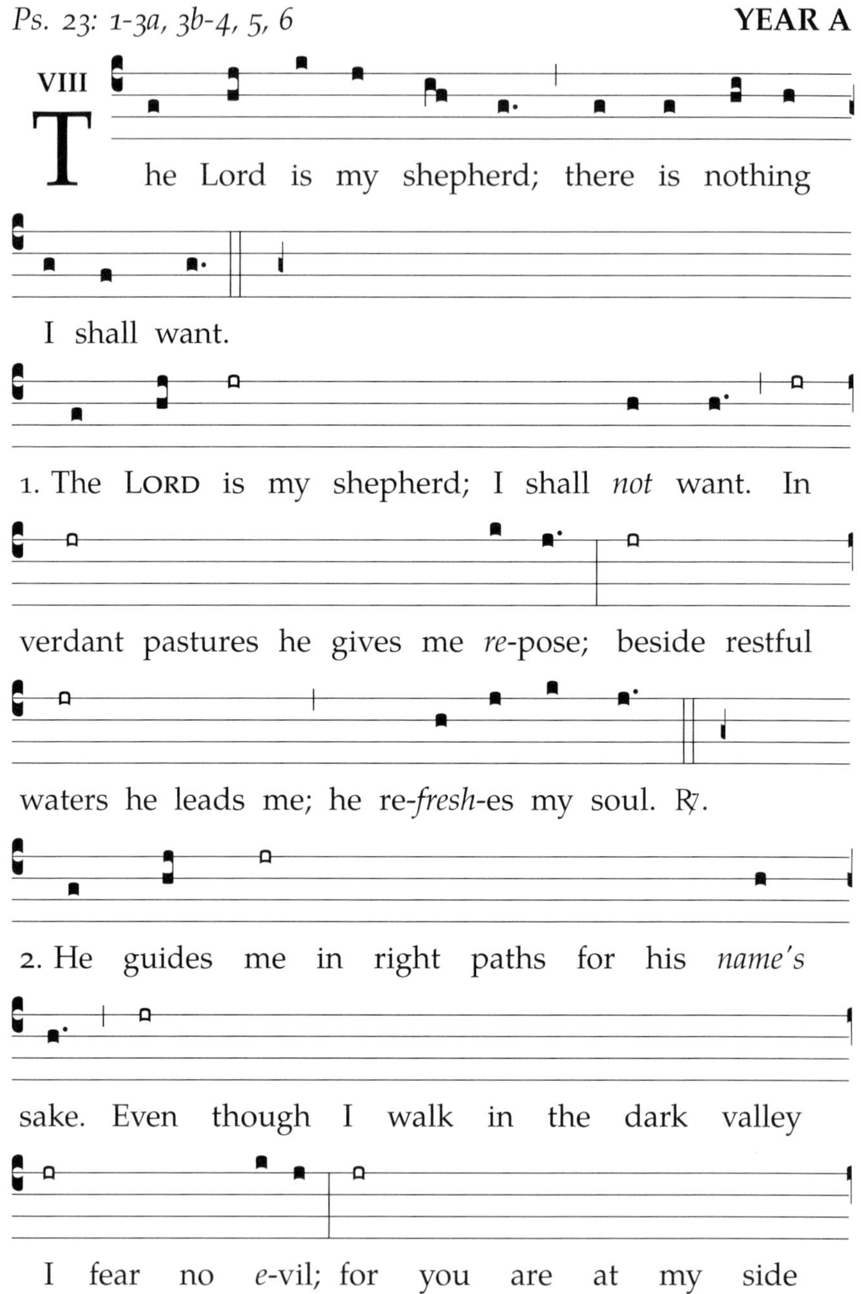

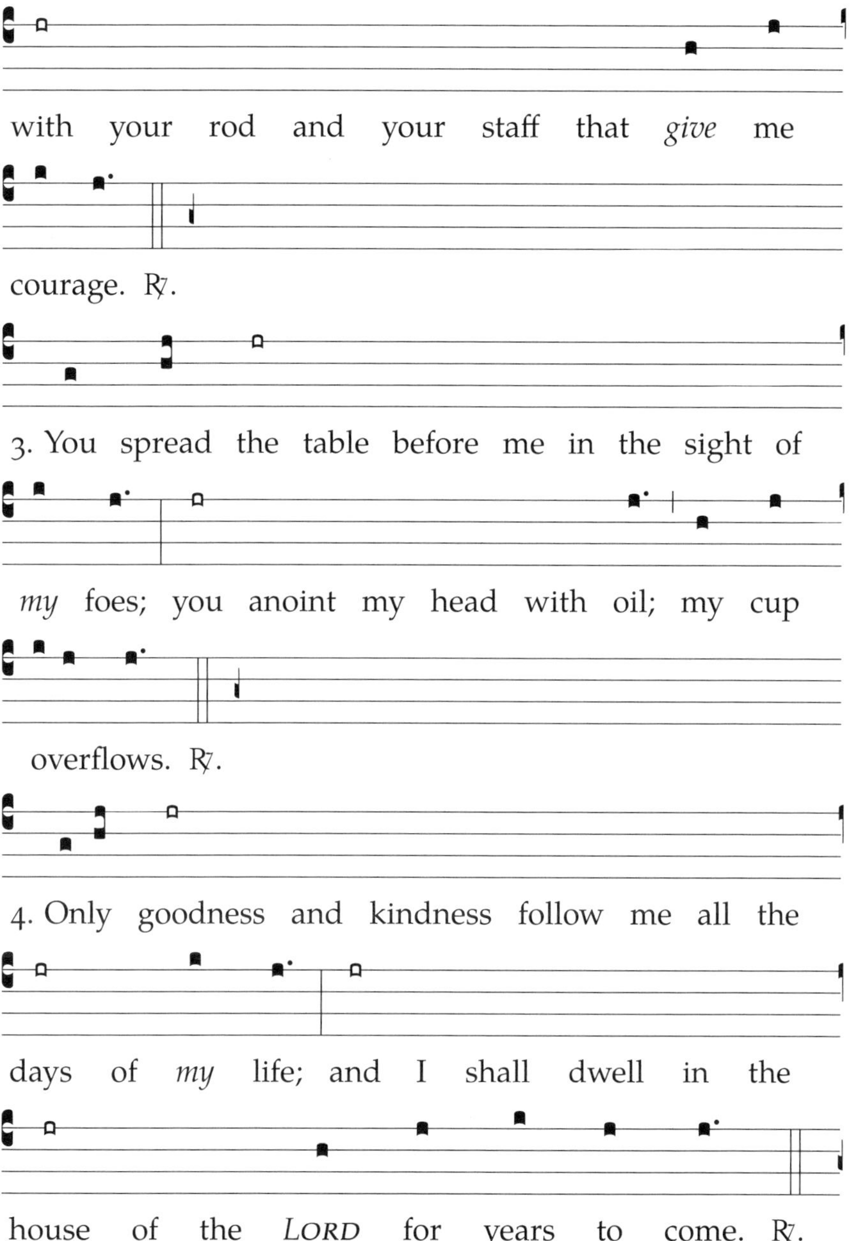
with your rod and your staff that *give* me
courage. ℟.
3. You spread the table before me in the sight of
my foes; you anoint my head with oil; my cup
overflows. ℟.
4. Only goodness and kindness follow me all the
days of *my* life; and I shall dwell in the
house of the LORD for years to come. ℟.

FOURTH SUNDAY OF EASTER

Ps. 118: 1, 8-9, 21-23, 26, 28, 29 **YEAR B**

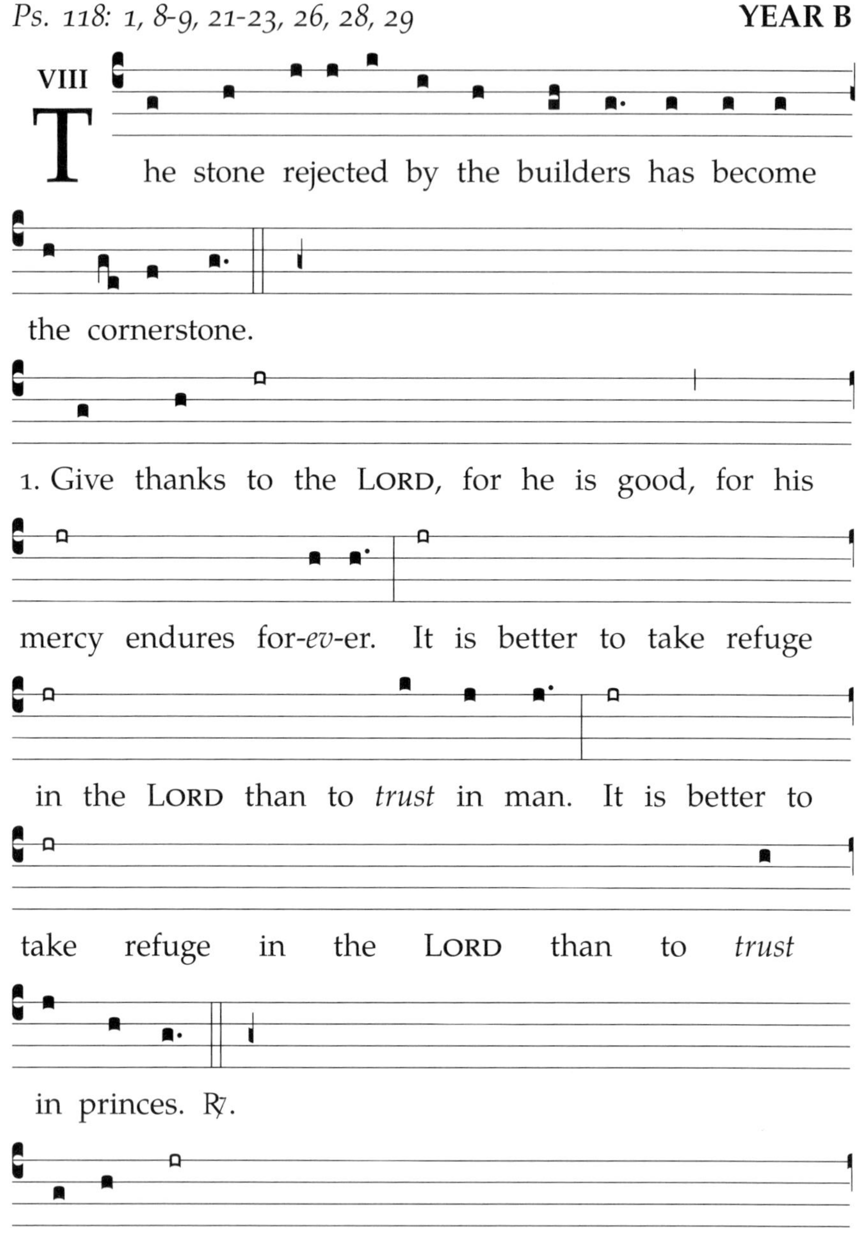

VIII
The stone rejected by the builders has become
the cornerstone.
1. Give thanks to the LORD, for he is good, for his
mercy endures for-*ev*-er. It is better to take refuge
in the LORD than to *trust* in man. It is better to
take refuge in the LORD than to *trust*
in princes. ℟.

2. I will give thanks to you, for you have answered me

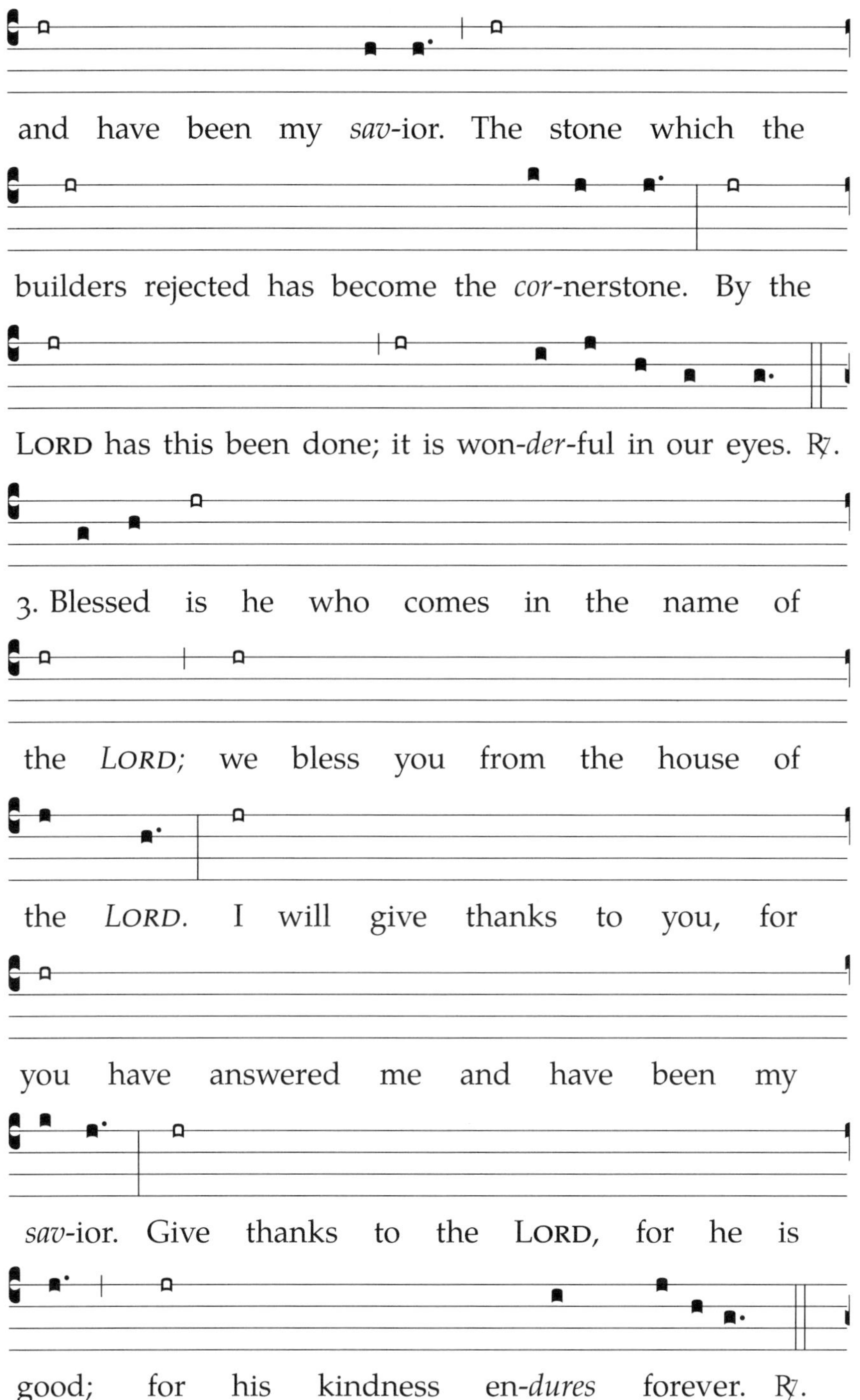
and have been my sav-ior. The stone which the
builders rejected has become the cor-nerstone. By the
LORD has this been done; it is won-der-ful in our eyes. ℟.
3. Blessed is he who comes in the name of
the LORD; we bless you from the house of
the LORD. I will give thanks to you, for
you have answered me and have been my
sav-ior. Give thanks to the LORD, for he is
good; for his kindness en-dures forever. ℟.

Fourth Sunday of Easter

Ps. 100: 1-2, 3, 5 **YEAR C**

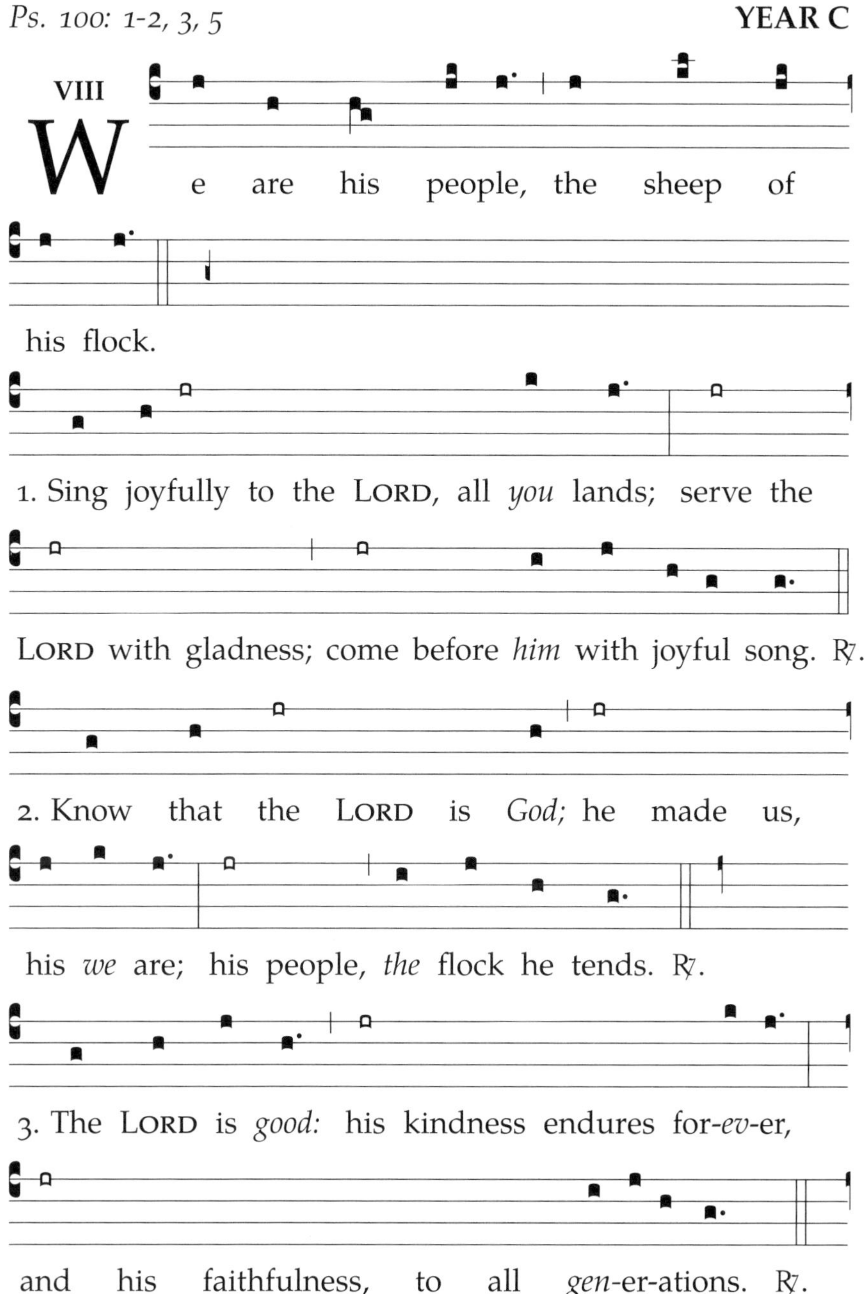

VIII
We are his people, the sheep of
his flock.
1. Sing joyfully to the LORD, all *you* lands; serve the
LORD with gladness; come before *him* with joyful song. ℟.
2. Know that the LORD is *God;* he made us,
his *we* are; his people, *the* flock he tends. ℟.
3. The LORD is *good:* his kindness endures for-*ev*-er,
and his faithfulness, to all *gen*-er-ations. ℟.

Fifth Sunday of Easter

Ps. 33: 1-2, 4-5, 18-19 **YEAR A**

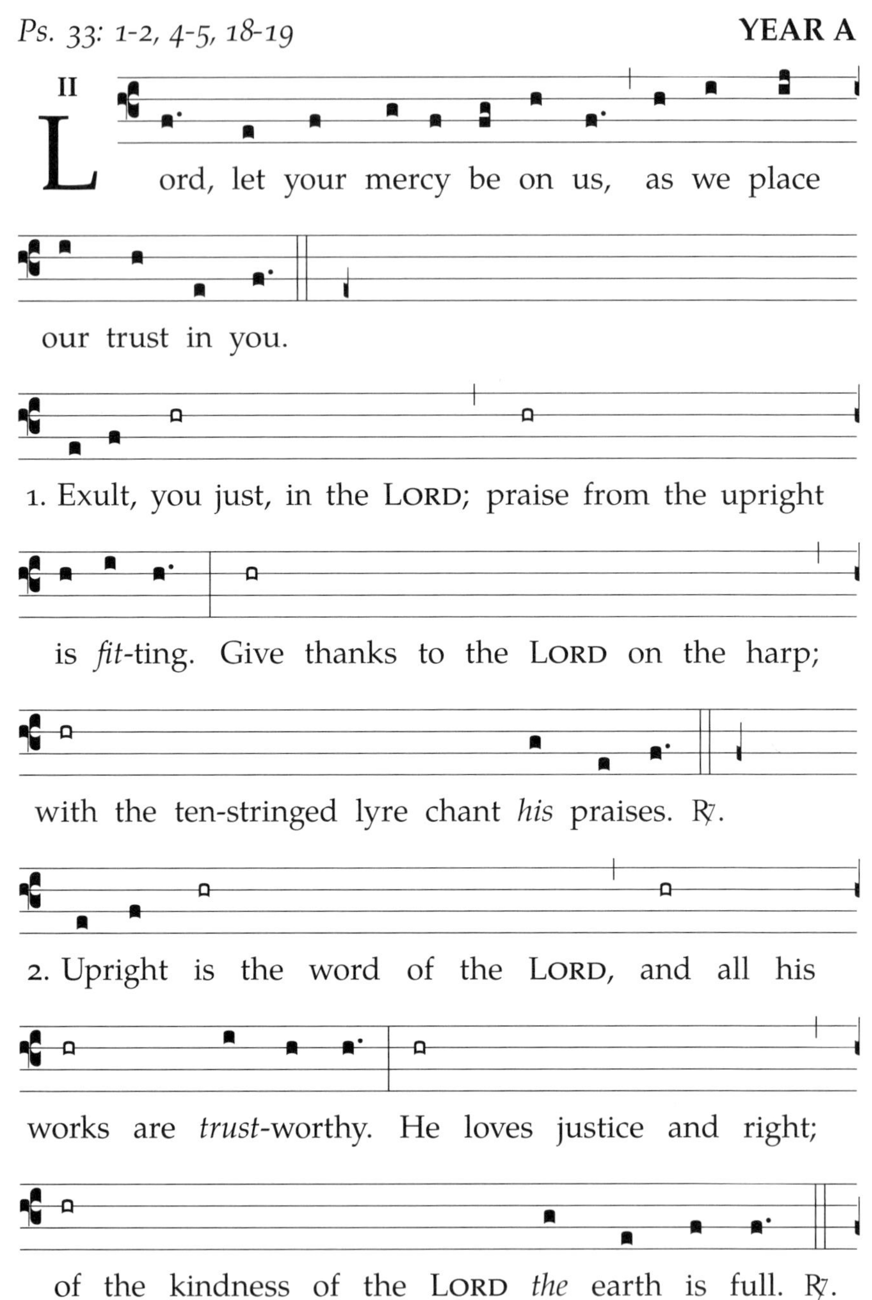

II
Lord, let your mercy be on us, as we place our trust in you.
1. Exult, you just, in the LORD; praise from the upright is *fit*-ting. Give thanks to the LORD on the harp; with the ten-stringed lyre chant *his* praises. ℟.
2. Upright is the word of the LORD, and all his works are *trust*-worthy. He loves justice and right; of the kindness of the LORD *the* earth is full. ℟.

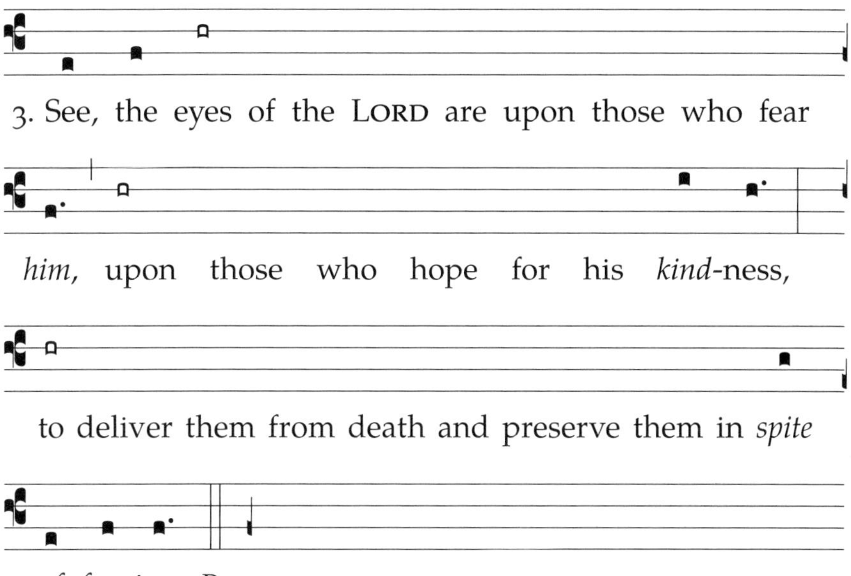
3. See, the eyes of the LORD are upon those who fear
him, upon those who hope for his *kind*-ness,
to deliver them from death and preserve them in *spite*
of famine. ℟.

Fifth Sunday of Easter

Ps. 22: 26-27, 28, 30, 31-32 **YEAR B**

VIII
I will praise you, Lord, in the assembly
of your people.
1. I will fulfill my vows before those who fear *the*
Lord. The lowly shall eat *their* fill; they who seek the
Lord shall praise him: "May your hearts *live* for-ev-er!" ℟.
2. All the ends of the earth shall remember and turn
to *the* Lord; all the families of the nations shall bow
down before him. ℟.

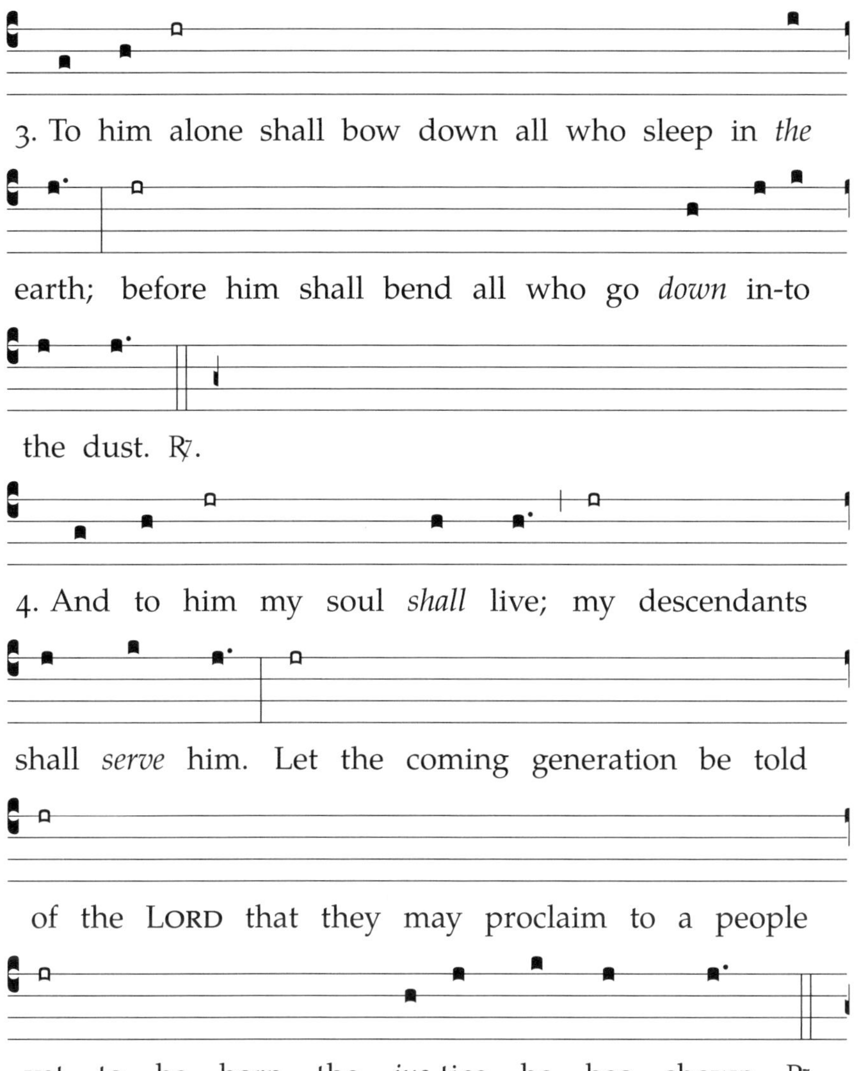
3. To him alone shall bow down all who sleep in *the*
earth; before him shall bend all who go *down* in-to
the dust. ℟.
4. And to him my soul *shall* live; my descendants
shall *serve* him. Let the coming generation be told
of the LORD that they may proclaim to a people
yet to be born the *jus*-tice he has shown. ℟.

Fifth Sunday of Easter

Ps. 145: 8-9, 10-11, 12-13 **YEAR C**

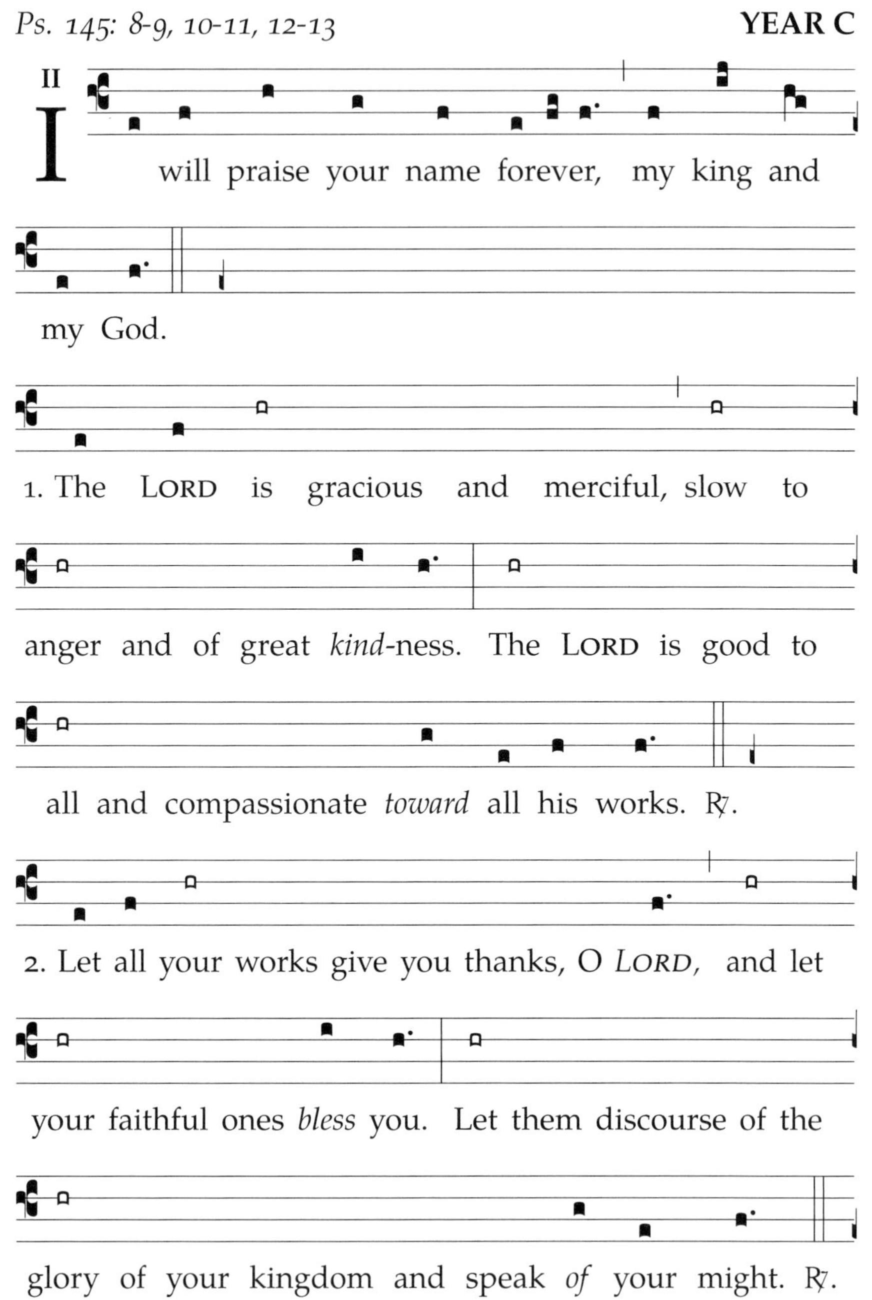
II
I will praise your name forever, my king and
my God.
1. The LORD is gracious and merciful, slow to
anger and of great *kind*-ness. The LORD is good to
all and compassionate *toward* all his works. ℟.
2. Let all your works give you thanks, O *LORD,* and let
your faithful ones *bless* you. Let them discourse of the
glory of your kingdom and speak *of* your might. ℟.

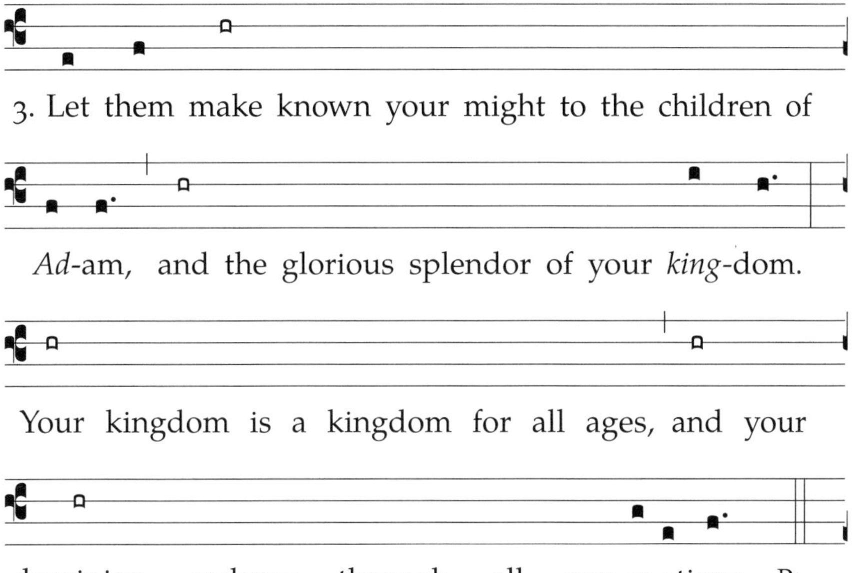
3. Let them make known your might to the children of
Ad-am, and the glorious splendor of your *king*-dom.
Your kingdom is a kingdom for all ages, and your
dominion endures through all gen-*er*-ations. ℟.

Sixth Sunday of Easter

Ps. 66: 1-3, 4-5, 6-7, 16, 20 **YEAR A**

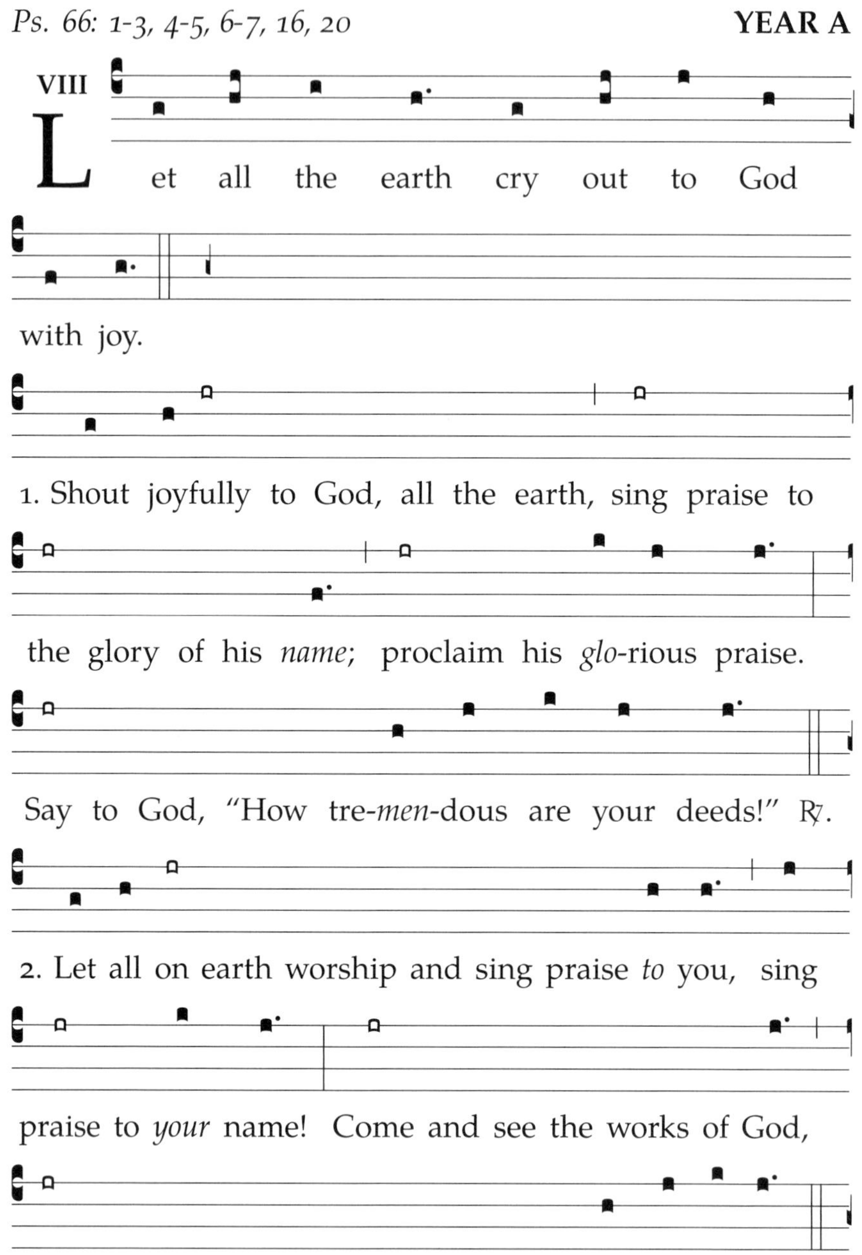

VIII
Let all the earth cry out to God with joy.
1. Shout joyfully to God, all the earth, sing praise to the glory of his *name;* proclaim his *glo*-rious praise.
Say to God, "How tre-*men*-dous are your deeds!" ℟.
2. Let all on earth worship and sing praise *to* you, sing praise to *your* name! Come and see the works of God,
his tremendous deeds among the chil-*dren* of Adam. ℟.

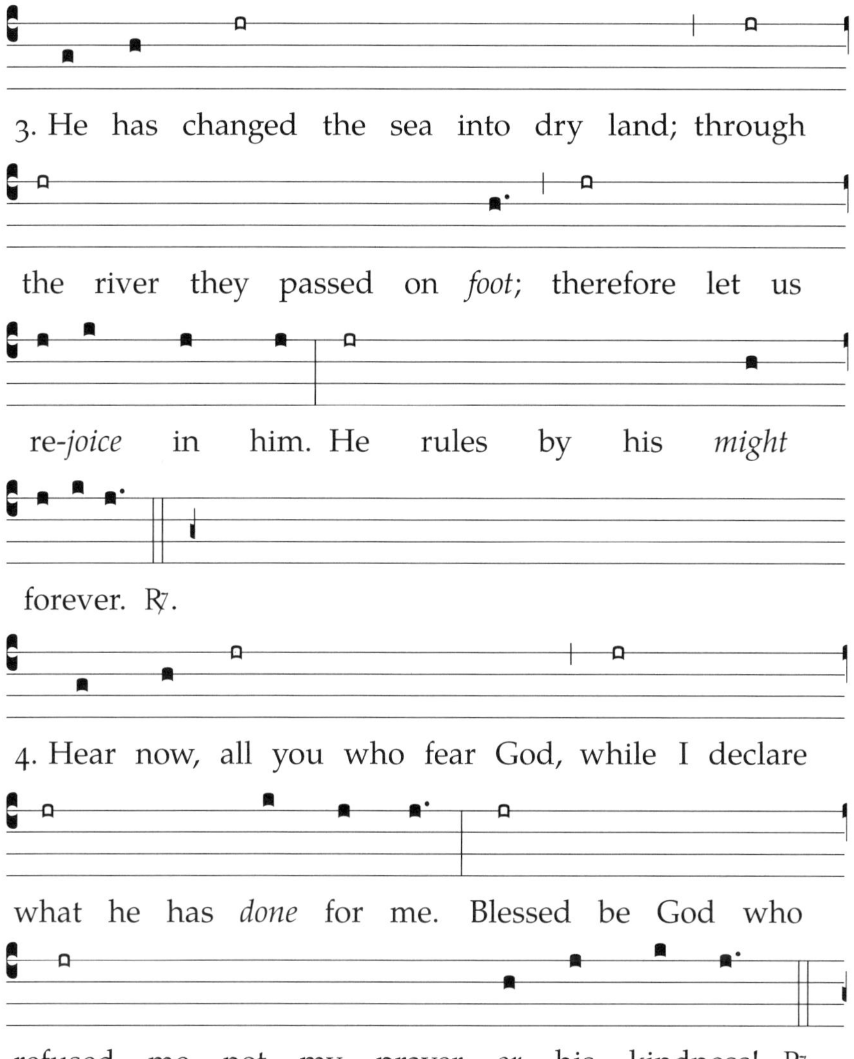
3. He has changed the sea into dry land; through
the river they passed on *foot*; therefore let us
re-*joice* in him. He rules by his *might*
forever. ℟.
4. Hear now, all you who fear God, while I declare
what he has *done* for me. Blessed be God who
refused me not my prayer *or* his kindness! ℟.

Sixth Sunday of Easter

Ps. 98: 1, 2-3, 3-4 **YEAR B**

III
The Lord has revealed to the nations his
saving power.
1. Sing to the LORD a new song, for he has *done*
wondrous deeds; his right hand has won victory for
him, his *ho*-ly arm. ℟.
2. The LORD has made his salvation *known*: in the sight
of the nations he has re-*vealed* his justice. He has
remembered his kindness and his faithfulness toward

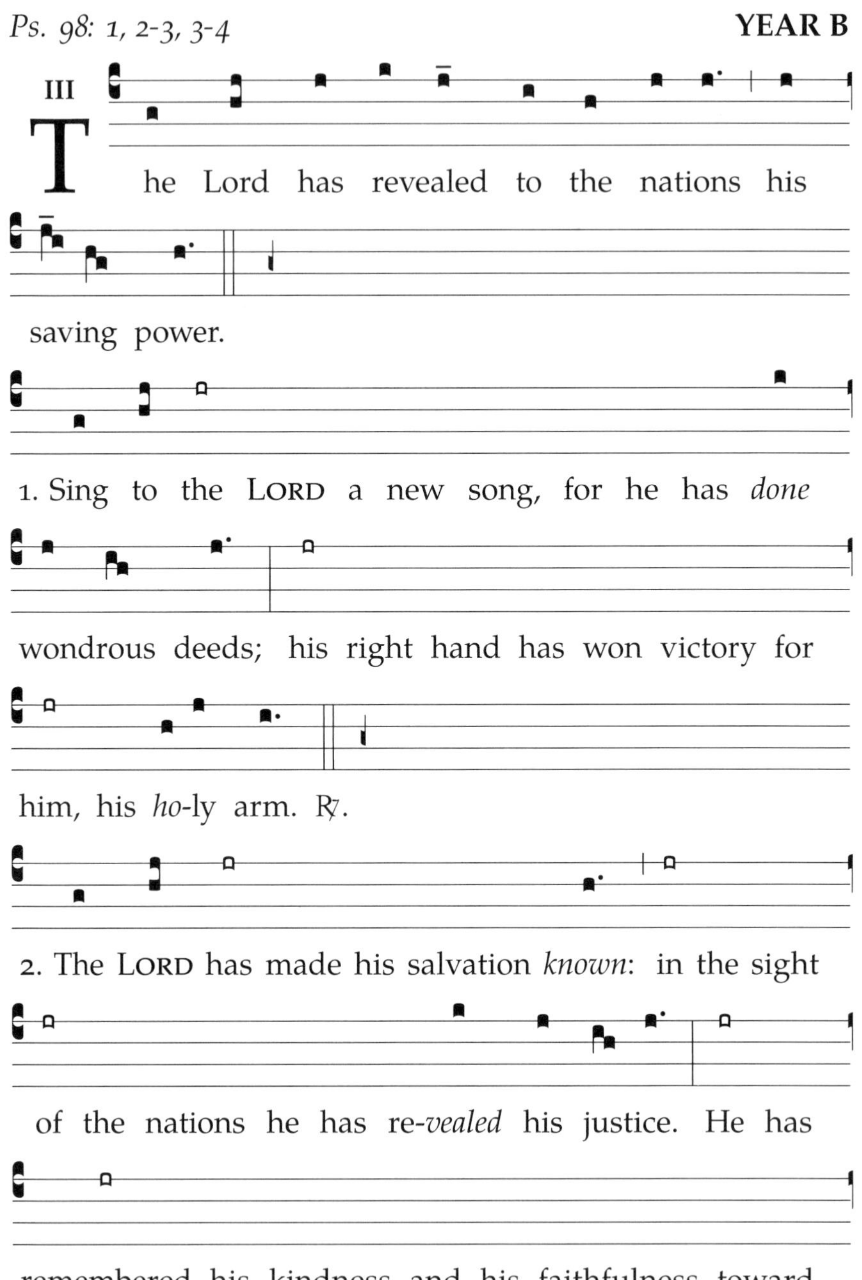

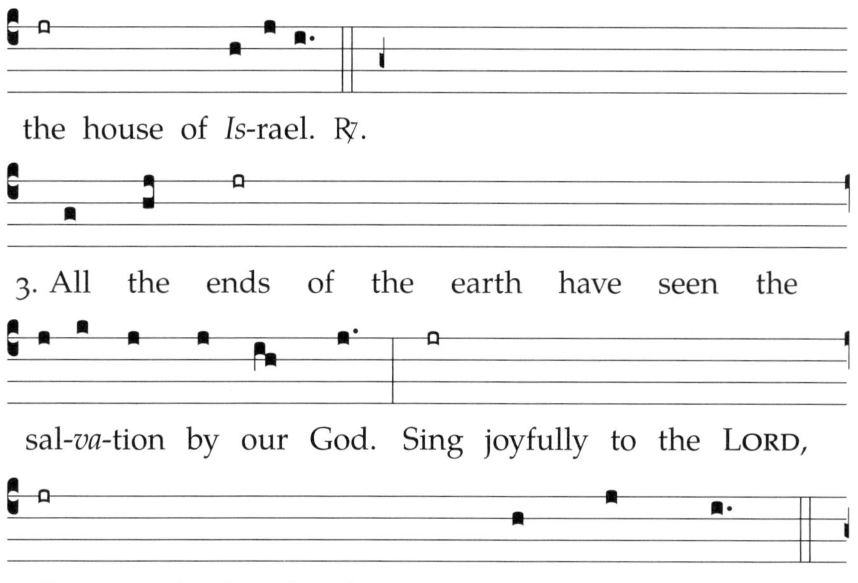
the house of *Is*-rael. ℟.
3. All the ends of the earth have seen the
sal-*va*-tion by our God. Sing joyfully to the LORD,
all you lands: break into *song*; sing praise. ℟.

Sixth Sunday of Easter

Ps. 67: 2-3, 5, 6, 8 **YEAR C**

VIII
O God, let all the nations praise you!
1. May God have pity on us and bless us; may he
let his face shine up-*on* us. So may your way
be known upon earth; among all nations, *your*
salvation. ℟.
2. May the nations be glad and exult because you rule
the peoples in *eq*-uity; the nations *on* the earth you
guide. ℟.

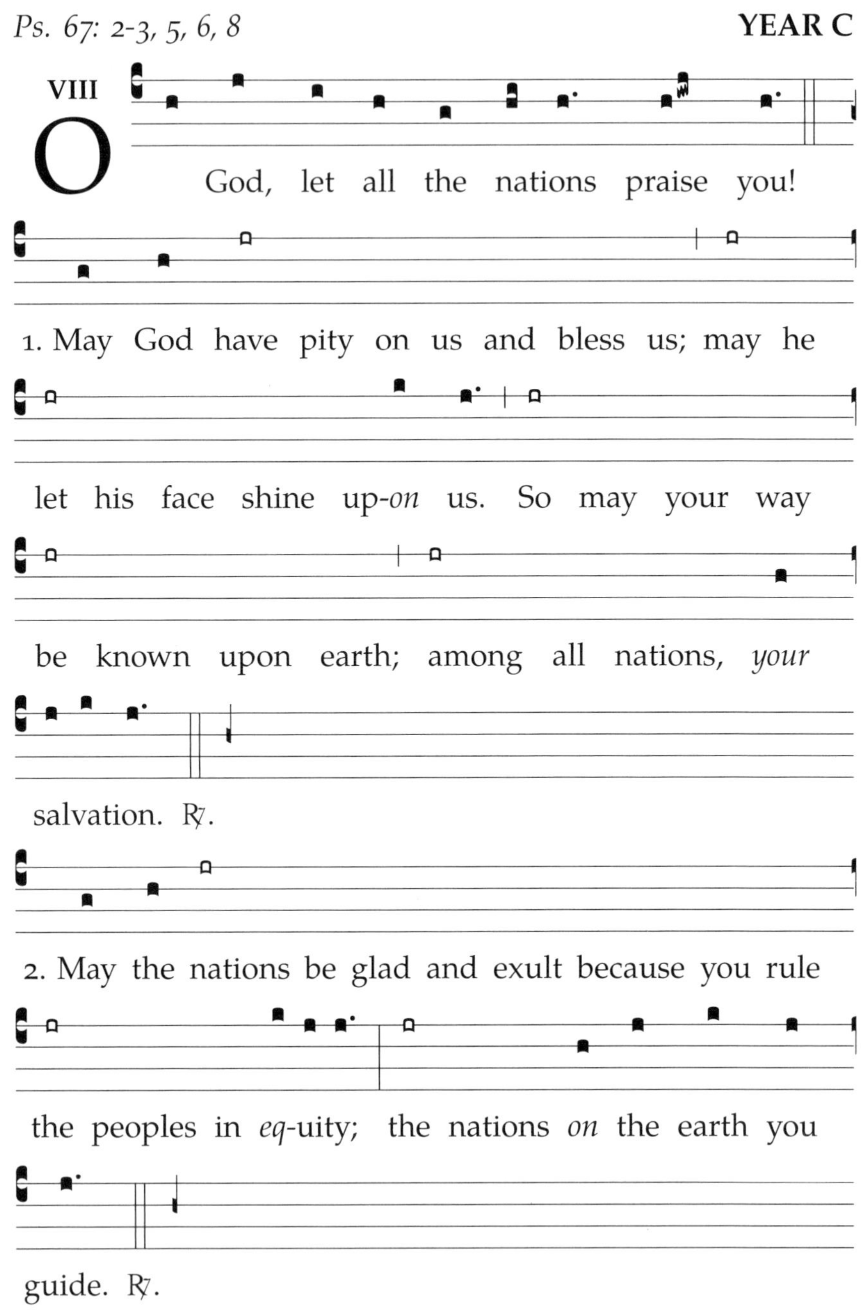

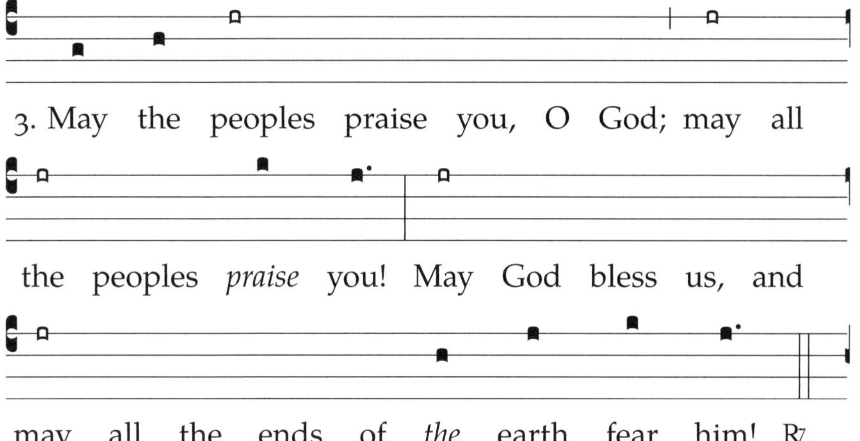
3. May the peoples praise you, O God; may all
the peoples *praise* you! May God bless us, and
may all the ends of *the* earth fear him! ℟.

The Ascension of the Lord

Ps. 47: 2-3, 6-7, 8-9 **YEAR ABC**

℣
God mounts his throne to shouts of joy:
a blare of trumpets for the Lord.
1. All you peoples, clap your hands, shout to God
with cries of *glad*-ness, For the LORD, the Most
High, the awesome, is the great king *o*-ver all the earth. ℟.
2. God mounts his throne amid shouts *of* joy;
the LORD, amid *trum*-pet blasts. Sing praise to God,
sing praise; sing praise *to* our king, sing praise. ℟.

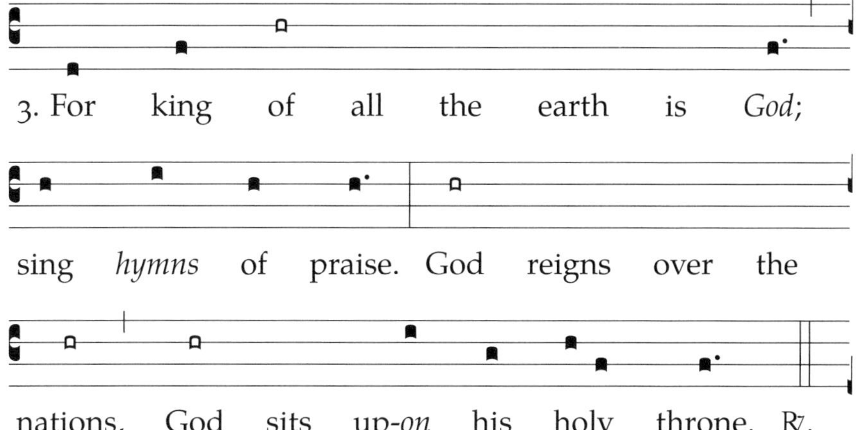
3. For king of all the earth is *God;*
sing *hymns* of praise. God reigns over the
nations, God sits up-*on* his holy throne. ℟.

Seventh Sunday of Easter

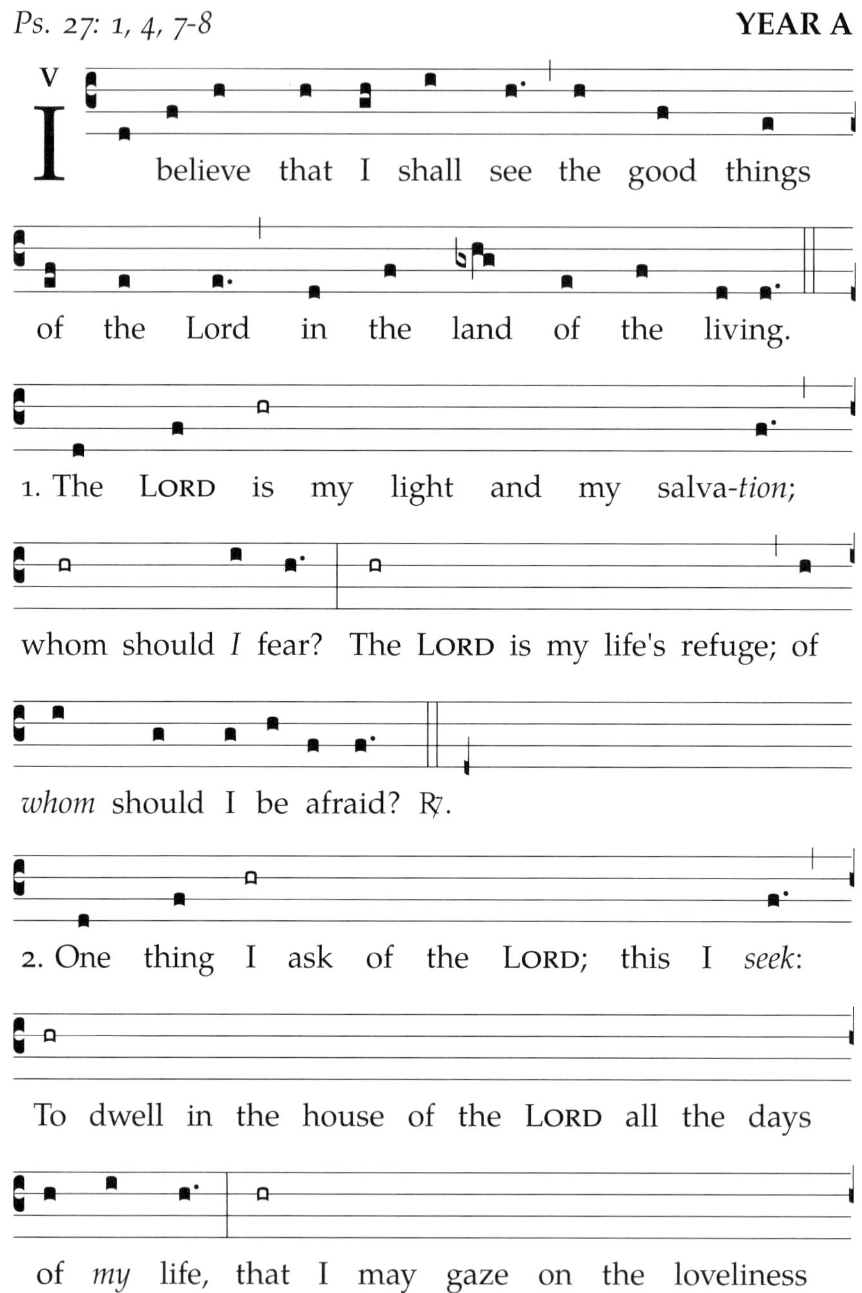

Ps. 27: 1, 4, 7-8
YEAR A
V
I believe that I shall see the good things
of the Lord in the land of the living.
1. The Lord is my light and my salva-*tion*;
whom should *I* fear? The Lord is my life's refuge; of
whom should I be afraid? ℟.
2. One thing I ask of the Lord; this I *seek*:
To dwell in the house of the Lord all the days
of *my* life, that I may gaze on the loveliness

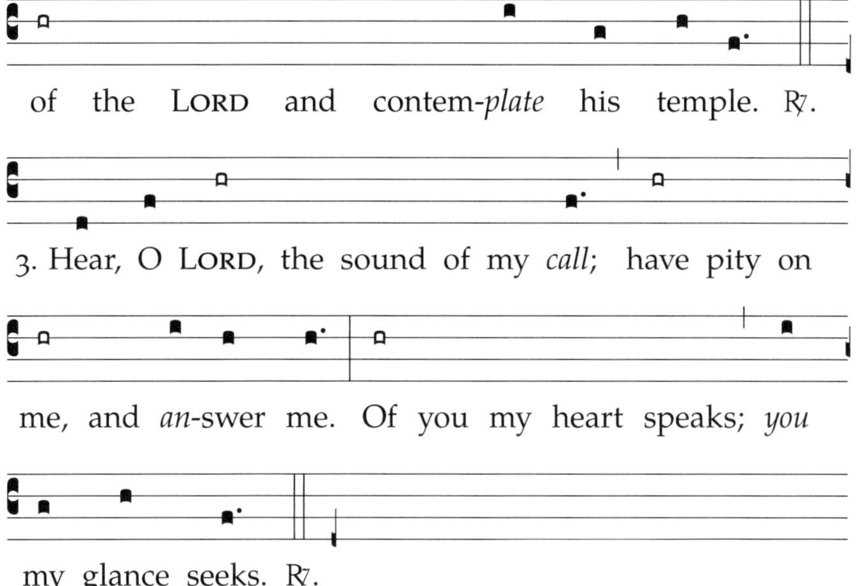
of the LORD and contem-*plate* his temple. ℟.
3. Hear, O LORD, the sound of my *call;* have pity on
me, and *an*-swer me. Of you my heart speaks; *you*
my glance seeks. ℟.

Seventh Sunday of Easter

Ps. 103: 1-2, 11-12, 19-20
YEAR B
V
The Lord has set his throne in heaven.
1. Bless the Lord, O my soul; and all my being, bless
his ho-ly name. Bless the Lord, O my soul, and forget
not all his benefits. ℟.
2. For as the heavens are high above the earth,
so surpassing is his kindness toward those who
fear him. As far as the east is from the west,
so far has he put our trans-gres-sions from us. ℟.

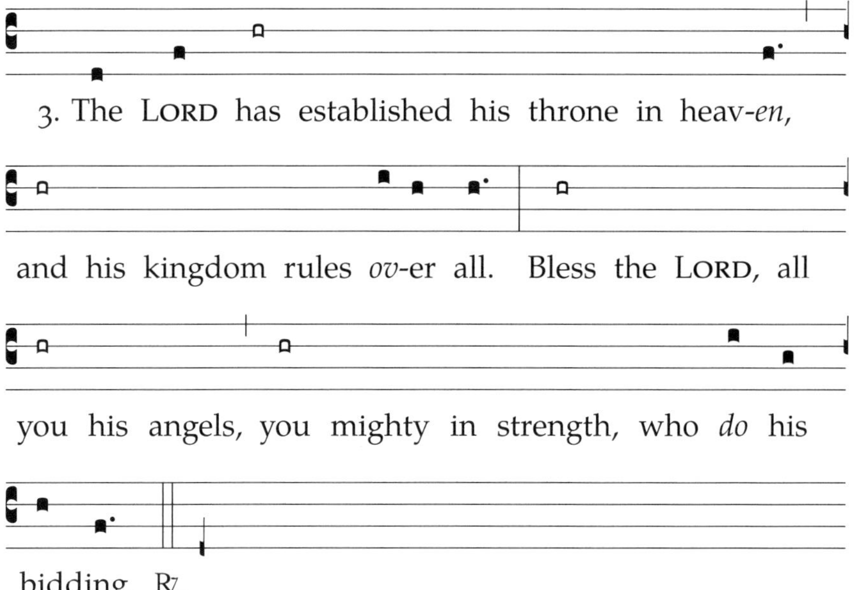
3. The LORD has established his throne in heav-*en*,
and his kingdom rules *ov*-er all. Bless the LORD, all
you his angels, you mighty in strength, who *do* his
bidding. ℟.

Seventh Sunday of Easter

Ps. 97: 1-2, 6-7, 9 **YEAR C**

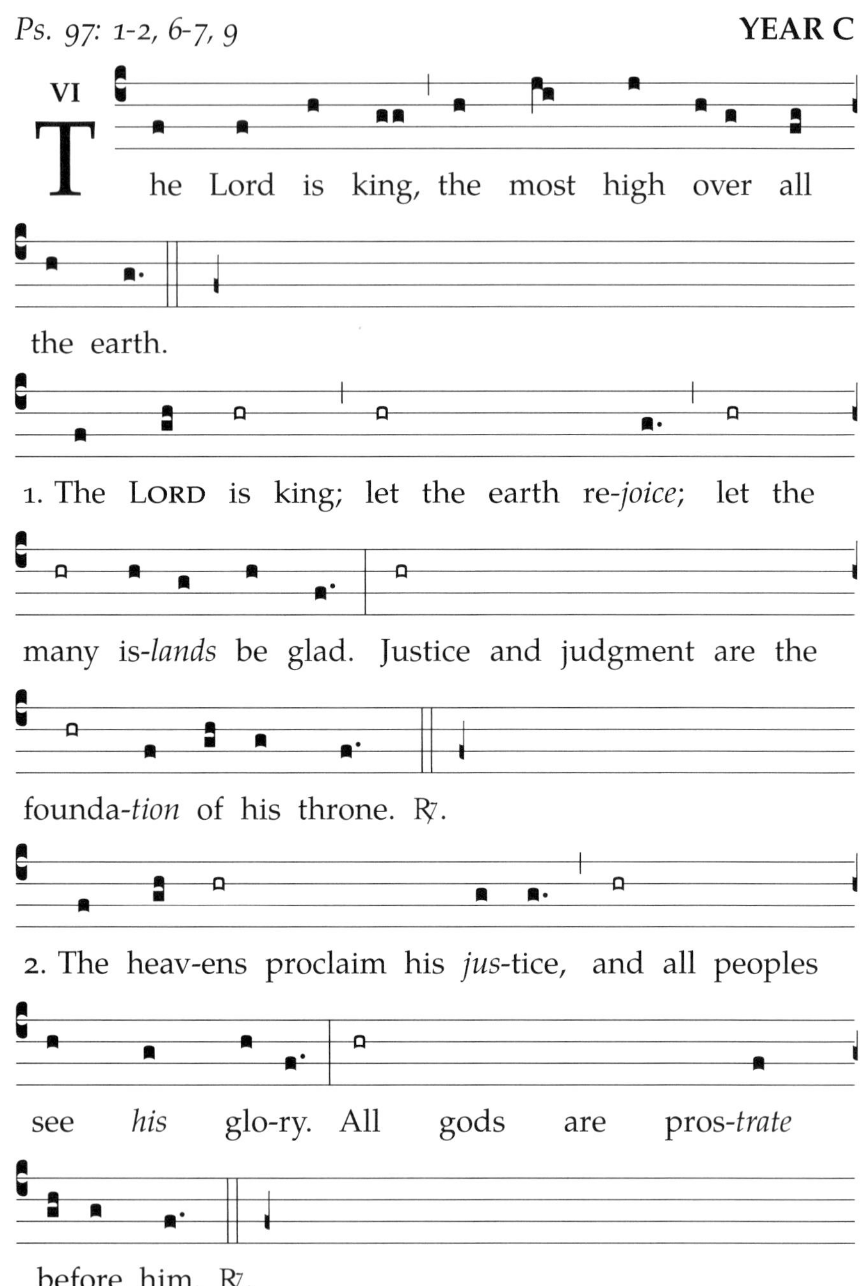
VI
The Lord is king, the most high over all the earth.
1. The LORD is king; let the earth re-*joice*; let the many is-*lands* be glad. Justice and judgment are the founda-*tion* of his throne. ℟.
2. The heav-ens proclaim his *jus*-tice, and all peoples see *his* glo-ry. All gods are pros-*trate* before him. ℟.

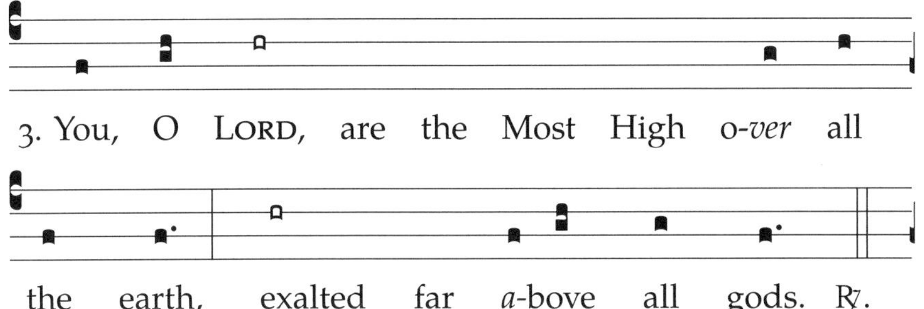
3. You, O LORD, are the Most High o-*ver* all
the earth, exalted far *a*-bove all gods. ℟.

Pentecost Sunday
Vigil Mass (simple form)

Ps. 104: 1-2, 24, 35, 27-28, 29, 30 **YEAR ABC**

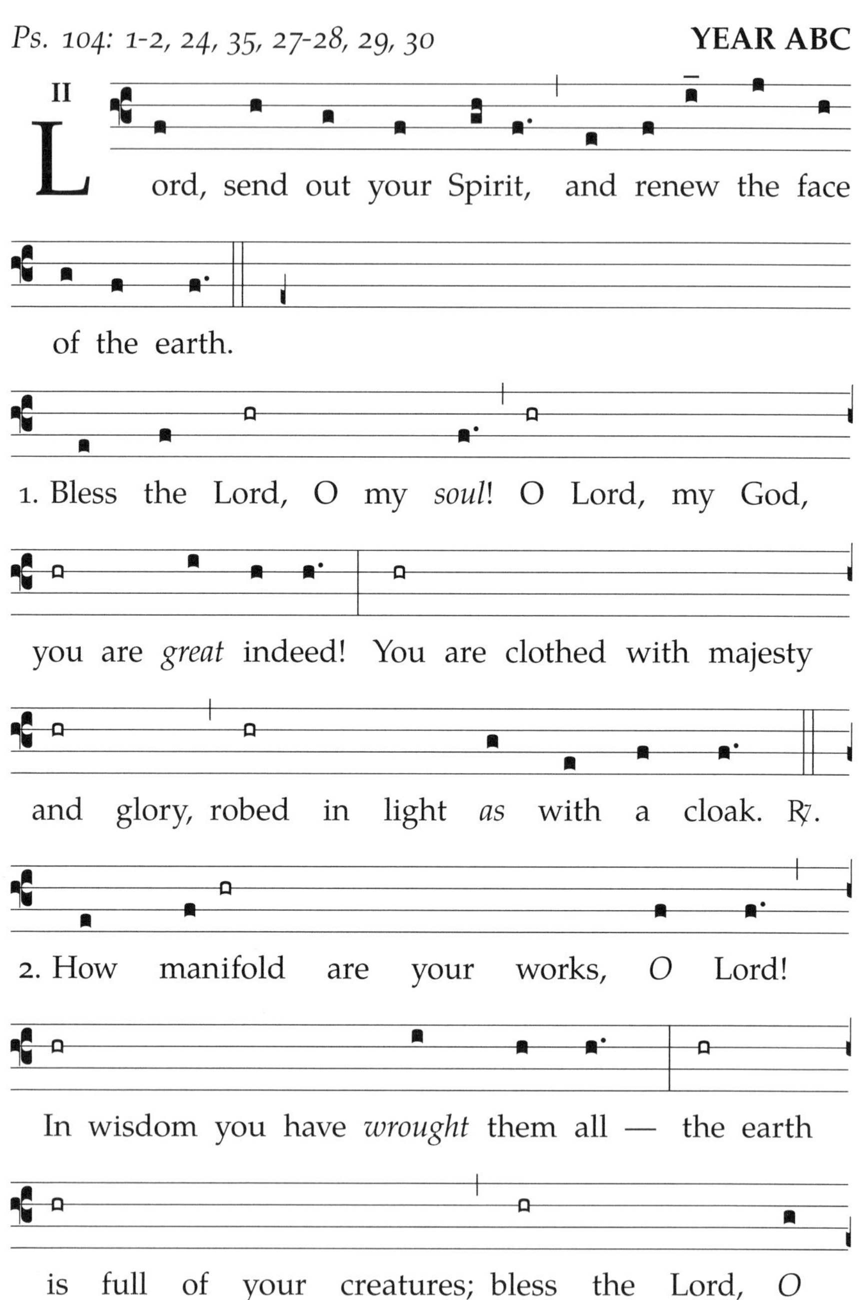

II
Lord, send out your Spirit, and renew the face
of the earth.
1. Bless the Lord, O my *soul*! O Lord, my God,
you are *great* indeed! You are clothed with majesty
and glory, robed in light *as* with a cloak. ℟.
2. How manifold are your works, *O* Lord!
In wisdom you have *wrought* them all — the earth
is full of your creatures; bless the Lord, *O*

my soul! ℟.
3. Crea-tures all look to you to give them food in due
time. When you give it to them, they *gath*-er it;
when you open your hand, they are filled *with*
good things. ℟.
4. If you take away their breath, they perish and return
to *their* dust. When you send forth your spirit, they
are created, and you renew the face *of* the earth. ℟.

Pentecost Sunday
Vigil Mass, extended form, after Reading 1

Ps. 33: 10-11, 12-13, 14-15 **YEAR ABC**

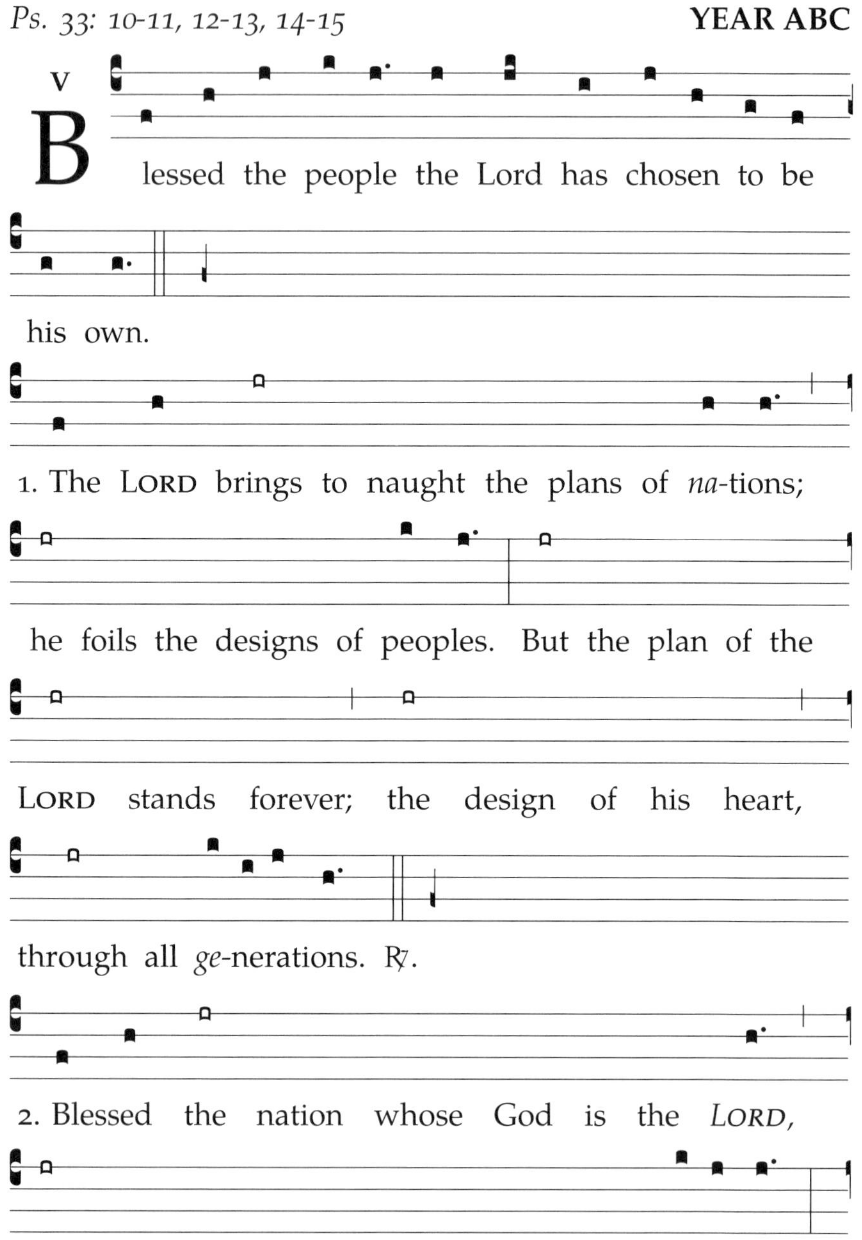

℟
Blessed the people the Lord has chosen to be
his own.
1. The LORD brings to naught the plans of *na*-tions;
he foils the designs of peoples. But the plan of the
LORD stands forever; the design of his heart,
through all *ge*-nerations. ℟.
2. Blessed the nation whose God is the *LORD*,
the people he has chosen for his own in-*her*-itance.

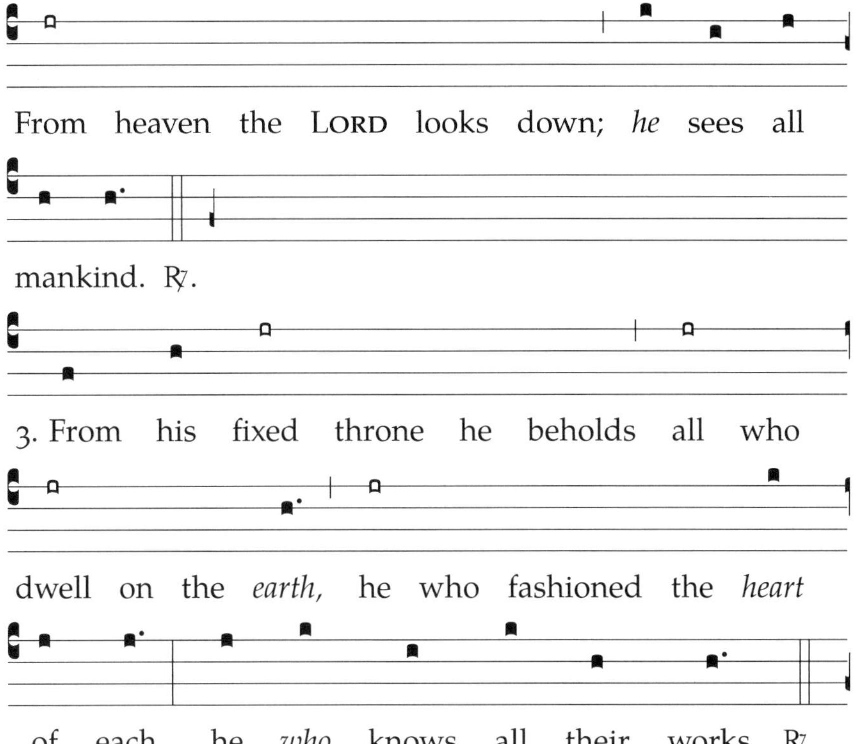
From heaven the LORD looks down; he sees all
mankind. ℟.
3. From his fixed throne he beholds all who
dwell on the earth, he who fashioned the heart
of each, he who knows all their works. ℟.

Pentecost Sunday Vigil Mass, extended form, after Reading 2 (Option 1)

Dn. 3: 52, 53, 54, 55 **YEAR ABC**

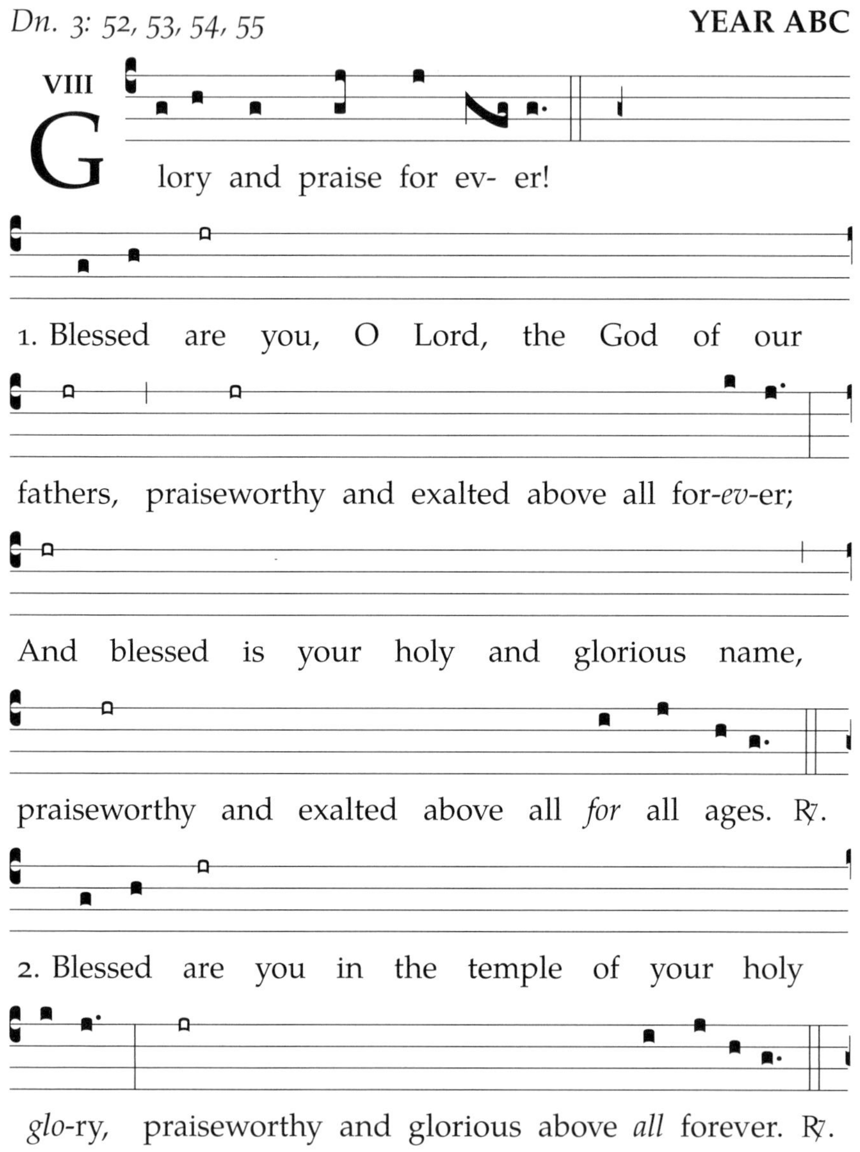

VIII
Glory and praise for ev- er!
1. Blessed are you, O Lord, the God of our
fathers, praiseworthy and exalted above all for-*ev*-er;
And blessed is your holy and glorious name,
praiseworthy and exalted above all *for* all ages. ℟.
2. Blessed are you in the temple of your holy
glo-ry, praiseworthy and glorious above *all* forever. ℟.

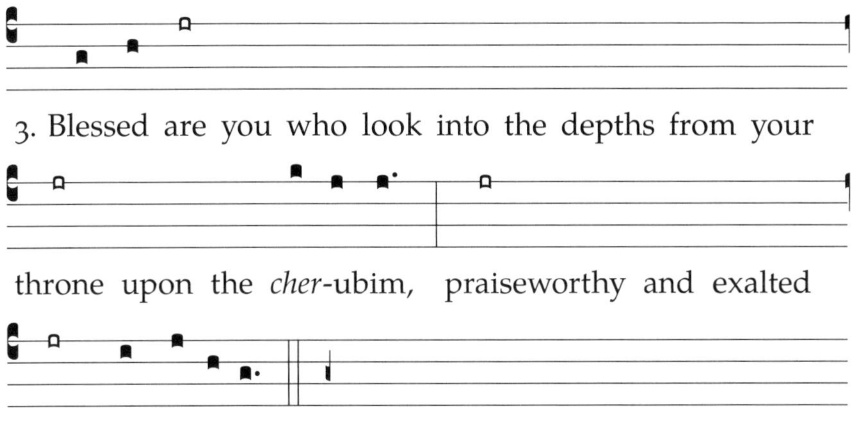
3. Blessed are you who look into the depths from your
throne upon the *cher*-ubim, praiseworthy and exalted
above *all* forever. ℟.

Pentecost Sunday Vigil Mass, extended form, after Reading 2 (option 2)

Ps. 19: 8, 9, 10, 11 **YEAR ABC**

V
Lord, you have the words of everlasting life.
1. The law of the LORD is perfect, refreshing *the* soul;
the decree of the LORD is trustworthy, giving wisdom
to the simple. ℟.
2. The precepts of the LORD are right, rejoicing *the* heart;
the command of the LORD is clear, en-*light*-ening
the eye. ℟.
3. The fear of the LORD is pure, enduring for-*ev*-er;

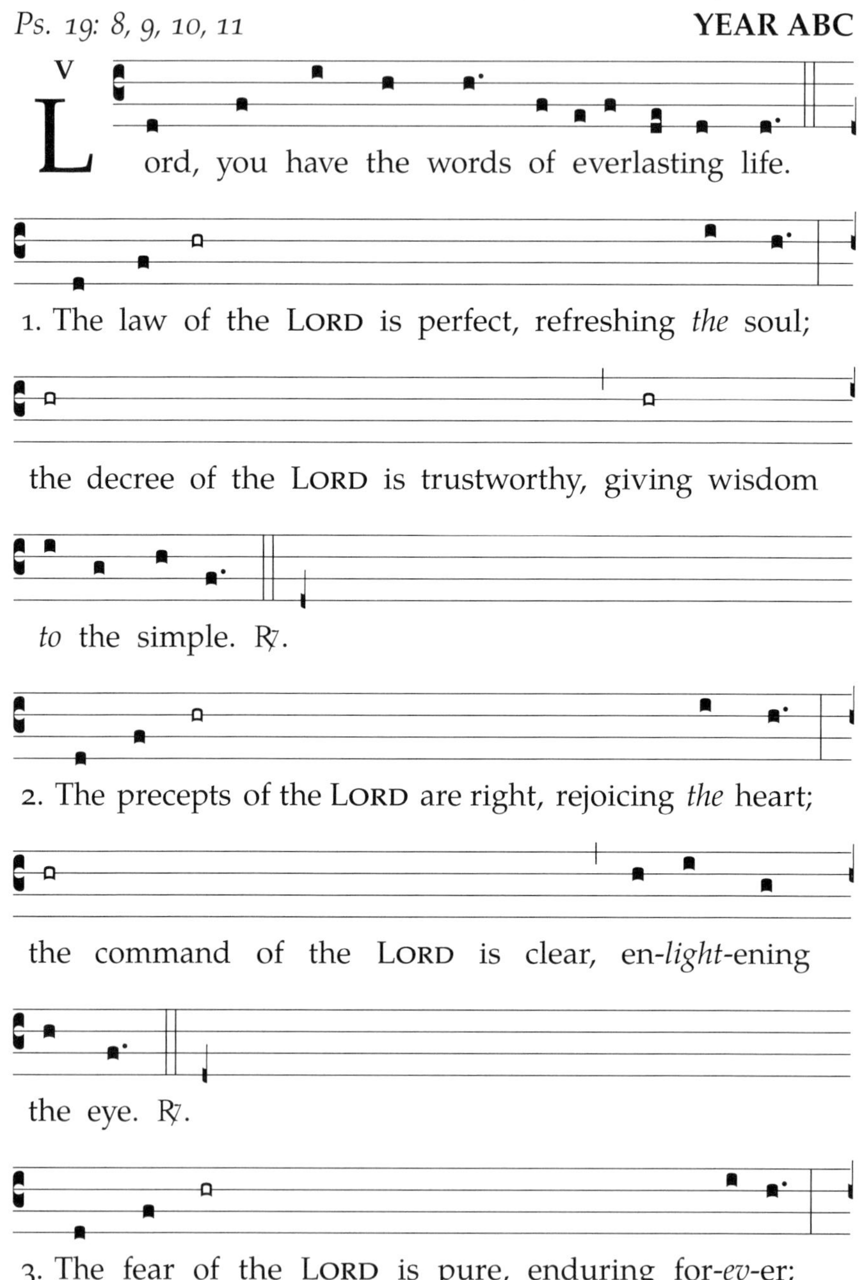

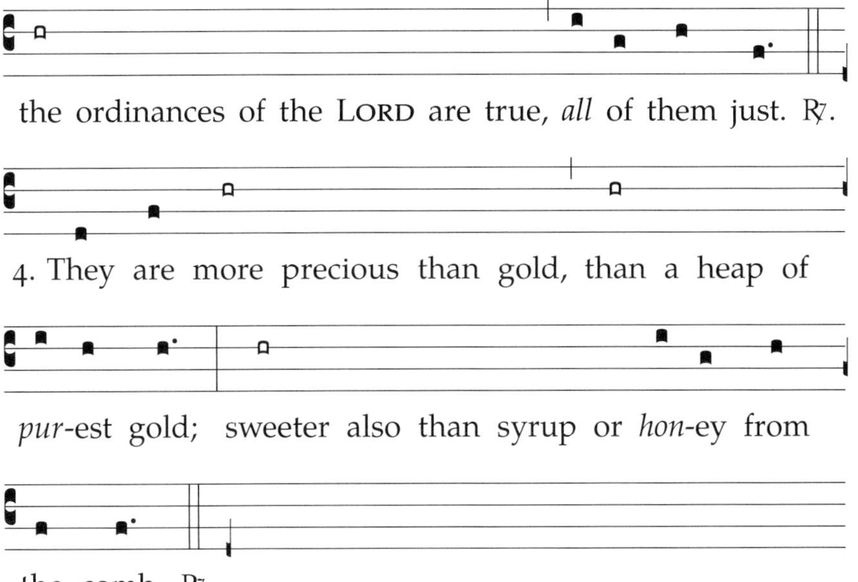
the ordinances of the LORD are true, *all* of them just. ℟.
4. They are more precious than gold, than a heap of
pur-est gold; sweeter also than syrup or *hon*-ey from
the comb. ℟.

Pentecost Sunday
Vigil Mass, extended form, after Reading 3

Ps. 107: 2-3, 4-5, 6-7, 8-9 **YEAR ABC**

III
Give thanks to the Lord; his love is everlast-ing.
1. Let the redeemed of the LORD *say,* those whom
he has redeemed from the hand of the foe
and *gath*-ered from the lands, from the east and
the west, from the north *and* the south. ℟.
2. They went astray in the desert wil-*der*-ness; the way

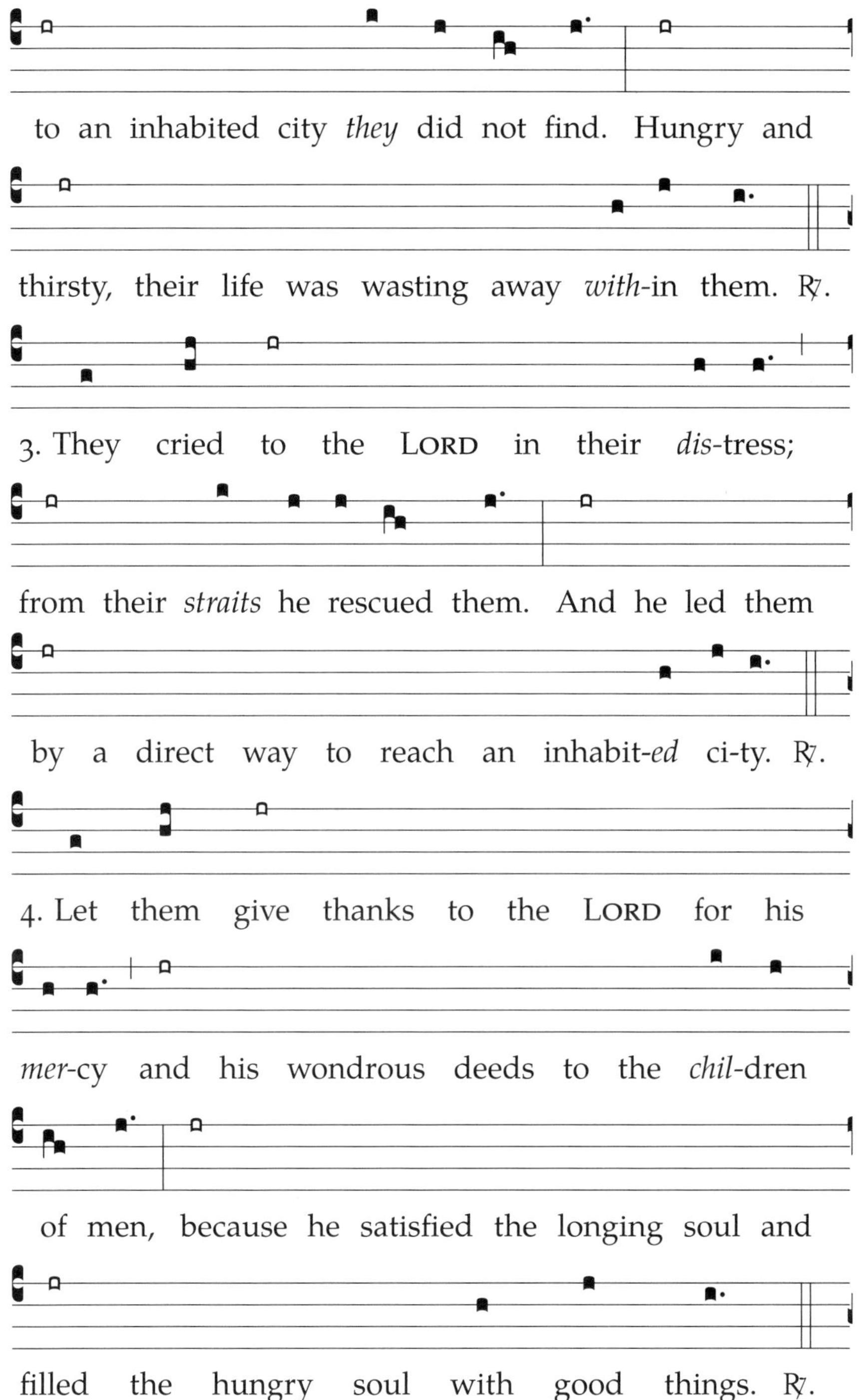
to an inhabited city *they* did not find. Hungry and
thirsty, their life was wasting away *with*-in them. ℟.
3. They cried to the LORD in their *dis*-tress;
from their *straits* he rescued them. And he led them
by a direct way to reach an inhabit-*ed* ci-ty. ℟.
4. Let them give thanks to the LORD for his
mer-cy and his wondrous deeds to the *chil*-dren
of men, because he satisfied the longing soul and
filled the hungry soul with good things. ℟.

Pentecost Sunday Vigil Mass, extended form, after Reading 4

Ps. 104: 1-2, 24, 35, 27-28, 29, 30 **YEAR ABC**

II
Lord, send out your Spirit, and renew the face
of the earth.
1. Bless the Lord, O my *soul*! O Lord, my God,
you are *great* indeed! You are clothed with majesty
and glory, robed in light *as* with a cloak. ℟.
2. How manifold are your works, *O* Lord!
In wisdom you have *wrought* them all — the earth

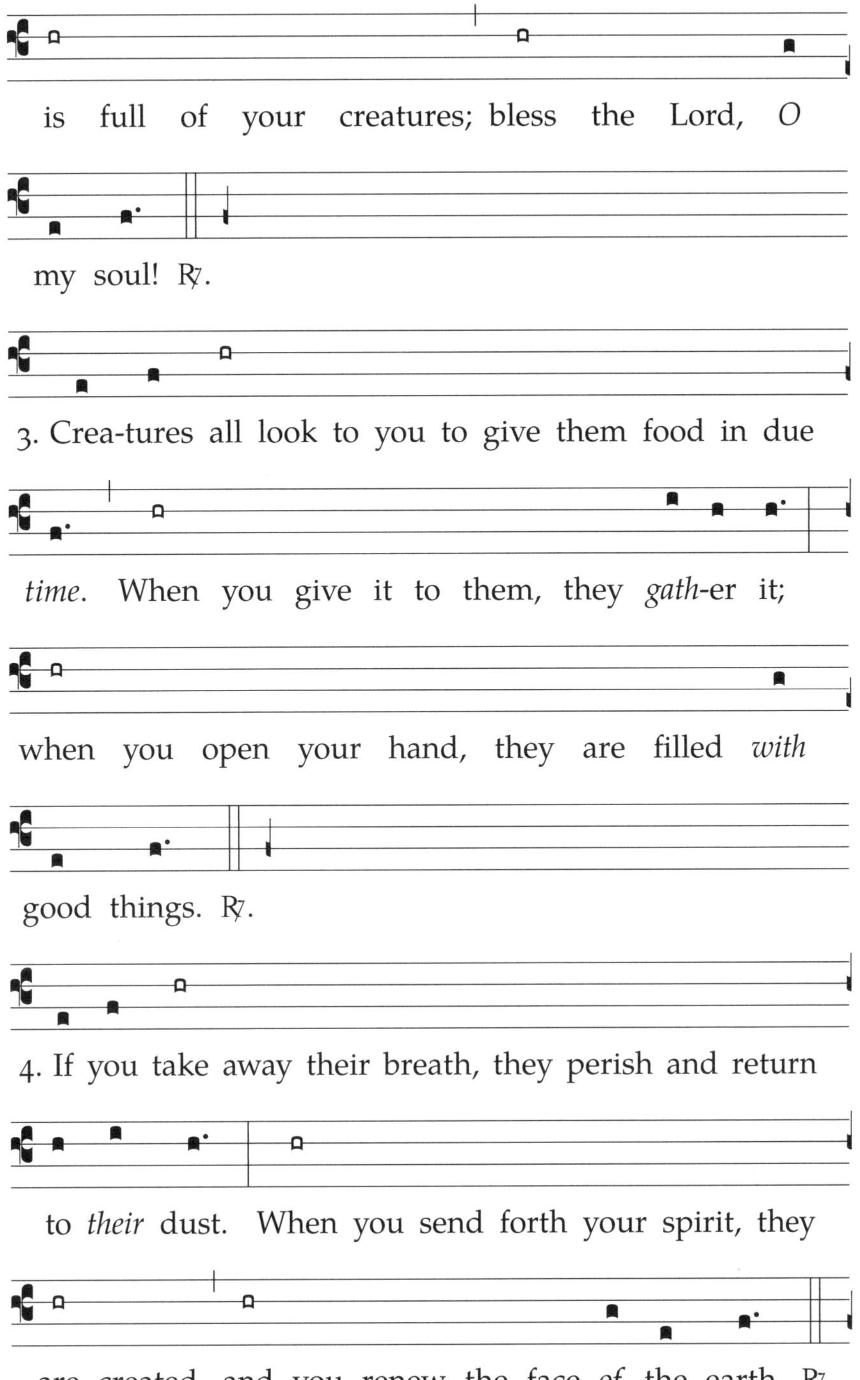
is full of your creatures; bless the Lord, *O*
my soul! ℟.
3. Crea-tures all look to you to give them food in due
time. When you give it to them, they *gath*-er it;
when you open your hand, they are filled *with*
good things. ℟.
4. If you take away their breath, they perish and return
to *their* dust. When you send forth your spirit, they
are created, and you renew the face *of* the earth. ℟.

Pentecost Sunday
Mass during the Day

Ps. 104: 1, 24, 29-30, 31, 34 **YEAR ABC**

II
Lord, send out your Spirit, and renew the
face of the earth.
1. Bless the LORD, O my *soul!* O LORD, my God,
you are *great* indeed! How manifold are your
works, O LORD! The earth is full *of* your
creatures. ℟.
2. If you take away their breath, they perish and return
to *their* dust. When you send forth your spirit,

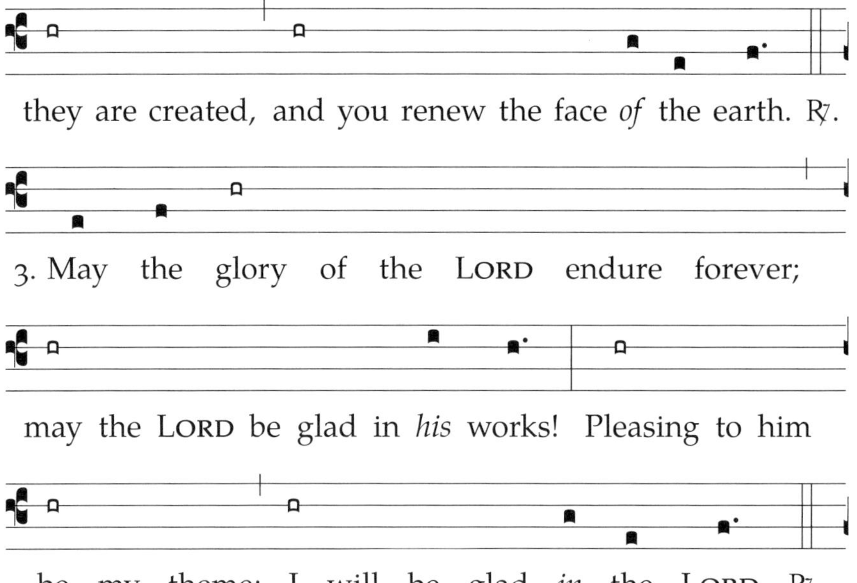
they are created, and you renew the face *of* the earth. ℟.
3. May the glory of the LORD endure forever;
may the LORD be glad in *his* works! Pleasing to him
be my theme; I will be glad *in* the LORD. ℟.

The Most Holy Trinity

Dn. 3: 52, 53, 54, 55 **YEAR A**

VIII
Glory and praise for ev- er!
1. Blessed are you, O Lord, the God of our
fathers, praiseworthy and exalted above all for-*ev*-er;
and blessed is your holy and glorious name,
praiseworthy and exalted above all *for* all ages. ℟.
2. Blessed are you in the temple of your holy
glo-ry, praiseworthy and glorious above *all* forever. ℟.
3. Blessed are you who look into the depths from your

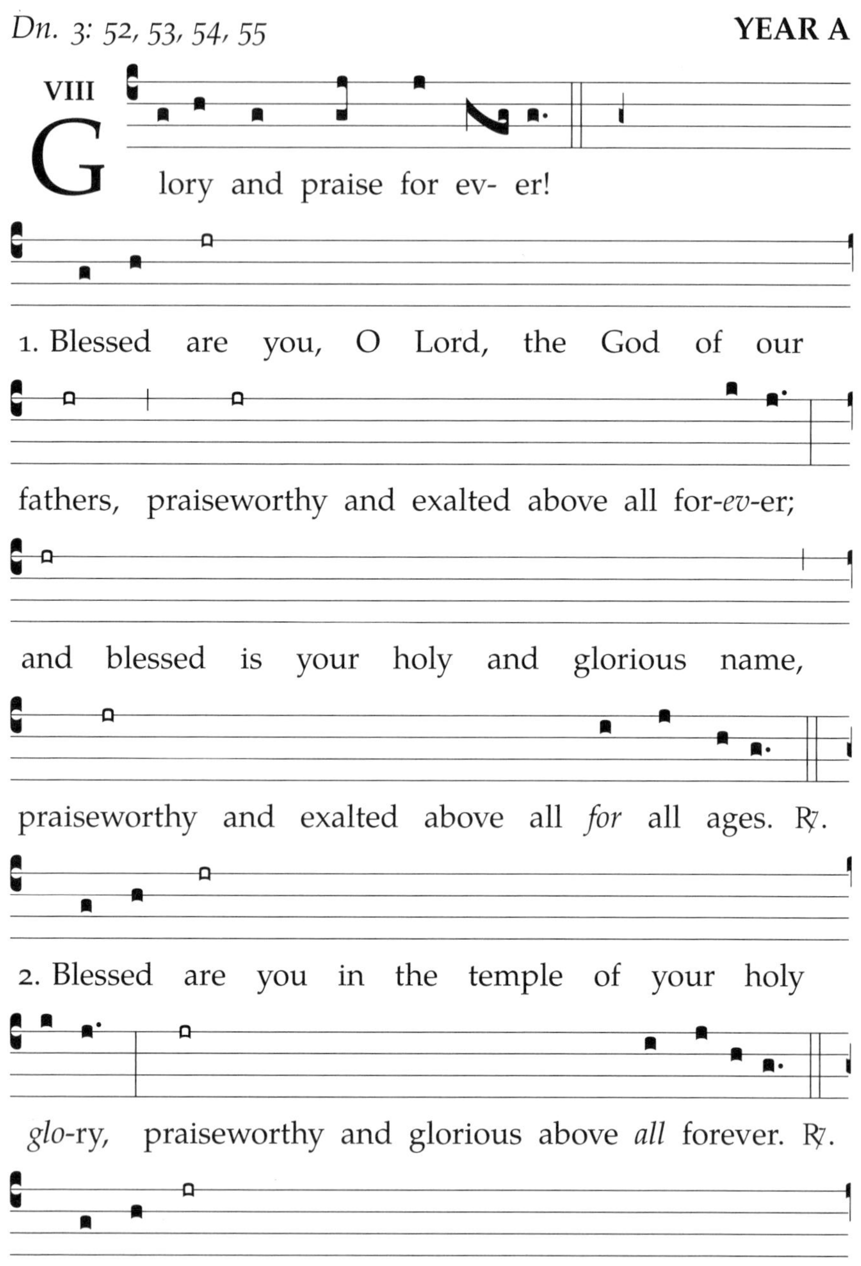

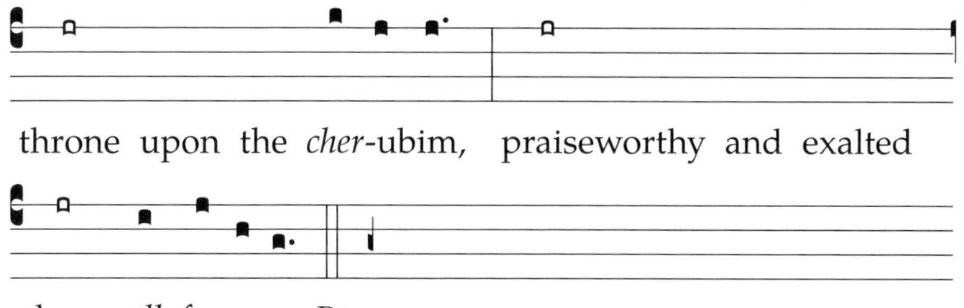
throne upon the *cher*-ubim, praiseworthy and exalted
above *all* forever. ℟.

The Most Holy Trinity

Ps. 33: 4-5, 6, 9, 18-19, 20, 22 **YEAR B**

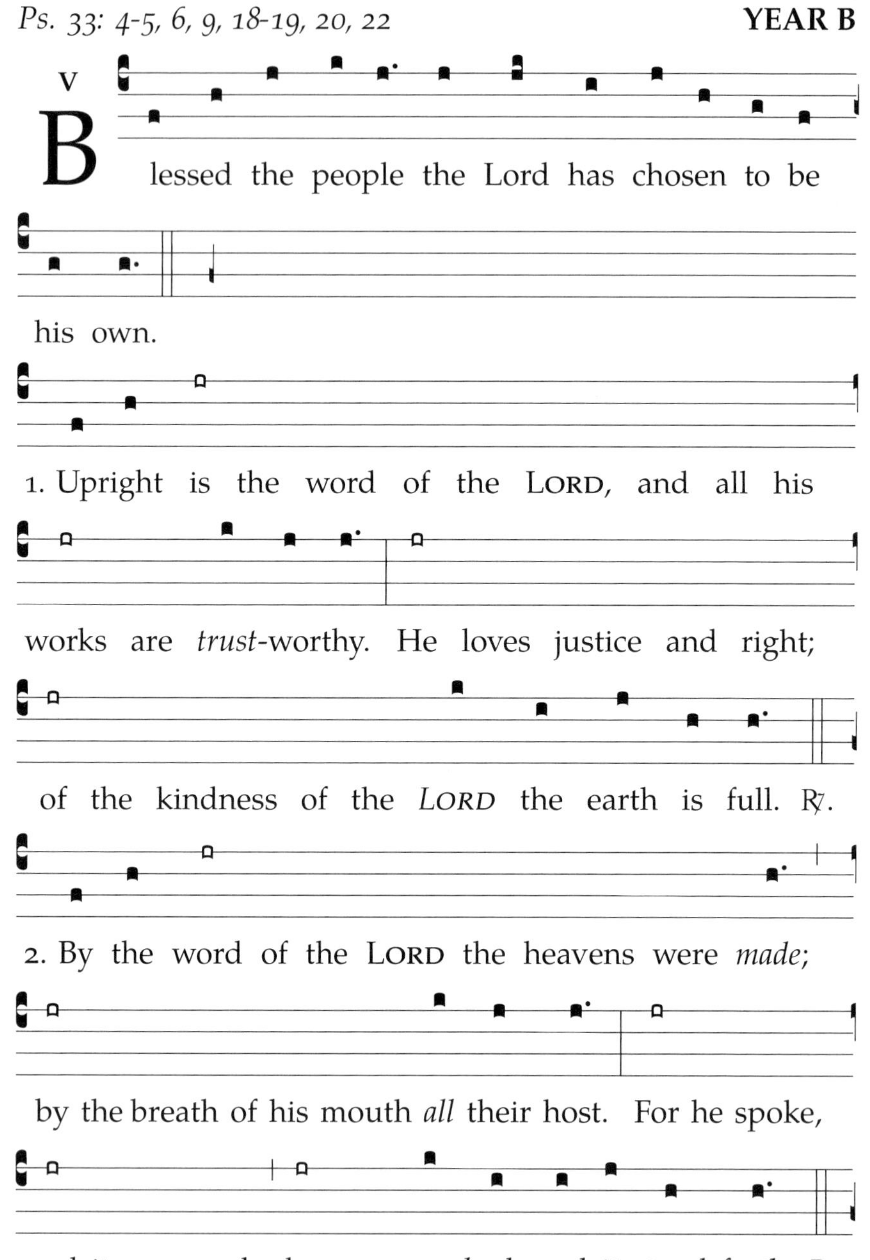

V
Blessed the people the Lord has chosen to be
his own.
1. Upright is the word of the LORD, and all his
works are *trust*-worthy. He loves justice and right;
of the kindness of the *LORD* the earth is full. ℟.
2. By the word of the LORD the heavens were *made;*
by the breath of his mouth *all* their host. For he spoke,
and it was made; he com-*mand*-ed, and it stood forth. ℟.

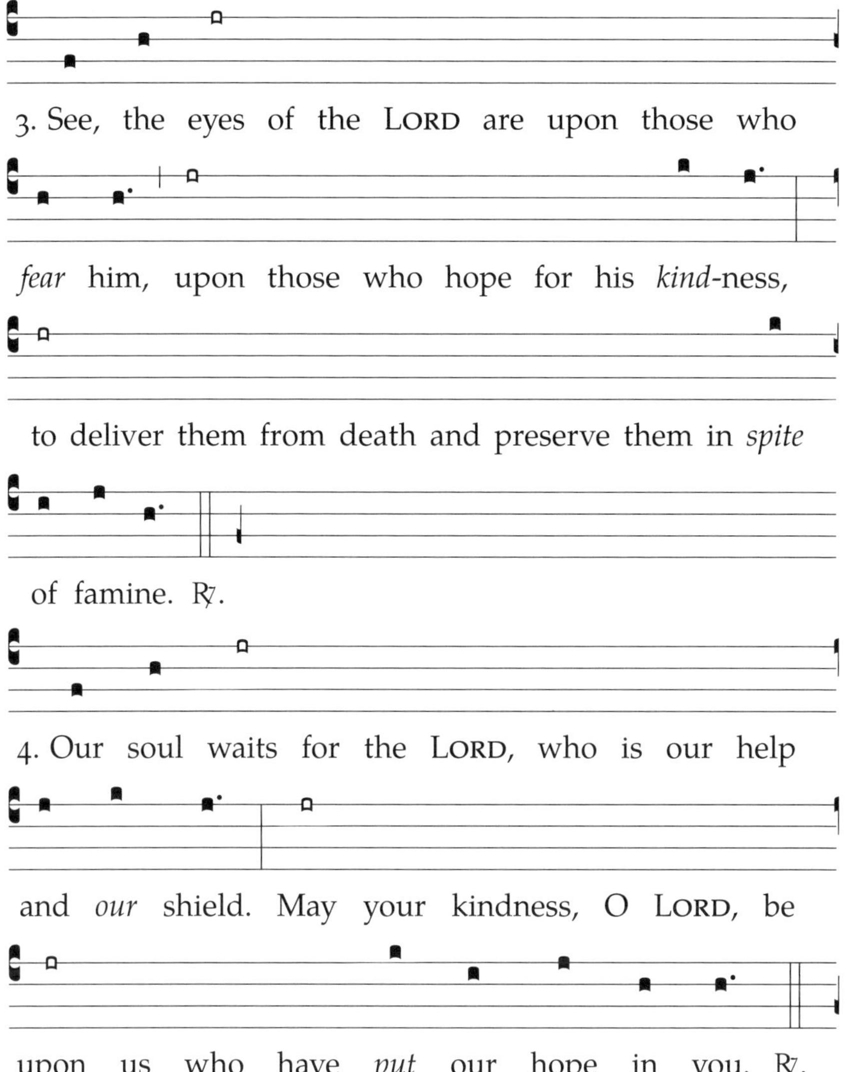
3. See, the eyes of the LORD are upon those who
fear him, upon those who hope for his kind-ness,
to deliver them from death and preserve them in spite
of famine. ℟.
4. Our soul waits for the LORD, who is our help
and our shield. May your kindness, O LORD, be
upon us who have put our hope in you. ℟.

The Most Holy Trinity

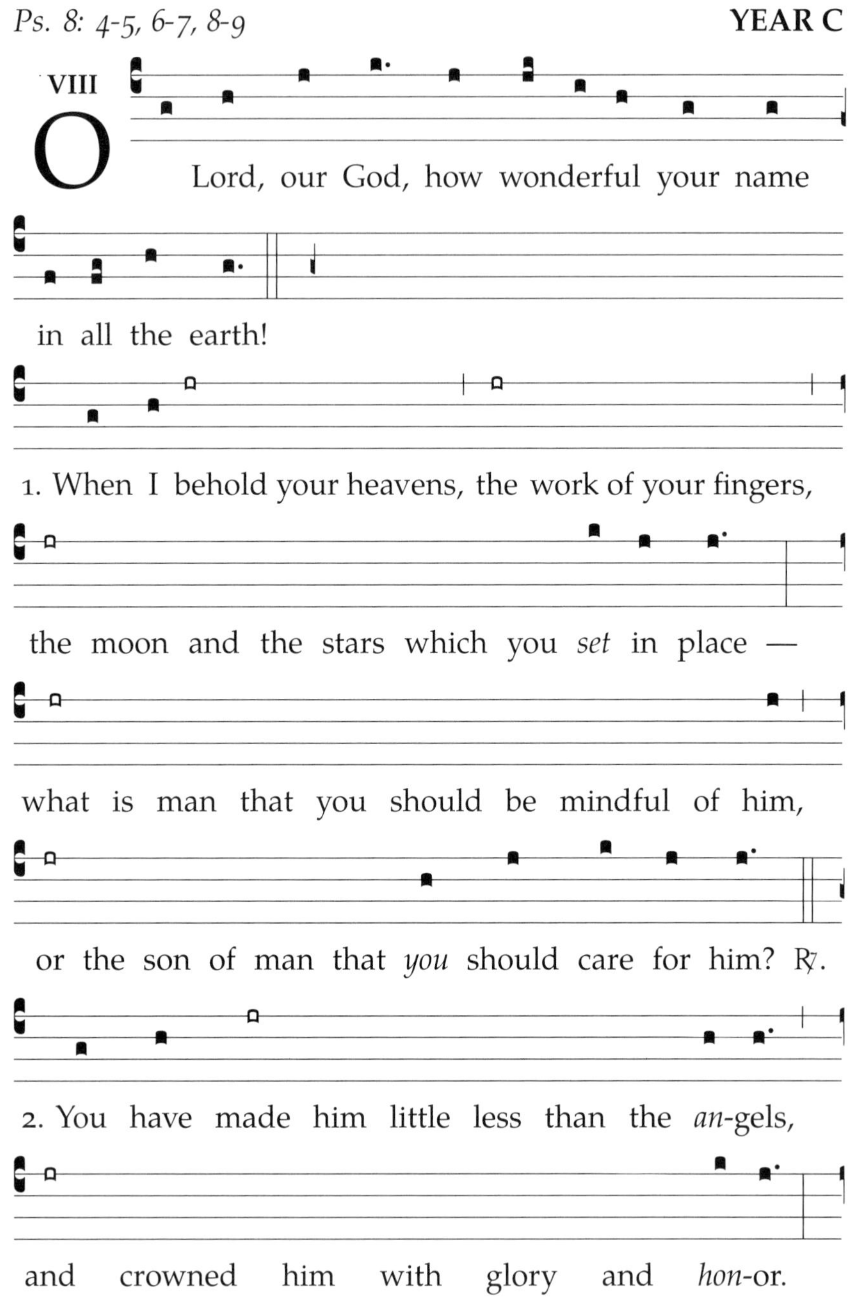
Ps. 8: 4-5, 6-7, 8-9
YEAR C
VIII
O Lord, our God, how wonderful your name
in all the earth!
1. When I behold your heavens, the work of your fingers,
the moon and the stars which you *set* in place —
what is man that you should be mindful of him,
or the son of man that *you* should care for him? ℟.
2. You have made him little less than the *an*-gels,
and crowned him with glory and *hon*-or.

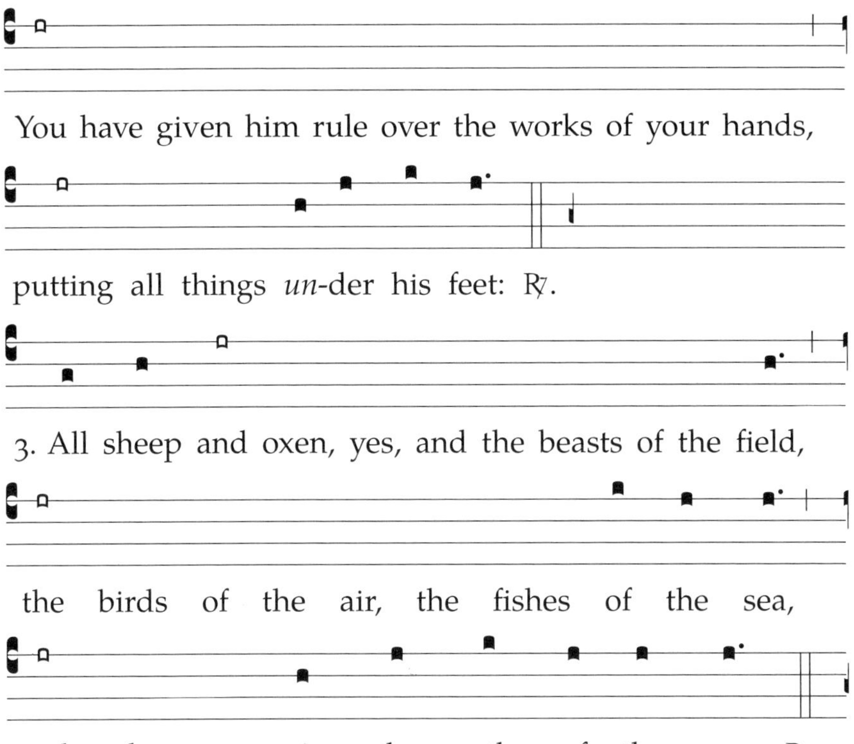
You have given him rule over the works of your hands,
putting all things *un*-der his feet: ℟.
3. All sheep and oxen, yes, and the beasts of the field,
the birds of the air, the fishes of the sea,
and whatever *swims* the paths of the seas. ℟.

The Most Holy Body and Blood of Christ

Ps. 147: 12-13, 14-15, 19-20 **YEAR A**

VIII
Praise the Lord, Je-rusalem.
1. Glori-fy the LORD, O Je-*ru*-sa-lem; praise your God,
O *Zi*-on. For he has strengthened the bars of your
gates; he has blessed your chil-*dren* within you. ℟.
2. He has granted peace in your *bor*-ders; with the
best of wheat he *fills* you. He sends forth his
command to the earth; swift-*ly* runs his word! ℟.
3. He has proclaimed his word to Ja-*cob*,

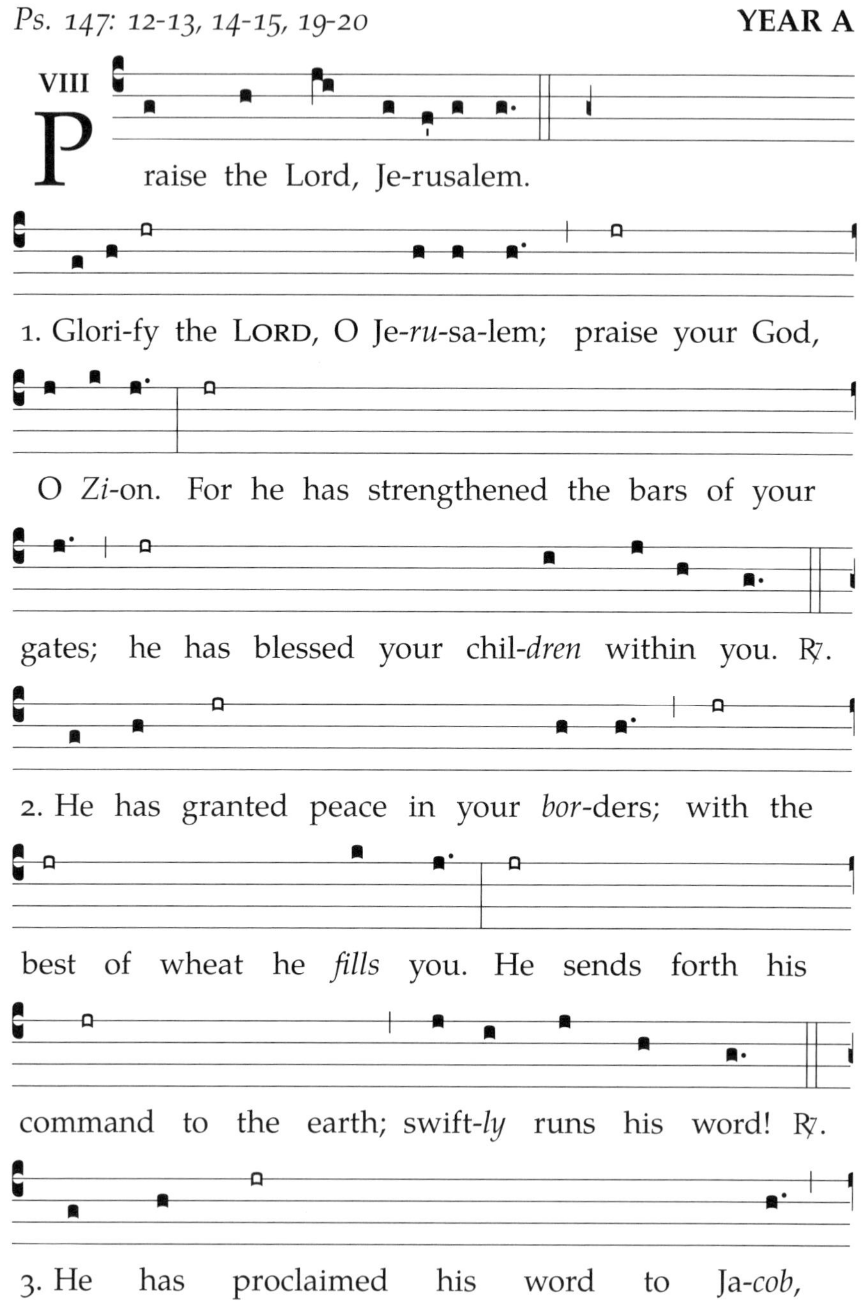

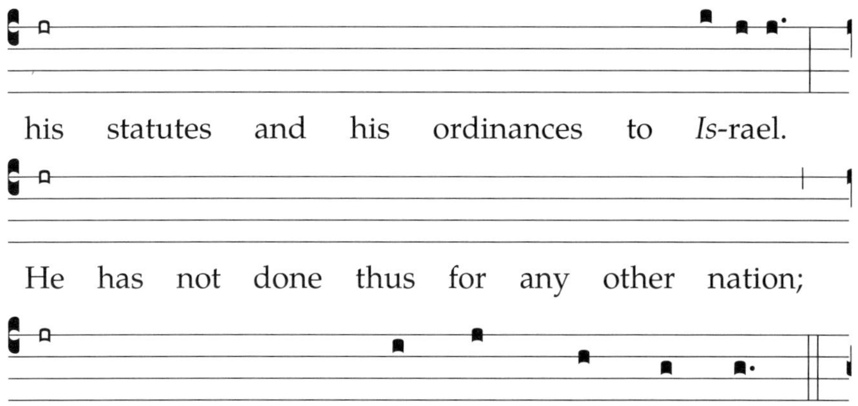
his statutes and his ordinances to *Is*-rael.
He has not done thus for any other nation;

his ordinances he has *not* made known to them. ℟.

The Most Holy Body and Blood of Christ

Ps. 116: 12-13, 15-16, 17-18 **YEAR B**

VIII
I will take the cup of salvation, and call
on the name of the Lord.
1. How shall I make a return to the LORD for all the
good he has *done* for me? The cup of salvation I
will take up, and I will call upon the *name* of the
LORD. ℟.
2. Precious in the eyes of the LORD is the death
of his *faith*-ful ones. I am your servant, the son

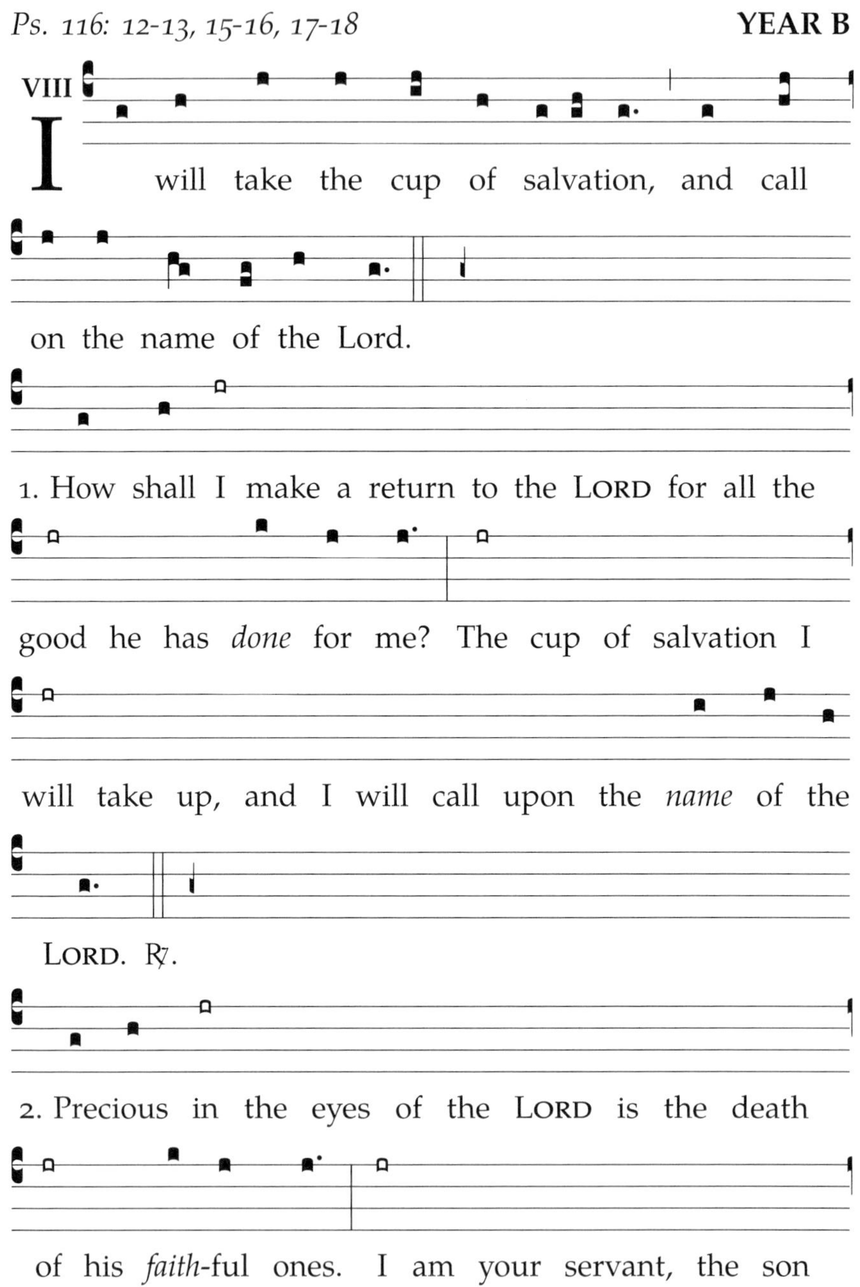

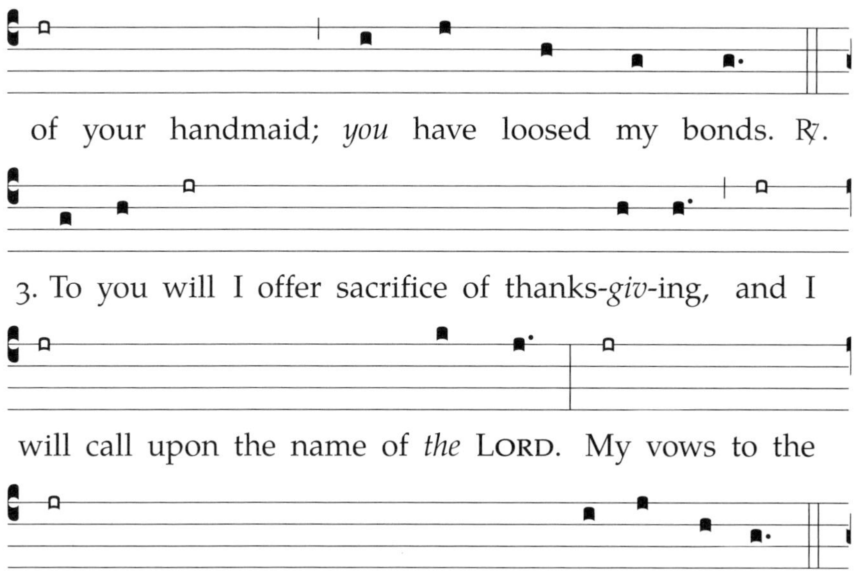
of your handmaid; *you* have loosed my bonds. ℟.
3. To you will I offer sacrifice of thanks-*giv*-ing, and I
will call upon the name of *the* LORD. My vows to the
LORD I will pay in the presence of *all* his people. ℟.

The Most Holy Body and Blood of Christ

Ps. 110: 1, 2, 3, 4 **YEAR C**

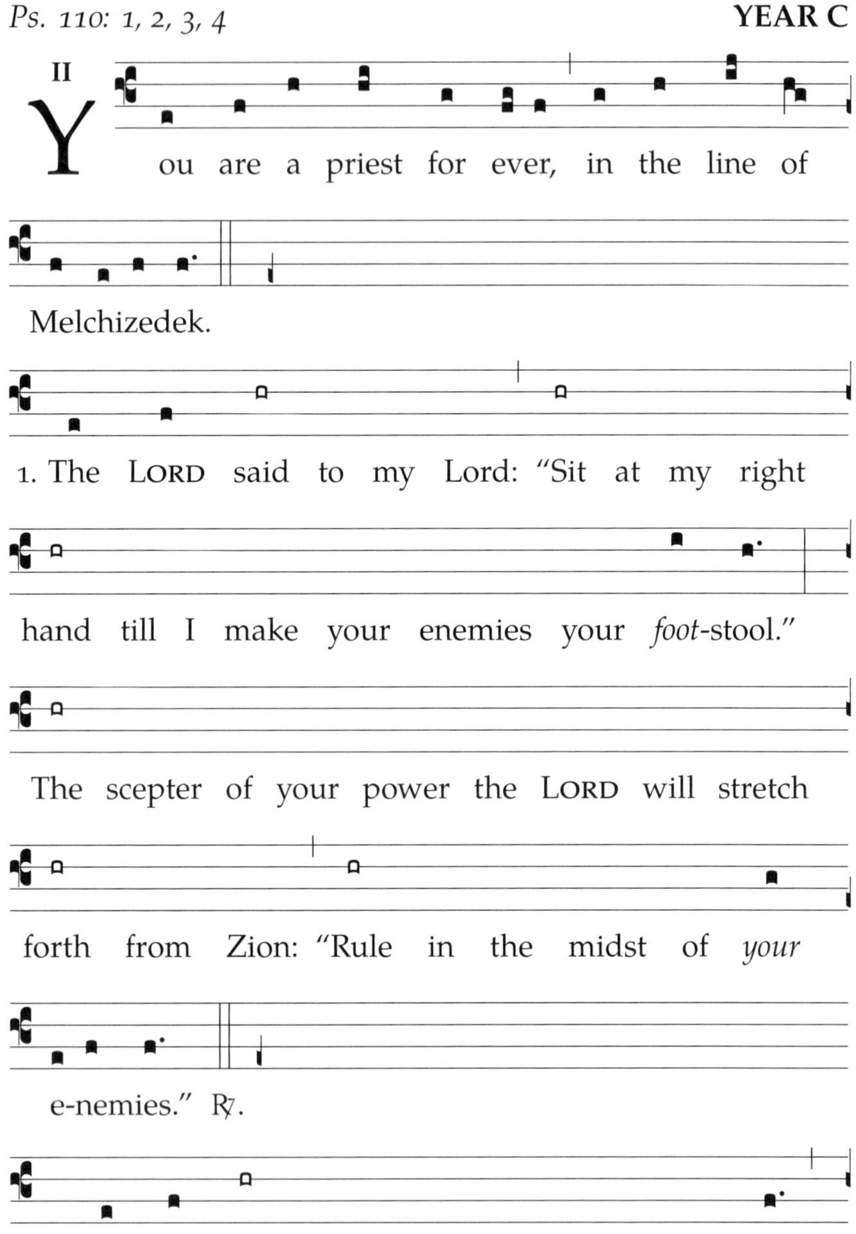
II
You are a priest for ever, in the line of Melchizedek.
1. The LORD said to my Lord: "Sit at my right hand till I make your enemies your *foot*-stool."
The scepter of your power the LORD will stretch forth from Zion: "Rule in the midst of *your* e-nemies." ℟.
2. "Yours is princely power in the day of your *birth,*

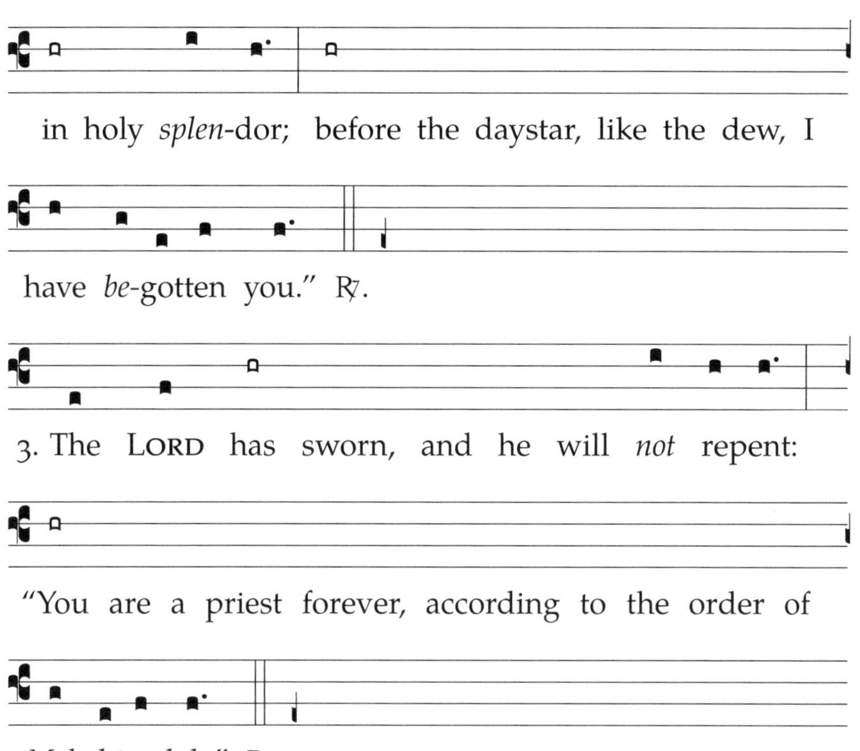
in holy splen-dor; before the daystar, like the dew, I
have be-gotten you." ℟.
3. The LORD has sworn, and he will not repent:
"You are a priest forever, according to the order of
Mel-chizedek." ℟.

The Sacred Heart of Jesus

Ps. 103: 1-2, 3-4, 6-7, 8, 10 **YEAR A**

VI
The Lord's kindness is everlasting to those who fear him.
1. Bless the LORD, O my *soul;* all my being, bless his holy name. Bless the LORD, O my soul; and forget not *all* his benefits. ℟.
2. He pardons all your iniquities, *heals* all your ills.
He redeems your life from destruction, crowns you with kindness *and* compassion. ℟.

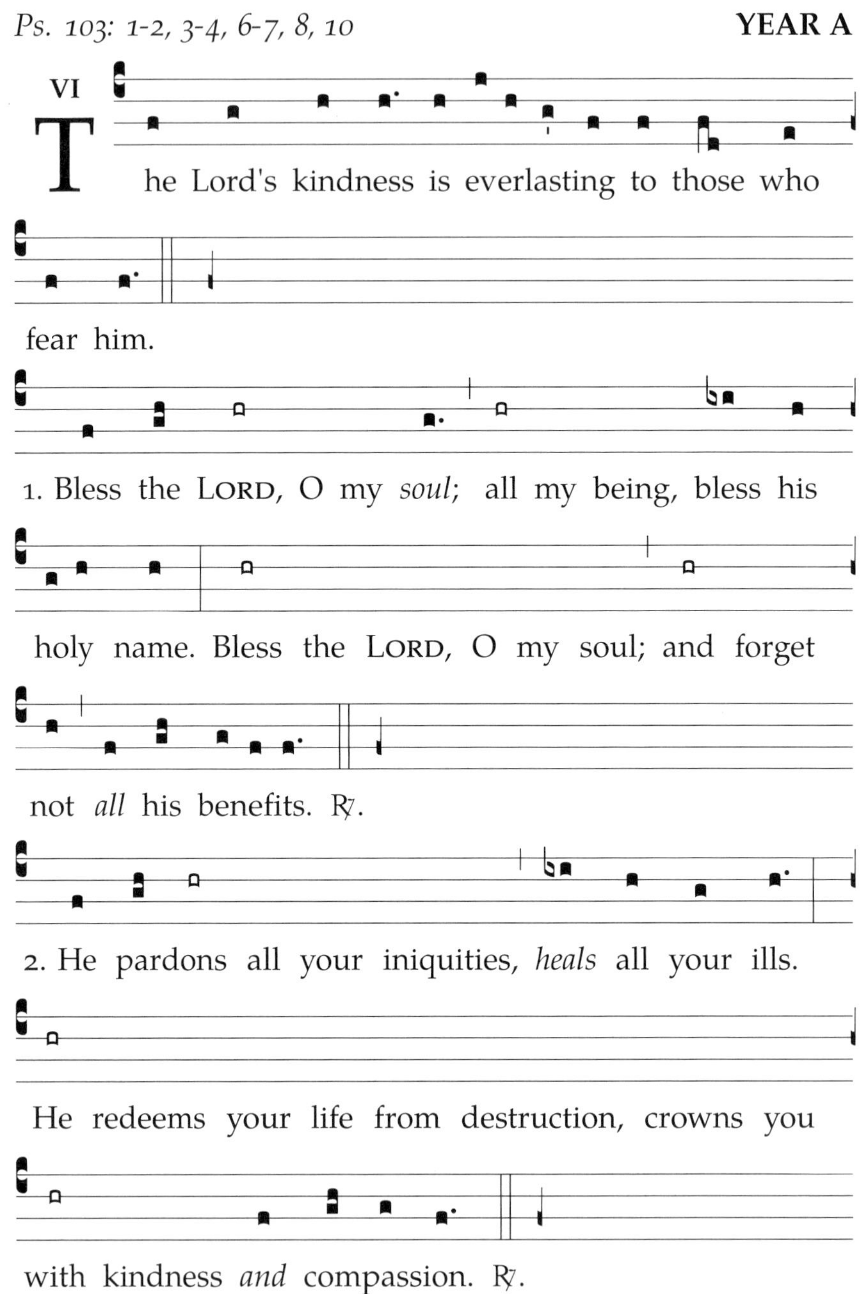

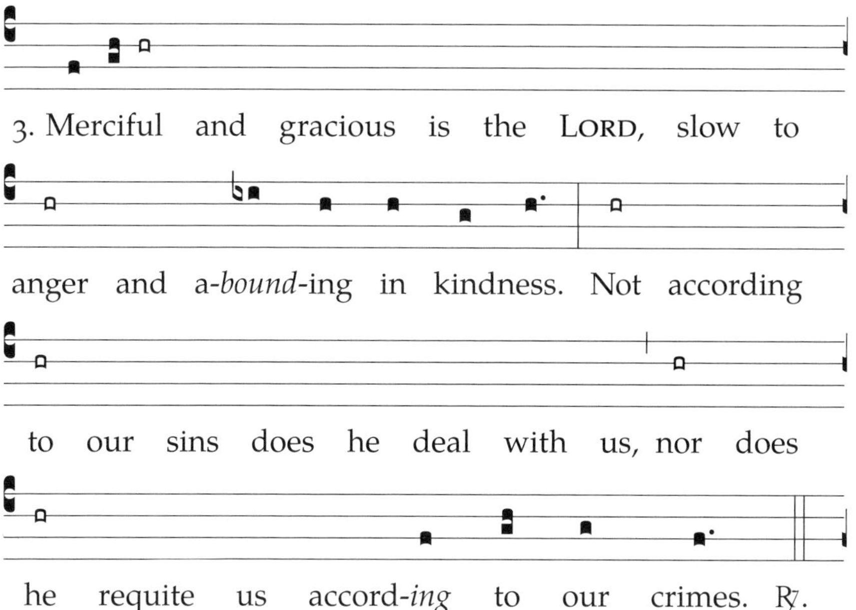
3. Merciful and gracious is the LORD, slow to
anger and a-*bound*-ing in kindness. Not according
to our sins does he deal with us, nor does
he requite us accord-*ing* to our crimes. ℟.

The Sacred Heart of Jesus

Is. 12: 2-3, 4, 5-6 **YEAR B**

V
You will draw water joyfully from the springs
of salvation.
1. God indeed is my savior; I am confident and
un-*a*-fraid. My strength and my courage is the
LORD, and he has been my *sav*-ior. With joy
you will draw water at the fountain *of* salvation. ℟.
2. Give thanks to the LORD, acclaim *his* name; among
the nations make known his deeds, proclaim how

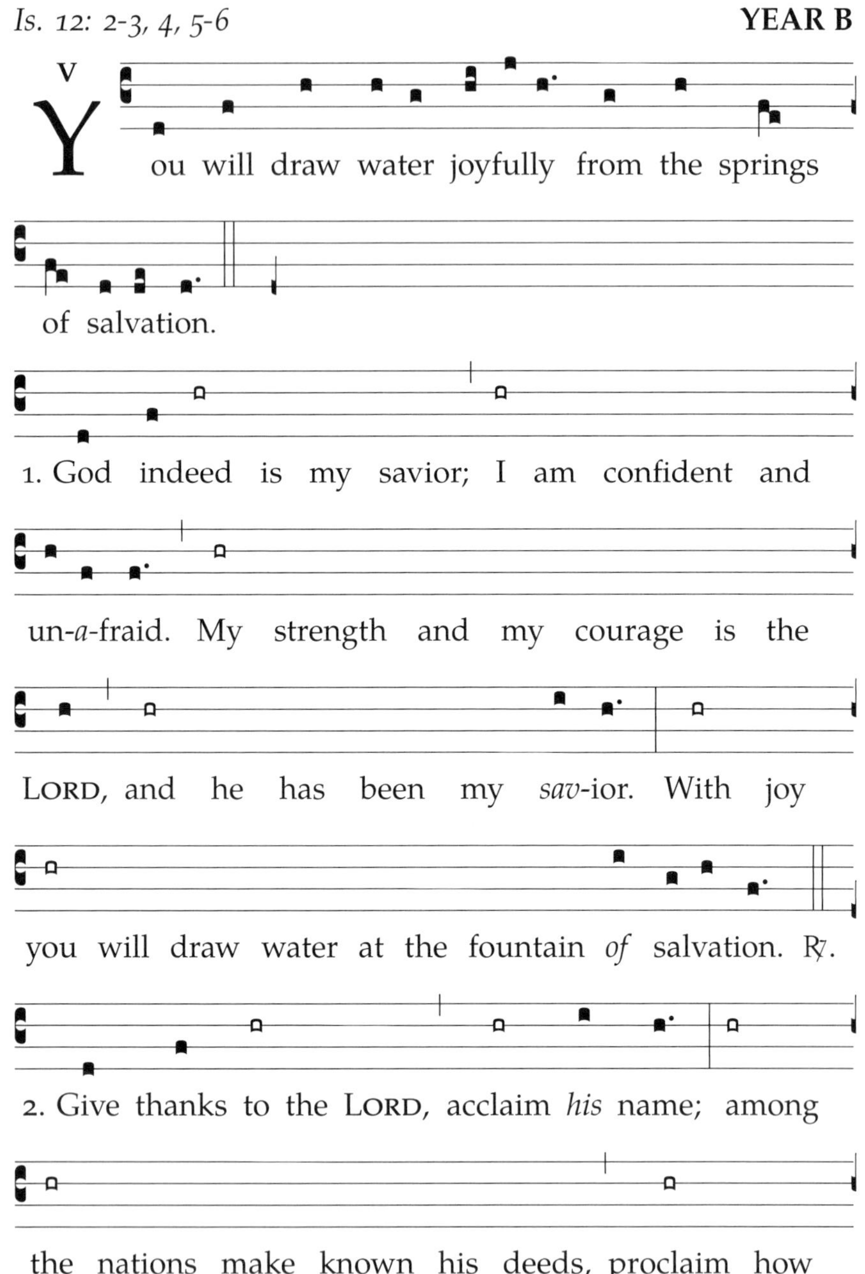

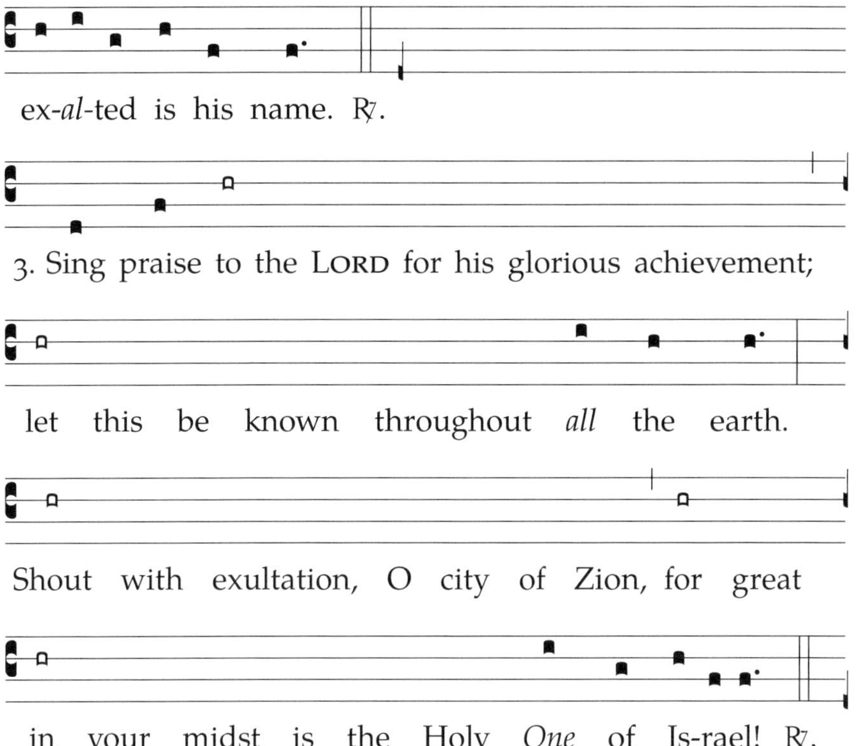
ex-*al*-ted is his name. ℟.
3. Sing praise to the LORD for his glorious achievement;
let this be known throughout *all* the earth.
Shout with exultation, O city of Zion, for great
in your midst is the Holy *One* of Is-rael! ℟.

The Sacred Heart of Jesus

Ps. 23: 1-3a, 3b-4, 5, 6 **YEAR C**

VIII
The Lord is my shepherd; there is nothing I shall want.
1. The LORD is my shepherd; I shall *not* want. In verdant pastures he gives me *re*-pose; beside restful waters he leads me; he re-*fresh*-es my soul. ℟.
2. He guides me in right paths for his *name's* sake. Even though I walk in the dark valley I fear no *e*-vil; for you are at my side

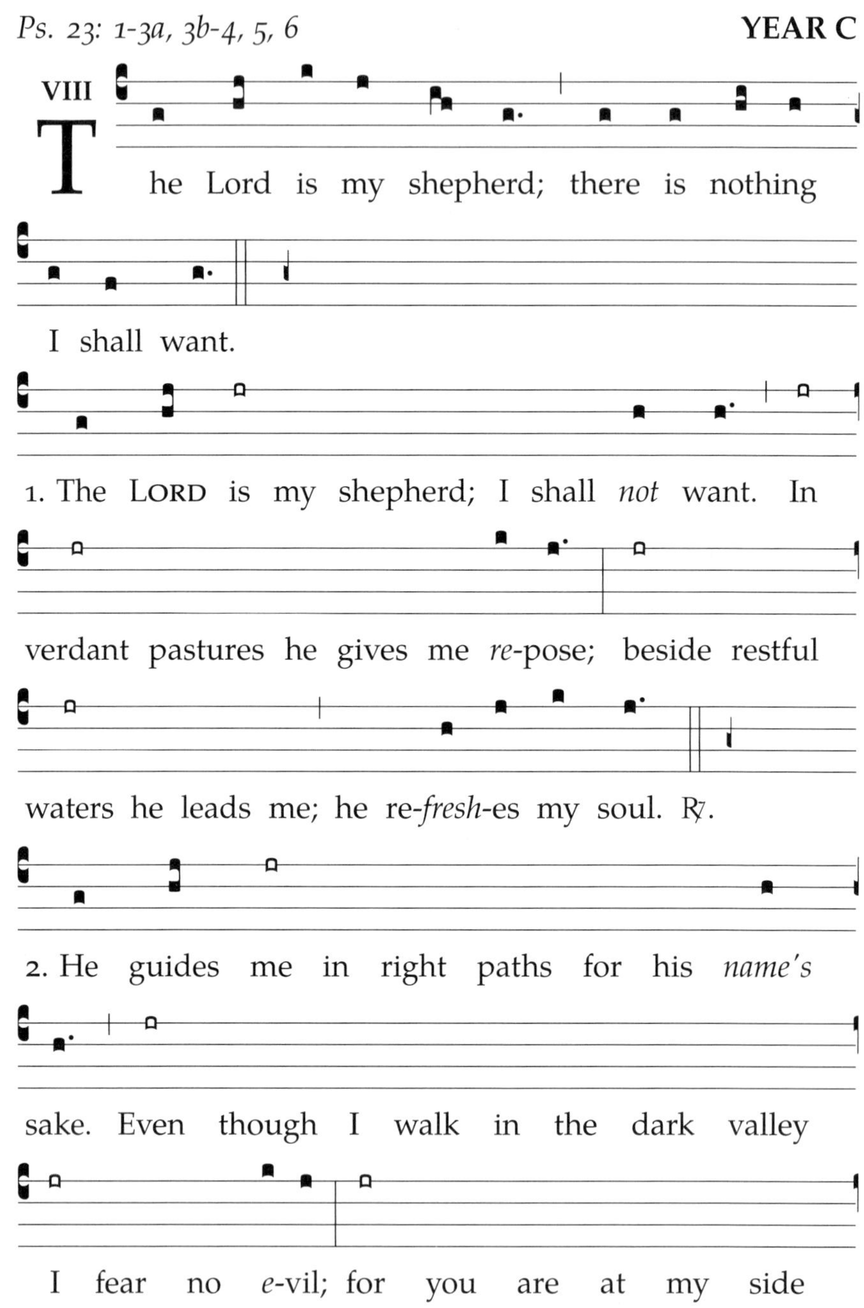

with your rod and your staff that give me
courage. ℟.
3. You spread the table before me in the sight of
my foes; you anoint my head with oil; my cup
overflows. ℟.
4. Only goodness and kindness follow me all the
days of my life; and I shall dwell in the
house of the LORD for years to come. ℟.

Ordinary Time

Second Sunday in Ordinary Time

Ps. 40: 2, 4, 7-8, 8-9, 10 **YEAR AB**

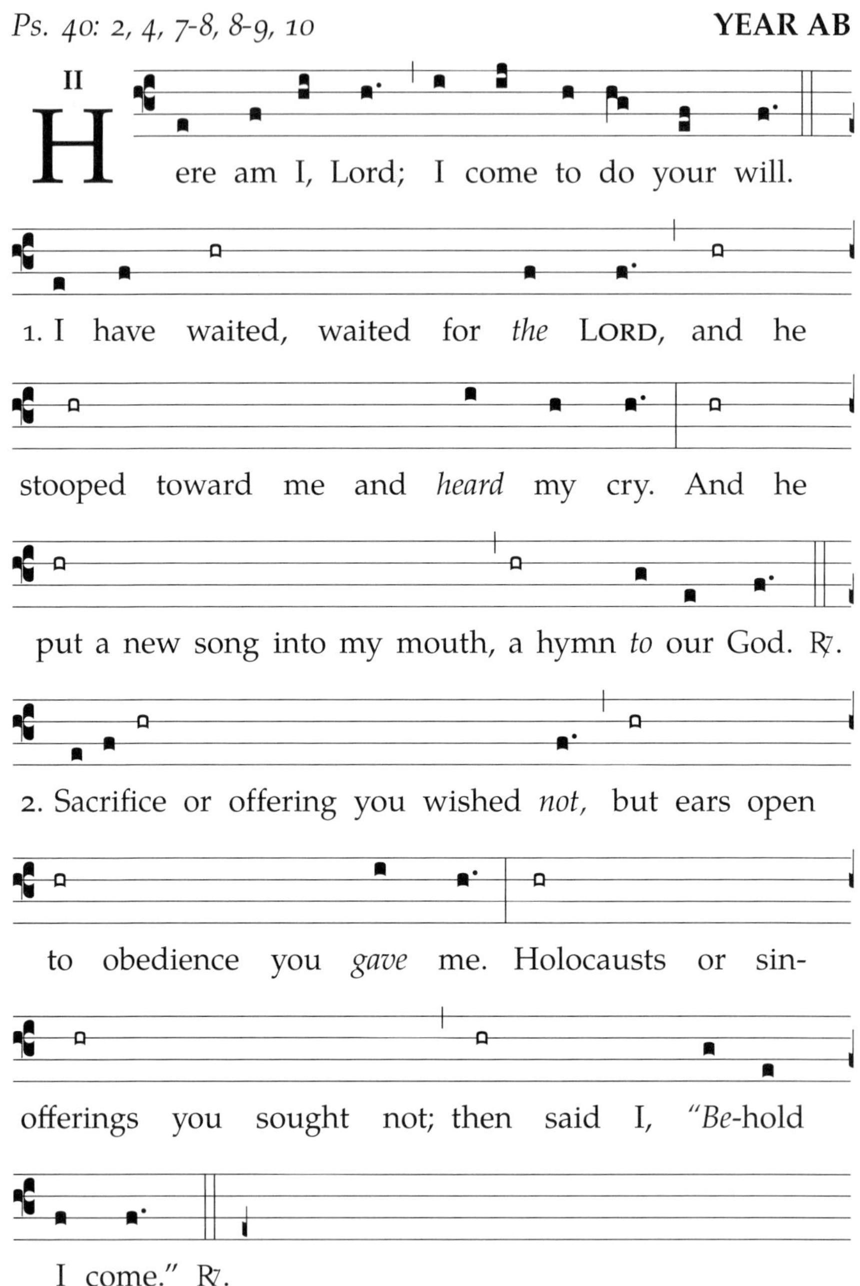
II
Here am I, Lord; I come to do your will.
1. I have waited, waited for *the* Lord, and he
stooped toward me and *heard* my cry. And he
put a new song into my mouth, a hymn *to* our God. ℟.
2. Sacrifice or offering you wished *not,* but ears open
to obedience you *gave* me. Holocausts or sin-
offerings you sought not; then said I, "*Be*-hold
I come." ℟.

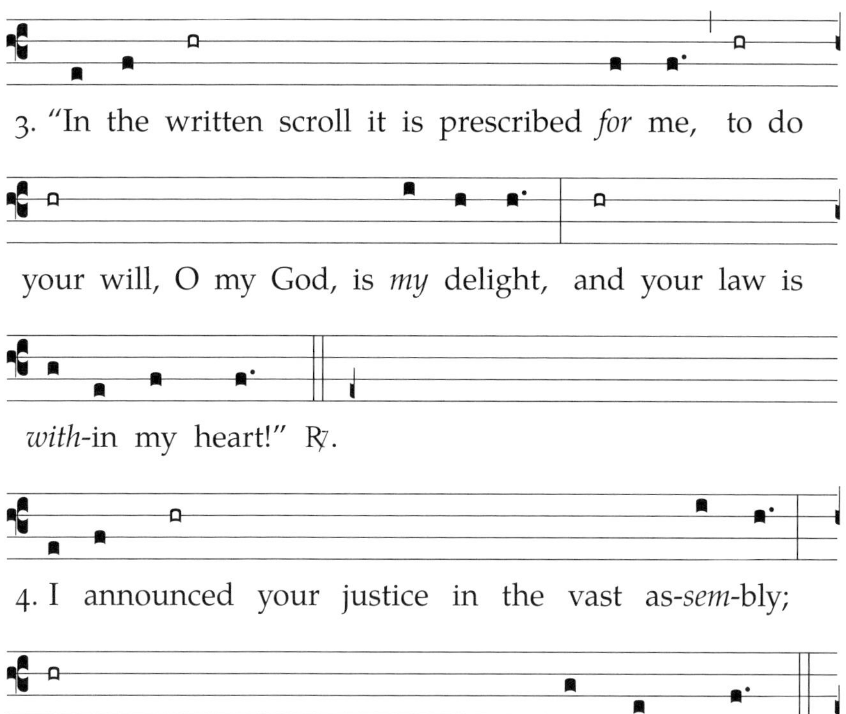
3. "In the written scroll it is prescribed for me, to do
your will, O my God, is my delight, and your law is
with-in my heart!" ℟.
4. I announced your justice in the vast as-sem-bly;
I did not restrain my lips, as you, O LORD, know. ℟.

Second Sunday in Ordinary Time

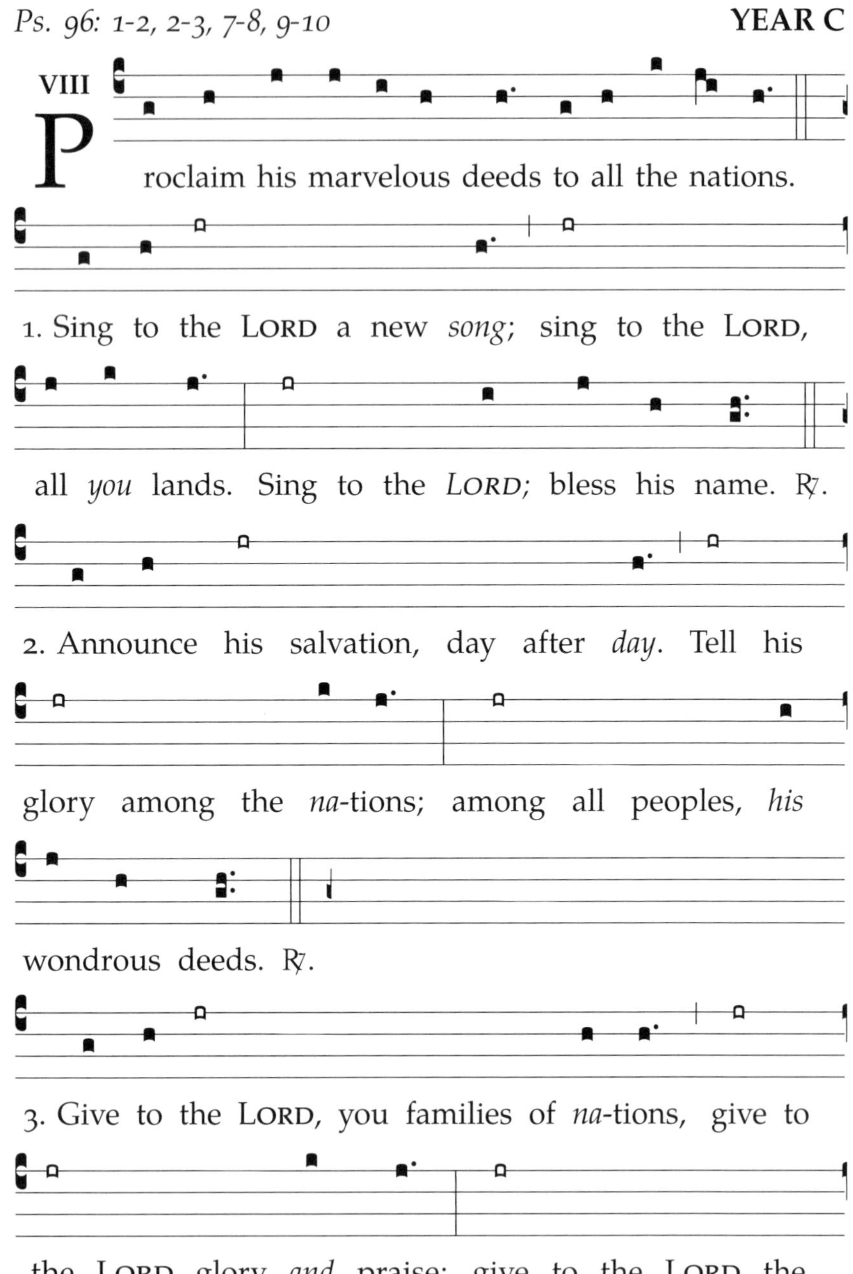
Ps. 96: 1-2, 2-3, 7-8, 9-10
YEAR C
VIII
Proclaim his marvelous deeds to all the nations.
1. Sing to the Lord a new *song;* sing to the Lord,
all *you* lands. Sing to the *Lord;* bless his name. ℟.
2. Announce his salvation, day after *day.* Tell his
glory among the *na*-tions; among all peoples, *his*
wondrous deeds. ℟.
3. Give to the Lord, you families of *na*-tions, give to
the Lord glory *and* praise; give to the Lord the

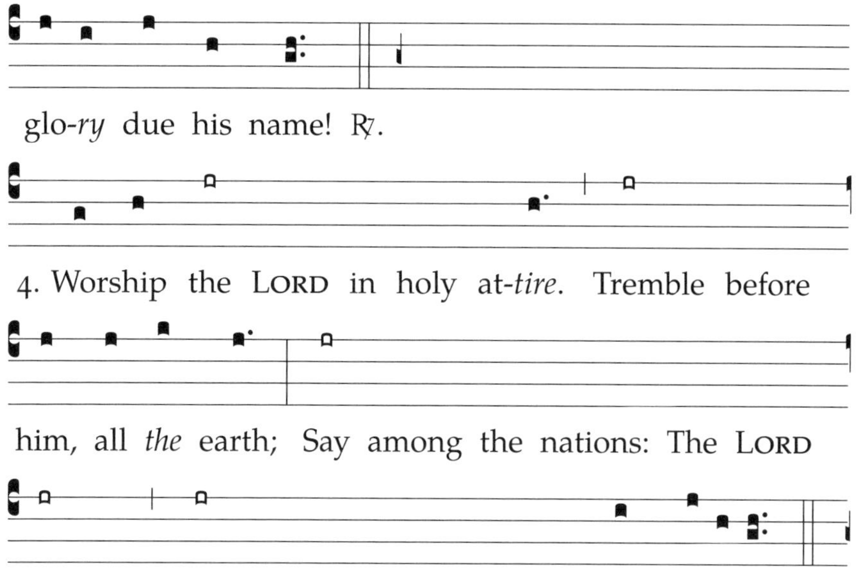
glo-*ry* due his name! ℟.
4. Worship the LORD in holy at-*tire*. Tremble before
him, all *the* earth; Say among the nations: The LORD
is king. He governs the peoples *with* equity. ℟.

Third Sunday in Ordinary Time

Ps. 27: 1, 4, 13-14 **YEAR A**

℣
The Lord is my light and my salvation.
1. The LORD is my light and my salvation; whom
should *I* fear? The LORD is my life's refuge; of *whom*
should I be afraid? ℟.
2. One thing I ask of the LORD; this *I* seek:
to dwell in the house of the LORD all the days
of my life, that I may gaze on the loveliness of the
LORD and contem-*plate* his temple. ℟.

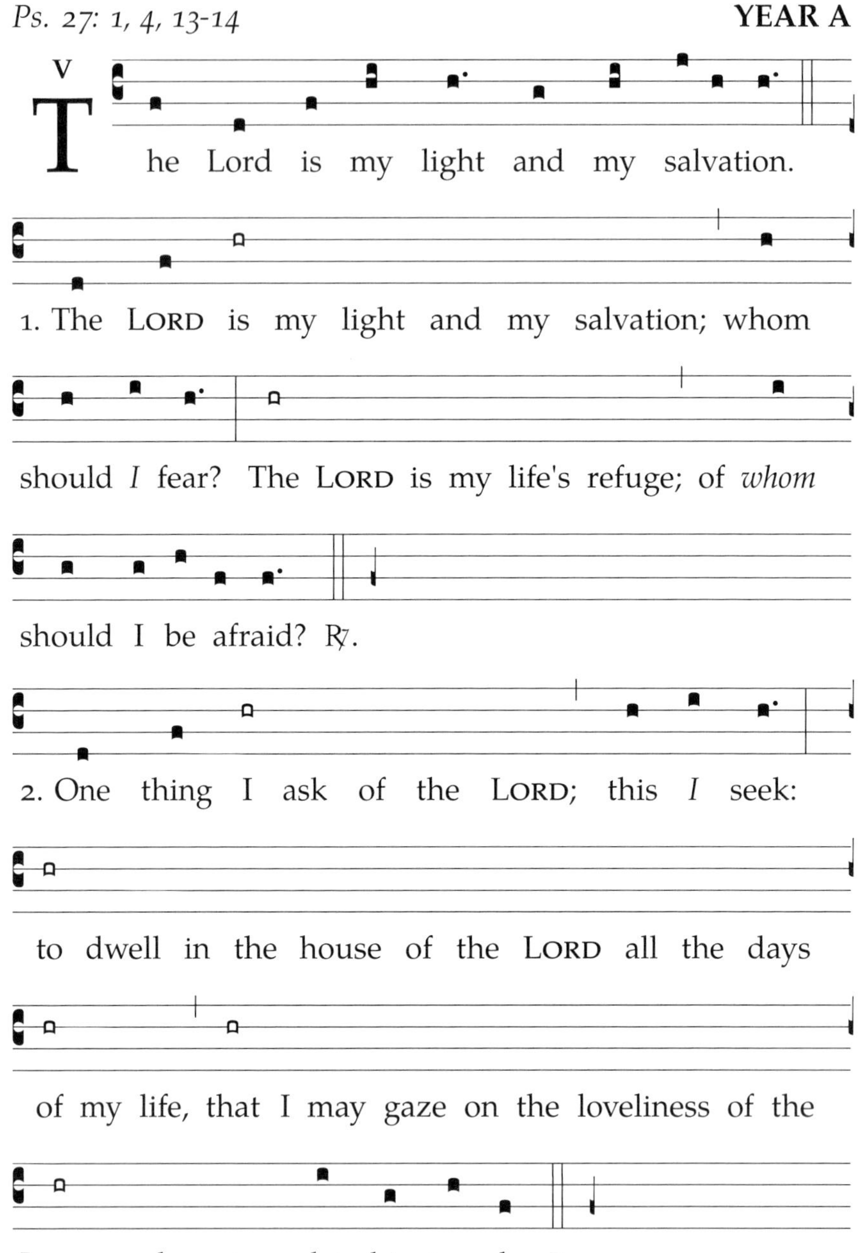

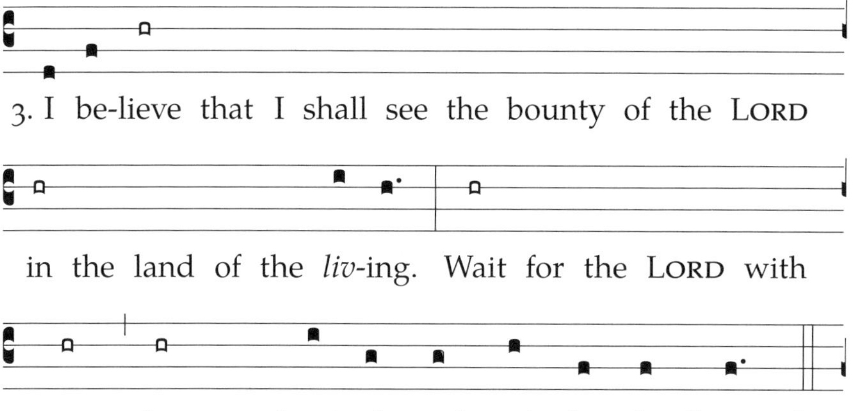
3. I be-lieve that I shall see the bounty of the LORD
in the land of the *liv*-ing. Wait for the LORD with
courage; be stout-*heart*-ed, and wait for the LORD. ℟.

THIRD SUNDAY IN ORDINARY TIME

Ps. 25: 4-5, 6-7, 8-9 **YEAR B**

I
Teach me your ways, O Lord.
1. Your ways, O LORD, make known to *me;*
teach me your paths, guide me in your truth
and teach me, for you are *God* my savior. ℟.
2. Remember that your compassion, O *LORD,* and your
love are from of old. In your kindness
remember me, because of your *good*-ness,
O LORD. ℟.

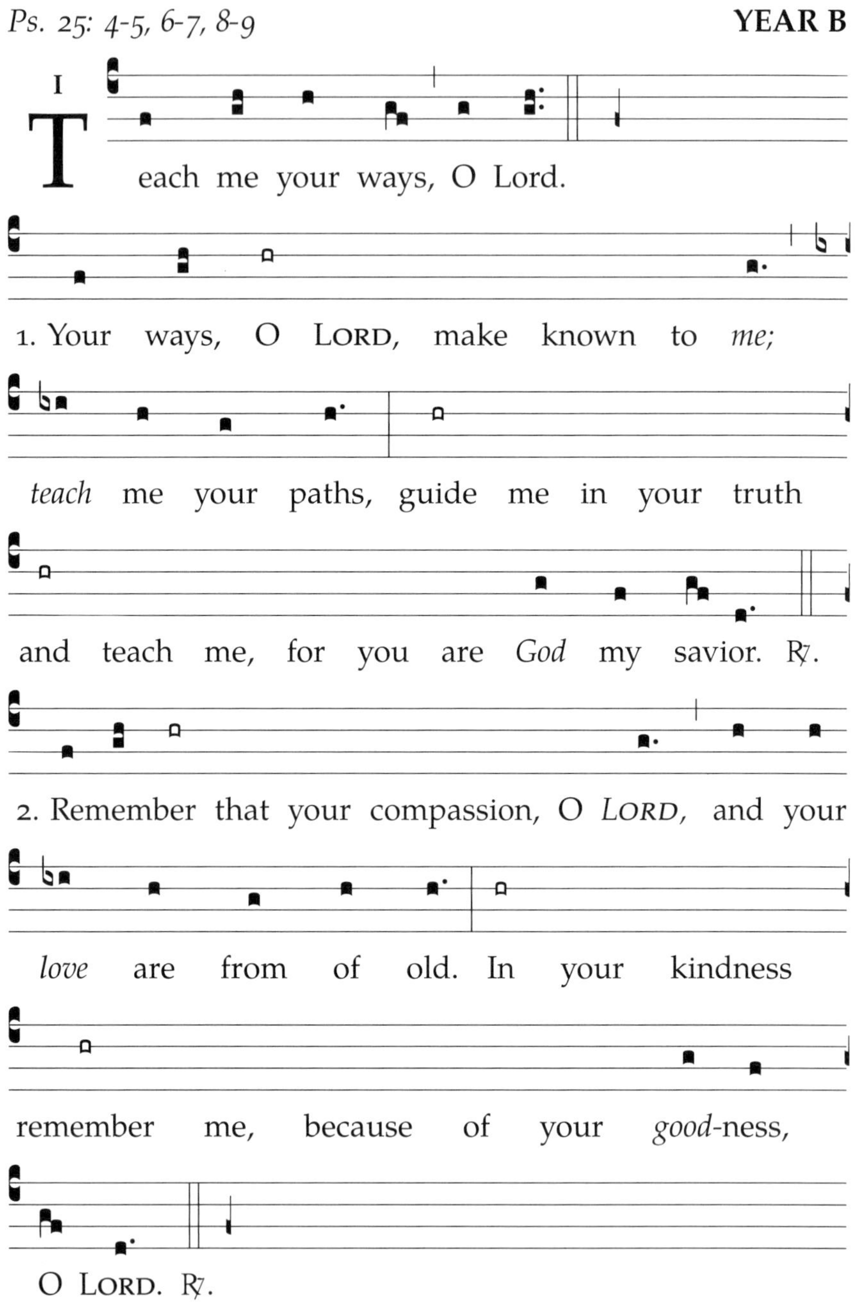

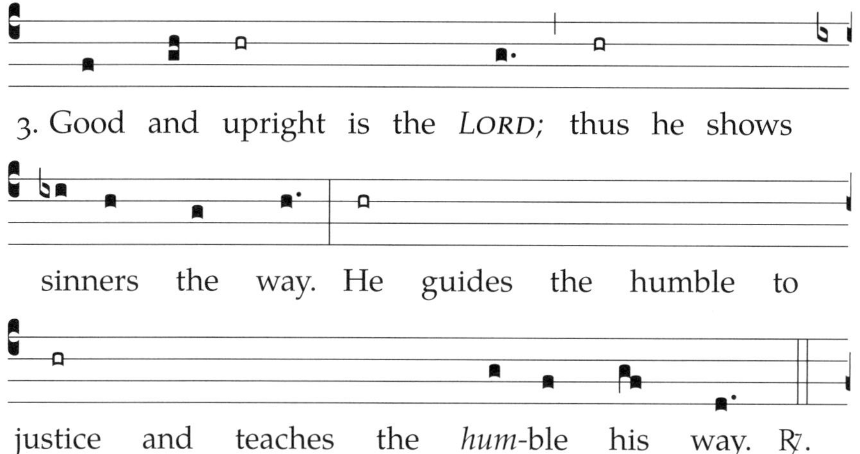
3. Good and upright is the *LORD;* thus he shows
sinners the way. He guides the humble to
justice and teaches the *hum*-ble his way. ℟.

Third Sunday in Ordinary Time

Ps. 19: 8, 9, 10, 15 **YEAR C**

VIII
Your words, Lord, are Spirit and life.
1. The law of the LORD is perfect, refreshing *the* soul;
the decree of the LORD is trustworthy, giving wisdom
to the simple. ℟.
2. The precepts of the LORD are right, rejoicing
the heart; the command of the LORD is clear,
en-*light*-ening the eye. ℟.
3. The fear of the LORD is pure, enduring for-*e*-ver; the

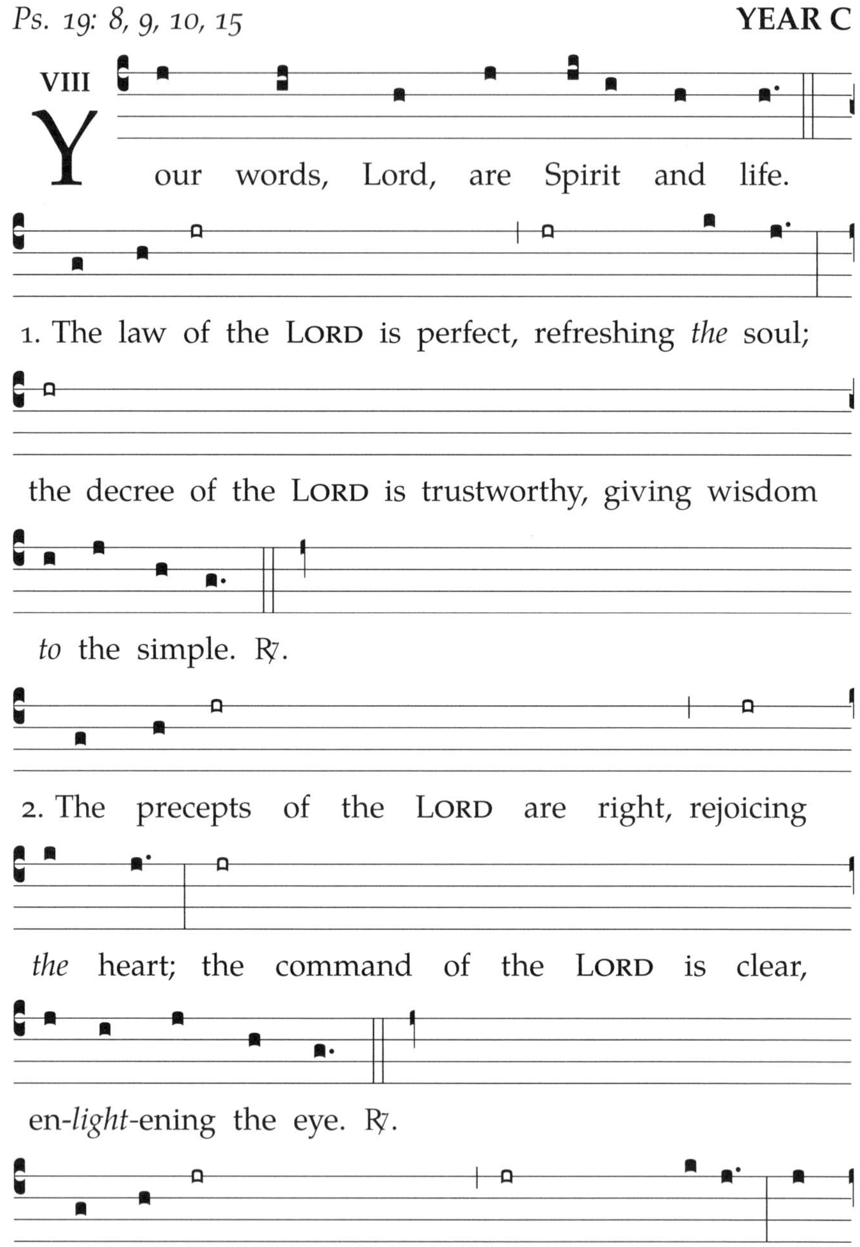

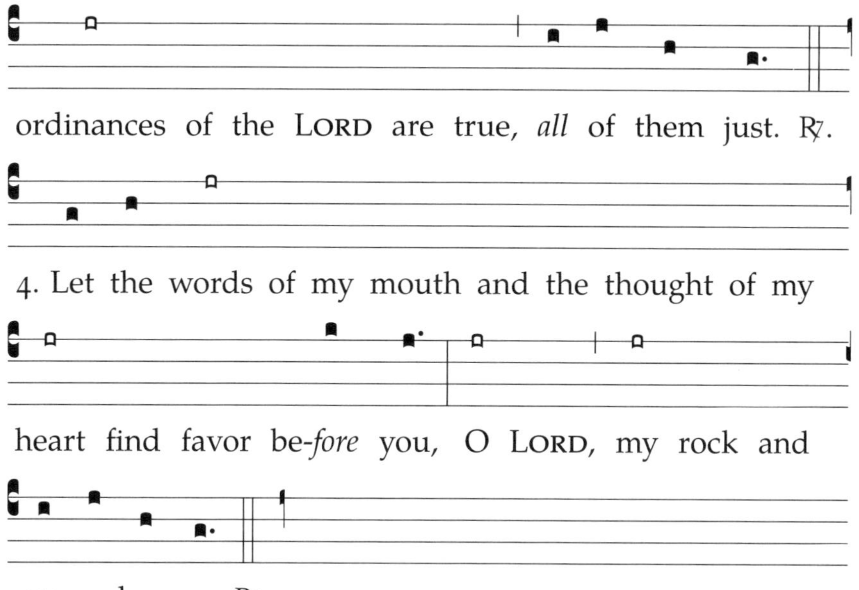
ordinances of the LORD are true, *all* of them just. ℟.
4. Let the words of my mouth and the thought of my
heart find favor be-*fore* you, O LORD, my rock and
my redeemer. ℟.

Fourth Sunday in Ordinary Time

Ps. 146: 6-7, 8-9, 9-10 **YEAR A**

VIII
Blessed are the poor in spirit; the kingdom of heaven is theirs.
1. The LORD keeps faith for-*ev*-er, secures justice for the oppressed, gives food to the *hun*-gry. The LORD sets captives free. ℟.
2. The LORD gives sight to the blind; the LORD raises up those who were *bowed* down. The LORD loves the just; the LORD *pro*-tects strang-ers. ℟.

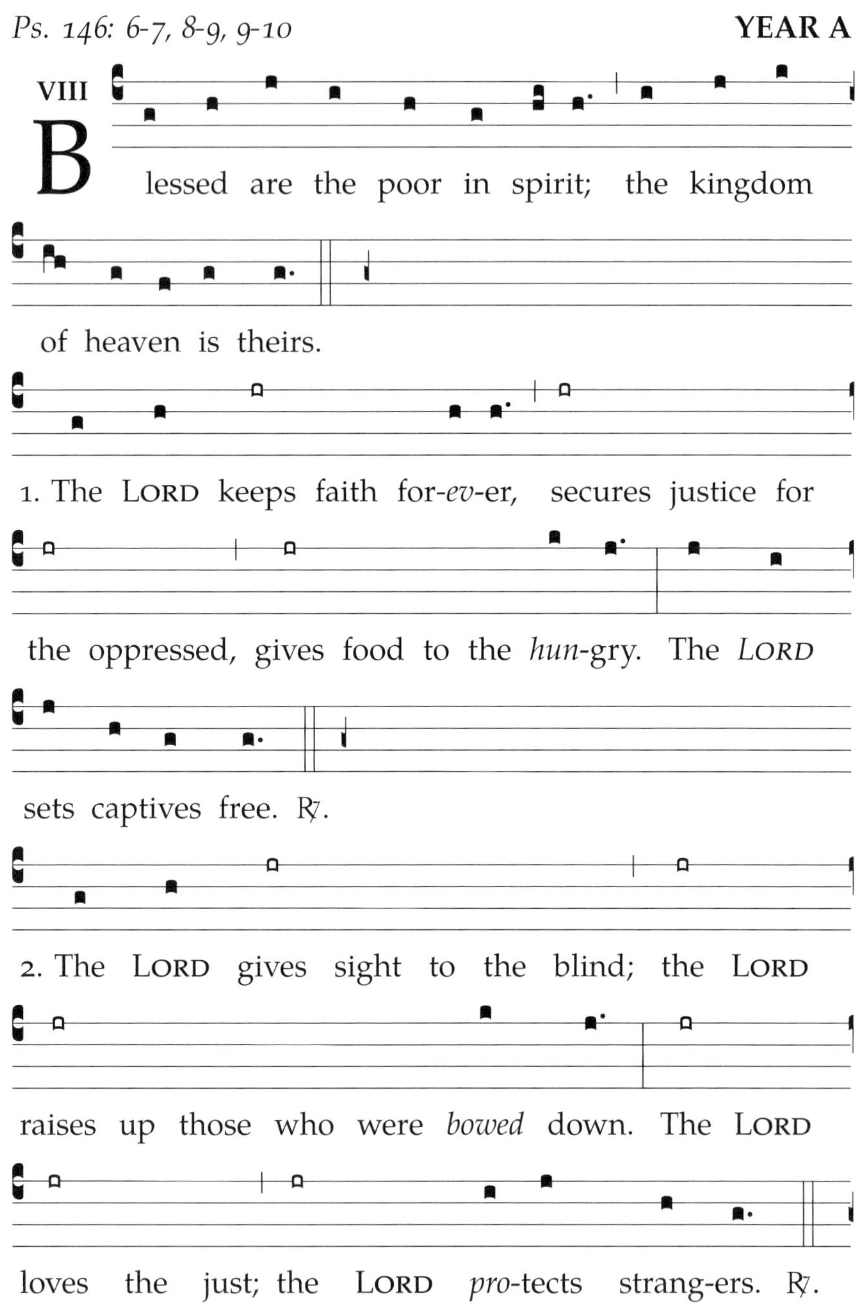

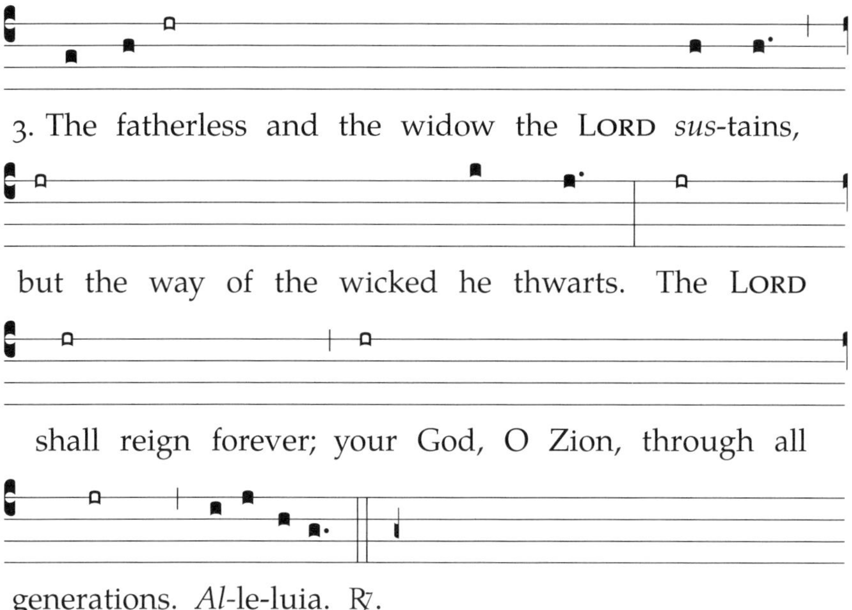
3. The fatherless and the widow the LORD *sus*-tains,
but the way of the wicked he thwarts. The LORD
shall reign forever; your God, O Zion, through all
generations. *Al*-le-luia. ℟.

Fourth Sunday in Ordinary Time

Ps. 95: 1-2, 6-7, 8-9 **YEAR B**

VIII
If today you hear his voice, harden not
your hearts.
1. Come, let us sing joyfully to the LORD; let us
acclaim the Rock of our sal-*va*-tion. Let us come into
his presence with thanksgiving; let us joyful-*ly* sing
psalms to him. ℟.
2. Come, let us bow down in worship; let us kneel
before the LORD who *made* us. For he is our God,

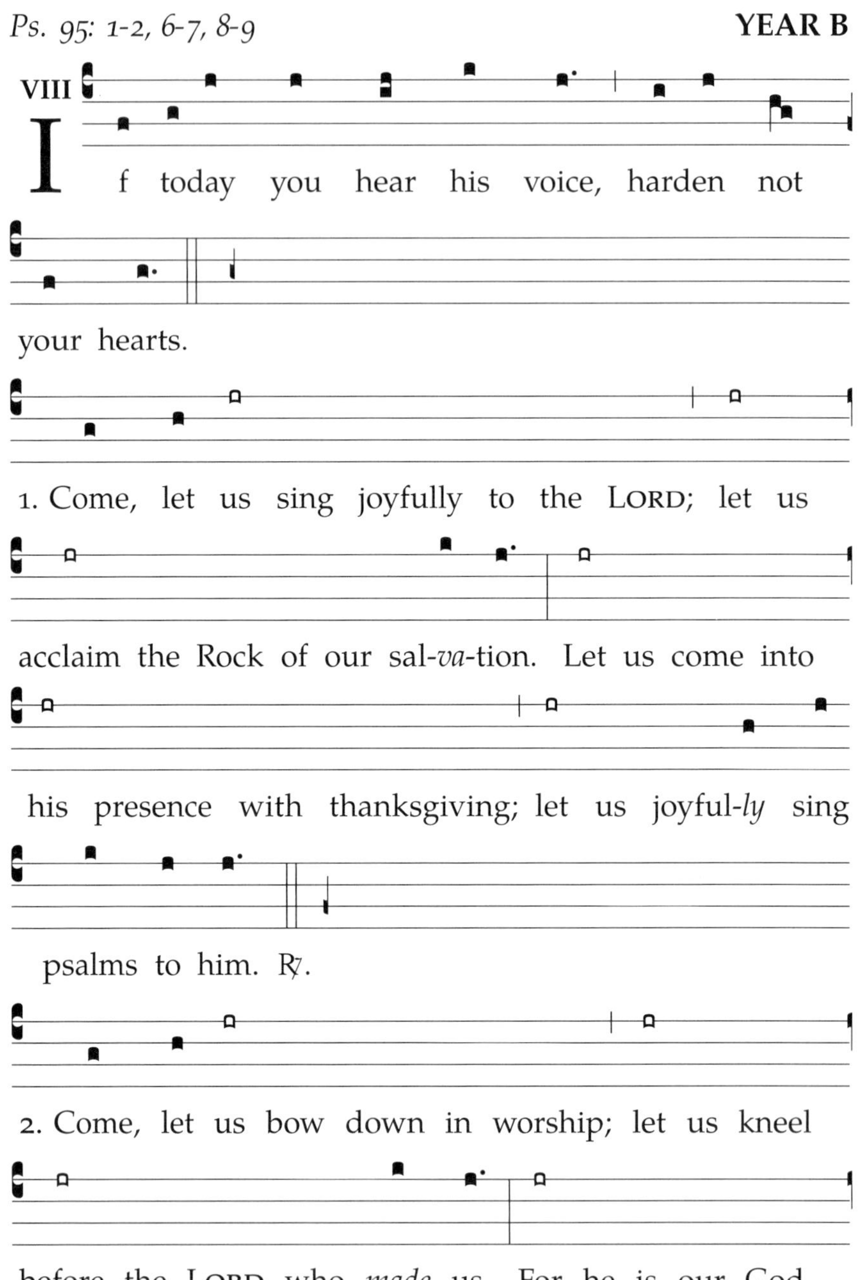

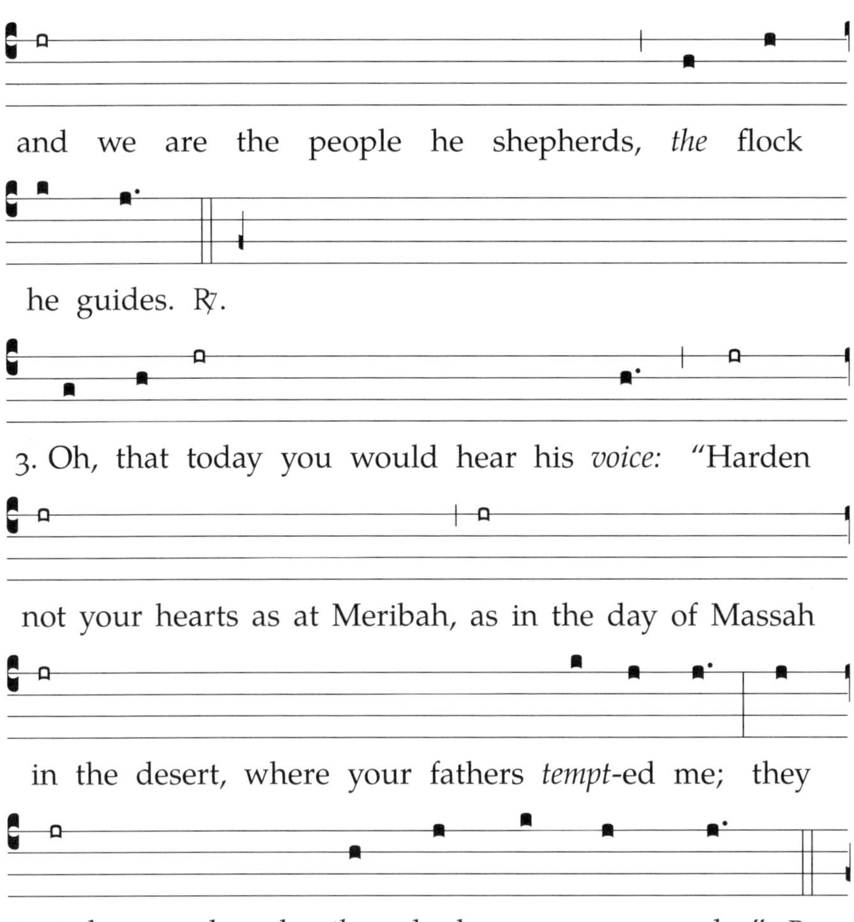
and we are the people he shepherds, *the* flock
he guides. ℟.
3. Oh, that today you would hear his *voice:* "Harden
not your hearts as at Meribah, as in the day of Massah
in the desert, where your fathers *tempt*-ed me; they
tested me though *they* had seen my works." ℟.

Fourth Sunday in Ordinary Time

Ps. 71: 1-2, 3-4, 5-6, 15-17 **YEAR C**

II
I will sing of your salvation.
1. In you, O LORD, I take *re*-fuge; let me never
be put *to* shame. In your justice rescue me, and
deliver me; incline your ear to me, *and* save me. ℟.
2. Be my rock of refuge, a stronghold to give me
safe-ty, for you are my rock and my *fort*-ress. O my
God, rescue me from the hand of *the* wicked. ℟.
3. For you are my hope, O Lord; my trust, O God,

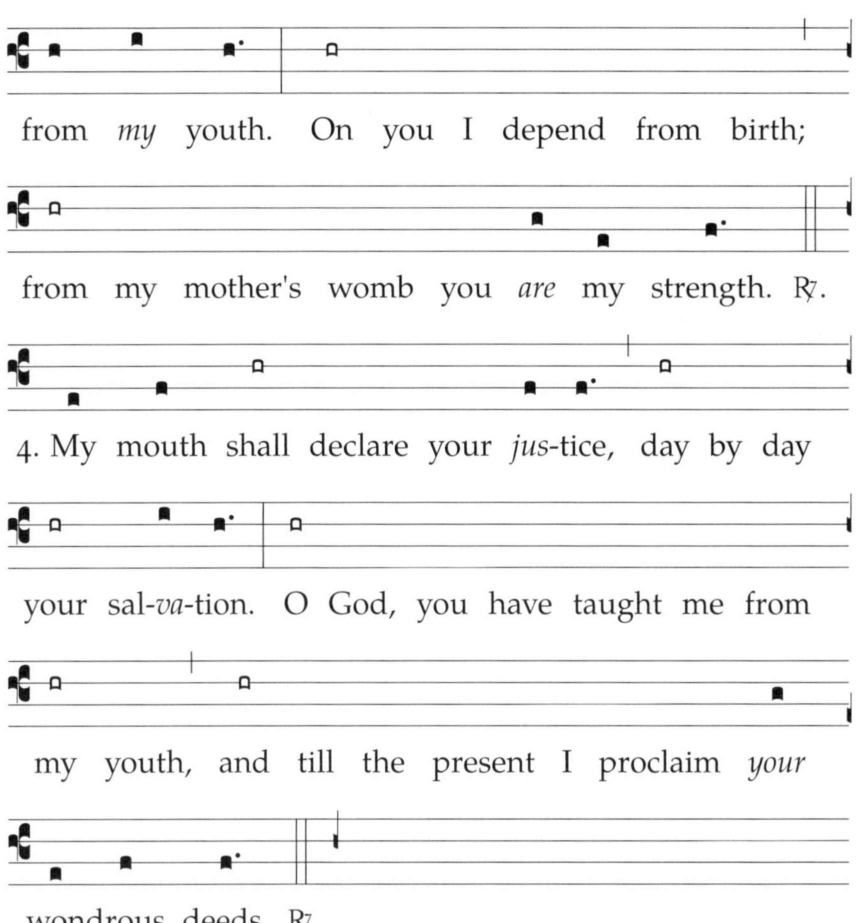
from my youth. On you I depend from birth;
from my mother's womb you are my strength. ℟.
4. My mouth shall declare your jus-tice, day by day
your sal-va-tion. O God, you have taught me from
my youth, and till the present I proclaim your
wondrous deeds. ℟.

Fifth Sunday in Ordinary Time

Ps. 112: 4-5, 6-7, 8-9 **YEAR A**

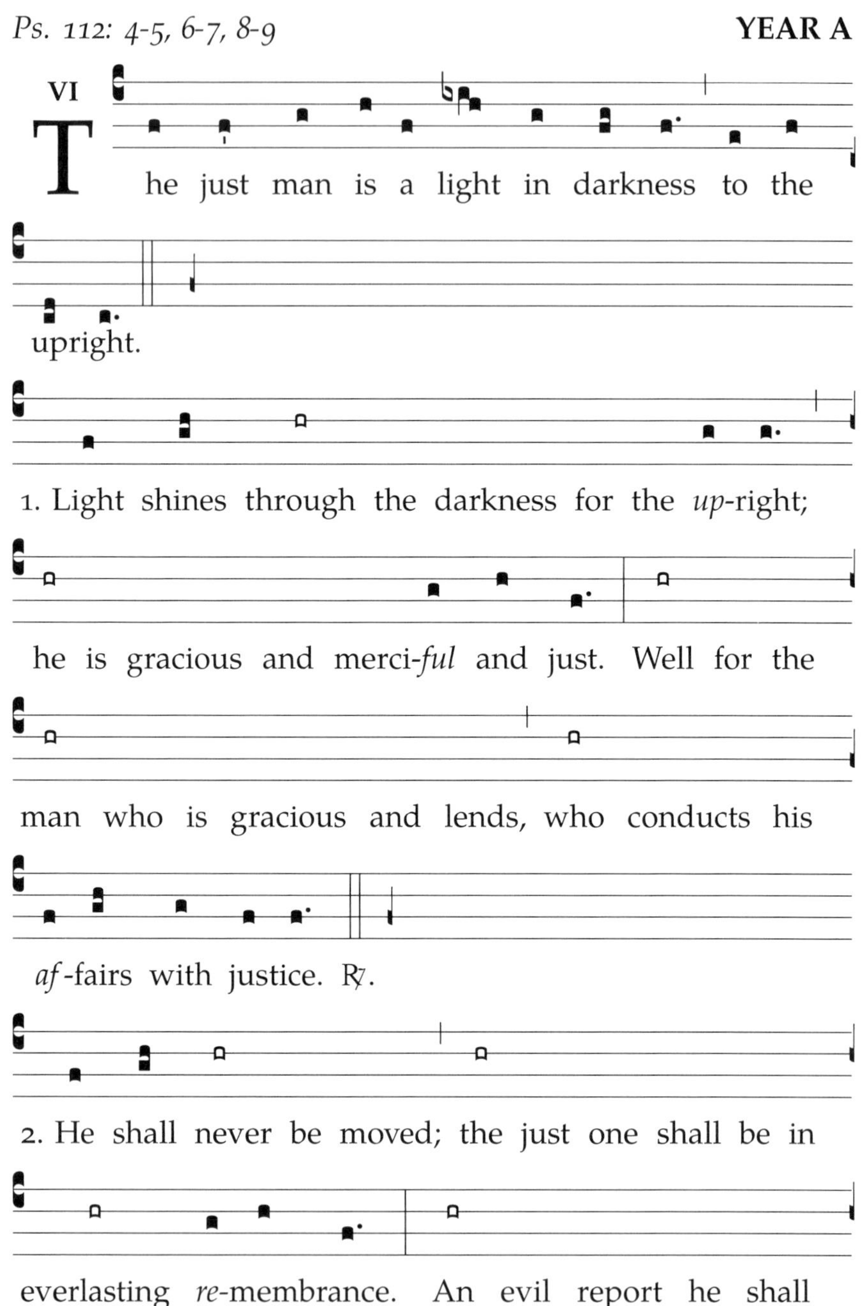
VI
The just man is a light in darkness to the
upright.
1. Light shines through the darkness for the *up*-right;
he is gracious and merci-*ful* and just. Well for the
man who is gracious and lends, who conducts his
af-fairs with justice. ℟.
2. He shall never be moved; the just one shall be in
everlasting *re*-membrance. An evil report he shall

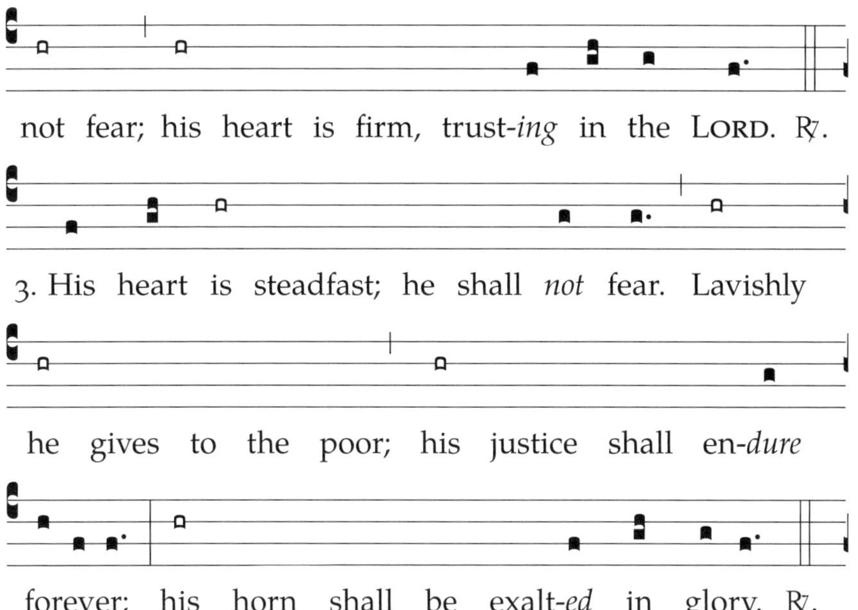
not fear; his heart is firm, trust-*ing* in the LORD. ℟.
3. His heart is steadfast; he shall *not* fear. Lavishly
he gives to the poor; his justice shall en-*dure*
forever; his horn shall be exalt-*ed* in glory. ℟.

Fifth Sunday in Ordinary Time

Ps. 147: 1-2, 3-4, 5-6 **YEAR B**

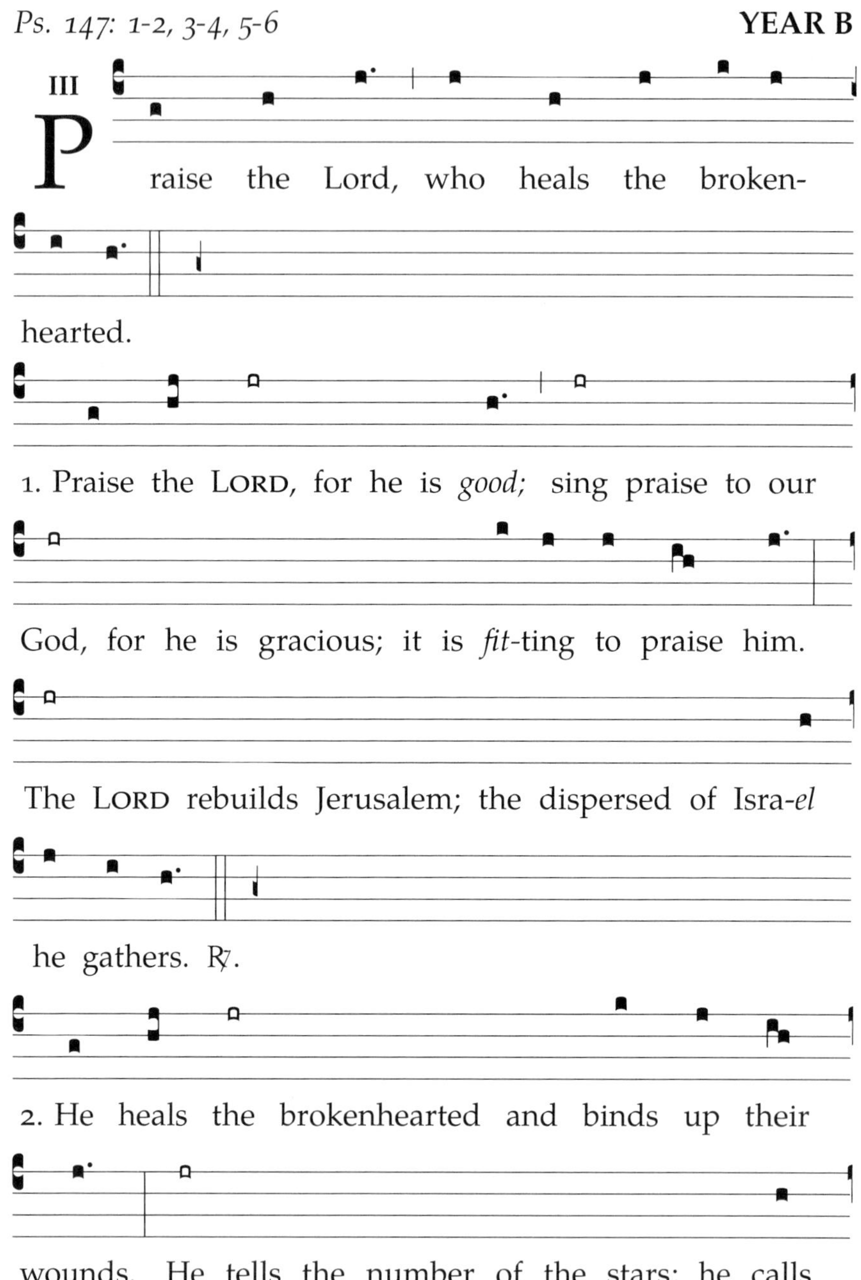
III
Praise the Lord, who heals the brokenhearted.
1. Praise the LORD, for he is *good;* sing praise to our
God, for he is gracious; it is *fit*-ting to praise him.
The LORD rebuilds Jerusalem; the dispersed of Isra-*el*
he gathers. ℟.
2. He heals the brokenhearted and binds up their
wounds. He tells the number of the stars; he calls

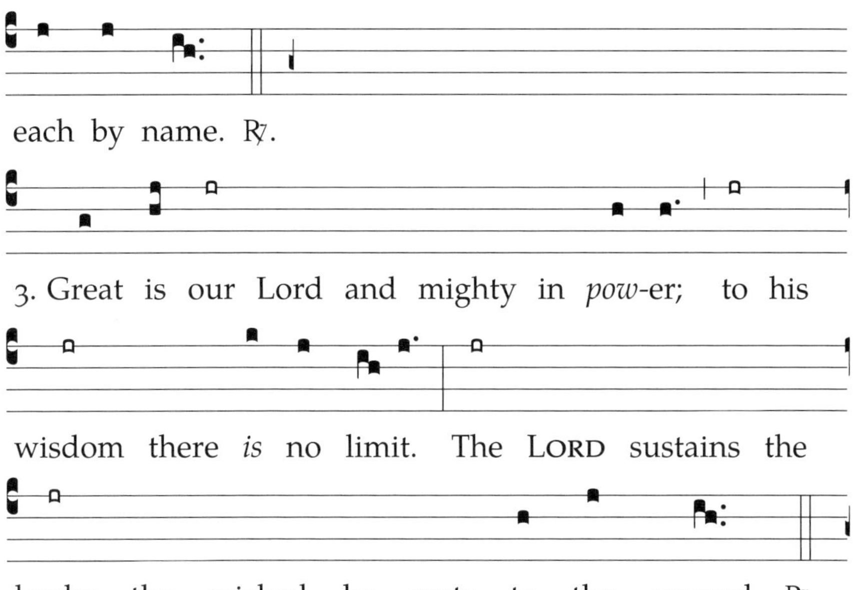
each by name. ℟.
3. Great is our Lord and mighty in *pow*-er; to his
wisdom there *is* no limit. The LORD sustains the
lowly; the wicked he casts to the ground. ℟.

Fifth Sunday in Ordinary Time

Ps. 138: 1-2, 2-3, 4-5, 7-8 **YEAR C**

II
In the sight of the angels I will sing your
praises, Lord.
1. I will give thanks to you, O Lord, with all my heart,
for you have heard the words of my mouth; in the
presence of the angels I will sing your praise; I will worship at your holy temple and give thanks to your name. ℟.
2. Because of your kindness and your truth; for you
have made great above all things your name and your

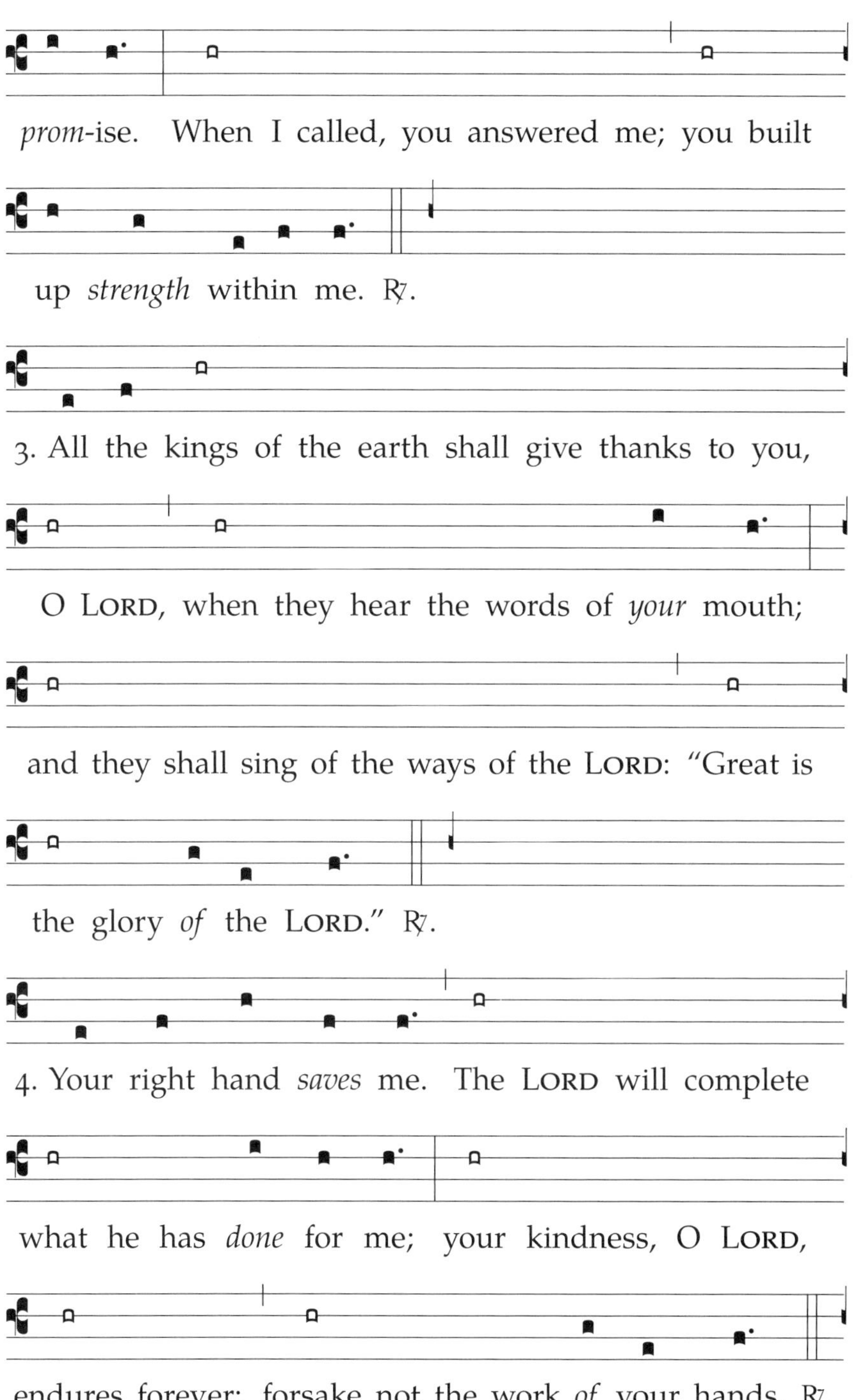
prom-ise. When I called, you answered me; you built
up *strength* within me. ℟.
3. All the kings of the earth shall give thanks to you,
O LORD, when they hear the words of *your* mouth;
and they shall sing of the ways of the LORD: "Great is
the glory *of* the LORD." ℟.
4. Your right hand *saves* me. The LORD will complete
what he has *done* for me; your kindness, O LORD,
endures forever; forsake not the work *of* your hands. ℟.

Sixth Sunday in Ordinary Time

Ps. 119: 1-2, 4-5, 17-18, 33-34 **YEAR A**

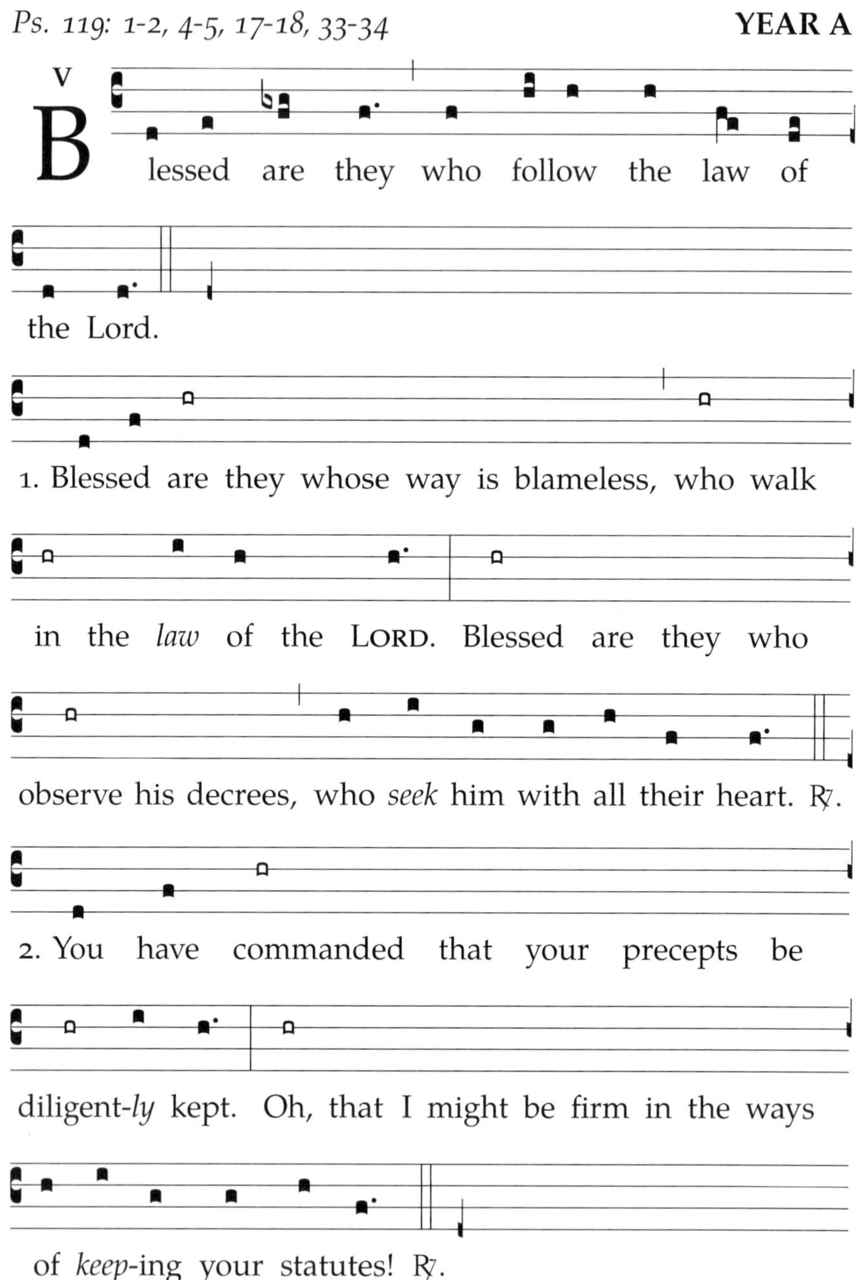
V
Blessed are they who follow the law of the Lord.
1. Blessed are they whose way is blameless, who walk
in the *law* of the LORD. Blessed are they who
observe his decrees, who *seek* him with all their heart. ℟.
2. You have commanded that your precepts be
diligent-*ly* kept. Oh, that I might be firm in the ways
of *keep*-ing your statutes! ℟.

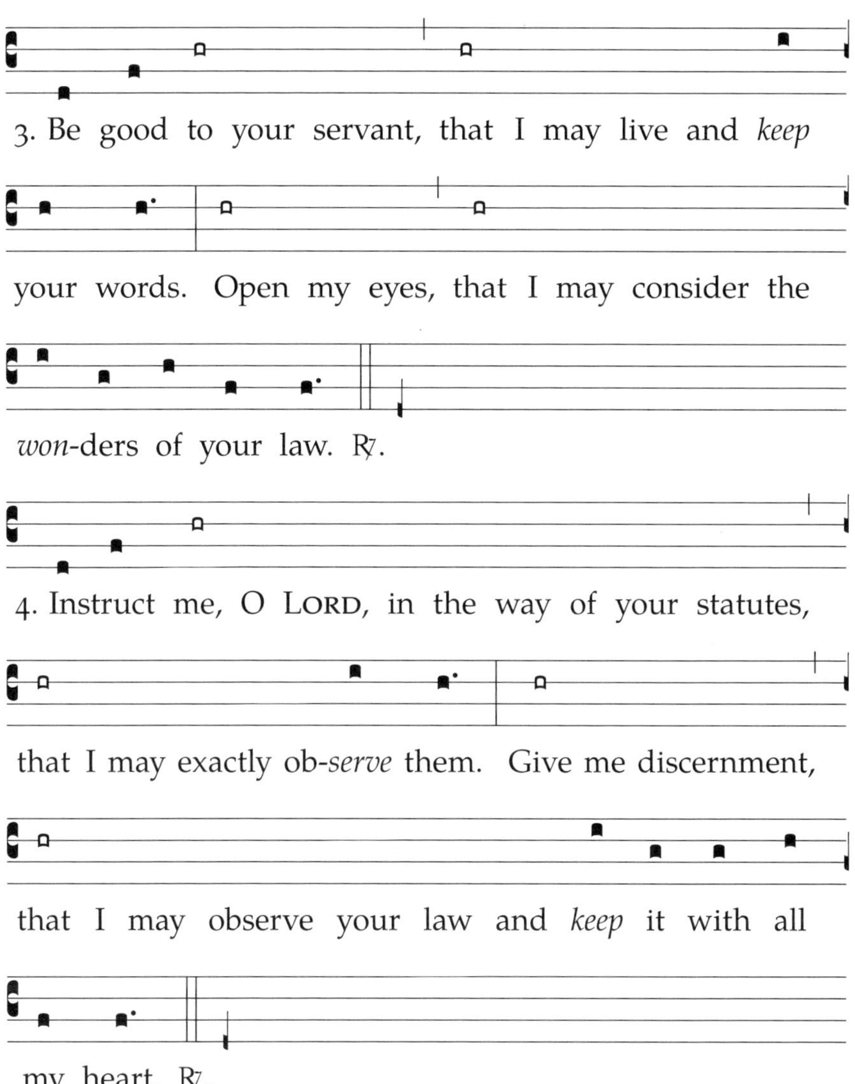
3. Be good to your servant, that I may live and keep
your words. Open my eyes, that I may consider the
won-ders of your law. ℟.
4. Instruct me, O LORD, in the way of your statutes,
that I may exactly ob-serve them. Give me discernment,
that I may observe your law and keep it with all
my heart. ℟.

Sixth Sunday in Ordinary Time

Ps. 32: 1-2, 5, 11 **YEAR B**

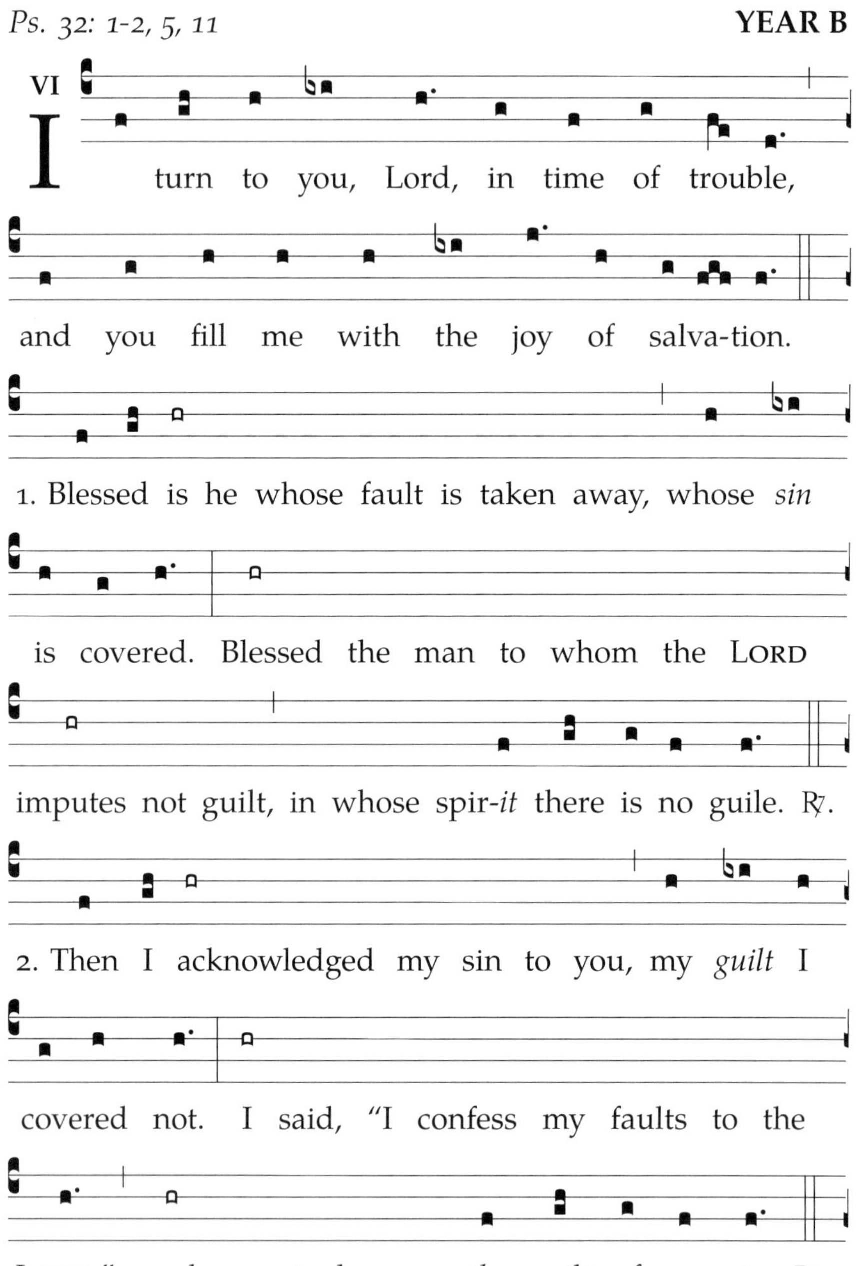
VI
I turn to you, Lord, in time of trouble,
and you fill me with the joy of salva-tion.
1. Blessed is he whose fault is taken away, whose *sin*
is covered. Blessed the man to whom the Lord
imputes not guilt, in whose spir-*it* there is no guile. ℟.
2. Then I acknowledged my sin to you, my *guilt* I
covered not. I said, "I confess my faults to the
Lord," and you took away *the* guilt of my sin. ℟.

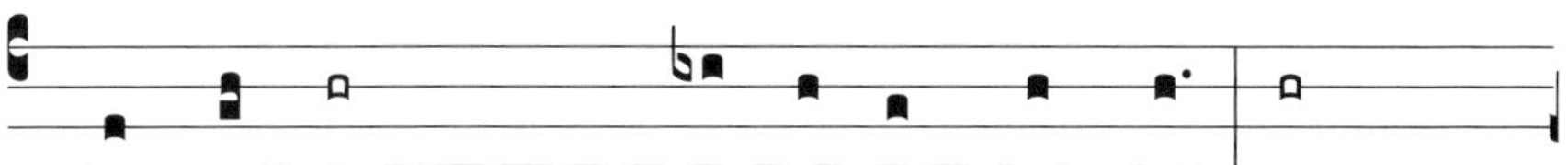

3. Be glad in the LORD *and* rejoice, you just; exult, all

you upright of heart. ℟.

Sixth Sunday in Ordinary Time

Ps. 1: 1-2, 3, 4, 6 **YEAR C**

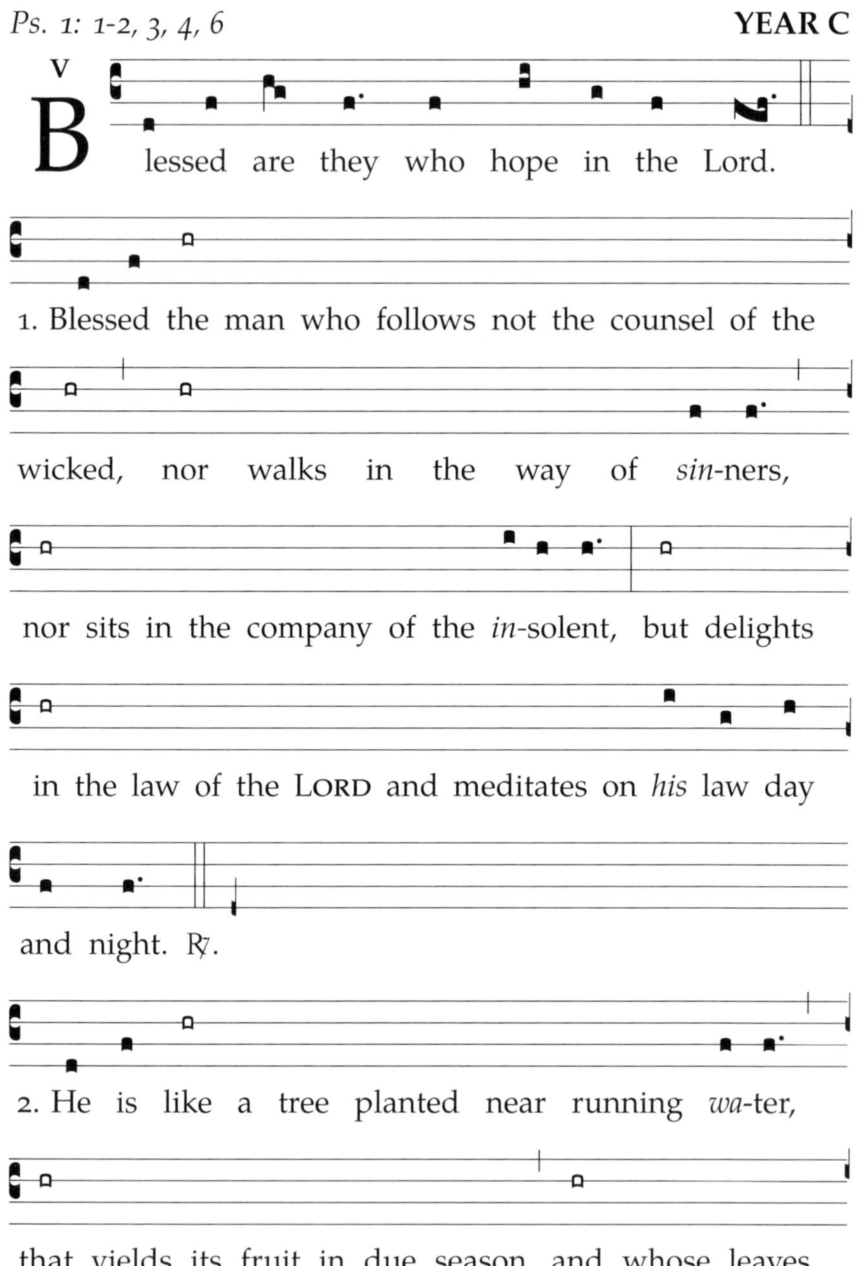

V
Blessed are they who hope in the Lord.
1. Blessed the man who follows not the counsel of the
wicked, nor walks in the way of *sin*-ners,
nor sits in the company of the *in*-solent, but delights
in the law of the LORD and meditates on *his* law day
and night. ℟.
2. He is like a tree planted near running *wa*-ter,
that yields its fruit in due season, and whose leaves

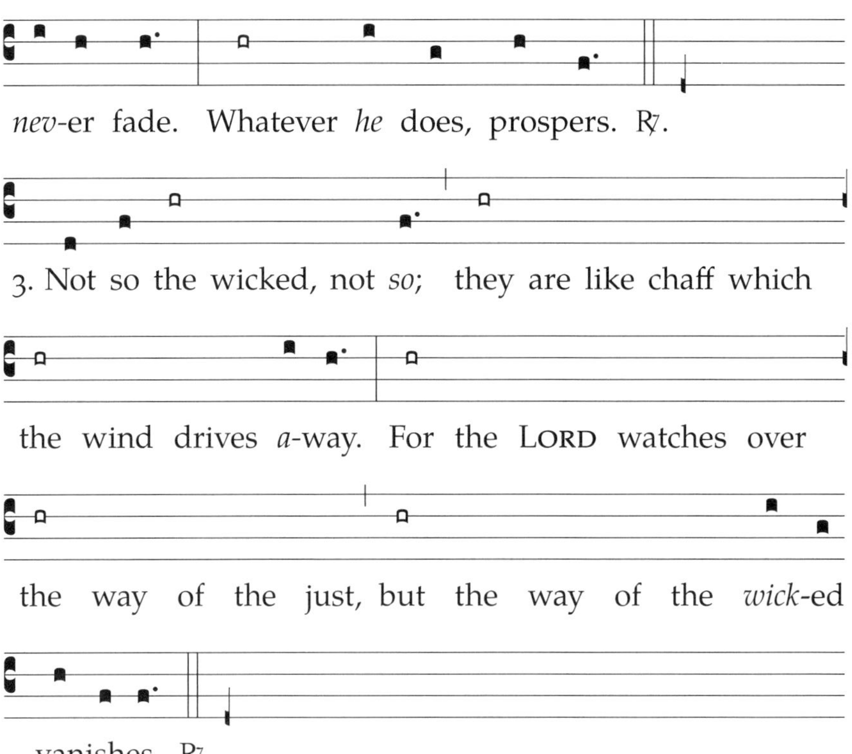

nev-er fade. Whatever *he* does, prospers. ℟.
3. Not so the wicked, not *so;* they are like chaff which
the wind drives *a*-way. For the LORD watches over
the way of the just, but the way of the *wick*-ed
vanishes. ℟.

Seventh Sunday in Ordinary Time

Ps. 103: 1-2, 3-4, 8, 10, 12-13 **YEAR AC**

VIII
The Lord is kind and merciful.
1. Bless the LORD, O my soul; and all my being, bless
his *ho*-ly name. Bless the LORD, O my soul, and
forget not *all* his benefits. ℟.
2. He pardons all your iniquities, heals all *your* ills.
He redeems your life from destruction, crowns you
with kindness *and* compassion. ℟.
3. Merciful and gracious is the LORD, slow to

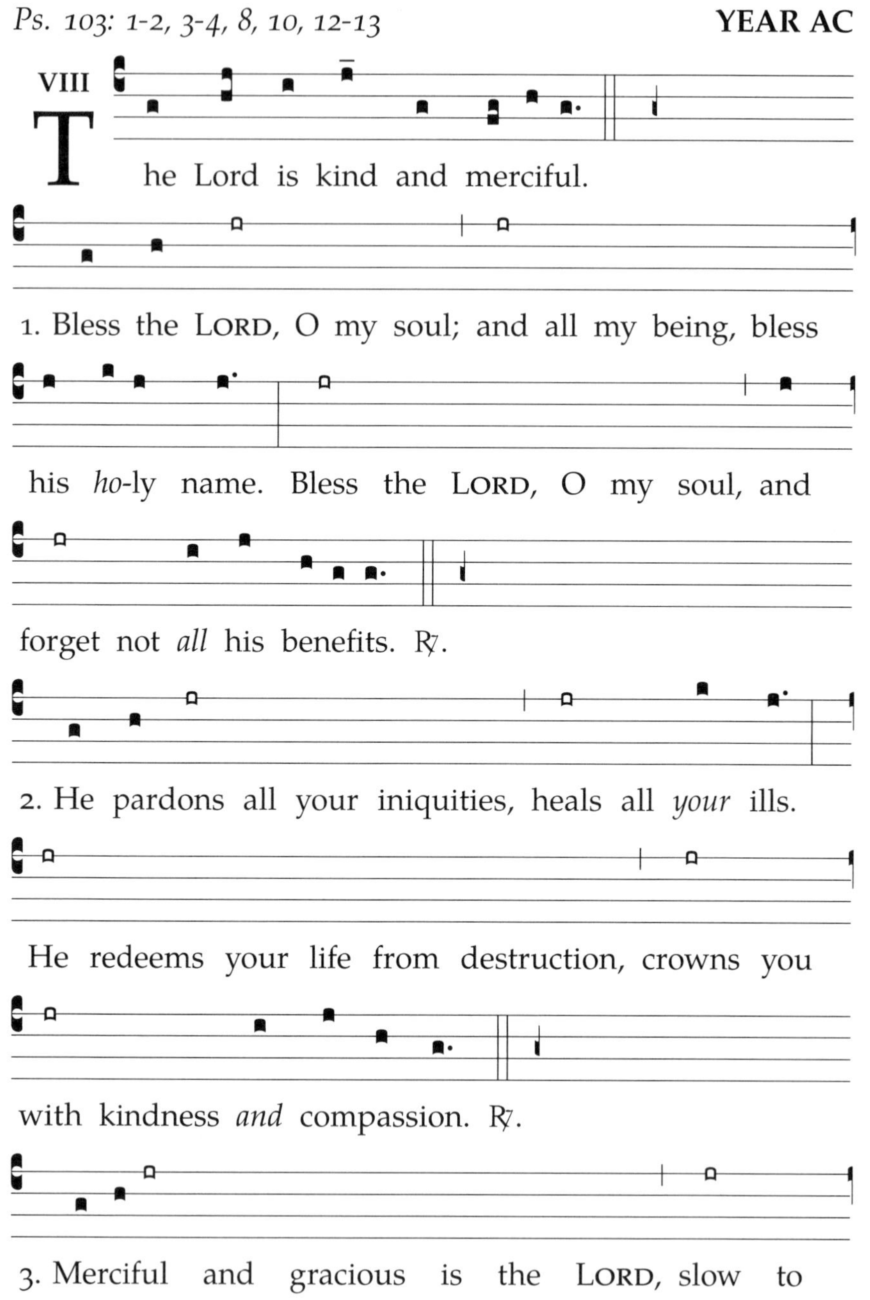

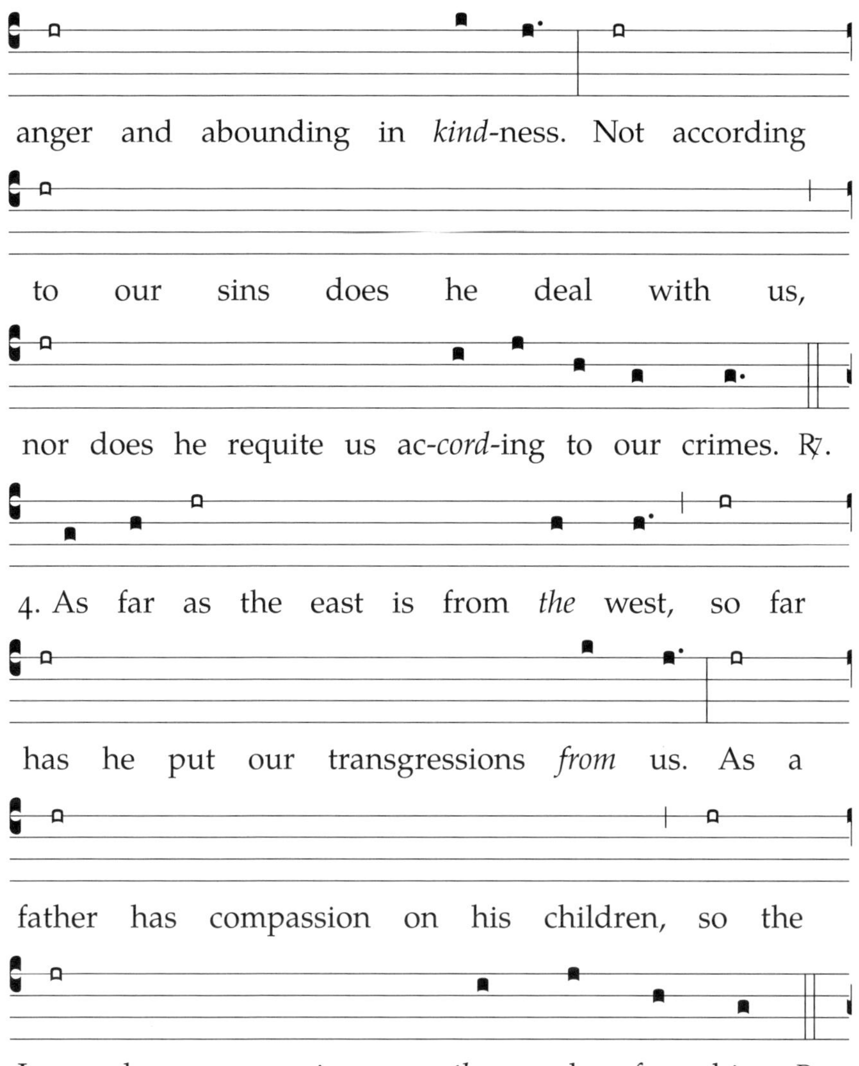
anger and abounding in kind-ness. Not according
to our sins does he deal with us,
nor does he requite us ac-cord-ing to our crimes. ℟.
4. As far as the east is from the west, so far
has he put our transgressions from us. As a
father has compassion on his children, so the
LORD has compassion on those who fear him. ℟.

Seventh Sunday in Ordinary Time

Ps. 41: 2-3, 4-5, 13-14 **YEAR B**

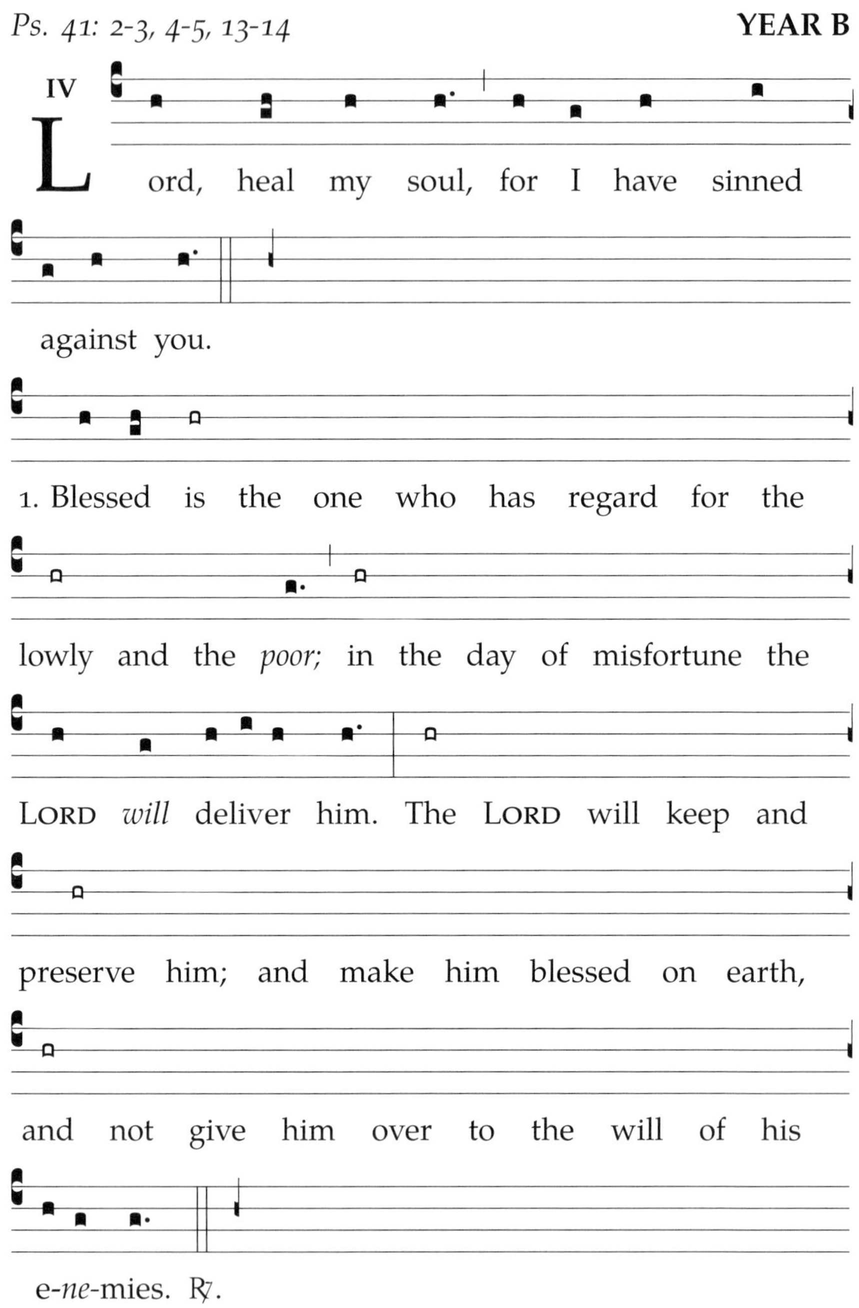
IV
Lord, heal my soul, for I have sinned
against you.
1. Blessed is the one who has regard for the
lowly and the *poor;* in the day of misfortune the
LORD *will* deliver him. The LORD will keep and
preserve him; and make him blessed on earth,
and not give him over to the will of his
e-*ne*-mies. ℟.

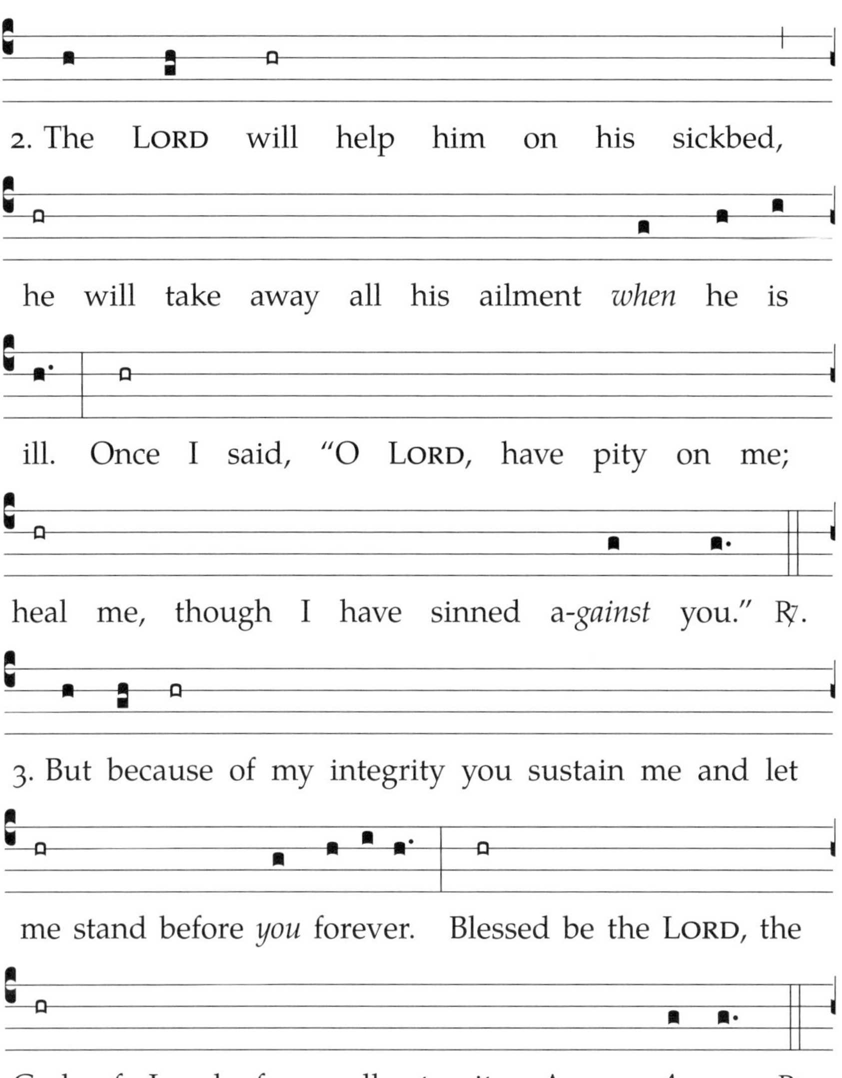
2. The LORD will help him on his sickbed,
he will take away all his ailment *when* he is
ill. Once I said, "O LORD, have pity on me;
heal me, though I have sinned a-*gainst* you." ℟.
3. But because of my integrity you sustain me and let
me stand before *you* forever. Blessed be the LORD, the
God of Israel, from all eternity. Amen. *A*-men. ℟.

Eighth Sunday in Ordinary Time

Ps. 62: 2-3, 6-7, 8-9 **YEAR A**

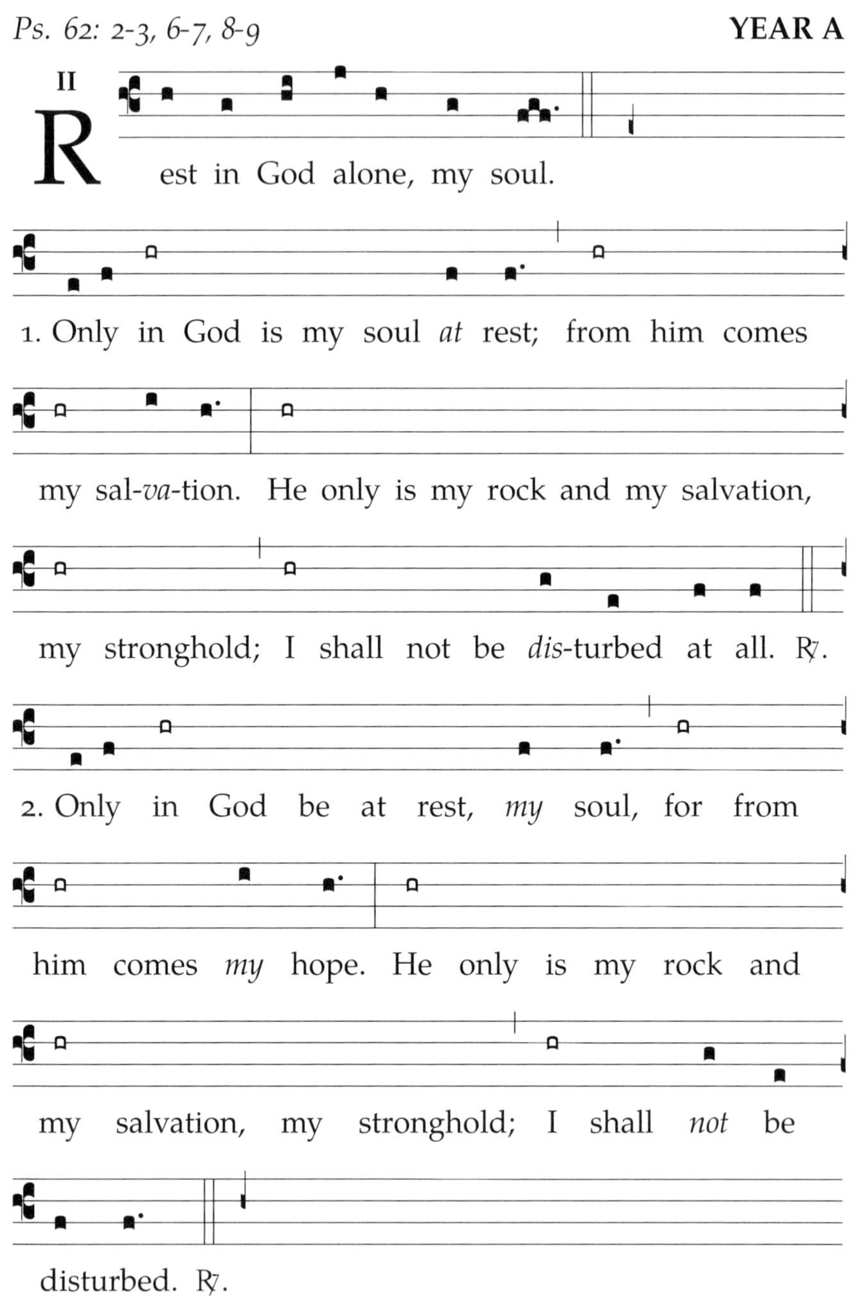
II
R est in God alone, my soul.
1. Only in God is my soul *at* rest; from him comes
my sal-*va*-tion. He only is my rock and my salvation,
my stronghold; I shall not be *dis*-turbed at all. ℟.
2. Only in God be at rest, *my* soul, for from
him comes *my* hope. He only is my rock and
my salvation, my stronghold; I shall *not* be
disturbed. ℟.

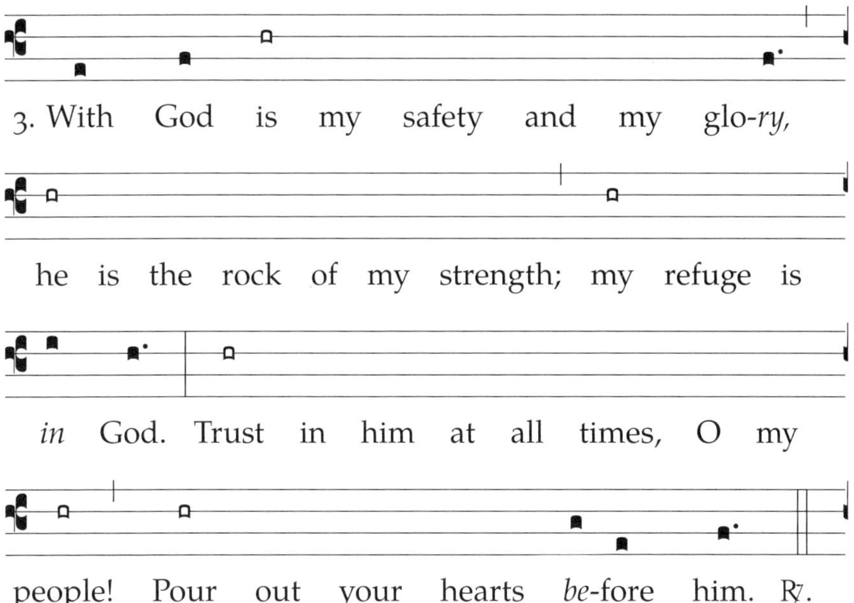
3. With God is my safety and my glo-*ry,*
he is the rock of my strength; my refuge is
in God. Trust in him at all times, O my
people! Pour out your hearts *be*-fore him. ℟.

Eighth Sunday in Ordinary Time

Ps. 103: 1-2, 3-4, 8, 10, 12-13 **YEAR B**

VIII
The Lord is kind and merciful.
1. Bless the LORD, O my soul; and all my being, bless
his *ho*-ly name. Bless the LORD, O my soul, and
forget not *all* his benefits. ℟.
2. He pardons all your iniquities, heals all *your* ills. He
redeems your life from destruction, crowns you with
kindness *and* compassion. ℟.
3. Merciful and gracious is the LORD, slow to

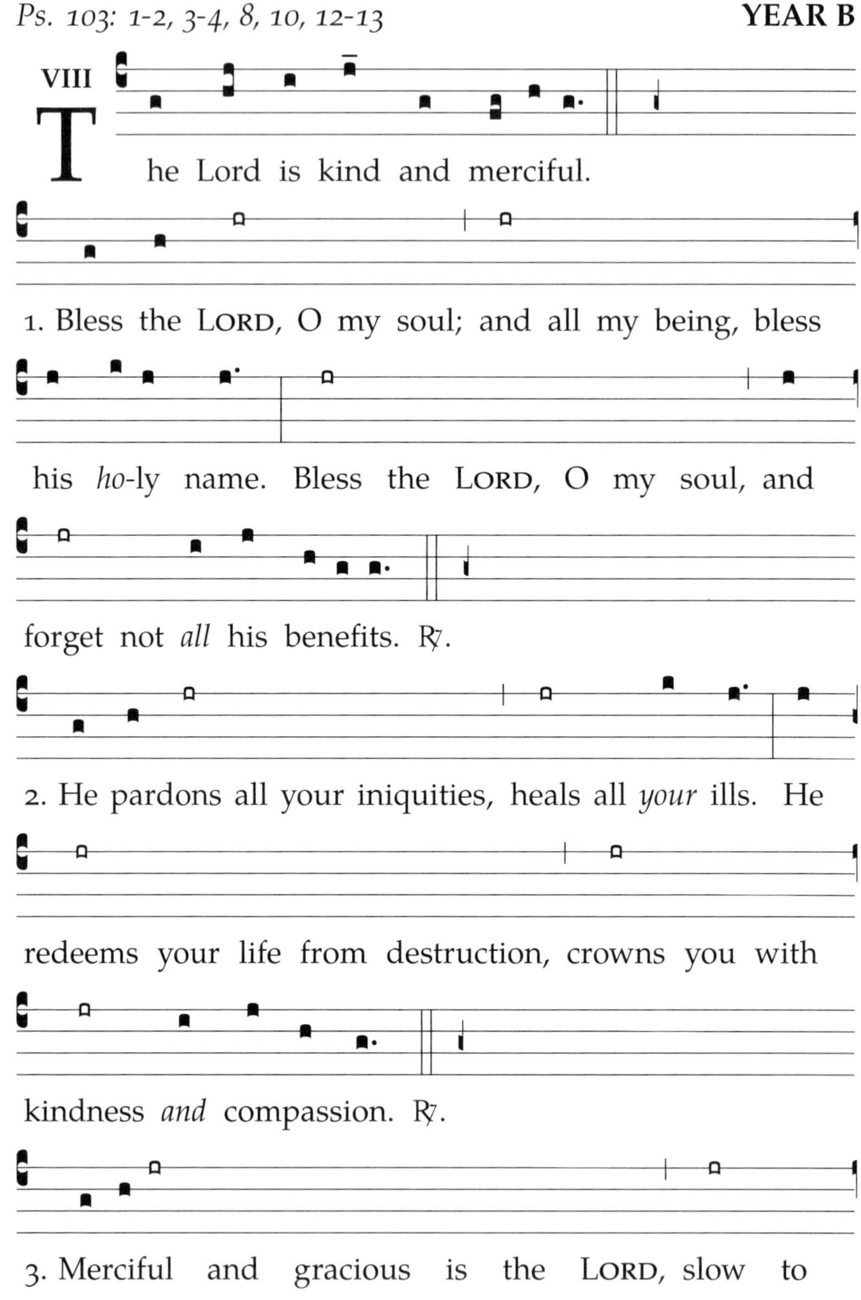

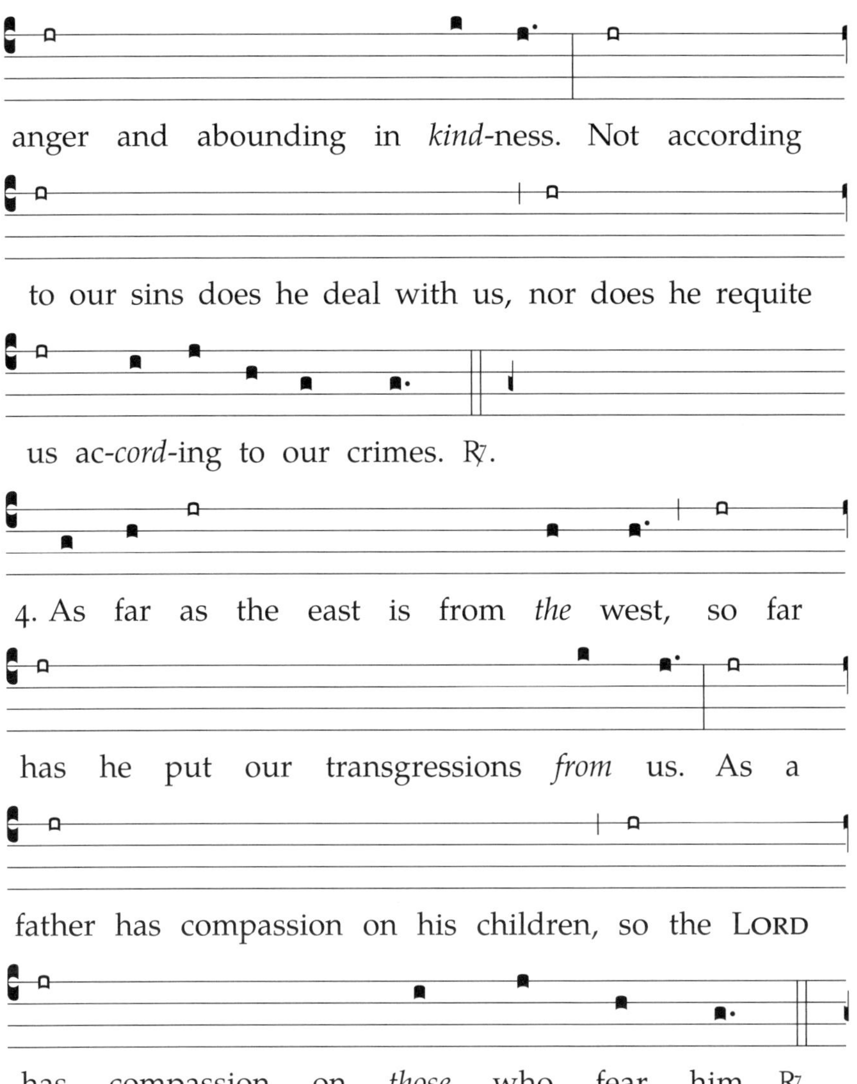
anger and abounding in *kind*-ness. Not according
to our sins does he deal with us, nor does he requite
us ac-*cord*-ing to our crimes. ℟.
4. As far as the east is from *the* west, so far
has he put our transgressions *from* us. As a
father has compassion on his children, so the LORD
has compassion on *those* who fear him. ℟.

Eighth Sunday in Ordinary Time

Ps. 92: 2-3, 13-14, 15-16 **YEAR C**

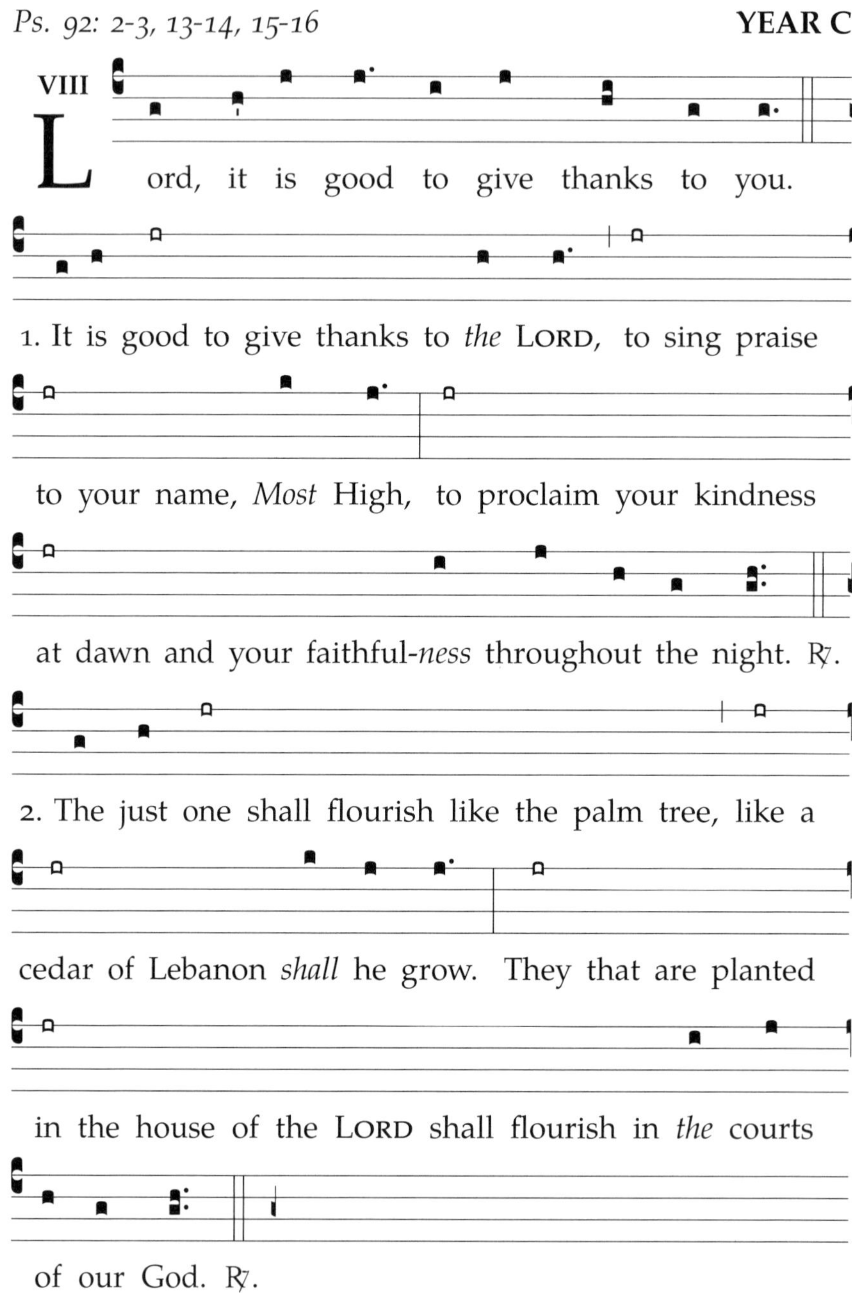

VIII
Lord, it is good to give thanks to you.

1. It is good to give thanks to *the* Lord, to sing praise
to your name, *Most* High, to proclaim your kindness
at dawn and your faithful-*ness* throughout the night. ℟.

2. The just one shall flourish like the palm tree, like a
cedar of Lebanon *shall* he grow. They that are planted
in the house of the Lord shall flourish in *the* courts
of our God. ℟.

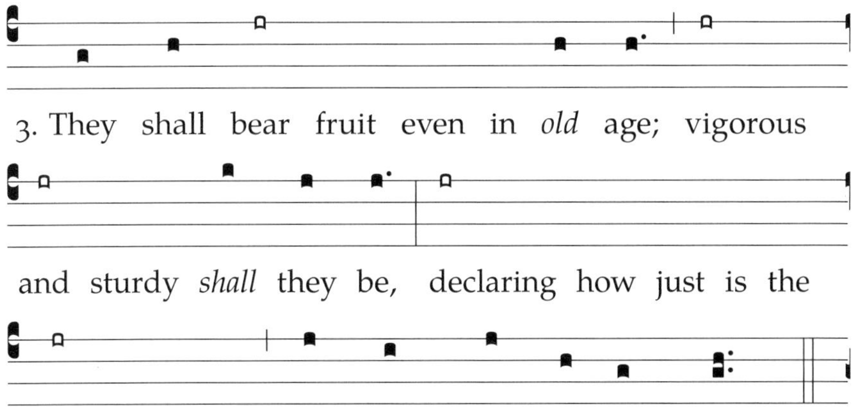
3. They shall bear fruit even in *old* age; vigorous
and sturdy *shall* they be, declaring how just is the
LORD, my rock, in *whom* there is no wrong. ℟.

Ninth Sunday in Ordinary Time

Ps. 31: 2-3, 3-4, 17, 25 **YEAR A**

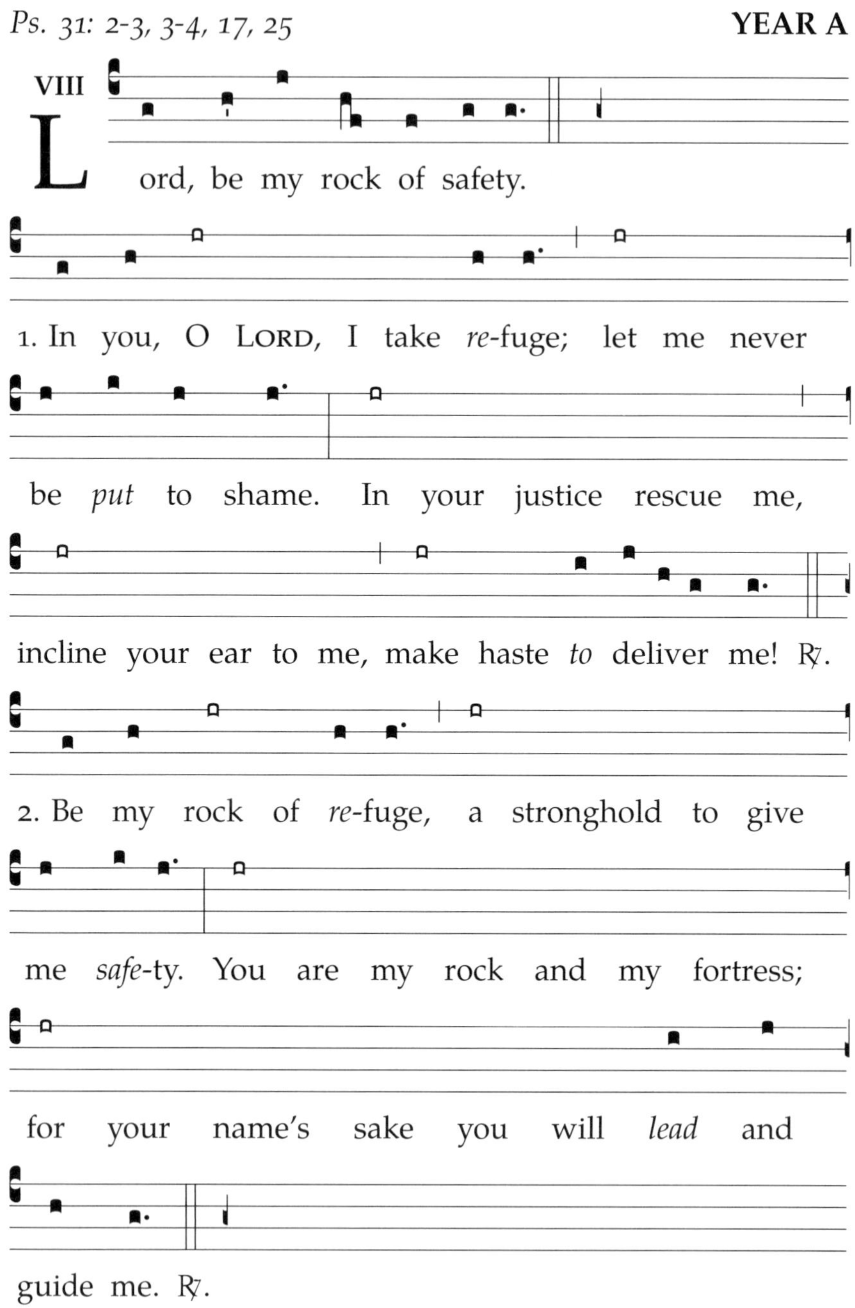
VIII
Lord, be my rock of safety.
1. In you, O Lord, I take *re*-fuge; let me never
be *put* to shame. In your justice rescue me,
incline your ear to me, make haste *to* deliver me! ℟.
2. Be my rock of *re*-fuge, a stronghold to give
me *safe*-ty. You are my rock and my fortress;
for your name's sake you will *lead* and
guide me. ℟.

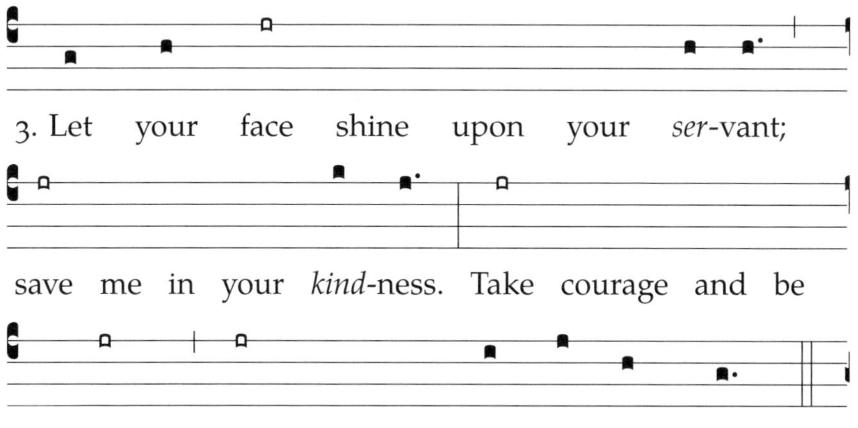
3. Let your face shine upon your ser-vant;
save me in your kind-ness. Take courage and be
stouthearted, all you who hope in the LORD. ℟.

Ninth Sunday in Ordinary Time

Ps. 81: 3-4, 5-6, 6-8, 10-11 **YEAR B**

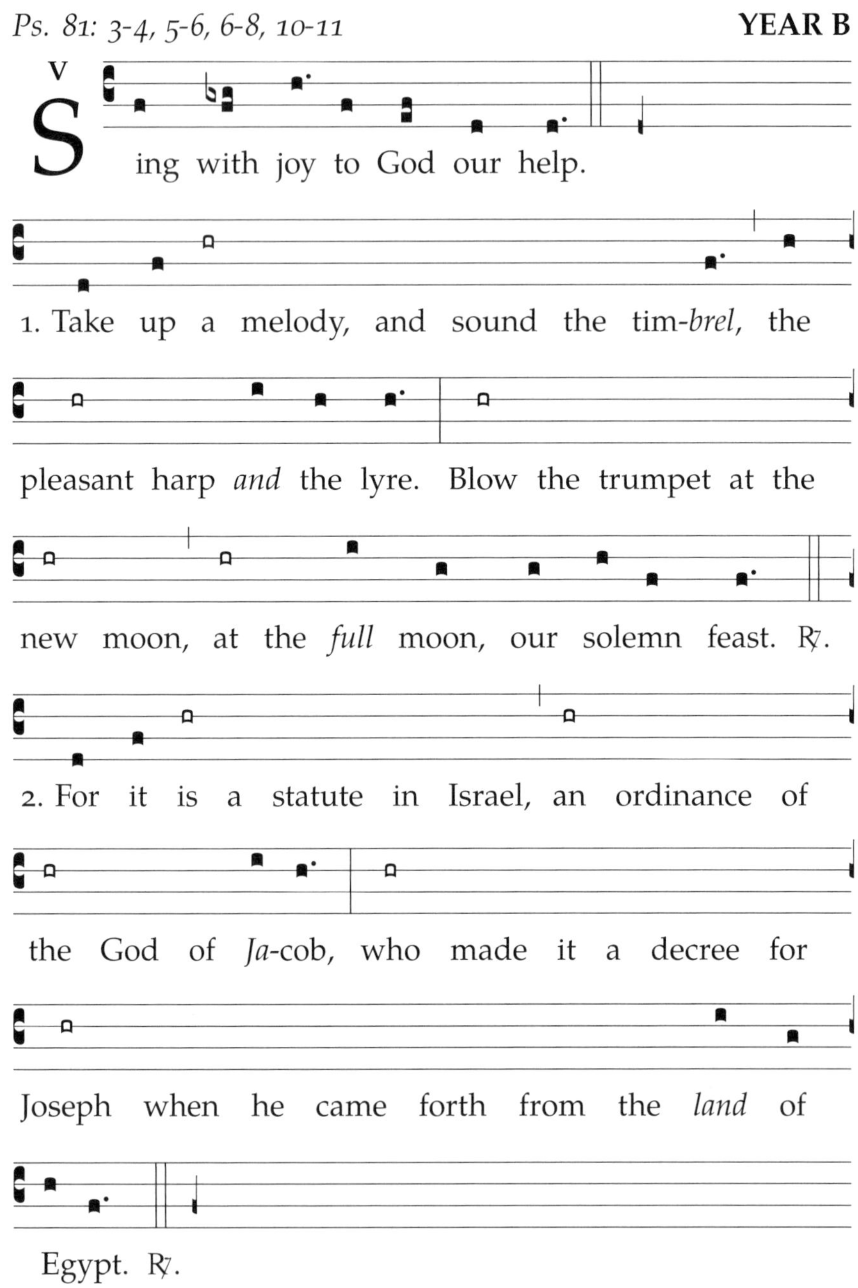

V
Sing with joy to God our help.
1. Take up a melody, and sound the tim-*brel,* the
pleasant harp *and* the lyre. Blow the trumpet at the
new moon, at the *full* moon, our solemn feast. ℟.
2. For it is a statute in Israel, an ordinance of
the God of *Ja*-cob, who made it a decree for
Joseph when he came forth from the *land* of
Egypt. ℟.

3. An unfamiliar speech *I* hear: "I relieved his shoulder
of the burden; his hands were freed from the *bas*-ket.
In distress you called, *and* I rescued you." ℟.
4. "There shall be no strange god among you nor shall
you worship any *a*-lien god. I, the Lord, am your
God who led you forth from the *land* of Egypt." ℟.

Ninth Sunday in Ordinary Time

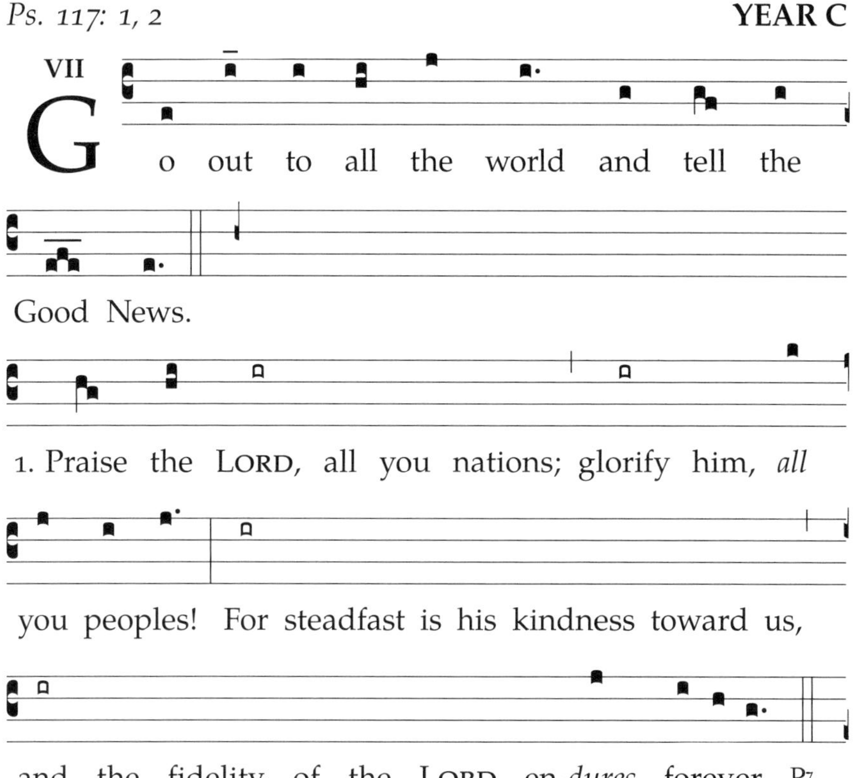
Ps. 117: 1, 2
YEAR C
VII
Go out to all the world and tell the Good News.
1. Praise the LORD, all you nations; glorify him, all you peoples! For steadfast is his kindness toward us,
and the fidelity of the LORD en-dures forever. R.

10TH SUNDAY IN ORDINARY TIME

Ps. 50: 1, 8, 12-13, 14-15 **YEAR A**

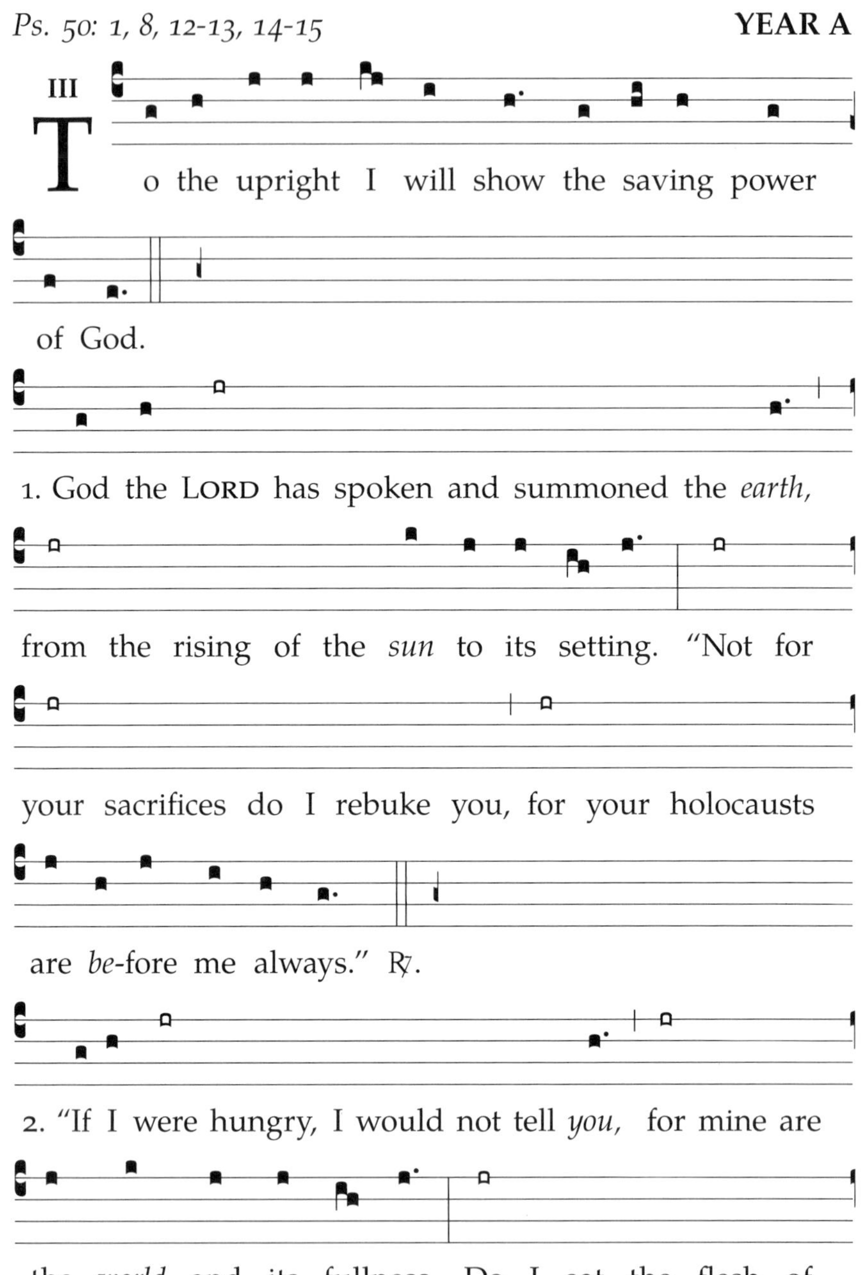

III
To the upright I will show the saving power
of God.
1. God the LORD has spoken and summoned the *earth,*
from the rising of the *sun* to its setting. "Not for
your sacrifices do I rebuke you, for your holocausts
are *be*-fore me always." ℟.
2. "If I were hungry, I would not tell *you,* for mine are
the *world* and its fullness. Do I eat the flesh of

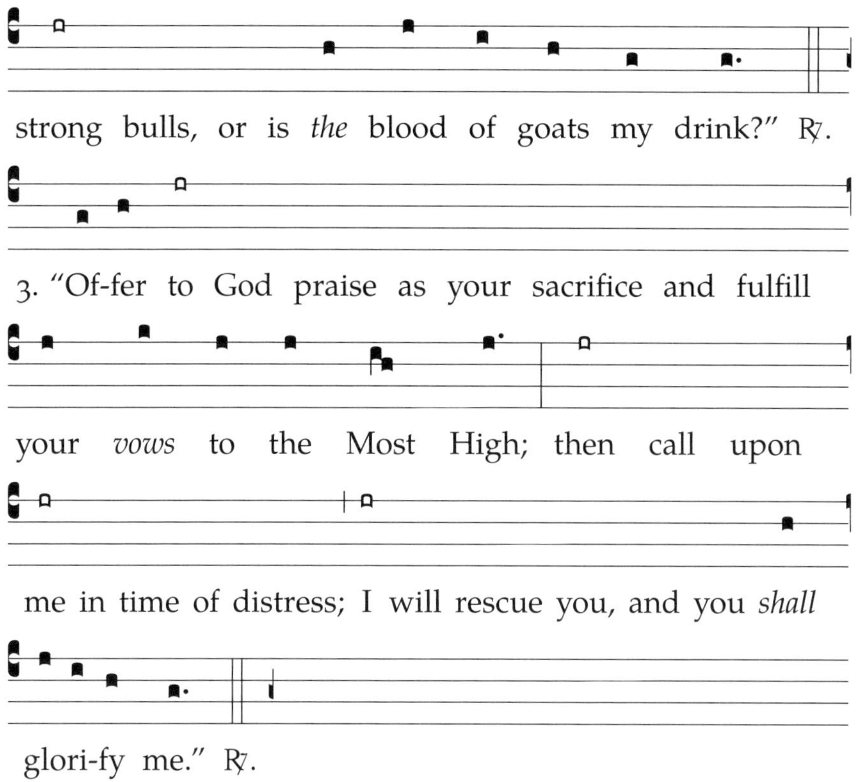
strong bulls, or is *the* blood of goats my drink?" ℟.
3. "Of-fer to God praise as your sacrifice and fulfill
your *vows* to the Most High; then call upon
me in time of distress; I will rescue you, and you *shall*
glori-fy me." ℟.

10th Sunday in Ordinary Time

Ps. 130: 1-2, 3-4, 5-6, 7-8 **YEAR B**

II
W
ith the Lord there is mercy and fullness
of redemption.
1. Out of the depths I cry to you, *O* LORD; LORD, *hear*
my voice! Let your ears be attentive to my voice in
sup-*pli*-cation. ℟.
2. If you, O LORD, mark iniquities, LORD, *who* can
stand? But with you is forgiveness, that you *may* be
revered. ℟.

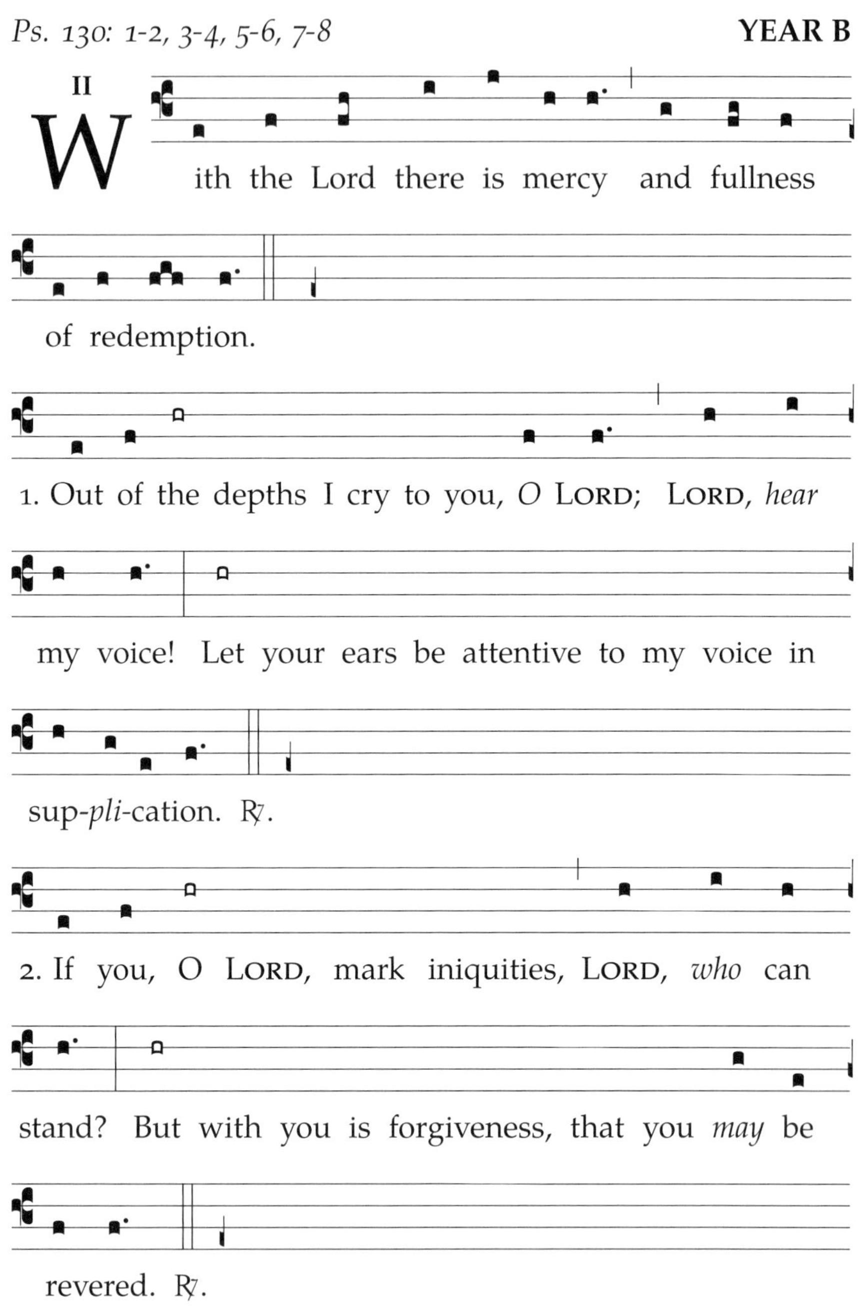

3. I trust in the LORD; my soul trusts in *his* word.
More than sentinels wait for the dawn, let Israel *wait*
for the LORD. ℟.
4. For with the LORD is kindness and with
him is plenteous re-*demp*-tion; And he will redeem
Israel from all their *in*-iq-uities. ℟.

10TH SUNDAY IN ORDINARY TIME

Ps. 30: 2, 4, 5-6, 11-12, 13 **YEAR C**

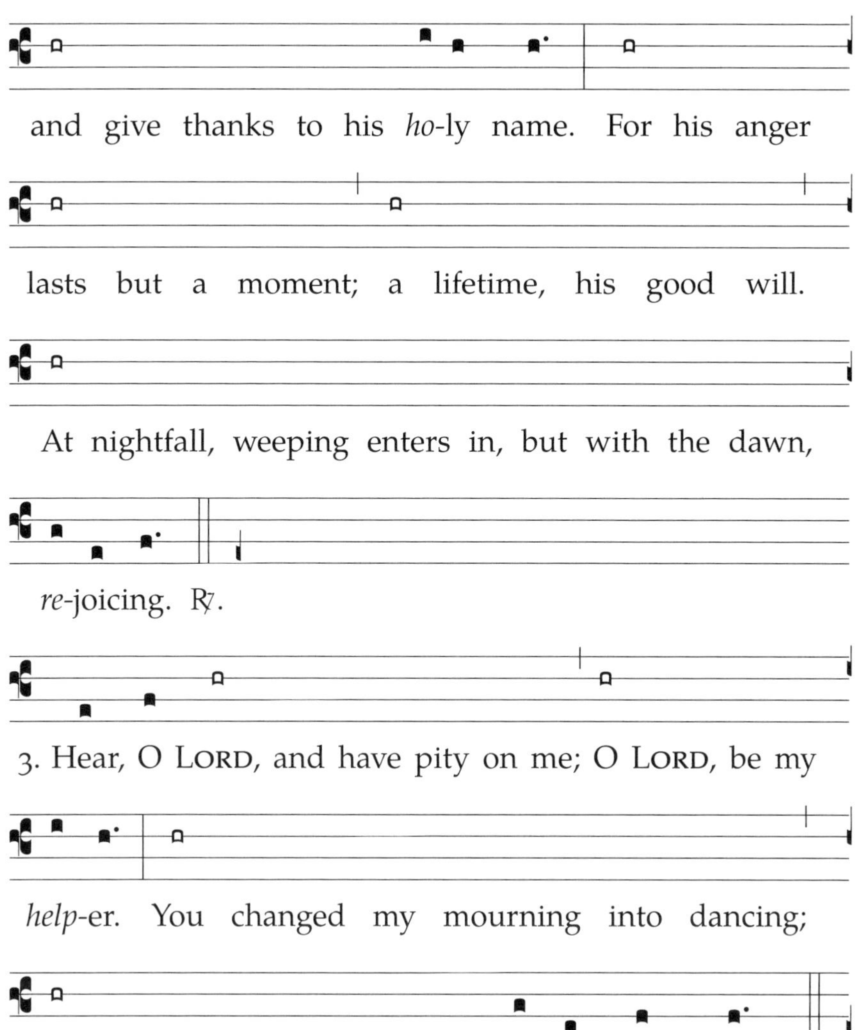
and give thanks to his ho-ly name. For his anger
lasts but a moment; a lifetime, his good will.
At nightfall, weeping enters in, but with the dawn,
re-joicing. ℟.
3. Hear, O Lord, and have pity on me; O Lord, be my
help-er. You changed my mourning into dancing;
O Lord, my God, forever will I give you thanks. ℟.

11TH SUNDAY IN ORDINARY TIME

Ps. 100: 1-2, 3, 5 **YEAR A**

VIII
We are his people: the sheep of his flock.
1. Sing joyfully to the LORD, all *you* lands; serve the
LORD with gladness; come before *him* with joyful song. ℟.
2. Know that the LORD is *God;* he made us,
his *we* are; his people, *the* flock he tends. ℟.
3. The LORD is *good:* his kindness endures for-*ev*-er,
and his faithfulness, to all *gen*-er-ations. ℟.

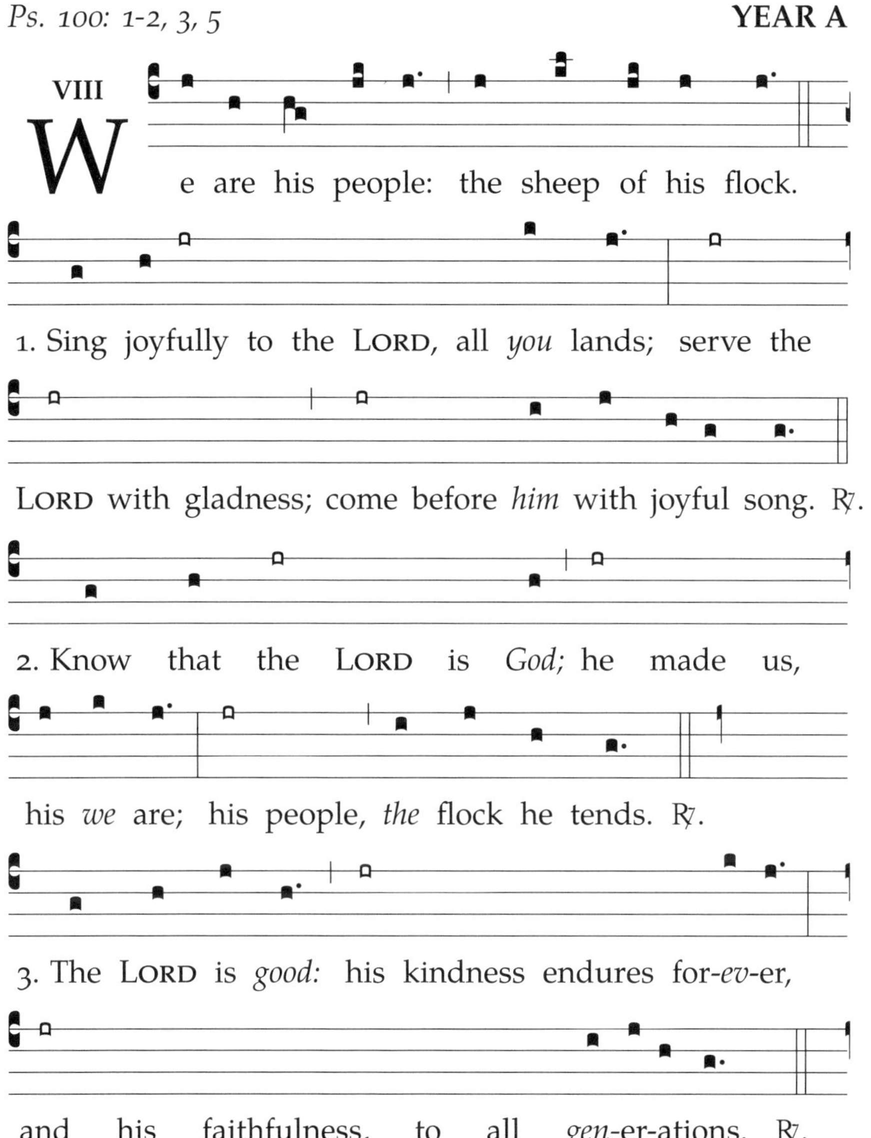

11th Sunday in Ordinary Time

Ps. 92: 2-3, 13-14, 15-16 **YEAR B**

VIII
Lord, it is good to give thanks to you.
1. It is good to give thanks to *the* Lord, to sing praise
to your name, *Most* High, to proclaim your kindness
at dawn and your faithful-*ness* throughout the night. ℟.
2. The just one shall flourish like the palm tree, like a
cedar of Lebanon *shall* he grow. They that are planted
in the house of the Lord shall flourish in *the* courts
of our God. ℟.

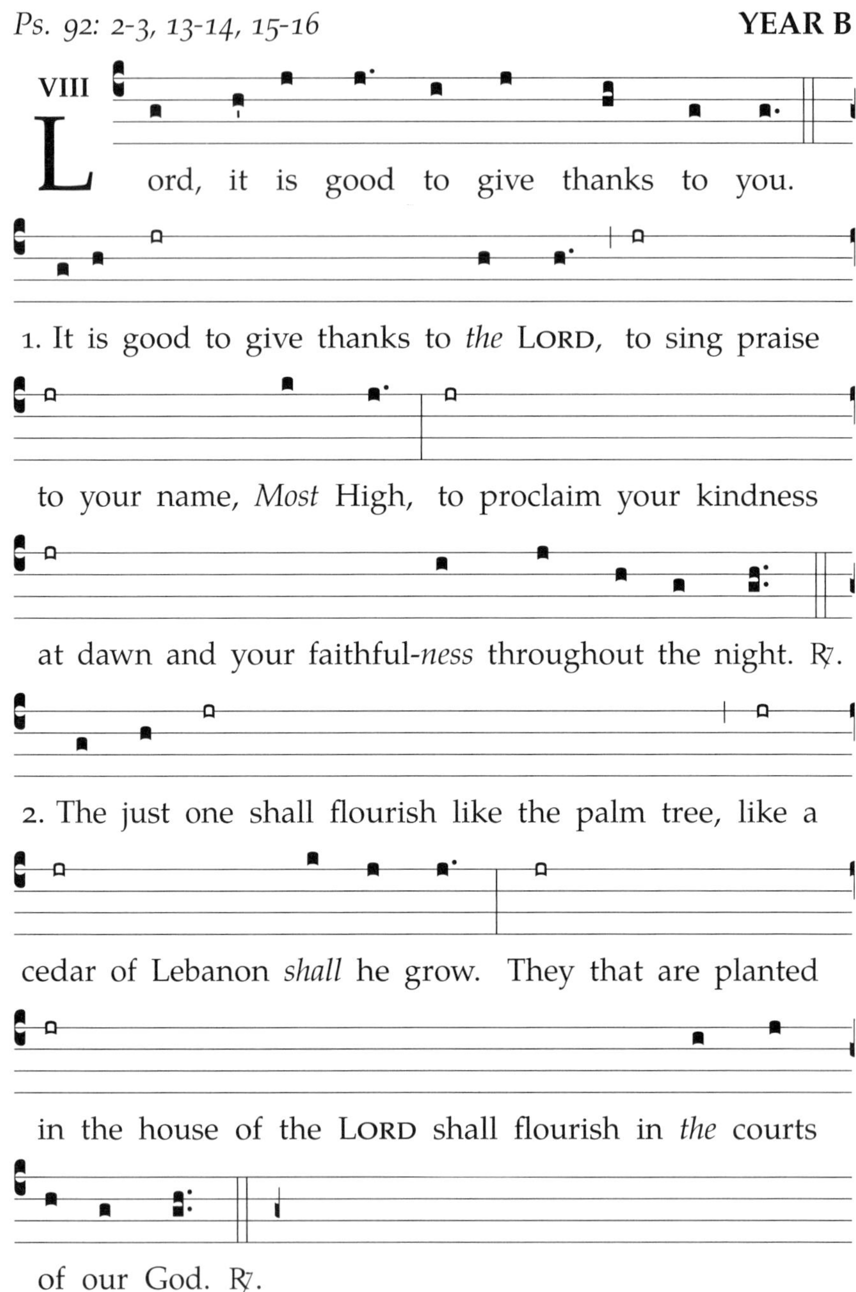

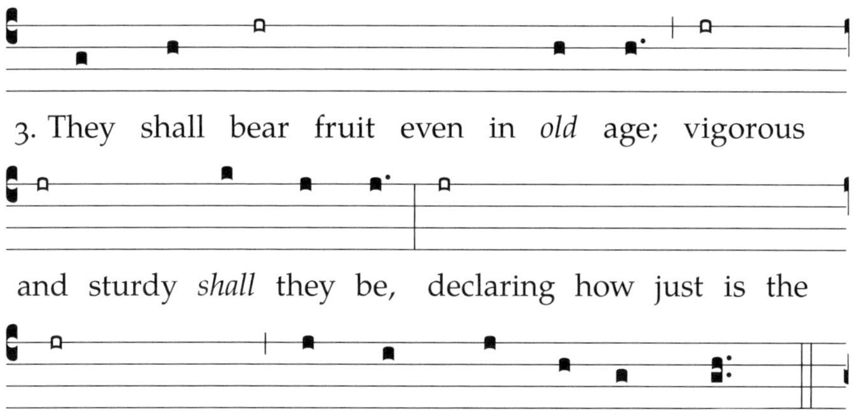
3. They shall bear fruit even in *old* age; vigorous
and sturdy *shall* they be, declaring how just is the
LORD, my rock, in *whom* there is no wrong. ℟.

11TH SUNDAY IN ORDINARY TIME

Ps. 32: 1-2, 5, 7, 11 **YEAR C**

IV
Lord, forgive the wrong I have done.
1. Blessed is the one whose fault is taken away, whose
sin is covered. Blessed the man to whom the LORD
imputes not guilt, in whose spirit there is *no* guile. ℟.
2. I acknowledged my sin to you, my *guilt* I covered
not. I said, "I confess my faults to the LORD,"
and you took away the guilt of my *sin*. ℟.
3. You are my shelter; from distress you will preserve

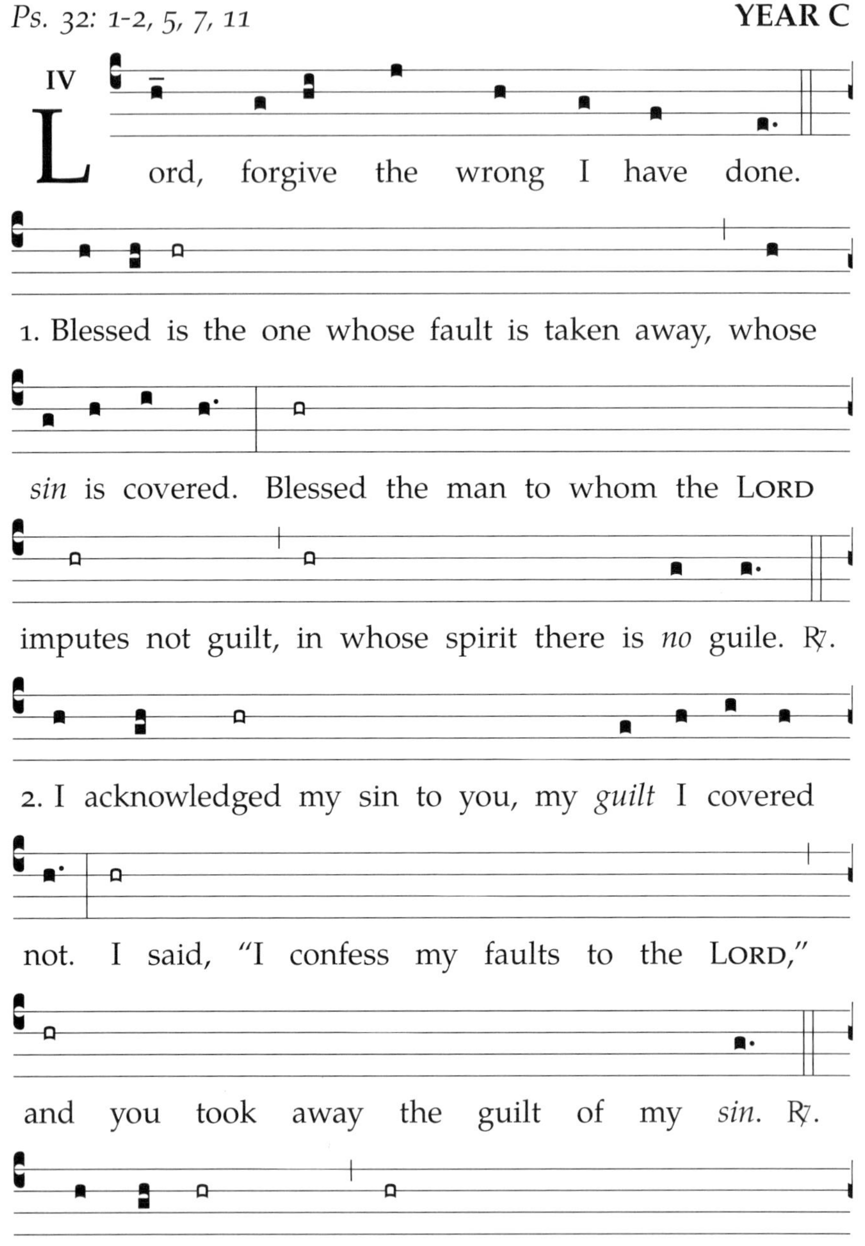

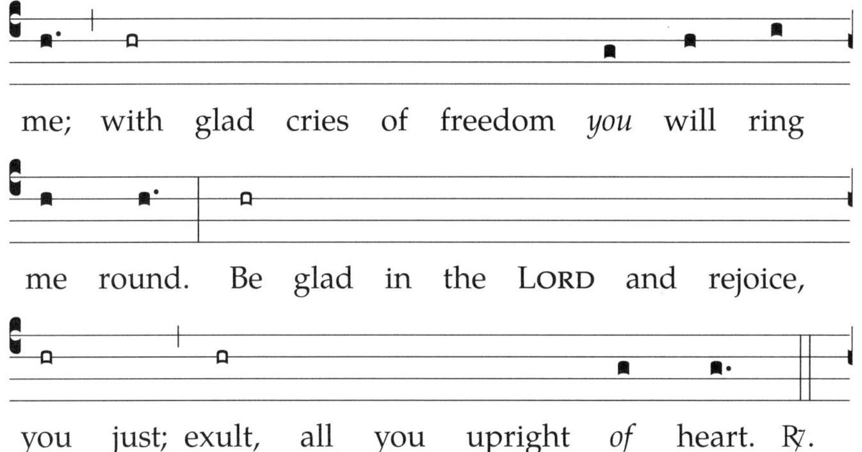
me; with glad cries of freedom *you* will ring
me round. Be glad in the LORD and rejoice,
you just; exult, all you upright *of* heart. ℟.

12th Sunday in Ordinary Time

Ps. 69: 8-10, 14, 17, 33-35 **YEAR A**

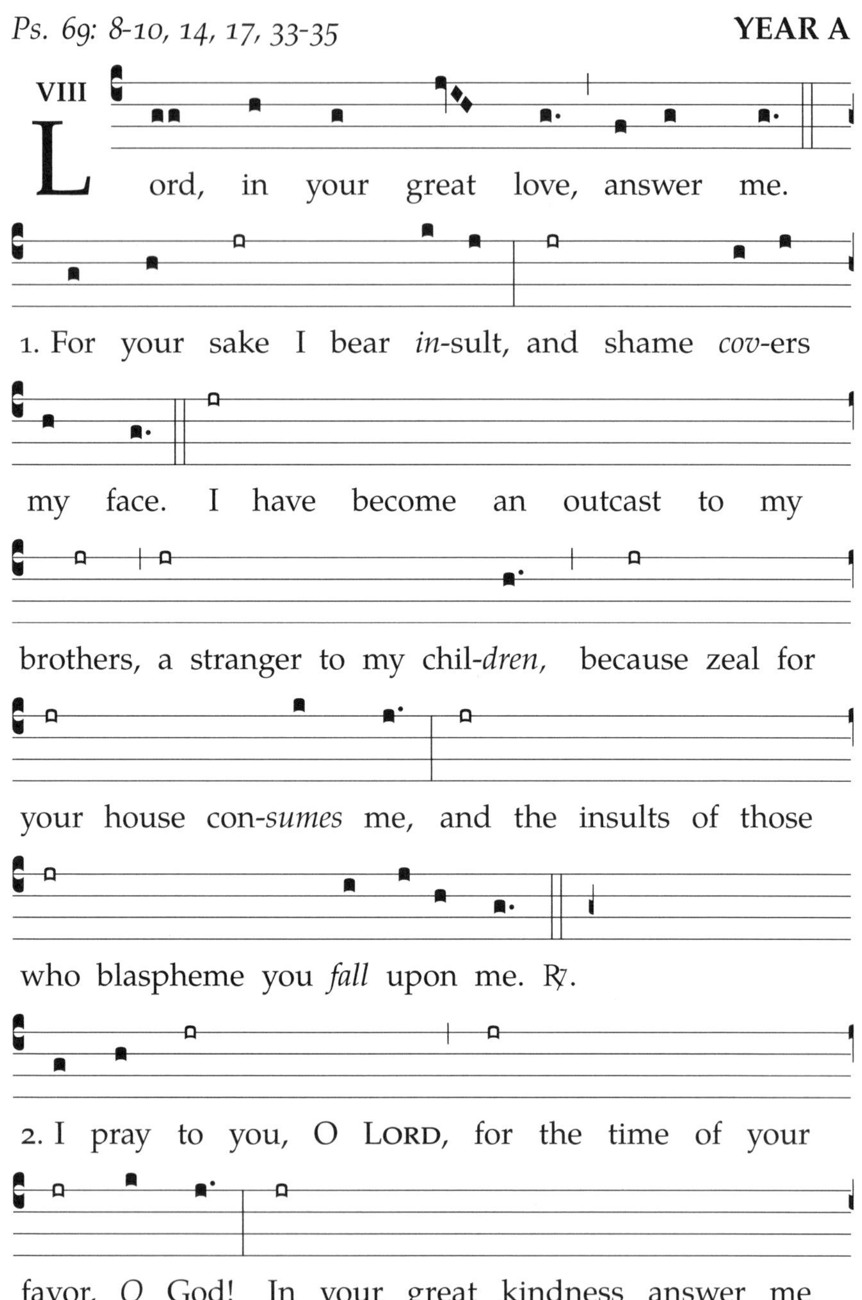

VIII
Lord, in your great love, answer me.
1. For your sake I bear *in*-sult, and shame *cov*-ers
my face. I have become an outcast to my
brothers, a stranger to my chil-*dren,* because zeal for
your house con-*sumes* me, and the insults of those
who blaspheme you *fall* upon me. ℟.
2. I pray to you, O Lord, for the time of your
favor, *O* God! In your great kindness answer me

with your constant help. Answer me, O LORD,
for bounteous is your kind-ness; in your great mer-cy
turn toward me. ℟.
3. "See, you lowly ones, and be glad; you who seek
God, may your hearts revive! For the LORD hears
the poor, and his own who are in bonds he spurns
not. Let the heavens and the earth praise him,
the seas and what-ev-er moves in them!" ℟.

12th Sunday in Ordinary Time

Ps. 107: 23-24, 25-26, 28-29, 30-31 **YEAR B**

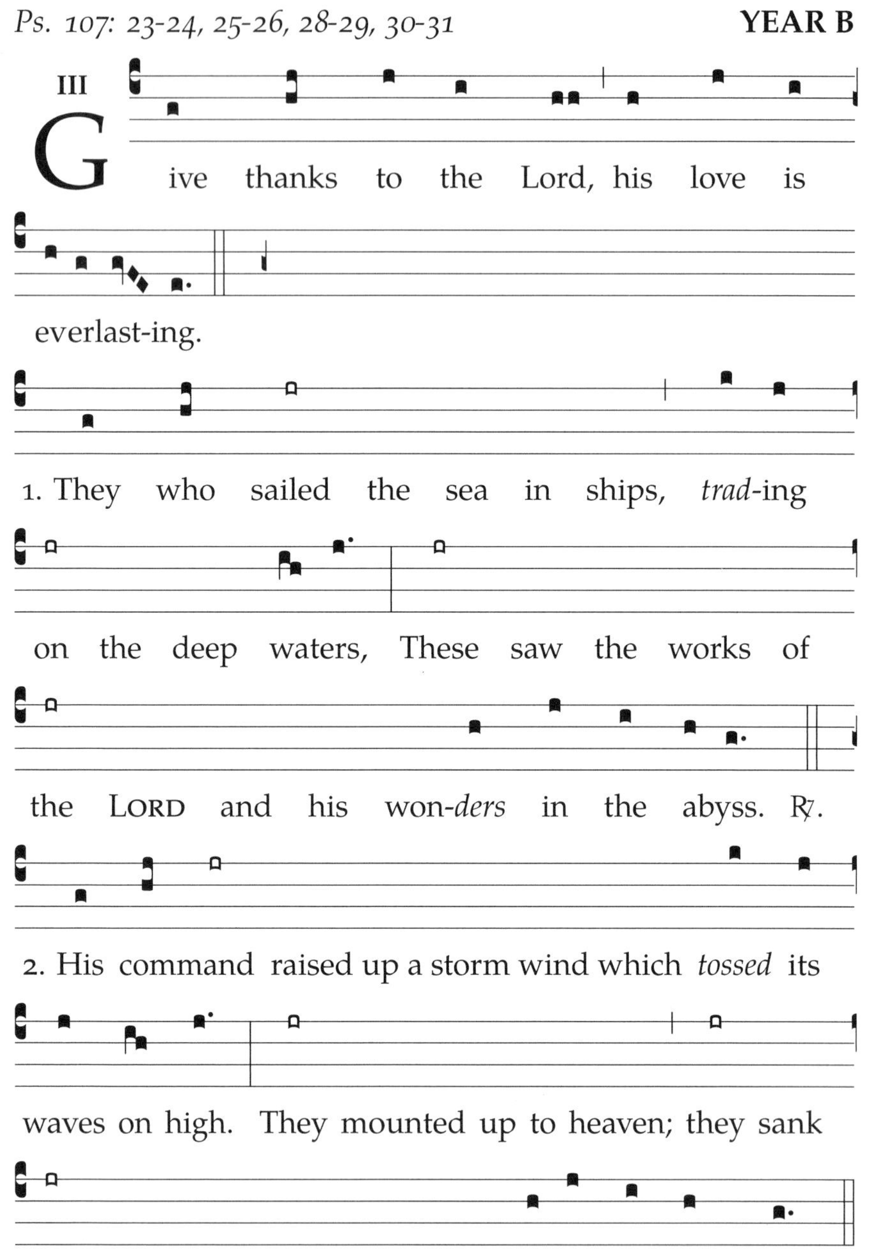
III
Give thanks to the Lord, his love is
everlast-ing.
1. They who sailed the sea in ships, trad-ing
on the deep waters, These saw the works of
the LORD and his won-ders in the abyss. ℟.
2. His command raised up a storm wind which tossed its
waves on high. They mounted up to heaven; they sank
to the depths; their hearts melted a-way in their plight. ℟.

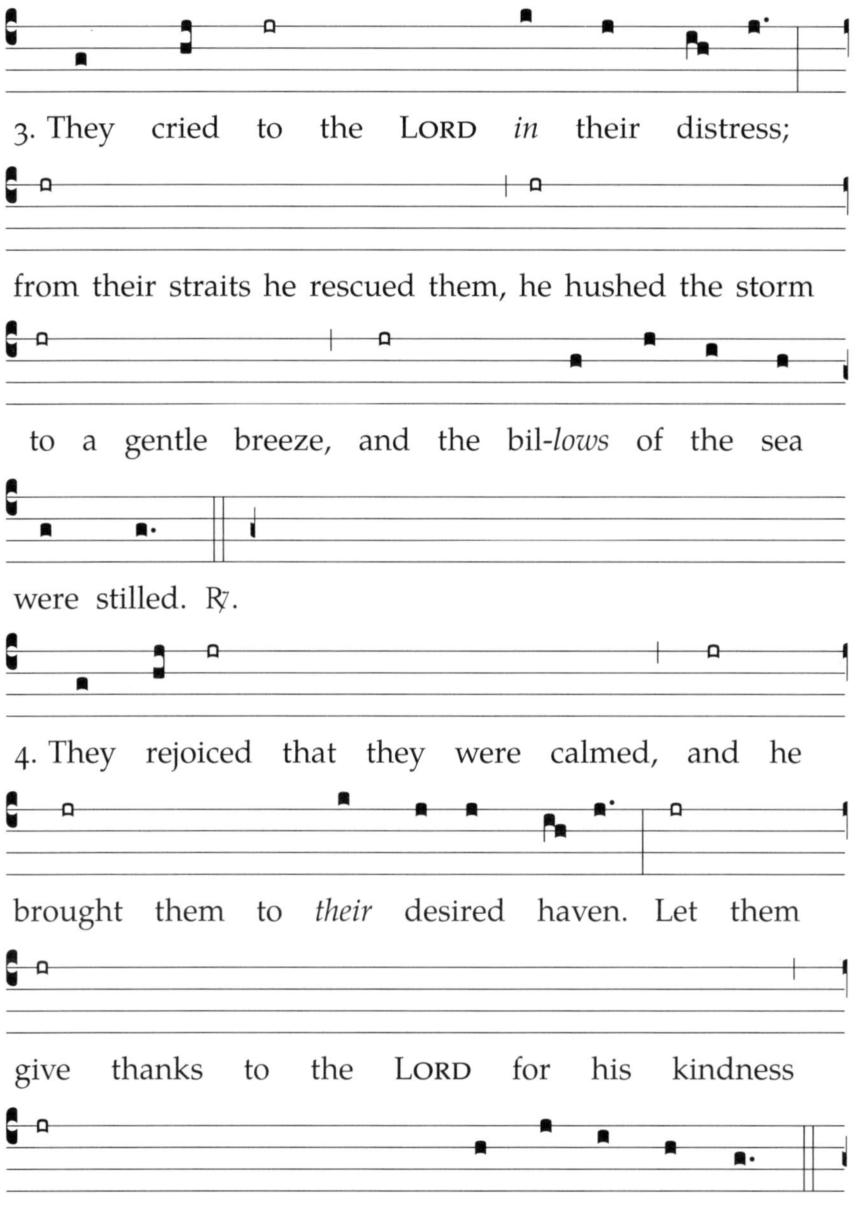
3. They cried to the LORD *in* their distress;
from their straits he rescued them, he hushed the storm
to a gentle breeze, and the bil-*lows* of the sea
were stilled. ℟.
4. They rejoiced that they were calmed, and he
brought them to *their* desired haven. Let them
give thanks to the LORD for his kindness
and his wondrous deeds to *the* children of men. ℟.

12TH SUNDAY IN ORDINARY TIME

Ps. 63: 2, 3-4, 5-6, 8-9 **YEAR C**

VI
My soul is thirsting for you, O Lord my God.
1. O God, you are my God *whom* I seek;
for you my flesh pines and my soul thirsts like
the earth, parched, lifeless *and* without water. ℟.
2. Thus have I gazed toward you in the sanctuary to
see your power and *your* glory, for your kindness is a
greater good than life; my lips *shall* glori-fy you. ℟.

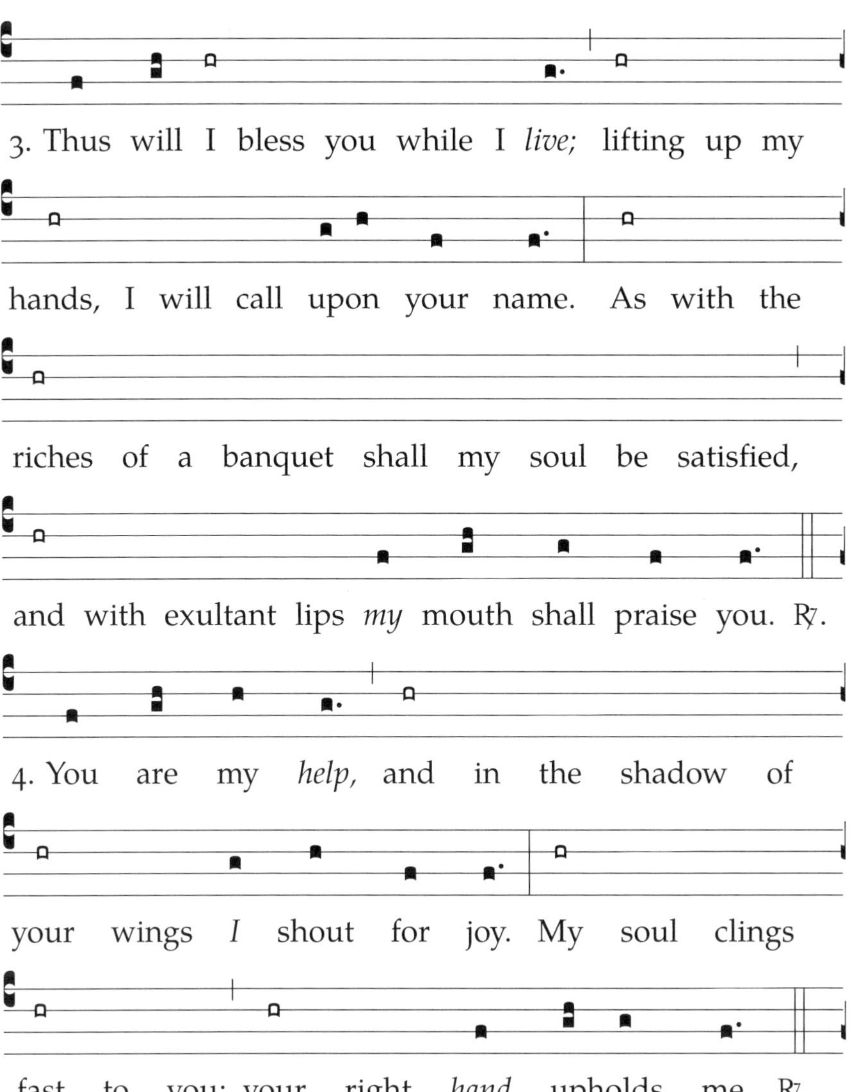
3. Thus will I bless you while I *live;* lifting up my
hands, I will call upon your name. As with the
riches of a banquet shall my soul be satisfied,
and with exultant lips *my* mouth shall praise you. ℟.
4. You are my *help,* and in the shadow of
your wings *I* shout for joy. My soul clings
fast to you; your right *hand* upholds me. ℟.

13TH SUNDAY IN ORDINARY TIME

Ps. 89: 2-3, 16-17, 18-19 **YEAR A**

VII
Forever I will sing the goodness of the Lord.
1. The promises of the LORD I will *sing* forever,
through all generations my mouth shall pro-*claim* your
faithfulness. For you have said, "My kindness is
es-*tab*-lished forever"; in heaven you have con-*firmed*
your faithfulness. ℟.
2. Blessed the people who *know* the joyful shout;
in the light of your countenance, *O* LORD,

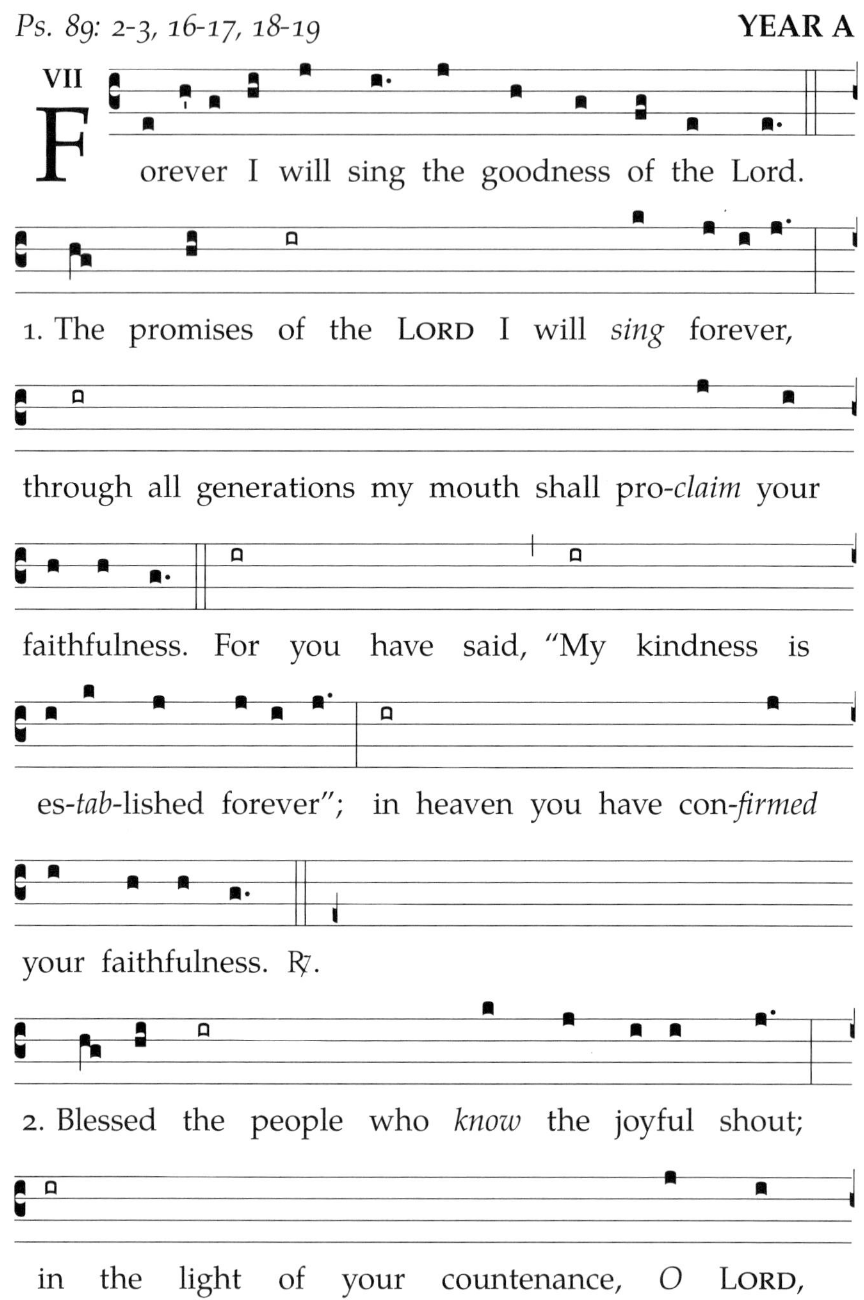

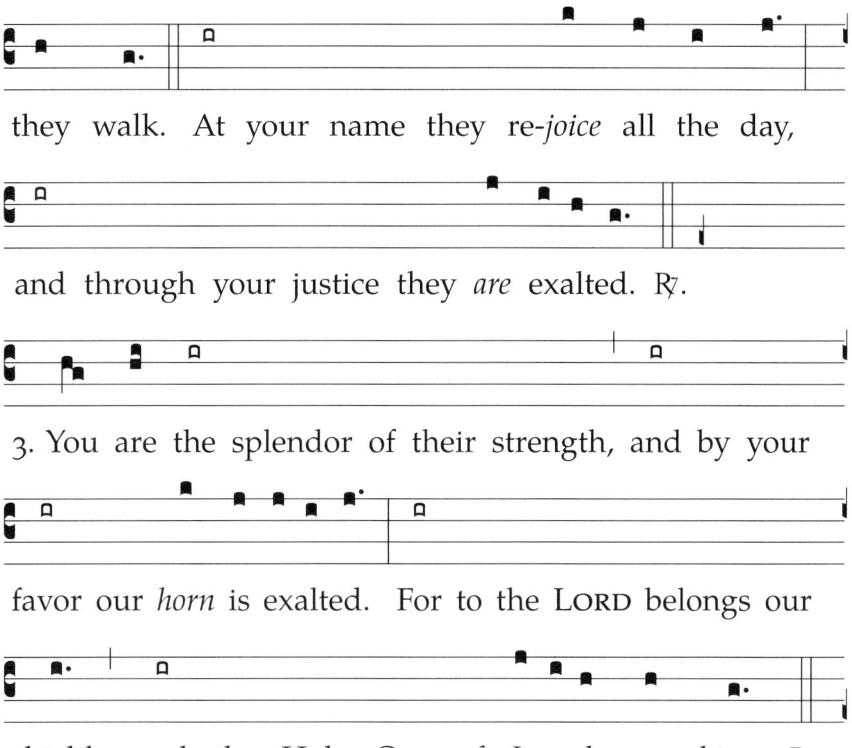
they walk. At your name they re-*joice* all the day,
and through your justice they *are* exalted. ℟.
3. You are the splendor of their strength, and by your
favor our *horn* is exalted. For to the LORD belongs our
shield, and the Holy One of *Is*-rael, our king. ℟.

13th Sunday in Ordinary Time

Ps. 30: 2, 4, 5-6, 11-12, 13 **YEAR B**

II
I will praise you, Lord, for you have rescued me.
1. I will extol you, O Lord, for you drew me clear
and did not let my enemies rejoice *o*-ver me.
O Lord, you brought me up from the netherworld;
you preserved me from among those going down
in-to the pit. ℟.
2. Sing praise to the Lord, you his faith-*ful* ones,

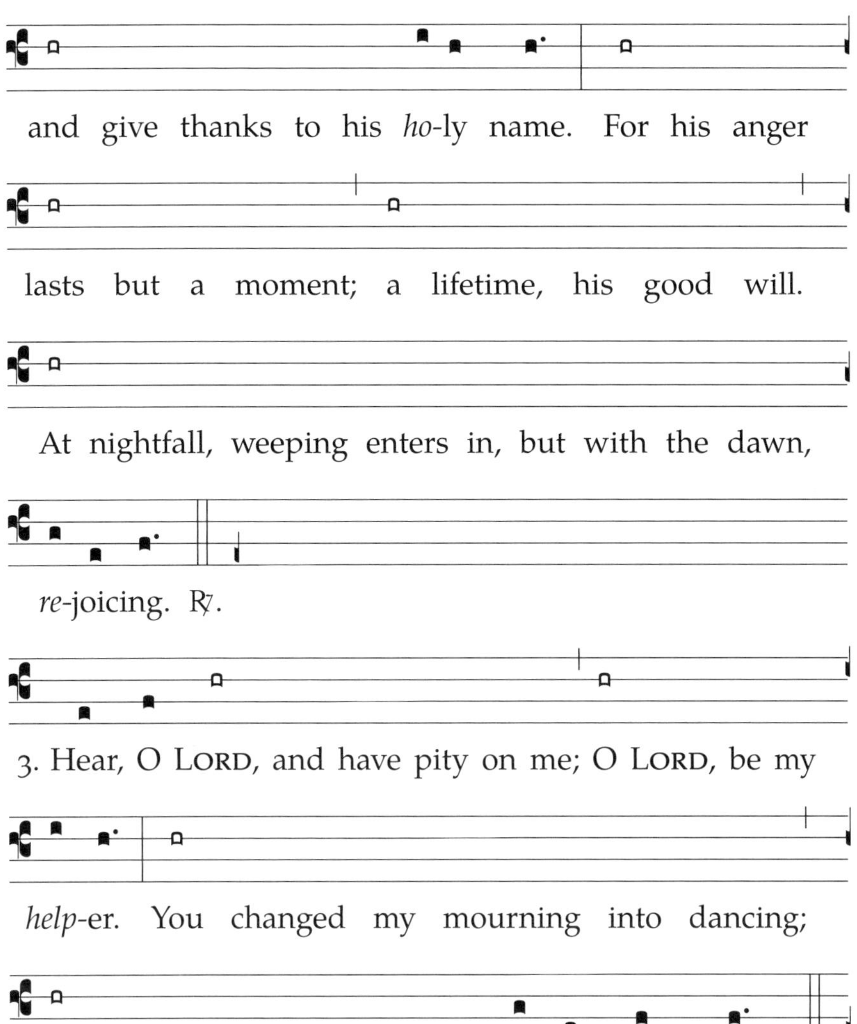

O LORD, my God, forever will *I* give you thanks. ℟.

13th Sunday in Ordinary Time

Ps. 16: 1-2, 5, 7-8, 9-10, 11 **YEAR C**

II
You are my inher-itance, O Lord.
1. Keep me, O God, for in you I take *ref*-uge; I say
to the Lord, "My Lord *are* you. O Lord, my allotted
portion and my cup, you it is who *hold* fast my lot." ℟.
2. I bless the Lord who counsels me; even in the night
my heart ex-*horts* me. I set the Lord ever before me;
with him at my right hand I shall *not* be disturbed. ℟.
3. Therefore my heart is glad and my soul re-*joic*-es,

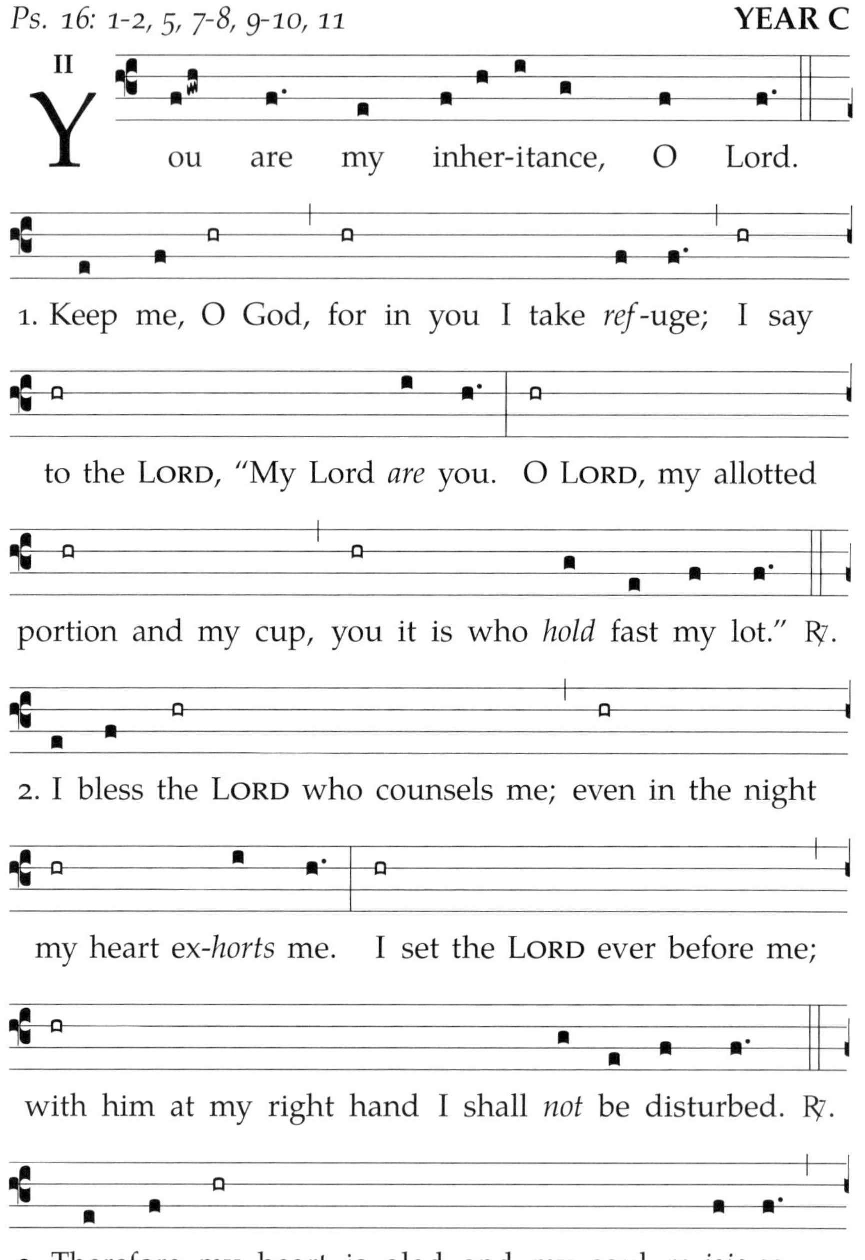

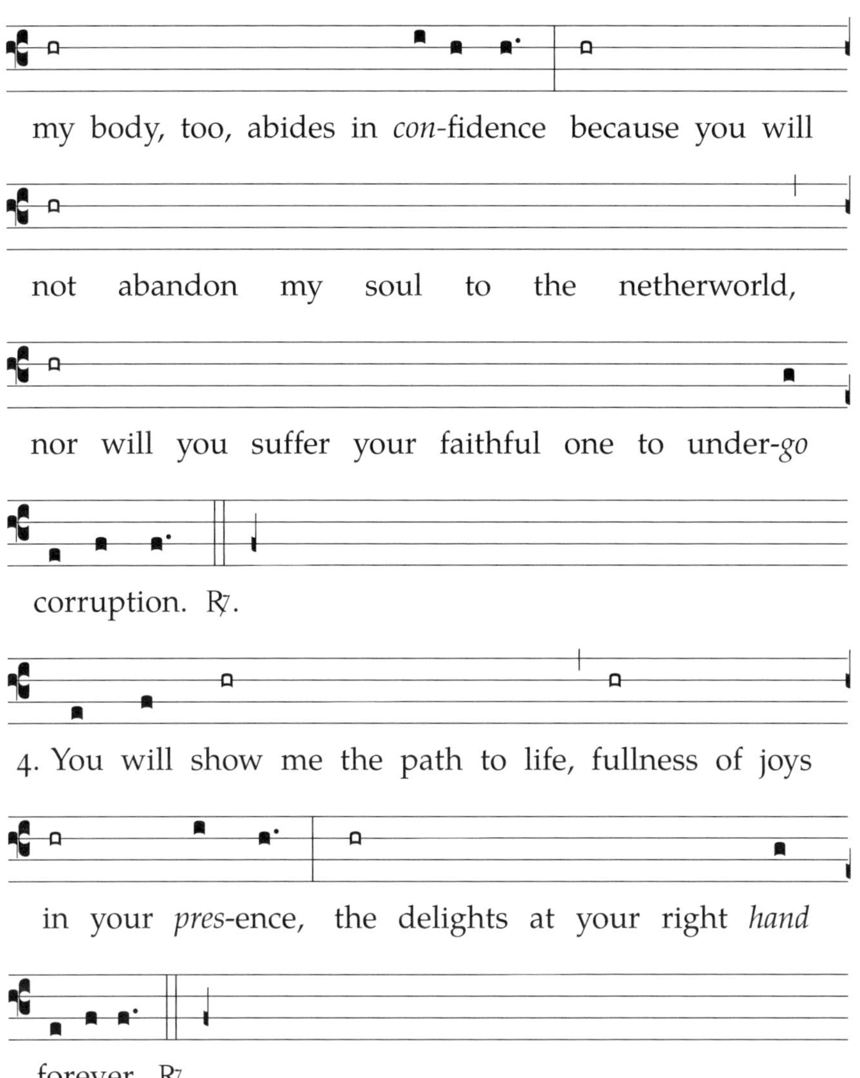
my body, too, abides in *con*-fidence because you will
not abandon my soul to the netherworld,
nor will you suffer your faithful one to under-*go*
corruption. ℟.
4. You will show me the path to life, fullness of joys
in your *pres*-ence, the delights at your right *hand*
forever. ℟.

14th Sunday in Ordinary Time

Ps. 145: 1-2, 8-9, 10-11, 13-14
YEAR A
II
I will praise your name forev- er, my king and
my God.
1. I will extol you, O my God and King, and I will
bless your name forever and *ev*-er. Every day will
I bless you, and I will praise your name forever *and*
ever. ℟.
2. The LORD is gracious and merciful, slow to
anger and of great *kind*-ness. The LORD is

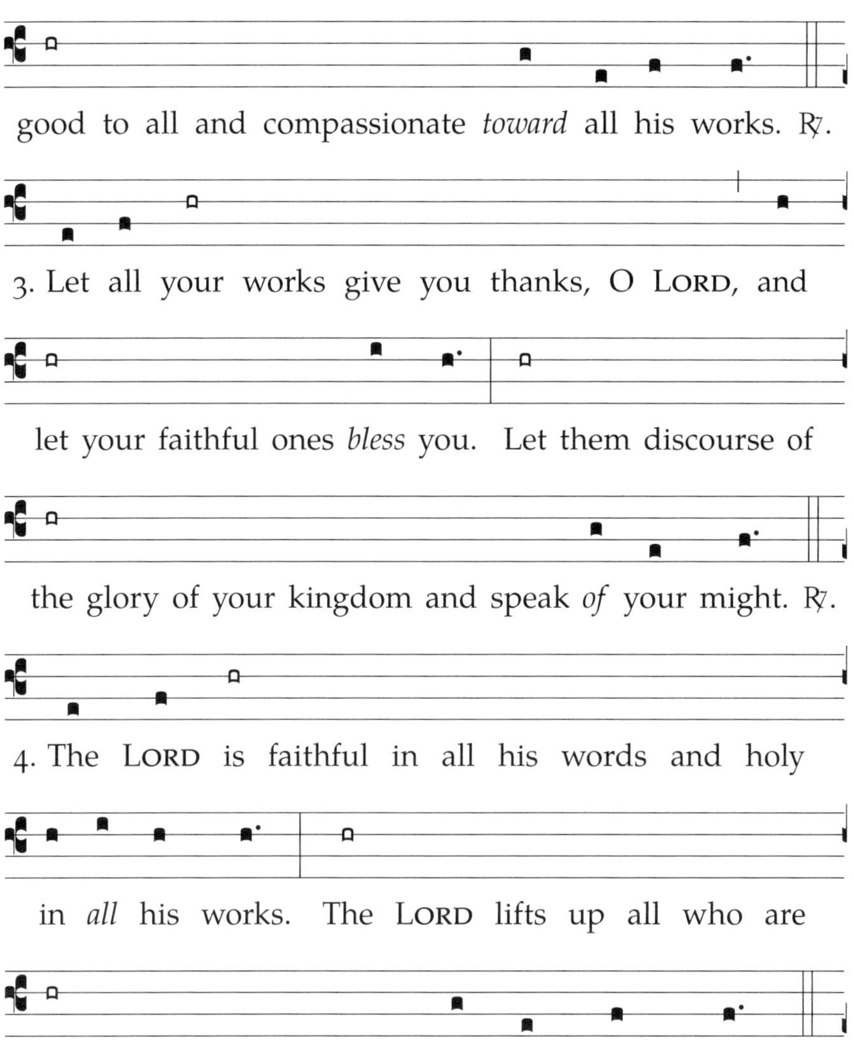
good to all and compassionate *toward* all his works. ℟.
3. Let all your works give you thanks, O LORD, and
let your faithful ones *bless* you. Let them discourse of
the glory of your kingdom and speak *of* your might. ℟.
4. The LORD is faithful in all his words and holy
in *all* his works. The LORD lifts up all who are
falling and raises up all *who* are bowed down. ℟.

14th Sunday in Ordinary Time

Ps. 123: 1-2, 2, 3-4 **YEAR B**

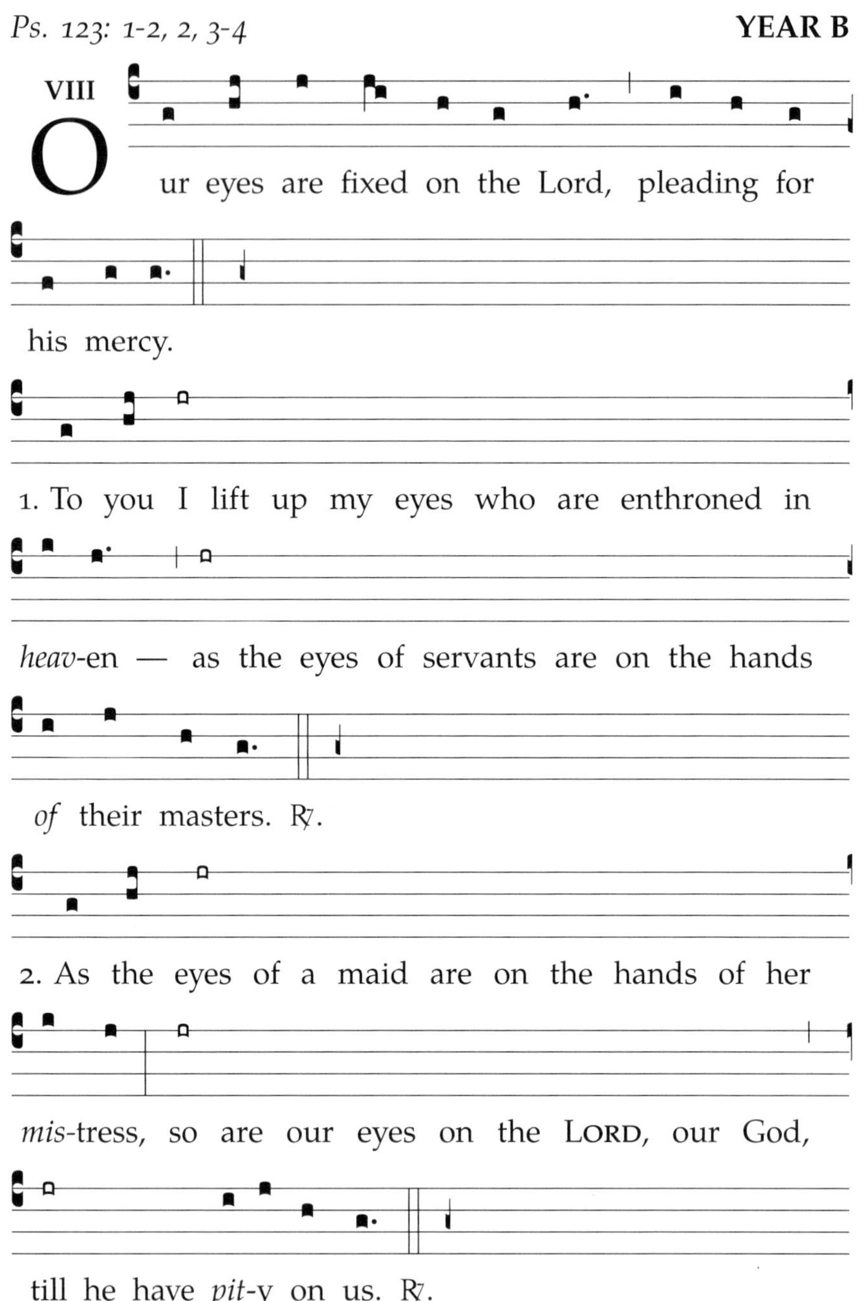
VIII
Our eyes are fixed on the Lord, pleading for his mercy.
1. To you I lift up my eyes who are enthroned in *heav*-en — as the eyes of servants are on the hands *of* their masters. ℟.
2. As the eyes of a maid are on the hands of her *mis*-tress, so are our eyes on the Lord, our God, till he have *pit*-y on us. ℟.

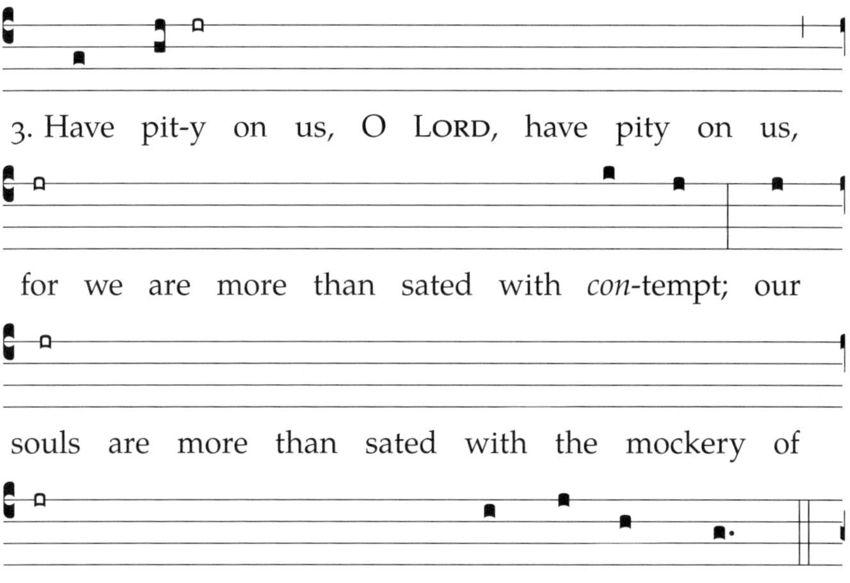
3. Have pit-y on us, O LORD, have pity on us,
for we are more than sated with *con*-tempt; our
souls are more than sated with the mockery of
the arrogant, with the con-*tempt* of the proud. ℟.

14th Sunday in Ordinary Time

Ps. 66: 1-3, 4-5, 6-7, 16, 20 **YEAR C**

VIII
Let all the earth cry out to God with joy.
1. Shout joyfully to God, all the earth, sing praise to
the glory of his *name;* proclaim his *glo*-rious praise.
Say to God, "How tre-*men*-dous are your deeds!" ℟.
2. "Let all on earth worship and sing praise *to* you,
sing praise to *your* name!" Come and see the works
of God, his tremendous deeds among the chil-*dren* of
Adam. ℟.

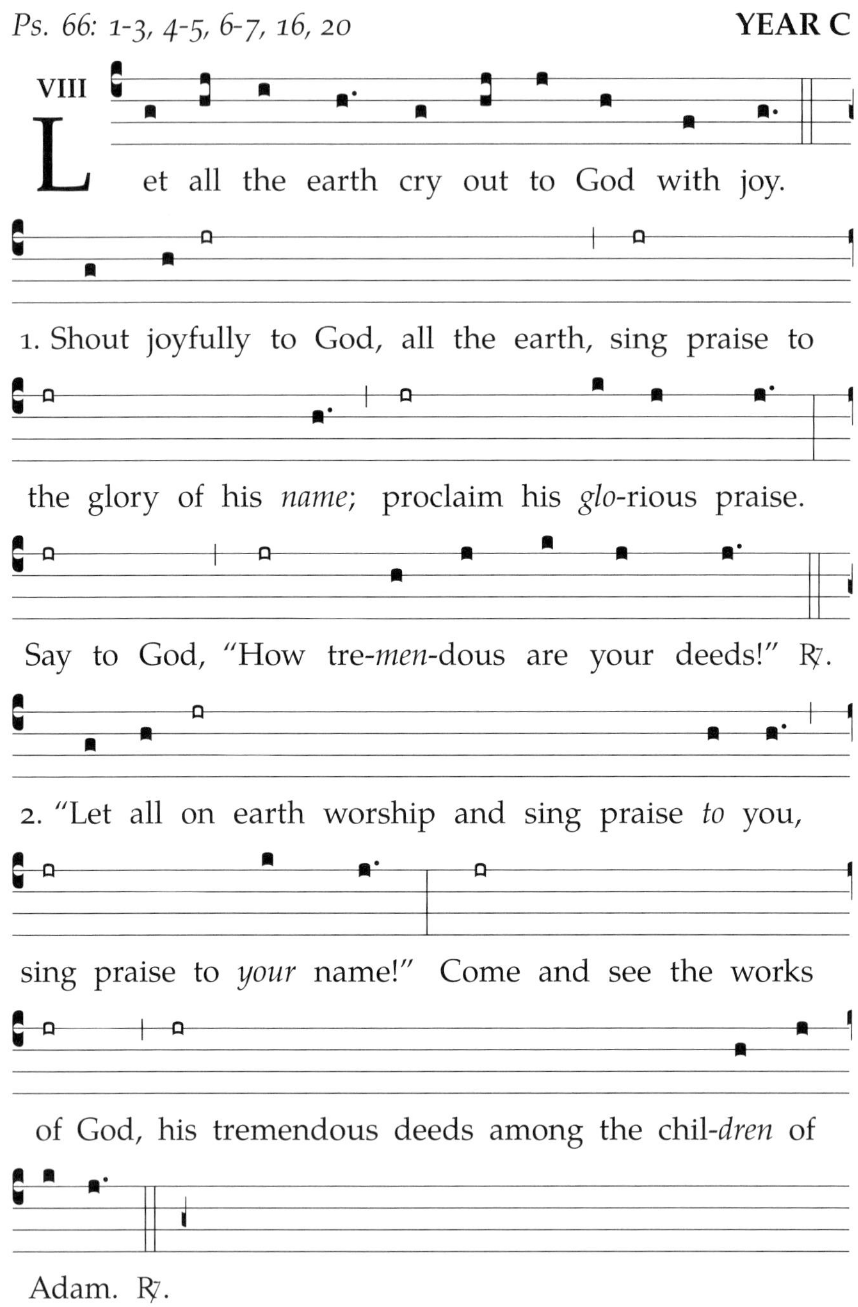

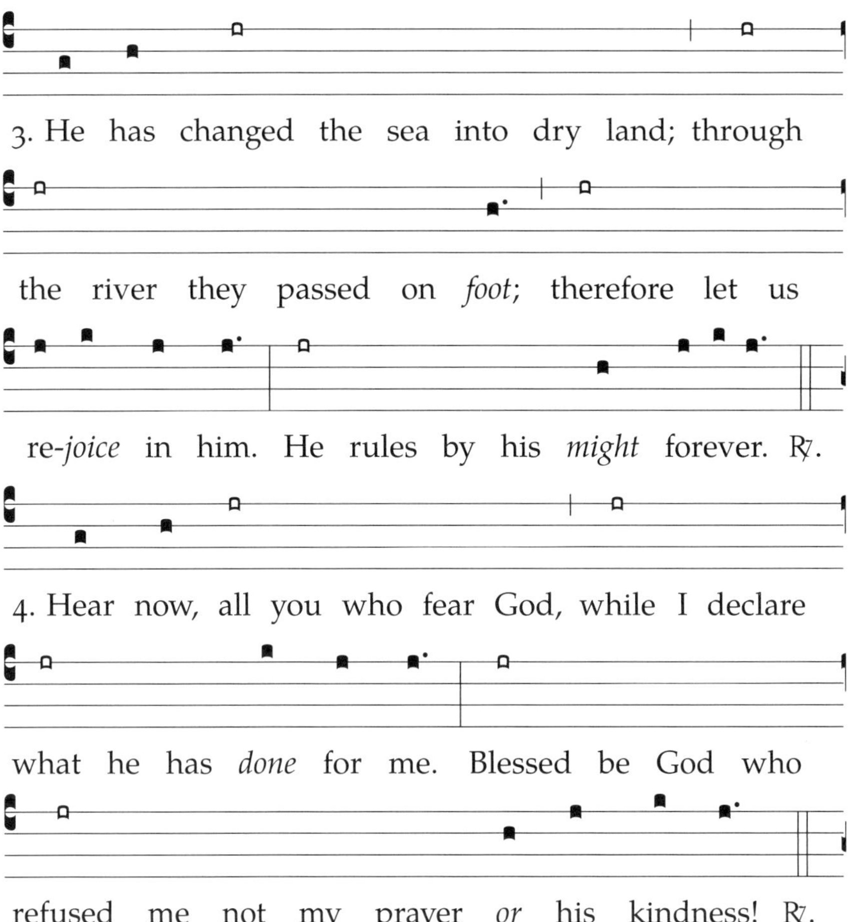
3. He has changed the sea into dry land; through
the river they passed on *foot*; therefore let us
re-*joice* in him. He rules by his *might* forever. ℟.
4. Hear now, all you who fear God, while I declare
what he has *done* for me. Blessed be God who
refused me not my prayer *or* his kindness! ℟.

15th Sunday in Ordinary Time

Ps. 65: 10, 11, 12-13, 14 **YEAR A**

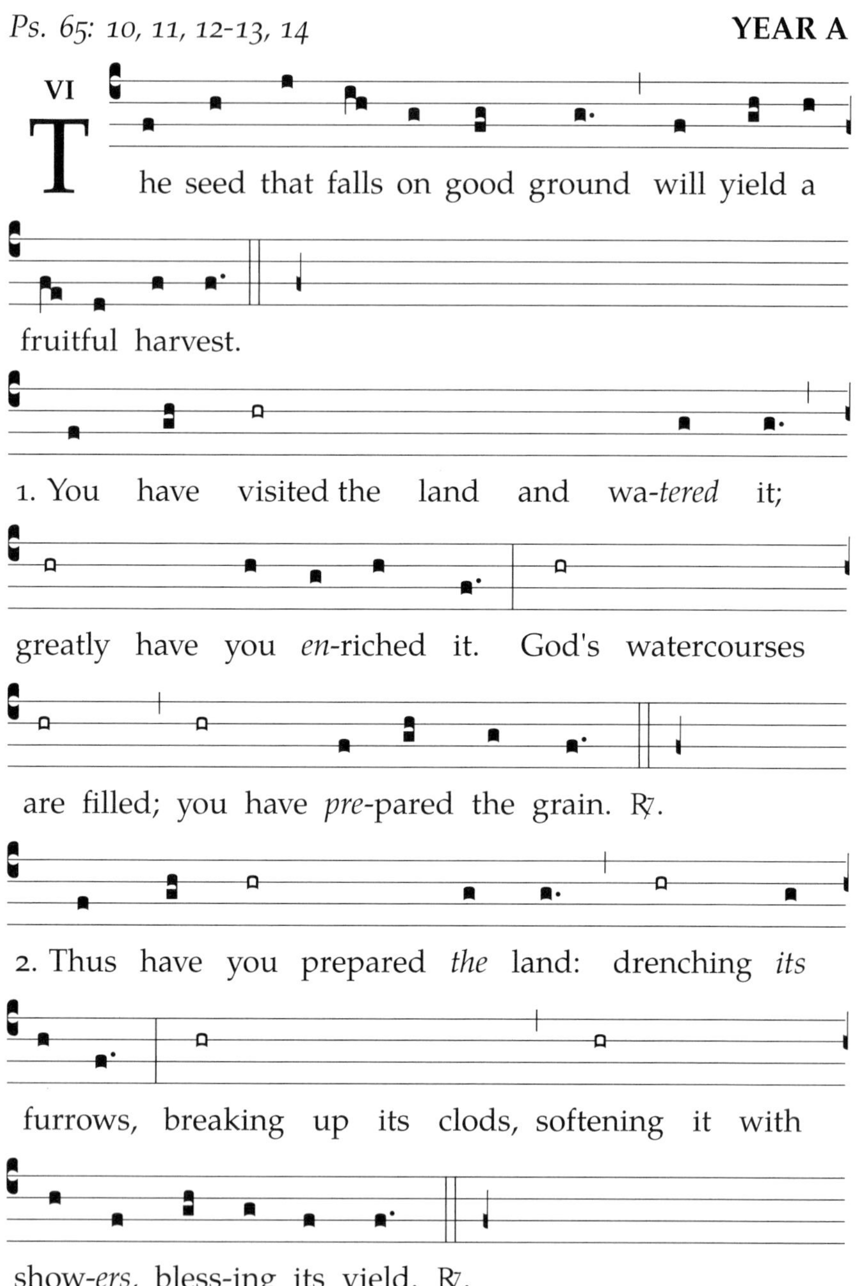
VI
The seed that falls on good ground will yield a
fruitful harvest.
1. You have visited the land and wa-*tered* it;
greatly have you *en*-riched it. God's watercourses
are filled; you have *pre*-pared the grain. ℟.
2. Thus have you prepared *the* land: drenching *its*
furrows, breaking up its clods, softening it with
show-*ers*, bless-ing its yield. ℟.

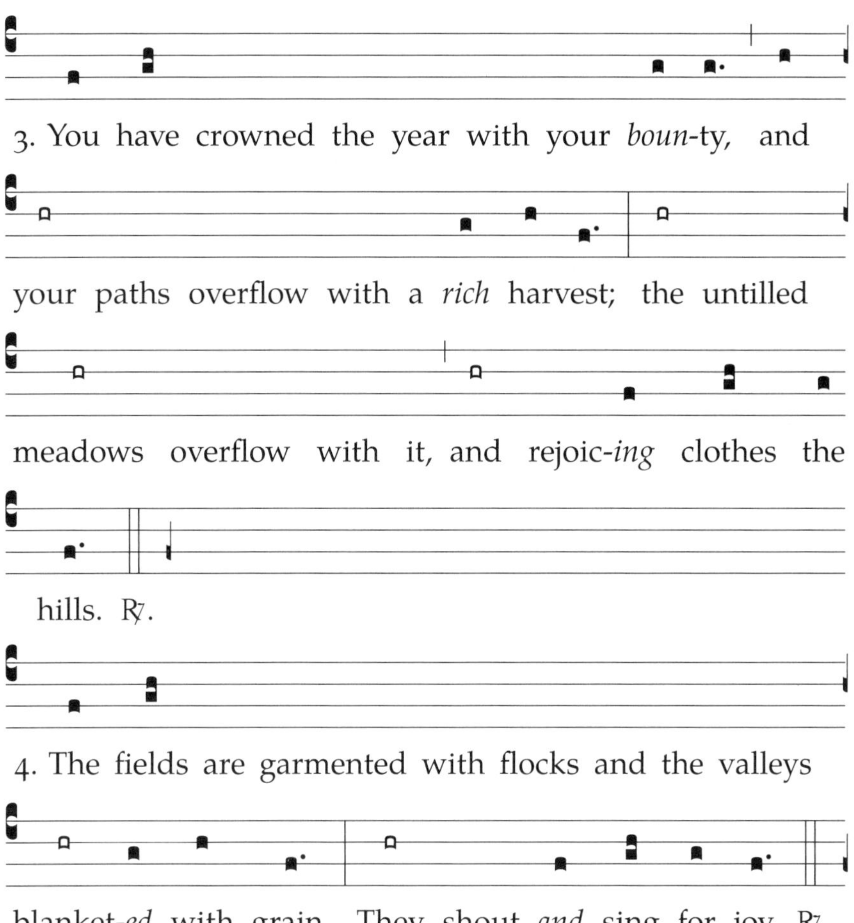
3. You have crowned the year with your *boun*-ty, and
your paths overflow with a *rich* harvest; the untilled
meadows overflow with it, and rejoic-*ing* clothes the
hills. ℟.
4. The fields are garmented with flocks and the valleys
blanket-*ed* with grain. They shout *and* sing for joy. ℟.

15th Sunday in Ordinary Time

Ps. 85: 9-10, 11-12, 13-14
YEAR B
V
Lord, let us see your kindness, and grant us your salva-tion.
1. I will hear what God *pro*-claims; the LORD — for he pro-*claims* peace. Near indeed is his salvation to those who fear him, glory *dwell*-ing in our land. ℟.
2. Kindness and truth shall meet; justice and *peace* shall kiss. Truth shall spring out of the earth, and justice shall look *down* from heaven. ℟.

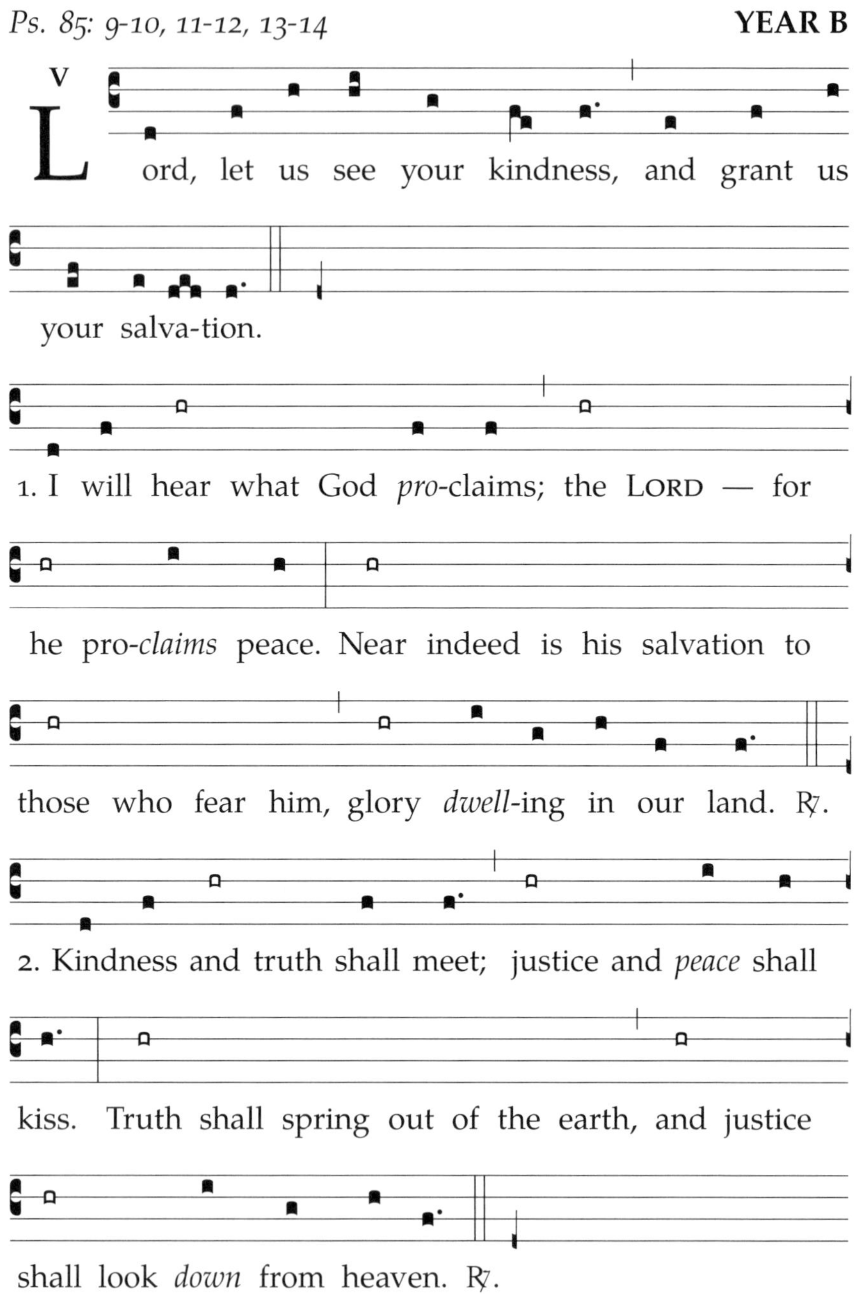

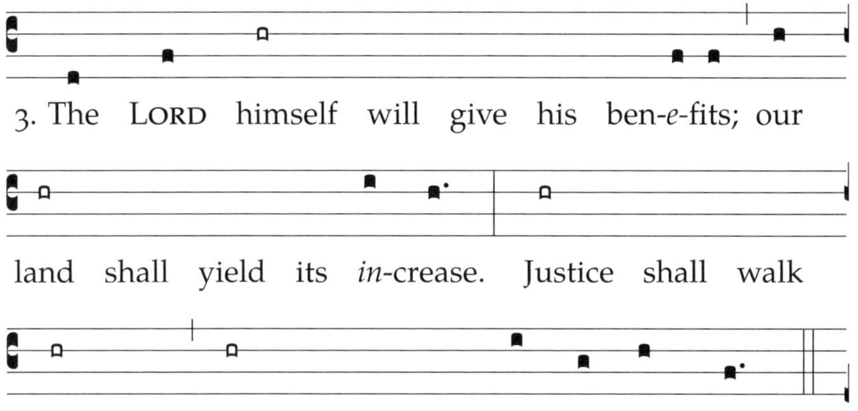
3. The LORD himself will give his ben-*e*-fits; our
land shall yield its *in*-crease. Justice shall walk
before him, and prepare the *way* of his steps. ℟.

15th Sunday in Ordinary Time (Option 1)

Ps. 69: 14, 17, 30-31, 33-34, 36, 37 **YEAR C**

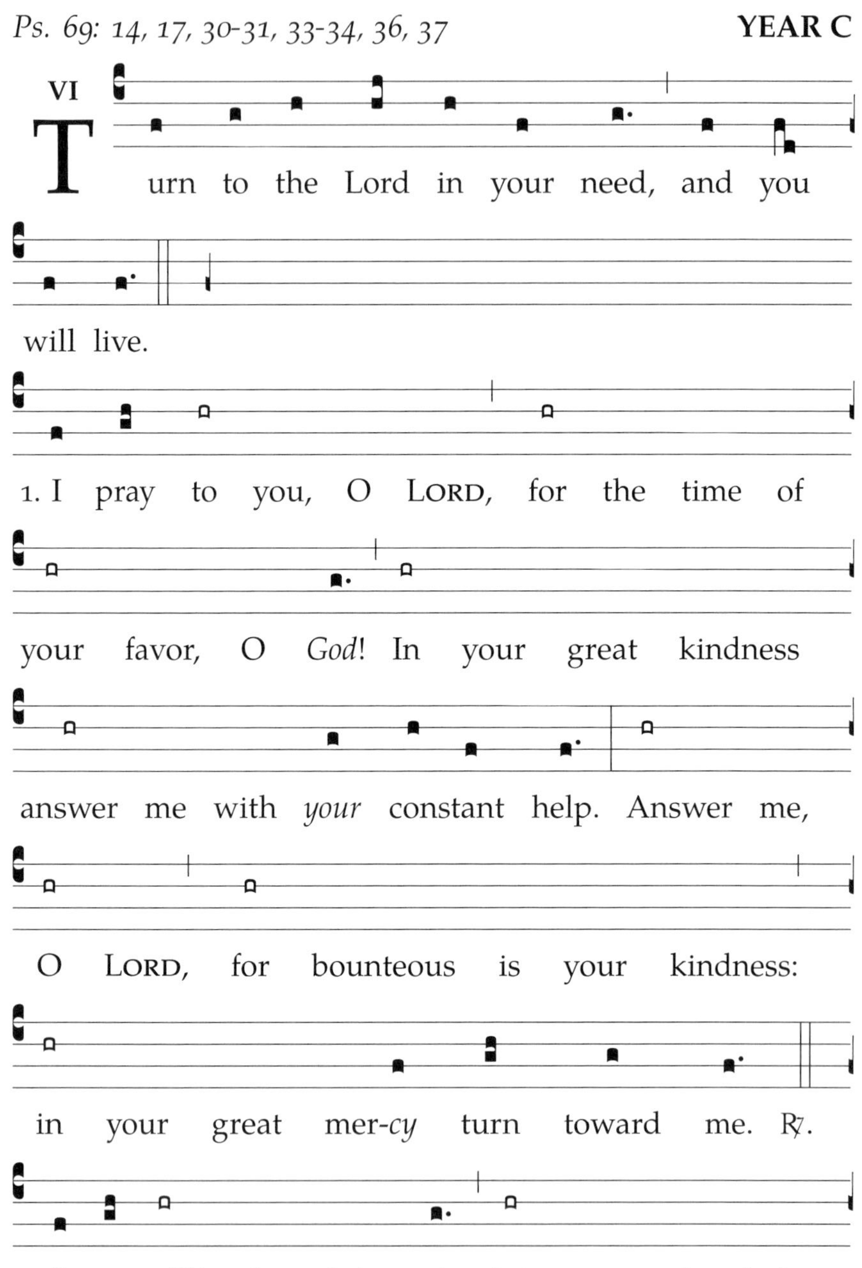
VI
Turn to the Lord in your need, and you
will live.
1. I pray to you, O LORD, for the time of
your favor, O *God*! In your great kindness
answer me with *your* constant help. Answer me,
O LORD, for bounteous is your kindness:
in your great mer-*cy* turn toward me. ℟.
2. I am afflicted and in *pain;* let your saving help,

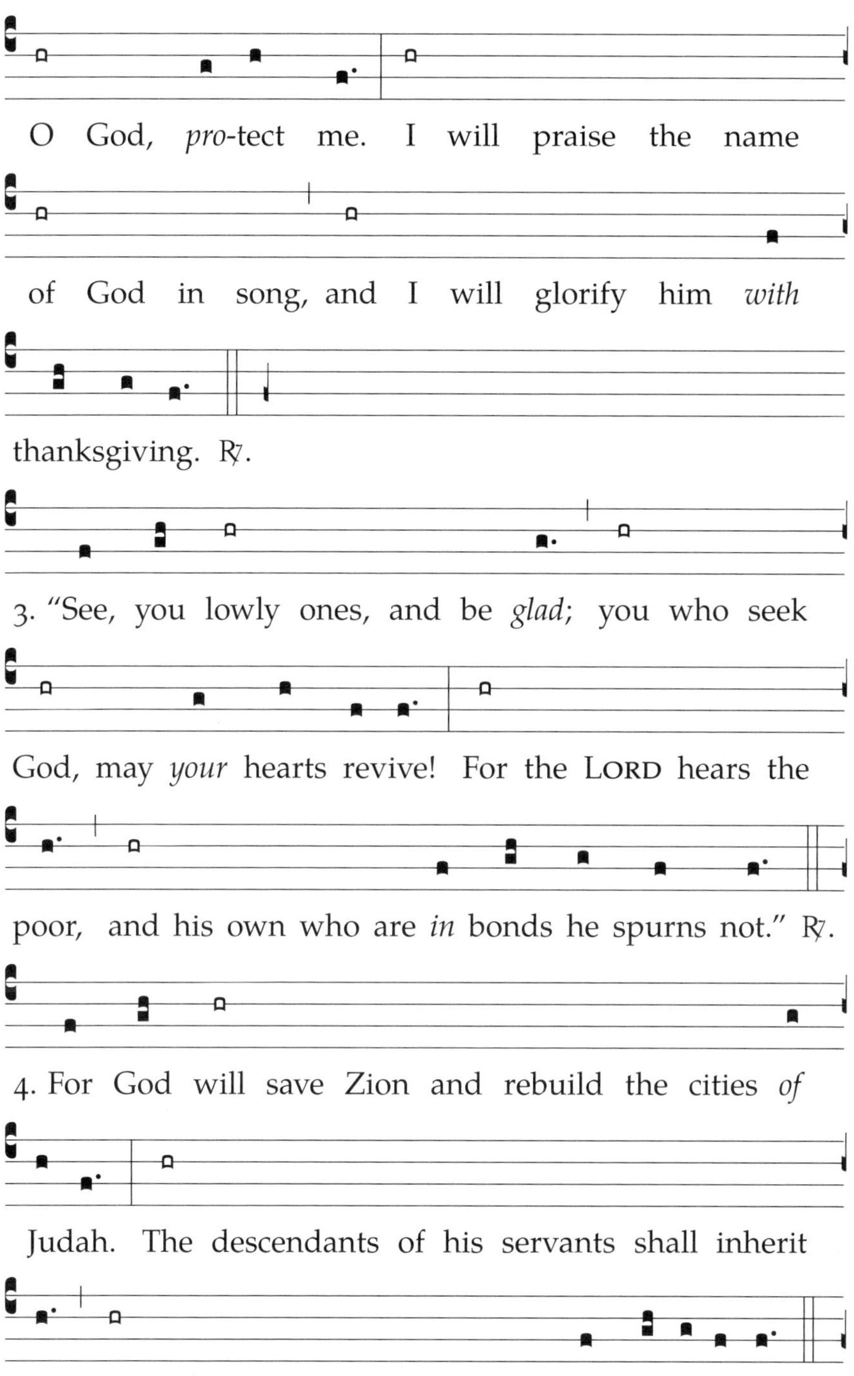
O God, pro-tect me. I will praise the name
of God in song, and I will glorify him with
thanksgiving. ℟.
3. "See, you lowly ones, and be glad; you who seek
God, may your hearts revive! For the LORD hears the
poor, and his own who are in bonds he spurns not." ℟.
4. For God will save Zion and rebuild the cities of
Judah. The descendants of his servants shall inherit
it, and those who love his name shall inhabit it. ℟.

15th Sunday in Ordinary Time (option 2)

Ps. 19: 8, 9, 10, 11 **YEAR C**

VIII
Your words, Lord, are Spirit and life.
1. The law of the LORD is perfect, refreshing *the* soul;
the decree of the LORD is trustworthy, giving wisdom
to the simple. ℟.
2. The precepts of the LORD are right, rejoicing *the*
heart; the command of the LORD is clear, en-*light*-ening
the eye. ℟.
3. The fear of the LORD is pure, enduring for-*ev*-er;

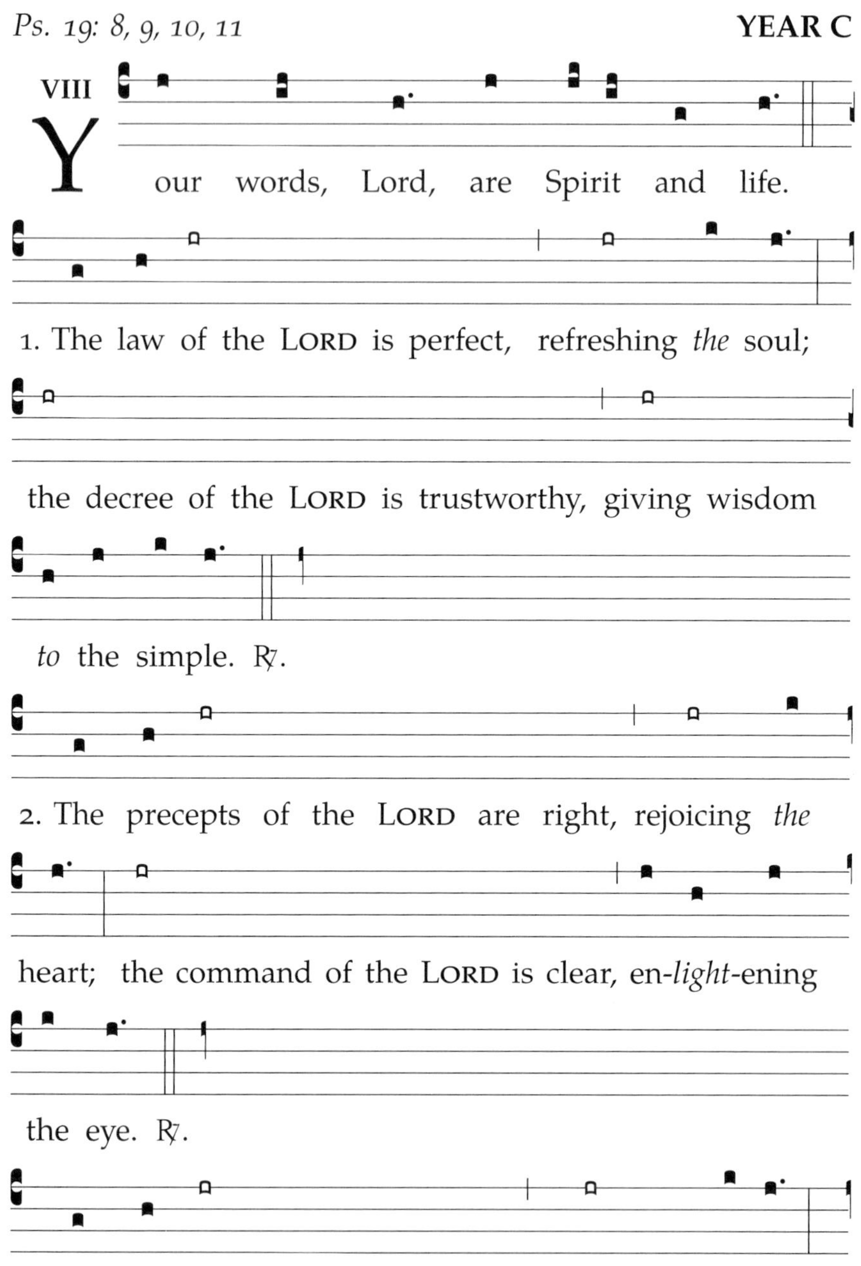

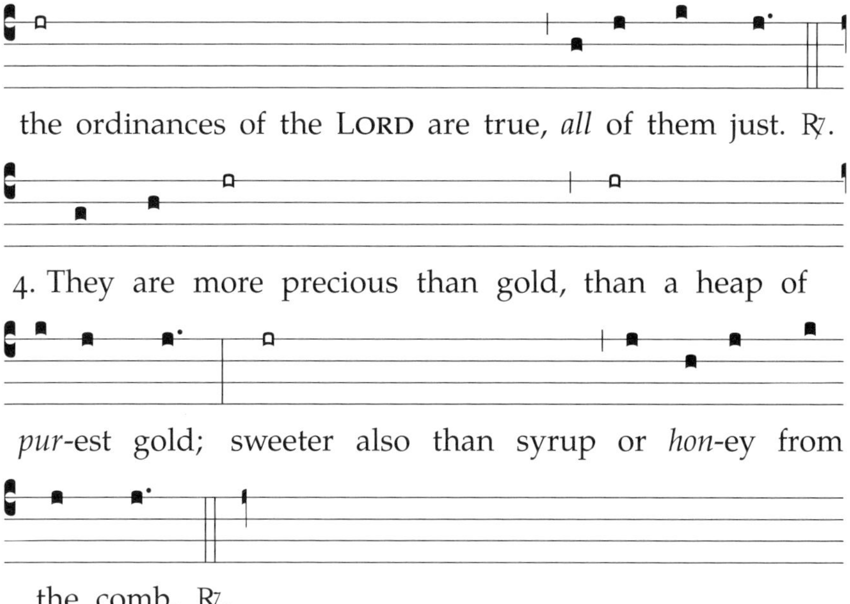
the ordinances of the LORD are true, *all* of them just. ℟.
4. They are more precious than gold, than a heap of
pur-est gold; sweeter also than syrup or *hon*-ey from
the comb. ℟.

16th Sunday in Ordinary Time

Ps. 86: 5-6, 9-10, 15-16 **YEAR A**

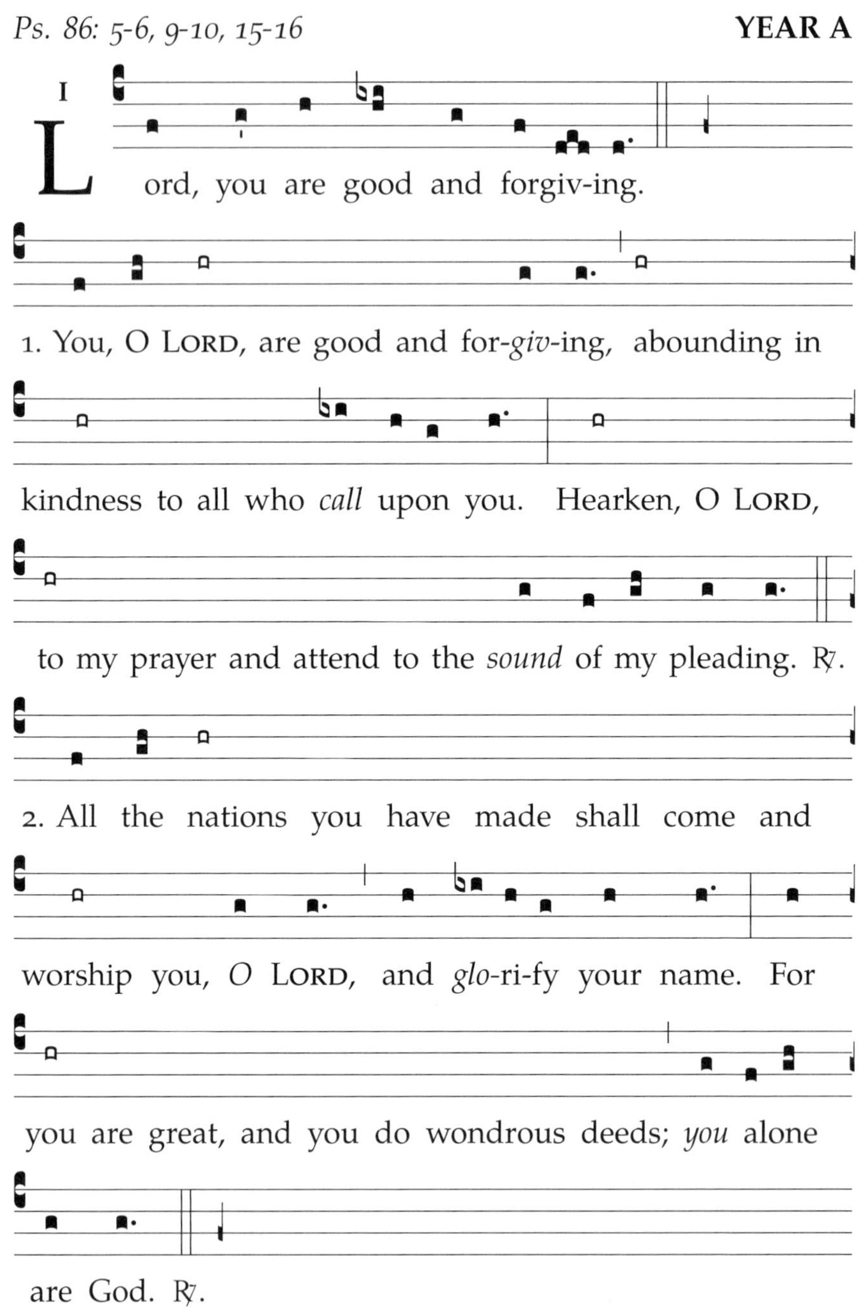
I
Lord, you are good and forgiv-ing.
1. You, O Lord, are good and for-*giv*-ing, abounding in
kindness to all who *call* upon you. Hearken, O Lord,
to my prayer and attend to the *sound* of my pleading. ℟.
2. All the nations you have made shall come and
worship you, *O* Lord, and *glo*-ri-fy your name. For
you are great, and you do wondrous deeds; *you* alone
are God. ℟.

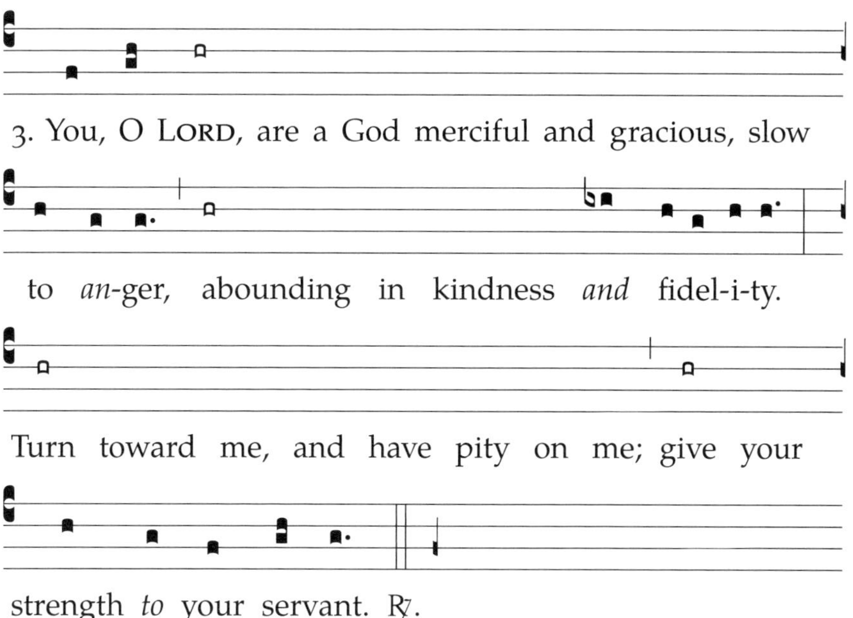
3. You, O LORD, are a God merciful and gracious, slow
to *an*-ger, abounding in kindness *and* fidel-i-ty.
Turn toward me, and have pity on me; give your
strength *to* your servant. ℟.

16TH SUNDAY IN ORDINARY TIME

Ps. 23: 1-3, 3-4, 5, 6 **YEAR B**

VIII
The Lord is my shepherd; there is nothing I
shall want.
1. The LORD is my shepherd; I shall *not* want.
In verdant pastures he gives me *re*-pose; beside
restful waters he leads me; he re-*fresh*-es my soul. ℟.
2. He guides me in right paths for his *name's* sake.
Even though I walk in the dark valley I fear
no *e*-vil; for you are at my side with your

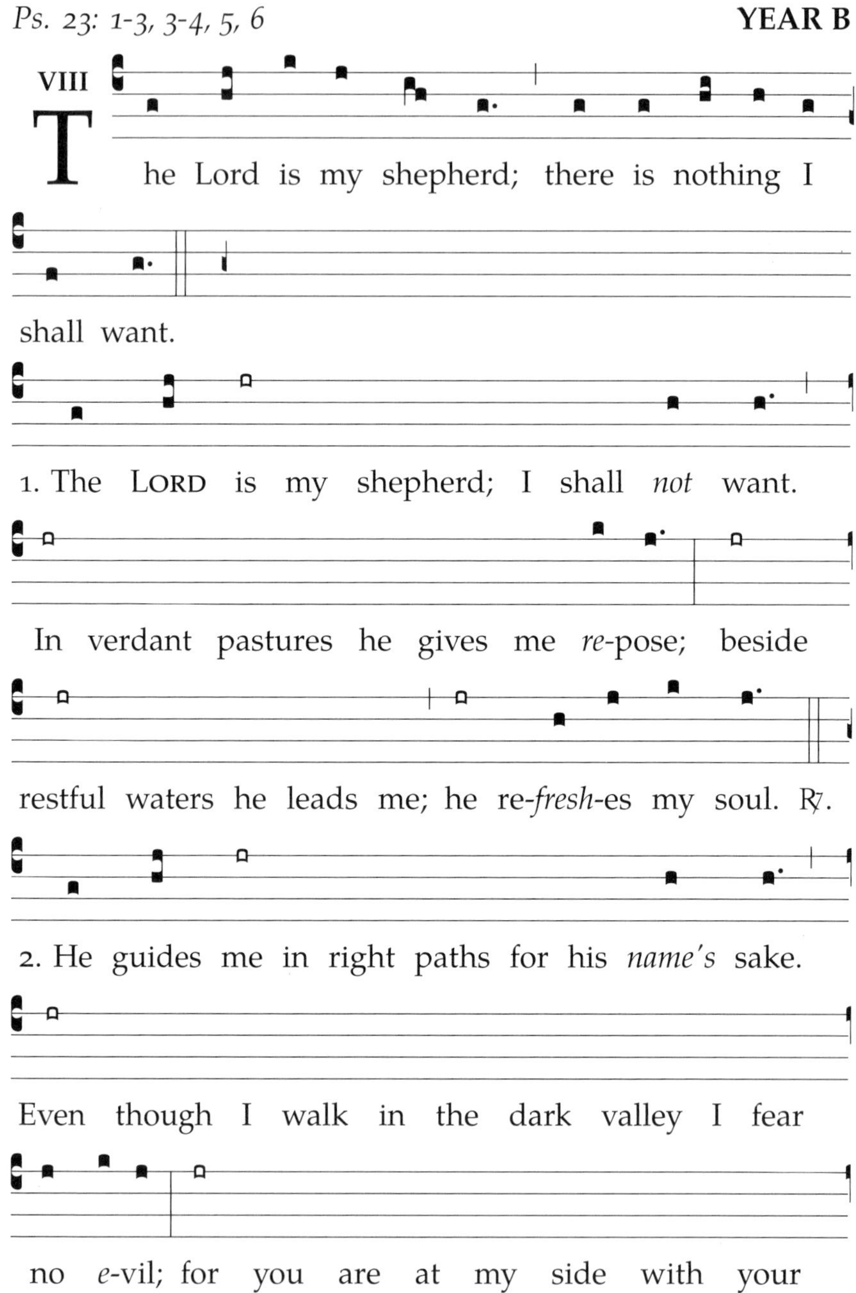

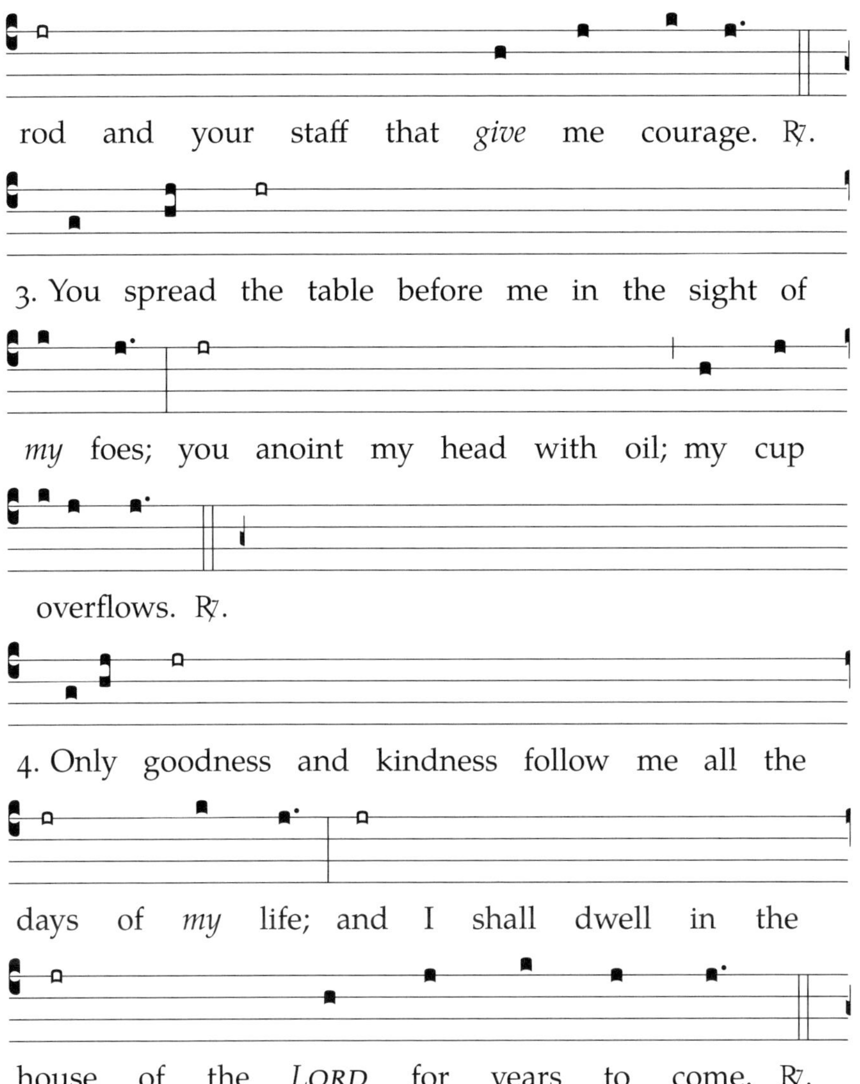
rod and your staff that give me courage. ℟.
3. You spread the table before me in the sight of
my foes; you anoint my head with oil; my cup
overflows. ℟.
4. Only goodness and kindness follow me all the
days of my life; and I shall dwell in the
house of the LORD for years to come. ℟.

16TH SUNDAY IN ORDINARY TIME

Ps. 15: 2-3, 3-4, 5 **YEAR C**

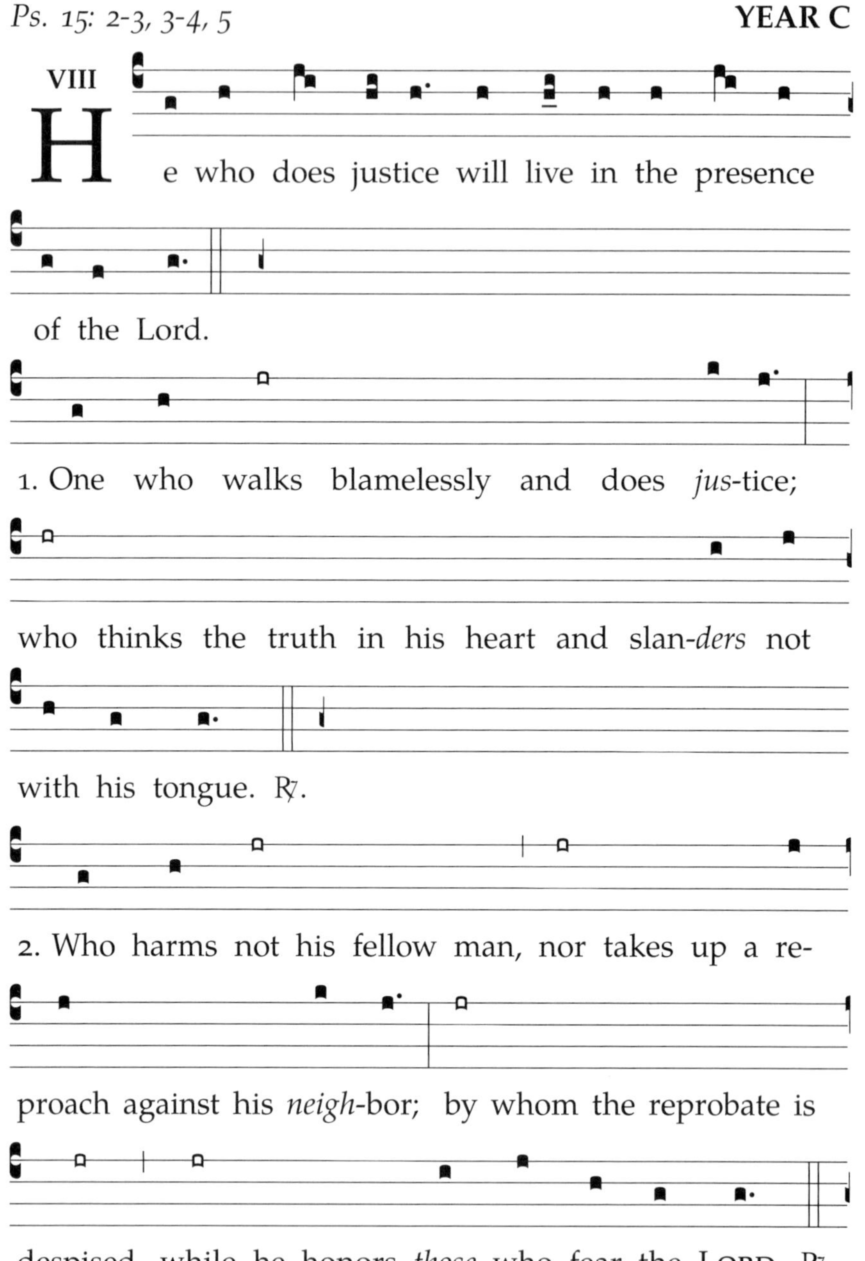

VIII
He who does justice will live in the presence
of the Lord.
1. One who walks blamelessly and does *jus*-tice;
who thinks the truth in his heart and slan-*ders* not
with his tongue. ℟.
2. Who harms not his fellow man, nor takes up a reproach against his *neigh*-bor; by whom the reprobate is
despised, while he honors *those* who fear the LORD. ℟.

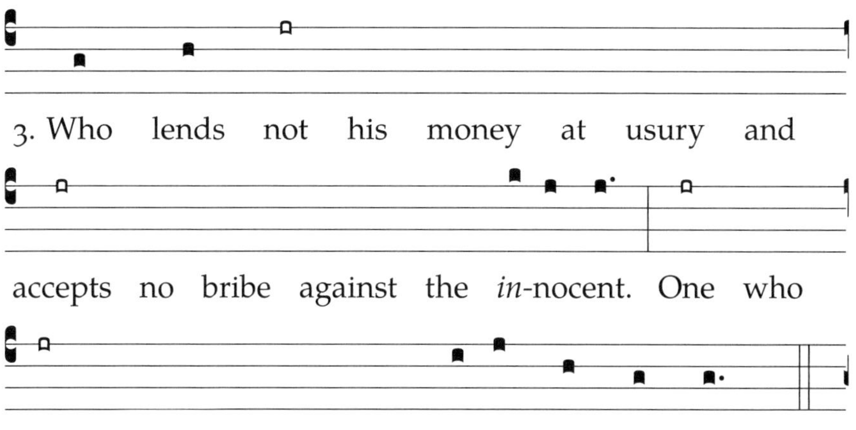
3. Who lends not his money at usury and
accepts no bribe against the *in*-nocent. One who
does these things shall *nev*-er be disturbed. ℟.

17TH SUNDAY IN ORDINARY TIME

Ps. 119: 57, 72, 76-77, 127-128, 129-130 **YEAR A**

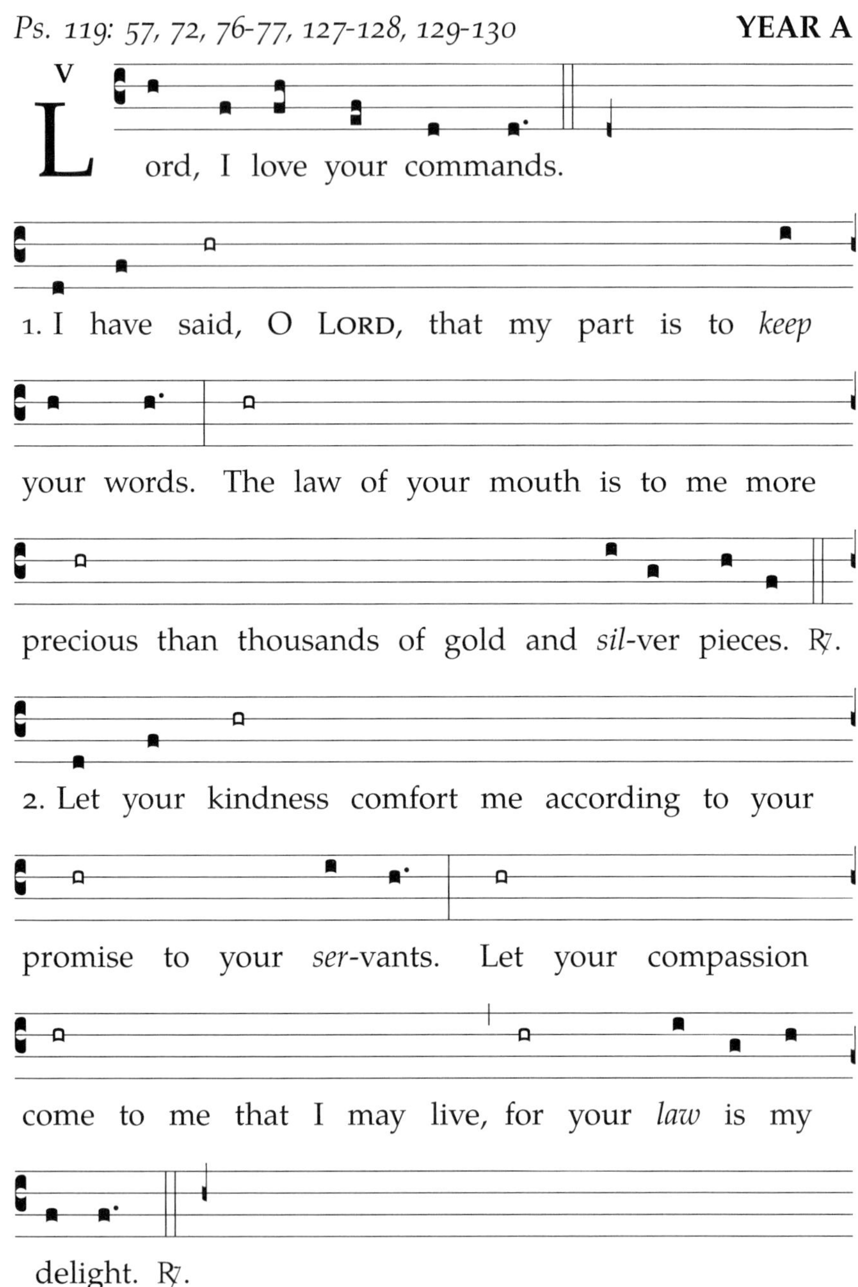

℣
Lord, I love your commands.
1. I have said, O LORD, that my part is to *keep*
your words. The law of your mouth is to me more
precious than thousands of gold and *sil*-ver pieces. ℟.
2. Let your kindness comfort me according to your
promise to your *ser*-vants. Let your compassion
come to me that I may live, for your *law* is my
delight. ℟.

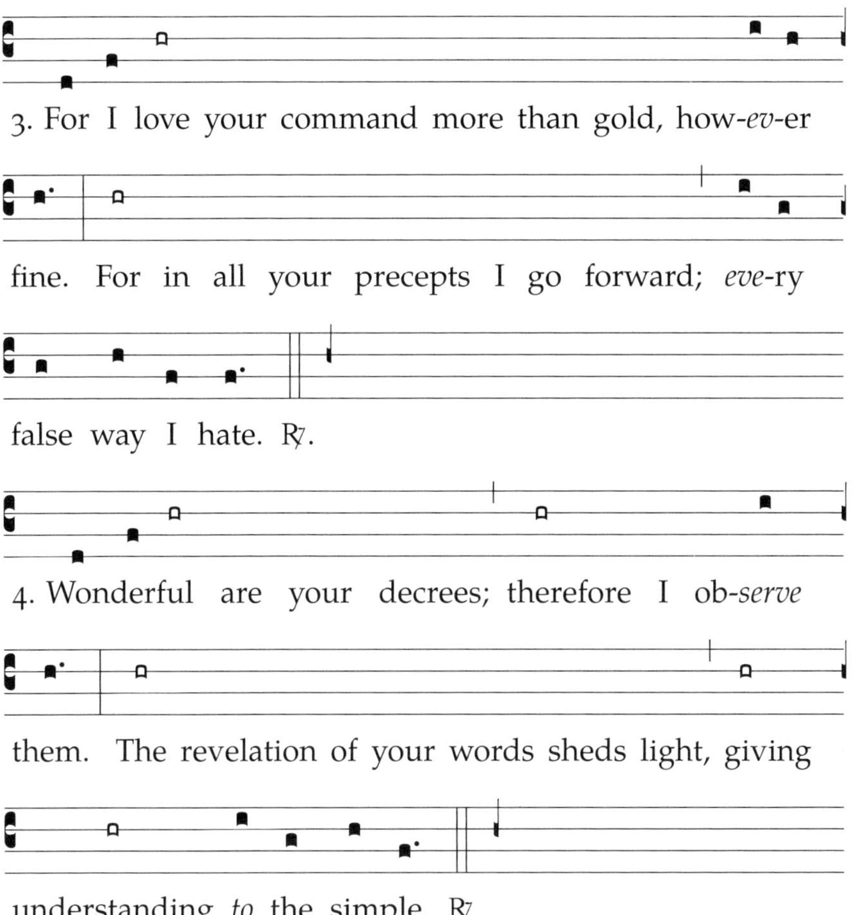
3. For I love your command more than gold, how-*ev*-er
fine. For in all your precepts I go forward; *eve*-ry
false way I hate. ℟.
4. Wonderful are your decrees; therefore I ob-*serve*
them. The revelation of your words sheds light, giving
understanding *to* the simple. ℟.

17TH SUNDAY IN ORDINARY TIME

Ps. 145: 10-11, 15-16, 17-18 **YEAR B**

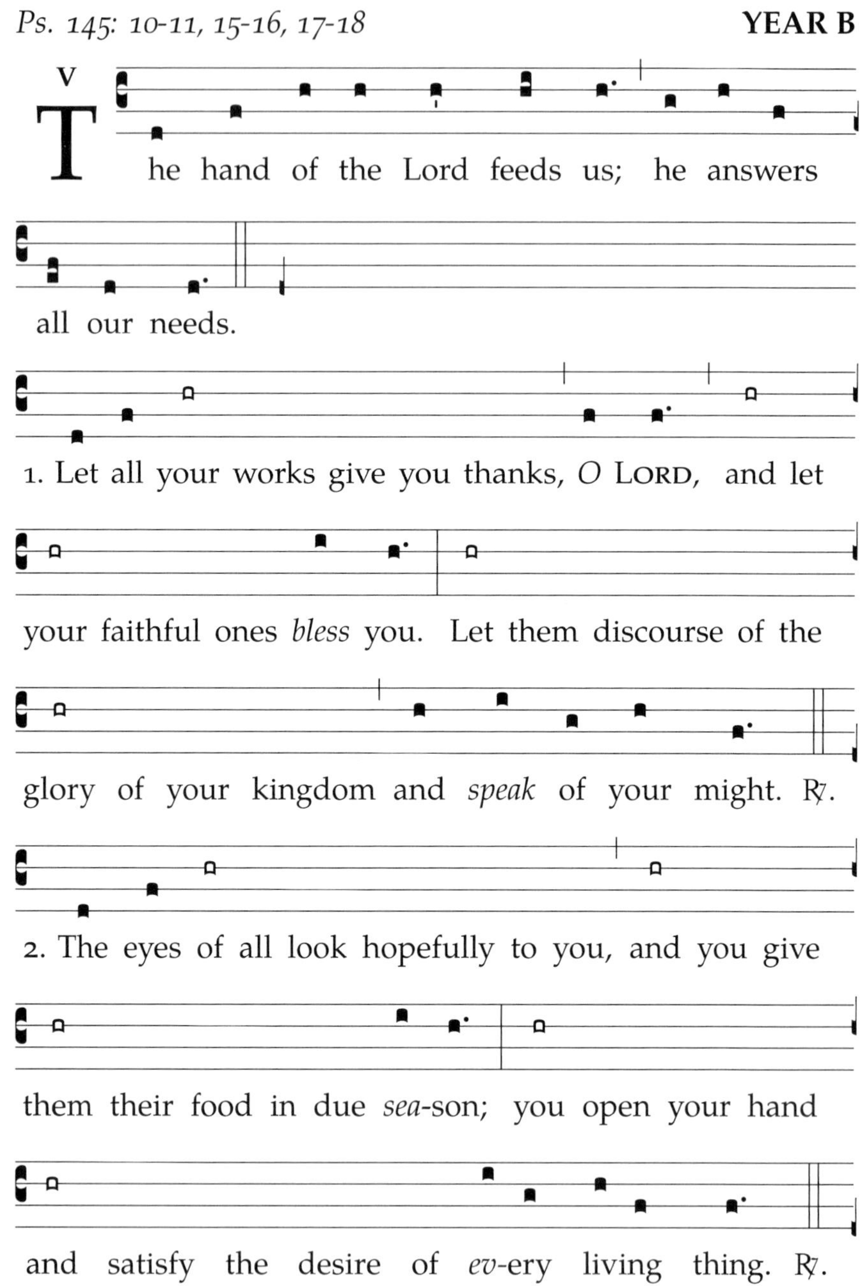

℟.
The hand of the Lord feeds us; he answers all our needs.
1. Let all your works give you thanks, *O* LORD, and let your faithful ones *bless* you. Let them discourse of the glory of your kingdom and *speak* of your might. ℟.
2. The eyes of all look hopefully to you, and you give them their food in due *sea*-son; you open your hand and satisfy the desire of *ev*-ery living thing. ℟.

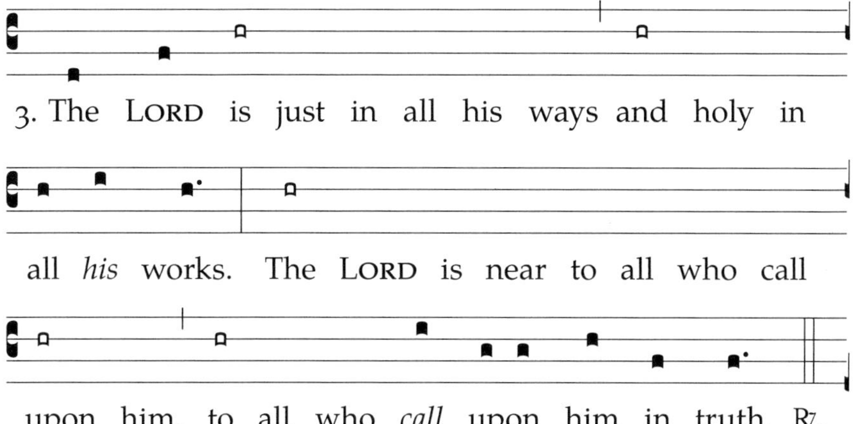
3. The LORD is just in all his ways and holy in
all *his* works. The LORD is near to all who call
upon him, to all who *call* upon him in truth. ℟.

17th Sunday in Ordinary Time

Ps. 138: 1-2, 2-3, 6-7, 7-8 **YEAR C**

II
Lord, on the day I called for help, you
answered me.
1. I will give thanks to you, O LORD, with
all my *heart*, for you have heard the words
of *my* mouth; in the presence of the angels
I will sing your praise; I will worship at
your holy temple and give thanks *to*
your name. ℟.

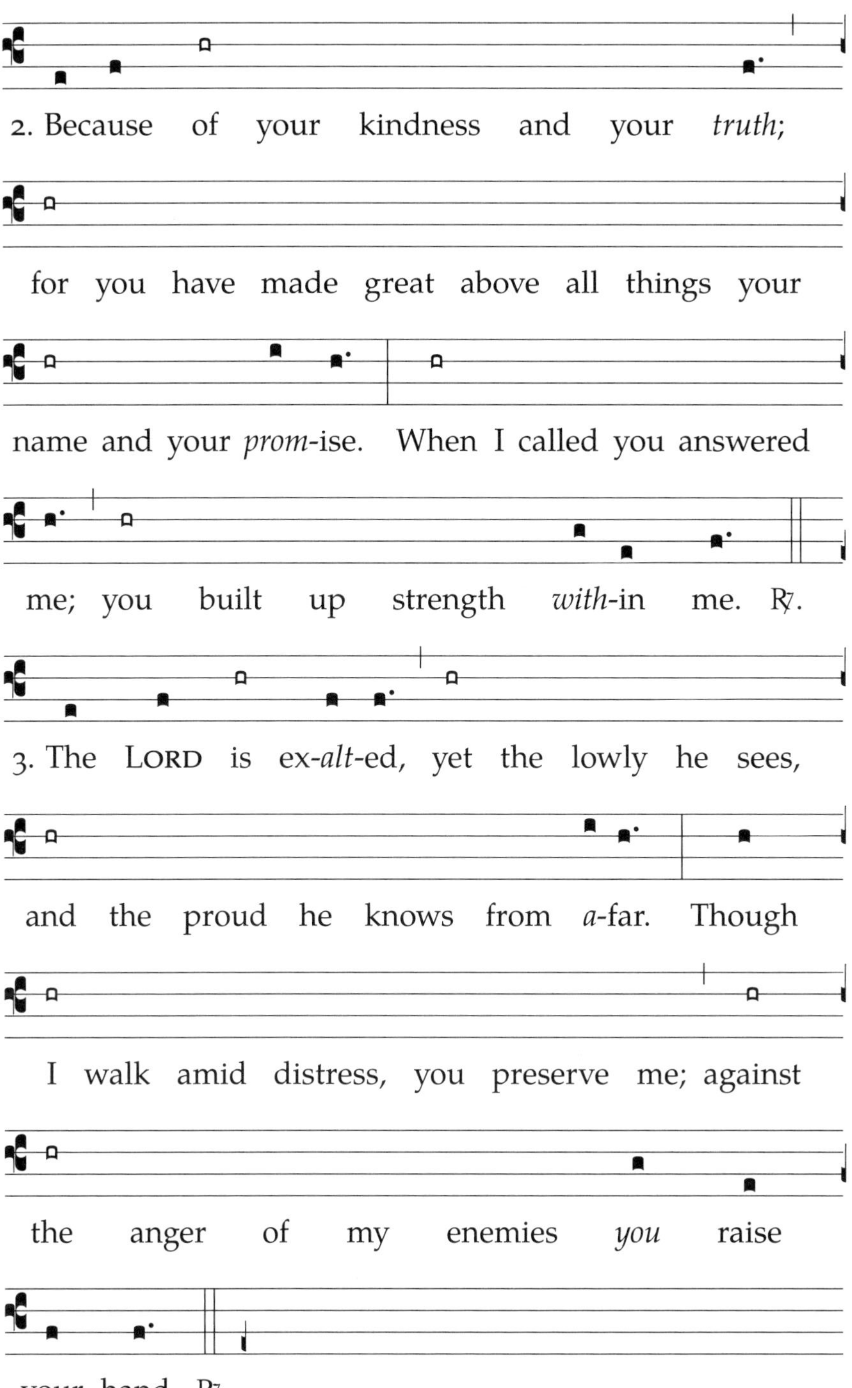
2. Because of your kindness and your *truth;*
for you have made great above all things your
name and your *prom*-ise. When I called you answered
me; you built up strength *with*-in me. ℟.
3. The LORD is ex-*alt*-ed, yet the lowly he sees,
and the proud he knows from *a*-far. Though
I walk amid distress, you preserve me; against
the anger of my enemies *you* raise
your hand. ℟.

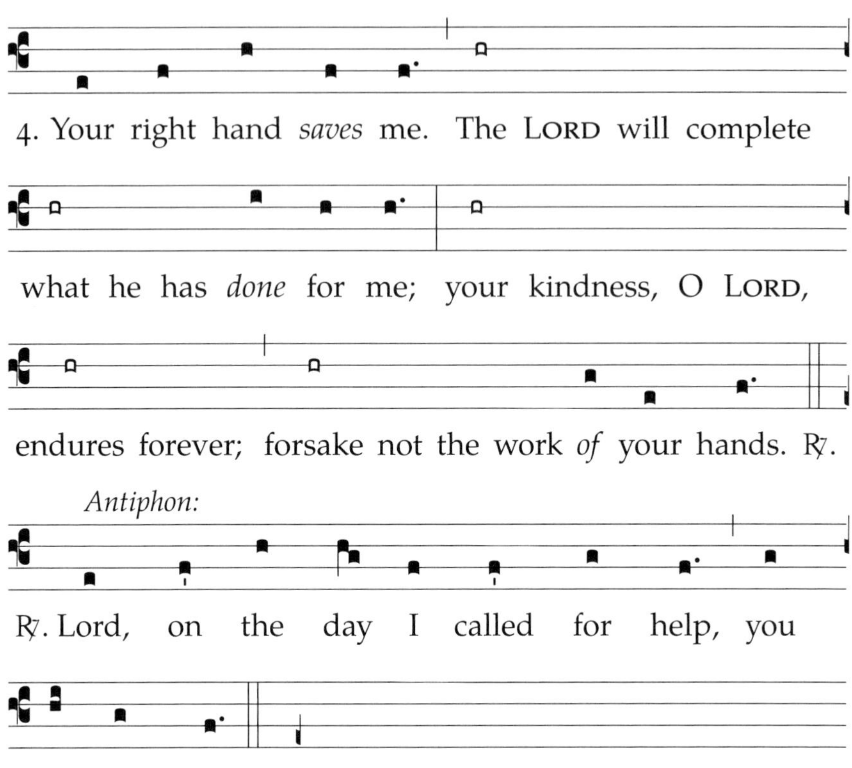
4. Your right hand *saves* me. The LORD will complete
what he has *done* for me; your kindness, O LORD,
endures forever; forsake not the work *of* your hands. ℟.
Antiphon:
℟. Lord, on the day I called for help, you
answered me.

18th Sunday in Ordinary Time

Ps. 145: 8-9, 15-16, 17-18 **YEAR A**

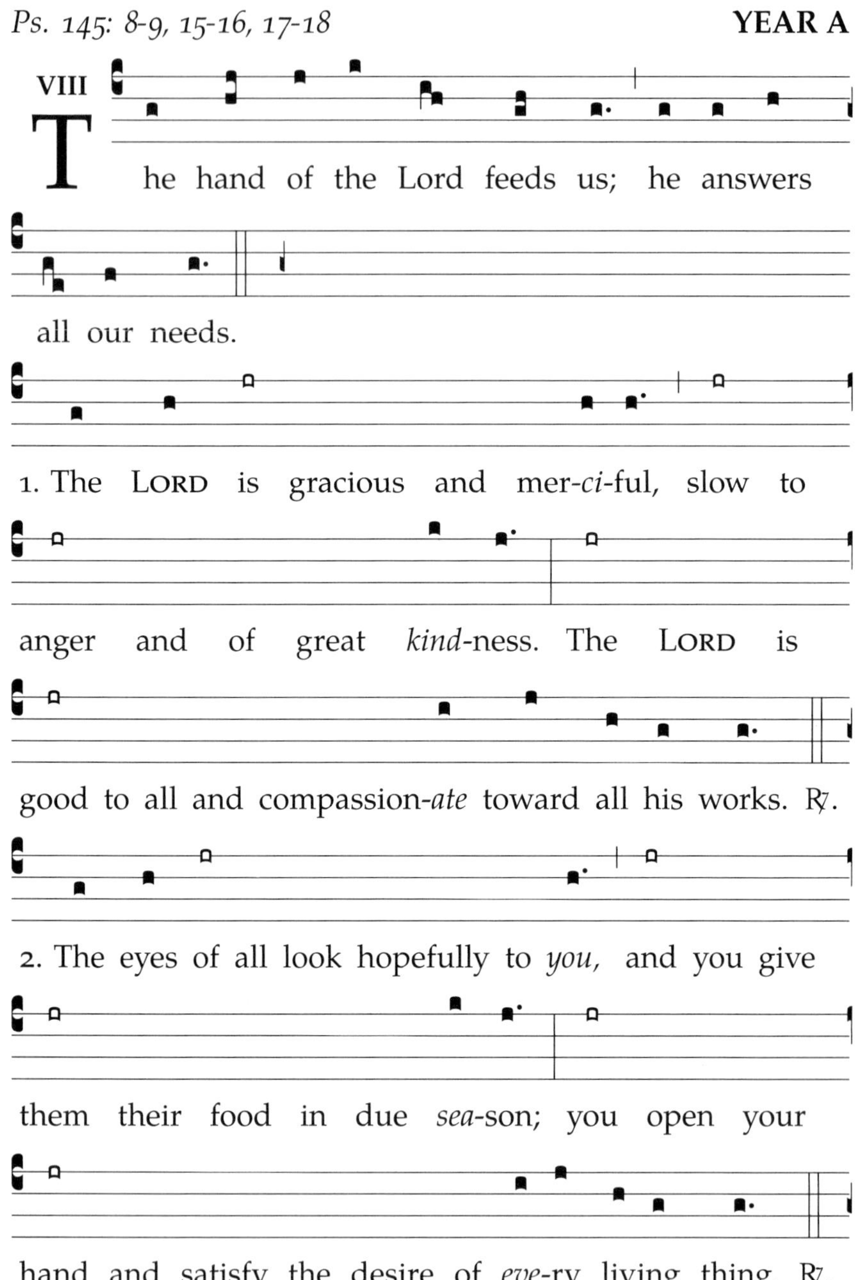
VIII
The hand of the Lord feeds us; he answers all our needs.
1. The LORD is gracious and mer-*ci*-ful, slow to anger and of great *kind*-ness. The LORD is good to all and compassion-*ate* toward all his works. ℟.
2. The eyes of all look hopefully to *you,* and you give them their food in due *sea*-son; you open your hand and satisfy the desire of *eve*-ry living thing. ℟.

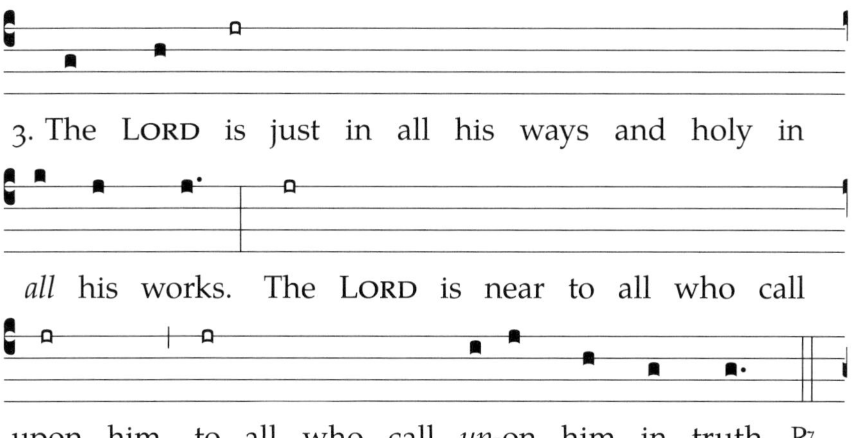
3. The LORD is just in all his ways and holy in
all his works. The LORD is near to all who call
upon him, to all who call *up*-on him in truth. ℟.

18th Sunday in Ordinary Time

Ps. 78: 3-4, 23-24, 25, 54 **YEAR B**

III
The Lord gave them bread from heaven.
1. What we have heard and know, and what our
fathers have declared *to* us, we will declare to the
gener-*a*-tion to come, the glorious deeds of the Lord
and his strength and the wonders *that* he wrought. ℟.
2. He commanded the skies above and opened the
doors of heaven; he rained manna upon them
for food and gave them *heaven*-ly bread. ℟.

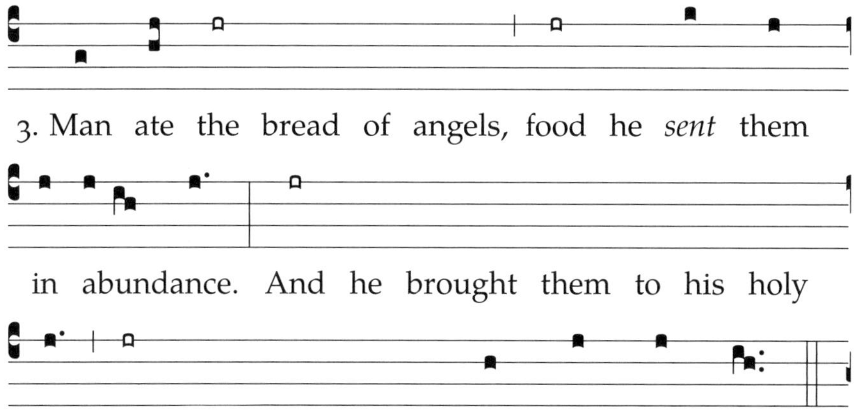
3. Man ate the bread of angels, food he *sent* them
in abundance. And he brought them to his holy

land, to the mountains his *right* hand had won. ℟.

18th Sunday in Ordinary Time

Ps. 90: 3-4, 5-6, 12-13, 14, 17 **YEAR C**

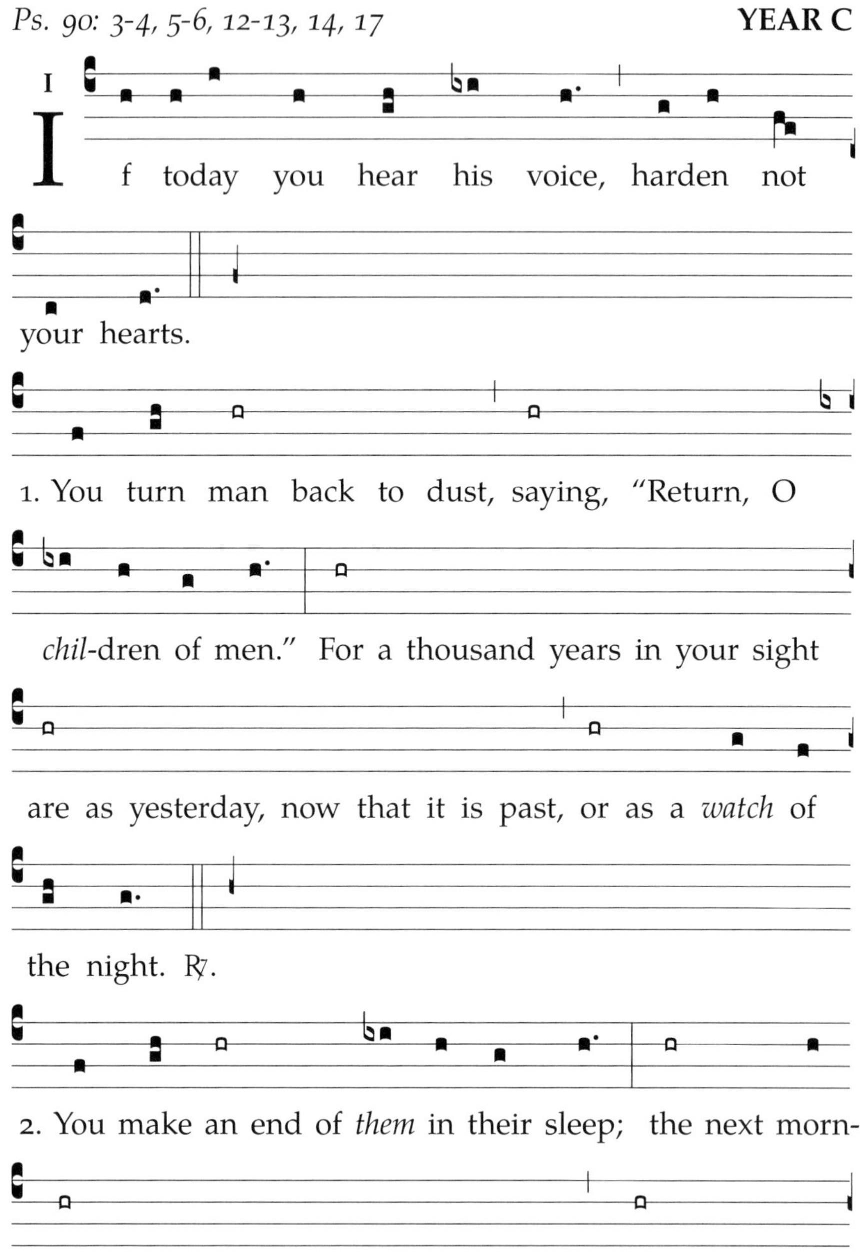

I
If today you hear his voice, harden not
your hearts.
1. You turn man back to dust, saying, "Return, O
chil-dren of men." For a thousand years in your sight
are as yesterday, now that it is past, or as a *watch* of
the night. ℟.
2. You make an end of *them* in their sleep; the next morning they are like the changing grass, which at dawn

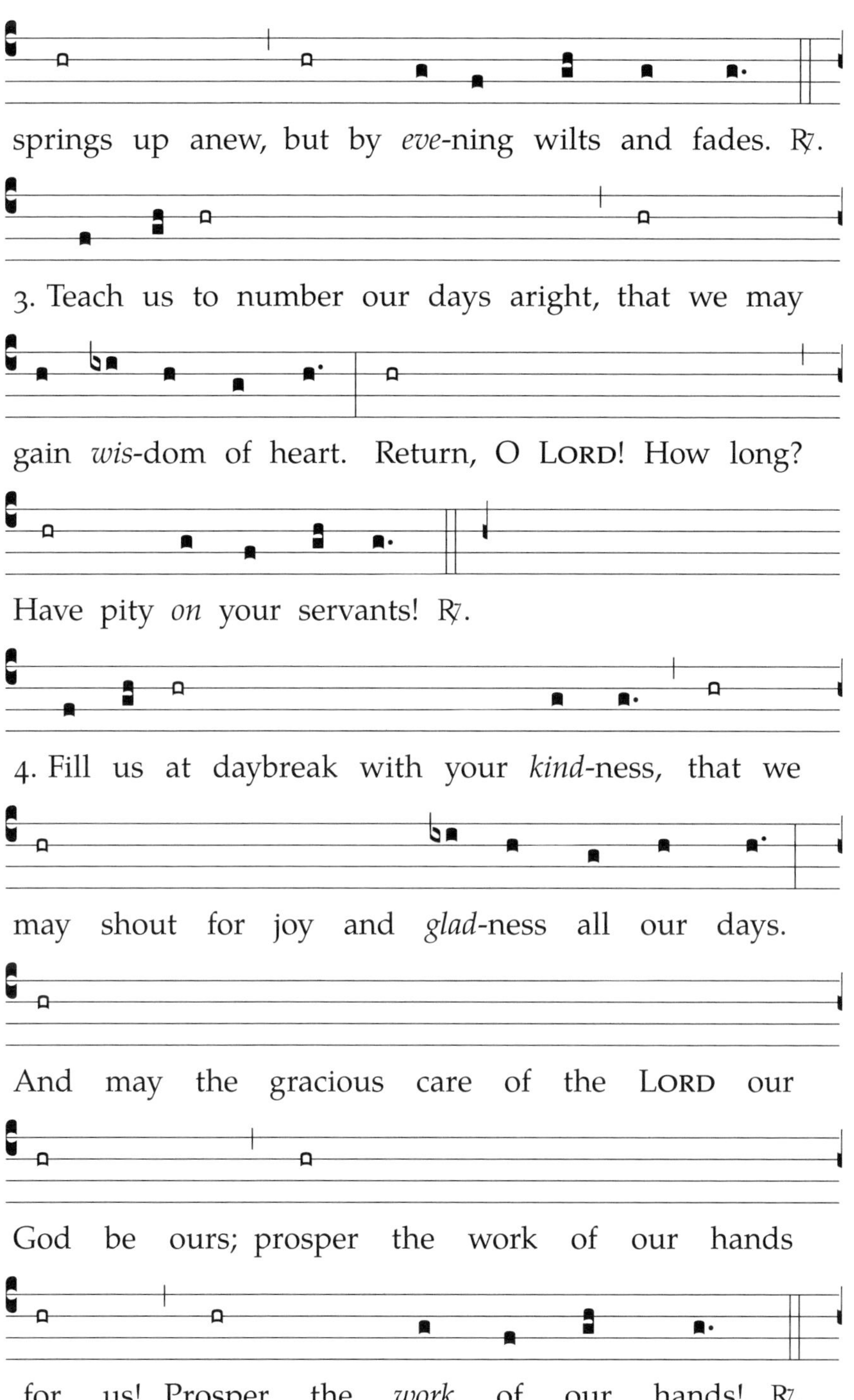
springs up anew, but by eve-ning wilts and fades. ℟.
3. Teach us to number our days aright, that we may
gain wis-dom of heart. Return, O LORD! How long?
Have pity on your servants! ℟.
4. Fill us at daybreak with your kind-ness, that we
may shout for joy and glad-ness all our days.
And may the gracious care of the LORD our
God be ours; prosper the work of our hands
for us! Prosper the work of our hands! ℟.

19TH SUNDAY IN ORDINARY TIME

Ps. 85: 9, 10, 11-12, 13-14 **YEAR A**

II
Lord, let us see your kindness, and grant us
your salvation.
1. I will hear what God proclaims; the LORD — for
he pro-*claims* peace. Near indeed is his salvation
to those who fear him, glory dwelling *in* our land. ℟.
2. Kind-ness and truth shall meet; justice and peace
shall kiss. Truth shall spring out of the earth, and
justice shall look *down* from heaven. ℟.

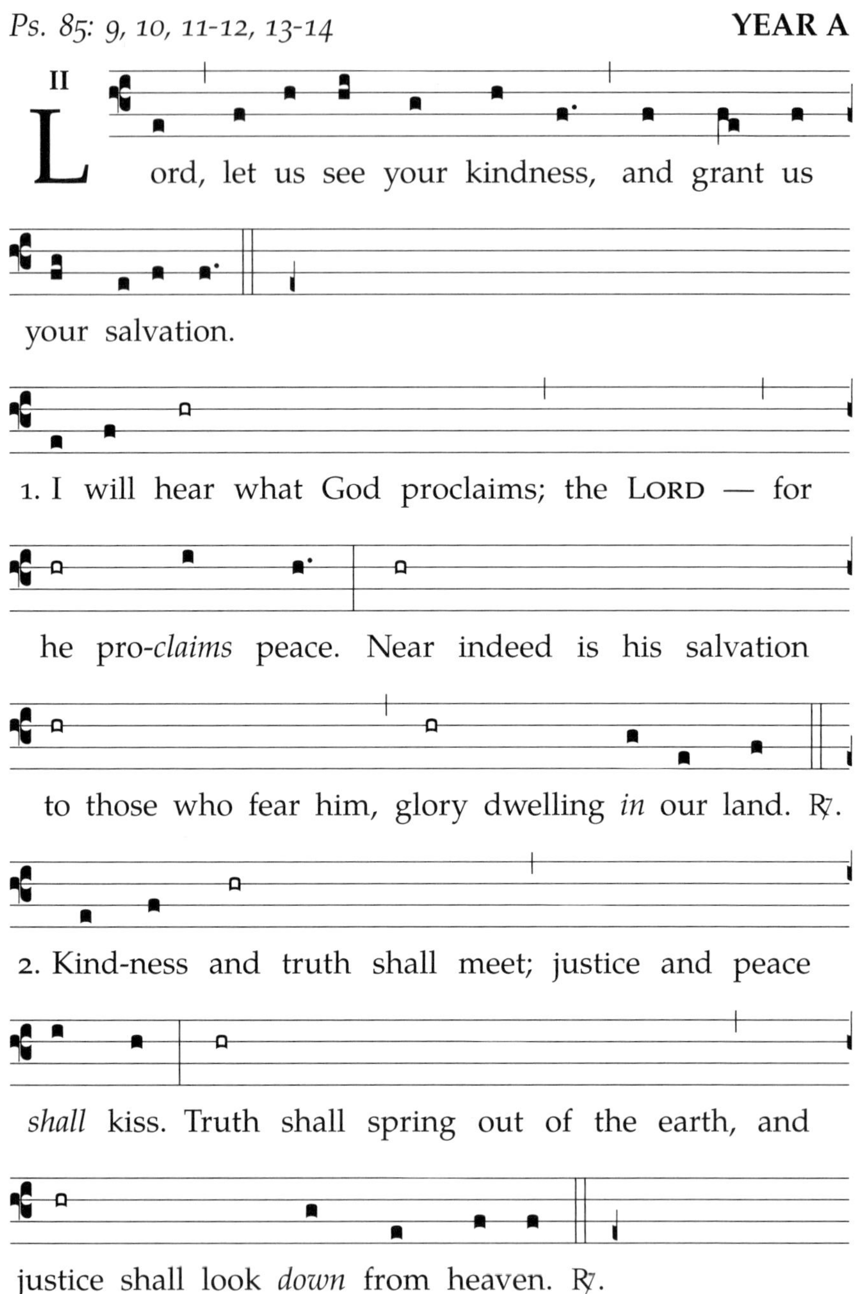

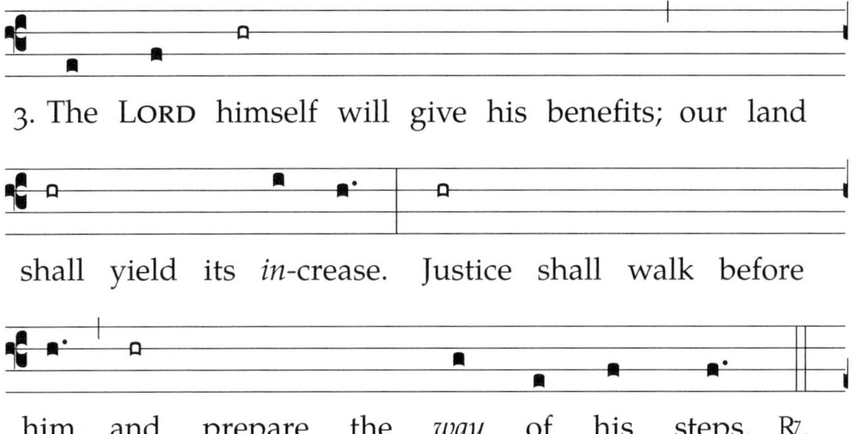
3. The LORD himself will give his benefits; our land
shall yield its *in*-crease. Justice shall walk before
him, and prepare the *way* of his steps. ℟.

19th Sunday in Ordinary Time (alternate setting)

Ps. 85: 9, 10, 11-12, 13-14 **YEAR A**

V
Lord, let us see your kindness, and grant us
your salva-tion.
1. I will hear what God *pro*-claims; the LORD — for
he pro-*claims* peace. Near indeed is his salvation to
those who fear him, glory *dwell*-ing in our land. ℟.
2. Kindness and truth shall meet; justice and *peace*
shall kiss. Truth shall spring out of the earth,
and justice shall look *down* from heaven. ℟.

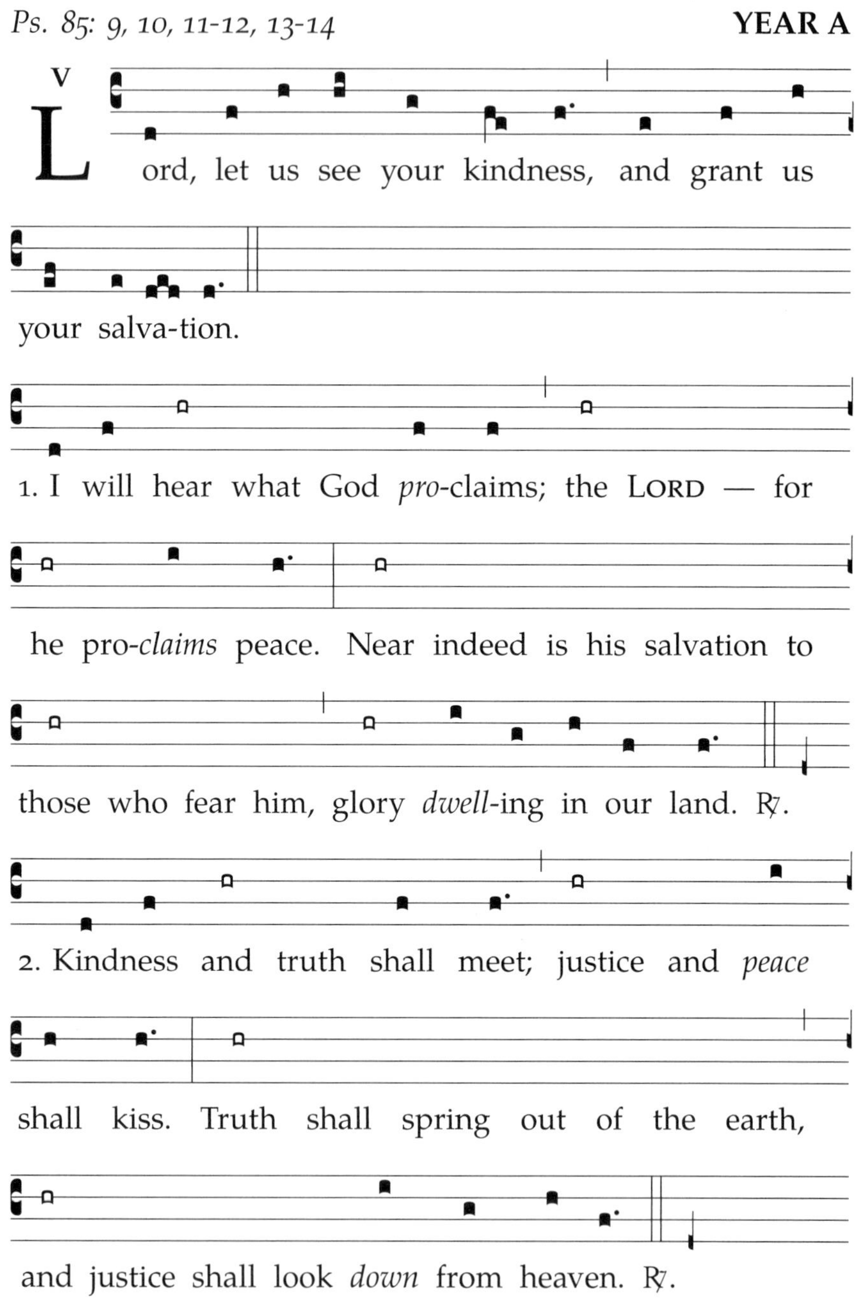

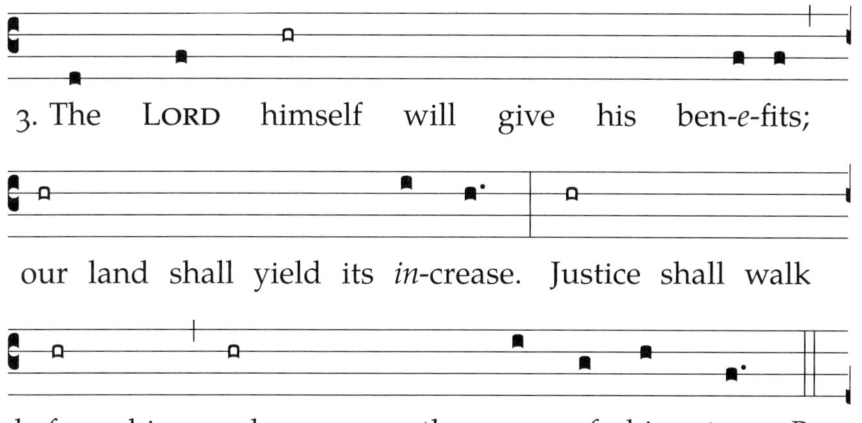
3. The LORD himself will give his ben-*e*-fits;
our land shall yield its *in*-crease. Justice shall walk
before him, and prepare the *way* of his steps. ℟.

19TH SUNDAY IN ORDINARY TIME

Ps. 34: 2-3, 4-5, 6-7, 8-9 **YEAR B**

VIII
Taste and see the goodness of the Lord.
1. I will bless the LORD at all times; his praise shall
be ever in *my* mouth. Let my soul glory in
the LORD; the lowly will *hear* me and be glad. ℟.
2. Glori-fy the LORD with me, let us together
extol *his* name. I sought the LORD, and he
answered me and delivered *me* from all
my fears. ℟.

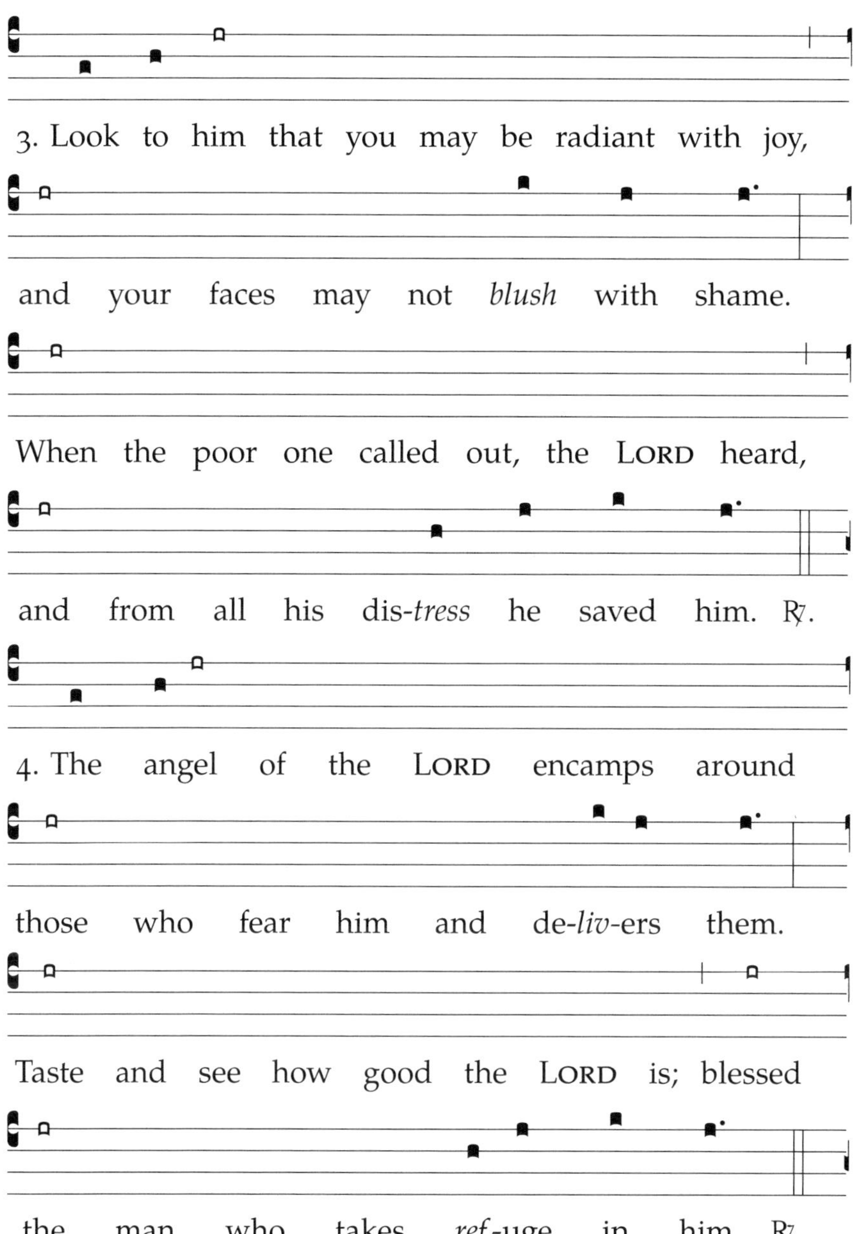
3. Look to him that you may be radiant with joy,
and your faces may not *blush* with shame.
When the poor one called out, the LORD heard,
and from all his dis-*tress* he saved him. ℟.
4. The angel of the LORD encamps around
those who fear him and de-*liv*-ers them.
Taste and see how good the LORD is; blessed
the man who takes *ref*-uge in him. ℟.

19th Sunday in Ordinary Time

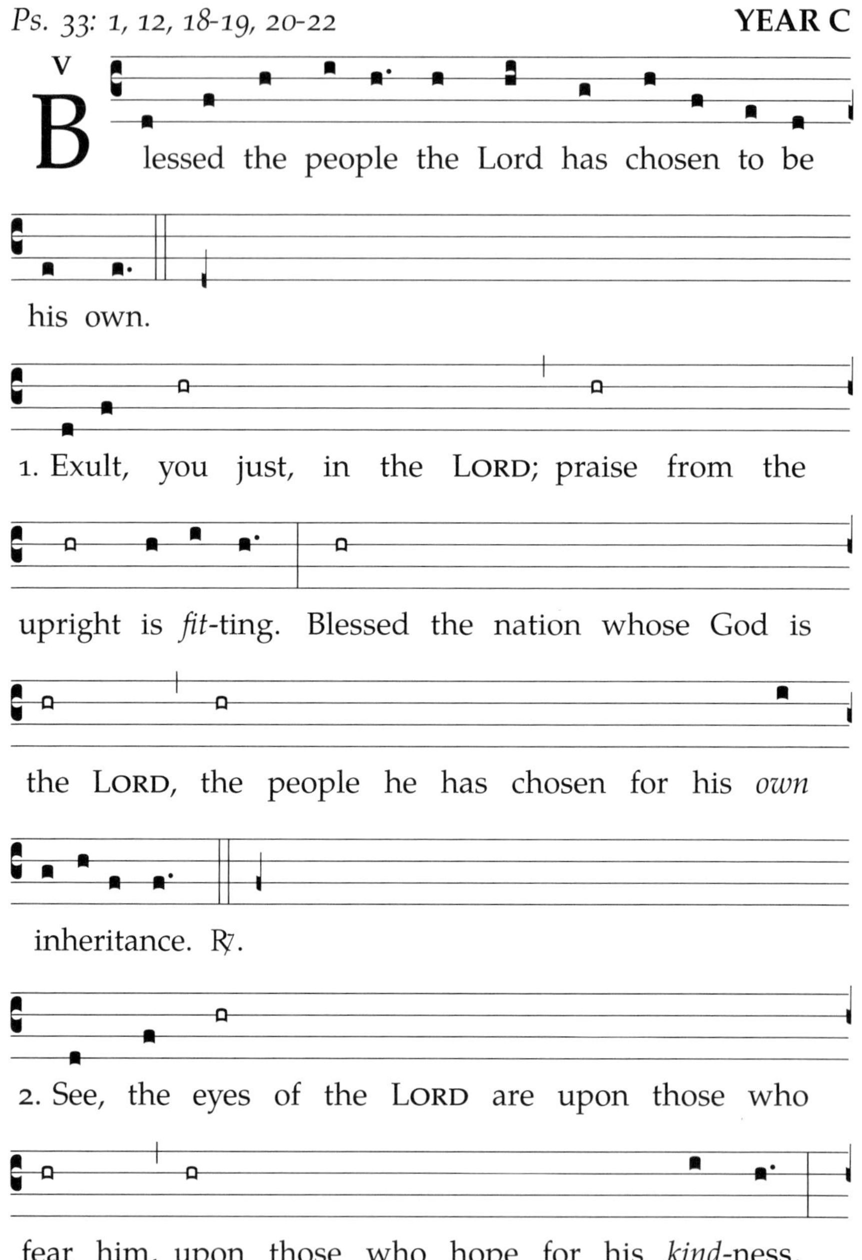
Ps. 33: 1, 12, 18-19, 20-22
YEAR C
V
Blessed the people the Lord has chosen to be
his own.
1. Exult, you just, in the LORD; praise from the
upright is fit-ting. Blessed the nation whose God is
the LORD, the people he has chosen for his own
inheritance. ℟.
2. See, the eyes of the LORD are upon those who
fear him, upon those who hope for his kind-ness,

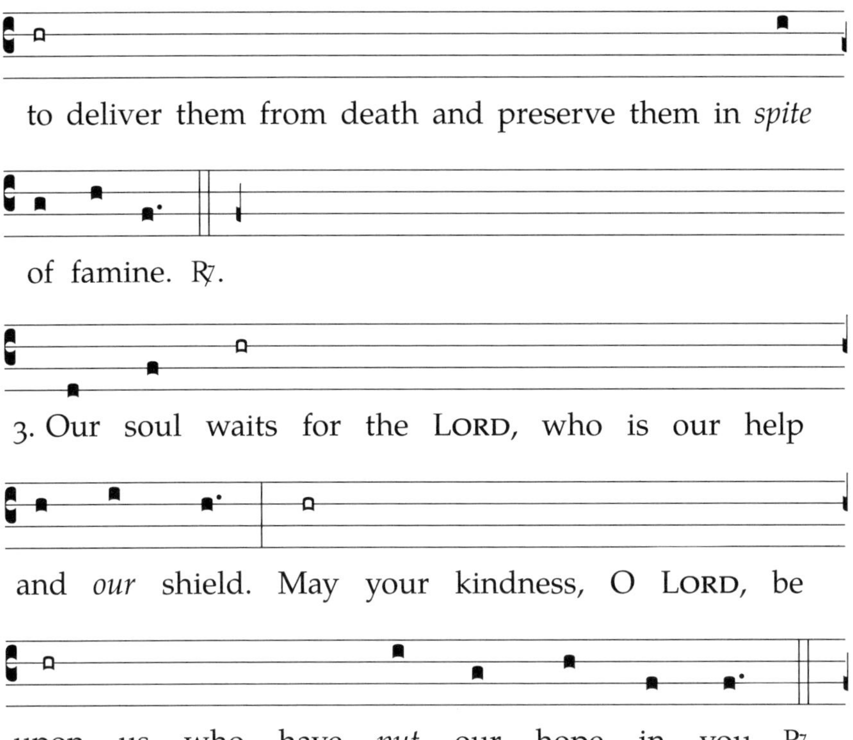
to deliver them from death and preserve them in *spite*
of famine. ℟.
3. Our soul waits for the LORD, who is our help
and *our* shield. May your kindness, O LORD, be
upon us who have *put* our hope in you. ℟.

20TH SUNDAY IN ORDINARY TIME

Ps. 67: 2-3, 5, 6, 8 **YEAR A**

VIII
O God, let all the nations praise you!
1. May God have pity on us and bless us; may he
let his face shine up-*on* us. So may your way
be known upon earth; among all nations, *your*
salvation. ℟.
2. May the nations be glad and exult because you rule
the peoples in *eq*-uity; the nations *on* the earth you
guide. ℟.

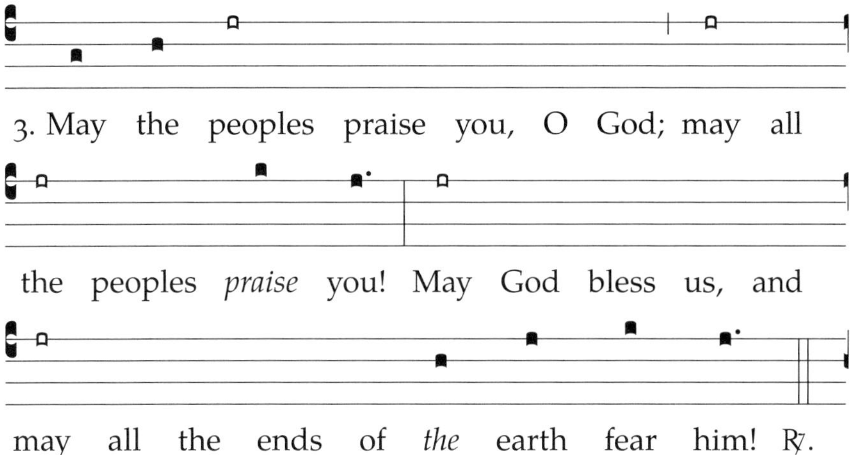
3. May the peoples praise you, O God; may all
the peoples praise you! May God bless us, and
may all the ends of the earth fear him! ℟.

20TH SUNDAY IN ORDINARY TIME

Ps. 34: 2-3, 4-5, 6-7 **YEAR B**

VIII
Taste and see the goodness of the Lord.
1. I will bless the LORD at all times; his praise shall
be ever in *my* mouth. Let my soul glory in
the LORD; the lowly will *hear* me and be glad. ℟.
2. Glori-fy the LORD with me, let us together
extol *his* name. I sought the LORD, and he
answered me and delivered *me* from all
my fears. ℟.

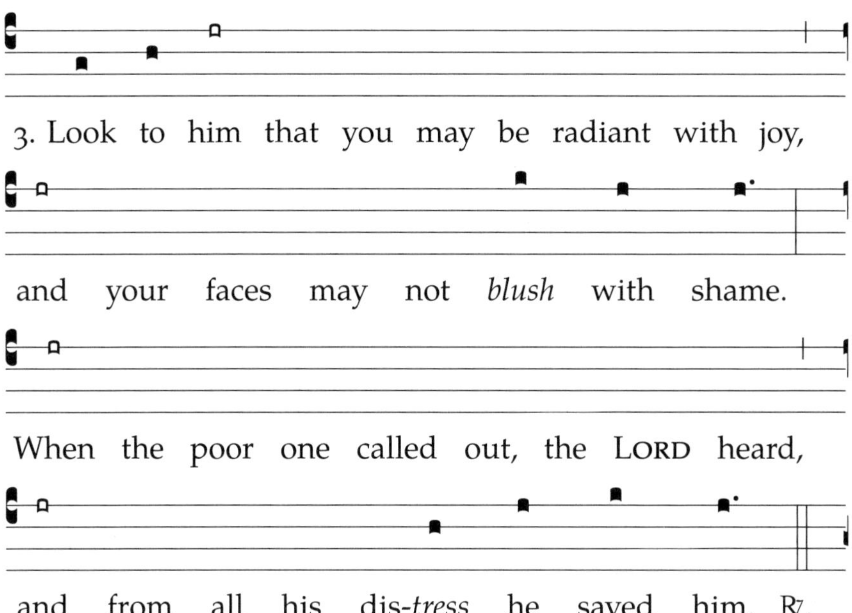
3. Look to him that you may be radiant with joy,
and your faces may not *blush* with shame.
When the poor one called out, the LORD heard,
and from all his dis-*tress* he saved him. ℟.

20th Sunday in Ordinary Time

Ps. 40: 2, 3, 4, 18 **YEAR C**

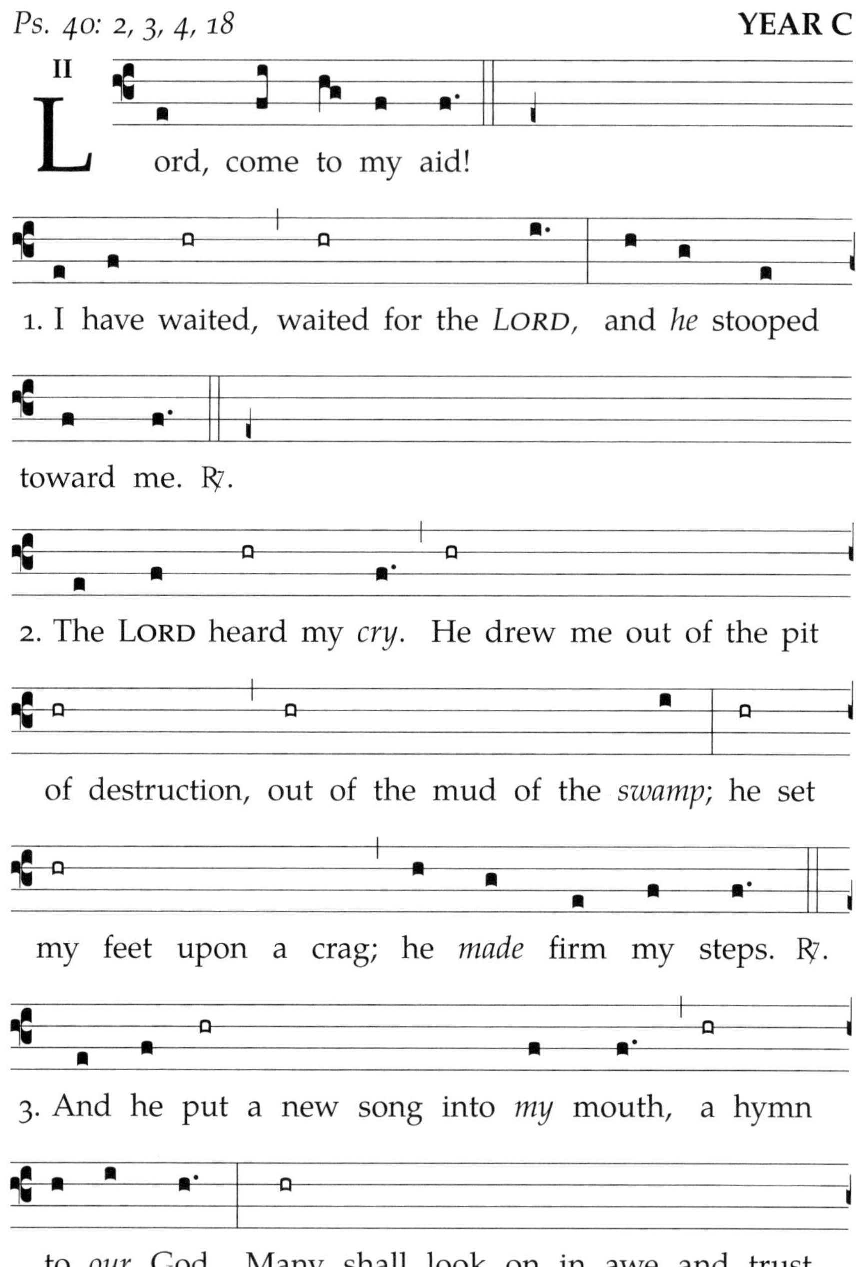
II
Lord, come to my aid!
1. I have waited, waited for the *Lord,* and *he* stooped
toward me. ℟.
2. The Lord heard my *cry.* He drew me out of the pit
of destruction, out of the mud of the *swamp;* he set
my feet upon a crag; he *made* firm my steps. ℟.
3. And he put a new song into *my* mouth, a hymn
to *our* God. Many shall look on in awe and trust

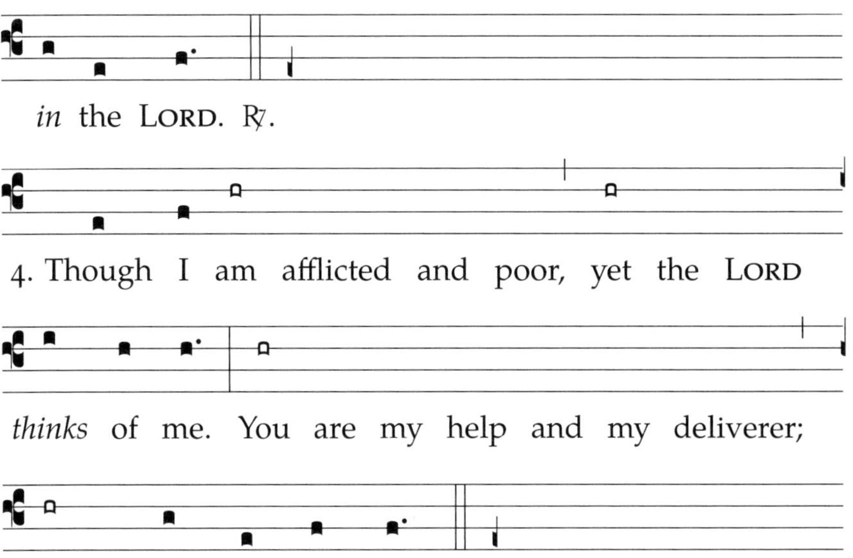
in the LORD. ℟.
4. Though I am afflicted and poor, yet the LORD
thinks of me. You are my help and my deliverer;
O my *God*, hold not back! ℟.

21st Sunday in Ordinary Time

Ps. 138: 1-2, 2-3, 6, 8 **YEAR A**

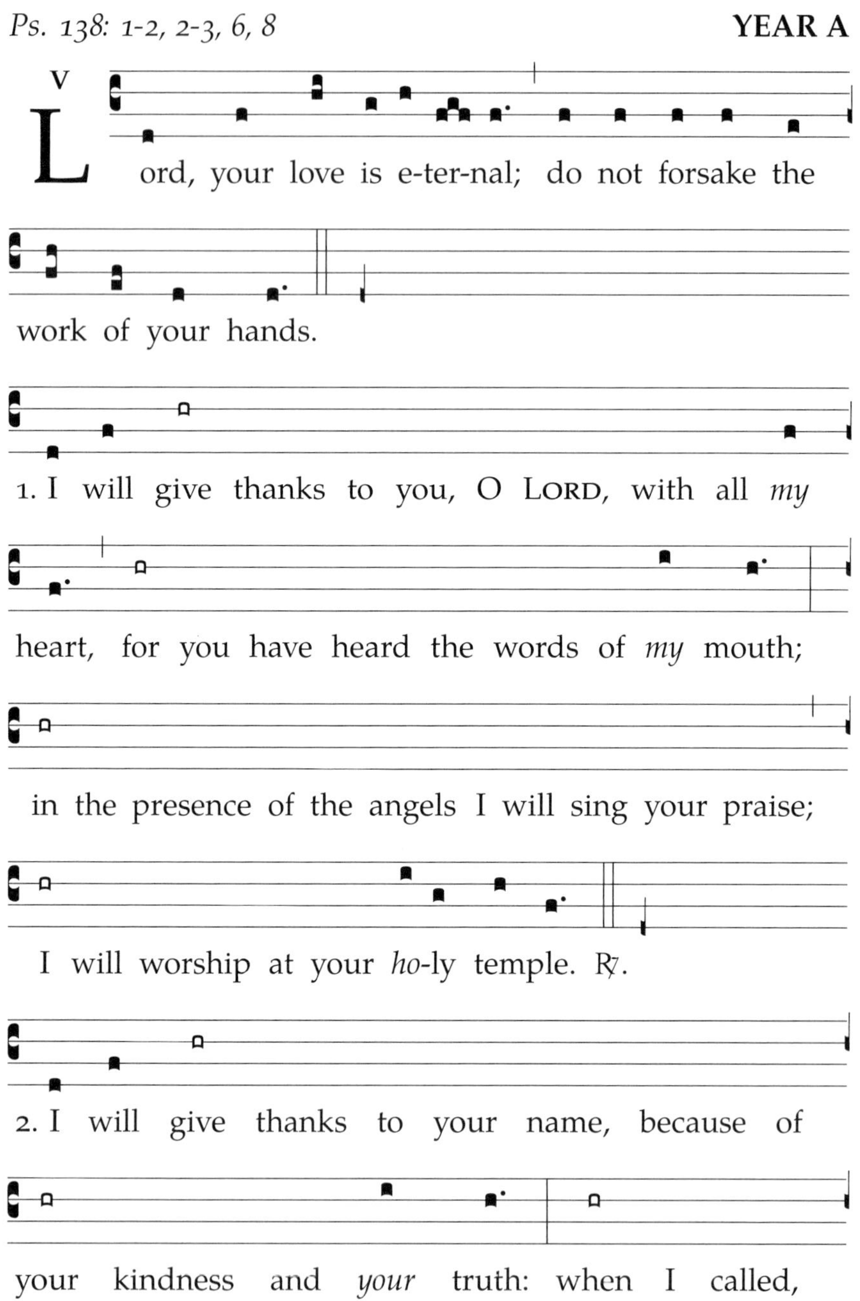

℟
Lord, your love is e-ter-nal; do not forsake the
work of your hands.
1. I will give thanks to you, O Lord, with all *my*
heart, for you have heard the words of *my* mouth;
in the presence of the angels I will sing your praise;
I will worship at your *ho*-ly temple. ℟.
2. I will give thanks to your name, because of
your kindness and *your* truth: when I called,

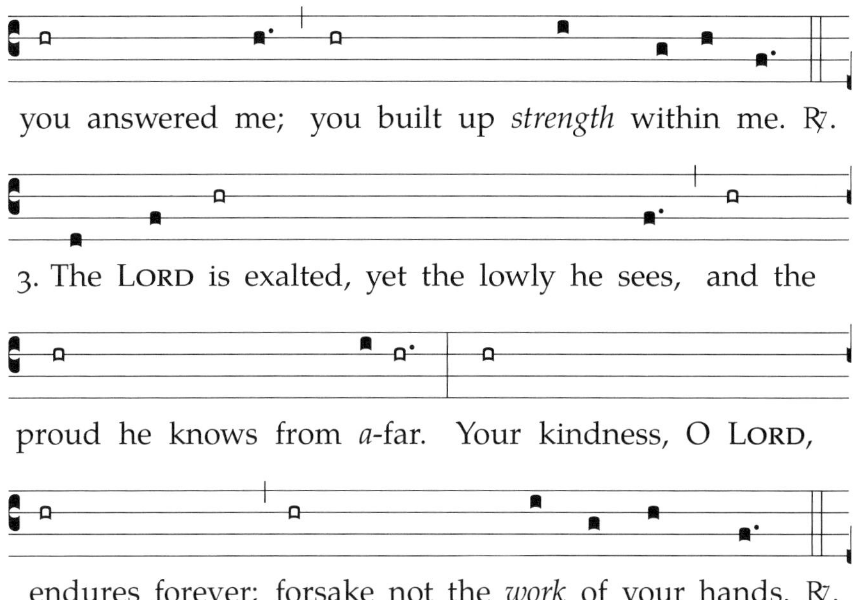
you answered me; you built up *strength* within me. ℟.
3. The LORD is exalted, yet the lowly he sees, and the
proud he knows from *a*-far. Your kindness, O LORD,
endures forever; forsake not the *work* of your hands. ℟.

21TH SUNDAY IN ORDINARY TIME

Ps. 34: 2-3, 16-17, 18-19, 20-21 **YEAR B**

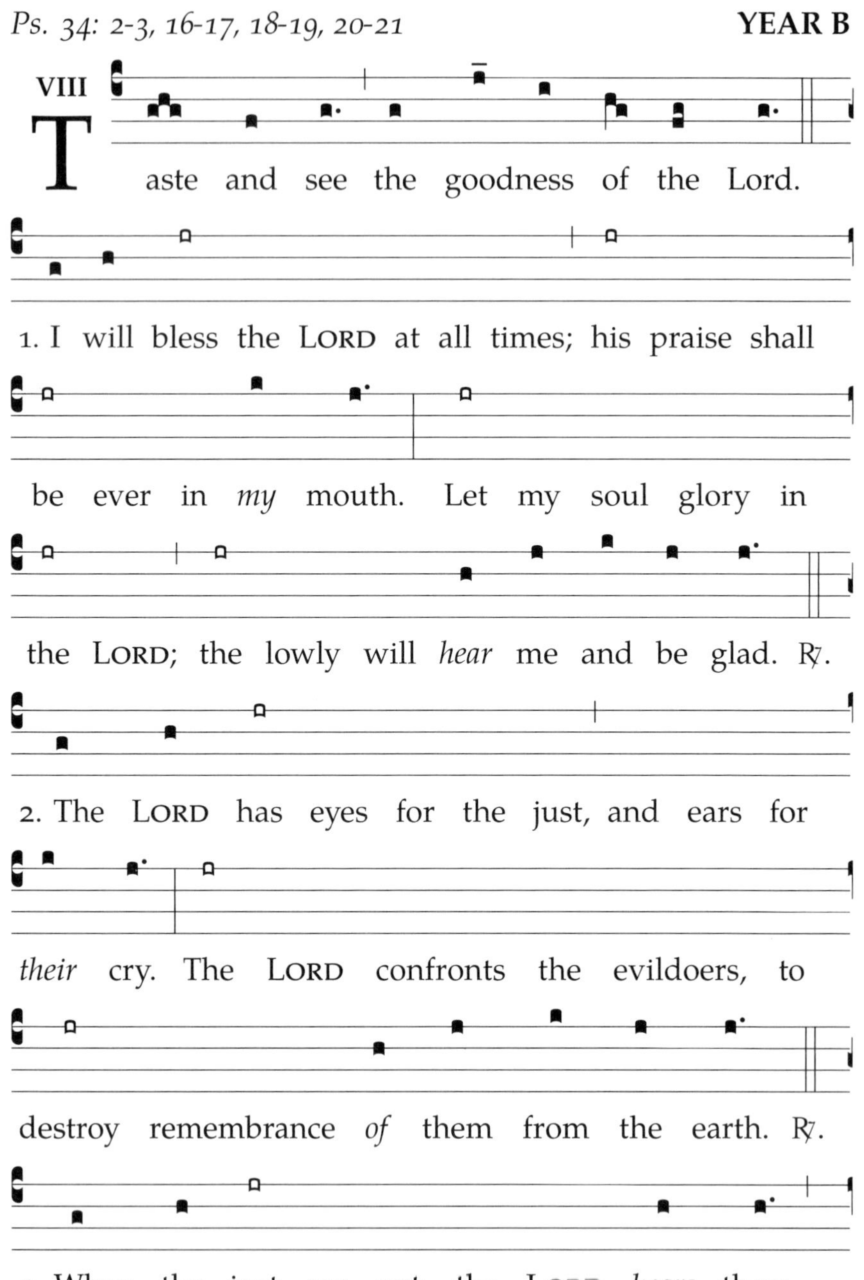
VIII
Taste and see the goodness of the Lord.
1. I will bless the LORD at all times; his praise shall
be ever in *my* mouth. Let my soul glory in
the LORD; the lowly will *hear* me and be glad. ℟.
2. The LORD has eyes for the just, and ears for
their cry. The LORD confronts the evildoers, to
destroy remembrance *of* them from the earth. ℟.
3. When the just cry out, the LORD *hears* them,

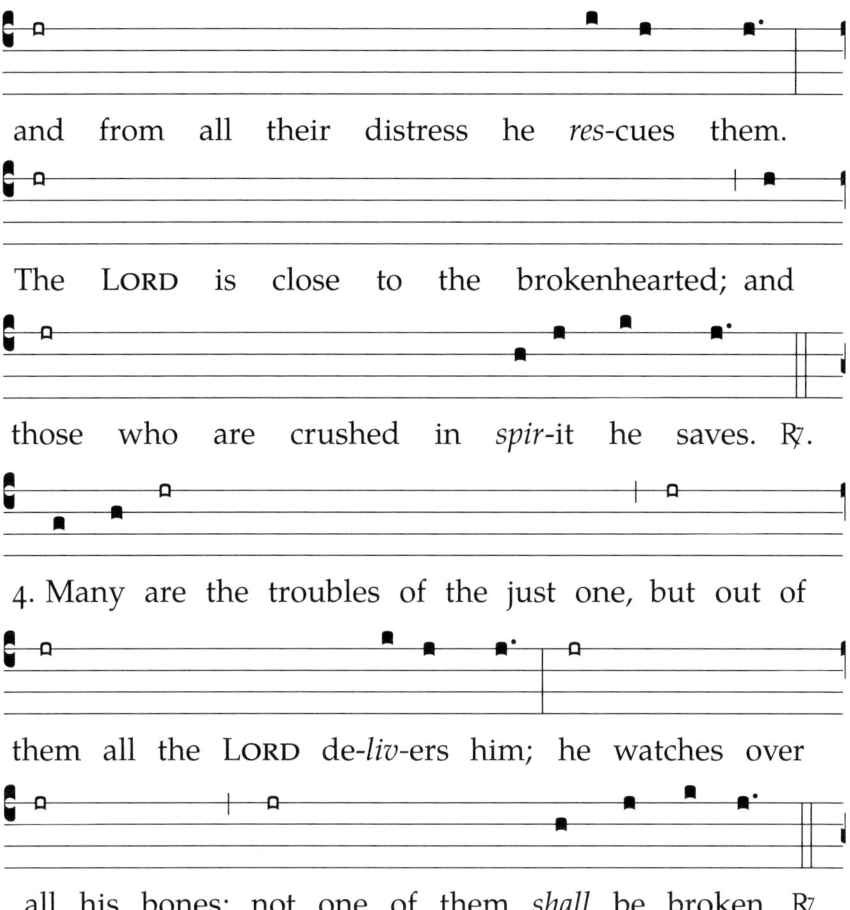
and from all their distress he res-cues them.
The LORD is close to the brokenhearted; and
those who are crushed in spir-it he saves. ℟.
4. Many are the troubles of the just one, but out of
them all the LORD de-liv-ers him; he watches over
all his bones; not one of them shall be broken. ℟.

21TH SUNDAY IN ORDINARY TIME

Ps. 117: 1, 2 **YEAR C**

VII
Go out to all the world and tell the
Good News.
1. Praise the LORD all you nations; glorify him, *all*
you peoples! For steadfast is his kindness toward us,
and the fidelity of the LORD en-*dures* forever. ℟.

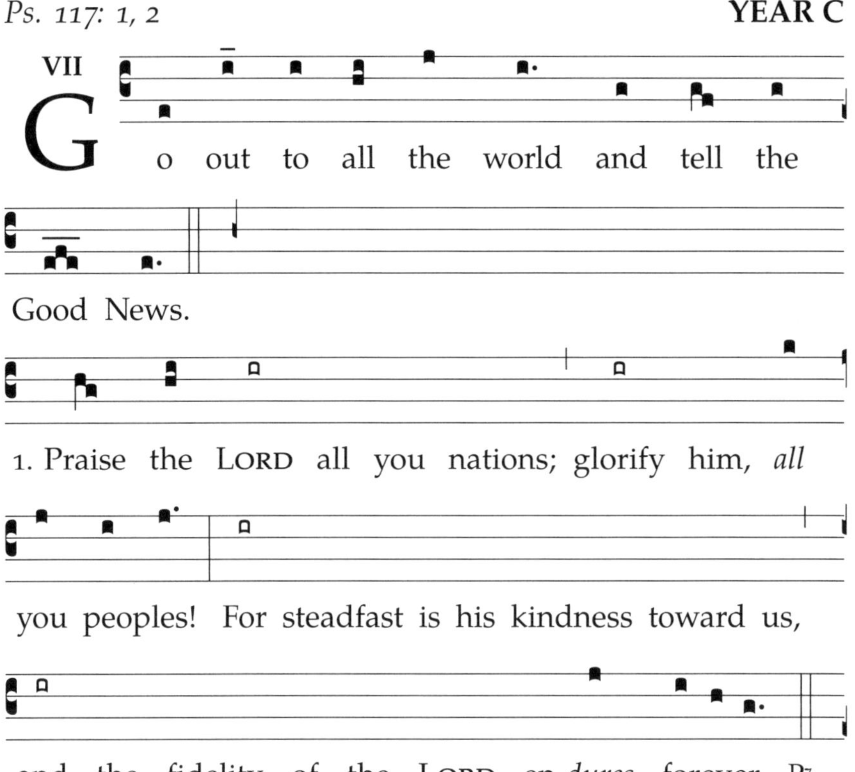

22nd Sunday in Ordinary Time

Ps. 63: 2, 3-4, 5-6, 8-9 **YEAR A**

VI
My soul is thirsting for you, O Lord
my God.
1. O God, you are my God *whom* I seek;
for you my flesh pines and my soul thirsts like
the earth, parched, lifeless *and* without water. ℟.
2. Thus have I gazed toward you in the sanctuary to
see your power and *your* glory, for your kindness is a
greater good than life; my lips *shall* glori-fy you. ℟.

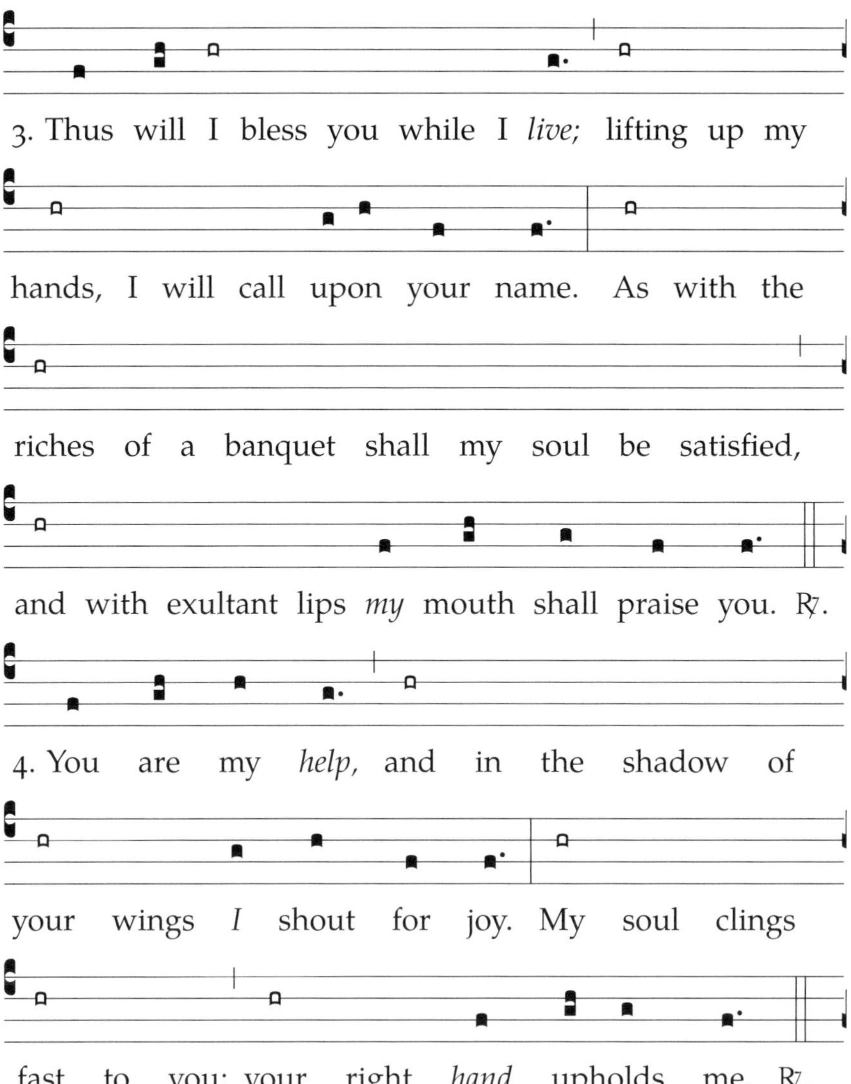
3. Thus will I bless you while I *live;* lifting up my
hands, I will call upon your name. As with the
riches of a banquet shall my soul be satisfied,
and with exultant lips *my* mouth shall praise you. ℟.
4. You are my *help,* and in the shadow of
your wings *I* shout for joy. My soul clings
fast to you; your right *hand* upholds me. ℟.

22nd Sunday in Ordinary Time

Ps. 15: 2-3, 3-4, 4-5 **YEAR B**

VIII
He who does justice will live in the presence
of the Lord.
1. Whoever walks blamelessly and does *jus*-tice;
who thinks the truth in his heart and slan-*ders* not with
his tongue. ℟.
2. Who harms not his fellow man, nor takes up a
reproach against his *neigh*-bor; by whom the reprobate
is despised, while he honors *those* who fear the Lord. ℟.

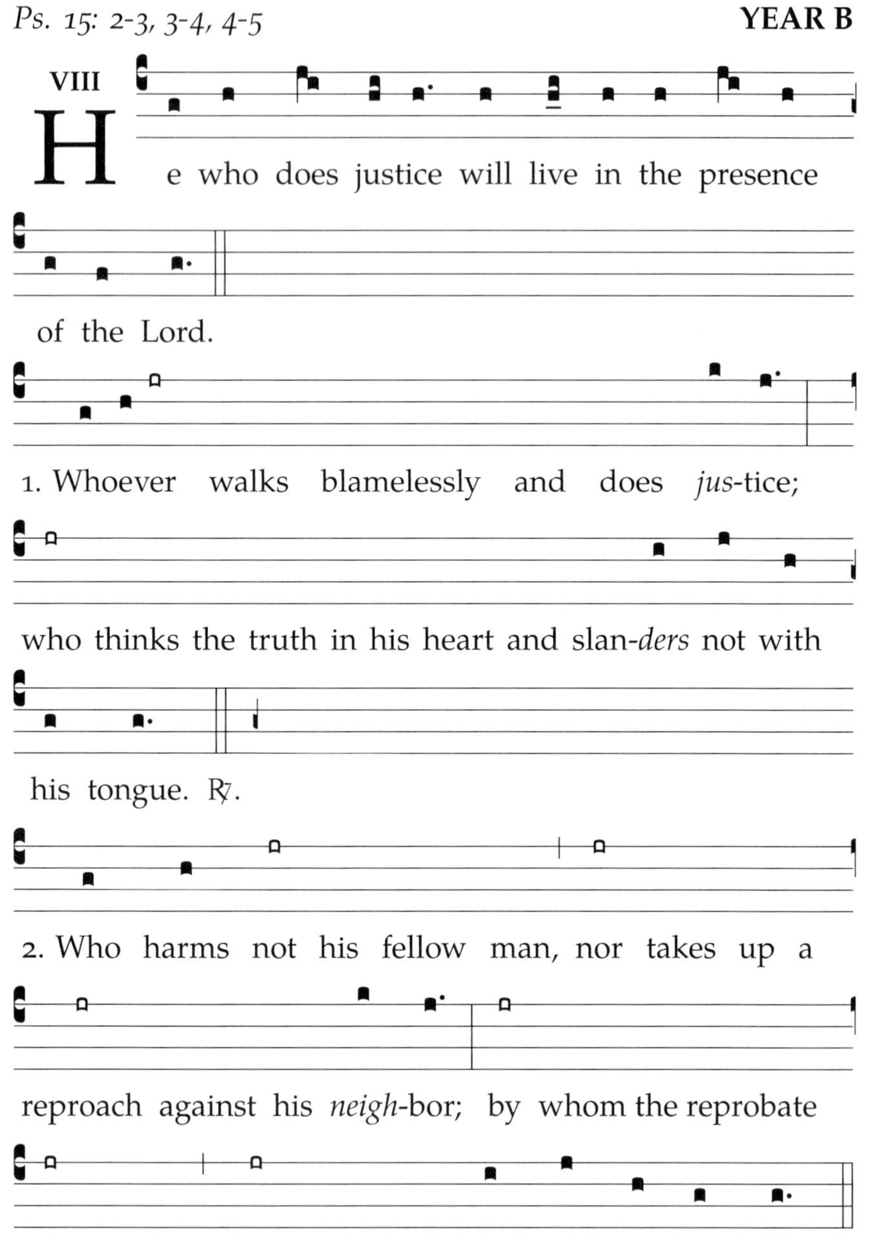

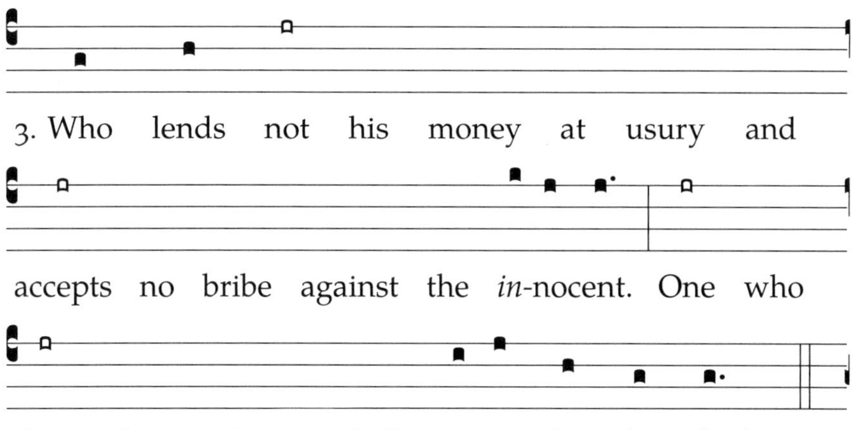
3. Who lends not his money at usury and
accepts no bribe against the *in*-nocent. One who
does these things shall *nev*-er be disturbed. ℟.

22th Sunday in Ordinary Time

Ps. 68: 4-5, 6-7, 10-11 **YEAR C**

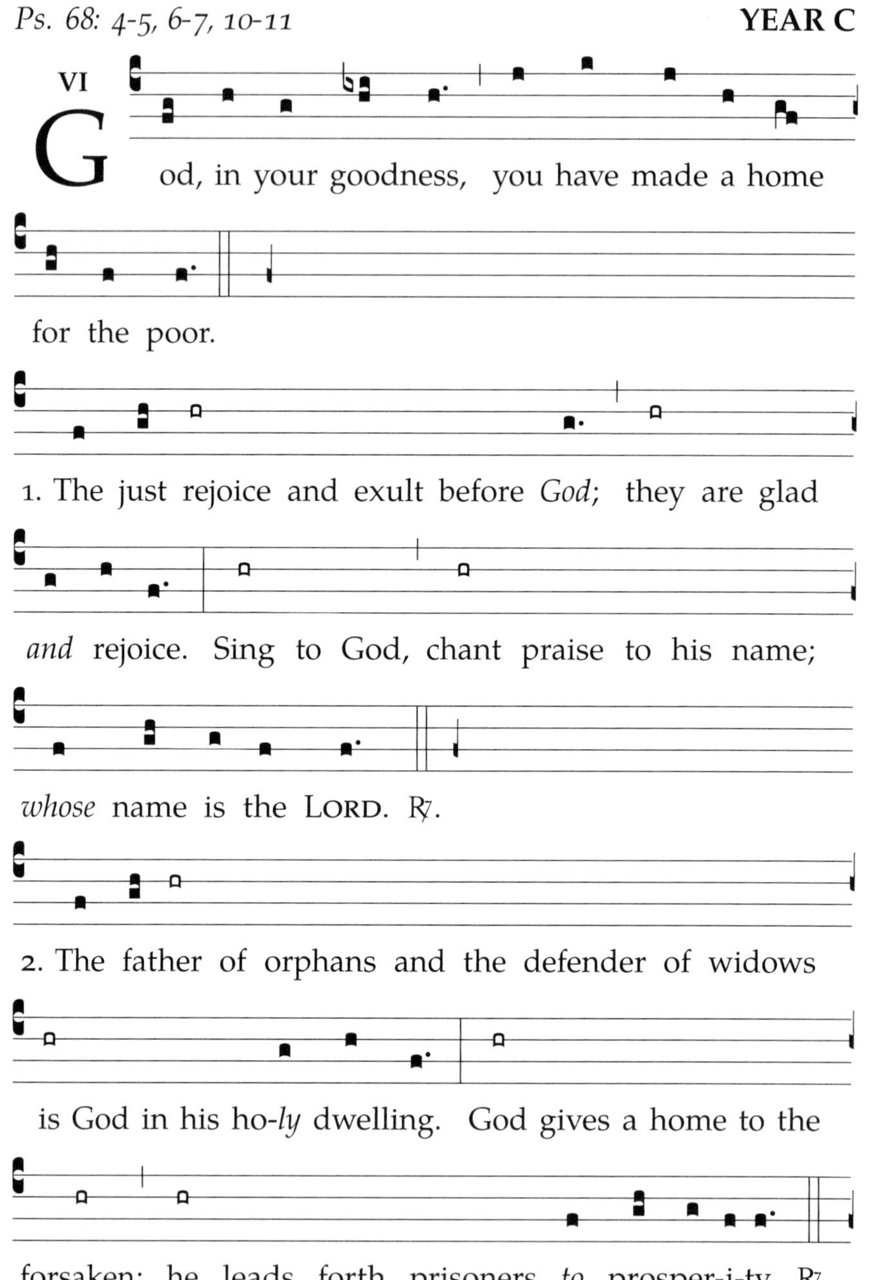
VI
God, in your goodness, you have made a home
for the poor.
1. The just rejoice and exult before *God;* they are glad
and rejoice. Sing to God, chant praise to his name;
whose name is the Lord. ℟.
2. The father of orphans and the defender of widows
is God in his ho-*ly* dwelling. God gives a home to the
forsaken; he leads forth prisoners *to* prosper-i-ty. ℟.

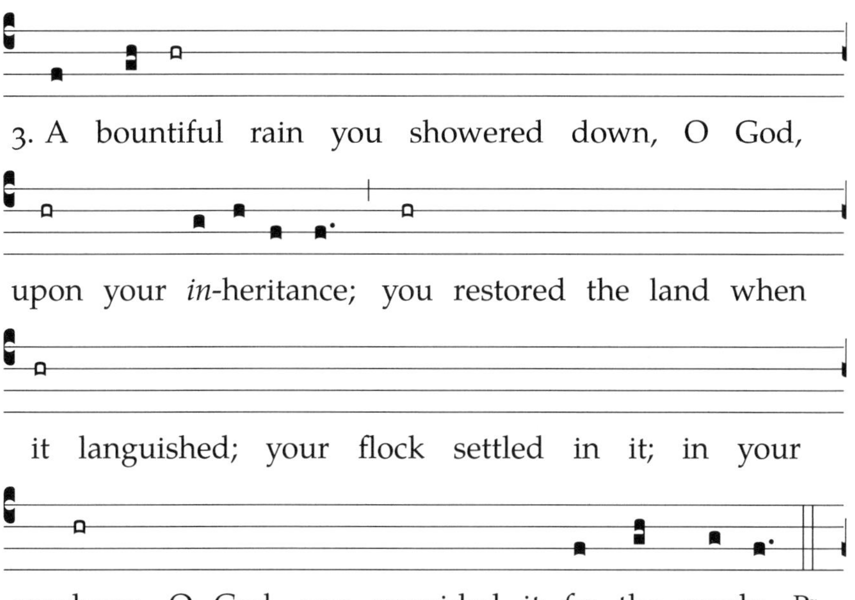
3. A bountiful rain you showered down, O God,
upon your *in*-heritance; you restored the land when
it languished; your flock settled in it; in your
goodness, O God, you provided it *for* the needy. ℟.

23rd Sunday in Ordinary Time

Ps. 95: 1-2, 6-7, 8-9 **YEAR A**

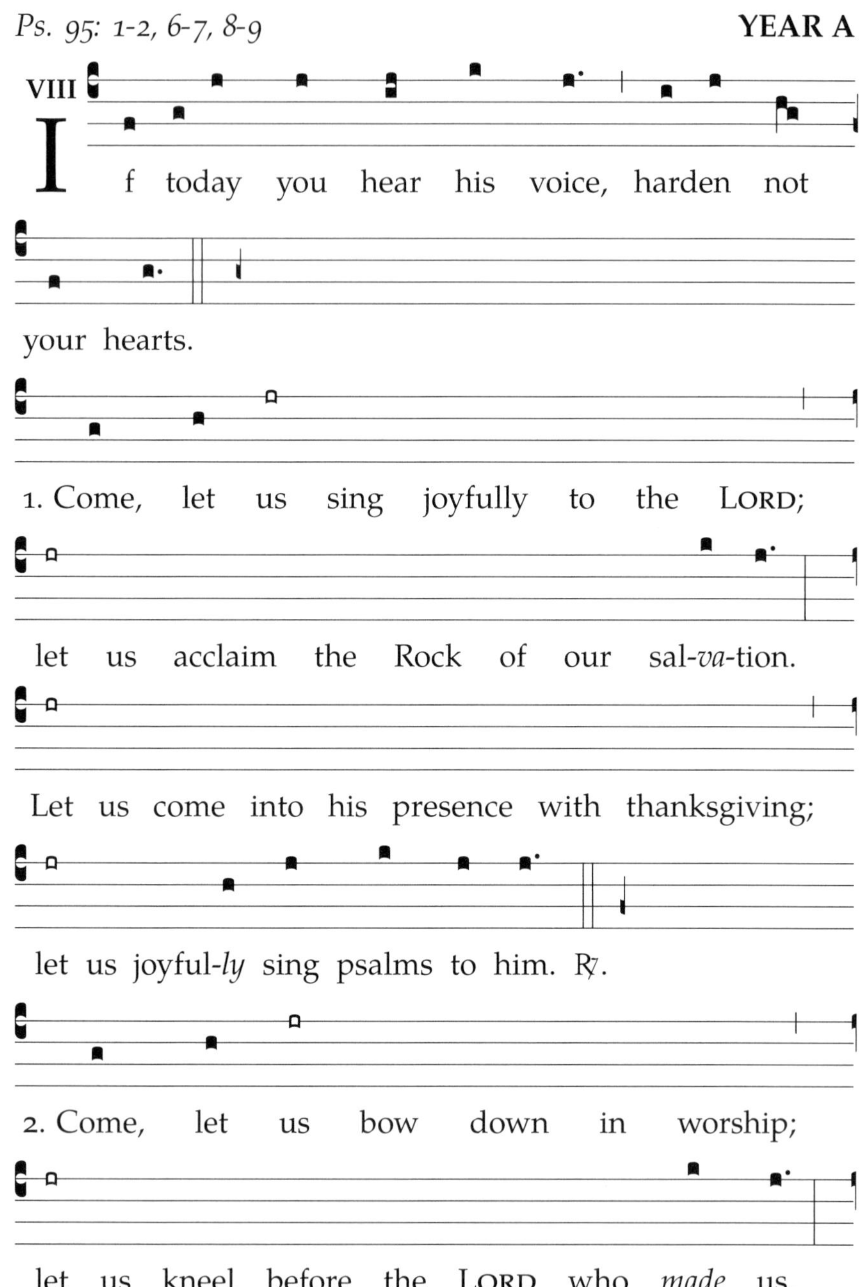

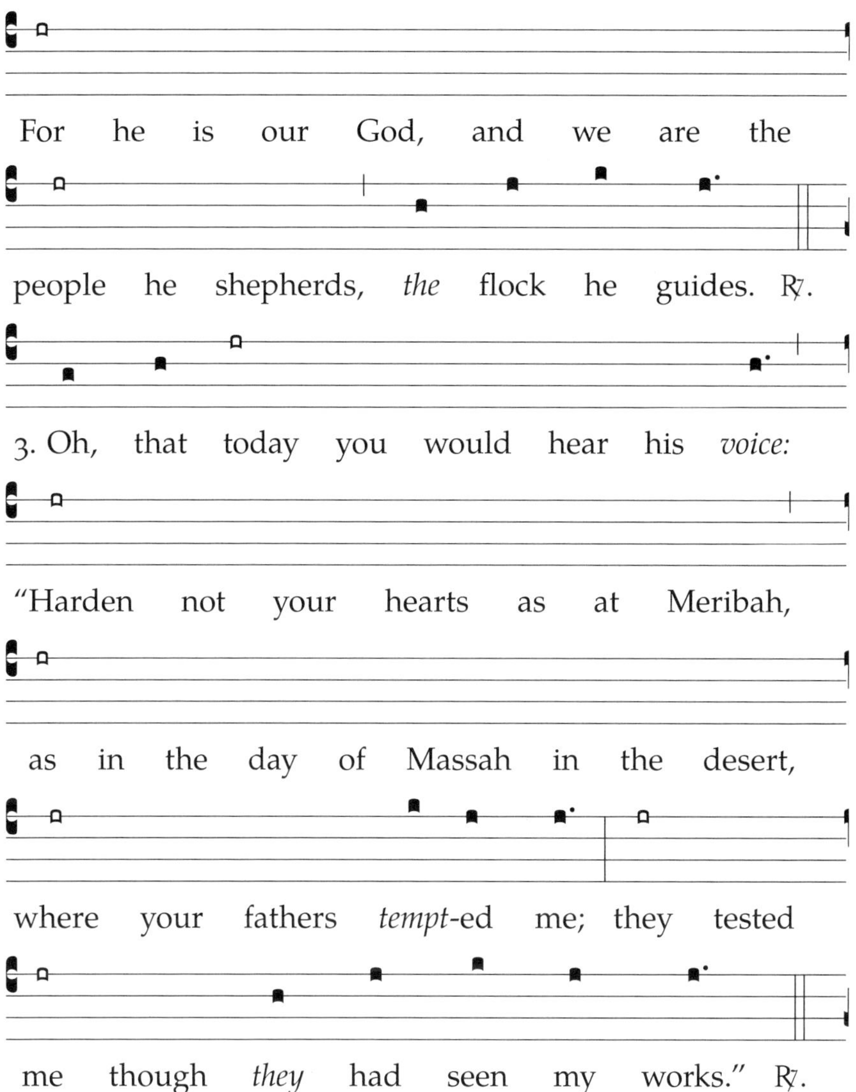
For he is our God, and we are the
people he shepherds, *the* flock he guides. ℟.
3. Oh, that today you would hear his *voice:*
"Harden not your hearts as at Meribah,
as in the day of Massah in the desert,
where your fathers *tempt*-ed me; they tested
me though *they* had seen my works." ℟.

23rd Sunday in Ordinary Time

Ps. 146: 7, 8-9, 9-10 **YEAR B**

VIII
Praise the Lord, my soul!
1. The God of Jacob keeps faith forever, secures justice
for the op-*pressed*, gives food to the *hun*-gry.
The *Lord* sets captives free. ℟.
2. The Lord gives sight to the blind;
the Lord raises up those who were *bowed* down.
The Lord loves the just; the Lord *pro*-tects
strangers. ℟.

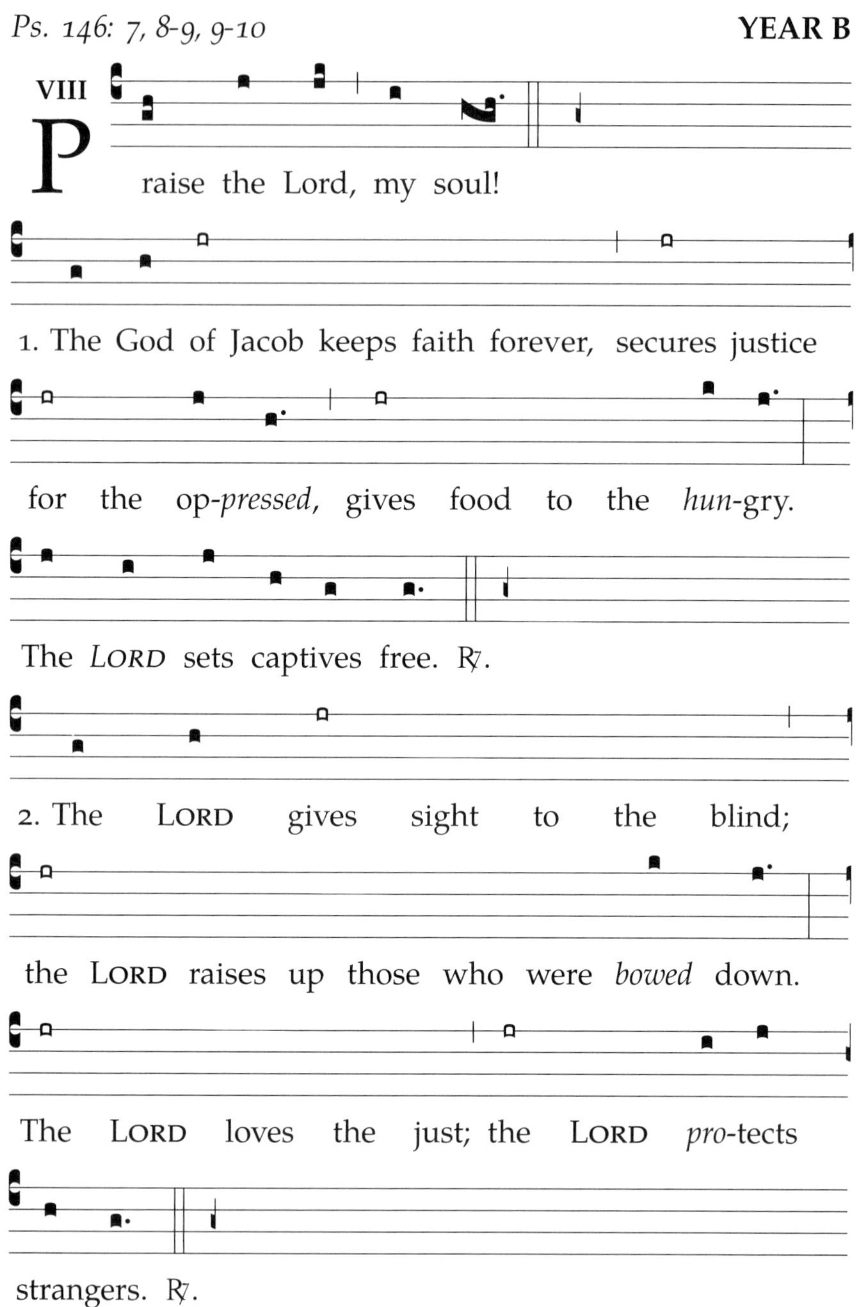

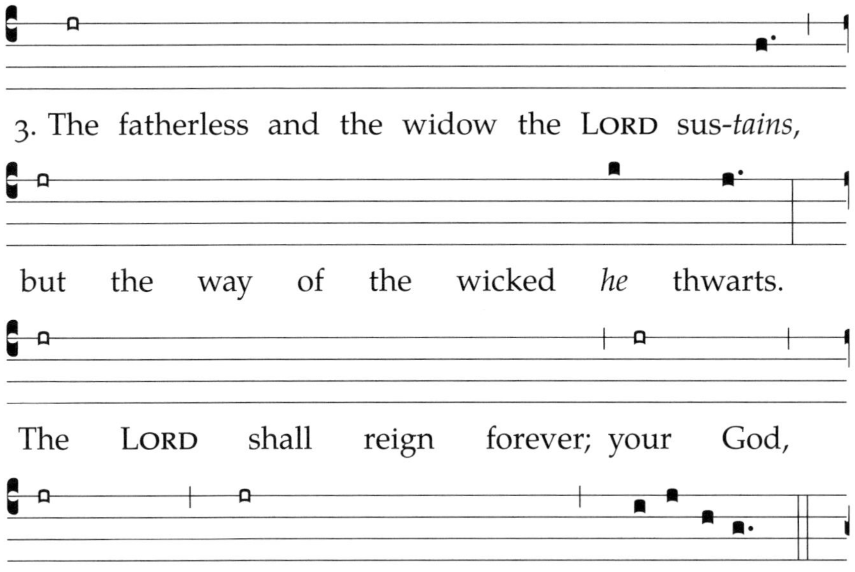
3. The fatherless and the widow the LORD sus-*tains*,
but the way of the wicked *he* thwarts.
The LORD shall reign forever; your God,
O Zion, through all generations. *Al*-le-luia. ℟.

23rd Sunday in Ordinary Time

Ps. 90: 3-4, 5-6, 12-13, 14-17 **YEAR C**

℣
In every age, O Lord, you have been our refuge.
1. You turn man back to dust, saying, "Return,
O children *of* men." For a thousand years
in your sight are as yesterday, now that it
is past, or as a *watch* of the night. ℟.
2. You make an end of them in their sleep;
the next morning they are like the

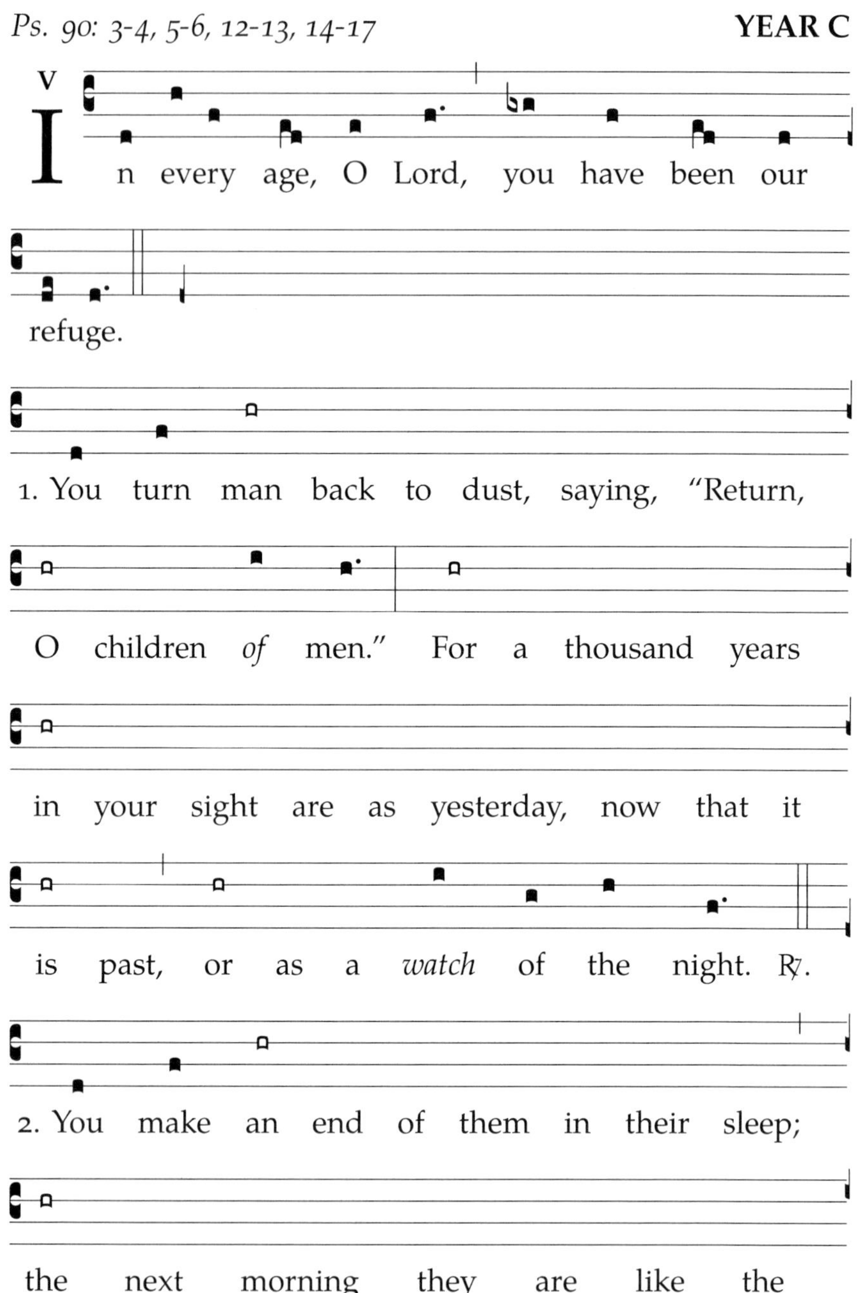

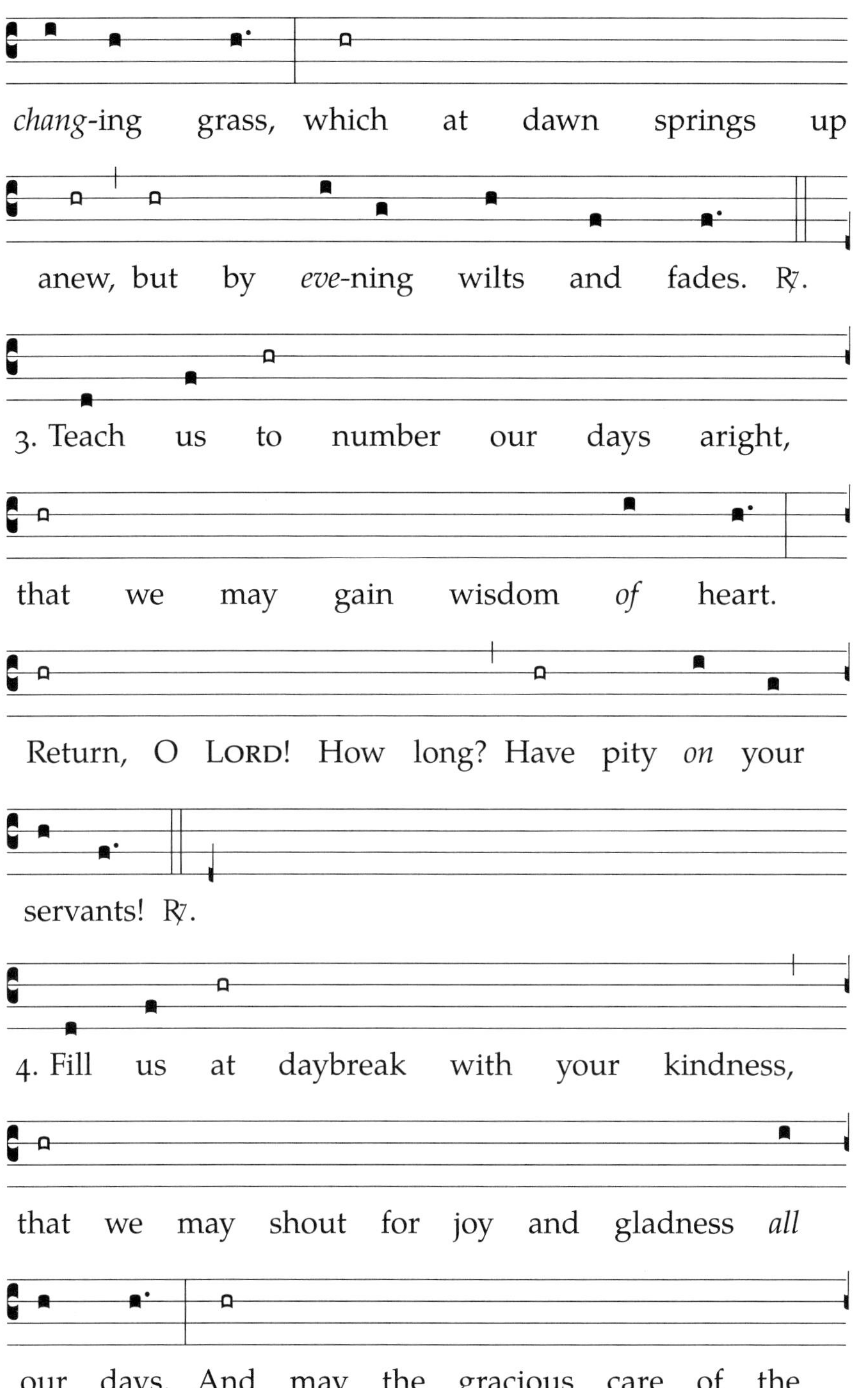
changing grass, which at dawn springs up
anew, but by evening wilts and fades. ℟.
3. Teach us to number our days aright,
that we may gain wisdom of heart.
Return, O LORD! How long? Have pity on your
servants! ℟.
4. Fill us at daybreak with your kindness,
that we may shout for joy and gladness all
our days. And may the gracious care of the

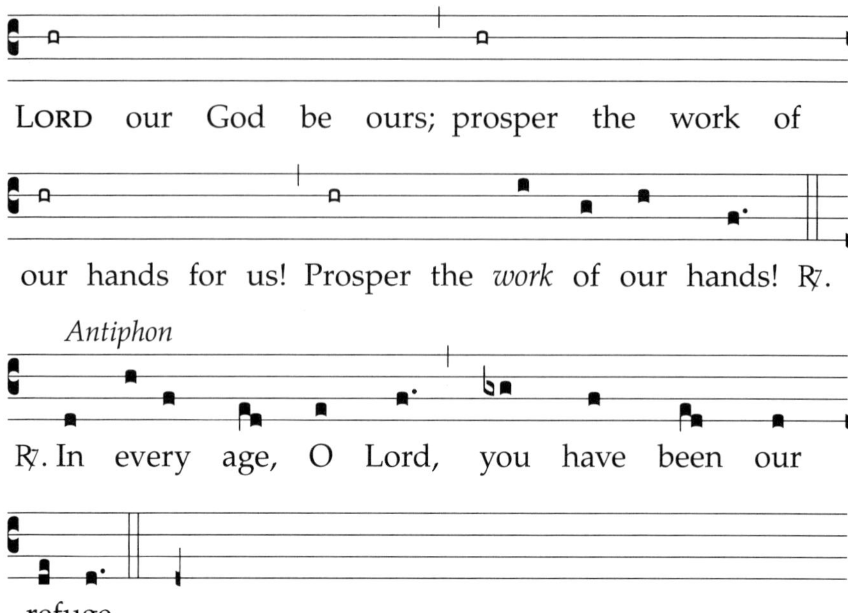
LORD our God be ours; prosper the work of
our hands for us! Prosper the *work* of our hands! ℟.
Antiphon
℟. In every age, O Lord, you have been our
refuge.

24th Sunday in Ordinary Time

Ps. 103: 1-2, 3-4, 9-10, 11-12 **YEAR A**

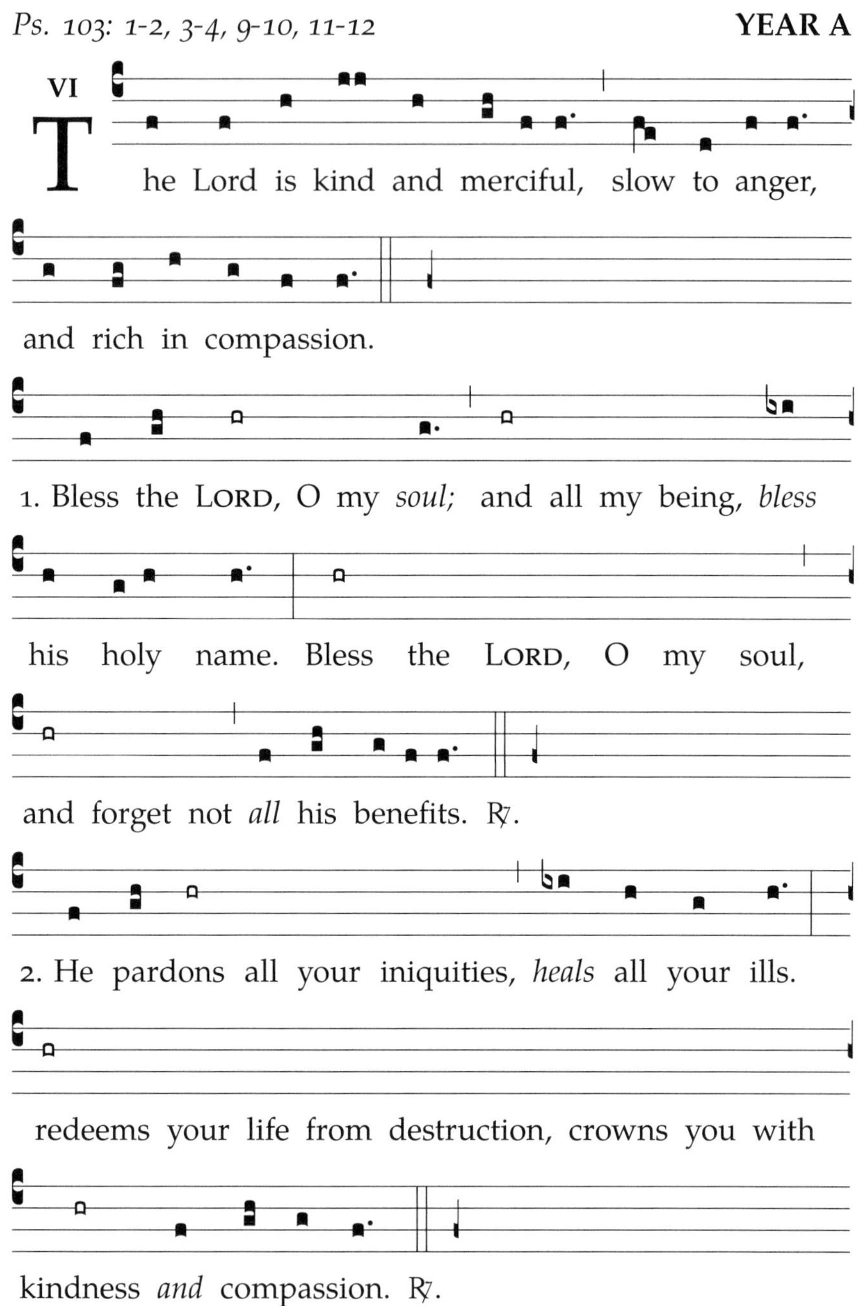

VI
The Lord is kind and merciful, slow to anger,
and rich in compassion.
1. Bless the Lord, O my *soul;* and all my being, *bless*
his holy name. Bless the Lord, O my soul,
and forget not *all* his benefits. ℟.
2. He pardons all your iniquities, *heals* all your ills.
redeems your life from destruction, crowns you with
kindness *and* compassion. ℟.

3. He will not always chide, nor does he keep his
wrath forever. Not according to our sins does he deal
with us, nor does he requite us accord-*ing* to our
crimes. ℟.
4. For as the heavens are high above the *earth,*
so surpassing is his kindness toward *those* who
fear him. As far as the east is from the west,
so far has he put our *trans*-gressions from us. ℟.

24th Sunday in Ordinary Time

Ps. 116: 1-2, 3-4, 5-6, 8-9 **YEAR B**

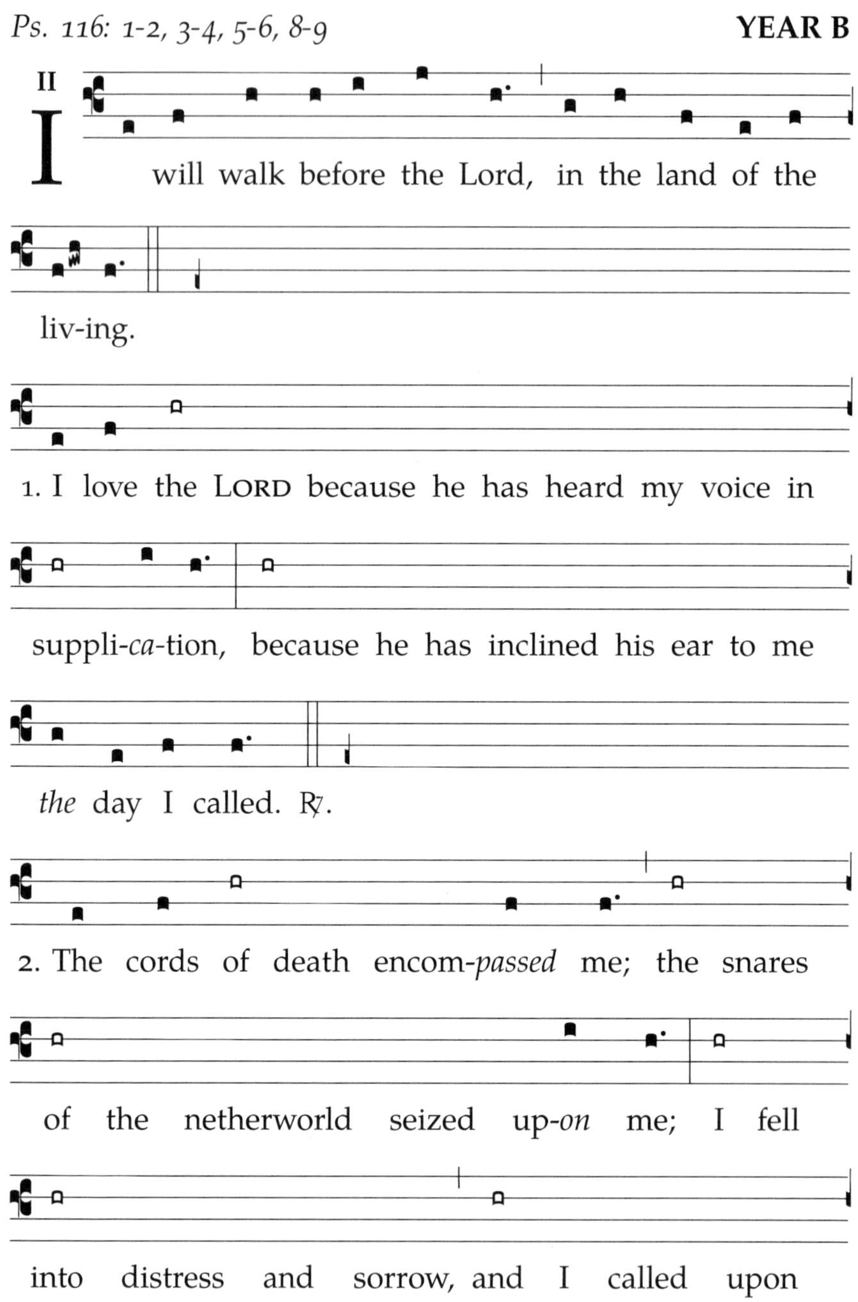

II
I will walk before the Lord, in the land of the
liv-ing.
1. I love the LORD because he has heard my voice in
suppli-*ca*-tion, because he has inclined his ear to me
the day I called. ℟.
2. The cords of death encom-*passed* me; the snares
of the netherworld seized up-*on* me; I fell
into distress and sorrow, and I called upon

the name of the LORD, "O *LORD*, save my life!" ℟.
3. Gracious is the LORD and just; yes, our God is
mer-ciful. The LORD keeps the little ones; I was
brought low, and *he* saved me. ℟.
4. For he has freed my soul *from* death, my eyes
from tears, my feet from *stum*-bling. I shall walk
before the LORD in the land of *the* living. ℟.

24rd Sunday in Ordinary Time

Ps. 51: 3-4, 12-13, 17, 19 **YEAR C**

VIII
I will rise and go to my father.
1. Have mercy on me, O God, in your goodness; in the
greatness of your compassion wipe out *my* offense.
Thoroughly wash me from my guilt and of *my* sin
cleanse me. ℟.
2. A clean heart create for me, O God, and a steadfast
spirit renew with-*in* me. Cast me not out from your
presence, and your Holy Spirit *take* not from me. ℟.

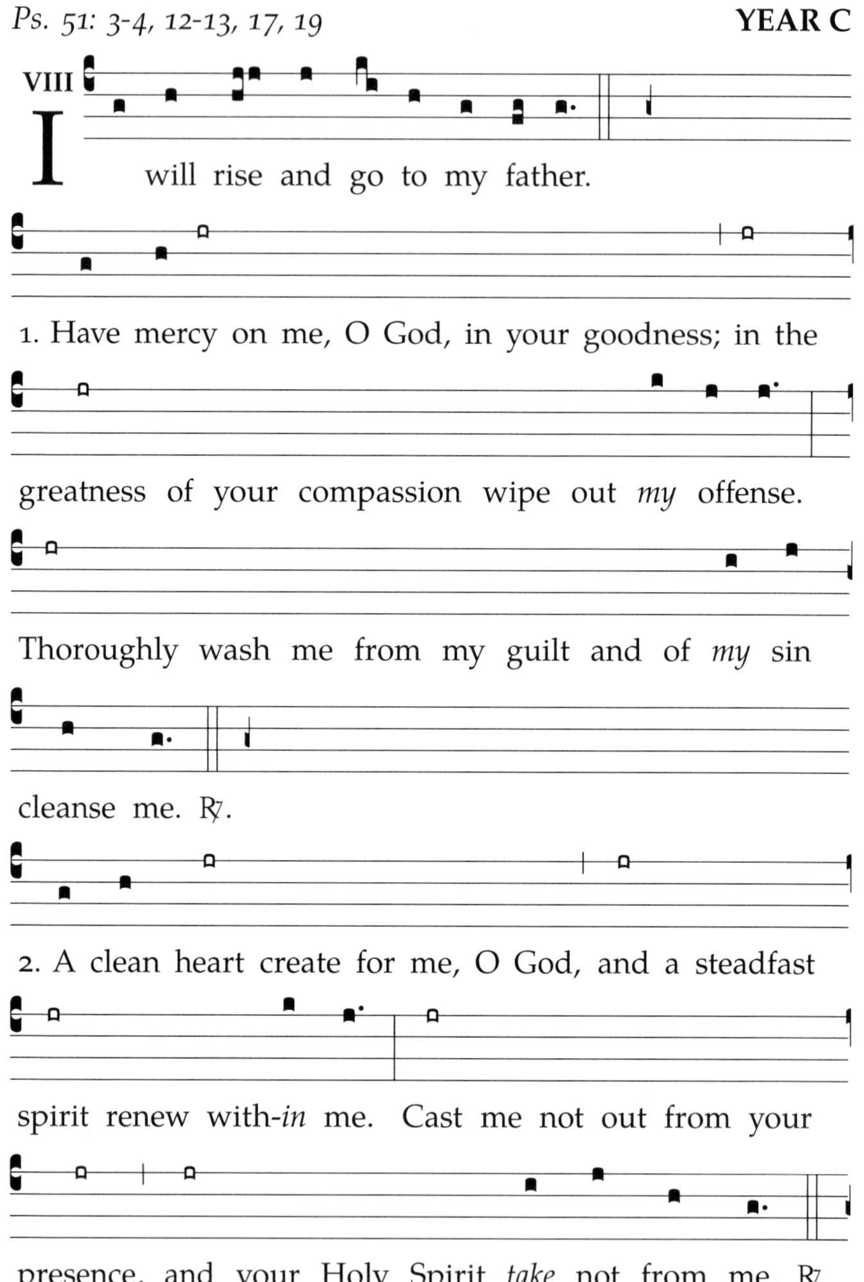

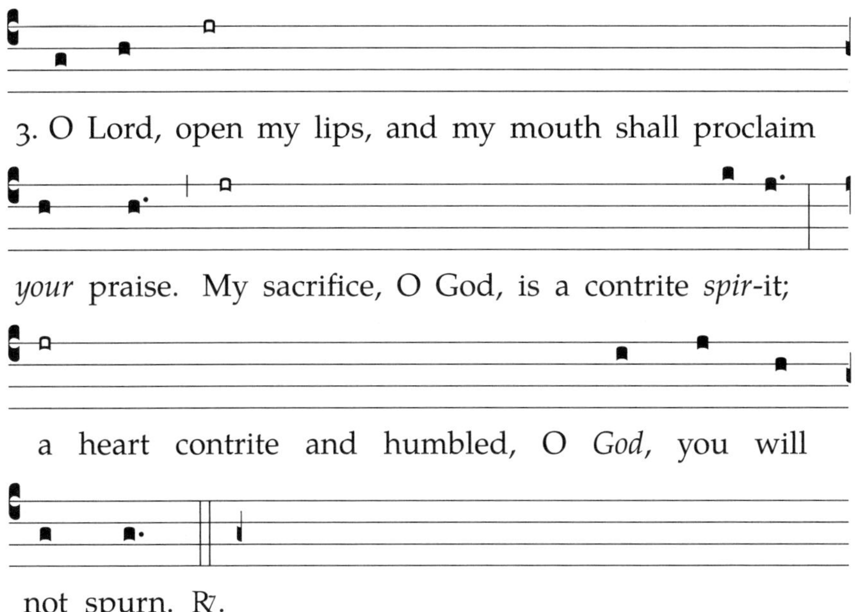
3. O Lord, open my lips, and my mouth shall proclaim
your praise. My sacrifice, O God, is a contrite *spir*-it;
a heart contrite and humbled, O *God,* you will
not spurn. ℟.

25th Sunday in Ordinary Time

Ps. 145: 2-3, 8-9, 17-18 **YEAR A**

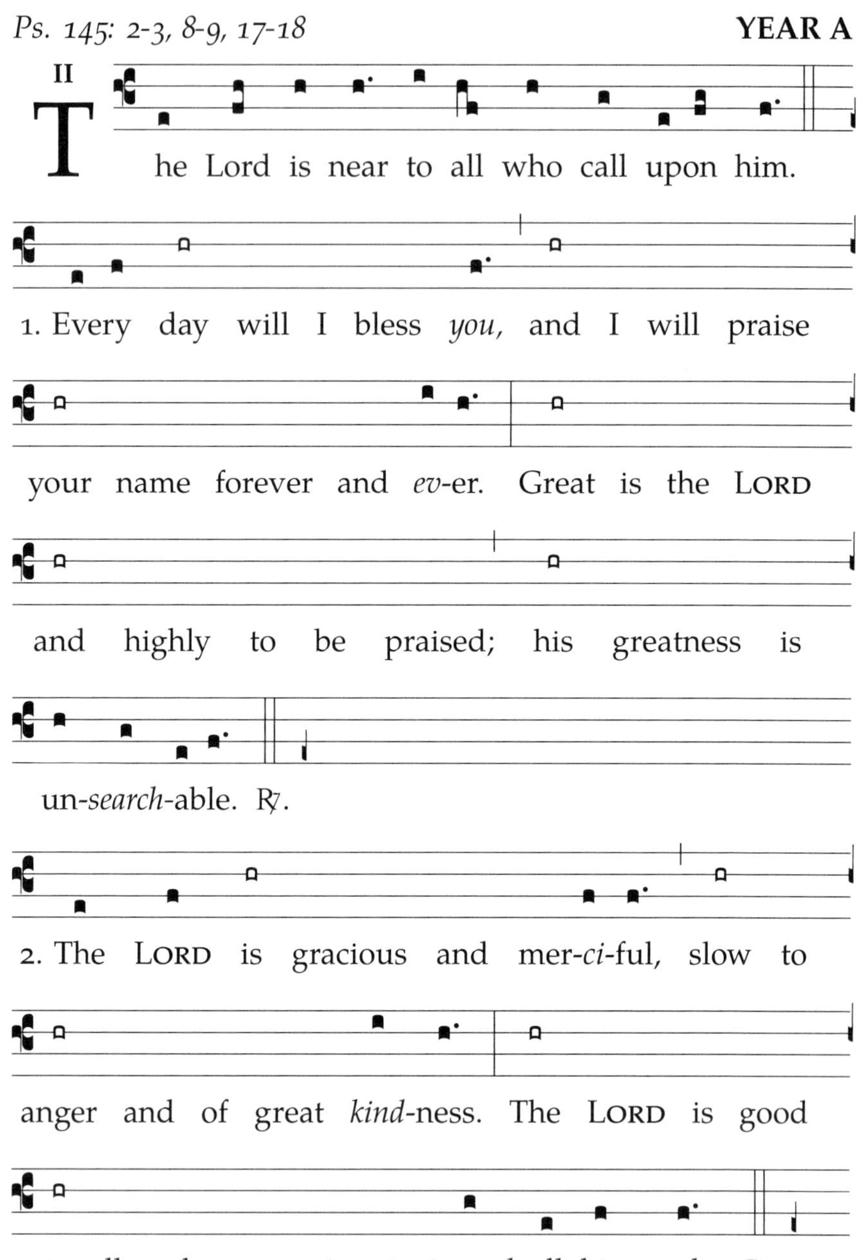
II
The Lord is near to all who call upon him.
1. Every day will I bless *you,* and I will praise
your name forever and *ev*-er. Great is the LORD
and highly to be praised; his greatness is
un-*search*-able. ℟.
2. The LORD is gracious and mer-*ci*-ful, slow to
anger and of great *kind*-ness. The LORD is good
to all and compassionate *toward* all his works. ℟.

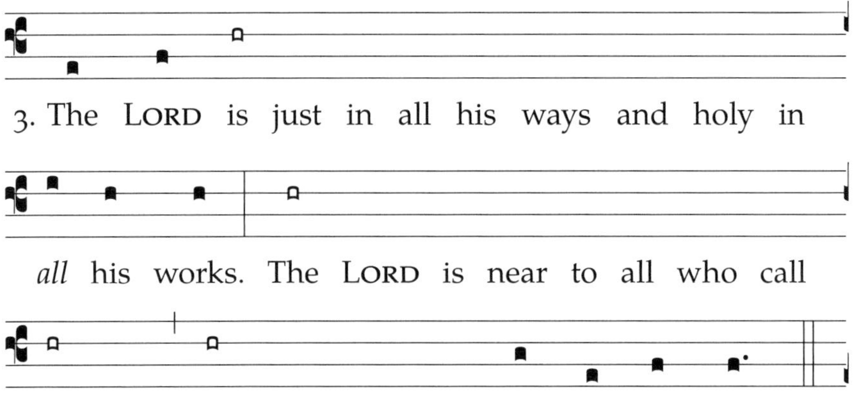
3. The LORD is just in all his ways and holy in
all his works. The LORD is near to all who call

upon him, to all who call up-*on* him in truth. ℟.

25th Sunday in Ordinary Time

Ps. 54: 3-4, 5, 6-8 **YEAR B**

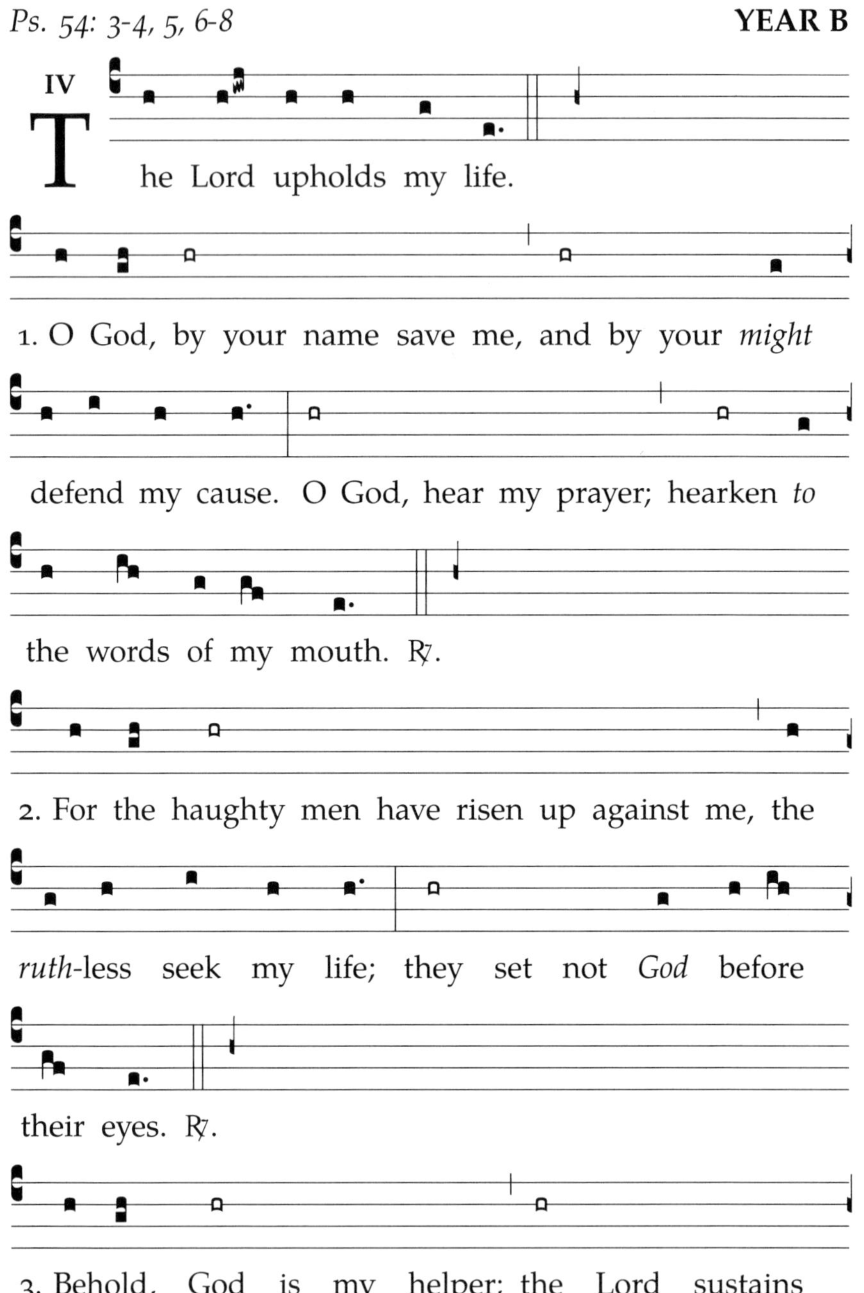
IV
The Lord upholds my life.
1. O God, by your name save me, and by your *might*
defend my cause. O God, hear my prayer; hearken *to*
the words of my mouth. ℟.
2. For the haughty men have risen up against me, the
ruth-less seek my life; they set not *God* before
their eyes. ℟.
3. Behold, God is my helper; the Lord sustains

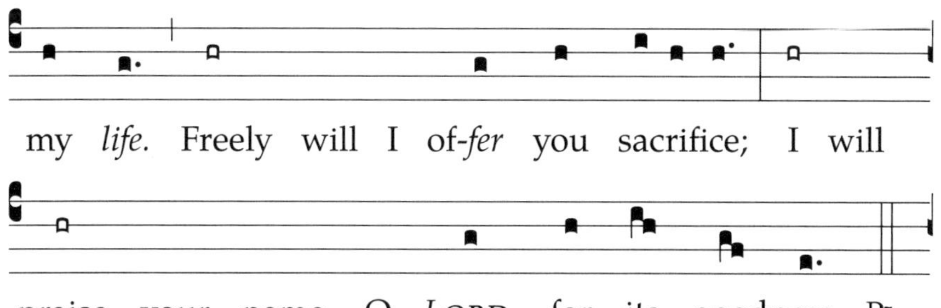
my *life.* Freely will I of-*fer* you sacrifice; I will
praise your name, O *LORD,* for its goodness. ℟.

25th Sunday in Ordinary Time

Ps. 113: 1-2, 4-6, 7-8 **YEAR C**

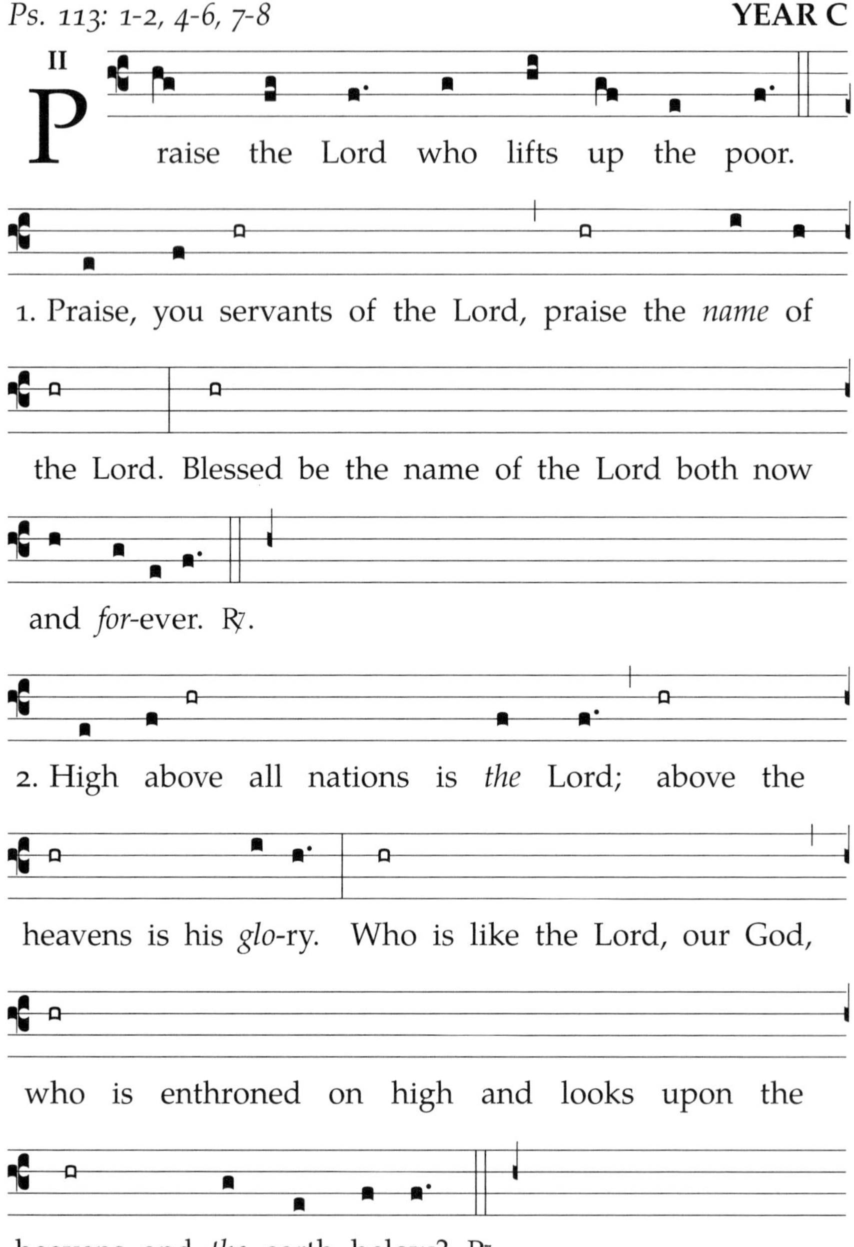
II
Praise the Lord who lifts up the poor.
1. Praise, you servants of the Lord, praise the *name* of
the Lord. Blessed be the name of the Lord both now
and *for*-ever. ℟.
2. High above all nations is *the* Lord; above the
heavens is his *glo*-ry. Who is like the Lord, our God,
who is enthroned on high and looks upon the
heavens and *the* earth below? ℟.

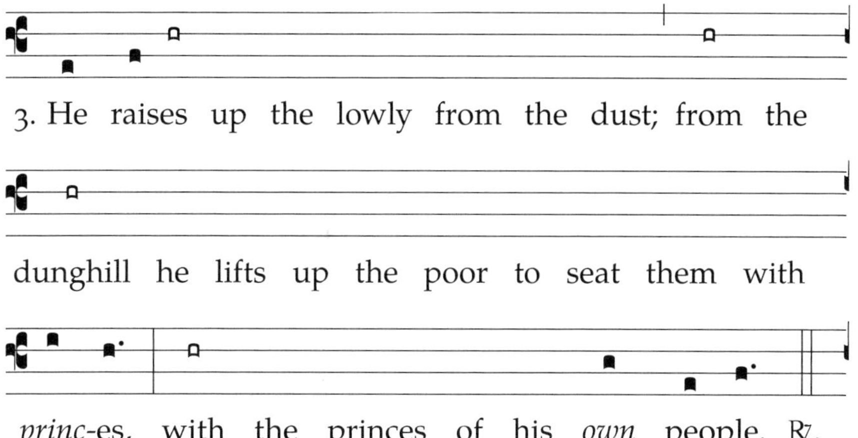
3. He raises up the lowly from the dust; from the
dunghill he lifts up the poor to seat them with
princ-es, with the princes of his *own* people. ℟.

26th Sunday in Ordinary Time

Ps. 25: 4-5, 6-7, 8-9 **YEAR A**

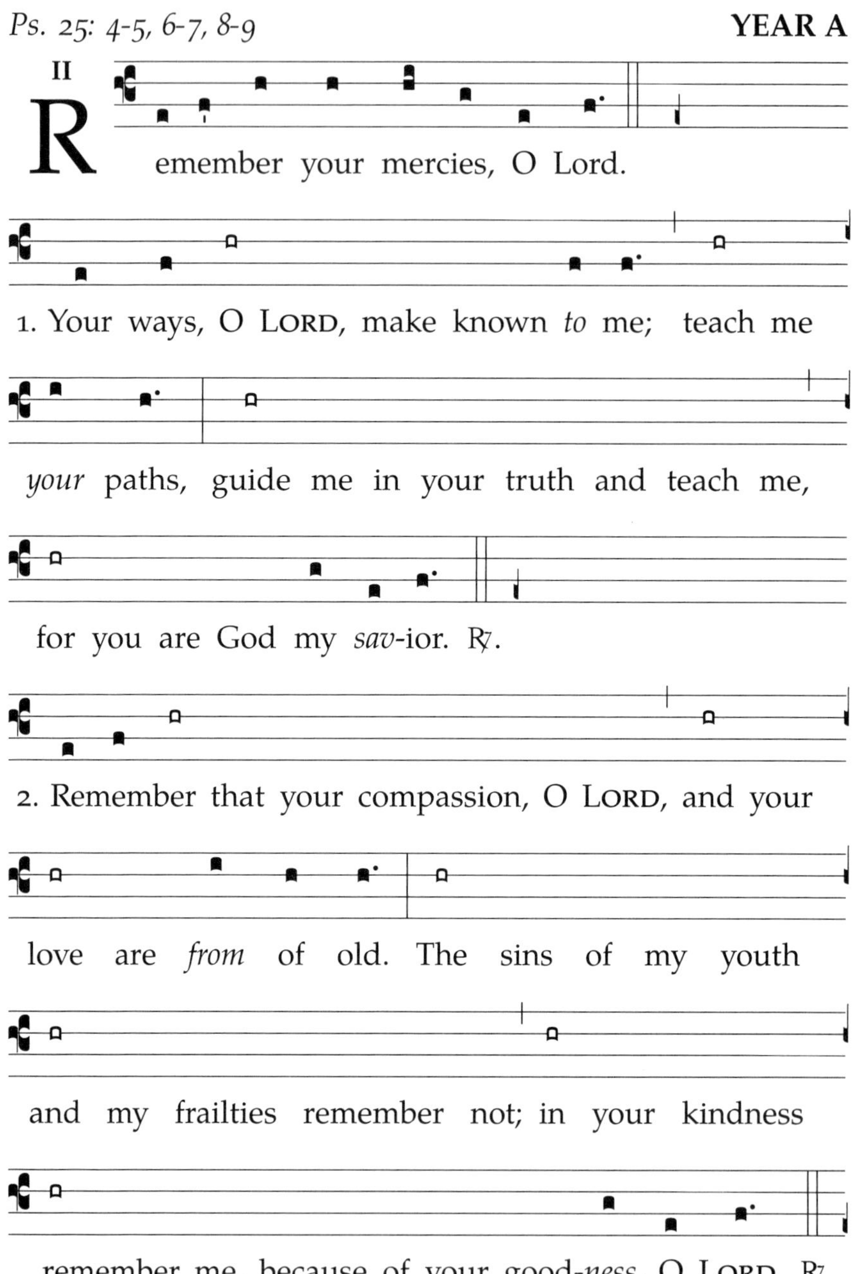

II
R emember your mercies, O Lord.
1. Your ways, O LORD, make known *to* me; teach me
your paths, guide me in your truth and teach me,
for you are God my *sav*-ior. ℟.
2. Remember that your compassion, O LORD, and your
love are *from* of old. The sins of my youth
and my frailties remember not; in your kindness
remember me, because of your good-*ness,* O LORD. ℟.

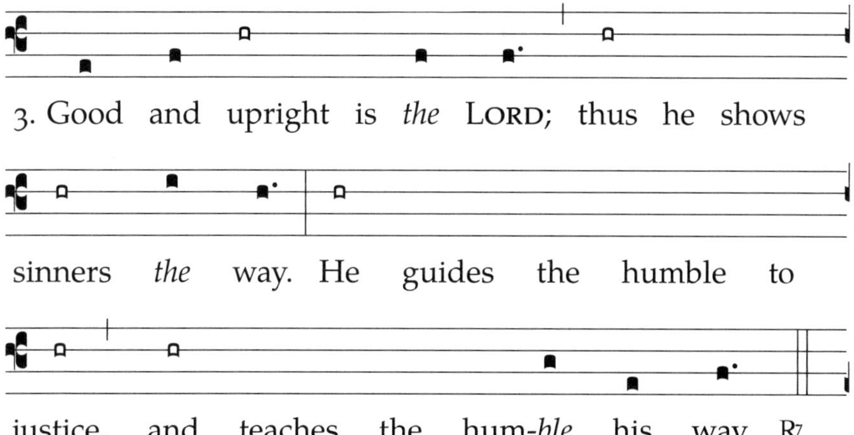
3. Good and upright is *the* LORD; thus he shows
sinners *the* way. He guides the humble to
justice, and teaches the hum-*ble* his way. ℟.

26th Sunday in Ordinary Time

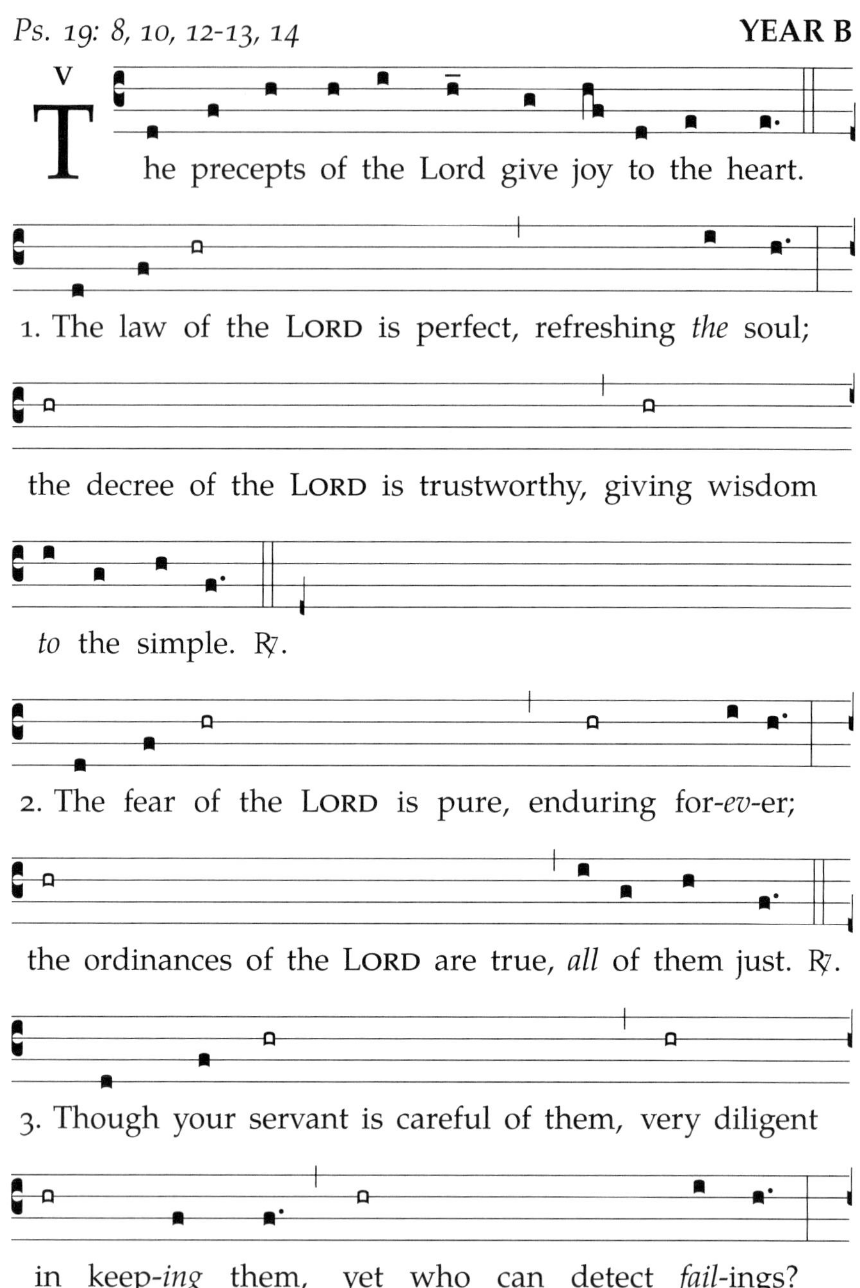
Ps. 19: 8, 10, 12-13, 14
YEAR B
℟
The precepts of the Lord give joy to the heart.
1. The law of the LORD is perfect, refreshing *the* soul;
the decree of the LORD is trustworthy, giving wisdom
to the simple. ℟.
2. The fear of the LORD is pure, enduring for-*ev*-er;
the ordinances of the LORD are true, *all* of them just. ℟.
3. Though your servant is careful of them, very diligent
in keep-*ing* them, yet who can detect *fail*-ings?

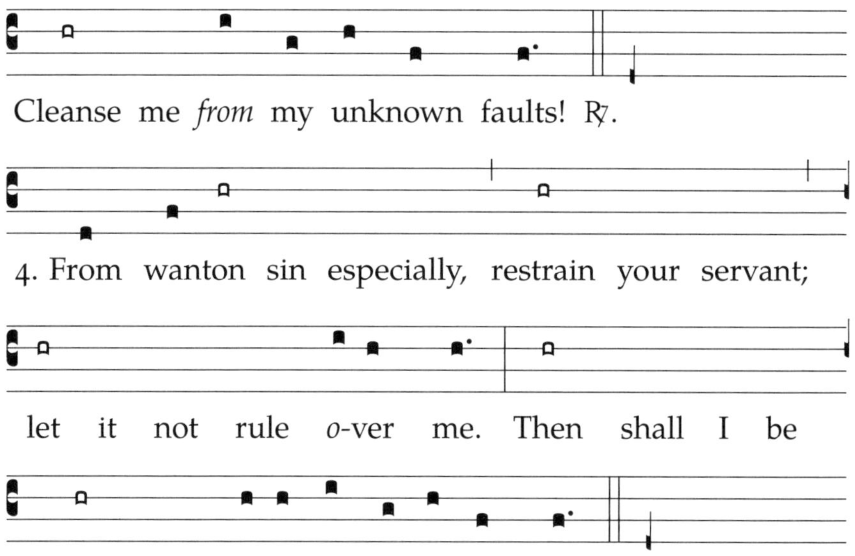
Cleanse me from my unknown faults! ℟.
4. From wanton sin especially, restrain your servant;
let it not rule o-ver me. Then shall I be
blameless and inno-cent of serious sin. ℟.

26th Sunday in Ordinary Time

Ps. 146: 7, 8-9, 9-10
YEAR C
VIII
Praise the Lord, my soul!
1. The God of Jacob keeps faith forever, secures justice
for the op-*pressed*, gives food to the *hun*-gry.
The *LORD* sets captives free. ℟.
2. The LORD gives sight to the blind;
the LORD raises up those who were *bowed* down.
The LORD loves the just; the LORD *pro*-tects
strangers. ℟.

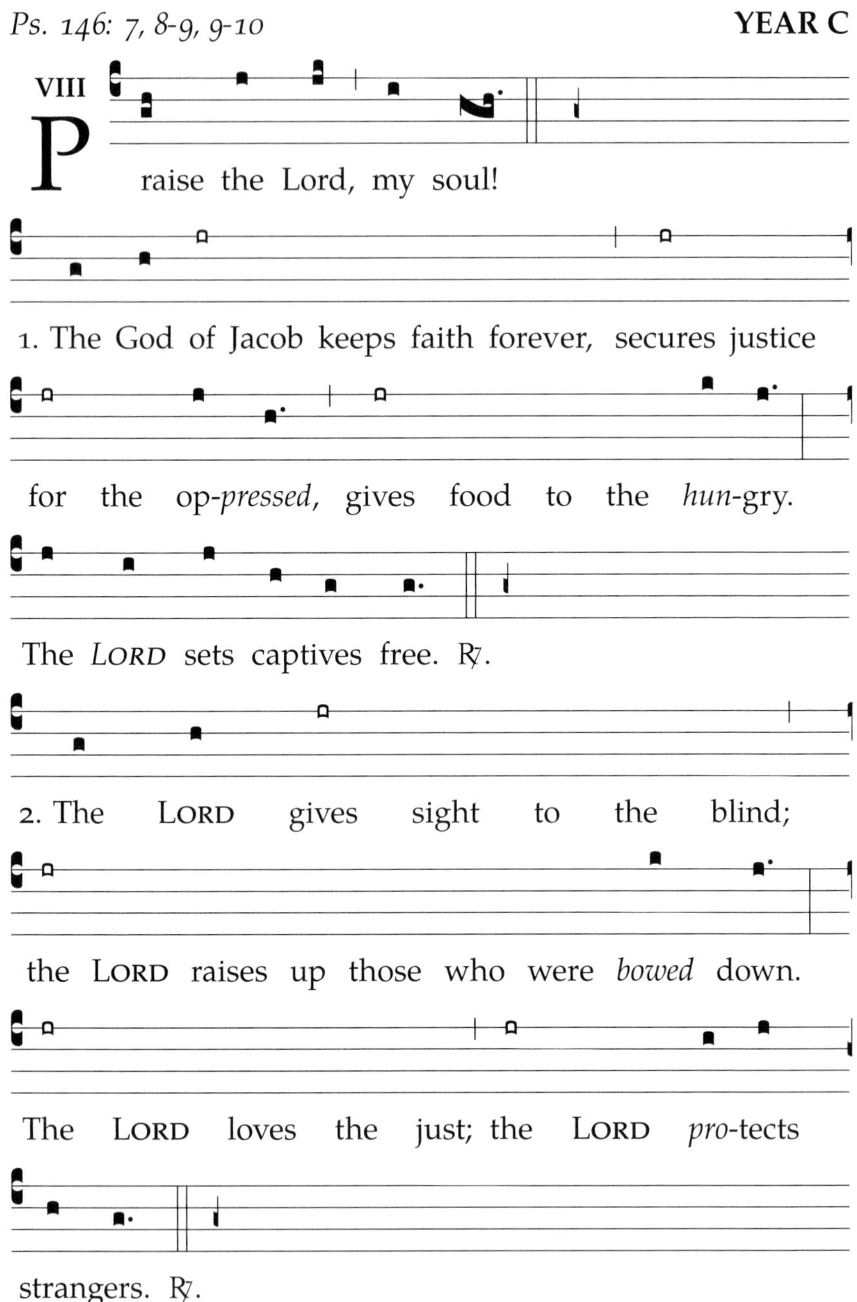

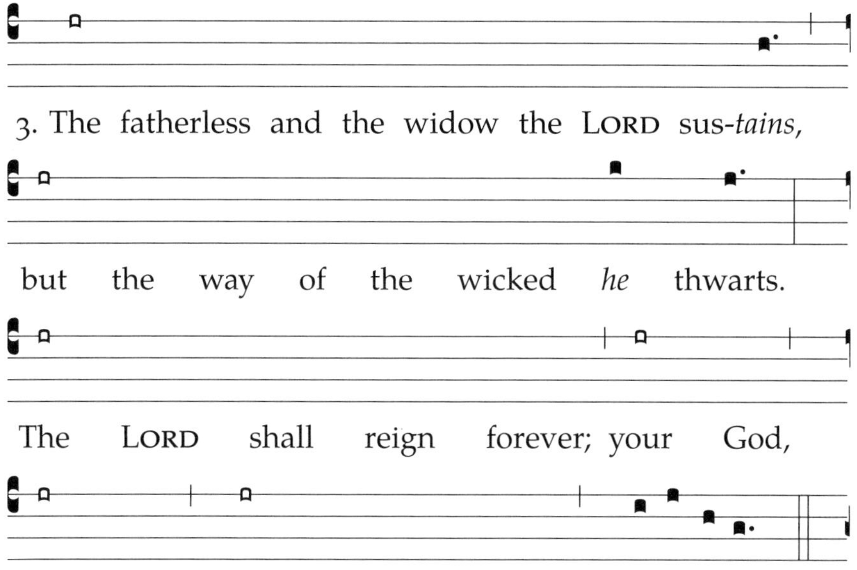
3. The fatherless and the widow the LORD sus-*tains,*
but the way of the wicked *he* thwarts.
The LORD shall reign forever; your God,
O Zion, through all generations. *Al*-le-luia. ℟.

27th Sunday in Ordinary Time

Ps. 80: 9, 12, 13-14, 15-16, 19-20 **YEAR A**

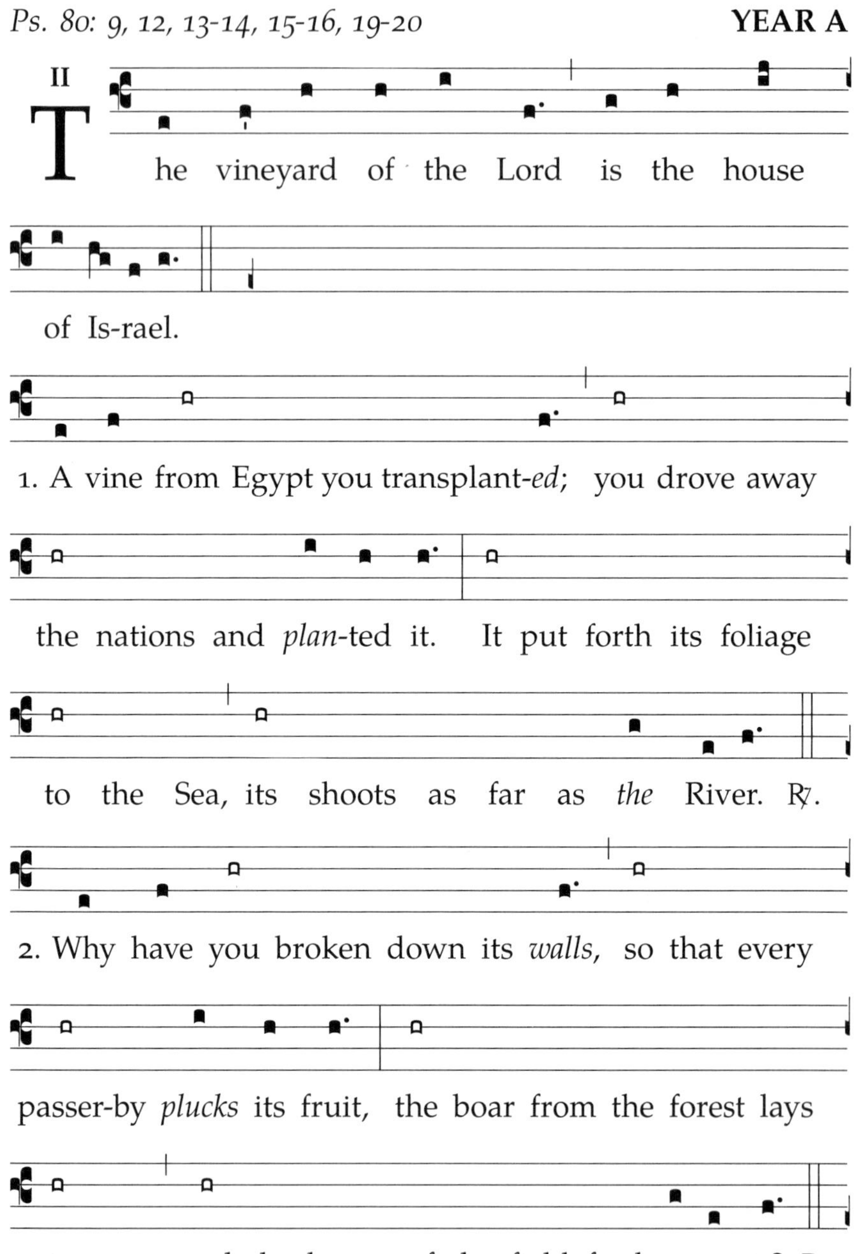
II
The vineyard of the Lord is the house
of Is-rael.
1. A vine from Egypt you transplant-*ed;* you drove away
the nations and *plan*-ted it. It put forth its foliage
to the Sea, its shoots as far as *the* River. ℟.
2. Why have you broken down its *walls,* so that every
passer-by *plucks* its fruit, the boar from the forest lays
it waste, and the beasts of the field feed *up*-on it? ℟.

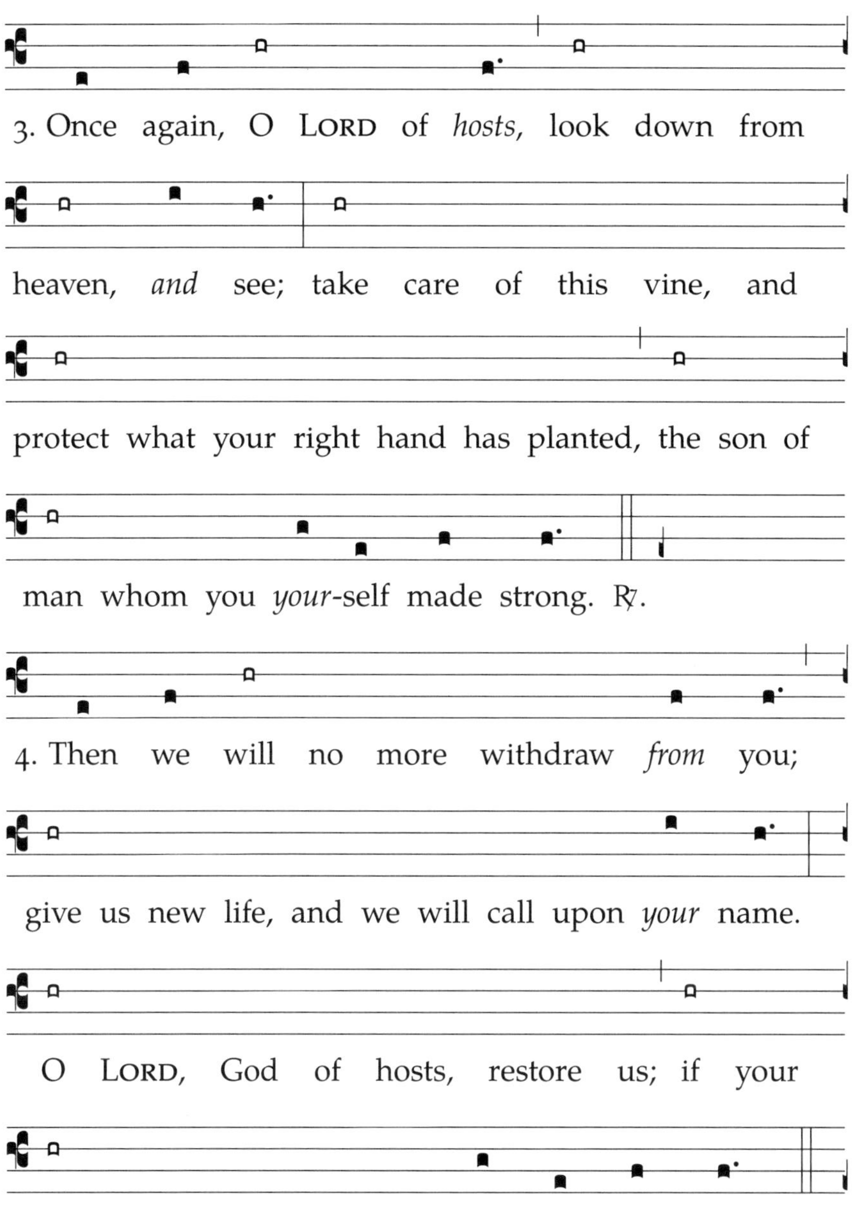
3. Once again, O LORD of *hosts,* look down from
heaven, *and* see; take care of this vine, and
protect what your right hand has planted, the son of
man whom you *your*-self made strong. ℟.
4. Then we will no more withdraw *from* you;
give us new life, and we will call upon *your* name.
O LORD, God of hosts, restore us; if your
face shine upon us, then *we* shall be saved. ℟.

27th Sunday in Ordinary Time

Ps. 128: 1-2, 3, 4-5, 6 **YEAR B**

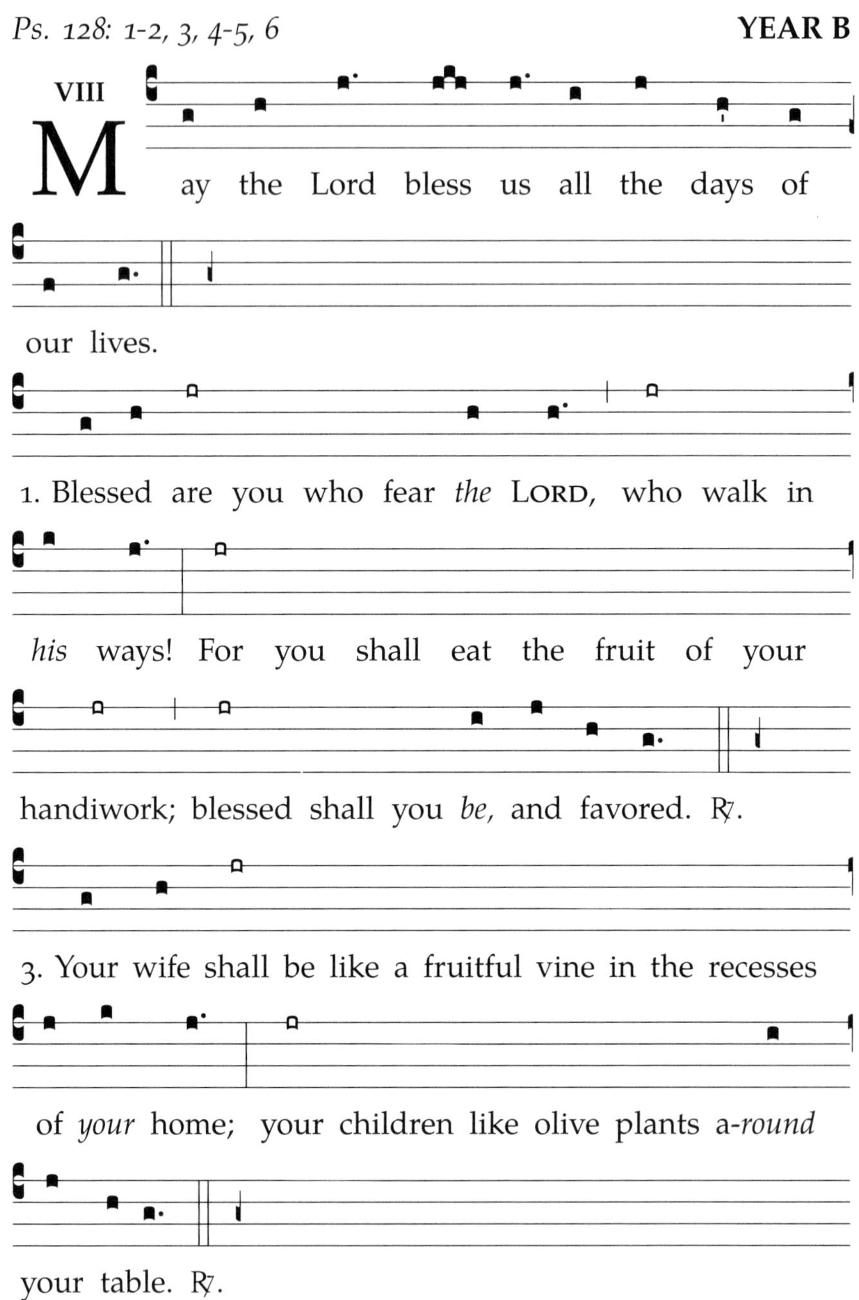
VIII
May the Lord bless us all the days of
our lives.
1. Blessed are you who fear *the* Lord, who walk in
his ways! For you shall eat the fruit of your
handiwork; blessed shall you *be,* and favored. ℟.
3. Your wife shall be like a fruitful vine in the recesses
of *your* home; your children like olive plants a-*round*
your table. ℟.

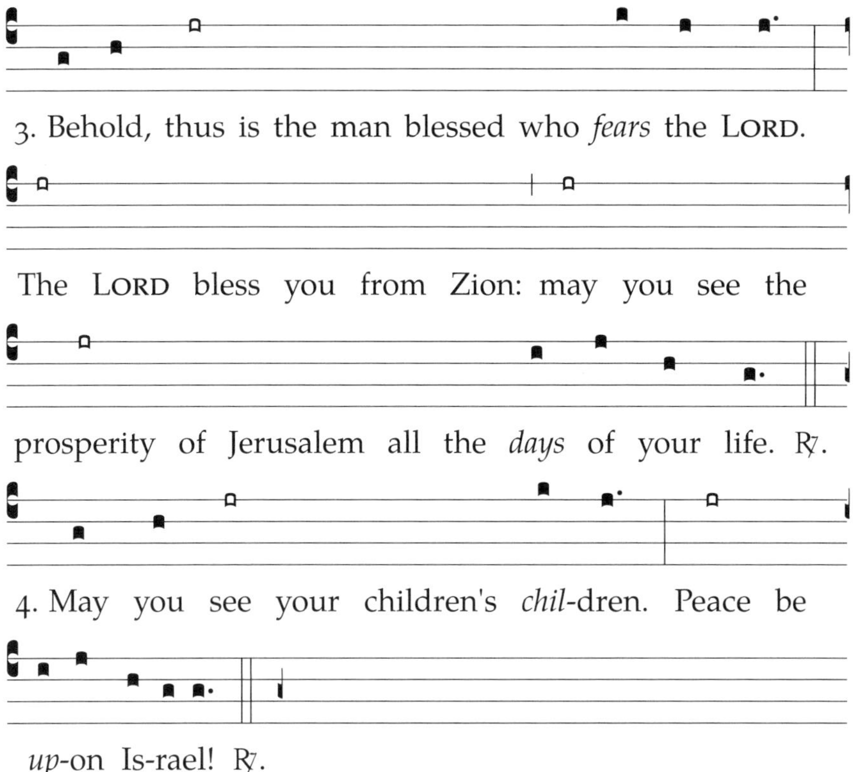
3. Behold, thus is the man blessed who *fears* the LORD.
The LORD bless you from Zion: may you see the
prosperity of Jerusalem all the *days* of your life. ℟.
4. May you see your children's *chil*-dren. Peace be
up-on Is-rael! ℟.

27TH SUNDAY IN ORDINARY TIME

Ps. 95: 1-2, 6-7, 8-9 **YEAR C**

VIII
If today you hear his voice, harden not your hearts.
1. Come, let us sing joyfully to the LORD; let us acclaim the Rock of our sal-*va*-tion. Let us come into his presence with thanksgiving; let us joyful-*ly* sing psalms to him. ℟.
2. Come, let us bow down in worship; let us kneel before the LORD who *made* us. For he is our God,

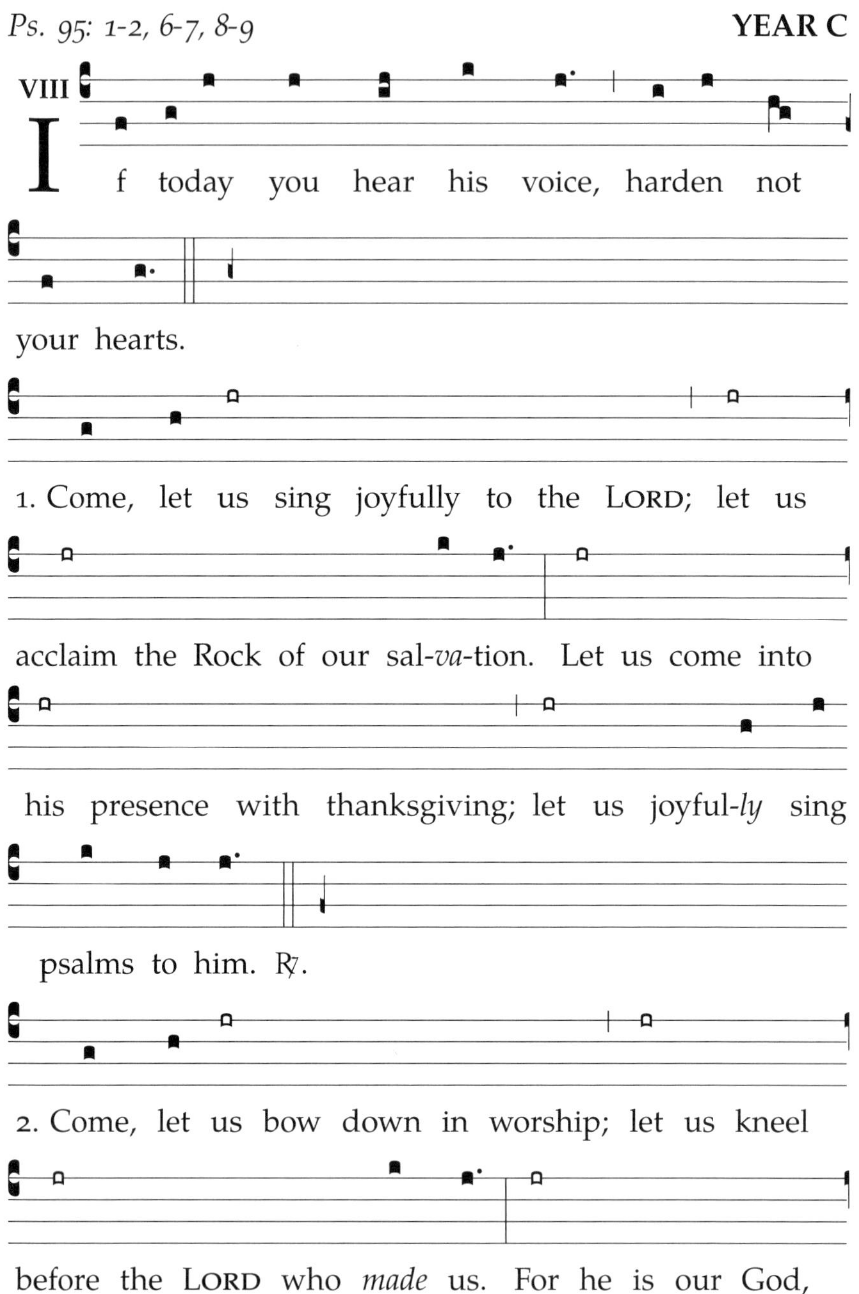

and we are the people he shepherds, the flock
he guides. ℟.
3. Oh, that today you would hear his voice: "Harden
not your hearts as at Meribah, as in the day of Massah
in the desert, where your fathers tempt-ed me; they
tested me though they had seen my works." ℟.

28th Sunday in Ordinary Time

Ps. 23: 1-3a, 3b-4, 5, 6 **YEAR A**

V
I shall live in the house of the Lord all the
days of my life.
1. The LORD is my shepherd; I shall not *want.*
In verdant pastures he gives *me* repose; beside
restful waters he leads me; he re-*fresh*-es my soul. ℟.
2. He guides me in right paths for his name's *sake.*
Even though I walk in the dark valley I fear
no *e*-vil; for you are at my side with your rod and

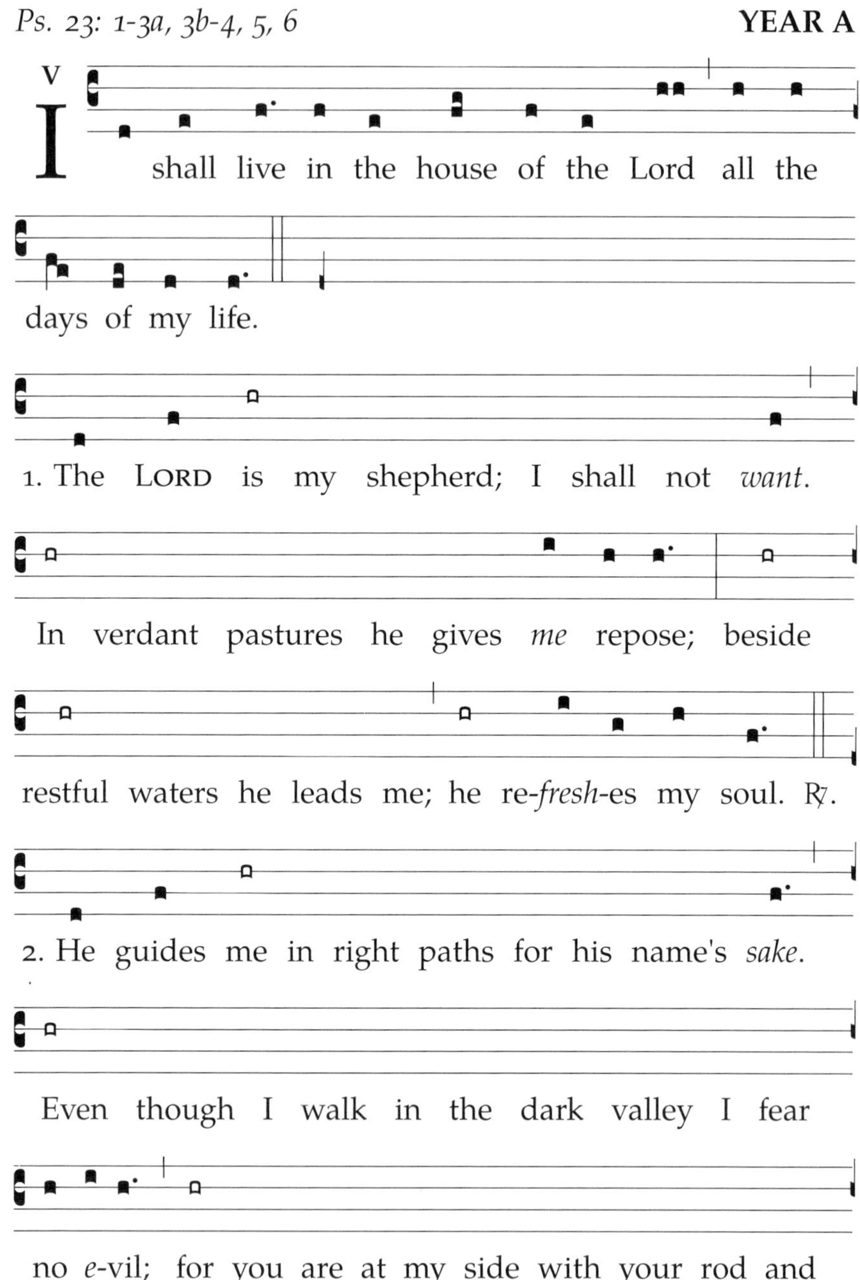

your staff that *give* me cour-age. ℟.
3. You spread the table before me in the sight of
my foes; you anoint my head with oil; *my* cup
overflows. ℟.
4. Only goodness and kindness follow me all the
days of *my* life; and I shall dwell in the
house of the *LORD* for years to come. ℟.

28TH SUNDAY IN ORDINARY TIME

Ps. 90: 12-13, 14-15, 16-17 **YEAR B**

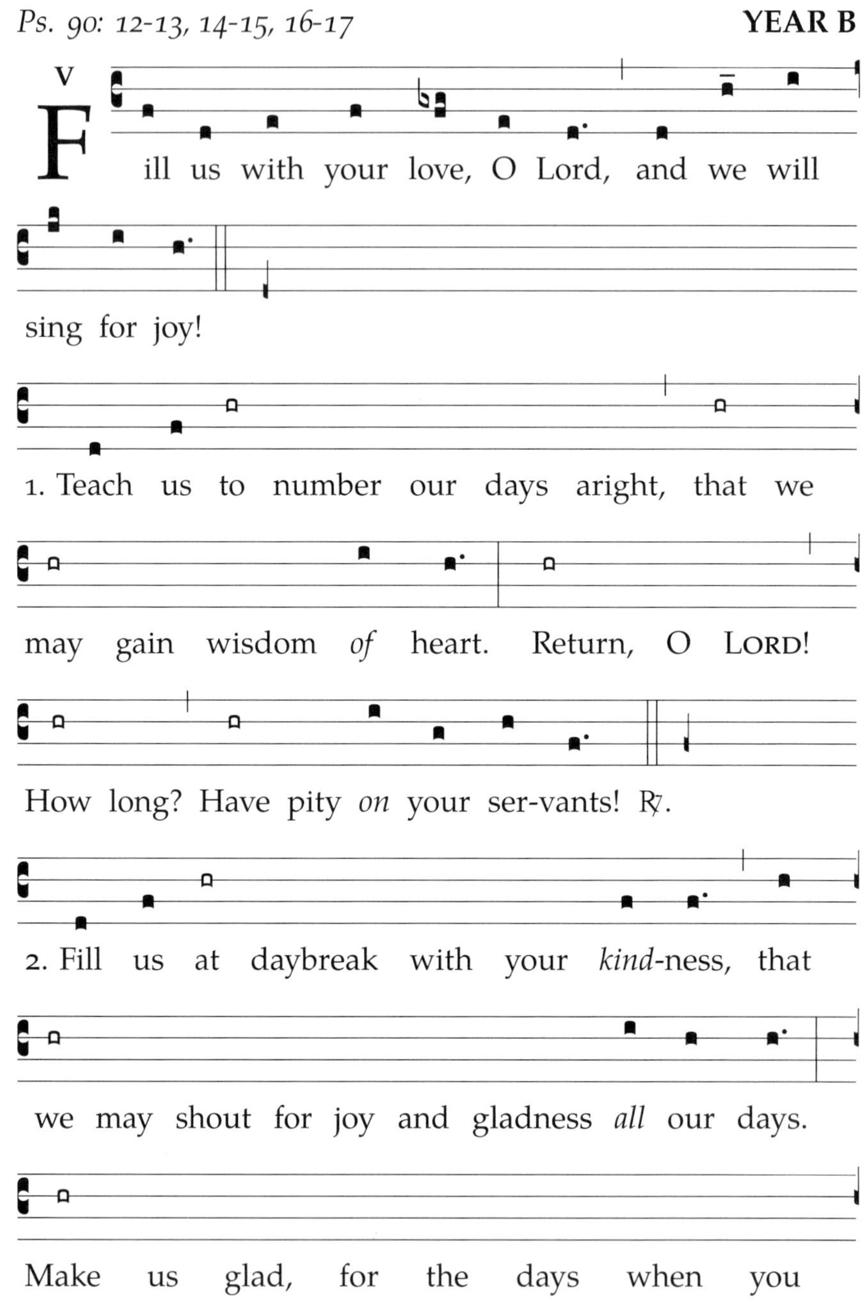

V
Fill us with your love, O Lord, and we will
sing for joy!
1. Teach us to number our days aright, that we
may gain wisdom *of* heart. Return, O LORD!
How long? Have pity *on* your ser-vants! ℟.
2. Fill us at daybreak with your *kind*-ness, that
we may shout for joy and gladness *all* our days.
Make us glad, for the days when you

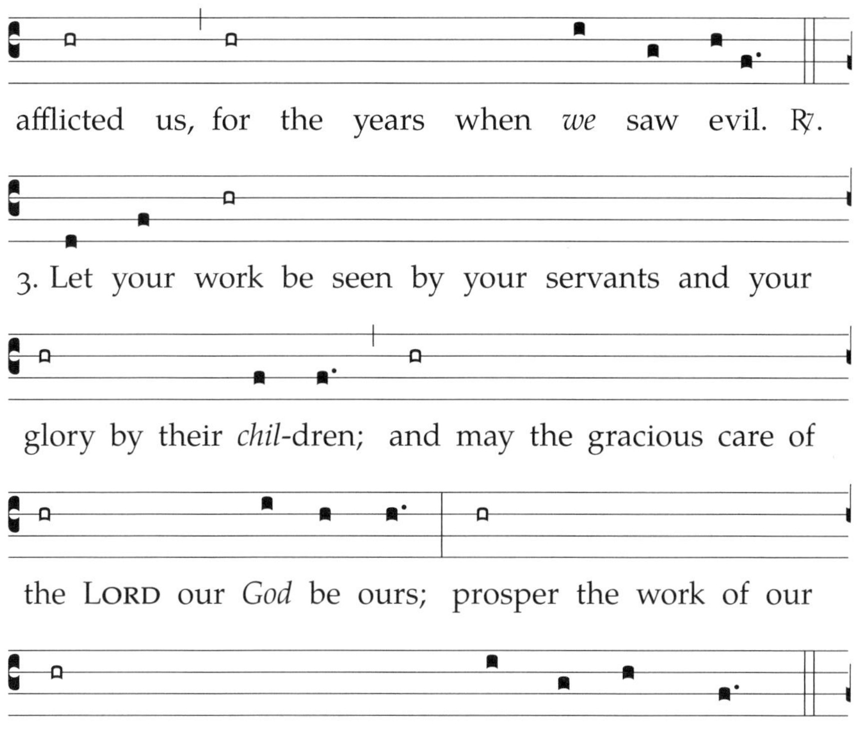
afflicted us, for the years when *we* saw evil. ℟.
3. Let your work be seen by your servants and your
glory by their *chil*-dren; and may the gracious care of
the LORD our *God* be ours; prosper the work of our
hands for us! Prosper the *work* of our hands! ℟.

28th Sunday in Ordinary Time

Ps. 98: 1, 2-3, 3-4 **YEAR C**

III
The Lord has revealed to the nations his
saving power.
1. Sing to the LORD a new song, for he has *done*
won-drous deeds; his right hand has won victory for
him, his *ho*-ly arm. ℟.
2. The LORD has made his salvation *known*: in the sight
of the nations he has re-*vealed* his justice. He has
remembered his kindness and his faithfulness toward

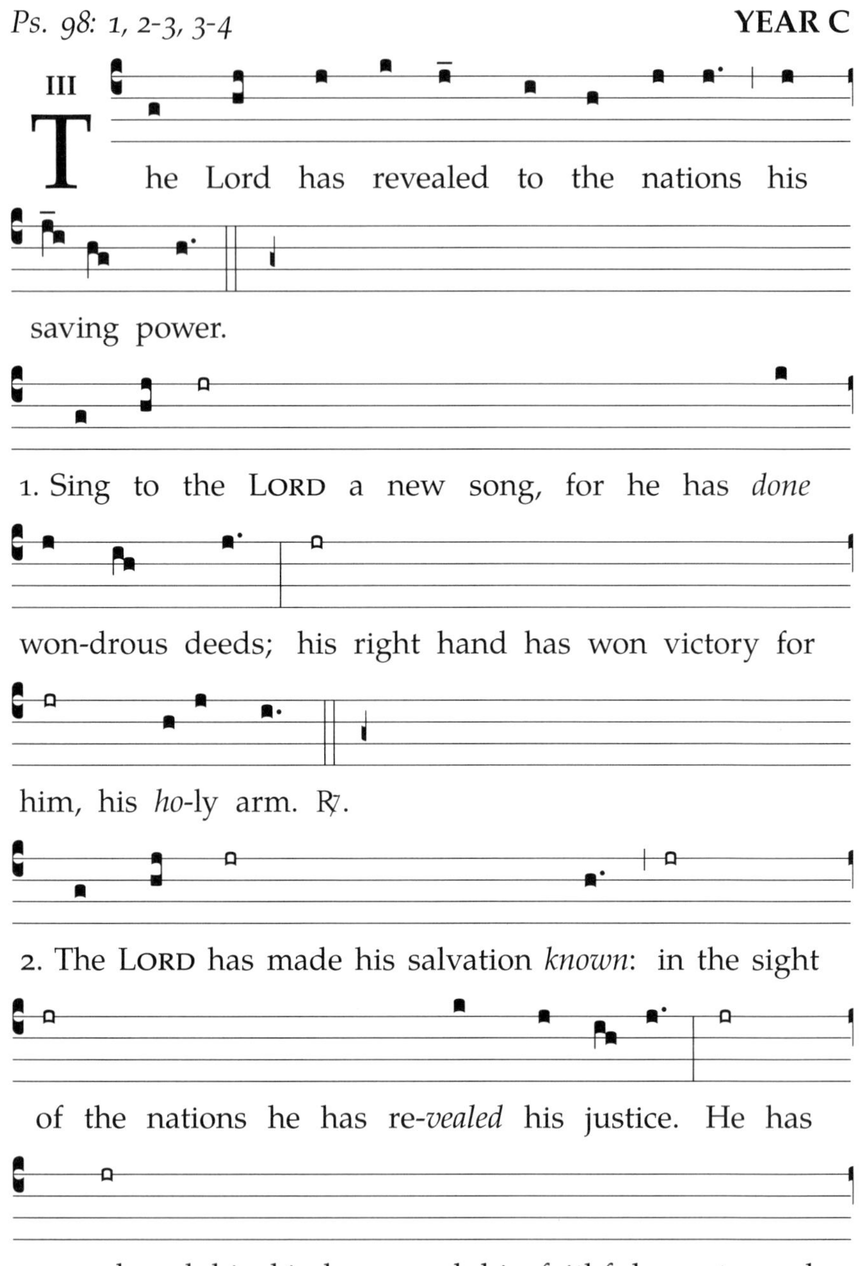

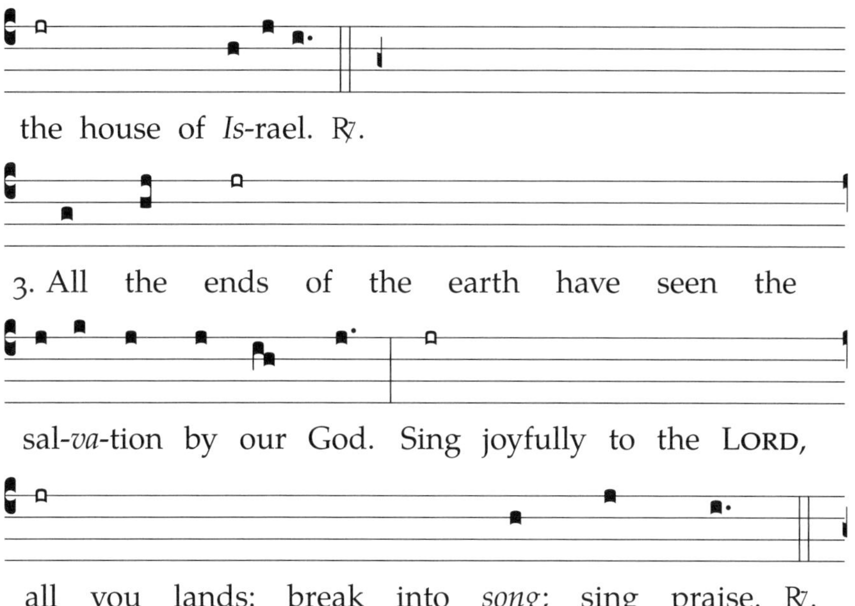
the house of *Is*-rael. ℟.
3. All the ends of the earth have seen the
sal-*va*-tion by our God. Sing joyfully to the LORD,
all you lands: break into *song;* sing praise. ℟.

29TH SUNDAY IN ORDINARY TIME

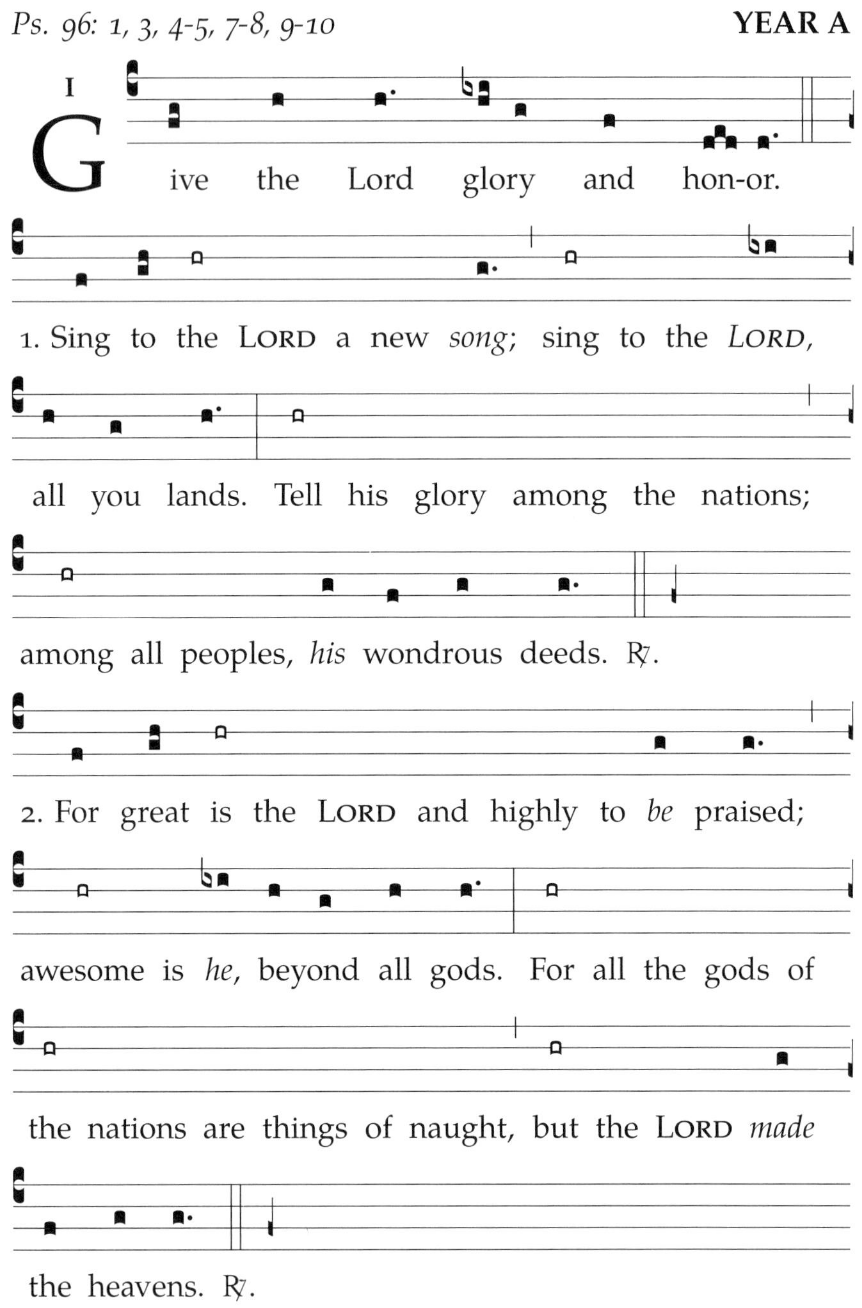
Ps. 96: 1, 3, 4-5, 7-8, 9-10
YEAR A
I
Give the Lord glory and hon-or.
1. Sing to the LORD a new song; sing to the LORD,
all you lands. Tell his glory among the nations;
among all peoples, his wondrous deeds. ℟.
2. For great is the LORD and highly to be praised;
awesome is he, beyond all gods. For all the gods of
the nations are things of naught, but the LORD made
the heavens. ℟.

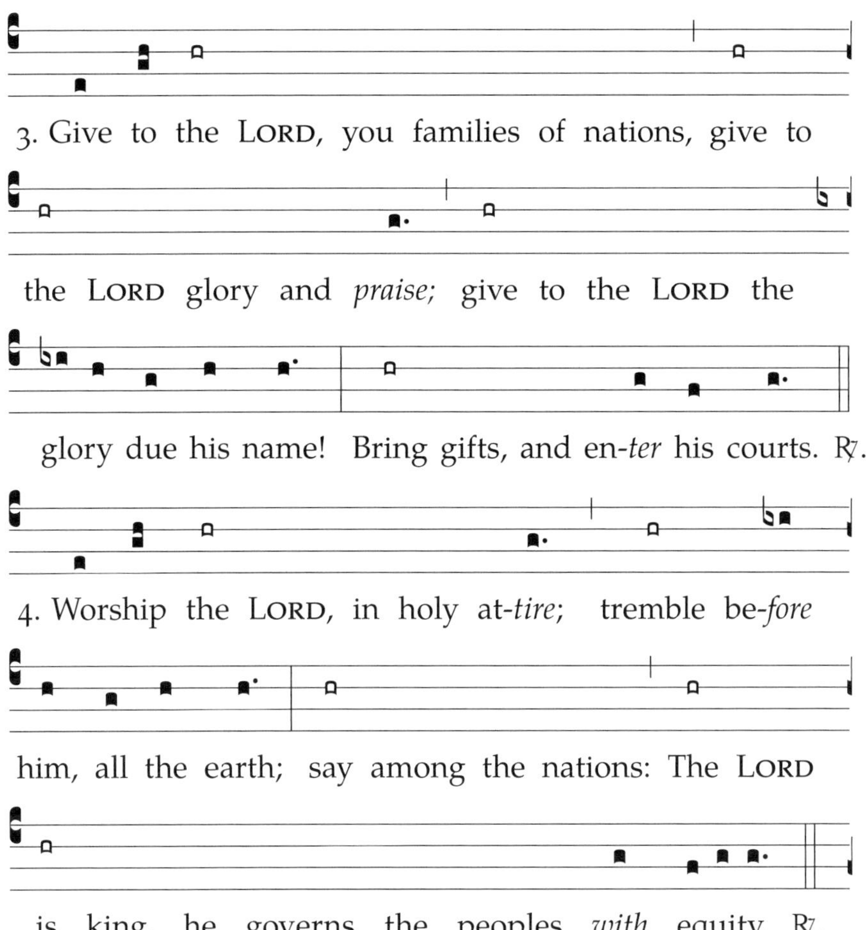
3. Give to the LORD, you families of nations, give to
the LORD glory and *praise;* give to the LORD the
glory due his name! Bring gifts, and en-*ter* his courts. ℟.
4. Worship the LORD, in holy at-*tire;* tremble be-*fore*
him, all the earth; say among the nations: The LORD
is king, he governs the peoples *with* equity. ℟.

29TH SUNDAY IN ORDINARY TIME

Ps. 33: 4-5, 18-19, 20, 22 **YEAR B**

II
Lord, let your mer-cy be on us, as we place
our trust in you.
1. Upright is the word of the LORD, and all his
works are *trust*-worthy. He loves justice and right;
of the kindness of the LORD *the* earth is full. ℟.
2. See, the eyes of the LORD are upon those who fear
him, upon those who hope for his *kind*-ness,
To deliver them from death and preserve them in *spite*

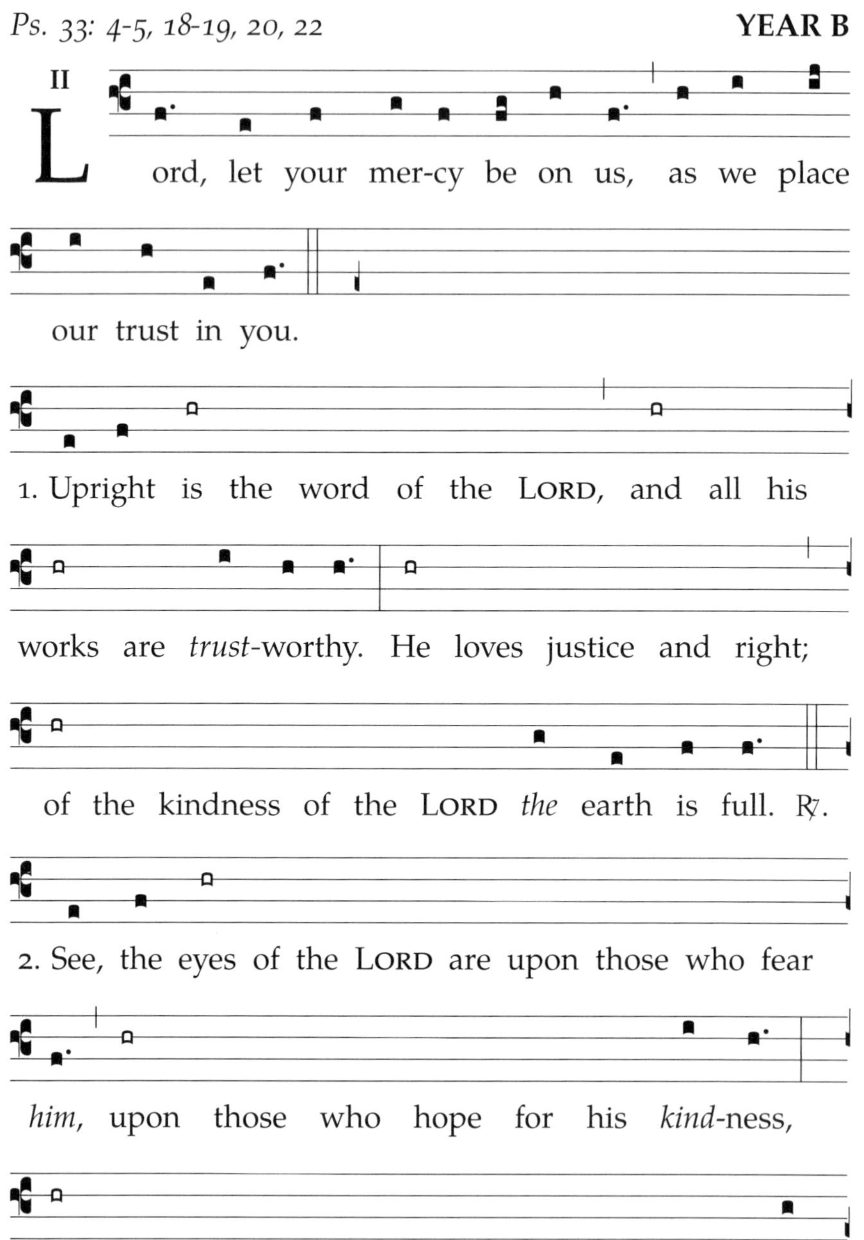

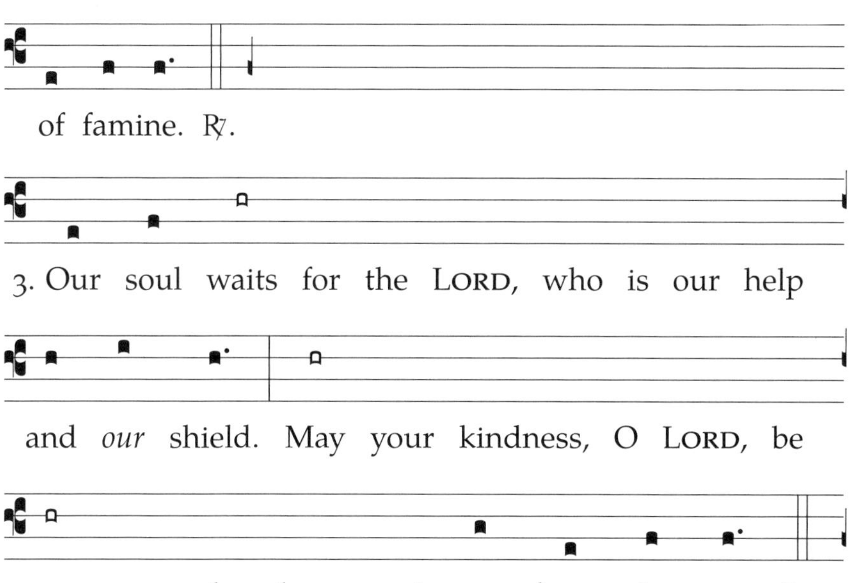
of famine. ℟.
3. Our soul waits for the LORD, who is our help
and *our* shield. May your kindness, O LORD, be
upon us who have put *our* hope in you. ℟.

29th Sunday in Ordinary Time

Ps. 121: 1-2, 3-4, 5-6, 7-8 **YEAR C**

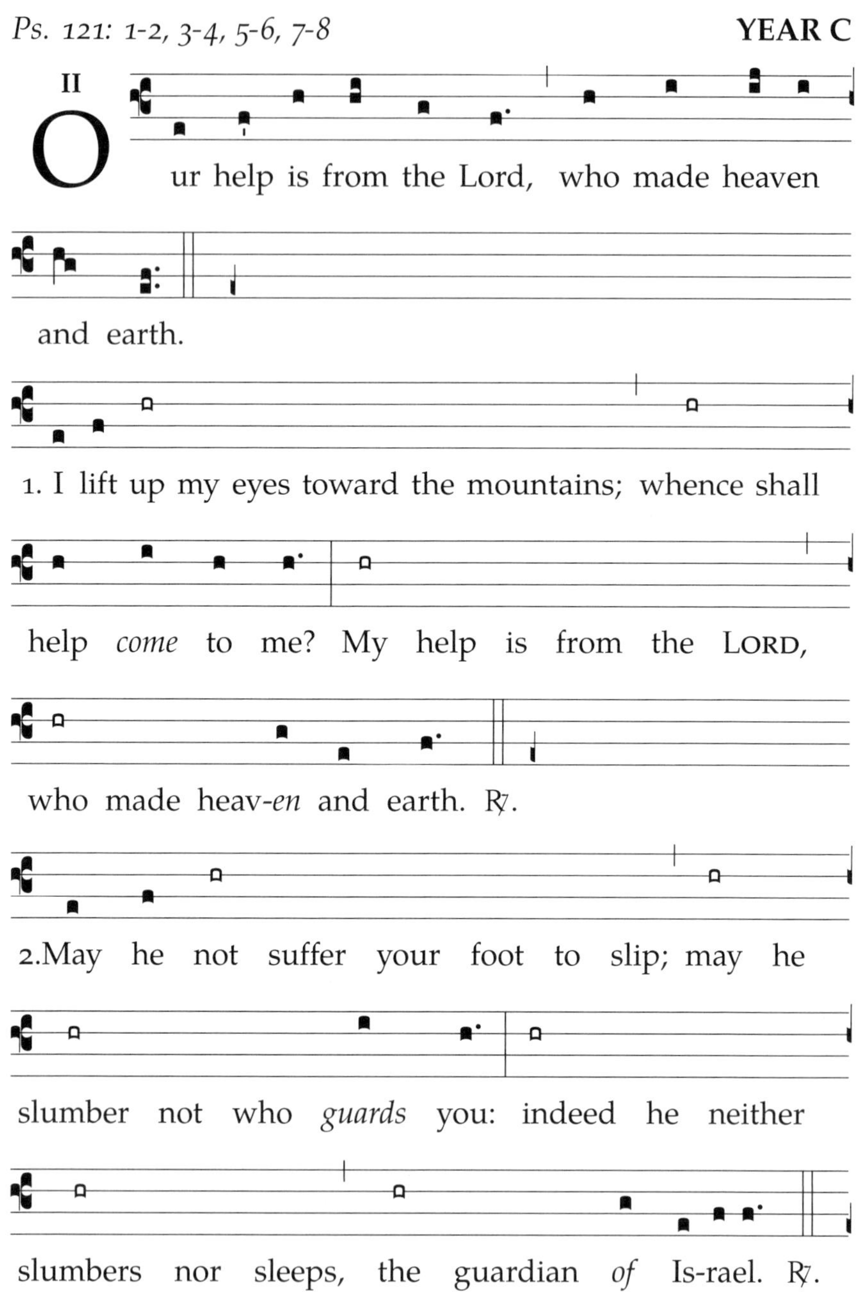
II
Our help is from the Lord, who made heaven and earth.
1. I lift up my eyes toward the mountains; whence shall help *come* to me? My help is from the LORD, who made heav-*en* and earth. ℟.
2.May he not suffer your foot to slip; may he slumber not who *guards* you: indeed he neither slumbers nor sleeps, the guardian *of* Is-rael. ℟.

3. The LORD is your guardian; the LORD is your shade;
he is beside you at your *right* hand. The sun shall
not harm you by day, nor *the* moon by night. ℟.
4. The LORD will guard you from all evil; he will
guard your life. The LORD will guard your coming
and your going, both now and *for*-ever. ℟.

30th Sunday in Ordinary Time

Ps. 18: 2-3, 3-4, 47, 51 **YEAR A**

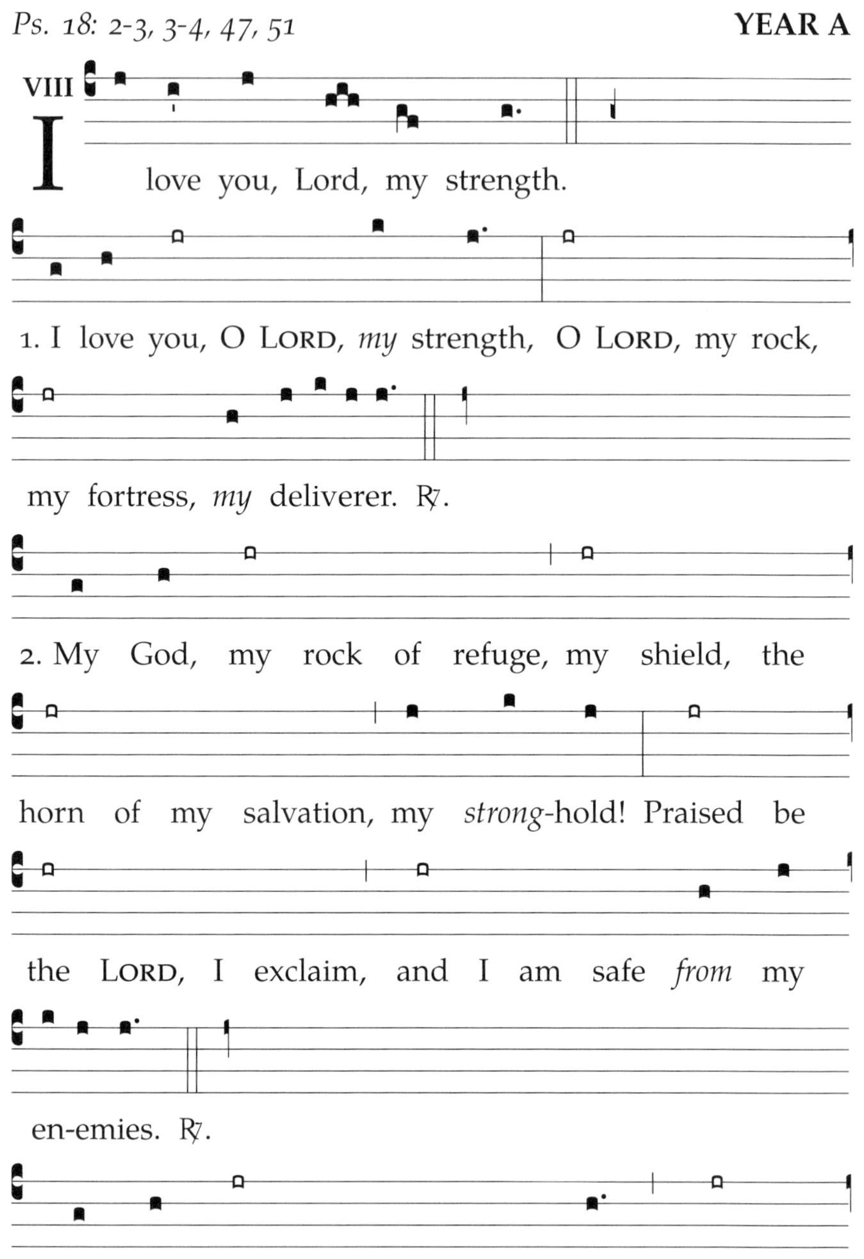
VIII
I love you, Lord, my strength.
1. I love you, O LORD, *my* strength, O LORD, my rock,
my fortress, *my* deliverer. ℟.
2. My God, my rock of refuge, my shield, the
horn of my salvation, my *strong*-hold! Praised be
the LORD, I exclaim, and I am safe *from* my
en-emies. ℟.
3. The LORD lives and blessed be my *rock!* Extolled be

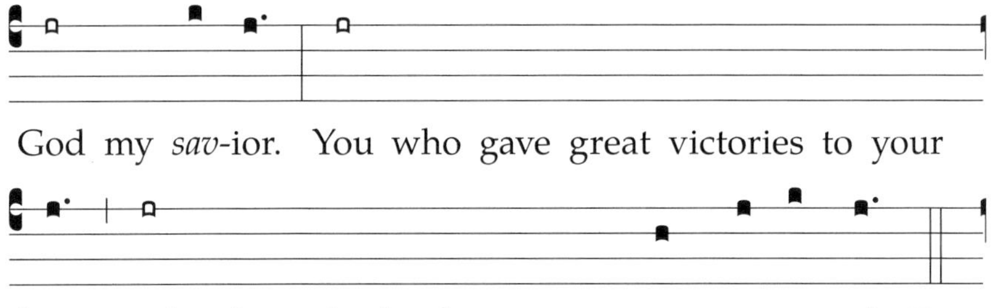

God my *sav*-ior. You who gave great victories to your king and showed kindness to *your* anointed. ℟.

30th Sunday in Ordinary Time

Ps. 126: 1-2, 2-3, 4-5, 6 **YEAR B**

VIII
The Lord has done great things for us; we are
filled with joy.
1. When the LORD brought back the captives of Zion,
we were like men *dream*-ing. Then our mouth was
filled with laughter, and our tongue *with* rejoicing. ℟.
2. Then they said among the nations, "The LORD has
done great *things* for them." The LORD has done
great things for us; *we* are glad indeed. ℟.

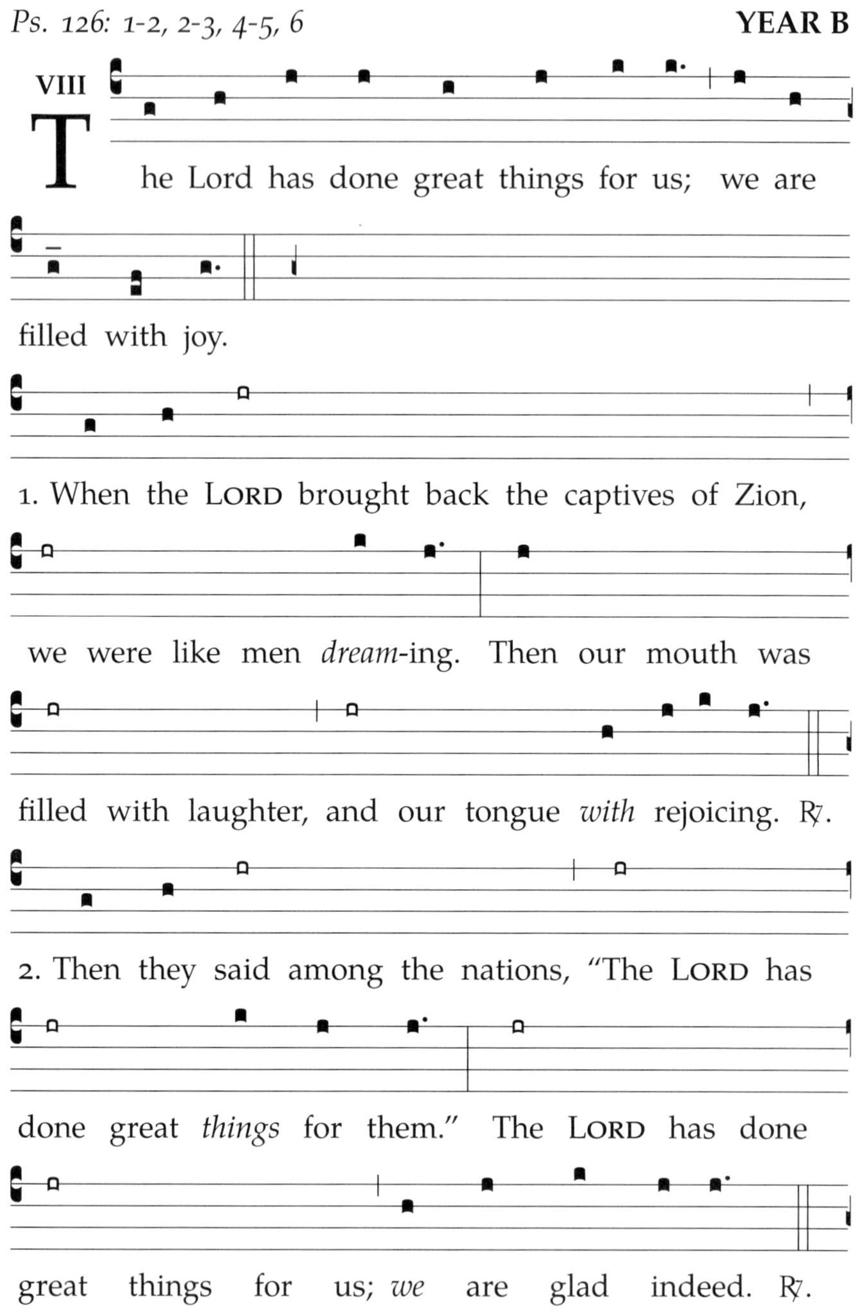

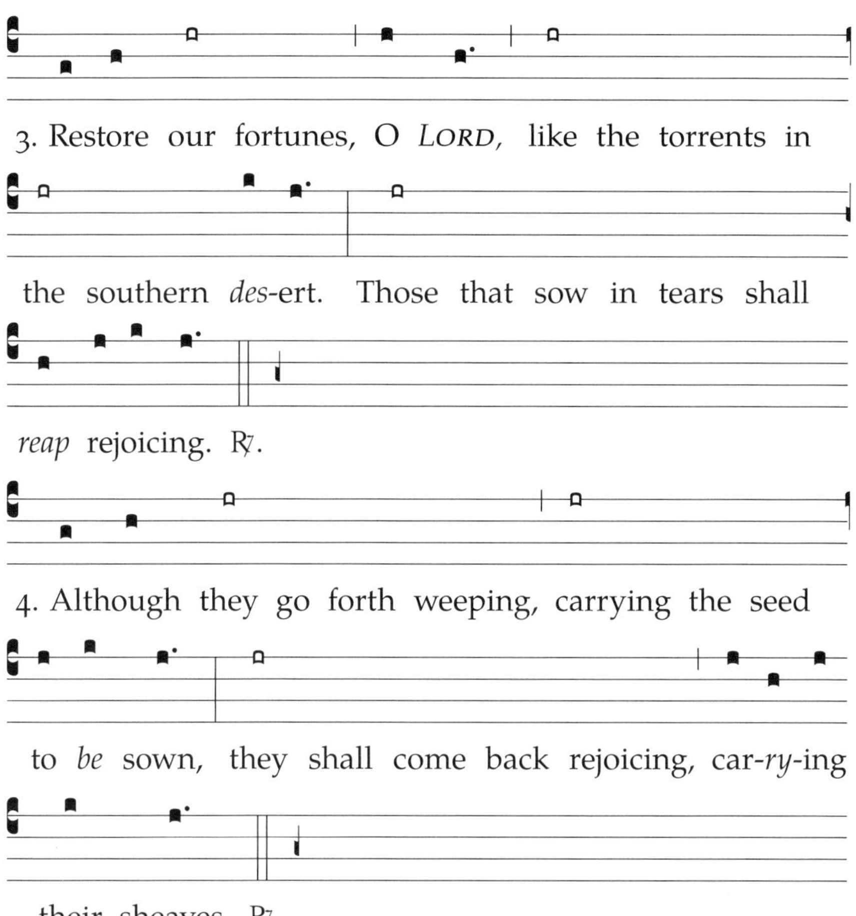
3. Restore our fortunes, O *Lord,* like the torrents in
the southern *des*-ert. Those that sow in tears shall
reap rejoicing. ℟.
4. Although they go forth weeping, carrying the seed
to *be* sown, they shall come back rejoicing, car-*ry*-ing
their sheaves. ℟.

30th Sunday in Ordinary Time

Ps. 34: 2-3, 17-18, 19, 23 **YEAR C**

IV
The Lord hears the cry of the poor.
1. I will bless the LORD at all times; his praise shall
be *ev*-er in my mouth. Let my soul glory in the
LORD; the lowly will hear me and *be* glad. ℟.
2. The LORD confronts the evildoers, to destroy
remembrance *of* them from the earth. When the just
cry out, the LORD hears them, and from all their
distress he res-*cues* them. ℟.

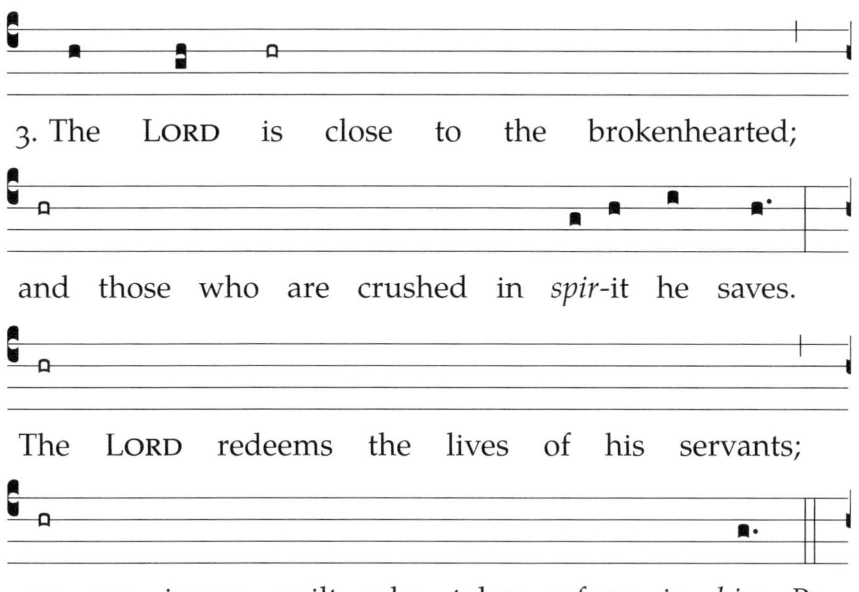
3. The LORD is close to the brokenhearted;
and those who are crushed in *spir*-it he saves.
The LORD redeems the lives of his servants;
no one incurs guilt who takes refuge in *him*. ℟.

31st Sunday in Ordinary Time

Ps. 131: 1, 2, 3 **YEAR A**

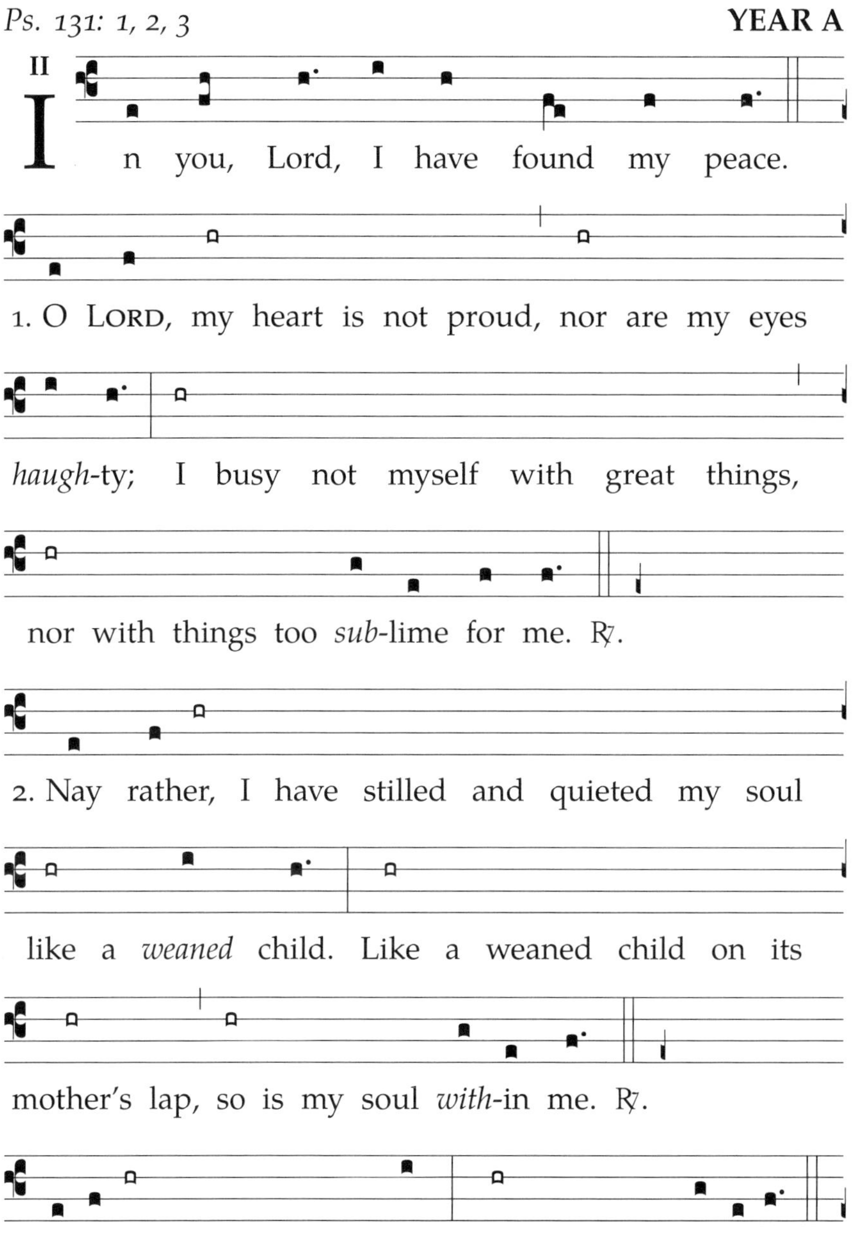

II
In you, Lord, I have found my peace.
1. O LORD, my heart is not proud, nor are my eyes
haugh-ty; I busy not myself with great things,
nor with things too *sub*-lime for me. ℟.
2. Nay rather, I have stilled and quieted my soul
like a *weaned* child. Like a weaned child on its
mother's lap, so is my soul *with*-in me. ℟.
3. O Is-rael, hope in the *LORD*, both now and *for*-ever. ℟.

31st Sunday in Ordinary Time

Ps. 18: 2-3, 3-4, 47, 51 **YEAR B**

VIII
I love you, Lord, my strength.
1. I love you, O LORD, *my* strength, O LORD,
my rock, my fortress, *my* deliverer. ℟.
2. My God, my rock of refuge, my shield, the
horn of my salvation, my *strong*-hold! Praised be
the LORD, I exclaim, and I am safe *from* my
en-emies. ℟.
3. The LORD lives and blessed be my *rock!* Extolled be

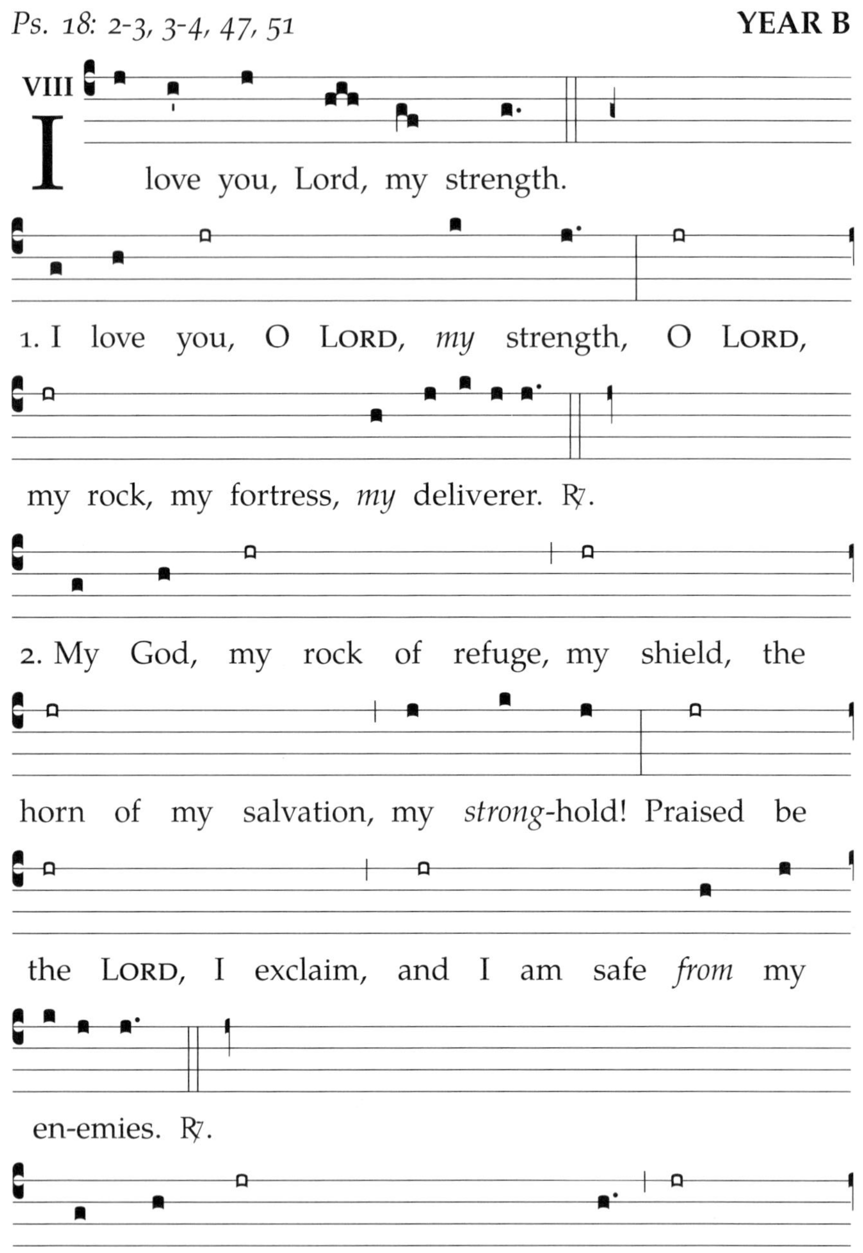

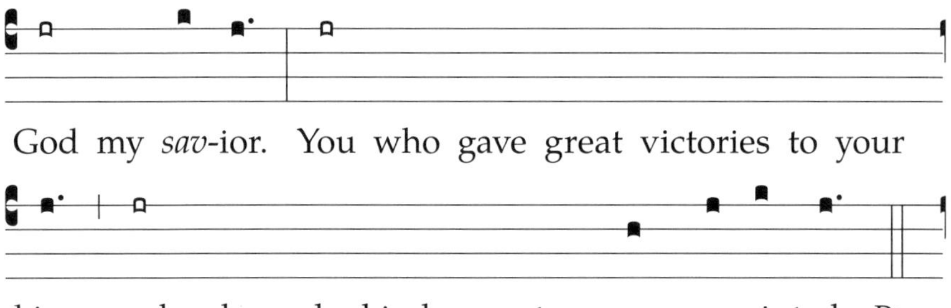
God my *sav*-ior. You who gave great victories to your
king and showed kindness to *your* anointed. ℟.

31st Sunday in Ordinary Time

Ps. 145: 1-2, 8-9, 10-11, 13-14 **YEAR C**

II
I will praise your name forev- er, my king and
my God.
1. I will extol you, O my God and King, and I will
bless your name forever and *ev*-er. Every day will
I bless you, and I will praise your name forever *and*
ever. ℟.
2. The Lord is gracious and merciful, slow to
anger and of great *kind*-ness. The Lord is

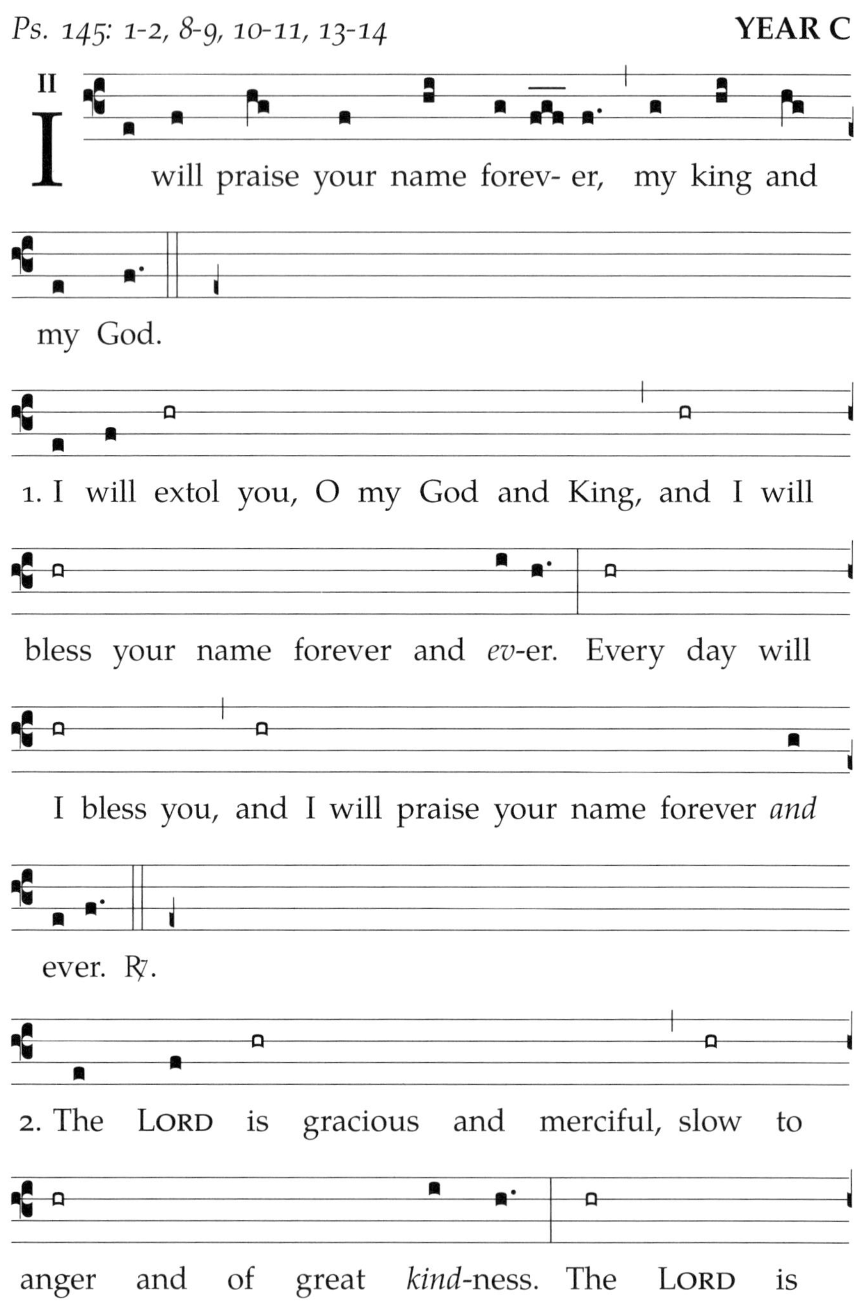

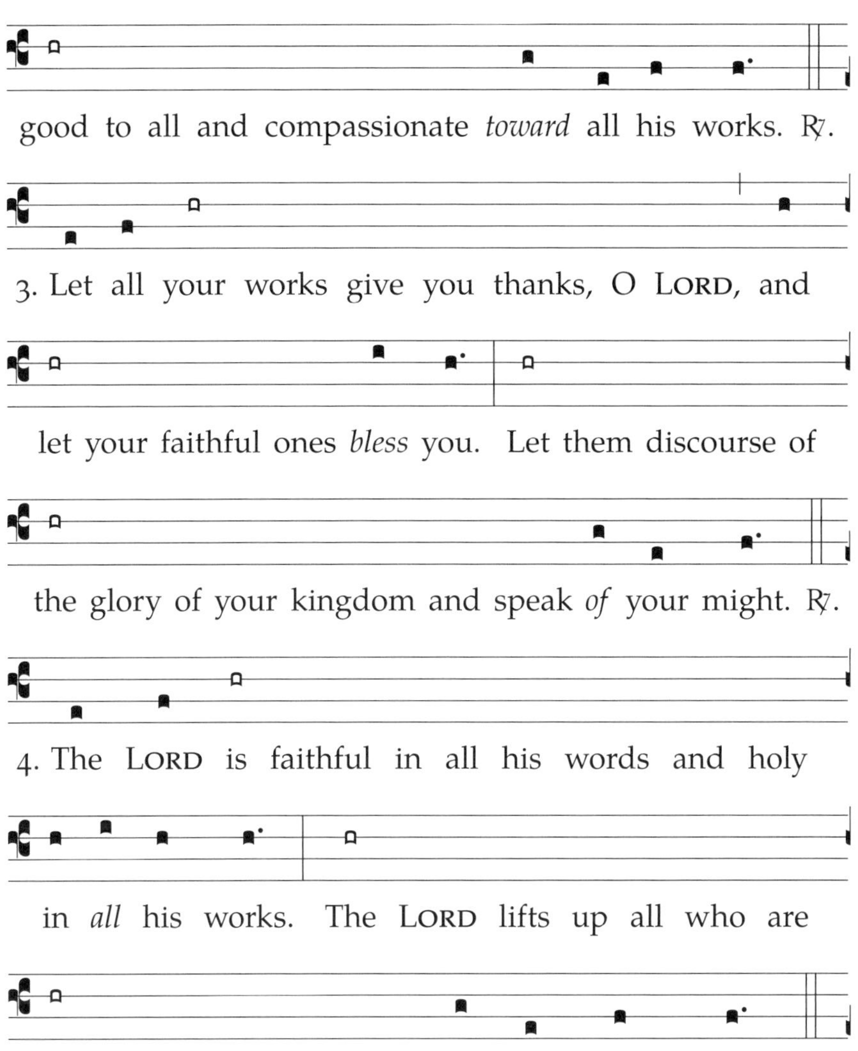
good to all and compassionate *toward* all his works. ℟.
3. Let all your works give you thanks, O LORD, and
let your faithful ones *bless* you. Let them discourse of
the glory of your kingdom and speak *of* your might. ℟.
4. The LORD is faithful in all his words and holy
in *all* his works. The LORD lifts up all who are
falling and raises up all *who* are bowed down. ℟.

32nd Sunday in Ordinary Time

Ps. 63: 2, 3-4, 5-6, 7-8 **YEAR A**

III
My soul is thirsting for you, O Lord my God.
1. O God, you are my *God* whom I seek;
for you my flesh pines and my soul thirsts
like the earth, parched, lifeless *and* without water. ℟.
2. Thus have I gazed toward you in the sanctuary to
see your power *and* your glory, for your kindness is a
greater good than life; my lips *shall* glori-fy you.

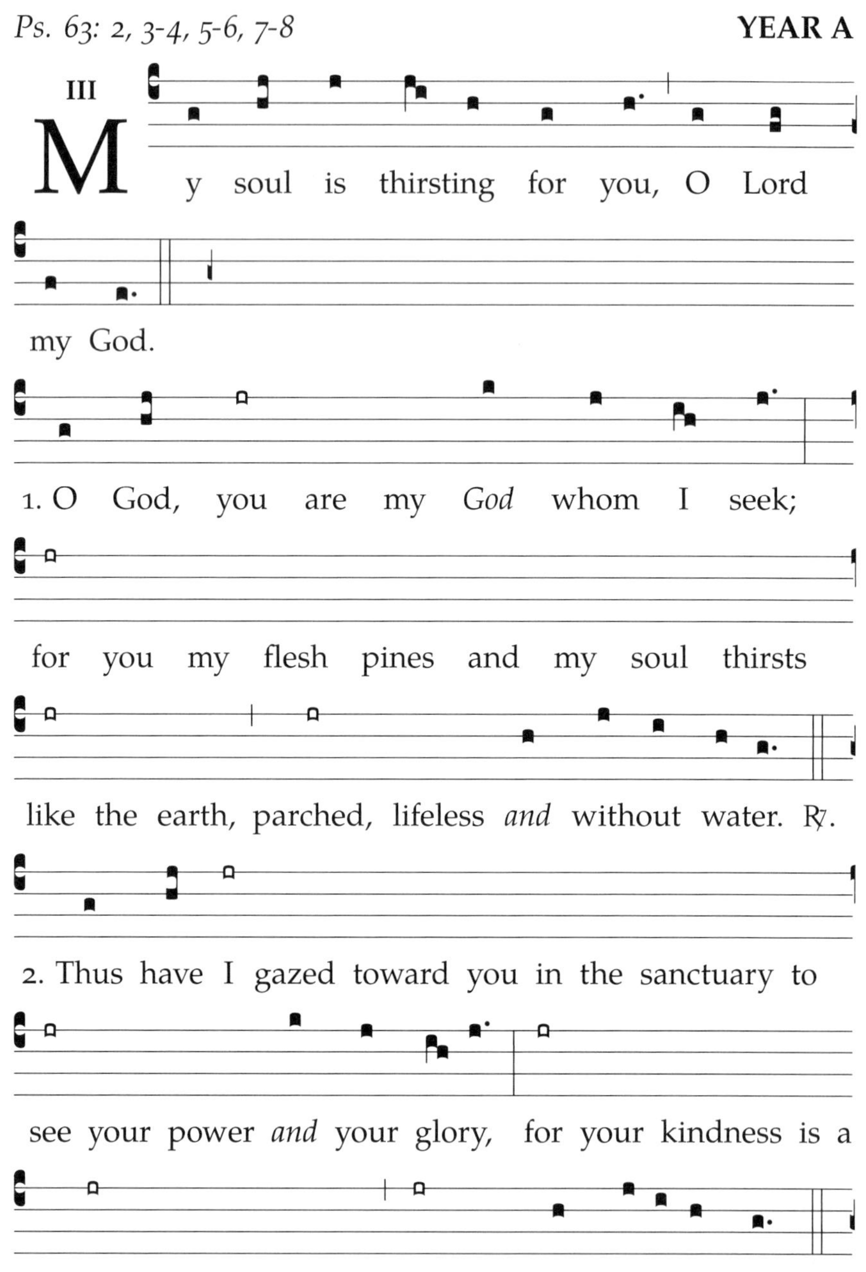

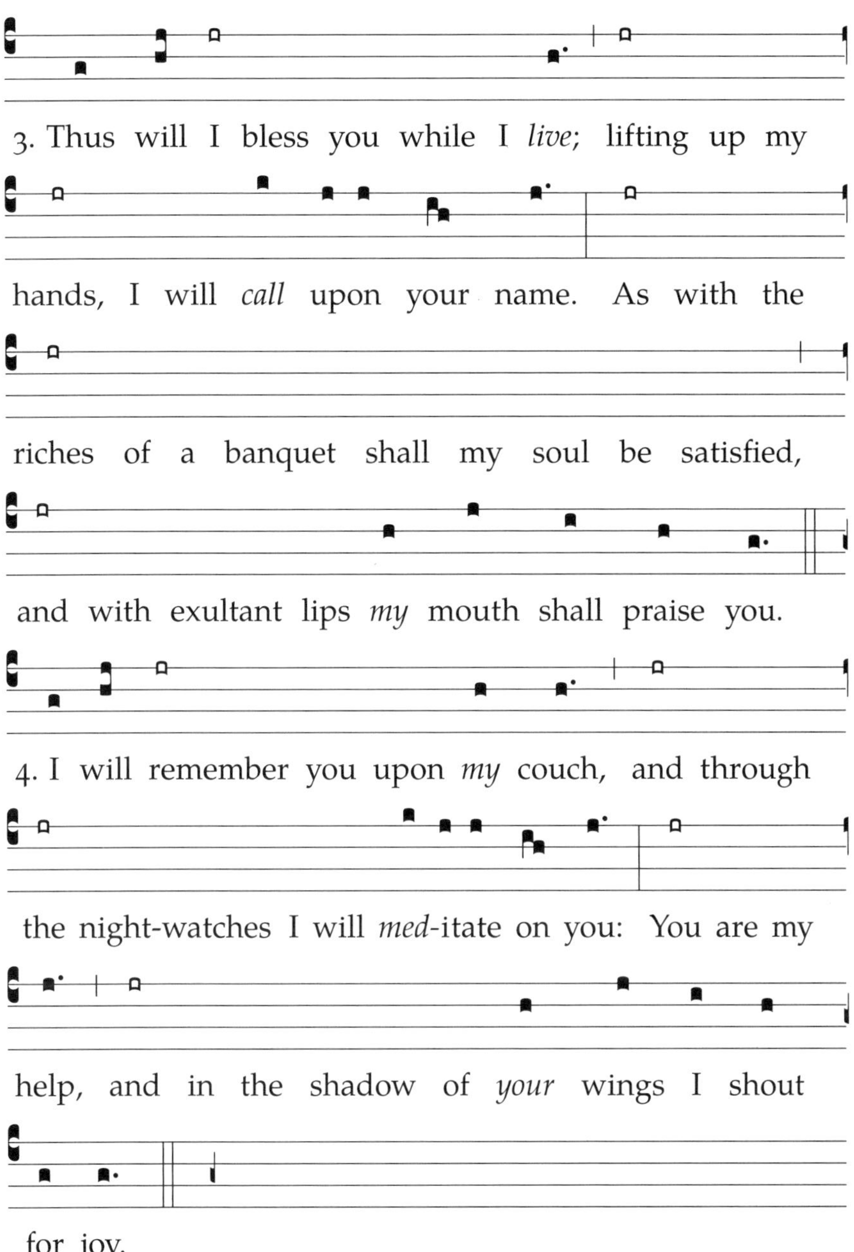
3. Thus will I bless you while I *live;* lifting up my
hands, I will *call* upon your name. As with the
riches of a banquet shall my soul be satisfied,
and with exultant lips *my* mouth shall praise you.
4. I will remember you upon *my* couch, and through
the night-watches I will *med*-itate on you: You are my
help, and in the shadow of *your* wings I shout
for joy.

32nd Sunday in Ordinary Time

Ps. 146: 7, 8-9, 9-10 **YEAR B**

VIII
Praise the Lord, my soul!
1. The LORD keeps faith forever, secures justice for the
op-*pressed*, gives food to the *hun*-gry. The *LORD* sets
captives free. ℟.
2. The LORD gives sight to the blind; the LORD
raises up those who were *bowed* down.
The LORD loves the just; the LORD *pro*-tects
strangers. ℟.

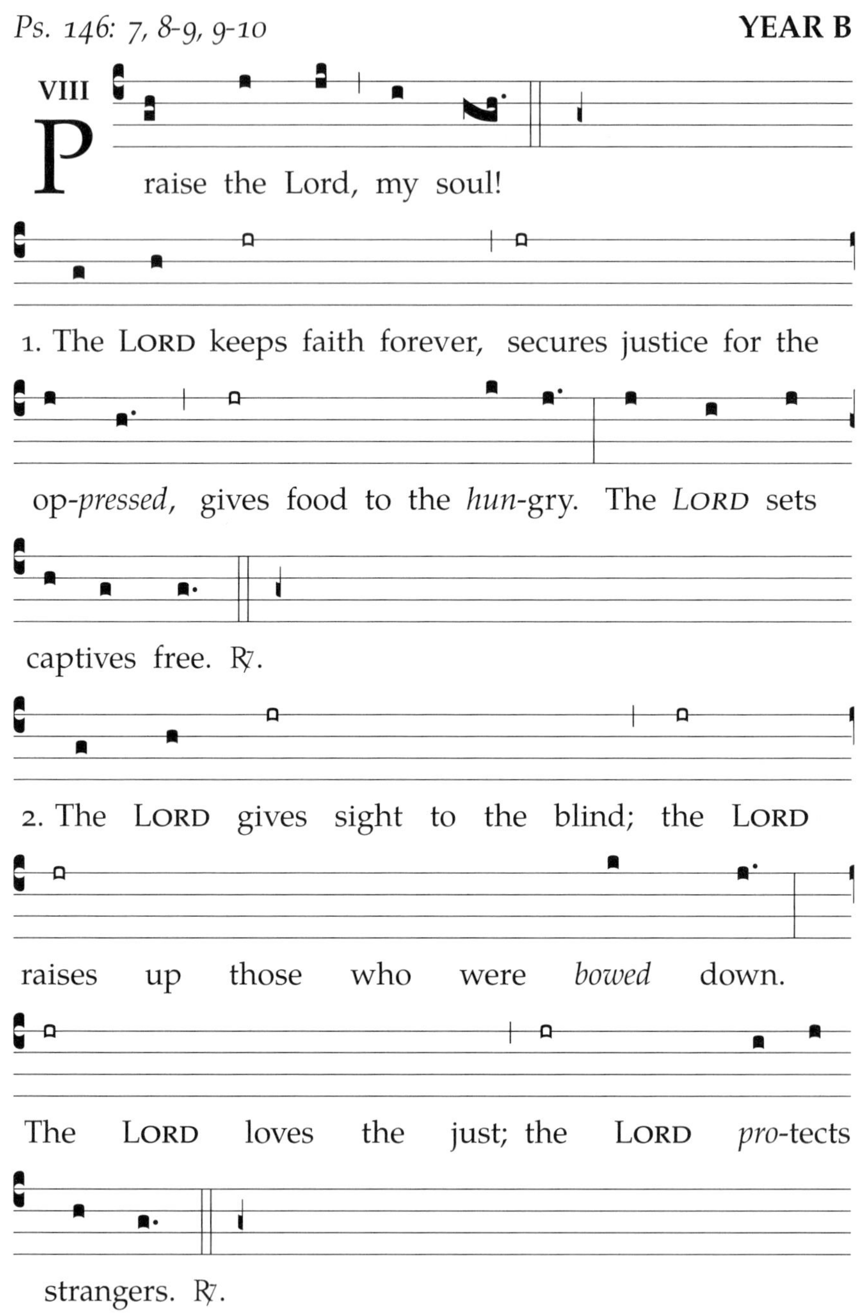

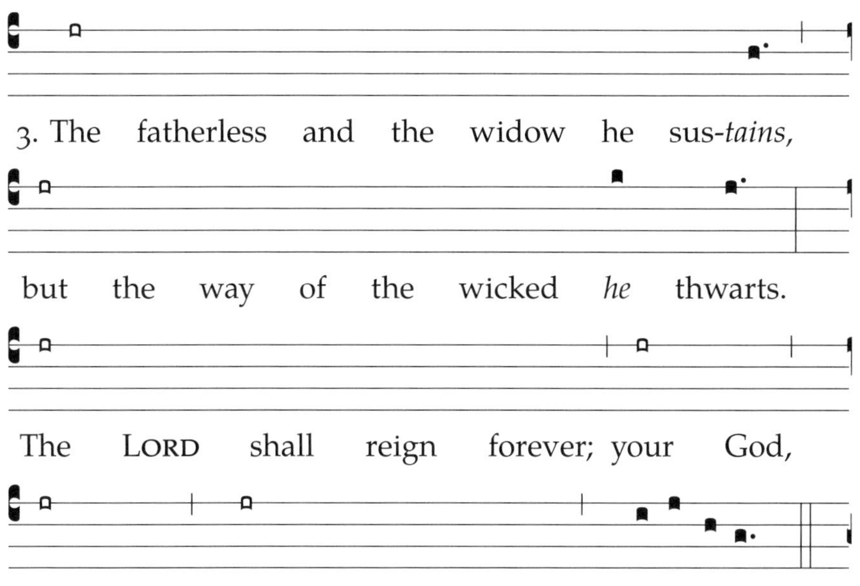
3. The fatherless and the widow he sus-*tains*,
but the way of the wicked *he* thwarts.
The LORD shall reign forever; your God,
O Zion, through all generations. *Al*-le-luia. ℟.

32nd Sunday in Ordinary Time

Ps. 17: 1, 5-6, 8, 15 **YEAR C**

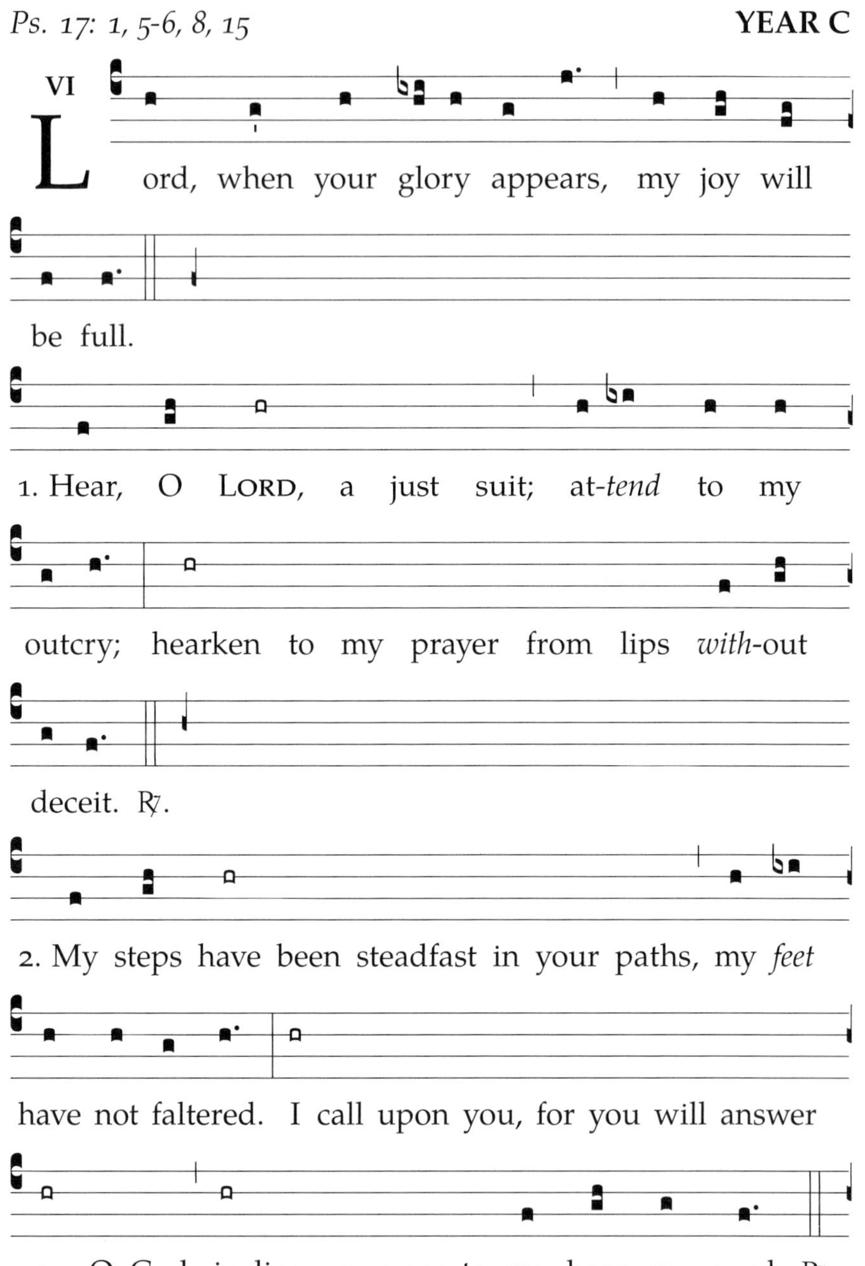
VI
Lord, when your glory appears, my joy will
be full.
1. Hear, O LORD, a just suit; at-*tend* to my
outcry; hearken to my prayer from lips *with*-out
deceit. ℟.
2. My steps have been steadfast in your paths, my *feet*
have not faltered. I call upon you, for you will answer
me, O God; incline your ear to *me*; hear my word. ℟.

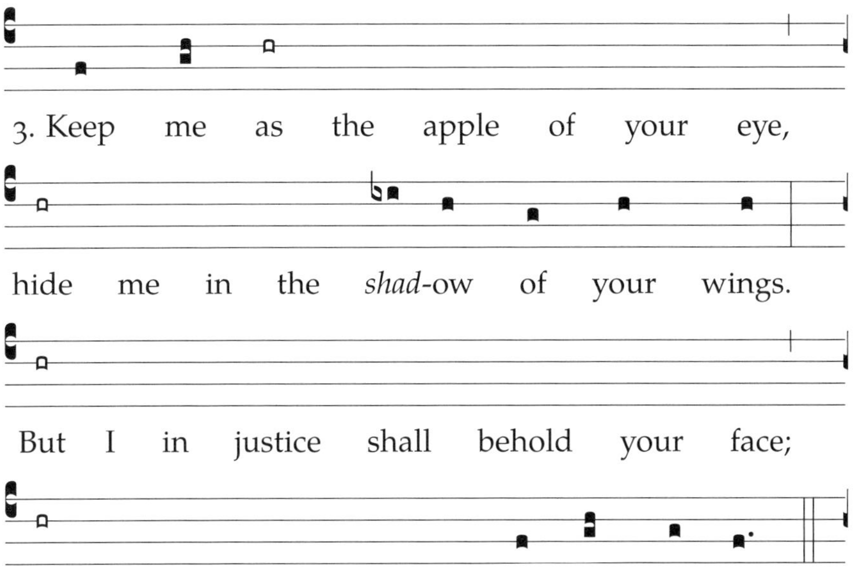
3. Keep me as the apple of your eye,
hide me in the *shad*-ow of your wings.
But I in justice shall behold your face;
on waking I shall be content *in* your presence. ℟.

33rd Sunday in Ordinary Time

Ps. 128: 1-2, 3, 4-5 **YEAR A**

II
Blessed are those who fear the Lord.
1. Blessed are you who fear the *Lord,* who walk
in *his* ways! For you shall eat the fruit of
your handiwork; blessed shall you be, *and* favored. ℟.
2. Your wife shall be like a fruitful vine in the recesses
of *your* home; your children like olive plants around
your table. ℟.
3. Behold, thus is the man blessed who *fears* the Lord.

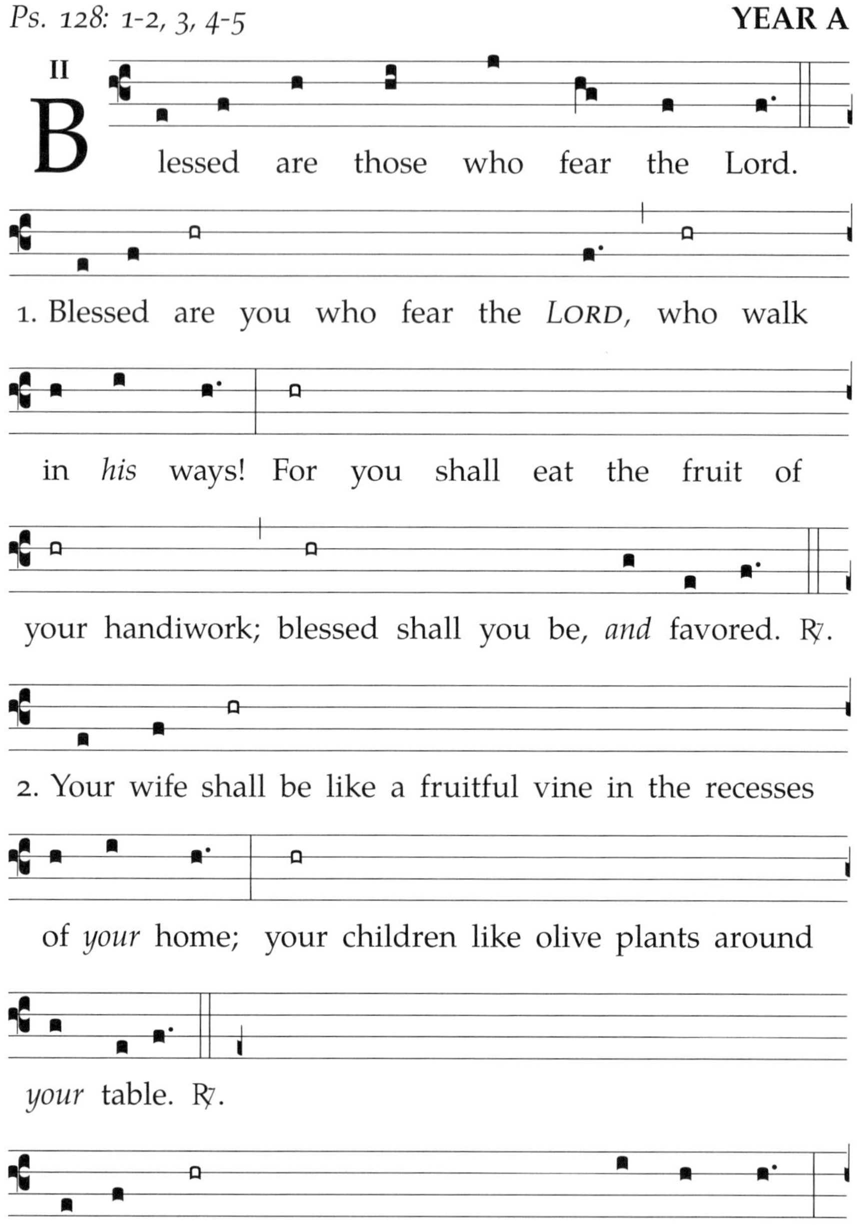

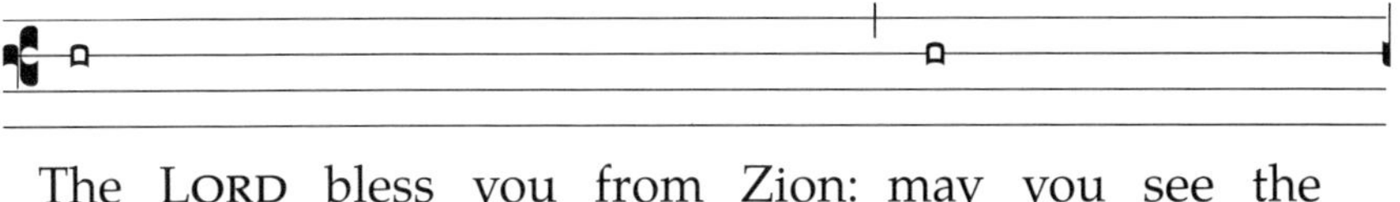

The LORD bless you from Zion: may you see the

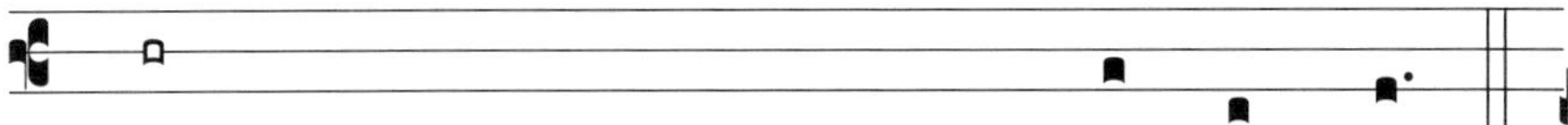

prosperity of Jerusalem all the days *of* your life. ℟.

33rd Sunday in Ordinary Time

Ps. 16: 5, 8, 9-10, 11 **YEAR B**

II
You are my inher-itance, O Lord.
1. O Lord, my allotted portion and my *cup*, you it is
who hold fast *my* lot. I set the Lord ever before
me; with him at my right hand I shall *not* be
disturbed. ℟.
2. Therefore my heart is glad and my soul re-*joic*-es,
my body, too, abides in *con*-fidence; because you
will not abandon my soul to the netherworld, nor

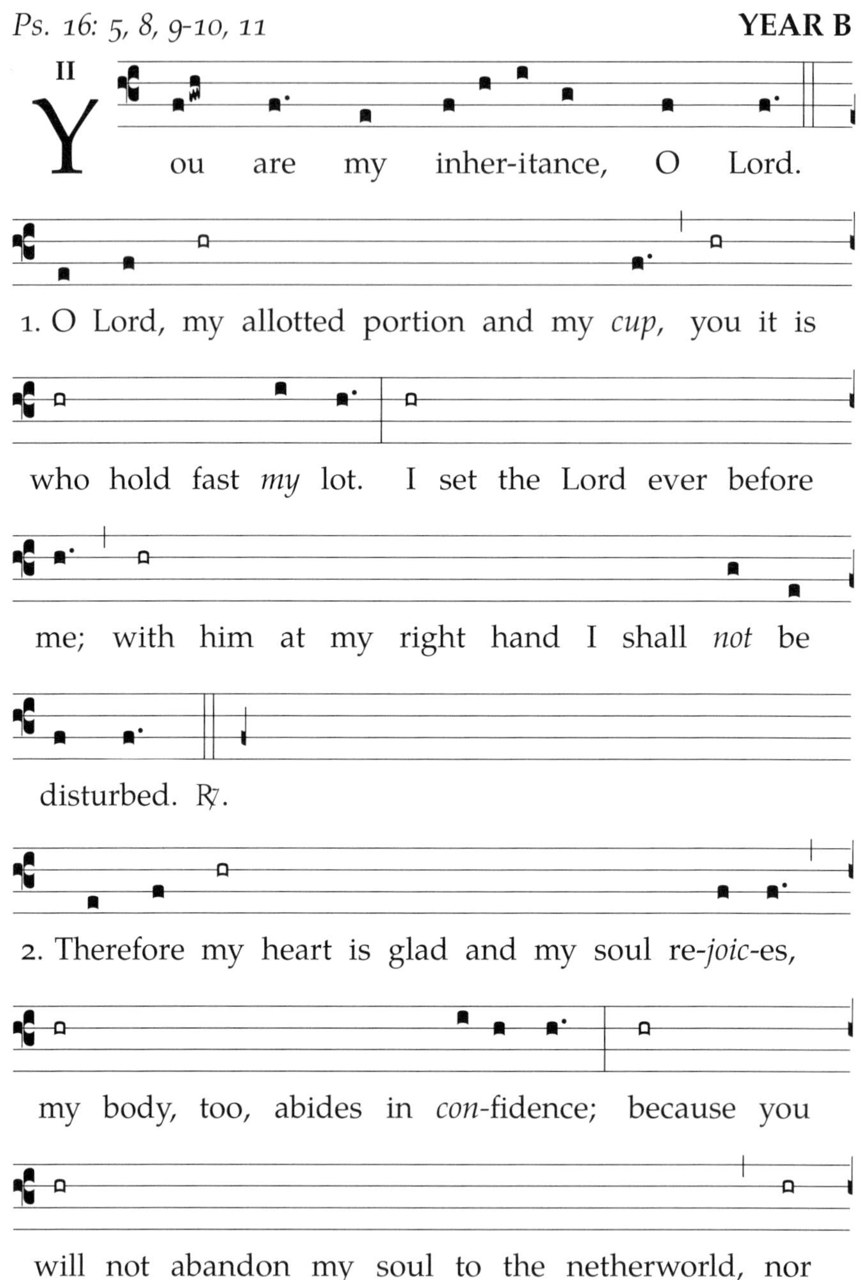

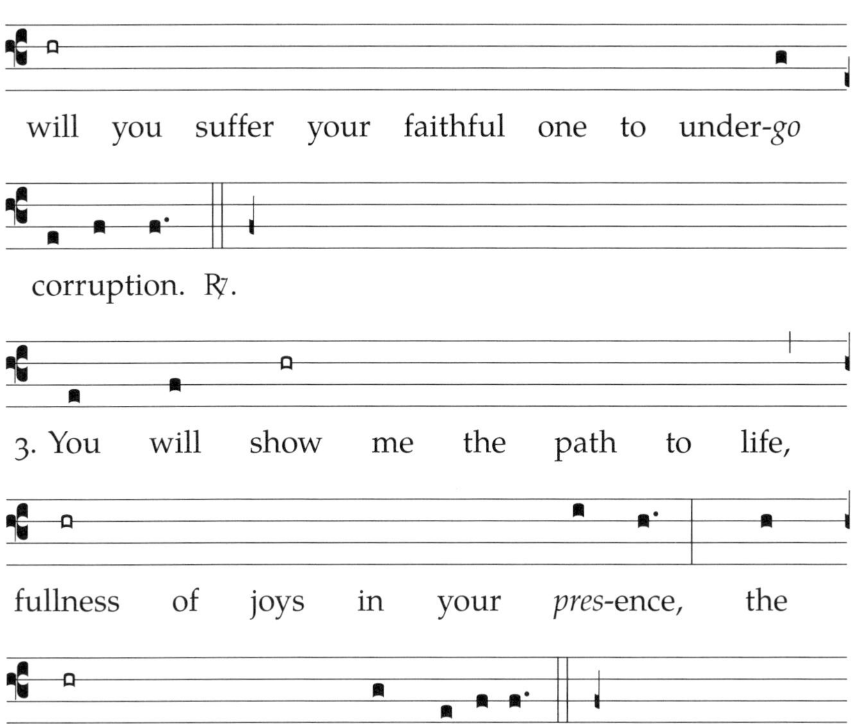
will you suffer your faithful one to under-*go*
corruption. ℟.
3. You will show me the path to life,
fullness of joys in your *pres*-ence, the
delights at your right *hand* forever. ℟.

33rd Sunday in Ordinary Time

Ps. 98: 5-6, 7-8, 9 **YEAR C**

VIII
The Lord comes to rule the earth with justice.
1. Sing praise to the LORD with the harp, with the
harp and me-*lo*-dious song. With trumpets and the
sound of the horn sing joyfully be-*fore* the King,
the LORD. ℟.
2. Let the sea and what fills it resound, the world
and those who *dwell* in it; let the rivers clap
their hands, the mountains *shout* with them for joy. ℟.

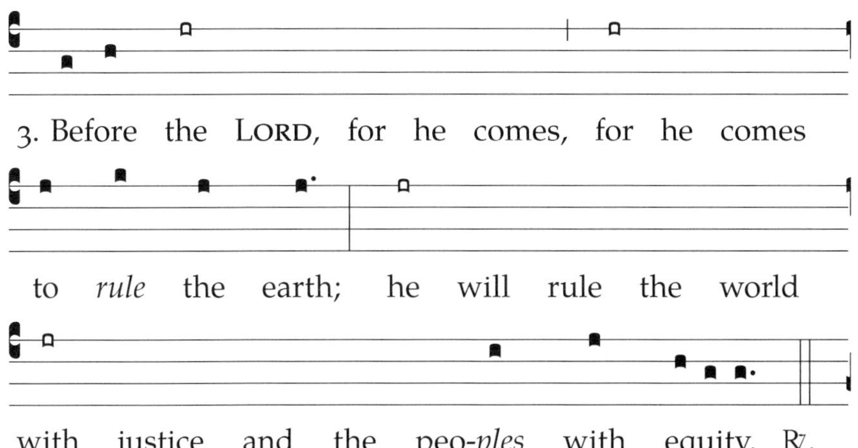
3. Before the LORD, for he comes, for he comes
to rule the earth; he will rule the world
with justice and the peo-ples with equity. ℟.

Christ the King

Ps. 23: 1-2, 2-3, 5-6 **YEAR A**

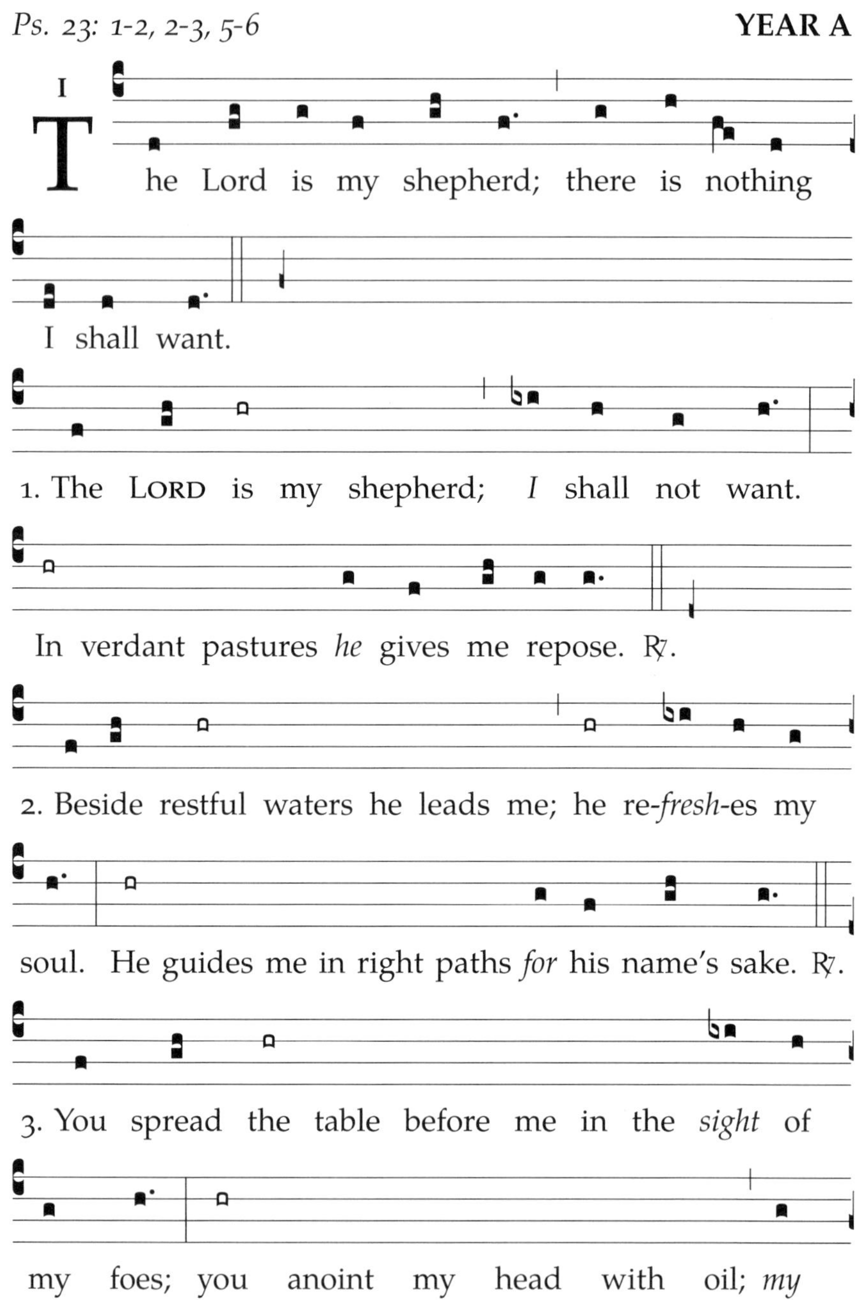
I
The Lord is my shepherd; there is nothing I shall want.
1. The LORD is my shepherd; *I* shall not want.
In verdant pastures *he* gives me repose. ℟.
2. Beside restful waters he leads me; he re-*fresh*-es my soul. He guides me in right paths *for* his name's sake. ℟.
3. You spread the table before me in the *sight* of my foes; you anoint my head with oil; *my*

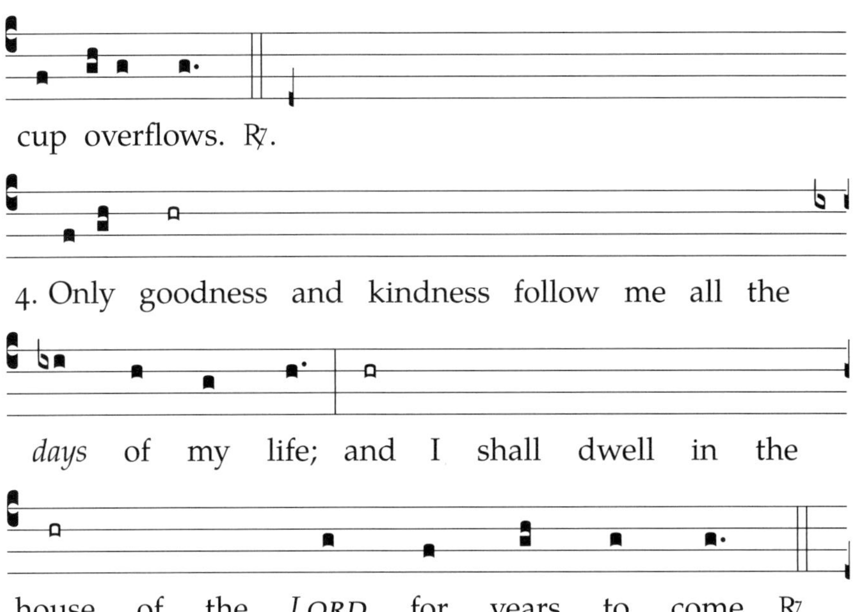
cup overflows. ℟.
4. Only goodness and kindness follow me all the
days of my life; and I shall dwell in the
house of the *LORD* for years to come. ℟.

Christ the King

Ps. 93: 1, 1-2, 5 **YEAR B**

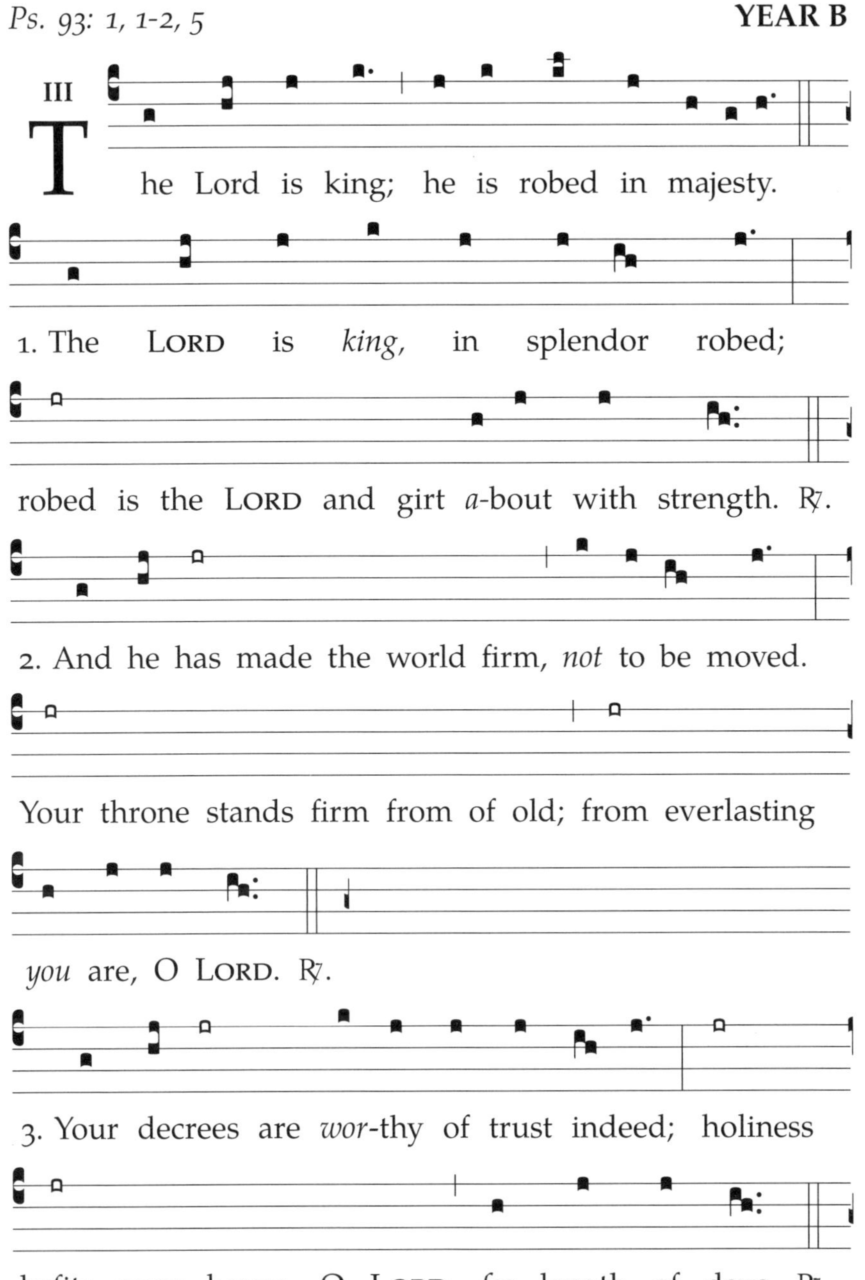
III
The Lord is king; he is robed in majesty.
1. The LORD is *king,* in splendor robed;
robed is the LORD and girt *a*-bout with strength. ℟.
2. And he has made the world firm, *not* to be moved.
Your throne stands firm from of old; from everlasting
you are, O LORD. ℟.
3. Your decrees are *wor*-thy of trust indeed; holiness
befits your house, O LORD, *for* length of days. ℟.

Christ the King

Ps. 122: 1-2, 3-4, 4-5 **YEAR C**

℣
Let us go rejoic-ing to the house of the Lord.
1. I rejoiced because they said to me, "We will go
up to the *house* of the LORD." And now we
have set foot within your gates, *O* Je-rusalem. ℟.
2. Je-rusalem, built as a city with compact *u*-nity.
To it the tribes go up, the *tribes* of the LORD. ℟.
3. According to the decree for Israel, to give thanks
to the *name* of the LORD. In it are set up

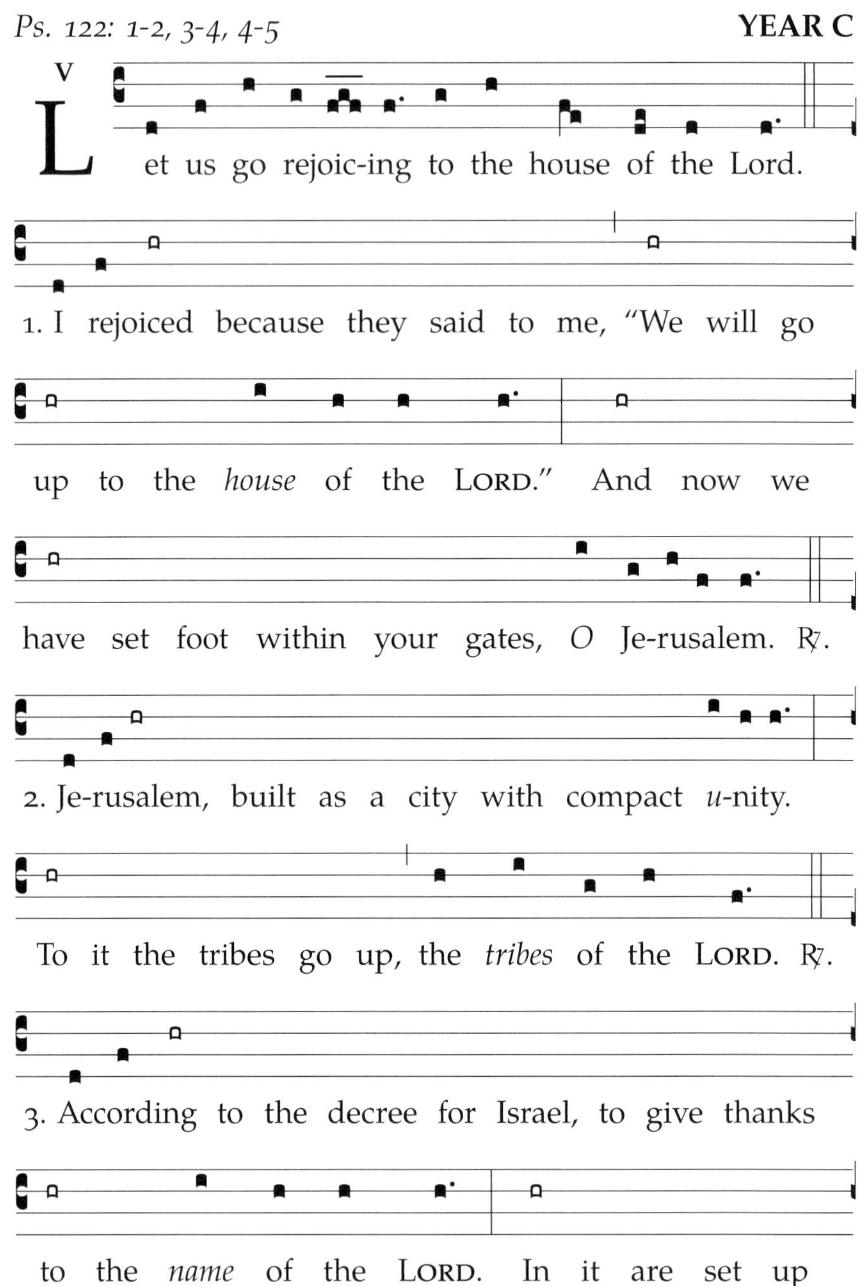

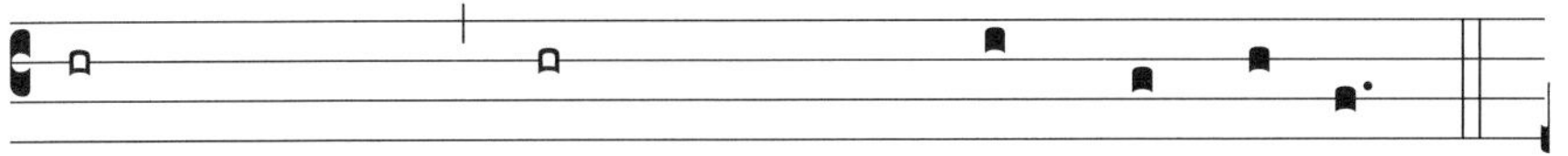

judgment seats, seats for the *house* of David. ℟.

Feasts and Solemnities

January 25: The Conversion of St. Paul the Apostle

Ps. 117: 1, 2 **YEAR ABC**

VII
Go out to all the world and tell the
Good News.
1. Praise the LORD all you nations; glorify him, *all*
you peoples! For steadfast is his kindness toward us,
and the fidelity of the LORD en-*dures* forever. ℟.

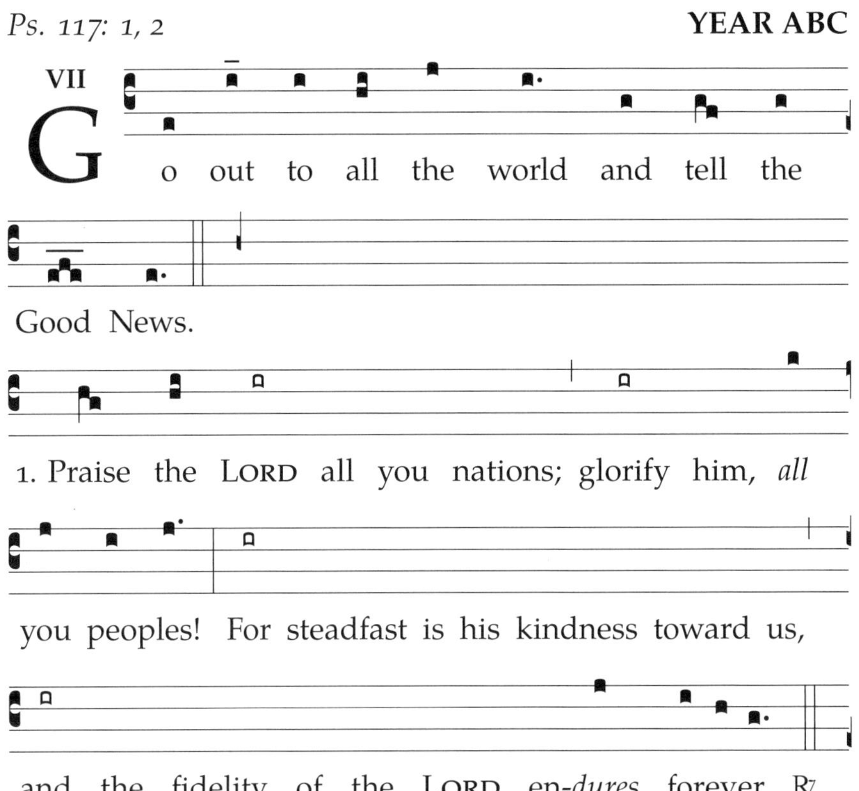

February 2: The Presentation of the Lord

Ps. 24: 7, 8, 9, 10 **YEAR ABC**

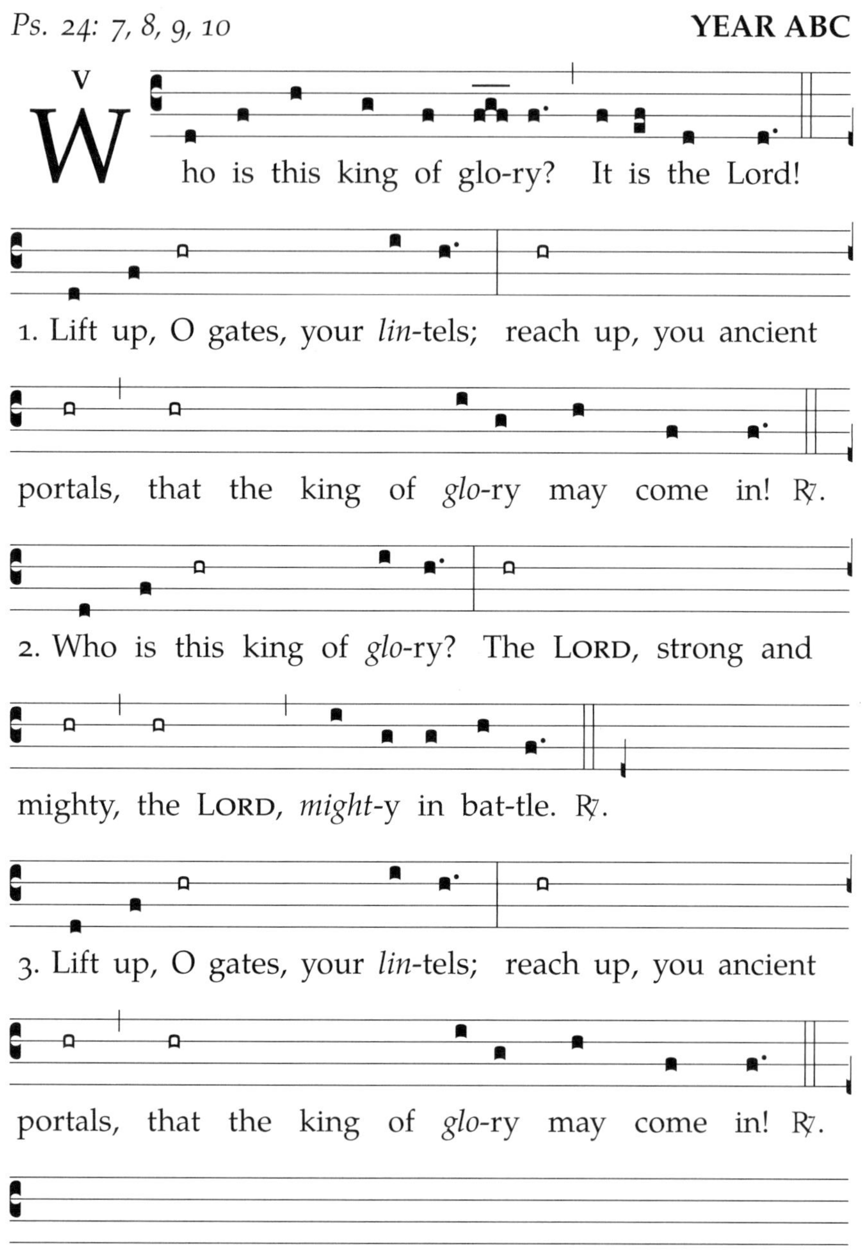

Who is this king of glo-ry? It is the Lord!
1. Lift up, O gates, your *lin*-tels; reach up, you ancient
portals, that the king of *glo*-ry may come in! ℟.
2. Who is this king of *glo*-ry? The Lord, strong and
mighty, the Lord, *might*-y in bat-tle. ℟.
3. Lift up, O gates, your *lin*-tels; reach up, you ancient
portals, that the king of *glo*-ry may come in! ℟.

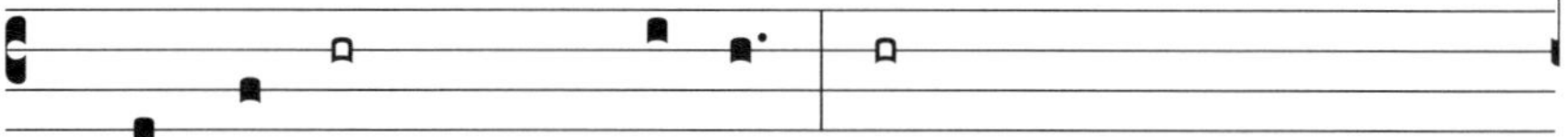

4. Who is this king of *glo*-ry? The LORD of hosts; he is

the *king* of glory. ℟.

March 19: St. Joseph, Husband of Mary

Ps. 89: 2-3, 4-5, 27, 29 **YEAR ABC**

II
The son of David will live for e- ver.
1. The promises of the LORD I will sing for-*ev*-er;
through all generations my mouth shall proclaim
your *faith*-fulness, for you have said, "My kindness is
established forever"; in heaven you have confirmed
your faithfulness. ℟.
2. "I have made a covenant with my cho-*sen* one,
I have sworn to David my *ser*-vant: Forever will I

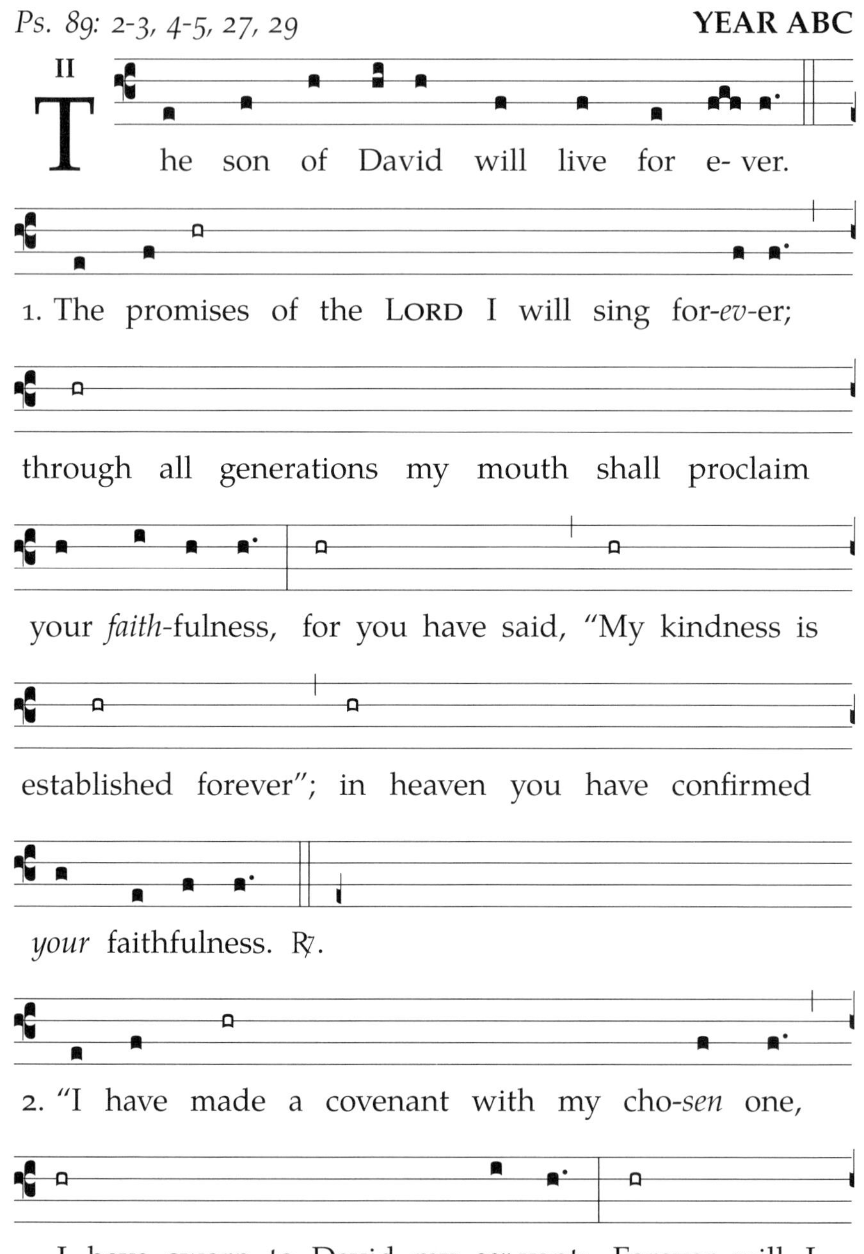

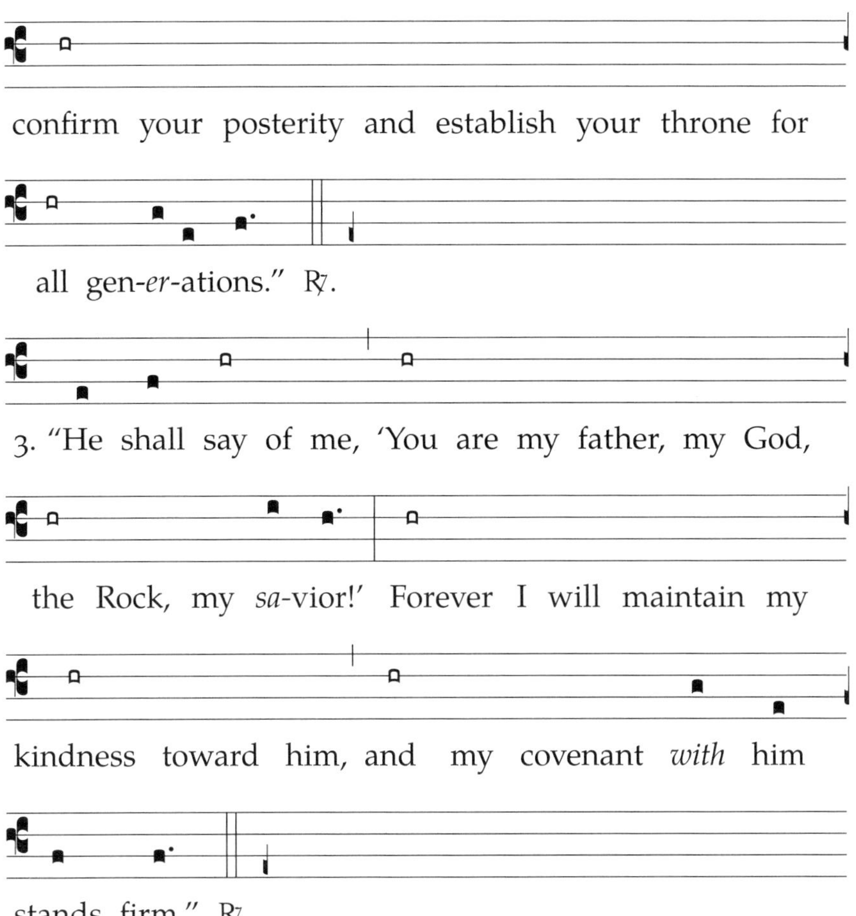
confirm your posterity and establish your throne for
all gen-*er*-ations." ℟.
3. "He shall say of me, 'You are my father, my God,
the Rock, my *sa*-vior!' Forever I will maintain my
kindness toward him, and my covenant *with* him
stands firm." ℟.

MARCH 25: THE ANNUNCIATION OF THE LORD

Ps. 40: 2, 4, 7-8, 8-9, 10 **YEAR ABC**

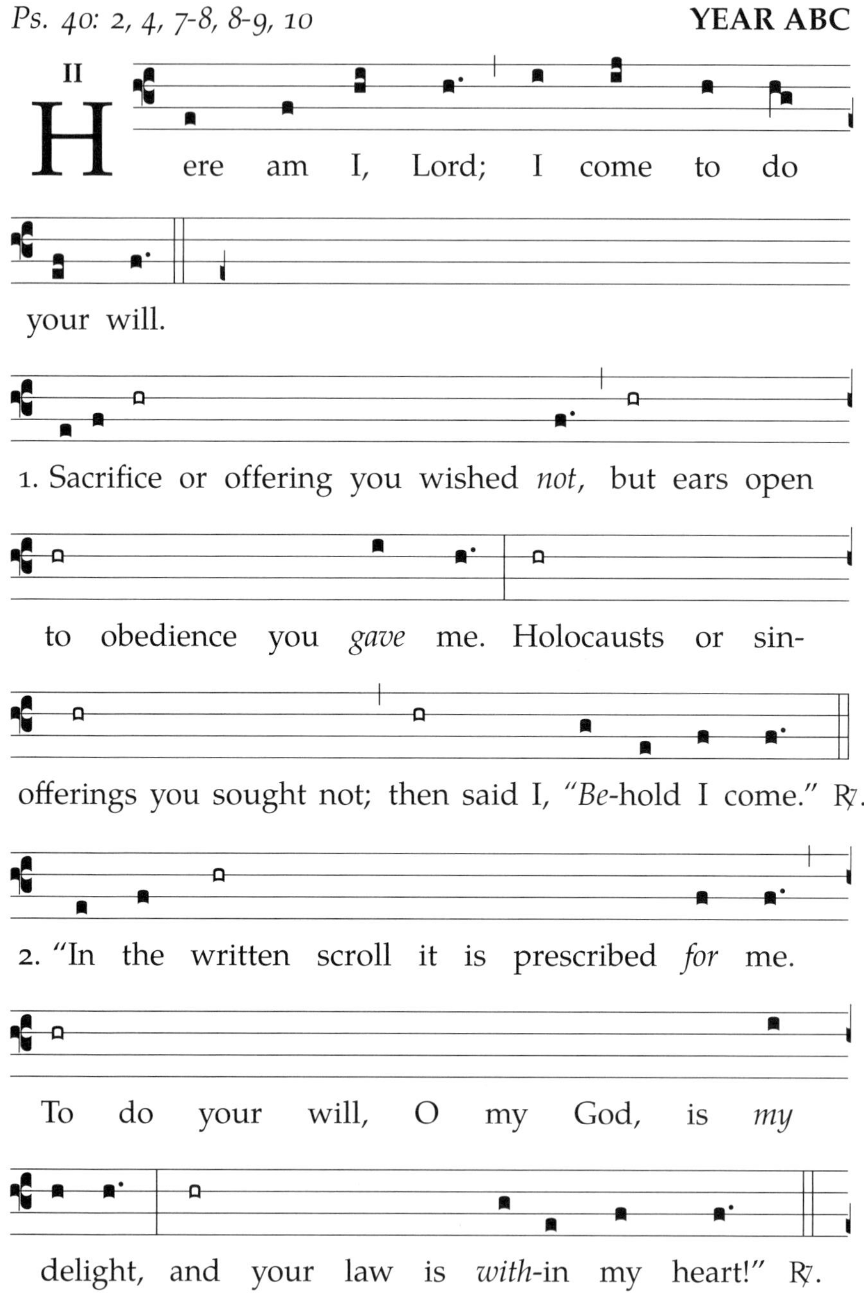
II
Here am I, Lord; I come to do
your will.
1. Sacrifice or offering you wished *not*, but ears open
to obedience you *gave* me. Holocausts or sin-
offerings you sought not; then said I, "*Be*-hold I come." ℟.
2. "In the written scroll it is prescribed *for* me.
To do your will, O my God, is *my*
delight, and your law is *with*-in my heart!" ℟.

3. I announced your justice in the vast as-*sem*-bly;
I did not restrain my lips, as you, *O* LORD, know. ℟.
4. Your justice I kept not hid within *my* heart;
your faithfulness and your salvation I have *spo*-ken of;
I have made no secret of your kindness
and your truth in the vast *as*-sembly. ℟.

June 23: Vigil of the Nativity of St. John the Baptist

Ps. 71: 1-2, 3-4a, 5-6ab, 15ab, 17 **YEAR ABC**

II
Since my mother's womb, you have been my strength.
1. In you, O LORD, I take *re*-fuge; let me never be *put* to shame. In your justice rescue me, and deliver me; incline your ear to me, *and* save me. ℟.
2. Be my rock of refuge, a stronghold to give me *safe*-ty, for you are my rock and my *for*-tress.
O my God, rescue me from the hand of *the* wicked. ℟.

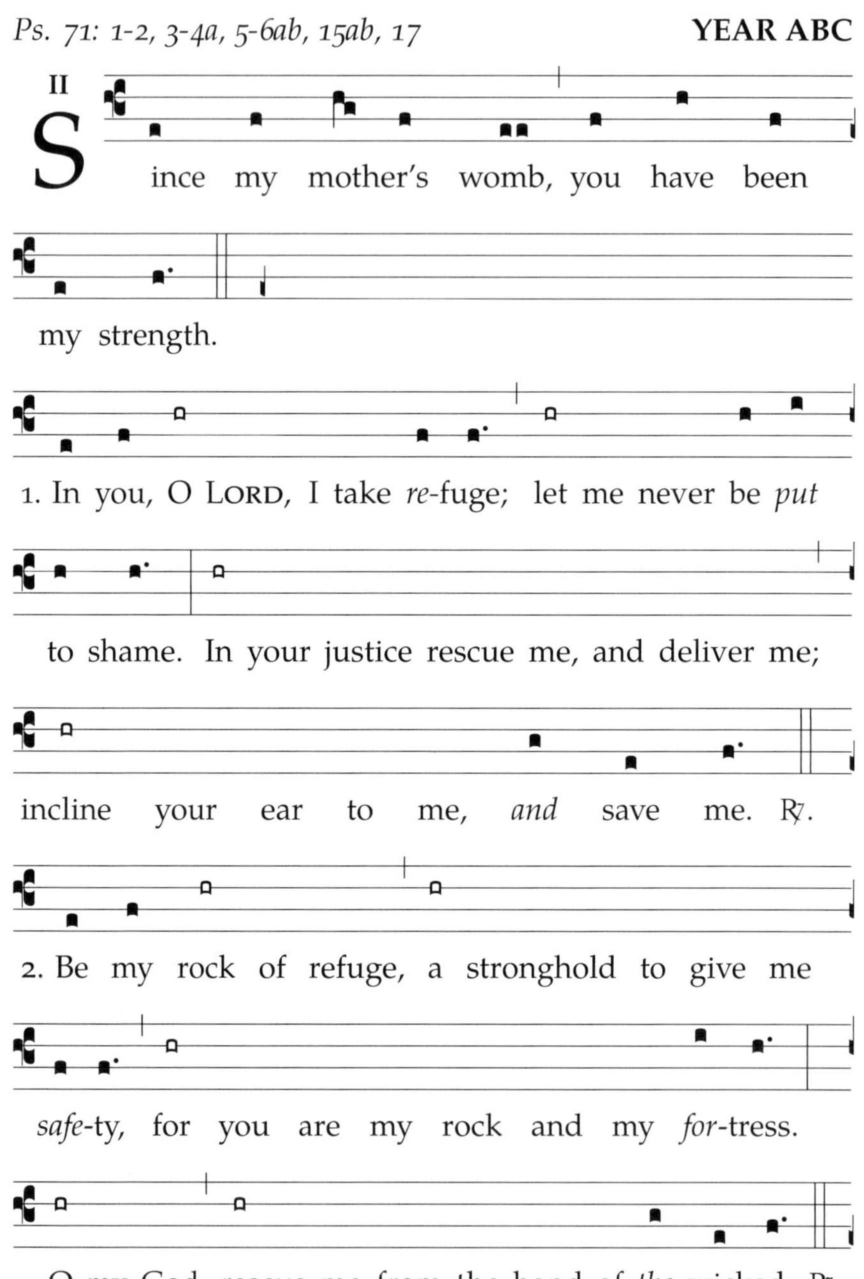

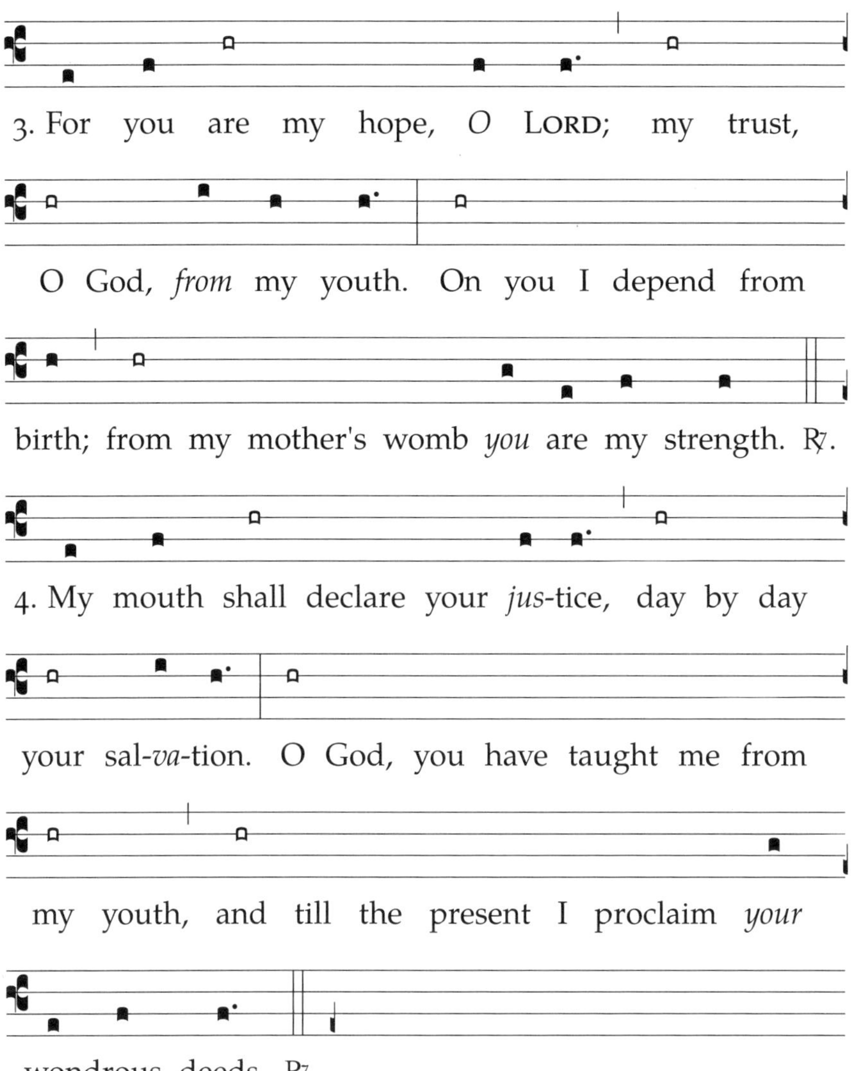
3. For you are my hope, *O* LORD; my trust,
O God, *from* my youth. On you I depend from
birth; from my mother's womb *you* are my strength. ℟.
4. My mouth shall declare your *jus*-tice, day by day
your sal-*va*-tion. O God, you have taught me from
my youth, and till the present I proclaim *your*
wondrous deeds. ℟.

June 24: The Nativity of St. John the Baptist

Ps. 139: 1b-3, 13-14ab, 14c-15 **YEAR ABC**

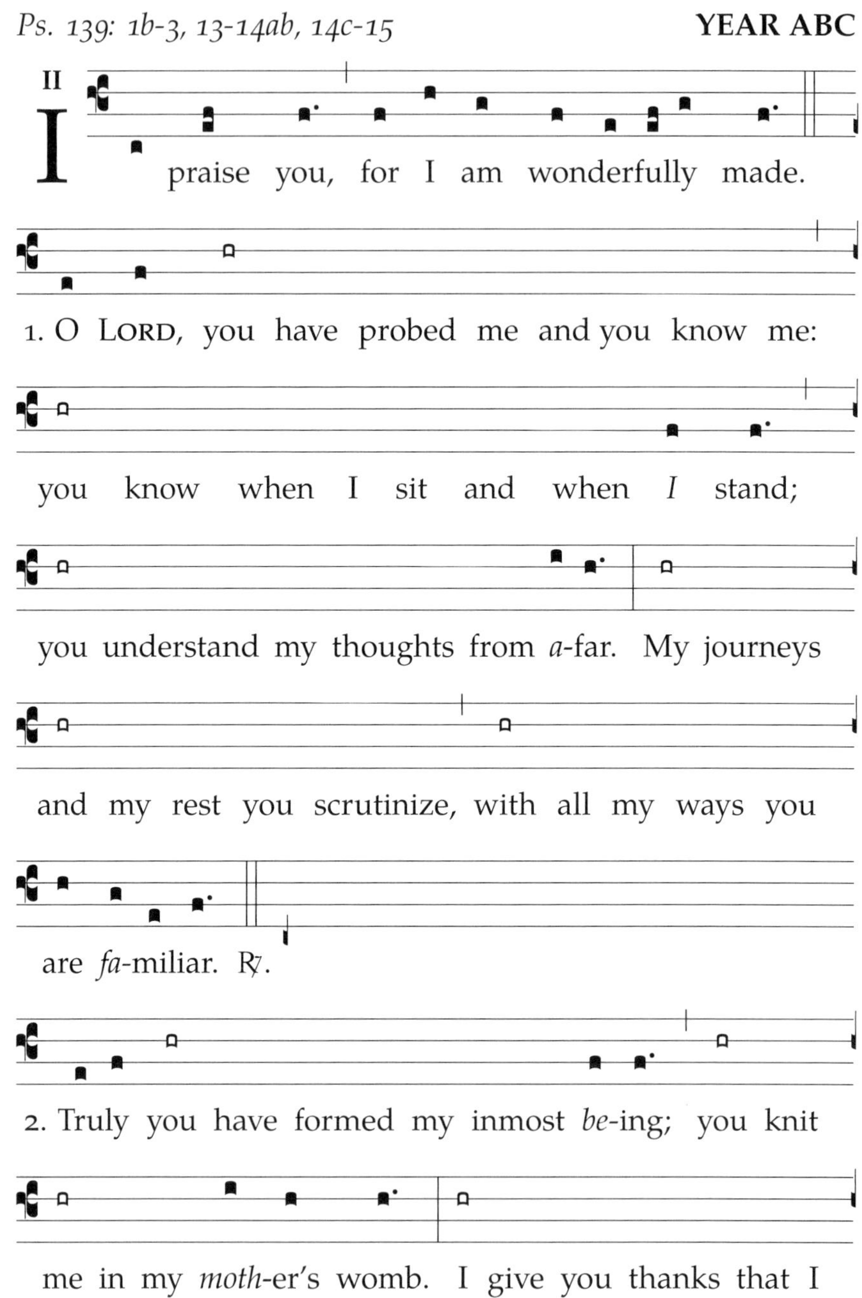
II
I praise you, for I am wonderfully made.
1. O LORD, you have probed me and you know me:
you know when I sit and when I stand;
you understand my thoughts from a-far. My journeys
and my rest you scrutinize, with all my ways you
are fa-miliar. ℟.
2. Truly you have formed my inmost be-ing; you knit
me in my moth-er's womb. I give you thanks that I

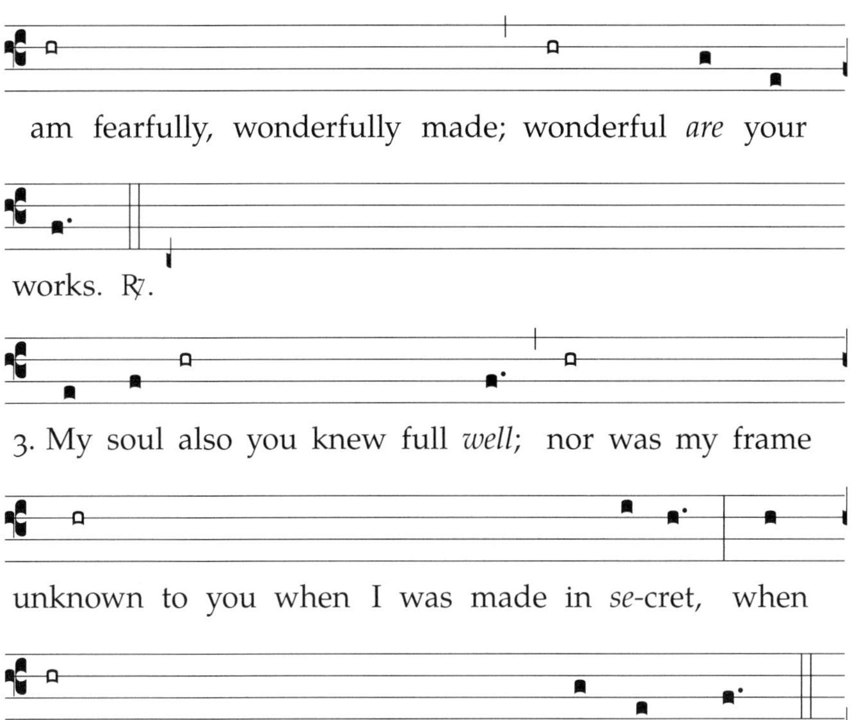
am fearfully, wonderfully made; wonderful *are* your
works. ℟.
3. My soul also you knew full *well;* nor was my frame
unknown to you when I was made in *se*-cret, when
I was fashioned in the depths *of* the earth. ℟.

June 29: Sts. Peter and Paul

Ps. 34: 2-3, 4-5, 6-7, 8-9 **YEAR ABC**

IV
The angel of the Lord will rescue those who
fear him.
1. I will bless the LORD at all times; his praise shall
be *ev*-er in my mouth. Let my soul glory in
the LORD; the lowly will hear me and *be* glad. ℟.
2. Glori-fy the LORD with me, let us togeth-*er*
extol his name. I sought the LORD, and he
answered me and delivered me from all *my* fears. ℟.

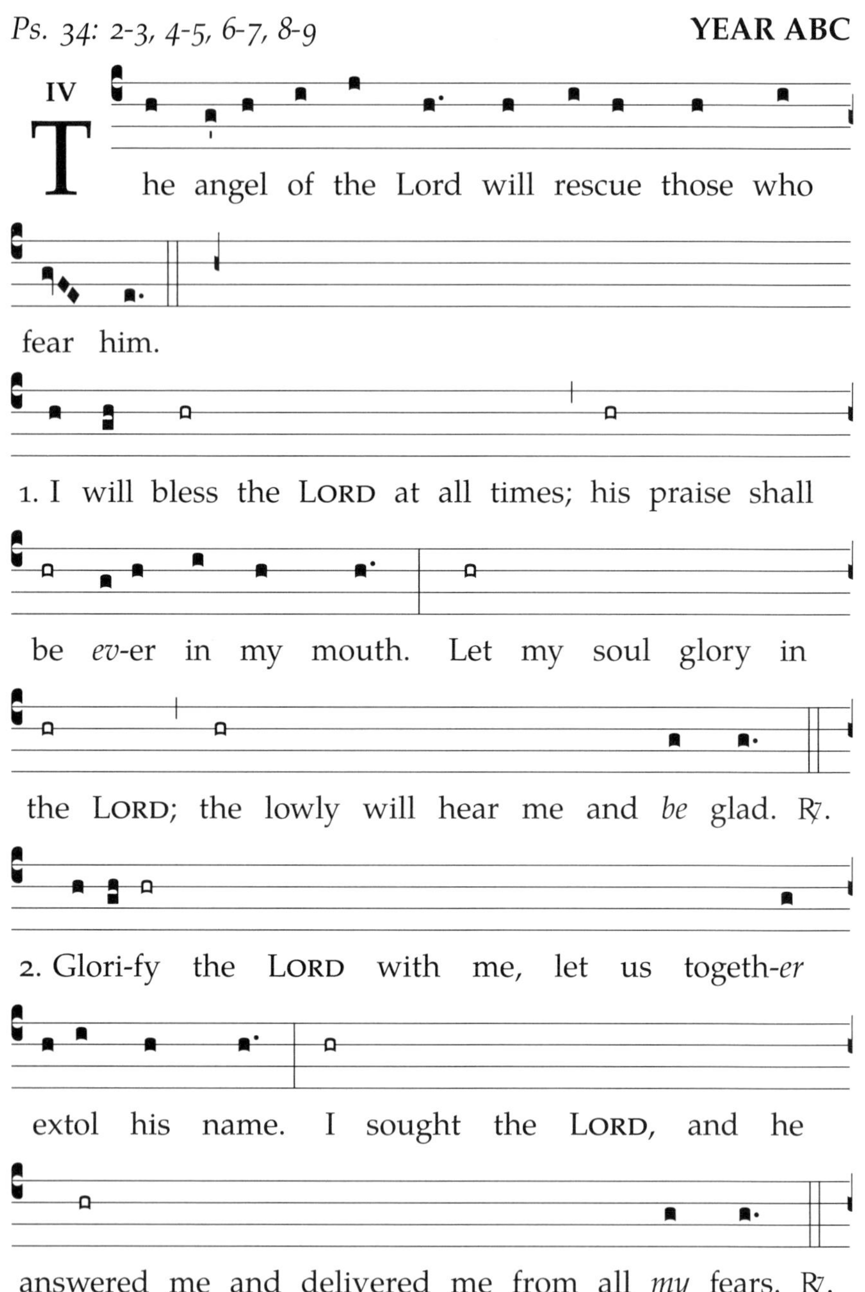

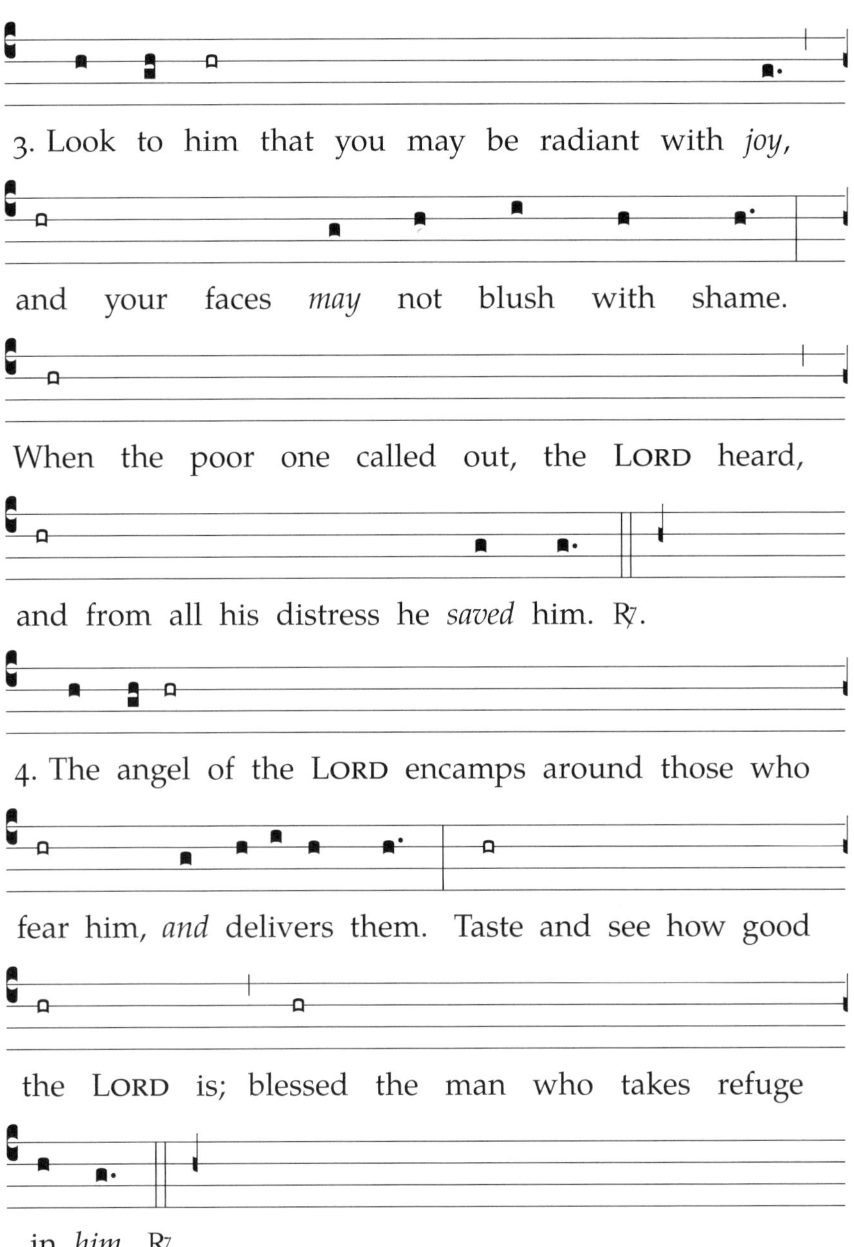
3. Look to him that you may be radiant with *joy*,
and your faces *may* not blush with shame.
When the poor one called out, the LORD heard,
and from all his distress he *saved* him. ℟.
4. The angel of the LORD encamps around those who
fear him, *and* delivers them. Taste and see how good
the LORD is; blessed the man who takes refuge
in *him*. ℟.

August 6: The Transfiguration of the Lord

Ps. 34: 2-3, 4-5, 6-7, 8-9 **YEAR ABC**

VI
The Lord is king, the most high over all
the earth.
1. The LORD is king; let the earth re-*joice*; let the
many is-*lands* be glad. Clouds and darkness are round
about him; justice and judgment are the founda-*tion*
of his throne. ℟.
2. The mountains melt like wax before the *LORD*,
before the LORD of *all* the earth. The heavens

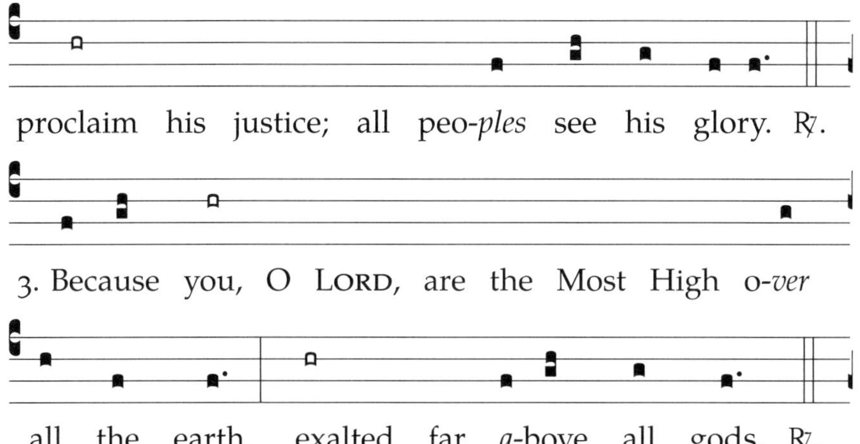
proclaim his justice; all peo-*ples* see his glory. ℟.
3. Because you, O LORD, are the Most High o-*ver*
all the earth, exalted far *a*-bove all gods. ℟.

August 14: The Assumption of the Blessed Virgin Mary, Vigil Mass

Ps. 132: 6-7, 9-10, 13-14 **YEAR ABC**

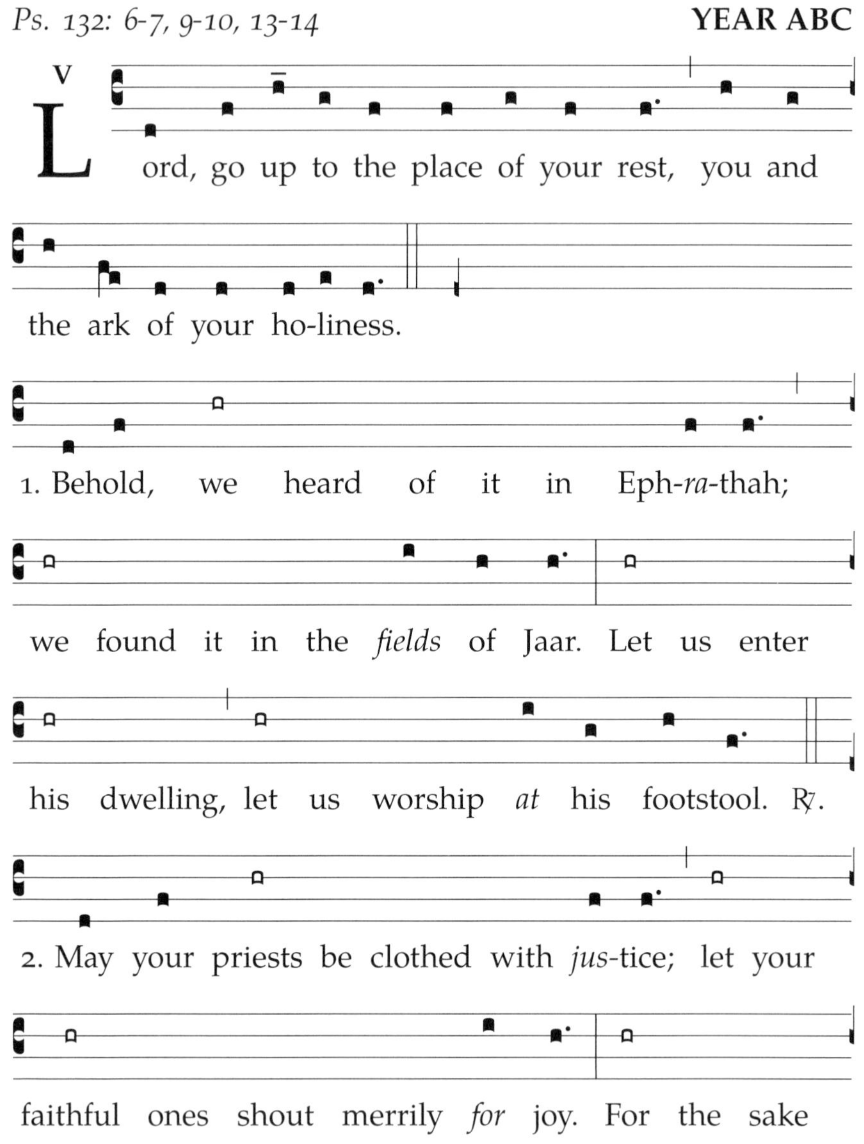

℣
Lord, go up to the place of your rest, you and
the ark of your ho-liness.
1. Behold, we heard of it in Eph-*ra*-thah;
we found it in the *fields* of Jaar. Let us enter
his dwelling, let us worship *at* his footstool. ℟.
2. May your priests be clothed with *jus*-tice; let your
faithful ones shout merrily *for* joy. For the sake

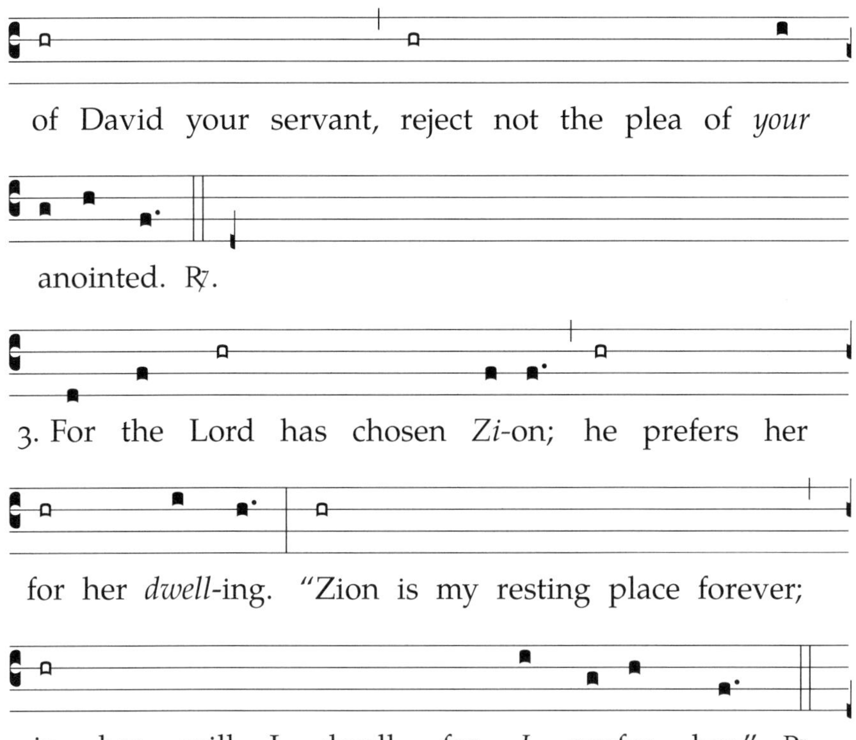
of David your servant, reject not the plea of your
anointed. ℟.
3. For the Lord has chosen Zi-on; he prefers her
for her dwell-ing. "Zion is my resting place forever;
in her will I dwell, for I prefer her." ℟.

August 15: The Assumption of the Blessed Virgin Mary

Ps. 45: 10, 11, 12, 16 **YEAR ABC**

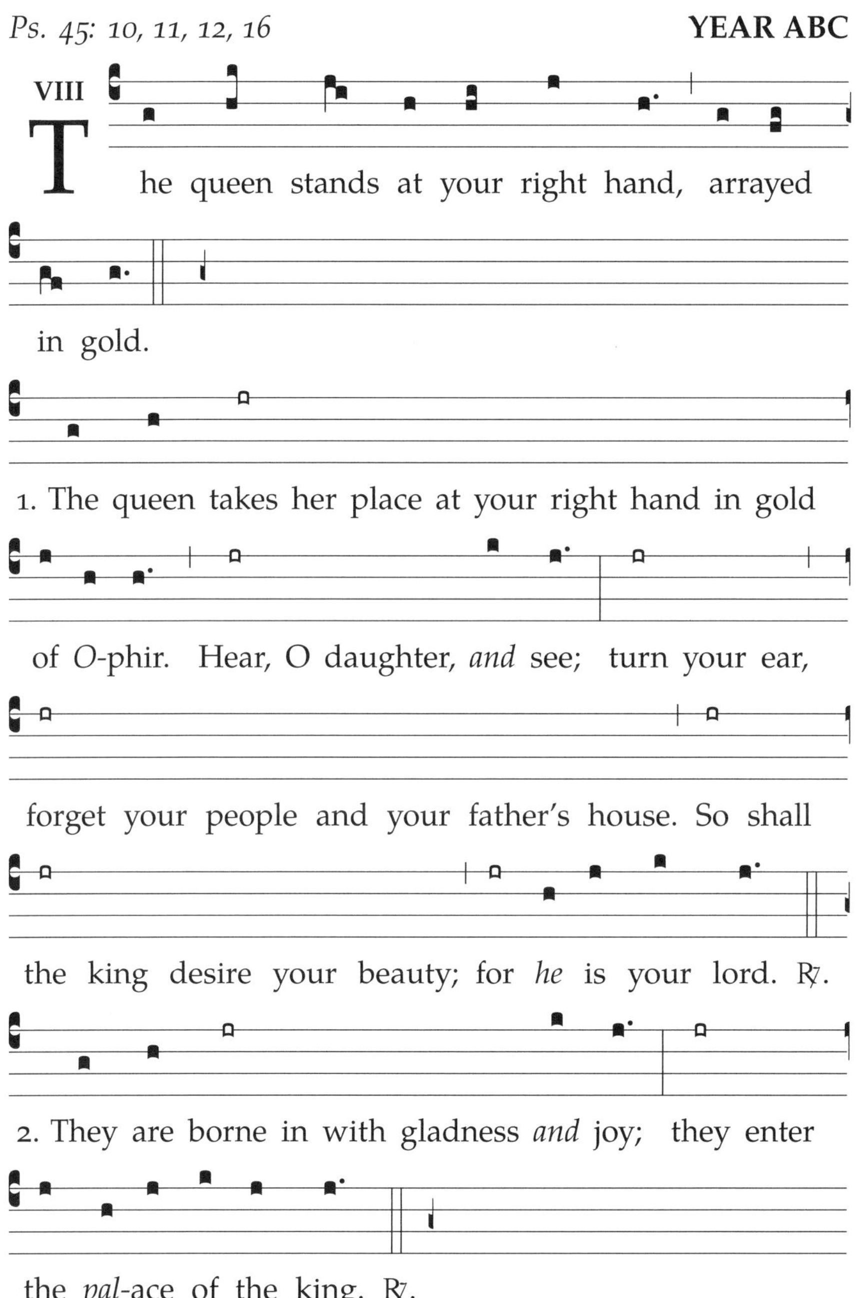
VIII
The queen stands at your right hand, arrayed
in gold.
1. The queen takes her place at your right hand in gold
of *O*-phir. Hear, O daughter, *and* see; turn your ear,
forget your people and your father's house. So shall
the king desire your beauty; for *he* is your lord. ℟.
2. They are borne in with gladness *and* joy; they enter
the *pal*-ace of the king. ℟.

September 14: The Exaltation of the Holy Cross

Ps. 78: 1bc-2, 34-35, 36-37, 38 **YEAR ABC**

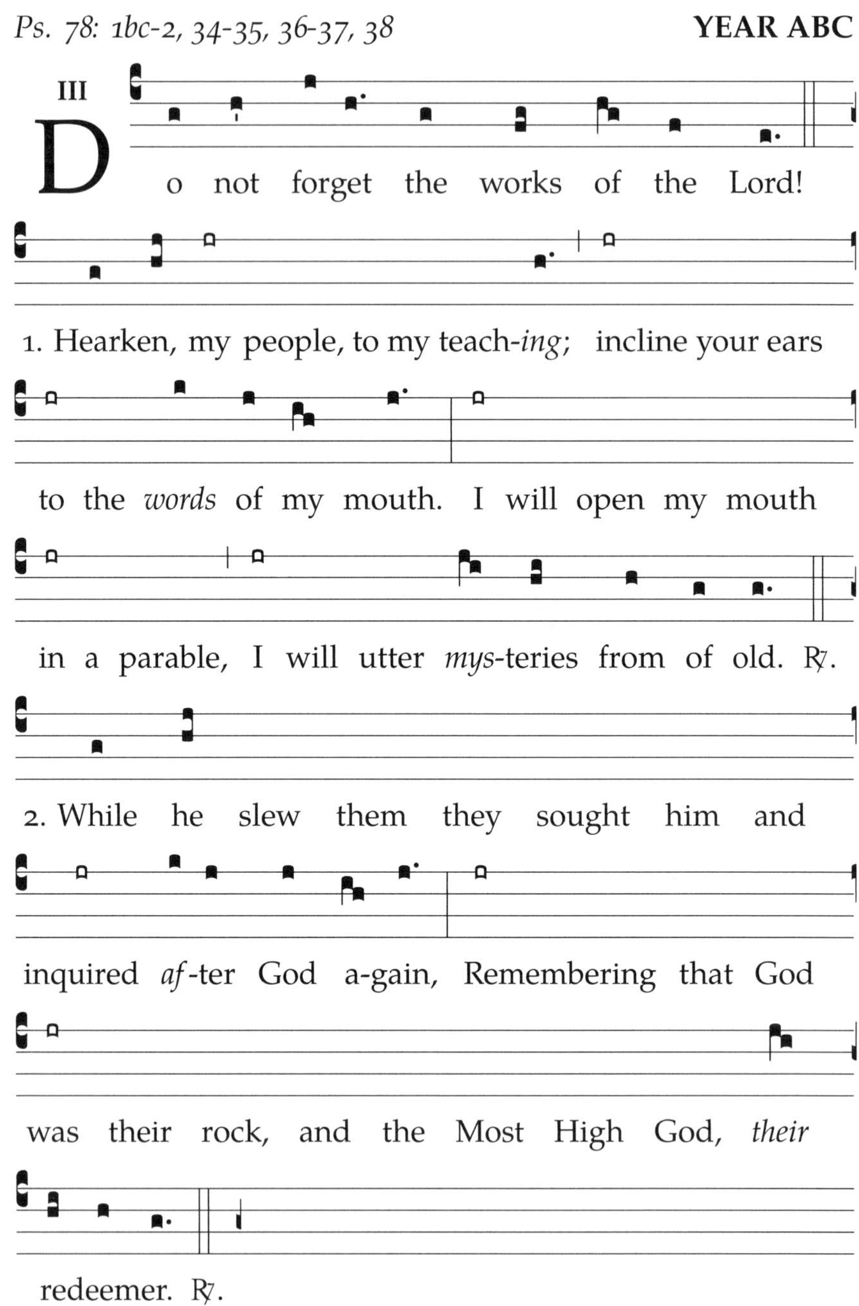
III
Do not forget the works of the Lord!
1. Hearken, my people, to my teach-*ing*; incline your ears
to the *words* of my mouth. I will open my mouth
in a parable, I will utter *mys*-teries from of old. ℟.
2. While he slew them they sought him and
inquired *af*-ter God a-gain, Remembering that God
was their rock, and the Most High God, *their*
redeemer. ℟.

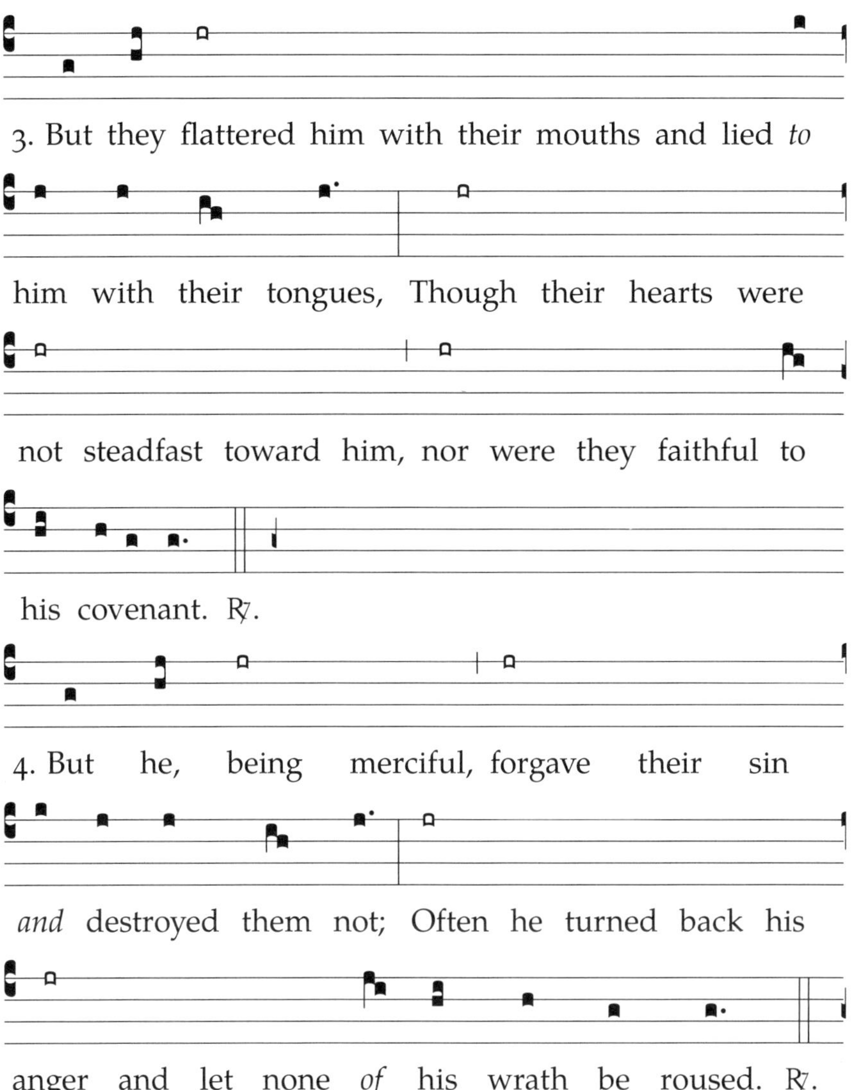
3. But they flattered him with their mouths and lied *to*
him with their tongues, Though their hearts were
not steadfast toward him, nor were they faithful to
his covenant. ℟.
4. But he, being merciful, forgave their sin
and destroyed them not; Often he turned back his
anger and let none *of* his wrath be roused. ℟.

November 1: All Saints

Ps. 24: 1bc-2, 3-4ab, 5-6 **YEAR ABC**

III
Lord, this is the people that longs to see
your face.
1. The LORD's are the earth and its fullness;
the world and those who dwell *in* it. For he
founded *it* upon the seas and established it *up*-on the
rivers. ℟.
2. Who can ascend the mountain of the *LORD?* or who
may stand in *his* ho-ly place? One whose hands are

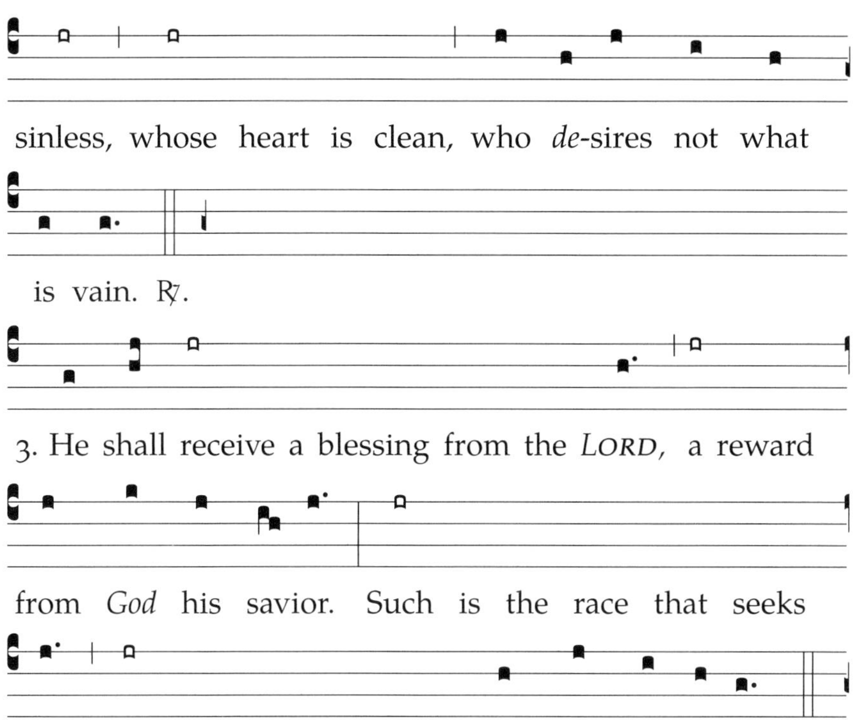

sinless, whose heart is clean, who *de*-sires not what
is vain. ℟.
3. He shall receive a blessing from the *LORD,* a reward
from *God* his savior. Such is the race that seeks
him, that seeks the face of *the* God of Jacob. ℟.

November 2: All Souls (option 1)

Ps. 23: 1-3a, 3b-4, 5, 6 **YEAR ABC**

VIII
The Lord is my shepherd; there is nothing I
shall want.
1. The LORD is my shepherd; I shall *not* want.
In verdant pastures he gives me *re*-pose;
beside restful waters he leads me; he re-*fresh*-es
my soul. ℟.
2. He guides me in right paths for his *name's*
sake. Even though I walk in the dark valley

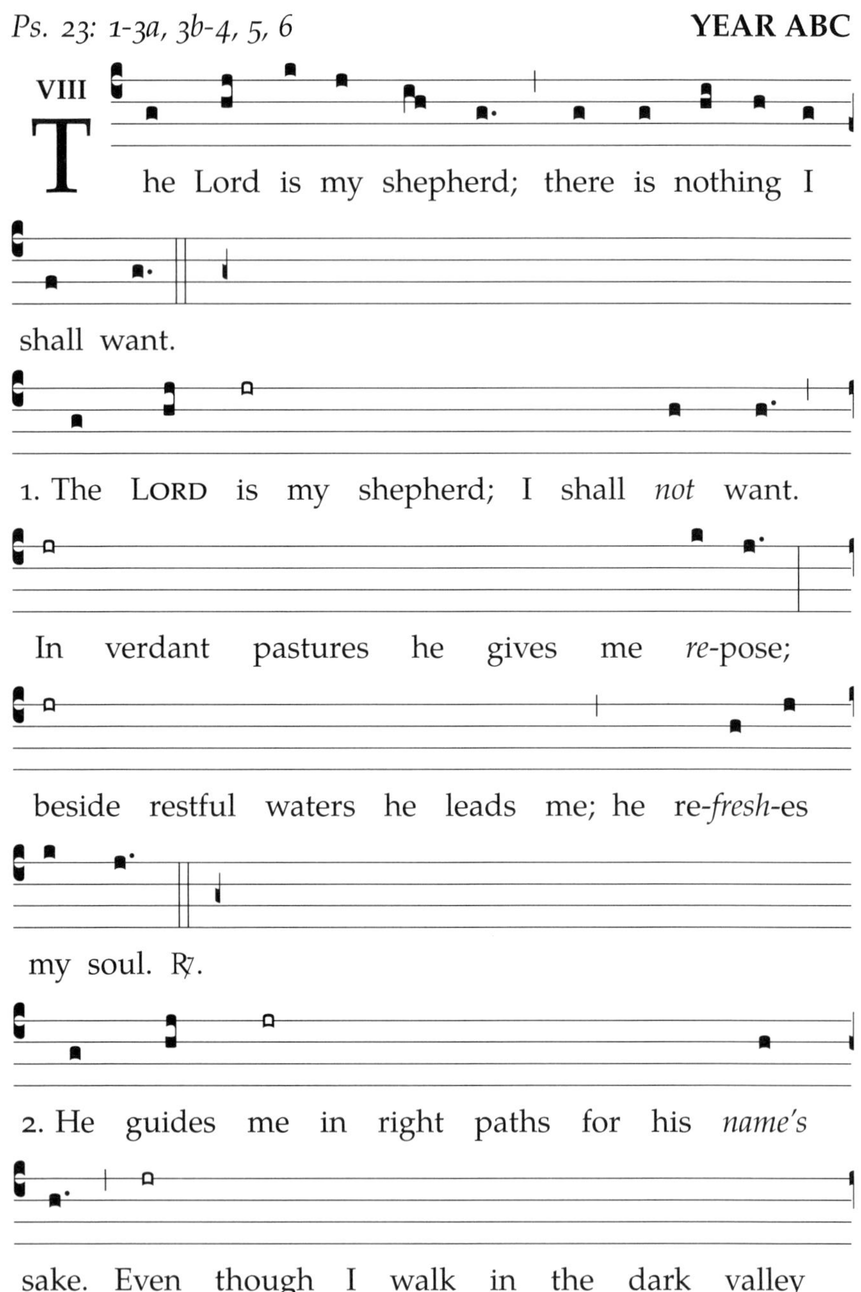

I fear no *e*-vil; for you are at my side
with your rod and your staff that *give* me courage. ℟.
3. You spread the table before me in the sight of
my foes; you anoint my head with oil; my cup
overflows. ℟.
4. Only goodness and kindness follow me all the
days of *my* life; and I shall dwell in the
house of the LORD for years to come. ℟.

November 2: All Souls (option 2)

Ps. 23: 1-3a, 3b-4, 5, 6 **YEAR ABC**

VIII
Though I walk in the valley of darkness,
I fear no evil, for you are with me.
1. The LORD is my shepherd; I shall not *want*.
In verdant pastures he gives me *re*-pose;
beside restful waters he leads me; he re-*fresh*-es
my soul. ℟.
2. He guides me in right paths for his *name's* sake.
Even though I walk in the dark valley I fear

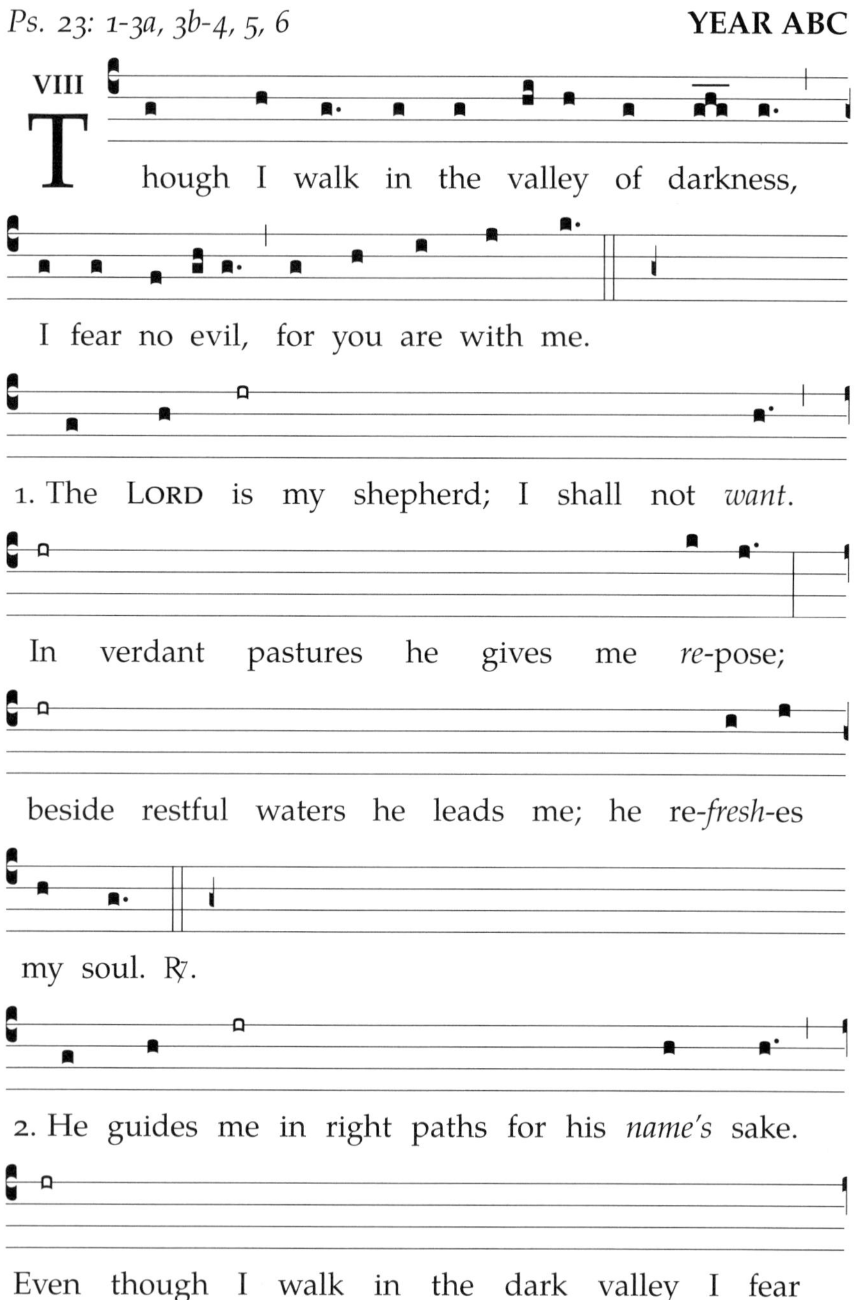

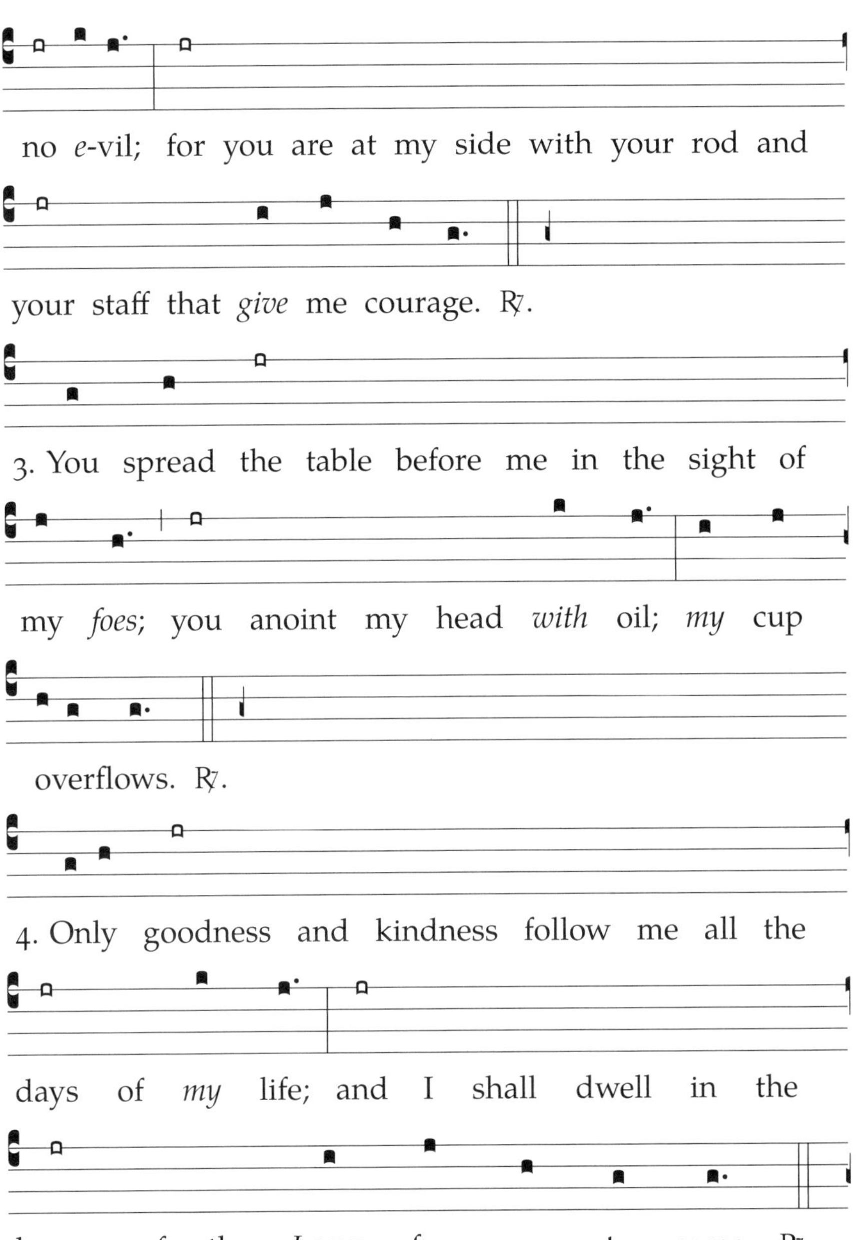
no e-vil; for you are at my side with your rod and
your staff that give me courage. ℟.
3. You spread the table before me in the sight of
my foes; you anoint my head with oil; my cup
overflows. ℟.
4. Only goodness and kindness follow me all the
days of my life; and I shall dwell in the
house of the LORD for years to come. ℟.

November 9: The Dedication of the Lateran Basilica

Ps. 46: 2-3, 5-6, 8-9 **YEAR ABC**

VIII
The waters of the riv-er gladden the ci-ty
of God, the holy dwelling of the Most High!
1. God is our refuge and our *strength,* an ever-present
help in *dis*-tress. Therefore, we fear not, though the
earth be shaken and mountains plunge into the *depths*
of the sea. ℟.
2. There is a stream whose runlets gladden the
city of *God,* the holy dwelling of the *Most* High.

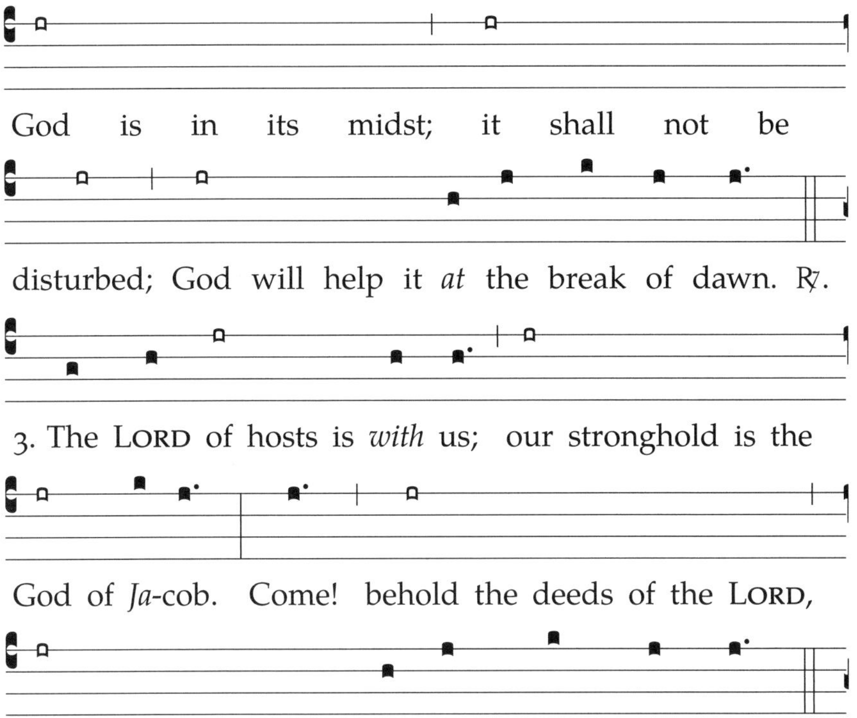
God is in its midst; it shall not be
disturbed; God will help it *at* the break of dawn. ℟.
3. The LORD of hosts is *with* us; our stronghold is the
God of *Ja*-cob. Come! behold the deeds of the LORD,
the astounding things *he* has wrought on earth. ℟.

December 8: The Immaculate Conception of the Blessed Virgin Mary

Ps. 98: 1, 2-3ab, 3cd-4 **YEAR ABC**

VIII
Sing to the Lord a new song, for he has done
marvelous deeds.
1. Sing to the LORD a new *song*, for he has done
marvel-*ous* deeds; his right hand has won victory for
him, his holy arm. ℟.
2. The LORD has made his salva-*tion* known:
in the sight of the nations he has revealed
his *jus*-tice. He has remembered his kindness

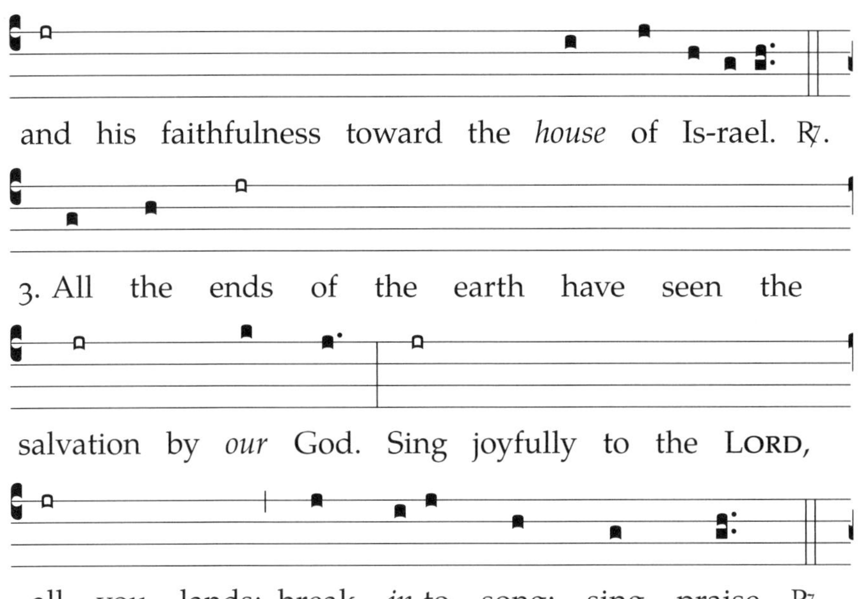
and his faithfulness toward the *house* of Is-rael. ℟.
3. All the ends of the earth have seen the
salvation by *our* God. Sing joyfully to the LORD,
all you lands; break *in*-to song; sing praise. ℟.

December 12: Our Lady of Guadalupe

Judith 15: 9d, 13: 18bcde, 19 **YEAR ABC**

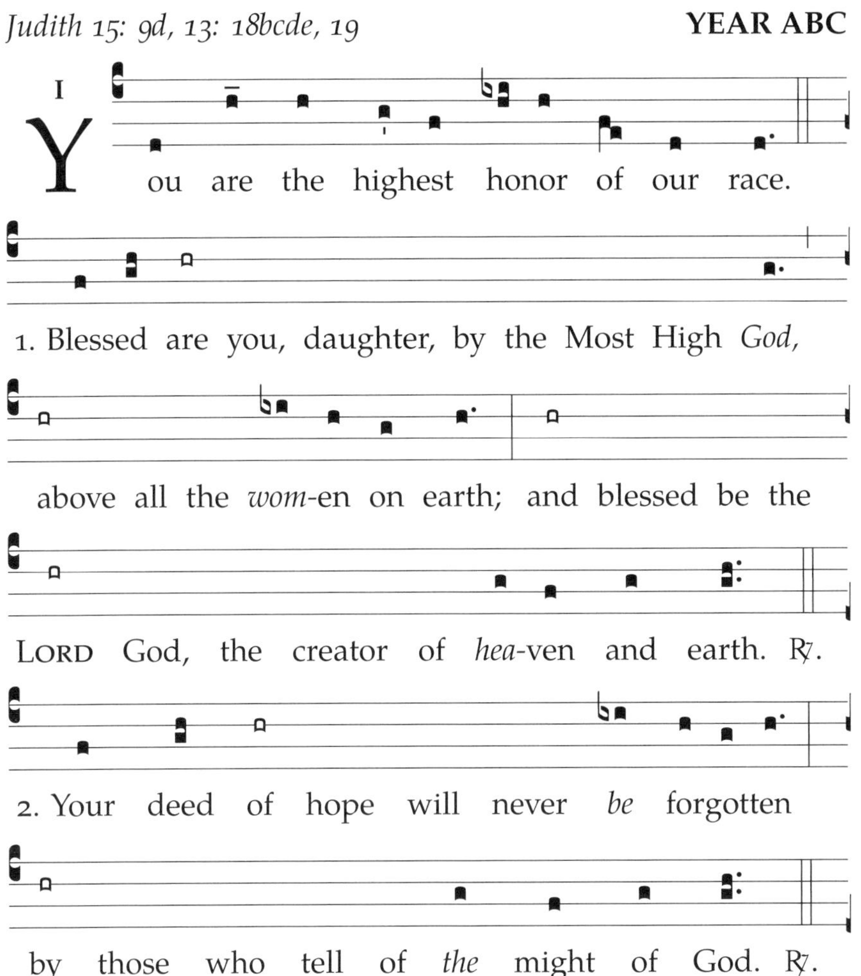
I
You are the highest honor of our race.
1. Blessed are you, daughter, by the Most High *God,*
above all the *wom*-en on earth; and blessed be the
LORD God, the creator of *hea*-ven and earth. ℟.
2. Your deed of hope will never *be* forgotten
by those who tell of *the* might of God. ℟.

Index

Antiphons

First Lines of Psalms and Canticles

Psalms and Canticles

Psalms

Each psalm was engraved using
open-source software and fonts
under a Linux operating system.
The chant-engraving program
Gregorio, originally invented
by Élie Roux, is a software add-on
for the document-processing
program LaTeX.
Information on the Gregorio project
is available on the internet at
home.gna.org/gregorio.